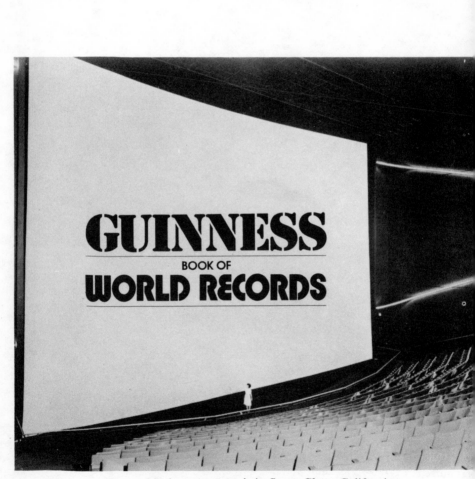

The world's largest screen is in Santa Clara, California.

1981 Edition

GUINNESS

BOOK OF

WORLD RECORDS

Editors and Compilers
NORRIS McWHIRTER
(ROSS McWHIRTER 1955-1975)

Sports Editor
STAN GREENBERG

American Editor
DAVID A. BOEHM

Associate American Editor
STEPHEN TOPPING

 STERLING PUBLISHING CO., INC. NEW YORK

World rights reserved
Revised American Edition © 1980, 1979, 1978, 1977, 1976, 1975, 1974,
1973, 1972, 1971, 1970, 1969, 1968, 1966, 1965, 1964, 1963, 1962
by Sterling Publishing Co., Inc.
Two Park Avenue, New York, N.Y. 10016.
© 1960 by Guinness Superlatives Ltd.

For information address: Sterling Publishing Company, Inc.
Library of Congress Catalog Card No.: 65-24391
ISBN 0-8069-0196-9 Trade
0197-7 Library
0198-5 Deluxe

CONTENTS

FOREWORD

Now that our *Guinness Book of World Records* has reached its 19th American edition it has long since moved from the status of an annual to that of a perennial.

When we first brought out this book, twenty-five years ago, we did so in the hope of providing a means for peaceful settling of arguments about record performances in this record-breaking world in which we live. We realize, of course, that much joy lies in the argument, but how exasperating it can be if there is no final means of finding the answer.

About a quarter of the many thousands of records listed have to be changed from one edition to the next. In this edition we are again obliged to revise our own entry that records that the global sales of this book, now being published in 23 languages, have surpassed the 40 million mark.

Whether the discussion concerns the highest that any man has jumped over his own height, the greatest weight lifted by a woman, the nationality of the first woman to climb Everest, or—an old bone of contention— the longest time for anyone to become a Saint, I can but quote the words used in introducing the first edition, "How much heat these innocent questions can raise: Guinness, in producing this book, hopes that it may assist in resolving many such disputes, and may, we hope, turn heat into light."

Iveagh
[BENJAMIN GUINNESS]
EARL OF IVEAGH, Chairman
September, 1980　　Arthur Guinness, Son & Co (Dublin) Ltd

PREFACE

This nineteenth US edition has been brought up to date and provided with new illustrations. We wish to thank correspondents from most of the countries of the world for raising and settling various editorial points. Strenuous efforts have been made to improve the value of the material presented and this policy will be continued in future editions.

NORRIS D. MCWHIRTER
General Editor

Guinness Superlatives, Ltd.,
Main Editorial Office,
2 Cecil Court,
London Road, Enfield,
Middlesex, England.

GUINNESS MUSEUMS

Empire State Building — New York City
Ocean Boulevard — Myrtle Beach, S.C.
Clifton Hill — Niagara Falls, Ont.
Parkway — Gatlinburg, Tenn.
Lake of the Ozarks — Missouri
Fisherman's Wharf — San Francisco, Calif.
Tivoli — Stockholm, Sweden

IS IT A RECORD?

We are likely to publish only those records which improve upon previous records or which are newly significant in having become the subject of widespread and preferably international competitiveness. It should be stressed that unique occurrences and interesting peculiarities are not in themselves necessarily records. Records in our sense essentially have to be both measureable and comparable. Records which are *qualified* in some way, for example, by age, day of the week, etc. cannot be accommodated in a reference work so general as *The Guinness Book of World Records*.

The authors and publishers reserve the right to determine in their sole discretion the record to be published and the name of the record holder for purposes of inclusion in the book. The publishers do *not* normally supply personnel to invigilate record attempts but reserve the right to do so.

Claimants should send independent corroboration in the form of local or national newspaper cuttings, radio or TV coverage reports and signed authentication by independent adult witnesses or representatives of organizations of standing in their community. Signed log books should show there has been unremitting surveillance in the case of endurance events. Action photographs in color or black-and-white should also be supplied.

Five-minute rest intervals (optional but aggregable) are *permitted after* each completed hour in marathon events except for those few "non-stop" categories in which minimal intervals may be taken only for purposes other than for resting.

If an activity is one controlled by a recognized world or national governing body that body should be consulted and involved in ratifying it.

The publishers do not publish gratuitously dangerous categories, such as the lowest height for a handcuffed free-fall parachutist to dive from or the thinnest burning rope suspending a man in a straitjacket from a helicopter.

There has been in recent years a marked increase in efforts to establish records for sheer endurance in many activities. In the very nature of record breaking the duration of such "marathons" will tend to be pushed to greater and greater extremes and it should be stressed that marathon attempts are not without possible dangers. Organizers of marathon events would be well counselled to seek medical advice before and surveillance during marathons which involve extended periods with little or no sleep. (See above for notes on rest periods.)

Notwithstanding the best efforts of the editors, errors in publication, while rare, may occur. In the event of such errors, the sole responsibility of the publishers will be to correct such errors in subsequent editions of the book.

Finally the editorial office, which is concerned with maintaining and improving the quality of each succeeding edition, is unable to perform also the function of a free general information bureau for quiz competitions and the like, by telephone or by correspondence.

VALUABLE ANIMAL: "Orky," the largest killer whale in captivity, is worth at least $250,000, making him the most valuable marine animal. The 14,000-lb mammal can be seen at Marineland of the Pacific, Palos Verdes, Calif, where he cavorts in the world's largest saltwater tank.

Chapter 1
The Human Being

1. DIMENSIONS

Tallest Giants

The height of human giants is a subject in which accurate information is frequently obscured by exaggeration and commercial dishonesty. The only admissible evidence on the true height of giants is that collected in the last 100 years under impartial medical supervision. Some medical papers have themselves, however, published fanciful, as opposed to measured, heights as recently as 1962.

The assertion that Goliath of Gath (*c.* 1060 BC) stood 6 cubits and a span (9 ft 6½ in) suggests a confusion of units or some over-enthusiastic exaggeration by the Hebrew chroniclers. The Hebrew historian Flavius Josephus (b 37 or 38 AD, d after 93 AD) and some of the manuscripts of the Septuagint (the earliest Greek translation of the Old Testament) attribute to Goliath the quite credible height of 4 Greek cubits and a span (6 ft 10 in).

Extreme medieval data, taken from bone measurements, invariably refer to specimens of extinct whale, giant cave bear, mastodon, woolly rhinoceros or other prehistoric non-human remains.

An extreme case of exaggeration concerned Siah Khan ibn Kashmir Khan (b 1913) of Bushehr (Bushire), Iran. Prof D. H. Fuchs showed photographs of him at a meeting of the Society of Physicians in Vienna, Austria, in Jan 1935 claiming that he was 10 ft 6 in tall. Later, when Siah Khan entered the Imperial Hospital in Teheran for an operation, it was revealed that his actual height was 7 ft 2.6 in, a full meter (39.4 in) less.

The tallest recorded "true" (non-pathological) giant was Angus MacAskill (1825–63), born on the island of Berneray, in the Sound of Harris, in the Western Isles, Scotland. He stood 7 ft 9 in tall and died in St. Ann's, on Cape Breton Island, Nova Scotia, Canada.

Modern opinion is that the tallest recorded man of whom there is irrefutable evidence was the pre-acromegalic giant Robert Pershing Wadlow, born at 6:30 a.m. in Alton, Ill, on Feb 22, 1918. Weighing 8½ lb at birth, his abnormal growth started at the age of 2, following a double hernia operation.

Dr C. M. Charles, Associate Professor of Anatomy at Washington University School of Medicine, in St Louis, and Dr Cyril MacBryde measured him at 8 ft 11.1 in, on June 27, 1940. He died 18 days later, at 1:30 a.m. on July 15, 1940, in Manistee, Mich, as a result of cellulitis (inflammation of cellular tissue) of the right ankle aggravated by a poorly fitted brace, which had been fitted only a week earlier. He was buried in Oakwood Cemetery, Alton, Ill, in a coffin measuring 10 ft 9 in in length, 32 in in width, and 30 in in depth.

His greatest recorded weight was 491 lb on his 21st birthday. He weighed 439 lb at the time of death. His shoes were size 37AA (18½ in long) and his hands measured 12¾ in from the wrist to the tip of the middle finger. His arm span was 9 ft 5¾ in and he consumed 8,000 calories daily. At the age of 9 he was able to carry his father, the mayor of Alton, who stood 5 ft 11 in tall and weighed 170 lb, up the stairs of the family home.

His height progressed as follows:

Age in Years	Height ft	in	Weight in lb	Age in Years	Height ft	in	Weight in lb
5	5	4	105	15	7	8	355
8	6	0	169	16	7	10½	374
9	6	2½	180	17	8	0½	315*
10	6	5	210	18	8	3½	—
11	6	7	—	19	8	5½	480
12	6	10½	—	20	8	6¾	—
13	7	1¾	255	21	8	8¼	491
14	7	5	301	22.4†	8	11.1	439

* Following severe influenza and infection of the foot.
† He was still growing during his terminal illness.

The only other men for whom heights of 8 ft or more have been reliably reported are those listed next. In six cases gigantism was followed by acromegaly, a disorder which causes an enlargement of the nose, lips, tongue, lower jaw, hands and feet, due to renewed activity by an already swollen pituitary gland, which is located at the base of the brain.

		ft	in
John F. Carroll (1932–69) of Buffalo, NY	(a)	8	7¾
John William Rogan (1871–1905) of Gallatin, Tenn	(b)	8	6
Don Koehler (1925–fl. 1980) of Denton, Mont, now living in Chicago	(c)	8	2
Bernard Coyne (1897–1921) of Anthon, Iowa	(d)	8	2
Vainö Myllyrinne (1909–63) of Helsinki, Finland	(e)	8	1.2
Patrick Cotter O'Brien (1760–1806) of Kinsale, County Cork, Ireland	(f)	8	1
"Constantine" (1872–1902) of Reutlingen, W. Germany	(g)	8	0.8
Sulaiman 'Ali Nashnush (1943–fl. 1979) of Tripoli, Libya	(h)	8	0.4
Gabriel Estevao Monjane (b 1944–fl. 1980) of Monjacaze, Mozambique	(i)	8	0

(a) Carroll was a victim of severe kypho-scoliosis (two-dimensional spinal curvature). The figure represents his height with assumed normal spinal curvature, calculated from a standing height of 8 ft 0 in, measured Oct 14, 1959. His standing height was 7 ft 8¼ in shortly before his death.

(b) Measured in a sitting position. Unable to stand owing to ankylosis (stiffening of the joints through the formation of adhesions) of the knees and hips.

(c) Some spinal curvature. Recent standing height c. 7 ft 10 in. He has a twin sister who is 5 ft 9 in tall. His father was 6 ft 2 in tall, his mother 5 ft 10 in. He lives a normal life.

(d) Eunuchoidal giant ("daddy-longlegs" syndrome). He was rejected by the US Army in 1918 when he stood 7 ft 9 in.

(e) Stood 7 ft 3½ in at the age of 21. Experienced a second phase of growth in his late thirties and may have stood 8 ft 3 in at one time.

(f) Revised height based on skeletal remeasurement in 1975.

(g) Height estimated, as both legs were amputated after they turned gangrenous. He claimed a height of 8 ft 6 in. Eunuchoidal.

(h) Operation in Rome in 1960 to correct abnormal growth was successful.

(i) Measured 7 ft 5 in at age of 16, and 7 ft 10 in Dec 1965. Eunuchoidal. Has not been anthropometrically assessed since joining a Portuguese circus, billed as 8 ft 8 in.

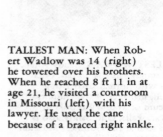

TALLEST MAN: When Robert Wadlow was 14 (right) he towered over his brothers. When he reached 8 ft 11 in at age 21, he visited a courtroom in Missouri (left) with his lawyer. He used the cane because of a braced right ankle.

In Apr 1978, a height of 8 ft 3 in was reported for Mangalsingh Sahu, 24, who entered a hospital in Bombay, India, for glandular treatment. Although not anthropometrically assessed, photographic evidence suggested his standing height to be at least 7 ft 9 in.

Tallest Twins

The tallest (identical) twins ever recorded were the Knipe brothers (b 1761) of Magherafelt, near Londonderry, N Ireland, who both measured

TALLEST TWINS: Ronnie and Donnie Creamer (20 years old) measure 6 ft 10 in or more. They live in South Carolina.

TALLEST WOMAN: Sandy Allen, who stands 7 ft 7¼ in tall, often visits with normal-sized Doug Birrell, manager of the Guinness Museum of World Records in Niagara Falls, Ont. Sandy also is often seen at the Guinness Museum on Fisherman's Wharf, San Francisco.

7 ft 2 in. The world's tallest living twins (also identical) are Ronnie and Donnie Creamer (b 1960) of Williamston, SC, who measure 6 ft 10¾ in and 6 ft 10½ in respectively.

Circus giants and others who are exhibited are normally under contract not to be measured and are, almost traditionally, billed by their promoters at heights up to 18 in in excess of their true heights. Notable examples of such exaggeration are:

Name	Dates	Country	Claimed Height ft	Claimed Height in	Actual Height ft	Actual Height in
Gerrit Bastiaansz	1620–68	Netherlands	8	3	7	1
Cornelius Magrath	1736–60	Ireland	8	6	7	2¼
Bernardo Gigli	1736–62	Italy	8	0	7	6½
Charles Byrne	1761–83	Ireland	8	4	7	7
Sam McDonald	1762–1802	Scotland	8	0	6	10
"Lolly"	1783–1816	Russia	8	4½	7	3
James Toller	1795–1819	England	8	6	7	6
Arthur Caley	1829–53	Isle of Man	8	4	7	6
Patrick Murphy	1834–62	Ireland	8	10	7	3.4
Martin van Buren Bates	1845–1919	US	7	11½	7	2½
Chang Wu-gow	1846–93	China	9	2	7	8¾
Joseph Drazel	1847–86	Germany	8	3½	7	6.5
Paul Henoch	1852–76	Germany	8	3	7	2
Franz Winkelmeier	1867–89	Austria	8	9	7	5.7
Lewis Wilkins	1873–1902	US	8	2	7	4½
John Turner	1876–1911	US	8	3	7	3
Baptiste Hugo	1879–1916	France	8	10	7	6.5
Fyodor Machnov	1880–1906	Russia	9	3½	7	9.7
Johnny Aasen	1890–1937	US	8	0	7	0
Albert Johann Kramer	b 1897	Netherlands	9	3½	7	8¼
Clifford Thompson	b 1904	US	8	8	7	5
Jacob Ehrlich, *alias* Jack Earle	1906–52	US	8	7	7	7½
Aurelio Tomaini	1912–62	US	8	4½	7	4
Henry Mullens, *alias* Henry Hite	b 1915	US	8	2	7	6¾
Rigardus Riynhout	b 1922	Netherlands	9	1½	7	8.1
William Camper	1924–42	US	8	6	7	2
Edward Evans	1924–58	England	9	3	7	8½
Poolad Gurd	b 1927	Iran	8	2	7	3
Max Palmer	b 1928	US	8	0½	7	7
Eddie Carmel*	1938–1972	Israel/US	9	0⅝	7	6⅝

Note: The actual heights given above for John Turner, Clifford Thompson and Max Palmer are estimated from photographs. Each of the other heights given in the last column above was obtained by an independent medical authority, the first deduced from evidence of his leg bones.

* Billed as "The Tallest Man on Earth" in Ringling Bros. Barnum & Bailey's Circus (1961–68) died as severe kypho-scoliosis (two-dimensional spinal curvature).

Tallest Living Woman

The tallest is **Sandy Allen** (b June 18, 1955, in Chicago), who lives in Niagara Falls, Canada. On July 14, 1977, she measured 7 ft 7¼ in at age 22, when she underwent a pituitary gland operation to inhibit further growth. A 6½-lb baby, her acromegalic growth began soon after birth. She now weighs about 440 lb and takes a size 16EEE shoe.

Tallest Giantesses

Giantesses are rarer than giants but their heights are still spectacular. The tallest woman in medical history was the acromegalic giantess **Jane ("Ginny") Bunford**, born July 26, 1895, at Bartley Green, Northfield, West Midlands, England. Her abnormal growth started at the age of 11 following a head injury, and on her 13th birthday she measured 6 ft 6 in. Shortly before her death Apr 1, 1922, she stood 7 ft 7 in tall, but she had severe kypho-scoliosis (curvature of the spine) and would have measured about 7 ft 11 in with assumed normal spinal curvature. Her skeleton, now preserved in the Anatomical Museum in the Medical School at Birmingham University, England, has a mounted height of 7 ft 4 in.

Anna Hanen Swan (1846–88) of Nova Scotia, Canada, was billed at 8 ft 1 in but actually measured 7 ft 5½ in. In London, June 17, 1871, she married Martin van Buren Bates (1845–1919), of Whitesburg, Letcher County, Ky, who stood 7 ft 2½ in, making them the tallest married couple on record. The eunuchoidal giantess Ella Ewing (b March 1872) of Gorin, Mo, was billed at 8 ft 2 in and reputedly measured 6 ft 9 in at the age of 10 (*cf.* 6 ft 5 in for Robert Wadlow at this age). She measured 7 ft 4½ in at the age of 23 and may have attained 7 ft 6 in before her death in Jan 1913.

Shortest Dwarfs

The strictures which apply to giants apply equally to dwarfs, except that exaggeration gives way to understatement. In the same way 9 ft may be regarded as the limit toward which the tallest giants tend, so 23 in must be regarded as the limit toward which the shortest mature dwarfs tend (*cf.* the average length of new-born babies is 18 to 20 in). In the case of child dwarfs their *ages* are often enhanced by their agents or managers.

There are many forms of human dwarfism. Ateliotic dwarfs, known as midgets, have essentially normal proportions but suffer from a growth hormone deficiency. Such dwarfs tended to be even shorter at a time when human stature was generally shorter due to lower nutritional standards.

The shortest mature human of whom there is independent evidence was Pauline Musters ("Princess Pauline"), a Dutch midget. She was born

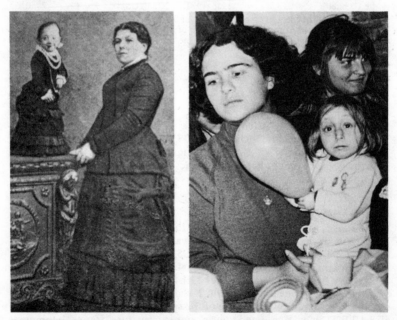

SHORTEST GIRLS: "Princess Pauline" (left) weighed 9 lb at her heaviest and reached 23.9 in at age 19. Stamatoula (right) the little Greek girl, aged 9, is destined never to grow to more than her present 19⅜ in. She weighs 4 lb 6 oz.

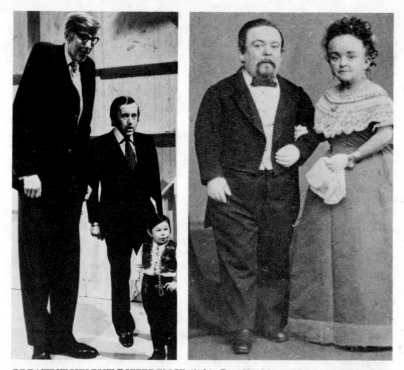

GREATEST HEIGHT DIFFERENCE (left): Don Koehler, tallest living man at 8 ft 2 in, is introduced on TV by David Frost to Mishu at 32⅝ in. The height difference was 5 ft 5⅜ in. FAMOUS MIDGET COUPLE (right): "General Tom Thumb" from Barnum's circus of the mid-1800's, with his wife.

at Ossendrecht Feb 26, 1876, and measured 12 in at birth. At the age of 9 she was 21.65 in tall and weighed only 3 lb 5 oz. She died, at the age of 19, of pneumonia, with meningitis, in New York City on March 1, 1895. Although she was billed at 19 in, she had earlier been medically measured and found to be 23.2 in tall. A *post mortem* examination showed her to be exactly 24 in (there was some elongation after death). Her mature weight varied from 7½ lb to 9 lb and her "vital statistics" were 18½–19–17, which suggests she was overweight.

Stamatoula, believed to be the survivor of twins, was left at the Lyrion Convent, Athens, in 1970. Aged 9, she is reported by Dr Paul Vlachos to be suffering from the Seckel syndrome and measures 19.68 in and weighs 4 lb 6 oz.

Shortest Male Dwarf

The shortest recorded adult male dwarf was Calvin Phillips, born in Bridgewater, Mass, Jan 14, 1791. He weighed 2 lb at birth and stopped growing at the age of 5. When he was 19 he measured 26½ in tall and weighed 12 lb with his clothes on. He died two years later, in Apr 1812, from progeria, a rare disorder characterized by dwarfism and premature senility.

The most famous midget in history was Charles Sherwood Stratton, *alias* "General Tom Thumb," born Jan 4, 1838. When he came into the clutches of the circus proprietor P. T. Barnum, his birth date was changed to Jan 4, 1832, so that when he was billed as standing 30½ in at the age of 18 he was in fact only 12 years old. He died of apoplexy on July 15, 1883 in his birthplace of Bridgeport, Ct, aged 45 (not 51), and was then 3 ft 4 in tall.

Another celebrated midget was Józef ("Count") Boruwalaski (b Nov 1739) of Poland. He measured only 8 in long at birth, growing to 14 in at the age of one year. He stood 17 in at 6 years, 21 in at 10, 25 in at 15, 35 in at 25 and 39 in at 30. He died near Durham, England, on Sept 5, 1837, aged 97.

William E. Jackson, *alias* "Major Mite," born Oct 2, 1864, in Dunedin, New Zealand, measured 9 in long and weighed 12 oz at birth. In Nov, 1880, he stood 21 in and weighed 9 lb. He died in New York City, on Dec 9, 1900, when he measured 27 in.

The shortest living mature human reported is Nruturam (b May 28, 1929), a rachitic dwarf of Naydwar, India, who measures 28 in. The circus aerobatic dancer Suleyman Eris (b Jan 24, 1955 in Turkey), was medically measured on March 3, 1977, and found to be 30.1 in tall and weighed 25 lb 2 oz. He, his brother (32.8 in) and his sister (38 in) are all primordial dwarfs.

Oldest Dwarf

There are only two centenarian dwarfs on record. The first was Miss Anne Clowes of Matlock, Derbyshire, England, who died Aug 5, 1784, at the age of 103. She was 3 ft 9 in tall and weighed 48 lb. On Apr 6, 1980, Hungarian-born Susanna Bokoyni ("Princess Susanna") of Newton, NJ, celebrated her 101st birthday. She is 3 ft 4 in tall and weighs 37 lb.

Most Variable Stature

Adam Rainer, born in 1899 in Graz, Austria, measured 3 ft 10.45 in at the age of 21. But then he suddenly started growing upwards at a rapid rate, and by 1931 he had reached 7 ft 1¾ in. He became so weak as a result that he was bedridden for the rest of his life. He died March 4, 1950, aged 51.

By constant practice in muscular manipulation of the vertebrae, the circus performer Clarence E. Willard (1882–1962) of the US was, at his prime, able to increase his apparent stature from 5 ft 10 in to 6 ft 4 in at will.

Tallest Tribes

The tallest major tribe is the Tutsi (also called Watussi), Nilotic herdsmen of Rwanda and Burundi, Central Africa, whose young males *average* 5 ft 10¾ in in height. The Tehuelches of Patagonia, long regarded as of gigantic stature (i.e. 7–8 ft) have in fact an average height (males) of 5 ft 10 in. The Montenegrins of Yugoslavia, with a male average of 5 ft 10 in (in the town of Trebinje the average height is 6 ft) compare with the men of Sutherland, South Africa, at 5 ft 9½ in.

Shortest Tribes

The smallest pygmies are the Mbuti, with an average height of 4 ft 6 in for men and 4 ft 5 in for women, with some groups averaging only 4 ft 4

OLDEST DWARF: At 100 years old, Princess Susanna was 3 ft 4 in tall.

HEAVIEST MAN: Robert Earl Hughes at 1,069 lb holds the record for the greatest undisputed weight.

in for men and 4 ft 1 in for women. They live in the forests near the river Ituri in the Congo (Kinshasa), Africa.

WEIGHT

Lightest Humans

The lightest recorded human on record was Lucia Zarate (b San Carlos, Mexico, Jan 2, 1863, d Oct 1889), an emaciated ateliotic dwarf of 26½ in who weighed 4.7 lb at the age of 17. She "fattened up" to 13 lb by her 20th birthday. At birth she had weighed 2½ lb.

The thinnest recorded adults of normal height are those suffering from Simmonds' disease (hypophyseal cachexia). Losses up to 65% of the original body weight have been recorded in females, with a "low" of 45 lb in the case of Emma Shaller (b St Louis, Mo, July 8, 1868, d Oct 4, 1890) who stood 5 ft 2 in tall.

Edward C. Hagner (1892–1962), *alias* Eddie Masher, is alleged to have weighed only 48 lb at a height of 5 ft 7 in. He was also known as "the Skeleton Dude." In Aug 1825 the biceps measurement of Claude-Ambroise Seurat (b Apr 10, 1797, d Apr 6, 1826), of Troyes, France, was 4 in and the distance between his back and his chest was less than 3 in. According to one report, he stood 5 ft 7½ in and weighed 78 lb, but in another account was described as 5 ft 4 in and only 36 lb.

It was recorded that the American exhibitionist Rosa Lee Plemons, (b 1873) weighed 27 lb at the age of 18. In March 1978 the death was reported of an anorexic 47-year-old woman in Hounslow, England, who scaled only 59 lb at a height of 5 ft 2 in.

Heaviest Men

The greatest weight ever attributed to a human has been 1187 lb, in the case of Francis John Lang (b 1934) *alias* Michael Walker of Clinton, Iowa. He could not be admitted for treatment for inflammation of the gall bladder to the Veteran's Administration Hospital, Houston, Tex because of the impossibility of getting him through the doors. He was treated in a trailer in the car park and discharged Jan 5, 1972 unweighed but estimated to be between 900 and 1000 lb. The more precise weight above was claimed for him, while suffering from drug-induced bulimia, in the summer of 1971 when he was working with the Christian Farms of Killeen, Tex. There is, however, no independent corroboration for the precise upper weight quoted, although photographic evidence suggests the weight was possibly reliable. By Feb 1980 Lang (6 ft 2 in) had reduced to 369 lb.

Jon Brower Minnoch (b 1941) of Bainbridge Island, Wash, was carried, immobile, into the University Hospital, Seattle on plywood planking in March 1978. Dr. Robert Schwartz, the endocrinological consultant, estimated (from extrapolating his intake and elimination rates) that he weighed 1400 lb and "probably more." By July 1979 he was down to 475 lb after nearly 16 months on a 1200-calorie-per-day diet.

The highest undisputed weight for a human remains at 1069 lb in Feb 1958 for 6-foot-0½-inch tall Robert Earl Hughes (b June 4, 1926), Monticello, Mo. An 11¼-lb baby, he weighed 203 lb at 6 years, 378 lb at 10, 546 lb at 13, 693 lb at 18, 896 lb at 25, and 945 lb at 27. He weighed 1041 lb at the time of his death. His claimed waist of 122 in, his chest of 124 in and his upper arm of 40 in were the greatest on record. Hughes died of uremia (condition caused by retention of urinary matter in the blood) in a trailer at Bremen, Ind, July 10, 1958, aged 32, and was buried in Binville Cemetery, near Mt Sterling, Ill. His coffin, as large as a piano case measuring 7 ft by 4 ft 4 in and weighing more than 1100 lb, had to be lowered by crane. It was once claimed by a commercial interest that Hughes had weighed 1500 lb—a 40% exaggeration.

The only other men for whom weights of 800 lb or more have been *reliably* reported are listed below:

Mills Darden (1798–1857) US (7ft 6 in)	1,020 lb
John Hanson Craig (1856–94) US (6 ft 5 in)	907 (b)
Arthur Knorr (1914–60) US (6 ft 1 in)	900 (a)
Toubi (b 1946) Cameroon	857½
T. A. Valenzuela (1895–1937) Mexico (5 ft 11 in)	850

(a) Gained 300 lb in the last 6 months of his life.
(b) Won $1,000 in a "Bonny Baby" contest in New York City in 1858.

Heaviest Twins

The heaviest were the performers Billy Leon and Benny Loyd McCrary, *alias* Billy and Benny McGuire (b Dec 7, 1946) of Hendersonville, NC. In Nov, 1978, they were weighed at 743 lb (Billy) and 723 lb (Benny) and had 84-in waists. Billy died of heart failure on July 13, 1979,

HEAVIEST TWINS: Benny and Billy McGuire weighed almost 1,500 lb together. They were normal weight at birth.

in Niagara Falls, Canada, after falling from his mini-bike (shown in photo). He was buried in a square coffin with a total weight of over 1000 lb in Hendersonville. A hydraulic lift was needed to lower the coffin to its final resting place. After one 6-week slimming course in a hospital, they emerged weighing 5 lb more each.

Heaviest Woman

The heaviest ever recorded was the late Mrs Percy Pearl Washington (b Louisiana, 1926) who died in a hospital in Milwaukee, Wis, Oct 9, 1972. The hospital scales registered only up to 800 lb, but she was believed to weigh about 880 lb. The previous weight record for a woman was set 84 years earlier at 850 lb although a wholly unsubstantiated report exists of a woman, Mrs Ida Maitland (1898–1932) of Springfield, Miss, who reputedly weighed 911 lb.

A more reliable and better documented case was that of Mrs Flora Mae (or May) Jackson (*née* King), a 5-ft-9-in black woman born in 1930 at Shuqualak, Miss. She weighted 10 lb at birth; 267 lb at the age of 11; 621 lb at 25; and 840 lb shortly before her death in Meridian, Miss, on Dec 9, 1965. She was known in show business as "Baby Flo."

Greatest Weight Differential

The greatest recorded for a married couple is 922 lb in the case of Mills Darden (1,020 lb) of North Carolina and his wife Mary (98 lb). Despite her diminutiveness, however, Mrs Darden bore her husband at least three (and possibly five) children before her death in 1837.

Slimming

The greatest recorded slimming feat was that of William J. Cobb (b 1926), *alias* "Happy Humphrey," a professional wrestler of Macon, Ga. It was reported in July 1965, that he had reduced from 802 lb to 232 lb, a

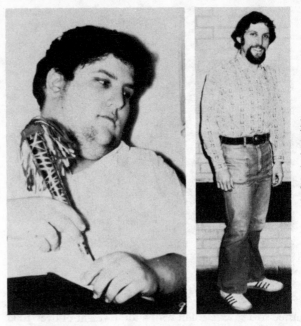

FASTEST
WEIGHT LOSS:
Paul Kimelman,
who weighed
487 lb, lost 357
lb in 8 months,
ending at 130
lb.

loss of 570 lb, in 3 years. His waist measurement declined from 101 to 44 in. In Oct 1973, "Happy" was reported back to a normal 650 lb.

The US circus fat lady Mrs Celesta Geyer (b 1901), *alias* Dolly Dimples, reduced from 553 lb to 152 lb 1950–51, a loss of 401 lb in 14 months. Her vital statistics diminished *pari passu* from 79–84–84 to a *svelte* 34–28–36. Her book "How I Lost 400 lb" was not a best seller. In Dec 1967, she was reportedly down to 110 lb.

The speed record for slimming was established by Paul M. Kimelman, 21, of Pittsburgh, Pa, who from Dec 25, 1966, to Aug 1967, went on a crash diet of 300 to 600 calories per day to reduce from 487 lb to 130 lb, a total loss of 357 lb. He has now stabilized at 175 lb. Between Feb 4th and 8th, 1951, Mrs Gertrude Levandowski of Burnips, Mich, successfully underwent a series of operations to reduce her weight from 616 lb to 308 lb.

Weight Gaining

A probable record for gaining weight was set by Arthur Knorr (b May 17, 1914), who died July 7, 1960, aged 46, in Reseda, Calif. He gained 300 lb in the last 6 months of his life and weighed 900 lb when he died. Miss Doris James of San Francisco is alleged to have gained 325 lb in the 12 months before her death in Aug 1965, aged 38, at a weight of 675 lb. She was only 5 ft 2 in tall.

2. ORIGINS

EARLIEST MAN

Earliest Primate

The earliest known primates appeared in the Paleocene period about 80 million years ago. The sub-order of higher primates, called Simiae (or Anthropoidea), evolved from the catarrhine or old-world sect more than 40 million years later in the Lower Oligocene period. During the Middle and Upper Oligocene the super-family Hominoidea emerged. This contains three accepted families, *viz.* Hominidae (bipedal, ground-dwelling man or near man), Pongidae (brachiating forest apes) and Oreopithecidae. The earliest known hominoid (man-like) fossil found is the *Oligopithecus savagei*, found in El Faiyum, Egypt, dated to *c.* 33 million years ago.

Scale of Time

If the age of the earth-moon system (latest estimate at least 4,700 million years) is likened to a single year, Handy Man appeared on the scene at about 8:35 p.m., on Dec 31, Britain's earliest known inhabitants arrived at about 11:32 p.m., the Christian era began about 13 seconds before midnight and the life span of a 114-year-old man (see *Oldest Centenarian*) would be about three-quarters of a second. Present calculations indicate that the sun's increased heat, as it becomes a "red giant," will make life insupportable on earth in about 10,000 million years. Meanwhile there may well be colder epicycles. The period of 1,000 million years is sometimes referred to as an eon.

Earliest Hominid (Near Man)

The characteristics of the Hominidae, such as a large brain, very fully distinguish them from any of the other Hominoidea. Evidence published in Aug 1969, indicated that *Ramapithecus,* discovered by G. Edward Lewis at Siwalik Hills in northern India in 1932, can be dated from 8 million to 13 million years ago.

Earliest Genus Homo (True Man)

The greatest age attributed to fossils of the genus *Homo* is for the remains of 8 adults and 3 children discovered in the summer of 1975 at Laetolil, Tanzania, by Dr Mary Leakey, and dated by the University of Calif at Berkeley to between 3,350,000 and 3,750,000 BC. An arm-bone fragment from Kanapoi has been tentatively regarded as from *Homo* and has been dated from *c.* 4 million years ago.

The most complete of the earliest skeletons of *Homo* is that of "Lucy" (40% complete) found by Dr Donald C. Johanson and named *Australopithecus afarensis,* found in the Afar region of Ethiopia in Nov 1974, and dating 3–4 million years before the present day.

Seven proto-human footprints dating from 1.5 million years ago were reported from Lake Turkana, Kenya, in Nov 1979. They were 10½ in long.

Earliest Homo Sapiens

Man (*Homo sapiens*) is a species in the sub-family Homininae of the family Hominidae of the super-family Hominoidea of the suborder Simiae (or Anthropoidea) of the order Primates of the infra-class Eutheria of the sub-class Theria of the class Mammalia of the sub-phylum Vertebrata (Craniata) of the phylum Chordata of the sub-kingdom Metazoa of the animal kingdom.

The earliest recorded remains of the species *Homo sapiens*, variously dated from 300,000 to 450,000 years ago, in the middle Pleistocene period, were discovered Aug 24, 1965, by Dr László Vértes in a limestone quarry at Vértasszöllös, about 30 miles west of Budapest, Hungary. The remains, designated *Homo sapiens palaeo-hungaricus*, comprised an almost complete occipital bone, part of a skull with an estimated cranial capacity of nearly 1,400 cc (85 cu in).

Earliest man in the Americas dates from at least 50,000 BC and "more probably 100,000 BC" according to the late Dr Louis Leakey after the examination of some hearth stones found in the Mojave Desert, Calif, and announced in Oct, 1970. The earliest human relic is a skull found in the area of Los Angeles, dated Dec, 1970, to be from 22,000 BC.

3. LONGEVITY

Oldest Centenarian

No single subject is more obscured by vanity, deceit, falsehood and deliberate fraud than the extremes of human longevity. Extreme claims are generally made on behalf of the very aged rather than *by* them.

Many hundreds of claims throughout history have been made for persons living well into their second century and some, insulting to the intelligence, for people living even into their third. The facts are that centenarians surviving beyond their 110th year are of the extremest rarity and the present absolute limit of proven human longevity does not admit of anyone living to celebrate a 116th birthday.

It is highly significant that in Sweden, where alone proper and thorough official investigations follow the death of every allegedly very aged citizen, none has been found to have surpassed 110 years. The most reliably pedigreed large group of people in the world, the British peerage, has, after ten centuries, produced only two peers who reached their 100th birthdays, and only one reached his 101st. However, this is possibly not unconnected with the extreme draftiness of many of their residences and the amount of lead in the game they consume.

Scientific research into extreme old age reveals that the correlation between the claimed density of centenarians in a country and its regional illiteracy is 0.83 ± 0.03. In late life, very old people often tend to advance their ages at the rate of about 17 years per decade. This was nicely corroborated by an analysis of the 1901 and 1911 censuses of England and Wales. Early claims must necessarily be without the elementary corroboration of birth dates. England was among the earliest of all countries to introduce local registers (1538) and official birth registration (July 1, 1837), which was made fully compulsory only in 1874. Even in the US, 45% of births occurring between 1890 and 1920 were unregistered.

OLD BEFORE HIS TIME: Charlie Smith convinced the Social Security Board that he was born in 1842, but it turned out when his bones were analyzed after death that he was 99 5/6 years old when he died in 1979.

Charlie Smith of Bartow, Fla obtained a Social Security card in 1955 when claiming to have been born in Liberia on July 4, 1842. The US Dept. of Health, Education and Welfare stated that they were "unable to disclose the type of evidence used" to determine Mr. Smith's age because such disclosure "would infringe on the confidentiality of the individual's record." He celebrated what he reckoned to be his 137th birthday on July 4, 1979. However, a reference to the county records at Arcadia, Florida (Book 2, page 392) revealed a marriage contracted at age 35 Jan 8, 1910, and hence an exaggeration of at least 33 years. He died Oct 7, 1979. According to research by A. Ross Eckler, he was most probably two months short of his 100th birthday.

Several celebrated super-centenarians are believed to have been double lives (father and son, relations with the same names or successive bearers of a title). The most famous example is Christian Jakobsen Drackenberg, allegedly born in Stavanger, Norway, Nov 18, 1626, and died in Aarhus, Denmark, aged seemingly 145 years 326 days on Oct 9, 1772. A number of instances have been commercially sponsored, while a fourth category of recent claims are those made for political ends, such as the 100 citizens of the Russian Soviet Federated Socialist Republic (population about 132,000,000 at mid-1967), claimed in March 1960 to be between 120 and 156. From data on documented centenarians, actuaries have shown that only one 115-year life can be expected in 2,100 million lives (cf. world population was estimated to be 4,205 million at mid-1978).

The height of credulity was reached May 5, 1933, when a news agency solemnly filed a story from China with a Peking dateline that Li Chung-yun, the "oldest man on earth," born in 1680, had just died aged 256 years (sic). Recently the most extreme case of longevity claimed has been 168 years for Shirali Mislimov of Azerbaijan, USSR, who died Sept 2,

1973 and was reputedly born on March 26, 1805. No interview with this man has ever been permitted to any Western journalist or scientist. He was said to have celebrated the 100th birthday of his third wife, Hartun, in 1966 and that of one of his grandchildren in Aug, 1973. It was reported in 1954 that in the Abkhasian Republic of Georgia, USSR, where aged citizens are invested with an almost saint-like status, 2.58% of the population was aged over 90—some 25 times the proportion in the US.

Dr Zhores A. Medvedev, the exiled Soviet gerontologist, on April 30, 1974, in Washington, DC, referring to the claims of the USSR, stated: "The whole phenomenon looks like a falsification . . . He (Stalin) liked the idea that (other) Georgians lived to be 100 or more . . . Local officials tried hard to find more and more cases for Stalin." He points out that the *average* life span in the regions claiming the highest incidence of centenarians is lower than the USSR's average, and that the number of centenarians claimed in the Caucasus has declined rapidly, from 8,000 in 1950 to 4,500 in 1970. Dr I. M. Spector, of the Institute of Traumatology, Kazan, USSR, quoted the maximum lifespan of man in Apr 1974 as "110–115 years," though Dr Medvedev in Dec 1977, put the *proven* limit in the USSR as low as 108 years.

After 4 years the Andean valley of Vilcabamba in Ecuador has ceased to be the source of highly publicized and uncritical reports about very aged humans. These, it was said, lived up to 25 years beyond the so far acceptable limit of about 115 years. The discovery by Mazess and Forman was published in March 1978 that inhabitants had been pointing to baptismal entries of their fathers, and even their grandfathers, as their own reduced the age of the valley's oldest man from 140 to 96. The lucrative income from tourism is expected to decline to a similar degree.

The 1900 US Federal census for Crawfish Springs Militia District of Walker County, Ga, records an age of 77 for a Mark Thrash. If the Mark Thrash (reputedly born in Ga in Dec 1822) who died near Chattanooga, Tenn on Dec 17, 1943, was he, and the age attributed being accepted, then he would have survived for 121 years.

The national records in the table on the next page can be taken as authentic:

In the face of authenticated data the claim published in the April, 1961 issue of the Soviet Union's *Vestnik Statistiki* ("Statistical Herald") that there were 224 male and 368 female Soviet citizens aged in excess of 120 recorded at the census of Jan 15, 1959, indicates a reliance on hearsay rather than evidence. Official Soviet insistence in 1961 on the unrivalled longevity of the country's citizenry is curious in view of the fact that the 592 persons in their unique "over 120" category must have spent at least the first 78 years of their prolonged lives under Czarism. It has recently been suggested that the extreme ages claimed by men in Georgia, USSR, are the result of attempts to avoid military service when younger, by assuming the identities of older men.

AUTHENTICATED NATIONAL LONGEVITY RECORDS

	Years	Days		Born		Died	
Japan	115	0	Shigechiyo Izumi	June 29, 1865	*fl.*	June 29, 1980	
US (d)	113	214	Delina Filkins (*née* Ecker)	May 4, 1815		Dec 4, 1928	
Canada (a)	113	124	Pierre Joubert	July 15, 1701		Nov 16, 1814	
UK (c)	112	39	Alice Stevenson	July 10, 1861		Aug 18, 1973	
Morocco	112	+	El Hadj Mohammed el Mokri (Grand Vizier)	1844		Sept 16, 1957	
Ireland	111	327	The Hon. Katherine Plunket	Nov 22, 1820		Oct 14, 1932	
France	111 *c.*	210	Virginie Duhem	Aug 1866		May 1, 1978	
S. Africa (b)	111	151	Johanna Booyson	Jan 17, 1857		June 16, 1968	
Czechoslovakia	111	+	Marie Bernatkova	Oct 22, 1857		*fl.* Oct 1968	
Channel Islands	110	321	Margaret Ann Neve (*née* Harvey)	May 18, 1792		Apr 4, 1903	
Northern Ireland	110	234	Elizabeth Watkins (Mrs)	Mar 10, 1863		Oct 31, 1973	
Yugoslavia	110	150+	Demitrius Philipovitch	Mar 9, 1818		*fl.* Aug 1928	
Netherlands	110	113	Geert Adrians Boomgaard	Sept 23, 1788		Feb 3, 1899	
Australia (f)	110	39	Ada Sharp (Mrs)	Apr 6, 1861		May 15, 1971	
USSR (i)	110	+	Khasako Dzugayev	Aug 7, 1860		*fl.* Aug 1970	
Tasmania	109	179	Mary Ann Crow (Mrs)	Feb 2, 1836		July 31, 1945	
Italy	109	179	Rosalia Spoto	Aug 25, 1847		Feb 20, 1957	
Scotland	109	14	Rachel MacArthur (Mrs)	Nov 26, 1827		Dec 10, 1936	
Norway	109	+	Marie Olsen (Mrs)	May 1, 1850		*fl.* May 1959	
Belgium	108	327	Mathilda Vertommen-Hellemans	Aug 12, 1868		July 4, 1977	
Germany (g)	108	128	Luise Schwarz	Sept 27, 1849		Feb 2, 1958	
Portugal (e)	108	+	Maria Luisa Jorge	June 7, 1859		*fl.* July 1967	
Finland	107	221	Amalia Wellenius (Mrs)	Aug 6, 1867		Mar 24, 1975	
Sweden	107	94	Anna Johansson	Nov 21, 1865		Feb 23, 1973	
Austria	106	231	Anna Migschitz	Feb 3, 1850		Nov 1, 1956	
Spain (h)	106	14	José Palido	Mar 15, 1866		Mar 29, 1972	
Malaysia	106	+	Hassan Bin Yusoff	Aug 14, 1865		*fl.* Jan 1972	
Isle of Man	105	221	John Kneen	Nov 12, 1852		June 9, 1958	

(a) Mrs Ellen Carroll died in North River, Newfoundland, Canada, Dec 8, 1943, reputedly aged 115 years 49 days.

(b) Mrs Susan Johanna Deporter of Port Elizabeth, South Africa, was reputedly 114 years old when she died Aug 4, 1954. Mrs Sarah Lawrence of Capetown, South Africa, was reputedly 112 on June 3, 1968.

(c) London-born Miss Isabella Shepheard was allegedly 115 years old when she died at St. Asaph, North Wales, Nov 20, 1948, but her actual age was believed to have been 109 years 90 days. Charles Alfred Nuñez Arnold died in Liverpool, England, Sept 15, 1941, reputedly 112 years 66 days (based on a baptismal claim in London on Nov 10, 1829). Mrs Elizabeth Cornish (*née* Veale), who was buried at Stratton, Cornwall, March 10, 1691 or 1692, was reputedly baptized on Oct 16, 1578, 112 or 113 years 4 months earlier.

(d) Ex-slave Mrs Martha Graham died in Fayetteville, NC, June 25, 1959, reputedly aged 117 or 118. Census researches by Eckler show that she was seemingly born in Dec 1844, and hence aged 114 years 6 months. Mrs Rena Glover Brailsford died in Summerton, SC, Dec 6, 1977, reputedly aged 118 years.

(e) Senhora Jesuina da Conçeicão of Lisbon was reputedly 113 years old when she died June 10, 1965.

(f) Reginald Beck of Sydney was allegedly 111 years old when he died Apr 13, 1928.

(g) Friedrich Sadowski of Heidelberg reputedly celebrated his 111th birthday Oct 31, 1936. Franz Joseph Eder died in Spitzburg May 3, 1911, allegedly aged 116.

(h) Juana Ortega Villarin, Madrid, was allegedly 112 years in Feb 1962. Ana Maria Parraga of Murcia was reportedly 107 in Nov 1969.

(i) There are allegedly 21,700 centenarians in the USSR compared with 7,000 in the US. Of these, 21,000 are ascribed to the Georgian SSR, or one out of every 232 people. In July 1962 it was reported that 128, mostly male, resided in the one village of Medini.

OLDEST MAN: On June 29, 1980, Shegechiyo Izumi of Japan celebrated his 115th birthday. Here he is having tea, but he prefers hard liquor, drinks ½ pint every night before he goes to sleep at 8. He wakes at 7 and takes the dog for a walk.

Oldest Authentic Centenarian

The greatest *authenticated* age to which any human has ever lived is a unique 115th birthday in the case of Shigechiyo Izumi of Asomon, Tokunoshima Island, Japan. He was born June 29, 1865, and recorded as a 6-year-old in Japan's first census of 1871. He watches television and says the best way to a long life is "not to worry."

4. REPRODUCTIVITY

MOTHERHOOD

Most Children

The greatest officially recorded number of children produced by a mother is 69 by the first of the 2 wives of Feodor Vassilyev (b 1707–*fl.* 1782), a peasant from Shuya, 150 miles east of Moscow, who, in 27 confinements, gave birth to 16 pairs of twins, 7 sets of triplets and 4 sets of quadruplets. The children, of whom almost all survived to their majority, were born in the period *c.* 1725–1765. At least 67 survived infancy. The case was reported to Moscow by the Monastery of Nikolskiy Feb 27, 1782. Empress Ekaterina II (The Great) (1762–96) was reputed to have evinced interest.

Currently the highest reliably reported figure is a 32nd child born to Raimundo Carnauba and his wife Madalena, of Ceilandia, Brazil. She was married at 13 and so far has had 24 sons and 8 daughters. In May 1972, the mother said, "They have given us a lot of work and worry but they are worth it," and the father, "I don't know why people make such a fuss." The figures given here are tentative, however, since no two published interviews with this family produce entirely consistent data.

Oldest Mother

Medical literature contains extreme but unauthenticated cases of septuagenarian mothers such as Mrs Ellen Ellis, aged 72, of Four Crosses, Clwyd, Wales, who allegedly produced a stillborn 13th child May 15, 1776, in her 46th year of marriage. Many cases are cover-ups for illegitimate grandchildren. The oldest recorded mother of whom there is certain evidence is Mrs Ruth Alice Kistler (*née* Taylor), formerly Mrs Shepard, of Portland, Ore. She was born at Wakefield, Mass, June 11, 1899, and gave birth to a daughter, Suzan, in Glendale, Calif, Oct 18, 1956, when her age was 57 years 129 days.

The incidence of quinquagenarian births varies widely, with the highest purported rate being in Albania (with nearly 5,500 per million) compared with 2 per million in England.

Descendants

In polygamous countries, the number of a person's descendants soon becomes incalculable. The last Sharifian Emperor of Morocco, Moulay Ismail (1672–1727), known as "The Bloodthirsty," was reputed to have fathered a total of 548 sons and 340 daughters.

Capt. Wilson Kettle (b 1860) of Grand Bay, Port Aux Basques, Newfoundland, Canada, died Jan 25, 1963, aged 102, leaving 11 children by 2 wives, 65 grandchildren, 201 great-grandchildren, and 305 great-great-grandchildren, a total of 582 living descendants. Mrs Johanna Booyson (see table, page 27), of Belfast, Transvaal, was estimated to have 600 living descendants in South Africa in Jan 1968.

Multiple Great-Grandparents

Theoretically a great-great-great-great-grandparent is a possibility, al-

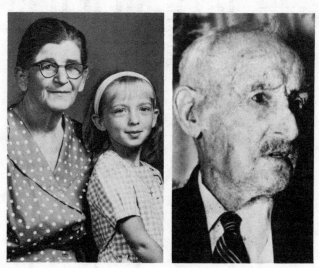

OLDEST MOTHER (left): Ruth Kistler first gave birth at age 57.
MOST DESCENDANTS (right): Capt Wilson Kettle had 582 when he died at age 102.

MULTIPLE BIRTHS

Highest number reported at single birth (Decaplets): 10 (2 male, 8 female), Bacacay, Brazil, Apr 22, 1946 (also report from Spain, 1924, and China, May 12, 1936).

Highest number medically recorded (Nonuplets): 9 (5 male, 4 female), to Mrs Geraldine Broderick at Royal Hospital, Sydney, Australia, June 13, 1971. 2 males were stillborn. Richard (12 oz) survived 6 days.
9 (all died), to patient at University of Penn, Philadelphia, May 29, 1972.
9 (all died) reported from Bagerhat, Bangladesh, c. May 1977, to 30-year-old mother.

Highest number surviving: 6 out of 6 sextuplets (3 males, 3 females), to Mrs Susan Rosenkowitz (*née* Scoones) at Capetown, South Africa, Jan 1, 1974. In order of birth they were: David, Nicolette, Jason, Emma, Grant and Elizabeth. They totaled 24 lb 1 oz.

Quintuplets (Heaviest): 25 lb to Mrs Lui Saulien, Chekiang, China, June 7, 1953.
25 lb to Mrs Kamalammal, Pondicherry, India, Dec 30, 1956.

(Most sets): No recorded case of more than a single set.

Quadruplets (Heaviest): 21 lb 9 oz to Mrs David Bergquist, Mountain Iron, Minn at University of Minn Hospital (4 girls), Sept 7, 1975.

(Most sets): 4, to Mme Feodor Vassilyev (d *ante* 1770), of Shuya, Russia.

Triplets (Heaviest): 26 lb 6 oz (unconfirmed), Iranian case (2 male, 1 female), March 18, 1968.

(Most sets): 15, to Maddalena Granata (1839—*fl.* 1886), Nocera Superiore, Italy.

Twins (Heaviest): 35 lb 8 oz (live-born), Warren's case (2 males, 17 lb 8 oz and 18 lb), reported in *The Lancet* from Derbyshire, England, Dec 6, 1884.
27 lb 12 oz (surviving), 14 lb and 13 lb 12 oz, to Mrs J. P. Haskin, Fort Smith, Ark, Feb 20, 1924.

(Most sets): 16, to Mme Vassilyev (see above).
15, to Mrs Mary Jonas (d Dec 4, 1899), of Chester, England—all sets were boy and girl.
Mrs Barbara Zulu of Barbeton, South Africa, bore 3 sets of girls and 3 mixed sets in 7 years (1967–73).

though, in practice, countries in which young mothers are common generally have a low life expectancy.

At least eleven cases of great-great-great-grandparents have been reported in the last 20 years. Of these cases the youngest person to learn that her great-granddaughter had become a grandmother was Mrs Ann V. Weirick (1888–1978) of Paxtonville, Pa, who received news of her great-great-great-grandson Matthew Stork (b Sept 9, 1976) when aged only 88. She died Jan 6, 1978.

Most Living Ascendants

Micheal Levion Moss (b March 23, 1979) of Underwood, Minn, had a full set of grandparents and great-grandparents, and three great-great-grandparents, making 17 direct ascendants.

Multiple Births

It was announced by Dr Gennaro Montanino of Rome that he had removed the fetuses of 10 girls and 5 boys from the womb of a 35-year-old housewife July 22, 1971. A fertility drug was responsible for this unique and unsurpassed instance of quindecaplets.

LIGHTEST TWINS (left): the Stimsons were 16 oz and 19 oz. SIAMESE TWINS (right): The Bunkers were the first well-known twins.

Lightest Twins

The lighest recorded birth weight for surviving twins is 2 lb 3 oz in the case of Mary (16 oz) and Margaret (19 oz) born to Mrs Florence Stimson of Peterborough, England, delivered by Dr Macaulay, Aug 16, 1931.

Oldest Twins

The oldest recorded twins were Eli and John Phipps, born Feb 14, 1803, in Affinghton, Virginia. Eli died at the age of 108 years 9 days Feb 23, 1911, in Hennessey, Okla, at which time John was still living, in Shenandoah, Iowa. The chances of identical twins both reaching 100 are said to be one in 700 million.

"Siamese" Twins

Conjoined twins derived this name from the celebrated Chang and Eng Bunker, born at Maklong, Thailand (Siam), May 11, 1811. They were joined by a cartilaginous band at the chest and married in Apr 1843 the Misses Sarah and Adelaide Yates. They fathered 10 and 12 children respectively. They died within three hours of each other Jan 17, 1874, aged 62.

The earliest successful separation of Siamese twins was performed on Prisna and Napit Atkinson (b May 1953 in Thailand) by Dr Dragstedt at the University of Chicago March 29, 1955.

The rarest form of conjoined twins is Dicephales tetrabrachius dipus (two heads, four arms and two legs) of which only two examples are known today. They are the pair Masha and Dasha, born on Jan 4, 1950, in the USSR, and an unidentified pair separated in a 10-hour operation June 23, 1977, in Washington, DC.

Oldest Surviving Triplets

The longest-lived triplets on record were Faith, Hope, and Charity Caughlin, born March 27, 1868, in Marlboro, Mass. Mrs (Ellen) Hope Daniels was the first to die, March 2, 1962, when 93.

Fastest Triplet Birth

The fastest recorded natural birth of triplets has been 2 minutes in the case of Mrs James E. Duck of Memphis, Tenn (Bradley, Christopher and Carmon) March 21, 1977.

BABIES

Heaviest Babies

The heaviest normal newborn child reported in modern times was a boy weighing 24 lb 4 oz, born June 3, 1961, to Mrs Saadet Cor of Cegham, southern Turkey. It was revealed in Jan 1978, however, that although this report was relayed by a major news agency, it cannot be considered reliable.

Mrs Anna Bates, *née* Swan (*see* Tallest Giantesses) produced a baby weighing 23 lb 12 oz according to a report in the *New York Medical Record* of March 22, 1879. A deformed baby weighing 29¼ lb was born in May 1939 in a hospital at Effingham, Ill but only lived for two hours.

Most Bouncing Baby

The most bouncing baby on record was probably James Weir (1819–21) whose headstone in the Old Parish Cemetery, Wishaw, Strathclyde, Scotland, lists him at 112 lb 3 ft 4 in in height, and 39 in around the waist at the age of 13 months.

Therese Parentean, who died in Rouyn, Quebec, Canada, aged 9, May 11, 1936, weighed 340 lb.

Lightest

The lowest birth weight for a surviving infant, of which there is definite evidence, is 10 oz in the case of Marion Chapman, born June 5, 1938, in South Shields, northwest England. She was 12¼ in long. By her first birthday her weight had increased to 13 lb 14 oz. She was born unattended, and was nursed by Dr D. A. Shearer, who fed her hourly through a fountain pen filler. Her weight on her 21st birthday was 106 lb.

The smallest viable baby reported born in the US has been Jacqueline Benson, who was born in Palatine, Ill, Feb 20, 1936, weighing 12 oz.

A weight of 8 oz was reported on March 20, 1938, for a baby born prematurely to Mrs John Womack, after she had been knocked down by a truck in East St. Louis, Ill. The baby was taken alive to St. Mary's Hospital, but further information is lacking. On Feb 23, 1952, it was reported that a 6 oz baby only 6½ in in length lived for 12 hours in a hospital in Indianapolis. A twin was stillborn.

Longest Pregnancy

Claims up to 413 days have been widely reported, but accurate data are bedevilled by the increasing use of oral contraceptive pills, which is a cause of amenorrhea. Some women on becoming pregnant erroneously add some preceding periodless months to their pregnancy. In the pre-pill era, English law had accepted pregnancies with extremes of 174 days (1939), and 349 days (1949).

Coincidental Birth Dates

The only verified example of a family producing five single children with coincidental birthdays is that of Catherine (1952), Carol (1953), Charles (1956), Claudia (1961) and Cecilia (1966), born to Ralph and Carolyn Cummins of Clintwood, Va, all on Feb 20th.

The random odds against five such births occurring singly on the same date would be 1 to 17,797,577,730—almost 4 times the world's population.

Most Proximate Births

Gloria Kuehn of Lemay, Mo gave birth to a daughter, Amy Elizabeth, June 9, 1978, and a son, Gregory Charles, Jan 19, 1979, only 224 days later.

Earliest Test Tube Baby

Louise Brown (5 lb 12 oz) was delivered by Caesarean section from Lesley Brown, 31, in Oldham General Hospital, Lancashire, England, at 11:47 p.m. July 25, 1978. She was externally conceived Nov 10, 1977.

5. PHYSIOLOGY AND ANATOMY

Hydrogen (63%) and oxygen (25.5%) are the commonest of the 24 elements in the human body. In 1972, four more trace elements were added—fluorine, silicon, tin and vanadium. The "essentiality" of nickel has not yet been finally pronounced upon.

Longest Bones

Excluding a variable number of sesamoids, there are 206 bones in the human body. The thigh bone or *femur* is the longest. It constitutes usually 27½% of a person's stature, and may be expected to be 19¾ in long in a 6-ft-tall man. The longest recorded bone was the *femur* of the German giant Constantine, who died in Mons, Belgium, March 30, 1902, aged 30. It measured 29.9 in. The *femur* of Robert Wadlow, the tallest man ever recorded, measured an estimated 29½ in.

Smallest Bones

The *stapes* or stirrup bone, one of the three auditory ossicles in the middle ear, is the smallest human bone, measuring from 2.6 to 3.4 mm (0.10 to 0.17 in) in length and weighing from 2.0 to 4.3 mg (0.03 to 0.065 of a grain).

Largest Muscles

Muscles normally account for 40% of the body weight and the bulkiest of the 639 muscles in the human body is the *gluteus maximus* or buttock muscle, which extends the thigh.

Smallest Muscles

The smallest muscle is the *stapedius,* which controls the *stapes* (see above), an auditory ossicle in the middle ear, and which is less than 1/20th in in length.

Smallest Waists

Queen Catherine de Medici (1519–89) decreed a standard waist measurement of 13 in for ladies of the French court. This was at a time when females were more diminutive. The smallest recorded waist among women of normal stature in the 20th century is a reputed 13 in in the cases of the French actress Mlle Polaire (1881–1939) and Mrs Ethel Granger (b Apr 12, 1905) of Peterborough, England, who reduced from a natural 22 in over the period 1929–39.

Largest Chest Measurements

The largest chest measurements are among endomorphs (those with a tendency toward globularity). In the extreme case of Robert Earl Hughes of Monticello, Mo (the heaviest recorded human), this was reportedly 124 in, but in the light of his known height and weight a figure of 104 in would be more supportable.

Among muscular subjects (mesomorphs) of normal height *expanded* chest measurements above 56 in are extremely rare. Louis Cyr (1865–1912), the famous French-Canadian strongman, had a chest measurement of 59 in at his best weight of 300 lb. Arnold Schwarzenegger (b 1948) of Graz, Austria, former Mr Universe and called "the most perfectly developed man in the history of the world," had a chest measurement of 57 in at a bodyweight of 235 lb. He also boasted a 22-in upper arm.

Largest Brains

The brain has 10×10^{10} nerve cells or neurons interconnected by dendrites or filaments and 10×10^{11} glia. Some of the brain's chemical reactions require only one millionth of a second.

After the age of 18 the brain loses some 10^3 cells every day. The brain of an average adult male (30–59 years) weighs 3 lb 1.73 oz, falling to 2 lb 4.31 oz. The heaviest brain ever recorded was that of a 50-year-old white male which weighed 4 lb 8.29 oz, reported by Dr Thomas F. Hegert, Chief Medical Examiner for District 9, Florida, Oct 23, 1975. The brain of Oliver Cromwell (1599–1658) reputedly weighed 4 lb 14.8 oz, but the size of his head in portraits does not support this extreme figure. The

SMALLEST BRAIN AND SMALLEST WAIST: Writer Anatole France (left) and Ethel Granger (right). His brain weighed 35.8 oz, her waist measured 13 in.

brain of Lord Byron, who died in Greece in 1824, aged 36, reportedly weighed 6 Neapolitan pounds (4 lb 3.86 oz), but this figure also included a certain amount of blood. In January, 1891, the *Edinburgh Medical Journal* reported a case of a 75-year-old man in the Royal Edinburgh Asylum whose brain weighed 4 lb 0.5 oz.

Smallest Brain

The non-atrophied brain of the writer Anatole France (1844–1924) weighed only 35.8 oz without the membrane. Brains in extreme cases of microcephaly may weigh as little as 10.6 oz (*cf.* 20 oz for the adult male gorilla, and 16–20 oz for other anthropoid apes).

Human Memory

Mehmed Ali Halici of Ankara, Turkey, on Oct 14, 1967, recited 6,666 verses of the Koran from memory in 6 hours. The recitation was followed by six Koran scholars. Rare instances of eidetic memory, the ability to reproject and thus "visually" recall material, are known to science.

Highest I.Q.

On the Terman index for Intelligence Quotients, 150 represents genius level. The indices are sometimes held to be immeasurable above a level of 200, but a figure of 210 has been attributed to Kim Ung-Yong of Seoul, South Korea (b March 7, 1963). He composed poetry and spoke four languages (Korean, English, German and Japanese), and performed integral calculus at the age of 4 years 8 months on television in Tokyo on "The World Surprise Show" Nov 2, 1967. Both his parents, Dr and Mrs Kim Soo Sun, are university professors and both were born at 11 a.m. on May 23, 1934. The International Society for Philosophical Enquiry has 239 members, of whom all have mean IQ of 160, none below 148, and some above 183. Only 100 persons in a million have I.Q.'s above 160.

The highest mean I.Q. published for a national population is 106.6 for the Japanese.

(Reading clockwise) HUMAN COMPUTER: Willem Klein took 2 min 5 sec to extract 13th root. PERFECTLY DEVELOPED MAN: Arnold Schwarzenegger shows his form. LONGEST FINGER NAILS: Five nails total 100 in long. LONGEST MOUSTACHE: 8 ft 6 in is still the record. LONGEST NECKS: The Padaung women of Burma used copper coils to stretch their muscles, but tend to asphyxiate themselves.

Human Computer

The fastest extraction of a 13th root from a 100-digit number is in 2 min 5 sec by Willem Klein (b 1914, Netherlands) on May 6, 1980 in London.

Memorizing Pi

The greatest number of places to which π (Pi) has been memorized and recited is 20,000 by Hideaki Tomoyori of Japan, an electronics company worker from Yokohama, Japan, on Oct 2, 1979 on Channel 8 Tokyo TV. (Note: It is only the *approximation* of π at 22/7 which recurs after its sixth decimal place and can, of course, be recited *ad nauseam*. The true value is a string of random numbers fiendishly difficult to memorize after only the fourth decimal place.)

Longest Necks

The maximum measured extension of the neck by the successive fitting of copper coils, as practiced by the Padaung or Karen people of Burma, is 15¾ in. The neck muscles become so atrophied that the removal of the support of the rings produces asphyxiation.

Most Fingers

In 1938, the extreme case of a baby girl with 14 fingers and 12 toes was reported by St. George's Hospital, Hyde Park, London.

Touch Sensitivity

The extreme sensitivity of the fingers is such that a vibration with a movement of 0.02 of a micron can be detected.

Longest Finger Nails

The longest finger nail ever grown is one of 25½ in, grown in 13 years by Romesh Sharma of Delhi, India, measured Feb 15, 1979.

The longest known set of nails now belongs to the left hand of Shridhar Chillal, 43, of Poona, India. The five nails on his left hand, by March 22, 1980, had achieved a measured aggregate length of 100 in (thumb 25 in) uncut since 1952. Human nails normally grow from cuticle to cutting length in from 117 to 138 days.

Longest Hair

Swami Pandarasannadhi, the head of the Tirudaduturai monastery, India, was reported in 1949 to have hair 26 ft in length. From photographs it appears that he was afflicted with the disease Plica caudiformis. Hiroko Yamazaki (b 1940) of Komae-shi, Japan, grew her hair to a length of 8½ ft from 1961 to Nov 1979.

Longest Moustache

The longest moustache on record was that of Masuriya Din (b 1908), a Brahmin of the Partabgarh district in Uttar Pradesh, India. It grew to an extended span of 102 in between 1949 and 1962. Karna Ram Bheel (b 1928) was granted permission by a New Delhi prison governor in Feb 1979 to keep his 7-ft-10-in moustache, grown since 1949, during his life sentence.

Longest Beard

The longest beard preserved was that of Hans N. Langseth (1846–1927) of Norway, which measured 17½ ft at the time of his burial in Kensett, Iowa, in 1927 after 15 years residence in the US. The beard was presented to the Smithsonian Institution, Washington, DC in 1967.

The beard of the bearded lady Janice Deveree (b Bracken County, Ky, 1842) was measured at 14 in in 1884.

Earliest Dentition

The first deciduous or milk teeth normally appear in infants at 5 to 8 months, these being the mandibular and maxillary first incisors. There are many records of children born with teeth, the most distinguished example being Prince Louis Dieudonné, later Louis XIV of France, who was born with two teeth on Sept 5, 1638. Molars usually appear at 24 months, but in Pindborg's case published in Denmark in 1970, a 6-week premature baby was documented with 8 natal teeth of which 4 were in the molar region.

Most Teeth

Cases of the growth in late life of a third set of teeth have been recorded several times. A reference to an extreme case in France of a fourth dentition known as Lison's case was published in 1896. A triple row of teeth was noted in 1680 by Albertus Hellwigius.

Most Dedicated Dentist

Brother Giovanni Battista Orsenigo of the Ospedale Fatebenefratelli, Rome, Italy, a religious dentist, conserved all the teeth he extracted in three enormous boxes during the time he exercised his profession from 1868 to 1904. In 1903, the number was counted and found to be 2,000,744 teeth.

Smallest Visible Object

The resolving power of the human eye is 0.0003 of a radian or an arc of one minute (1/60th of a degree), which corresponds to 100 microns at 10 in. A micron is a thousandth of a millimeter, hence 100 microns is 0.003937, or less than four thousandths of an inch. The human eye can, however, detect a bright light source shining through an aperture of only 3 to 4 microns across. In Oct 1972, the University of Stuttgart, West Germany reported that their student Frl Veronica Seider (b 1953) possessed a visual acuity 20 times better than average. She could identify people at a distance of more than a mile.

Color Sensitivity

The unaided human eye, under the best possible viewing conditions, comparing large areas of color, in good illumination, using both eyes, can distinguish 10,000,000 different color surfaces. The most accurate photoelectric spectrophotometers possess a precision probably only 40% as good as this.

Color Blindness

The most extreme form of color blindness, monochromatic vision, is very rare. The highest rate of red-green color blindness exists in Czecho-

FASTEST TALKER (above): In public life the highest speed recorded was 327 words per minute for John F. Kennedy. LONGEST BEARD: Hans Langseth had this picture of his 17½-foot-long beard taken in Barney, ND.

slovakia and the lowest rate among Fijians and Brazilian Indians. About 7.5% of men and 0.1% of women are color blind.

Fastest Talker

Extremely few people are able to speak *articulately* at a sustained speed above 300 words per min. The fastest broadcaster has usually been regarded to be Gerry Wilmot (b Oct 6, 1914, Victoria, BC, Canada), the ice hockey commentator in the post World War II period. Raymond Glendenning (1907–74), the BBC horse racing commentator, once spoke 176 words in 30 seconds while reporting a greyhound race. In public life the highest speed recorded is a 327-words-per-min burst in a speech made in Dec 1961, by John Fitzgerald Kennedy (1917–63), then President. Tapes of attempts to recite Hamlet's 262-word soliloquy in under 24 sec (655 wpm) have proved indecipherable. Patricia Keeling-Andrich delivered 403 words from W. S. Gilbert's "The Nightmare" in a test in 60 sec at Chabot College, Hayward, Calif, March 16, 1978.

Voice

The highest and lowest recorded notes attained by the human voice before this century were a staccato E in *alt-altissimo* (*e″″*) by Ellen Beach Yaw (US, 1869–1947) in Carnegie Hall, New York City, Jan 19, 1896, and an *A′* (55 cycles per sec) by Kaspar Foster (1617–73).

Madeleine Marie Robin (1918–60), the French operatic coloratura, could produce and sustain the B flat above high C in the Lucia mad scene in *Lucia di Lammermoor.*

Since 1950 singers have achieved high and low notes far beyond the hitherto accepted extremes. Notes, however, at the bass and treble extremities of the register tend to lack harmonics and are of little musical value.

Fräulein Marita Günther, trained by Alfred Wolfsohn, has covered the range of the piano from the lowest note A'' to c' $''$ $''$. Of this range of 7¼ octaves, 6 octaves are considered to be of musical value.

Roy Hart, also trained by Wolfsohn, has reached notes below the range of the piano. Barry Girard of Canton, Ohio, in May 1975 reached the e (4,340 Hz) above the piano's top note.

The lowest note put into song is D'' by the singer Tom King, of King's Langley, Hertfordshire, England. The highest note put into song is G'' $''$ first occurring in *Popoli di Tessaglia* by Mozart. Stefan Zucker sang A in *alt-altissimo* for 3.8 sec in the tenor role of Salvini in the world premiere of Bellini's *Adelson e Salvini* in Carnegie Hall, New York City, Sept 12, 1972.

Greatest Range

The normal intelligible outdoor range of the male human voice in still air is 200 yards. The *silbo,* the whistled language of the Spanish-speaking Canary Island of La Gomera, is intelligible across the valleys, under ideal conditions, at 5 miles. There is a recorded case, under freak acoustic conditions, of the human voice being detectable at a distance of 10½ miles across still water at night. It was said that Mills Darden (see *Heaviest Man*) could be heard 6 miles away when he shouted at the top of his voice.

Lowest Detectable Sound

The intensity of noise or sound is measured in terms of pressure. The pressure of the quietest sound that can be detected by a person of normal hearing at the most sensitive frequency of *c.* 2,750 Hz (cycles per sec) is 2 × 10^{-5} pascal. One tenth of the logarithm to this standard provides a unit termed a decibel. Prolonged noise above 150 decibels will cause immediate permanent deafness while 200 decibels may be fatal. A noise of 30 decibels is negligible.

Highest Detectable Pitch

The upper limit of hearing by the human ear has been regarded as 20,000 Hz (cycles per sec), although children with asthma can often detect a sound of 30,000 cycles per sec. It was announced in Feb 1964 that experiments in the USSR had conclusively proved that oscillations as high as 200,000 cycles per sec can be heard if the oscillator is pressed against the skull.

Shouting

At the "World" Shouting Competition at Scarborough, Yorkshire, England, held Feb 17, 1973, the title was taken by Skipper Kenny Leader with 111 decibels at a distance of 2½ meters. Mrs Grace Hall hit the feminine record of 110 decibels Nov 19, 1976 at Pathfinder Village, Exeter, Devon, England.

Commonest Diseases

The commonest non-contagious disease is dental caries or tooth decay, known to afflict over 53% of the population of the US. In Great Britain 13% of the people have lost all their teeth before reaching 21. During their lifetime few completely escape its effects. Infestation with pinworm (*Enterobius vermicularis*) approaches 100% in some areas of the world.

The commonest contagious illness in the world is coryza (acute naso-pharyngitis) or the common cold. The case of the person most resistant to being infected by a cold was reported by the Medical Research Council Common Cold Unit, Salisbury, England, to be J. Brophy, who had only one mild reaction after being exposed 24 times.

Rarest Disease

Medical literature periodically records hitherto undescribed diseases. A disease as yet undescribed but predicted by a Norwegian is podocytoma of the kidney—a tumor of the epithelial cells lining the glomerulus of the kidney. The last case of endemic smallpox was recorded in Somalia on Oct 26, 1977.

Kuru, or laughing sickness, afflicts only the Fore tribe of eastern New Guinea and is 100% fatal. This was formally attributed to the cannibalistic practice of eating human brains.

Highest Mortality

Rabies in humans has been regarded as uniformly fatal when associated with the hydrophobia symptom. A 25-year-old woman, Candida de Sousa Barbosa of Rio de Janeiro, Brazil, was believed to be the first to survive the disease in Nov 1968, though some sources give priority to Matthew Winkler, 6, on Oct 10, 1970, who was bitten by a rabid bat.

Most and Least Infectious Diseases

The most infectious of all diseases is the pneumonic form of plague, with a mortality rate of 99.99%. Leprosy transmitted by *Mycobacterium leprae* is the least infectious and most bacilliferous of communicable diseases.

Leading Cause of Death

The leading cause of death in industrialized countries is arteriosclerosis (thickening of the arterial wall), which underlies much coronary and cerebrovascular disease.

Most Notorious Carriers

The most publicized of all typhoid carriers was Mary Mallon, known as Typhoid Mary, of New York City. She was the source of 9 outbreaks, notably that of 1903. Because of her refusal to leave employment, often under assumed names, involving the handling of food, she was placed under permanent detention from 1915 until her death in 1938. A still anonymous dairy farmer from Camden, NY, was the source of 407 cases (40 fatal) in Aug 1909.

Parkinson's Disease

The most protracted case of Parkinson's disease (named after Dr James Parkinson's essay of 1817) for which the earliest treatments were not published until 1946, is 56 years in the case of Frederick G. Humphries of Croydon, London, England, whose symptoms became detectable in 1923.

Most Durable Cancer Patient

The most extreme recorded case of survival from diagnosed cancer is that of Mrs Winona Mildred Melick (*née* Douglass) (b Oct 22, 1876) of Long Beach, Calif. She had four cancer operations, in 1918, 1933, 1966 and 1968, but celebrated her 103rd birthday in 1979.

Blood Groups

The preponderance of one blood group varies greatly from one locality to another. On a world basis Group O is the most common (46%), but in some areas, for example Norway, Group A predominates.

The rarest blood group on the ABO system, one of 14 systems, is AB, which occurs in less than 3% of the population in the British Isles. The rarest type in the world is a type of Bombay blood (sub-type A-h) found so far only in a Czechoslovak nurse in 1961 and in a brother (Rh positive) and sister (Rh negative) named Jalbert in Mass, reported in Feb 1968. The brother has started a blood bank for himself.

Champion Blood Donor and Greatest User

Ed "Spike" Howard (1877–1946), the professional strongman from Philadelphia, during his life is said to have donated a total of 1,056 pints of blood. The present-day normal limit on donations is 5 pints a year. Warren C. Jyrich, a 50-year-old hemophiliac, required 2,400 donor units (2,283 pints) of blood when undergoing open heart surgery at the Michael Reese Hospital, in Chicago, in Dec 1970.

Richest Natural Resources

Joe Thomas of Detroit was reported in Aug 1970 to have the highest known count of Anti-Lewis B, the rare blood antibody. A US biological supply firm pays him $1,500 per quart. The Internal Revenue Service regards this income as a taxable liquid asset.

Largest Vein

In the human body, the largest vein is the inferior *vena cava,* which returns most of the blood from the body below the level of the heart.

Longest Coma

The longest recorded coma was that of Elaine Esposito (b Dec 3, 1934) of Tarpon Springs, Fla. She never stirred after an appendectomy on Aug 6, 1941, when she was six, in Chicago. She died on Nov 25, 1978, aged 43 years 357 days, having been in a coma for 37 years 111 days.

Pulse Rate

A normal adult pulse rate is 70–72 beats per min at rest for males, and 78–82 for females. Rates increase to 200 or more during violent exercise or drop to as low as 12 in the extreme case of Dorothy Mae Stevens (see *Lowest Body Temperature*).

Highest Body Temperature

Sustained body temperatures of much over 109 °F are normally incompatible with life, although recoveries after readings of 111 °F have been noted. Marathon runners in hot weather attain 105.8 °F.

In a case reported in the British medical magazine *Lancet* (Oct 31, 1970), a woman following halothane anesthesia ran a temperature of 112 °F. She recovered after a procainamide infusion.

A temperature of 115 °F was recorded in the case of Christopher Legge in the Hospital for Tropical Diseases, London, England, on Feb 9, 1934. A subsequent examination of the thermometer disclosed a flaw in the bulb, but it is regarded as certain that the patient sustained a temperature of more than 110 °F.

Lowest Body Temperature

There are two recorded cases of patients surviving body temperatures as low as 60.8 °F. Dorothy Mae Stevens (1929–74) was found in an alley in Chicago Feb 1, 1951, and Vickie Mary Davis of Milwaukee, Wis, at age 2 years 1 month was admitted to the Evangelical Hospital, Marshalltown, Iowa, Jan 21, 1956, each with a temperature of 60.8 °F. The little girl had been found unconscious on the floor of an unheated house and the air temperature had dropped to −24 °F. Her temperature returned to normal (98.4 °F) after 12 hours and may have been as low as 59 °F when she was first found.

Heart Stoppage

The longest recorded heart stoppage is a minimum of 3 hours 32 min in the case of Miss Jean Jawbone, 20, who was revived by a team of 26, using peritoneal dialysis, in Winnipeg Medical Centre, Manitoba, Canada, Jan 19, 1977.

In Feb 1974 Vegard Slettmoen, 5, fell through the ice on the River Nitselv, Norway. He was found 40 min later, 8 ft down, but was revived in Akerhaus Central Hospital without brain damage.

The longest recorded interval in a post-mortem birth was one of at least 80 min in Magnolia, Miss. Dr Robert E. Drake found Fanella Anderson, aged 25, dead in her home at 11:40 p.m., Oct 15, 1966, and he delivered her of a son weighing 6 lb 4 oz by Caesarean operation in the Beacham Memorial Hospital at 1 a.m. Oct 16, 1966.

Heart Transplants

The first human heart transplant operation was performed on Louis Washkansky, aged 55, at the Groote Schuur Hospital, Capetown, South Africa, between 1:00 and 6:00 a.m. Dec 3, 1967, by a team of 30 headed by Prof Christiaan N. Barnard (b 1922). The donor was Miss Denise Ann Darvall, aged 25. Washkansky died Dec 21, 1967.

The longest surviving heart transplantee has been Emmanuel Vitria, 57, of Marseilles, France, who received a heart transplant Nov 28, 1968, and entered the 12th year of his new life in 1979.

Largest Stone

The largest stone or vesical calculus reported in medical literature was one of 13 lb 14 oz, removed from an 80-year-old woman by Dr Humphrey Arthure at Charing Cross Hospital, London, England, Dec 29, 1952.

Fastest Reflexes

The results of experiments published in 1966 have shown that the fastest messages transmitted by the human nervous system travel as fast as 180 mph. With advancing age, impulses are carried 15% more slowly.

Most Alcoholic Person

It is recorded that a hard drinker named Vanhorn (1750–1811), born in London, England, averaged more than four bottles of ruby port per day for 23 years prior to his death at 61. He is believed to have emptied 35,688 bottles.

The youngest recorded death from alcoholic poisoning was that of a 4-year-old boy, Joseph Sweet, in Wolverhampton, England, in 1827, reported in the Stafford Assizes case *R. v. Martin.*

The late Samuel Riley (b 1922) of Sefton Park, Merseyside, England, was found by a disbelieving pathologist to have a level of 1220 mg of alcohol per 100 milliliters in his blood (legal limit for motorists in the UK is 80 mg/100 ml) on March 28, 1979. He had expired in his home and had been an inspector at the plant of a well-known car manufacturer.

Hiccoughing

The longest recorded attack of hiccoughs is that afflicting Charles Osborne (b 1894) of Anthon, Iowa, from 1922 to date. He contracted it when slaughtering a hog. His first wife left him and he is unable to keep in his false teeth.

The infirmary at Newcastle upon Tyne, England, is recorded to have admitted a young man from Long Witton, Northumberland, March 25, 1769, suffering from hiccoughs which were reportedly audible at a range of more than a mile.

Sneezing

The most chronic sneezing fit ever recorded is that of Tricia Reay, aged 12, of Sutton Coldfield, West Midlands, England. She started sneezing Oct 15, 1979 after catching a cold. The sneezing stopped after treatment at a clinic in the French Pyrenees on April 25, 1980 after a record 194 days.

The highest speed at which expelled particles have been measured to travel is 103.6 mph.

Loudest Snore

Research at the Ear, Nose and Throat Department of St. Mary's Hospital, London, published in Nov 1968 shows that a rasping snore can attain a loudness of 69 decibels, as compared to 70 to 90 decibels for a pneumatic drill.

UNDERWATER LONGEST: Robert L. Foster of Calif, while he held his breath for a record 13 min 42½ sec in a swimming pool. Record-breaking of this kind is extremely dangerous.

Underwater Duration

The record for voluntarily staying underwater is 13 min 42.5 sec by Robert Foster, aged 32, an electronics technician of Richmond, Calif, who stayed under 10 ft of water in the swimming pool of the Bermuda Palms at San Rafael, Calif, on March 15, 1959. He hyperventilated with oxygen for 30 min before his descent. It must be stressed that record-breaking of this kind is *extremely* dangerous.

Yawning

In a case reported in 1888, a 15-year-old female patient yawned continuously for a period of five weeks.

Swallowing

The worst reported case of compulsive swallowing was an insane woman, Mrs H., aged 42, who complained of a "slight abdominal pain." She was found to have 2,533 objects in her stomach, including 947 bent pins. They were removed by Drs Chalk and Foucar in June 1927 at the Ontario Hospital, Canada.

The heaviest object ever extracted from a human stomach was a 5-lb 3-oz ball of hair, from a 20-year-old woman at the South Devon and East Cornwall Hospital, England, March 30, 1895.

Sword "Swallowing"

The longest length of sword able to be "swallowed" by a practiced exponent, after a heavy meal, is 30 in. King Daredevil (real name Dan Larsen) (b Copenhagen, Denmark, Dec 18, 1943) swallowed twelve 23-in blades below the xiphisternum.

Pill Taking

The highest recorded total of pills swallowed by a patient is 358,586 from June 9, 1967 to Jan 1, 1980, by C. H. A. Kilner (b 1926) of Malawi, following a successful pancreatectomy.

Most Injections

Mrs Evelyn Ruth Winder, a diabetic from Invercargill, New Zealand, injected herself with insulin an estimated 53,460 times over 49 years to May 1980.

Most Tattoos

Vivian "Sailor Joe" Simmons, a Canadian tattoo artist, had 4,831 tattoos on his body. He died in Toronto Dec 22, 1965, aged 77. George Zastrow of Justice, Ill, who appeared on TV on the "Guinness Spectacular #2" in Jan 1980, is believed to be the most illustrious example of the art now living. Even the soles of his feet are tattooed.

The most decorated woman is Rusty Skuse (*née* Field) (b 1944) of Aldershot, Hampshire, England, who, after 12 years under the needle of her husband, tattoo artist Bill Skuse, came within 15% of totality. He stated that he always had designs on her.

Fire-Eating

Jack Sholomir (GB) blew a flame from his mouth to a distance of 23 ft at the Eardisley & District Royal Legion Stampede at Kinnersley, Hereford, and Worcester, England, June 6, 1977.

Mrs Jean Chapman successively extinguished 4,593 flaming torches in her mouth in 120 min on Aug 25, 1979 in Stoke Poges, Buckinghamshire, England. Fire-eating is potentially a highly dangerous activity.

Longest Survival in Iron Lung

The longest recorded survival by an iron lung patient is Mrs Laurel Nisbet (b Nov 17, 1912) of La Crescenta, Calif. who has been in an iron lung continuously to date since June 25, 1948.

Longest Operation

The most protracted reported operation for surgical as opposed to medical control purposes was one of arterial surgery for 47 hours performed on James Boydston, 26, at the Veterans Administration Medical Center, Des Moines, Iowa, June 15–17, 1979.

Oldest Subject Operated On

The greatest recorded age at which a person has been subjected to an

FIRE-BLOWER: Jack Sholomir of Great Britain blew a flame a distance of 23 ft in 1977.

FIRE-EATER (left): Jean Chapman put out 4,593 flaming torches in her mouth in 2 hours. MOST TATTOOS: Rusty Skuse was tattooed by her husband so that almost all of her body is covered.

operation is 111 years 105 days in the case of James Henry Brett, Jr. (b July 25, 1849, d Feb 10, 1961) of Houston, Tex. He underwent a hip operation Nov 7, 1960.

Most Major Operations

On Aug 20, 1975, Charles Hill (b 1914) of Sydney, Australia, underwent his 87th major operation. Most of the surgery has been abdominal.

Earliest Appendectomy

The earliest recorded successful appendix operation was performed in 1736 by Claudius Amyand (1680–1740). He was Serjeant Surgeon to King George II (reigned 1727–60) of Great Britain.

Earliest Kidney Transplant

R. H. Lawler (b 1895, US) performed the first transplantation of a human kidney in 1950. The longest survival, as between identical twins, has been 20 years.

Fastest Amputation

The shortest time recorded for the amputation of a leg in the pre-anesthetic era was 13 to 15 sec by Napoleon's chief surgeon, Dominique Larrey. There could have been no ligation.

Laryngectomy

On July 24, 1924, John I. Poole of Plymouth, England, then aged 33, after diagnosis of carcinoma, underwent total laryngectomy in Edinburgh, Scotland. In July 1978 he entered his 55th year as a "neck-breather."

Earliest Anesthesia

The earliest recorded operation under general anesthesia was for the removal of a cyst from the neck of James Venable by Dr Crawford Williamson Long (1815–78), using diethyl ether $((C_2 H_5)_2 O)$, in Jefferson, Ga, March 30, 1842.

Surgical Instruments

The largest surgical instruments are robot retractors used in abdominal surgery introduced by Abbey Surgical Instruments of Chingford, Essex, England in 1968 that weigh 11 lb. Some bronchoscopic forceps measure 23½ in in length. The smallest is Elliot's eye trephine which has a blade 0.078 in in diameter, and "straight" stapes picks with a needle-type tip or blade 0.013 long.

Fasting

Most humans experience considerable discomfort after an abstinence from food for even 12 hours, but this often passes off after 24–48 hours. Records claimed without unremitting medical surveillance are of little value.

The longest period for which anyone has gone without solid food is 382 days by Angus Barbieri (b 1940) of Tayport, Fife, Scotland, who lived on tea, coffee, water, soda water and vitamins from June 1965 to July 1966 in Maryfield Hospital, Dundee, Angus, Scotland. His weight declined from 472 lb to 178 lb.

Sister Thérèse Neumann survived 35 years on the "bread" of the Holy Eucharist at mass each morning at Konnersreuth, Germany.

The longest recorded case of survival without food *and* water is 18 days by Andreas Mihavecz, 18, of Bregenz, Austria, who was put in a holding cell April 1, 1979, in a local government building in Höchst, Austria, but was totally forgotten by the police. On April 18, 1979, he was discovered close to death, having had neither food nor water. He had been a passenger in a car crash.

Hunger Strike

The longest recorded hunger strike was one of 94 days by John and Peter Crowley, Thomas Donovan, Michael Burke, Michael O'Reilly, Christopher Upton, John Power, Joseph Kenny and Sean Hennessy in Cork Prison, Ireland, from Aug 11 to Nov 12, 1920. These nine survivors owed their lives to expert medical attention and an appeal by Arthur Griffith.

Isolation

The longest recorded period for which any volunteer has been able to withstand total deprivation of all sensory stimulation (sight, hearing and touch) is 92 hours, recorded in 1962 at Lancaster Moor Hospital, England.

The farthest distance that any human has been isolated from all other humans has been when the lone pilots of the lunar command modules were antipodal to their Apollo missions, 2,200 miles away.

LIVING STATUE: William Fuqua, who holds the record for standing motionless for 6 hours 31 min, is interviewed by David Frost on an ABC Guinness TV show. Fuqua now has a body-guard after he was stabbed by a man who bet his wife that Fuqua was a mannequin and not real.

Motionlessness

The longest that any person has voluntarily remained motionless is 6 hours 31 min by William Fuqua at Dillard's Department Store, Fort Worth, Tex July 22, 1978.

The longest recorded time that anyone was involuntarily made to stand at attention was 53 hours when Staff Sgt. Samuel B. Moody, USAF, was so punished in Narumi prison camp, Nagoya, Japan, in the spring of 1945. He survived to write *Reprieve from Hell*.

Longest Dream

Dreaming sleep is characterized by rapid eye movements (known as REM). The longest recorded period of REM is 2 hours 23 min, set by Bill Carskadon on Feb 15, 1967, at the Department of Psychology, University of Illinois, Chicago. His previous sleep had been interrupted.

Sleeplessness

Researches indicate that on the Circadian cycle, for the majority, peak efficiency is attained between 8 p.m. and 9 p.m., and the low comes at 4 a.m.

The longest recorded period for which a person has voluntarily gone without sleep is 449 hours (18 days 17 hours) by Mrs Maureen Weston of Peterborough, England, in a rocking chair marathon from Apr 14 to May 2, 1977. Though she tended to hallucinate toward the end of this surely ill-advised test, surprisingly, she suffered no lasting aftereffects. W. Amanda Vpali of Sri Lanka voluntarily went without sleep for 353 hours 10 min (almost 15 days) from Aug 20 to Sept 4, 1979.

Extrasensory Perception

The highest consistent performer in tests to detect powers of extrasensory perception is Pavel Stepánek (Czechoslovakia), known in parapsychological circles as "P.S." His performance in correctly naming hidden white or green cards from May 1967 to March 1968 departed from a chance probability yielding a Chi^2 value corresponding to $P < 10^{-50}$ or

FIRE-WALKER: Vernon ("Komar") Craig was able to walk on hot coals tested at 1,494°F. (A steak broils at 325°F.)

odds of more than 100 octillion to one against the achievement being one of chance. One of the two appointed referees recommended that the results should not be published.

The highest published scores in any ESP test were those of a 26-year-old female tested by Prof Bernard F. Reiss of Hunter College, New York City, in 1936. In 74 runs of 25 guesses each, she scored one with 25 all correct, two with 24, and an average of 18.24, as against a random score of 5.00. Such a result would depart from chance probability by a factor $> 10^{700}$. This produced the comment that there might be a defect in the theory of probability.

Highest Temperature Endured

The highest dry-air temperature endured by naked men in US Air Force experiments in 1960 was 400°F and for heavily clothed men 500°F. (*Steaks require only 325°F.*) Temperatures of 248°F have been found quite bearable in sauna baths.

The highest temperature recorded by a pyrometer for the coals in any fire-walk is 1,494°F by "Komar" (Vernon E. Craig) of Wooster, Ohio, at the International Festival of Yoga and Esoteric Sciences, Maidenhead, England, on Aug 14, 1976.

g Forces

The acceleration due to gravity (g) is 32 ft 1.05 in per sec per sec at sea level at the Equator. A *sustained* force of 25 g was withstood in a dry capsule during astronautic research by Dr Carter Collins of California.

The highest g force endured was 82.6 g for 0.04 sec on a water-braked rocket sled by Eli L. Beeding, Jr., at Holloman Air Force Base, NM, May 16, 1958. He was put in the hospital for three days.

A man who fell off a 185-ft cliff has survived a *momentary* g force of 209 in decelerating from 68 mph to stationary in 0.015 sec.

Race car driver David Purley survived a deceleration from 108 mph to zero in 26 in in a crash at the Silverstone circuit, Northamptonshire, England, July 13, 1977, which involved a force of 179.8 g.

The land divers of Pentecost Island, New Hebrides, dive from 70-ft-high platforms with liana vines attached to their ankles. The resulting jerk can transmit a momentary force in excess of 100 g.

Electric Shock

Excluding lightning bolts, the highest reported voltage electric shock survived was one of 230,000 volts by Brian Latasa, 17, on the tower of an ultra-high-voltage power line in Griffith Park, Los Angeles, Nov 9, 1967. Highly insulated individuals have touched 1,200,000-volt cables in bare-hand live cable work without harm.

Chapter 2

The Animal & Plant Kingdoms

ANIMAL KINGDOM (ANIMALIA)

Largest and Heaviest Animal

The largest and heaviest animal is the blue or sulphur-bottom whale (*Balaenoptera musculus*), also called Sibbald's rorqual. The largest accurately measured specimen on record was a female landed at the Cia Argentina de Pesca shore station, South Georgia, Falkland Islands, in the South Atlantic, *c.* 1904–20 which measured 110 ft 2½ in in length. Another female measuring 96¾ ft brought into the shore station at Prince Olaf, South Georgia, *c.* 1931 was calculated to have weighed 183.34 tons, exclusive of blood and other body fluids, judging by the number of cookers that were filled by the animal's blubber, meat and bones. The total weight of this whale was believed to have been 195 tons.

On the principle that the weight should vary as the cube of the linear dimensions, a 100-ft blue whale in good condition should weigh about 179 tons, but in the case of pregnant females the weight could be as much as 200 or more tons, equivalent to 35 adult bull African elephants.

Longest Animal

The longest animal ever recorded is the ribbon worm *Lineus longissimus,* also known as the "boot-lace worm," which is found in the shallow coastal waters of the North Sea. In 1864 a specimen measuring more than 180 ft was washed ashore at St. Andrews, Fifeshire, Scotland, after a storm.

Tallest Animal

The tallest living animal is the giraffe (*Giraffa camelopardalis*), which is now found only in the dry savannah and semi-desert areas of Africa south of the Sahara. The tallest ever recorded was a Masai bull (*G. came-*

Note: For more information about animals, see "Animal Facts and Feats: One of the Guinness Family of Books." This work treats the dimensions and performances of the Classes of the Animal Kingdom in greater detail, giving also the sources and authorities for much of the material in this chapter.

TALLEST ANIMAL (above): George, the
tallest giraffe in captivity, licked the
telephone wires that ran past his pen,
disrupting the system.

lopardalis tippelskirchi) named "George," received at Chester Zoo, England, Jan 8, 1959 from Kenya. His head *almost* touched the roof of the 20-ft-high Giraffe House when he was 9 years old. George died July 22, 1969. Less credible heights of up to 23 ft between taxidermist's pegs have been claimed for bulls shot in the field.

Longest-Lived Animal

Few non-bacterial creatures live longer than humans. It would appear that tortoises are the longest-lived such animals. The greatest authentic age recorded for a tortoise is 152-plus years for a male Marion's tortoise (*Testudo sumeirii*), brought from the Seychelles Islands in the Indian Ocean to Mauritius in 1766 by the Chevalier de Fresne, who presented it to the Port Louis army garrison. This specimen (it went blind in 1908) was accidentally killed in 1918. When the famous Royal Tongan tortoise "Tu'malilia" (believed to be a specimen of *Testudo radiata*) died May 19, 1966, it was reputed to be over 200 years old, having been presented to the then King of Tonga by Captain James Cook (1728–79) Oct 22, 1773, but this record may well have been compiled from two (or more) overlapping residents.

The bacteria *Thermoactinomyces vulgaris* has been found alive in cores of mud taken from the bottom of Windermere Lake, northern England, which have been dated to 1,500 years before the present.

Fastest Flying Animal

The fastest reliably measured air speed of any animal is 106.25 mph for a spine-tailed swift (*Chaetura caudacuta*), reported from the USSR in 1942. In 1934, ground speeds ranging from 171.8 to 219.5 mph were recorded by stopwatch for spine-tailed swifts over a 2-mile course in the

FASTEST GROWTH: The blue whale grows from a fraction of a milligram to 29 tons in 22¾ months (10¾ months gestation and the first 12 months of life). This model of a blue whale is in the Museum of Natural History in New York City.

Cachar Hills of northeastern India, but scientific tests since have revealed that this species of bird cannot be seen at a distance of 1 mile, even with standard binoculars. This bird is the fastest-moving living creature and has a blood temperature of 112.5 °F. Speeds even higher than a free-fall maximum of 185 mph have been ascribed to peregrine falcons (*Falco peregrinus*) in a stoop, but in recent experiments in which miniature air speedometers were fitted, the maximum recorded diving speed has been 82 mph.

Most Valuable Animals

The most valuable animals in cash terms are thoroughbred race horses. It was announced in March 1980 that "Spectacular Bid" would be syndicated for $22 million. The most valuable zoo exhibit is the giant panda (*Ailuropoda melanoleuca*) for which the San Diego Zoological Gardens offered $250,000 in 1971 for a fertile pair. The most valuable marine exhibit is the killer whale (*Orcinus orca*) named "Orky" at Marineland of the Pacific, Palos Verdes, Calif. He has grown to 14,000 lb since 1964 and his value is at least $250,000.

Commonest Animal

It is estimated that man shares the earth with 3×10^{33} (or 3 followed by 33 zeros) other living things. The number of nematode sea-worms has been estimated at 4×10^{25}.

Rarest Animal

The best claimants to the title of the rarest land animal are those species which are known only from a single (type) specimen. One of these is the tenrec *Dasogale fontoynonti,* a placental mammal, which is known only from the specimen collected in eastern Madagascar (Malagasy Republic) and now preserved in the Paris (France) Museum of Natural History.

Among subspecies of mammals, the Javan tiger (*Panthera tigris sondaica*) was reduced to 4 specimens by 1977, all of them in the Meru Betiri reserve in eastern Java. The Arabian oryx (*Oryx leucoryx*) has not been reported in the wild since 3 were killed and 4 captured in South Oman in 1972. In Dec 1979 the World Wildlife Fund announced that scientists had uncovered the first evidence that the Bali leopard (*Panthera pandus balica*) still existed on the island.

Longest Gestation

The viviparous amphibian Alpine black salamander (*Salamandra atra*) can have a gestation period of up to 38 months at altitudes above 4,600 ft in the Swiss Alps, but this drops to 24–26 months at lower altitudes.

Fastest and Slowest Growth

The fastest growth in the animal kingdom is that of the blue whale calf. A barely visible ovum weighing a fraction of a milligram (0.000035 of an ounce) grows to a weight of *c.* 29 tons in 22¾ months, made up of 10¾ months gestation and the first 12 months of life. This is equivalent to an increase of 30,000 million fold.

The slowest growth in the animal kingdom is that of the deep-sea clam (*Tindaria callistiformis*) of the North Atlantic, which takes an estimated 100 years to reach a length of 0.31 in (8 mm).

Largest Egg

The largest egg of any living animal is that of the whale shark (*Rhiniodon typus*). One egg case measuring 12 in by 5.5 in by 3.5 in was picked up by the shrimp trawler "Doris" June 29, 1953 at a depth of 186 ft in the Gulf of Mexico, 130 miles south of Port Isabel, Tex. The egg contained a perfect embryo of a whale shark 13.78 in long.

Greatest Size Difference Between Sexes

The largest female deep-sea angler fish of the species *Ceratias holboelki* on record weighed half a million times as much as the smallest known parasitic male.

Heaviest Brain

The sperm whale (*Physeter catodon*) has the heaviest brain of all living animals. The brain of a 49-ft-long bull processed aboard the Japanese factory ship *Nissin Maru No. 1* in the Antarctic Dec 11, 1949 weighed 9.2 kg (20.24 lb), compared to 6.9 kg (15.38 lb) for a 90-ft blue whale. The heaviest brain recorded for an elephant was an exceptional 16.5 lb in the case of a 2.17-ton Asiatic cow. The normal brain weight for an adult African bull is 9¼–12 lb.

Largest Eye

The giant squid *Architeuthis sp.* has the largest eye of any living animal. The ocular diameter may exceed 15 in, compared to less than 12 in for a 33⅓-rpm long-playing record.

Most Acute Sense of Smell

The most acute sense of smell exhibited in nature is that of the male emperor moth (*Eudia pavonia*), which, according to German experiments in 1961, can detect the sex attractant of the virgin female at the almost unbelievable range of 6.8 miles upwind. This scent has been identified as one of the higher alcohols ($C_{16}H_{29}OH$) of which the female carries less than 0.0001 mg.

Highest g Force

The highest g force encountered in nature is the 400 g *averaged* by the click beetle (*Athous haemorrhoidalis*), a common British species, when jackknifing into the air to escape predators. One example measuring 0.47 in in length and weighing 0.00014 oz which jumped to a height of 11¾ in was calculated to have "endured" a peak brain deceleration of 2,300 g at the end of the movement.

1. MAMMALS (*MAMMALIA*)

Largest and Heaviest Animal

The blue whale (see details on page 52) holds the record. One whale, a female taken by the *Slava* whaling fleet of the USSR in the Antarctic March 17, 1947 measured 90 ft 8 in in length. Its tongue and heart weighed 4.73 tons and 1,540 lb respectively.

Blue whales inhabit the colder seas and migrate to warmer waters in winter for breeding. Observations made in the Antarctic in 1947–8 showed that a blue whale can maintain speeds of 20 knots (23 mph) for 10 minutes when frightened. This means a 90-ft blue whale traveling at 20 knots would develop 520 hp. Newborn calves measure 21–28.5 ft long and weigh up to 3.3 tons.

It has been estimated that there were between 17,500 and 19,000 blue whales living throughout the oceans in 1977. The species has been protected *de jure* since 1967 although non-member countries of the International Whaling Commission (Chile and Peru) are not bound by this agreement.

Deepest Dive

The greatest *recorded* depth to which a whale has dived is 620 fathoms (3,720 ft) by a 47-ft bull sperm whale (*Physeter catodon*) found with his jaw entangled with a submarine cable running between Santa Elena, Ecuador, and Chorillos, Peru, Oct 14, 1955. At this depth he withstood a pressure of 1,680 lb per sq in of body surface.

On Aug 25, 1969, a sperm whale was killed 100 miles south of Durban, South Africa, after it had surfaced from a dive lasting 1 hour 52 min, and inside its stomach were found two small sharks which had been swallowed about an hour earlier. These were later identified as *Scymnodon sp.*, a species found only on the sea floor. At this point from land the depth of water is in excess of 1,646 fathoms (10,476 ft) for a radius of 30–40 miles, which now suggests that the sperm whale sometimes may descend to a depth of over 10,000 ft when seeking food.

Largest Animal on Land

The largest living land animal is the African bush elephant (*Loxodonta africana africana*). The average adult bull stands 10 ft 6 in at the shoulder and weighs 6½ tons. The largest specimen ever recorded, and the largest land animal of modern times, was a bull shot 25 miles north-northeast of Mucusso, southern Angola, Nov 7, 1974. Lying on its side this elephant measured 13 ft 8 in in a projected line from the highest

FASTEST AND SLOWEST MAMMALS: The cheetah (left) has been clocked at over 60 mph, a figure 353 times faster than the top speed attained by the three-toed sloth (right).

point of the shoulder to the base of the forefoot, indicating that its standing height must have been about 13 ft. Other measurements included an over-all length of 35 ft (tip of extended trunk to tip of extended tail) and a forefoot circumference of 5 ft 11 in. The weight was computed to be 26,328 lb (see also Shooting, Chapter 12).

Smallest Mammals

The smallest recorded mammal is the rare Kitti's hog-nosed bat (*Craseonycteris thonglongyai*) or bumblebee bat, which is restricted to two caves near the forestry station at Ban Sai Yoke on the Kwae Noi River, Kanchanaburi, Thailand. Mature specimens of both sexes have a wing span of about 6.29 in and weigh between 0.062 and 0.071 oz.

The smallest totally marine mammal is probably Heaviside's dolphin (*Caephalorhynchus heavisidei*) of the South Atlantic. Adult specimens have an average length of 4 ft and weigh up to 90 lb. The sea otter (*Enhydra lutris*) is even smaller, weighing from 55 to 81.4 lb, but this species sometimes comes ashore during storms.

Fastest Land Animal

The fastest of all land animals over a short distance (*i.e.* up to 600 yd) is the cheetah or hunting leopard (*Acinonyx jubatus*) of the open plains of East Africa, Iran, Turkmenia and Afghanistan, with a probable maximum speed of 60–63 mph over suitably level ground. Speeds of 71, 84 and even 90 mph have been claimed for this animal, but these figures must be considered exaggerated. Tests in London in 1937 showed that on an oval greyhound track over 345 yd a female cheetah's average speed

ELEPHANTS' AGES: Full authentication has yet to be reported for the 78-year-old claims made for "Modoc" (below), the cow elephant that died in Santa Clara, Calif in 1975. "Jessie" (above) a gift to Australia from the King of Siam in 1882 may well have been 77 if she was 12 at the time of the gift. "Kyaw Thee" (not shown), a bull, in Burma was verified as age 70 when he died in 1965.

over three runs was 43.4 mph (compared with 43.26 mph for the fastest race horse), but this specimen was not running at its best.

The fastest land animal over a sustained distance (*i.e.* 1,000 yd or more) is the pronghorn antelope (*Antilocapra americana*) of the western US. Specimens have been observed to travel at 35 mph for 4 miles, at 42 mph for 1 mile and 55 mph for half a mile. On Aug 14, 1936, at Spanish Lake, Lake County, Ore, a hard-pressed buck was timed by a car speedometer at 61 mph over 200 yd.

Slowest Land Mammal

The slowest moving land mammal is the ai or three-toed sloth (*Bradypus tridactylus*) of tropical America. The average ground speed is 6–8 ft per min (0.068 to 0.098 mph), but in the trees it can "accelerate" to 15 ft per min (0.170 mph). (Compare these figures with the 0.03 mph of the common garden snail and the 0.17 mph of the giant tortoise.)

Longest-Lived Mammal

No other mammal can match the proven age of 115 years attained by man (*Homo sapiens*). It is probable that the closest approach is among blue and fin whales (*Balaenoptera musculus* and *B. physalas*). Studies of the annual growth layers or laminations found in the wax-like plug deposited in the outer ear of these whales indicate a maximum life span of 90–100 years.

The longest-lived land mammal, excluding man, is the Asiatic elephant (*Elephas maximus*). The greatest age that has been verified with certainty is 70 years in the case of a bull timber elephant "Kyaw Thee" (Tuskar 1342), who died in the Taunggyi Forest division, southern Shan States, Burma, in 1965. The age of 78 years reported for "Modoc," the circus cow elephant, when she died in Santa Clara, Calif July 17, 1975 has not yet been fully authenticated.

Highest-Living Mammal

The highest-living wild mammal in the world is probably the yak (*Bos grunniens*), of Tibet and the Szechwanese Alps, China, which occasionally, when foraging, climbs to an altitude of 20,000 ft. The Bharal (*Pseudois nayaur*) and the Pika or Mouse hare (*Ochotona thibetana*) may also reach this height in the Himalayas. In 1890, the tracks of an elephant were found at 15,000 ft on Mt Kilimanjaro, Tanzania.

Largest Herds

The largest herds on record were those of the South African springbok (*Antidorcas marsupialis*) during migration in the 19th century. In 1849, Sir John Fraser of Bloemfontein observed a herd that took three days to pass through the settlement of Beaufort West, Cape Province. Another herd seen in the same province in 1888 was estimated to contain 100 million head, although 10 million is probably a more realistic figure. A herd estimated to be 15 miles wide and more than 100 miles long was reported from Karree Kloof, Orange River, South Africa, in July 1896.

The largest concentration of wild mammals found living anywhere in the world today is that of the guano bat (*Tadarida mexicana*) in Bracan Cave, San Antonio, Tex, where 20 million animals assemble after migration from Mexico.

Longest and Shortest Gestation Periods

The longest of all mammalian gestation periods is that of the Asiatic elephant (*Elephas maximus*), with an average of 609 days (or just over 20 months) and a maximum of 760 days, more than 2½ times that of a human.

The gestation period of the American opossum (*Didelphis marsupialis*), also called the Virginian opossum, is normally 12 to 13 days, but it may be as short as 8 days.

The gestation periods of the rare water opossum or Yapok (*Chironectes minimus*) of Central and northern South America (average 12–13 days) and the Eastern native cat (*Dasyurus viverrinus*) of Australia (average 12 days) may also be as short as 8 days.

Largest Litter

The greatest recorded number of young born to a wild mammal at a single birth is 32 (not all of which survived), in the case or the common tenrec (*Centetes ecaudatus*), found in Madagascar and the Comoro Islands. The average litter is 12 to 16.

In March 1961 a litter of 32 was also reported for a house mouse (*Mus musculus*) at the Roswell Park Memorial Institute in Buffalo, NY (average litter size 13–21). (See also Chapter 9, prolificacy records—pigs.)

Youngest Breeder

The streaked tenrec (*Hemicentetes semispinosus*) of Madagascar is weaned after only 5 days, and females are capable of breeding 3–4 weeks after birth.

Largest Carnivore

The largest living terrestrial carnivore is the Kodiak bear (*Ursus arctos middendorffi*), which is found on Kodiak Island and the adjacent Afognak and Shuyak islands in the Gulf of Alaska. The average adult male has a nose-to-tail length of 8 ft (tail about 4 in), stands 52 in at the shoulder and weighs 1,050–1,175 lb.

In 1894 a weight of 1,656 lb was recorded for a male shot at English Bay, Kodiak Island, whose *stretched* skin measured 13 ft 6 in from the tip of the nose to the root of the tail. This weight was exceeded by a "cage-fat" male in the Cheyenne Mountain Zoological Park, Colorado Springs, which scaled 1,670 lb at the time of its death Sept 22, 1955.

Weights in excess of 1,600 lb have also been reported for the male polar bear (*Ursus maritimus*), which has an average nose-to-tail length of 7¾ ft and weighs 850–900 lb. In 1960 a polar bear allegedly weighing 2,-210 lb before skinning was shot at the polar entrance to Kotzebue Sound, northwest Alaska. The 11-ft-1½-in mounted specimen is now on display at the Anchorage Airport, Alaska.

Smallest Carnivore

The smallest living carnivore is the least weasel (*Mustela rixosa*), also called the dwarf weasel, which is circumpolar in distribution. Four races are recognized, the smallest of which is the *M. r. pygmaea* of Siberia. Mature specimens have an overall length (including tail) of 6.96–8.14 in and weigh between 1¼ and 2½ oz.

LARGEST FELINE (left): Head of this 857-lb tiger shot in India in 1967, which is on display at the Smithsonian Institution in Washington. SMALLEST CARNIVORE (below): The least (or dwarf) weasel weighs less than 2½ oz. See how it compares with a human finger.

Largest Marine Carnivore

The largest toothed mammal ever recorded is the sperm whale (*Physeter catodon*), also called the cachalot. The average adult bull is 47 ft long and weighs about 37 tons. The largest specimen ever to be measured accurately was a bull 67 ft 11 in long captured off the Kurile Islands, in the northwest Pacific, by a USSR whaling fleet in the summer of 1950.

Largest Feline

The largest member of the cat family (Felidae) is the long-furred Siberian tiger (*Panthera tigris altaica*), also known as the Amur or Manchurian tiger. Adult males average 10 ft 4 in in length (nose to tip of extended tail), stand 39–42 in at the shoulder, and weigh about 585 lb. A male weighing 846.5 lb was shot in the Sikhote Alin Mountains, Maritime Territory, USSR in 1950. In Nov 1967 an 857-lb Indian tiger (*Panthera tigris tigris*) was shot in northern Uttar Pradesh by David H. Hasinger of Philadelphia. It measured 10 ft 7 in long (between taxidermist's pegs), or 11 ft 1 in over the curves, compared with 9 ft 3 in and 420 lb for the average adult male. It is now on display in the US Museum of Natural History, Smithsonian Institution, Washington, DC.

The average adult African lion (*Panthera leo*) measures 9 ft overall, stands 36–38 in at the shoulder, and weighs 400–410 lb. The heaviest recorded specimen found in the wild was one weighing 690 lb, shot near Hectorspruit, in the eastern Transvaal, South Africa, in 1936. In July 1970 a weight of 826 lb was reported for an 11-year-old black-maned lion named "Simba" (b Dublin Zoo, 1959) at the Colchester Zoo, Essex, England. He died Jan 16, 1973 at Knaresborough Zoo, North Yorkshire, England, where his stuffed body is currently on display.

Smallest Feline

The smallest member of the cat family is the rusty-spotted cat (*Felis rubiginosa*) of southern India and Sri Lanka. The average adult male has an overall length of 25–28 in (tail 9–10 in) and weighs about 3 lb.

Largest Pinniped (Seal, Sea Lion, Walrus)

The largest of the 32 known species of pinnipeds is the southern elephant seal (*Mirounga leonina*) which inhabits the sub-Antarctic islands. Adult bulls average 16½ ft in length (tip of inflated snout to the extremities of the outstretched tail flippers), 12 ft in maximum body girth and weigh 5,000 lb. The largest accurately measured specimen on record was a bull killed in Possession Bay, South Georgia, Falkland Islands, South Atlantic, Feb 28, 1913, which measured *c.* 22½ ft in length or 21 ft 4 in after flensing and probably weighed 9,000 lb. There are old records of bulls measuring 25, 30 and even 35 ft, but these figures must be considered exaggerated.

LARGEST PINNIPED: The southern elephant seal can weigh up to 9,000 lb—this one weighed 5,000—and measure more than 25 ft in length—this one was 16 ft.

Smallest Pinniped

The smallest pinniped is the Baykal seal (*Pusa sibirica*) of Lake Baykal, USSR, and the ringed seal (*Pusa hispida*) of the Arctic. Adult specimens measure up to 5 ft 6 in and weigh up to 280 lb.

Fastest and Deepest Pinnipeds

The highest speed measured for a pinniped is 25 mph for a California sea lion (*Zalophus californianus*). The deepest dive recorded for a pinniped is 1,968 ft for a bull Weddell seal (*Leptonychotes weddelli*) in McMurdo Sound, Antarctica, in March 1966. At this depth, the seal withstood a pressure of 875 lb per sq in of body area.

The exceptionally large eyes of the southern elephant seal (see above) point to a deep-diving ability, and unconfirmed measurements down to 2,000 ft have been claimed.

Longest-Lived Pinniped

A female gray seal (*Halichoerus grypus*) shot at Shunni Wick in the Shetland Islands, Scotland, Apr 23, 1969 was believed to be at least 46 years old, based on a count of dental annuli.

Rarest Pinniped

The Caribbean or West Indian monk seal (*Monachus tropicalis*) was last seen on the beach of Isla Mujeres off the Yucatan Peninsula, Mexico, in 1962, and is now believed to be on the verge of extinction.

Largest Bat

The only flying mammals are bats (order Chiroptera), of which there are about 1,000 living species. The bat with the greatest wing span is the Kalong (*Pteropus vampyrus*), a fruit bat found in Malaysia and Indonesia. It has a wing span of up to 5 ft 7 in and weighs up to 31.7 oz.

Smallest Bat

The smallest species of bat is the rare Kitti's hog-nosed or bumblebee bat (see page 57).

Fastest Bat

Because of great practical difficulties, few data on bat speeds have been published. The greatest speed attributed to a bat is 32 mph in the case of a free-tailed or guano bat (*Tadarida mexicana). This speed is closely matched by the noctule bat (Nyctalus noctula)* and the long-winged bat (*Miniopterus schreibersi*), both of which have been timed at 31 mph.

Longest-Lived Bat

The greatest age reliably reported for a bat is "at least 24 years" for a female little brown bat (*Myotis lucifugus*) found Apr 30, 1960 in a cave on Mount Aeolis, East Dorset, Vt. It had been banded at a summer colony in Mashpee, Mass June 22, 1937.

There is an unconfirmed French report of a 26–27-year-old greater horseshoe bat (*Rhinolophus ferrumequinum*).

Highest Detectable Pitch

Because of their ultrasonic echolocation, bats have the most acute hearing of any land animal. Vampire bats (*Desmodontidae*) and fruit bats (*Pteropodidae*) can hear frequencies as high as 150,000 cycles per sec (150 kHz). Compare this with 20 kHz for the adult human limit but 153 kHz for the bottle-nosed dolphin (*Tursiopis truncatus*).

BETTER HEARING THAN MAN'S: Both the fruit bat and the dolphin can hear frequencies 7 times higher than humans.

LARGEST PRIMATE (left): The gorilla bull can weigh up to 670 lb and stand 6 ft 2 in high. OLDEST PRIMATES are orangutans. "Guas" (right, above) of the Philadelphia Zoo lived 57 years.

Largest Living Primates

The largest living primate is the eastern lowland gorilla (*Gorilla gorilla graueri*) which inhabits the lowlands of the eastern part of Zaïre and southwestern Uganda. The average adult bull stands 5 ft 9 in tall (including crest) and measures 58–60 in around the chest and weighs about 360 lb. The greatest height (top of crest to heel) recorded for a mountain gorilla (*Gorilla gorilla beringei*) is 6 ft 2 in for a bull shot in the eastern Congo *c*. 1921.

The heaviest gorilla ever kept in captivity was a bull of the eastern lowlands named "Mbongo," who died in San Diego Zoological Gardens, March 15, 1942. During an attempt to weigh him shortly before his death, the platform scales "fluctuated from 645 lb to nearly 670." This specimen measured 5 ft 7½ in in height and 69 in around the chest.

The heaviest gorilla living in captivity today is the western lowland (*Gorilla gorilla*) bull "Samson" (b 1949) of Milwaukee County Zoological Park. He has weighed as much as 658 lb but is now down to 485 lb.

Smallest Living Primate

The smallest known primate is the rare feather-tailed tree shrew (*Ptiolcercus lowii*) of Malaysia. Adult specimens have a total body length of 9–13 in, a head and body length of 3.9–5.5 in, a tail of 5.1–7.5 in and weighs 1.23–1.76 oz. The mouse lemur (*Microcebus murinus*) of Madagascar is approximately the same length (10.8–11.8 in overall) but heavier, adults weighing 1.58–2.82 oz.

Longest-Lived Primate

The greatest irrefutable age reported for a primate (excluding humans) is 57 years in the case of a male orangutan (*Pongo pygmaeus*) named "Guas," who was received by the Philadelphia Zoo May 1, 1931 after having been kept in Cuba for some time and died Feb 9, 1977.

The oldest living primate is the western lowland gorilla "Massa" of the Philadelphia Zoological Garden, a bull who was still alive in March 1980 aged 49 years 3 months. He was received as a 5-year-old Dec 30, 1935.

Rarest Primate

The rarest primate is the hairy-eared mouse lemur (*Cheirogaleus trichotis*) of Madagascar, which was known, until fairly recently, only from a type specimen and two skins. However, in 1966 a live one was found on the east coast near Mananara.

Primate Strength

"Boma," a 165-lb male chimpanzee at the Bronx Zoo, New York City, in 1924 recorded a right-handed pull (feet braced) of 847 lb on a dynamometer (compare with 210 lb for a man of the same weight). On another occasion an adult female chimpanzee named "Suzette" (estimated weight 135 lb) at the same zoo registered a right-handed pull of 1,260 lb while in a rage. A record of a 100-lb chimpanzee achieving a two-handed dead lift of 600 lb with ease suggests that a male gorilla could, with training, raise 1,800 lb!

Largest and Smallest Monkeys

The only species of monkey reliably credited with a weight of more than 100 lb is the mandrill (*Mandrillus sphinx*) of equatorial West Africa. The greatest reliable weight recorded is 119 lb but an unconfirmed weight of 130 lb has been reported.

The smallest monkey is the pygmy marmoset (*Cebuella pygmaea*) of Ecuador, northern Peru and western Brazil. Mature specimens have a maximum total length of 12 in, half of which is tail, and weigh 1.7–2.81 oz which means it rivals the mouse lemur for the title of *Smallest Living Primate*.

Largest Rodent

The largest rodent is the capybara (*Hydrochoerus hydrochaeris*), also called the carpincho or water hog, which is found in tropical South America. Mature specimens have a head and body length of 3¼–4½ ft and weigh up to 174 lb. In Britain, the largest rodent, the coypu (*Myo-*

SMALLEST MONKEY: The pygmy marmoset, a South American native, is half tail. It might also be the smallest (and cutest) living primate.

caster coypus) or nutria was introduced from Argentina by fur breeders in 1927. In 1937 four specimens escaped from a nutria-farm near Ipswich, and by 1978 there were an estimated 8,000 coypu living wild in Britain. Adult males measure 30–36 in and weigh up to 28 lb in the wild state.

Smallest Rodent

The smallest known rodent is the pygmy mouse (*Baiomys taglore*) of central Mexico, southern Ariz and Tex, which measures up to 4.3 in in total length and weighs 0.24–0.28 oz.

Rarest Rodent

The rarest is believed to be the James Island rice rat (*Oryzomys swarthi*), also called Swarth's rat. Four specimens were collected on this island in the Galápagos group in the eastern Pacific Ocean in 1906, and it was not heard of again until Jan 1966 when a recent skull was found.

Fastest Breeding Rodent

The female meadow vole (*Microtus agrestis*), found in Britain, can reproduce from the age of 25 days and have up to 17 litters of 6–8 young in a year.

Longest-Lived Rodent

The greatest reliable âge reported for a rodent is 22 years 10 months for a female bushtailed porcupine (*Atherurus africanus*), which died in the Philadelphia Zoological Garden May 6, 1933. It was received as a young adult July 5, 1910.

Largest Insectivore (Insect-Eating Mammal)

The largest insectivore is the moon rat (*Echinosorex gymnurus*), also known as Raffles' gymnure, found in Burma, Thailand, Malaysia, Sumatra and Borneo. Mature specimens have a head and body length of 10.43–17.52 in, a tail measuring 7.87–8.26 in, and weight up to 3.08 lb. Although anteaters feed on termites and other soft-bodied insects, they are not insectivores, but belong to the order Edentata which means "without teeth."

Smallest Insectivore

The smallest insectivore is Savi's white-toothed pygmy shrew (*Suncus etruscus*), also called the Etruscan shrew, which is found along the coast of the northern Mediterranean and southwards to Cape Province, South Africa. Mature specimens have a head and body length of 1.32–2.04 in, a tail length of 0.94–1.14 in, and weight of between 0.052 and 0.09 oz.

Longest-Lived Insectivore

The greatest reliable age recorded for an insectivore is 10½ years for a hedgehog tenrec (*Setifer setosus*), which died in the London Zoo in 1971. There is an unconfirmed record of a hedgehog (*Erinaceus europaeus*) living for 14 years.

RAREST ANTELOPE (left): Only 4 black-headed duikers are left in captivity. Here are 2 of them. SMALLEST ANTELOPE (above): About the size of a hare, this royal antelope weighs no more than 8 lb.

LARGEST ANTELOPE (left): The rare Derby eland is a giant of its species and may weigh more than a ton.

Largest Antelope

The largest of all antelopes is the rare Derby eland (*Taurotragus derbianus*), also called the giant eland, of west and north-central Africa, which may surpass 2,000 lb. The common eland (*T. oryx*) of east and south Africa has the same shoulder height of up to 70 in, but is not quite so massive, although there is one record of a 65-in bull being shot in Nyasaland (now Malawi) *c.* 1937 which weighed 2,078 lb.

Smallest Antelope

The smallest known antelope is the royal antelope (*Neotragus pygmaeus*) of West Africa. Mature specimens measure only 10–12 in at the shoulder, and weigh only 7–8 lb, which is the size of a large brown hare. The slenderer Swayne's dik-dik (*Madoqua swaynei*) of Somalia, East Africa, weighs only 5–6 lb when adult, but stands about 13 in at the shoulder.

Rarest Antelope

The rarest antelope is probably Jentink's duiker (*Cephalophus jentinki*), also known as the black-headed duiker, which is found only in a restricted area of tropical West Africa. There are only four in captivity, "Alpha," a female born Dec 1, 1971, "Beta," and their two offspring, in the Gladys Porter Zoo, Brownsville, Tex.

Largest Deer

The largest deer is the Alaskan moose (*Alces alces gigas*). A bull standing 7 ft 8 in at the withers and weighing 1,800 lb was shot in Sept 1897 in the Yukon Territory, Canada. Unconfirmed measurements of up to 8½ ft at the withers and 2,600 lb have been claimed. The record antler span is 78½ in.

Smallest Deer

The smallest true deer (family Cervidae) is the pudu (*Pudu mephistophiles*) of Ecuador, the male of which stands 13–15 in at the shoulder and weighs 18–20 lb. The smallest known ruminant is the lesser Malayan chevrotain or mouse deer (*Tragulus javanicus*) of southeastern Asia. Adult specimens measure 8–10 in at the shoulder and weigh 6–7 lb.

Rarest Deer

The rarest deer is Fea's muntjac (*Muntiacus feae*), which is known only from two specimens collected on the borders of Tenasserim (Lower Burma) and Thailand.

Oldest Deer

The greatest reliable age recorded for a deer is 26 years 6 months 2 days for a red deer (*Cervus elaphus*), which died in the National Zoological Park, Washington, DC, March 24, 1941.

Longest Tusks

The longest recorded elephant tusks (excluding prehistoric examples) are a pair from Zaïre preserved in the National Collection of Heads and Horns, kept by the New York Zoological Society, Bronx Park. The right tusk measures 11 ft 5½ in along the outside curve and the left measures 11 ft. Their combined weight is 293 lb. A single tusk of 11 ft 6 in has been reported, but details are lacking.

Heaviest Tusk

The greatest weight ever recorded for one elephant tusk is 258 lb for a specimen collected in Benin (formerly Dahomey), West Africa, and exhibited at the Paris Exposition in 1900.

Longest Horns

The longest recorded animal horn was one measuring 81¼ in on the outside curve, with a circumference of 18¼ in, found on a specimen of domestic Ankole cattle (*Bos taurus*) near Lake Ngami, Botswana.

The largest head (horns measured from tip to tip across the forehead) is one of 13 ft 11 in on a wild buffalo (*Bubalus bubalus*) shot in India in 1955. The maximum for a Texas longhorn steer is 9 ft 9 in tip to tip.

The longest recorded anterior horn of a rhinoceros is one of 62¼ in, found on a female southern race white rhinoceros (*Ceratotheriam simum simum*) shot in South Africa *c.* 1848. The interior horn measured 22¼ in. There is also an unconfirmed record of an anterior horn measuring 81 in.

Blood Temperatures

The highest mammalian blood temperature is that of the domestic goat (*Capra hircus*) with an average of 103.8 °F and a normal range of from

"COOLEST" MAMMAL: The spiny anteater (above) has the lowest blood temperature of any mammal. It is from Australia and New Guinea.

HEAVIEST TUSKS (right): The elephant that bore these tusks could hardly raise his head and had to walk backwards to avoid getting them stuck in the ground. The heavier tusk was reported to weight 258 lb.

101.7° to 105.3°F. The lowest mammalian blood temperature is that of the spiny anteater (*Tachyglossus aculeatus*), a monotreme found in Australia and New Guinea, with a normal range of 72° to 87°F. The blood temperature of the golden hamster (*Mesocricetus auratus*) sometimes falls as low as 38.3°F during hibernation, and an extreme figure of 29.6°F has been reported for a myotis bat (family Vespertilionidae) during a deep sleep.

Ambergris

The heaviest piece of ambergris (a fatty deposit in the intestine of the sperm whale) on record weighed 1,003 lb and was recovered from a sperm whale (*Physeter catodon*) Dec 3, 1912 by a Norwegian whaling company in Australian waters. The lump was sold in London for £23,000 (then $111,780).

Largest Marsupial

The largest of all marsupials is the red kangaroo (*Macropus rufus*) of southern and eastern Australia. Adult males or "boomers" stand 6–7 ft tall, weigh 150–175 lb and measure up to 8 ft 11 in in a straight line from the nose to the tip of the extended tail.

Smallest Marsupial

The smallest known marsupial is the rare Kimberley planigale or flat-skulled marsupial mouse (*Planigale subtilissima*), found only in the Kimberley district of Western Australia. Adult males have a head and body length of 1.75 in, a tail length of 2 in and weight of about 0.141 oz. Females are smaller than males.

Rarest Marsupial

The rarest marsupial is probably the thylacine (*Thylacinus cynocephalus*), also known as the "Tasmanian tiger," the largest of the carnivorous marsupials, which reportedly became extinct some time in the mid-1930's. The last captive specimen died in the Hobart Zoo, Tasmania, in 1934. However, in 1961 a fisherman at Sandy Cape, western Tasmania, accidentally killed a young male, and in July 1977 a positive sighting was made of another specimen near Derby on the northwestern side of the island.

Longest-Lived Marsupial

The greatest reliable age recorded for a marsupial is 19 years 7 months for a South Australian wallaroo (*Macropus robustus erubescens*), which died at the New York Zoological Park (Bronx Zoo) in 1968.

Highest and Longest Marsupial Jump

The greatest measured height cleared by a hunted kangaroo is 10 ft 6 in over a pile of timber. The longest recorded leap was reported in Jan 1951 when, in the course of a chase, a female red kangaroo (*Macropus rufus*) made a series of bounds which included one of 42 ft. There is an unconfirmed report of a great gray kangaroo (*Macropus canguru*) jumping 44 ft 8½ in on the flat.

Most Valuable Furs

The highest-priced animal pelts are those of the sea otter (*Enhydra lutris*), also known as the Kamchatka beaver, which fetched up to $2,700 each before their 55-year-long protection started in 1912. The protection ended in 1967, and at the first legal auction of sea otter pelts in Seattle, Wash, Jan 31, 1968, Neiman-Marcus, the famous Dallas department store, paid $9,200 each for four pelts from Alaska.

In May 1970 a Kojah (mink-sable cross) coat costing $125,000 was sold by Neiman-Marcus to Welsh actor Richard Burton for his then wife, Elizabeth Taylor.

DOMESTICATED ANIMALS

Horse Population

The world's horse population is estimated to be 75 million.

Oldest Horse and Pony

The greatest reliable age recorded for a horse is 62 years in the case of "Old Billy" (foaled 1760), believed to be a cross between a Cleveland and an Eastern blood, who was bred by Edward Robinson of Wild Grave

JUMPERS: The red kangaroo (above) is known to have leaped 42 ft in one bound when chased. The Himalayan ibex (right) escapes from hunters by leaping criss-cross down sheer cliffs, momentarily touching its hoofs down on rocky ledges. Movies of the ibex can be seen at the various Guinness Museums.

Farm in Woolston, Lancashire, England. In 1762 or 1763 he was sold to the Mersey and Irwell Navigation Company and remained with them in a working capacity, marshalling and towing barges, until 1819 when he was retired to a farm, where he died Nov 27, 1822. The skull of this horse is preserved in the Manchester Museum, and his stuffed head is now on display in the Bedford Museum.

The greatest reliable age recorded for a pony is 54 years for a stallion owned by a farmer in central France which was still alive in 1919.

The greatest age recorded for a thoroughbred racehorse is 42 years in the case of the bay gelding "Tango Duke" (foaled 1935), owned by Mrs Carmen J. Koper of Barongarook, Victoria, Australia. The horse died Jan 25, 1978.

Largest Horse

The heaviest horse ever recorded was "Brooklyn Supreme," a pure-bred Belgian stallion (foaled Apr 12, 1928) owned by Ralph Fogleman of Callender, Iowa, which was reported to weigh slightly in excess of 3,200 lb shortly before his death Sept 6, 1948, aged 20. He stood 19.2 hands (6 ft 6 in).

In Apr 1973 the Belgian mare "Wilma du Bos" (foaled July 15, 1966), owned by Mrs Virgie Arden of Reno, Nev was reported to weigh slightly in excess of 3,200 lb when in foal and being shipped from Antwerp. The mare stood 18.2 hands (6 ft 2 in) and normally weighed about 2,400 lb.

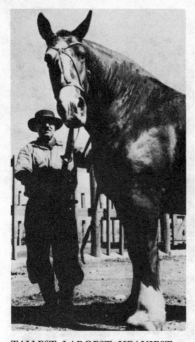

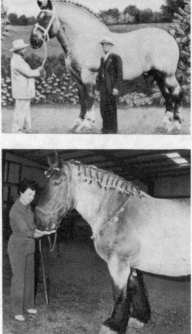

TALLEST, LARGEST, HEAVIEST
HORSES: "Firpon" (above) stood 7 ft 1 in high but weighed only 2,976 lb as compared to "Brooklyn Supreme" (top right) who tipped the scales at more than 3,200 lb. A mare "Wilma du Bos" (lower right) at the peak of her pregnancy weighed slightly more, though normally only 2,400 lb.

Tallest Horse

The tallest horse ever documented was the Percheron-Shire cross "Firpon" (foaled 1959) owned by Julio Falabella which stood 21.1 hands (7 ft 1 in) and weighed 2,976 lb. He died on Recco de Roca Ranch in Argentina, March 14, 1972. A height of 21.1 hands was also claimed for the Clydesdale gelding "Big Jim" (foaled 1950), bred by Lyall M. Anderson of West Broomley, Montrose, Scotland. "Big Jim" died in St Louis, Mo, in 1957.

A claim of 21.2 hands (7 ft 1½ in) was made in 1908 for "Morocco" of Allentown, Pa, weighing 2,835 lb.

Smallest Horse

The smallest breed of horse is the Falabella, bred by Julio Falabella (see *Tallest Horse*), developed over a period of 45 years by crossing and recrossing a small group of undersized English thoroughbreds with Shetland ponies. Adult specimens range from 15–30 in at the shoulder and weigh 40–80 lb. Foals standing 3 hands (12 in) have been recorded twice by Norman J. Mitchell of Glenorie, NSW, Australia, in the cases of "Tung Dynasty" (Feb 8, 1978) and "Quicksilver" (1975).

The upper accepted limit for the American Miniature Horse Breeders Association is 34 in.

Strongest Horses

The greatest load hauled by a pair of Clydesdale draught horses was 48 short tons (96,000 lb), equal to 50 pine logs (or 36,055 board-feet of lumber) hauled on a sledge litter 275 yd *pulled across snow* on the Nester Estate at Ewen, Mich, Feb 26, 1893. The two horses had a combined weight of 3,500 lb.

A pair of shire geldings owned by Liverpool Corporation registered a much more impressive *maximum* pull equivalent to a starting load of 56 tons on a dynamometer at the British Empire Exhibition at Wembley, London, Sept 4, 1924.

GREATEST LOAD EVER HAULED: These fifty logs weighing 96,000 lb were pulled 275 yd across snow by two Clydesdale horses in 1893 in Michigan. The horses themselves weighed a total of 3,500 lb.

Dog Population

In 1979 there were an estimated 41 million dogs in the US, compared to 5½ million in the UK.

Oldest Dogs

Authentic records of dogs living over 20 years are extremely rare, but even 34 years has been accepted by one authority. The greatest reliable age recorded for a dog is 29 years 5 months for a Queensland "heeler" named "Bluey," owned by Les Hall of Rochester, Vic, Australia. The dog was obtained as a puppy in 1910 and worked among cattle and sheep for nearly 20 years. He was put to sleep Nov 14, 1939.

Most Popular Dog Breed

The breed with the most American Kennel Club new registrations for the year 1979 was the poodle, with 57,700, down from 101,100 in 1978. Doberman Pinscher ran second. The earliest dog show was held in The

Town Hall, Newcastle upon Tyne, England, June 28–29, 1859, with 23 pointers and 27 setters.

Rarest Dog

The rarest breed of dog recognized by national kennel clubs is the Portuguese water dog (*Cao de Agua*). In Feb 1980, the world population was 334, including 297 in the US, and only 20 in Portugal.

Largest Dog

The heaviest breed of domestic dog (*Canis familiaris*) is the St Bernard. The heaviest example is "Benedictine," owned by Thomas C. and Ann E. Irwin of Grand Rapids, Mich. He was whelped Dec 17, 1970 and weighed 305 lb in May 1978 (height 39 in at shoulder).

Tallest Dogs

The tallest breeds of dog are the Great Dane and the Irish wolfhound, both of which can exceed 39 in at the shoulder. The extreme recorded example is the Great Dane "Shamgret Danzal" (whelped in 1975), owned by Mrs G. Comley of Milton Keynes, Buckinghamshire, England, which stands 40½ in and weighs 224 lb. The Irish wolfhound "Broadbridge Michael" (whelped in 1920), owned by Mrs Mary Beynon of Sutton-at-Hone, Kent, England, stood 39½ in at the age of two years.

Smallest Dogs

The smallest breeds of dog are the Yorkshire terrier, the Chihuahua and the toy poodle, *miniature* versions of which have been known to weigh less than 16 oz when adult. In Apr 1971 a weight of 10 oz was reliably reported for an adult Yorkshire terrier named "Sylvia," owned by Mrs Connie Hutchins of Walthamstow, Greater London, England.

Dog Strength and Endurance

The greatest load ever shifted by a dog was 6,400½ lb of railroad steel pulled by a 176-lb St Bernard named "Ryettes Brandy Bear," at Bothell, Wash, July 21, 1978. The 4-year-old dog, owned by Douglas Alexander of Monroe, Wash, pulled the weight on a four-wheeled carrier across a cement surface for a distance of 15 ft in less than 90 sec.

The strongest dog in the world in terms of most proportionate weight hauled is "Barbara-Allen's Dark Hans," a 97-lb Newfoundland, who pulled 5,045½ lb (= 52 lb per lb body weight) across a cement surface at Bothell, Wash, July 20, 1979. The dog, owned by Miss Terri Dickinson of Kenmore, Wash, was only 12 months old when he made the attempt.

In the annual 1,049-mile dog sled race from Anchorage to Nome, Alaska, the record time is 14 days 14 hours 43 min by "Emitt Peters" in the 1975 race.

Largest Litter

The largest recorded litter of puppies is one of 23 thrown on June 9, 1944, by "Lena," a foxhound bitch owned by Commander W. N. Ely of Ambler, Pa. On Feb 6–7, 1975, "Careless Ann," a St Bernard bitch owned by Robert and Alice Rodden of Lebanon, Mo, produced a litter of 23, of which 14 survived.

Most Prolific Dog

The dog who has sired the greatest recorded number of puppies was the greyhound "Low Pressure" nicknamed "Timmy," whelped in Sept 1957 and owned by Mrs Bruna Amhurst of Regent's Park, London. From Dec 1961 until he died in Nov 1969, he had fathered 2,414 registered puppies, with at least 600 others unregistered.

Most Valuable Dogs

Mrs Judith Thurlow of Great Ashfield, Suffolk, England, turned down an offer of £14,000 ($35,000) in June 1972 for her racing greyhound "Super Rory" (b Oct 1970). Show dogs have also fetched extremely high prices. In July 1976 Mrs Eiselle Banks of Rayleigh, Essex, England, turned down an American offer of $20,000 for her international champion Lowchen "Cluneen Adam Adamant" (b Aug 13, 1969). On June 27, 1972, August Belmont of Easton, Md, paid $22,000 for his Labrador retriever puppy, "Wanapum Lucky YoYo." This is the highest price *actually paid* for a dog.

Police Dogs

The top police dog is "Trep" of the Dade County Crime Force, Fla, who has sniffed out $63 million worth of narcotics. In a school demonstration looking for 10 hidden packets, Trep once found 11.

In Jan 1977 a "contract" worth $10,000 was put out on the life of a very successful drug-sniffing police dog named "Sergeant Blitz" by the underworld in Savannah, Ga. Shortly afterwards, an 8-ft-high concrete wall was built around the dog's kennel as a precautionary measure.

Guide Dog

The longest reported period of *active service* for a guide dog is 13 years 2 months, in the case of a Labrador retriever bitch named "Polly"

LARGEST LITTER: "Careless Ann," a St Bernard, tied the record of 23 puppies in 1975.

TALLEST DOG (left):
Standing 40½ in tall, this
Great Dane weighs 224 lb.
"TOP DOG": "Laika"
(right), a Samoyed husky was
rocketed in Sputnik II 1,050
miles into space in 1957.

(whelped Oct 10, 1956) owned by Rose Resnick of San Rafael, Calif. The
dog was put to sleep Dec 15, 1971.

"Top Dog"

The greatest altitude attained by a mammal other than man is 1,050
miles by the Samoyed husky bitch fired as a passenger in *Sputnik II* Nov
3, 1957. The dog was variously named "Kudryavka" (feminine form of
Curly), "Limonchik" (diminutive of lemon), "Malyshka," "Zhuchka" or
by the Russian breed name for husky "Laika."

Top Show Dog

The record number of "Best in Show" awards won by any dog in all-
breed shows is 127, compiled from Jan 1957 to Feb 1960 by the Peking-
ese International Champion "Chik T'Sun of Caversham," owned by Mr
and Mrs Charles C. Venable of Marietta, Ga.

Ratting Dog

The greatest ratter of all time was James Searle's bull terrier bitch
"Jenny Lind," who killed 500 rats in 1½ hours at "The Beehive" in Liverpool, England on July 12, 1853. Another bull terrier named "Jacko,"
owned by Mr Jemmy Shaw, was credited with killing 1,000 rats in 1 hour
40 min, but the feat was performed over a period of ten weeks in batches
of 100 at a time. The last 100 were accounted for in 5 min 28 sec in London on May 1, 1862.

Dog Tracking

The greatest tracking feat on record was performed by the Doberman
"Sauer" trained by Detective-Sergeant Herbert Kruger. In 1925 he
tracked a stock thief 100 miles across the Great Karroo, South Africa, by
scent alone.

In 1923 a collie named "Bobbie," lost by his owners while they were on
vacation in Wolcott, Ind, turned up at the family home in Silverton, Ore,

6 months later, after having covered a distance of close to 2,000 miles. The dog, later identified by people who had cared for him along the route, had apparently wandered back through Ill, Iowa, Neb, and Colo, before crossing the Rocky Mts in the depths of winter, then continuing through Wyo and Idaho.

Highest and Longest Dog Jumps

The canine "high jump" record for a leap and a scramble is held jointly by two German shepherd dogs named "Sabre" and "Harvey," who both scaled an 11-ft-6-in wall at the 22nd Annual Royal Air Force Police (UK) Working Dog Trials held at RAF Newton, Nottingham, England, on Aug 4, 1979.

The longest recorded canine long jump was one of 30 ft by a greyhound named "Bang," made in jumping a gate in coursing a hare at Brecon Lodge, Gloucestershire, England, in 1849.

Greatest Dog Funeral

The greatest dog funeral on record was for the mongrel "Lazaras," belonging to the eccentric, Emperor Norton I of the US, Protector of Mexico, held in San Francisco in 1862, which was attended by an estimated 10,000 people.

Top Dog Trainer

The most successful dog trainer—and the fastest—is Mrs Barbara Woodhouse of Rickmansworth, Hertfordshire, England, who has trained 17,028 dogs to a high standard from 1951 to March 25, 1980. Her record for a single day is 80 dogs in June 1973 in Denver, Colo.

Cat Population

The cat population in the US of 23 million is the largest in the world. It compares with 4.9 million in the UK.

Oldest Cats

Cats are generally longer-lived animals than dogs. Information on this subject is often obscured by two or more cats bearing the same nickname in succession. The oldest cat ever recorded was probably the tabby "Puss," owned by Mrs T. Holway of Clayhidon, Devon, England, who celebrated his 36th birthday on Nov 28, 1939 and died the next day. A more recent and better documented case was that of the female tabby "Ma," owned by Mrs Alice St George Moore, of Drewsteignton, Devon, England. She was put to sleep Nov 5, 1957, aged 34.

Largest Cat Litter

The largest litter ever recorded was one of 19 kittens (4 stillborn) delivered by Caesarean section to "Tarawood Antigone," a 4-year-old brown Burmese, on Aug 7, 1970. Her owner, Mrs Valerie Gane of Kingham, Oxfordshire, England, reported that the litter was the result of mismating with a half-Siamese. Of the 15 survivors, 14 were male.

The largest live litter of which all survived was one of 14 kittens born in Dec 1974 to the Persian cat "Bluebell," owned by Mrs Elenore Dawson of Wellington, Cape Province, South Africa.

Most Prolific Cat

A cat named "Dusty," aged 17, living in Bonham, Tex, gave birth to her 420th kitten June 12, 1952.

Heaviest Cat

The heaviest domestic cat (*Felix catus*) on record is a 10-year-old long-haired part-Persian named "Tiger," who until recently scaled 42–43 lb with a 12½-in neck, a 33-in waist and a 37-in length. He is owned by Mrs Phyllis Dacey of Billericay, Essex, England. In Sept 1979, however, he lost weight rapidly after being treated for a hormone imbalance and has since leveled out at 23 lb.

Smallest Cats

Because of the reproduction problems involved, there is no recognized smallest breed of cat. Adult weights of under 3 lb, however, have been reliably reported in cases of feline dwarfism (average weight 9–11 lb).

Richest Cats

Dr William Grier of San Diego, Calif, died in June 1963 leaving his entire estate of $415,000 to his two 15-year-old cats, "Hellcat" and "Brownie." When the cats died in 1965 the money went to George Washington University, Washington, DC.

Most Valuable Cat

In 1967 Miss Elspeth Sellar of Grafham, England, turned down an offer of 2,000 guineas (then $5,880) from an American breeder for her 2-year-old champion copper-eyed white Persian tom, "Coylum Marcus" (b March 28, 1965, d Apr 14, 1978).

Mousing Champion

The greatest mouser on record was a tabby named "Mickey," owned by Shepherd & Sons Ltd of Burscough, Lancashire, England, which killed more than 22,000 mice during 23 years with the firm. He died in Nov 1968.

Best Climbing Cat

On Feb 28, 1980 a female cat climbed 70 ft up the sheer outside wall of a 5-story apartment house in Bradford, Yorkshire, England, and took refuge in a roof space. She had been frightened by a dog.

Rabbits

The largest breed of domestic rabbit (*Oryctolagus cuniculus*) is the British giant. Adult specimens average 18–20 lb but weights up to 30 lb have been reliably reported for bucks. The heaviest recorded wild rabbit (average weight 3½ lb) is one of 6 lb 12 oz shot by Monty Forest on the Swinford Estate, Burford, Oxfordshire, England, in Feb 1976. The smallest breeds of domestic rabbit are the Netherlands dwarf and the Polish, both of which average 2¼ lb at maturity.

HEAVIEST CAT: Norris McWhirter, author of the "Guinness Book," checks for himself the weight of 42 lb (at his heaviest), claimed for "Tiger," a longhair part Persian. The cat is 37 in long, with a 33 in waist and a 12½ in neck.

Most Prolific Rabbits

The most prolific domestic breeds are the New Zealand white and the Californian. Does produce 5–6 litters a year, each containing 8–12 young (compare with 5 litters and 3–7 young for the wild rabbit).

Hares

In Nov 1956 a brown hare (*Lepus europaeus*), weighing a record 15 lb 1 oz, was shot near Welford, Northamptonshire, England. The average adult weight is 8 lb.

LARGEST PET LITTERS

Animal	Number	Breed	Owner
Cat	15	Burmese Siamese	Mrs Valerie Gane, Kingham, Oxfordshire, Eng
Dog	23	Foxhound	Cdr W. N. Ely, Ambler, Pa
	23	St Bernard	R. and A. Rodden, Lebanon, Mo
Rabbit	24	New Zealand White	Joseph Filek, Sydney, Cape Breton, Nova Scotia, Canada
Guinea Pig	12		Laboratory Specimen.
Hamster	18	Golden Hamster	Laboratory Specimen.
Mouse	32	House Mouse	Laboratory Specimen (US).
Gerbil	11		Steve Austin, Addington, Surrey, Eng

CAGED PET LONGEVITY TABLE

The greatest recorded ages for commonly kept pets are as follows:

	Years	Months	
Rabbit (*Oryctolagus cuniculus*)	18*		European rabbit *fl.* Aug 1977
Guinea Pig (*Cavia porcellus*)	14	10½	Snowball (M. A. Wall) Bingham, Eng Died Feb 14, 1979
Gerbil (*Gerbillus gerbillus*)	7	9½	Squirt (Tom Clouser) Brookfield, Wis. Died Sept 22, 1977
House Mouse (*Mus musculus*)	5	11	Hercules (R. Hair) Purley, Surrey, Eng Jan 1971–Dec 26, 1976
Rat (*Rattus sp.*)	5	8	Philadelphia *c.* 1924

* 18 years also reported for a doe still living in 1947.

Note: A report of 10 years 2 months for a hamster has been published but details are lacking.

2. BIRDS (*AVES*)

Largest Bird

The largest living bird is the North African ostrich (*Struthio camelus camelus*) which is found in reduced numbers south of the Atlas Mountains from Upper Senegal and Niger across to the Sudan and central Ethiopia. Male examples of this flightless or ratite subspecies have been recorded up to 9 ft in height and 345 lb in weight.

The heaviest flying bird, or *carinate,* is the Kori bustard or paauw (*Otis kori*) of East and South Africa. Weights up to 40 lb have been reliably reported for cock birds shot in South Africa. The mute swan (*Cygnus olor*) which is resident in Britain can also reach 40 lb on occasion, and there is a record from Poland of a cob weighing 49.5 lb which was probably too heavy to fly.

The heaviest bird of prey is the Andean condor (*Vultur gryphus*), which averages 20–25 lb as an adult. An unconfirmed weight of 31 lb has been claimed for a California condor (*Gymnogyps californianus*) (average weight 20 lb) now preserved in the California Academy of Sciences, Los Angeles.

Largest Wing Span

The wandering albatross (*Diomedea exulans*) of the southern oceans has the largest wing span of any living bird, adult males averaging 10 ft 4 in with wings tightly stretched. The largest recorded specimen was a male measuring 11 ft 10 in caught by banders in Western Australia *c.* 1957, but some unmeasured birds may exceed 13 ft.

The only other bird reliably credited with a wing spread in excess of 11 ft is the vulture-like marabou stork (*Leptoptilus crumeniferus*) of Africa. In the 1930's an extreme measurement of 13 ft 4 in was reported for a specimen shot in Central Africa, but this species rarely exceeds 9 ft.

Smallest Bird

The smallest bird is Helena's hummingbird (*Mellisuga helenae*) found in Cuba and the Isle of Pines. An average male adult measures 2.28 in in

LARGEST WING SPAN (left): The wandering albatross has a wing span that may exceed 13 ft. This one measures 11 ft 4 in. SMALLEST BIRD (right): Helena's hummingbird weighs 0.07 oz and is only 2¼ in long, including its bill.

total length—bill 0.59 in, head and body 0.59 in and tail 1.10 in—and weighs about 0.07 oz, which means it is lighter than a Sphinx moth (0.08 oz).

The smallest bird of prey is the 1¼-oz. Bornean falconet (*Microhierax latifrons*), which is about the size of a sparrow.

The smallest sea bird is the least storm petrel (*Halocyptena microsoma*), which breeds on many of the small islands in the Gulf of Calif, Mexico. Adult specimens average 5½ in in total length.

Rarest Bird

Because of the practical difficulties involved in assessing bird populations in the wild, it is virtually impossible to establish the identity of the rarest living bird. One of the strongest contenders, however, must be the Kauai O-o (*Moho braccatus*) of Kauai, Hawaii, of which only a single pair survived in 1976. In Jan 1978 a New Zealand ornithological expedition exploring Chatham Island positively identified and photographed three magenta petrels (*Pterodroma magentae*). The only previous *claimed* sighting had been in 1868, about 500 miles east of the island.

In 1979 only 8 Japanese ibis (*Nipponia nippon*) survived in a government nature reserve.

In Dec 1977 the white-winged guan (*Penelope albinennis*), thought to have become extinct about 100 years ago, was rediscovered in considerable numbers in northwestern Peru.

The world's rarest raptor (bird of prey) is the Mauritius kestrel (*Falco punctatus*). In Dec 1978 the total wild population was 18, with another 5 being raised in captivity.

Longest-Lived Bird

The greatest irrefutable age reported for any bird is 72 years in the case of a male Andean condor (*Vultur gryphus*) named "Kuzya," which died in Moskovskii Zoologicheskii Park, Moscow, in 1964. This bird had been received there as an adult in 1892. Other records which are regarded as *probably* reliable include 73 years (1818–91) for a greater sulphur-crested cockatoo (*Cacatua galerita*), 72 years (1797–1869) for an African

MOST ABUNDANT BIRD: About 10 billion red-billed queleas, shown alone and in a more social situation, inhabit sub-Saharan Africa.

gray parrot (*Psittacus erithacus*), 70 years (1770–1840) for a mute swan (*Cygnus olor*), and 69 years for a raven (*Corvus corax*). In 1972 a southern ostrich (*Struthio camelus australis*) aged 62 years 3 months was killed in the Ostrich Abattoir at Oudtshoorn, Cape Province, South Africa.

"Jimmy," a red and green Amazon parrot owned by Mrs Bella Ludford of Liverpool, England, was allegedly hatched in captivity on Dec 3, 1870, and lived 104 years in his original brass cage. He died Jan 5, 1975.

Most Abundant Birds

The most abundant species of wild bird is the red-billed quelea (*Quelea quelea*) of the drier parts of Africa south of the Sahara with a population estimated at 10,000 million of which a tenth are destroyed each year by pest control units.

The most abundant domesticated bird is the chicken, the domesticated form of the wild red jungle fowl (*Gallus gallus*) of Southeast Asia. In 1974 there were believed to be about 4,000 million chickens in the world, or about one chicken for every member of the human race.

The most abundant sea bird is Wilson's petrel (*Oceanites oceanicus*). No population estimates have been published, but the number runs into the hundreds—possibly thousands—of millions.

Fastest-Flying Bird

The spine-tailed swift (see page 53) is the fastest bird.

The bird which presents the hunter with the greatest difficulty is the red-breasted merganser (*Mergus serrator*). On May 29, 1960 a specimen flushed from the Kukpuk River, Cape Thompson, northern Alaska, by a light aircraft recorded an air speed of 80 mph in level flight for nearly 13 sec before turning aside.

Fastest and Slowest Wing Beat

The fastest recorded wing beat of any bird is 90 beats per sec by the hummingbird *Heliactin cornuta* of tropical South America. This rate is probably exceeded by the bee hummingbirds *Mellisuga helenae* and *Acestrura bombus,* but no figures have yet been published.

Large vultures (family Vulturidae) and albatrosses (family Diomedeidae) can soar for hours without beating their wings, and sometimes exhibit a flapping rate as low as one beat per sec.

Fastest Swimming and Deepest Diving Birds

The fastest swimmer is the Gentoo penguin (*Pygoscelis papua*). In Jan 1913 a small group was timed at 22.3 mph underwater near the Bay of Isles, South Georgia, Falkland Islands, South Atlantic. This is a respectable flying speed for some birds.

The deepest diver is the emperor penguin (*Aptenodytes forsteri*) of the Antarctic which can reach a depth of 870 ft and remain submerged for as long as 18 min.

Longest Bird Flights

The greatest distance covered by a ringed bird during migration is 12,-000 miles by an Arctic tern (*Sterna paradisaea*), which was banded as a nestling July 5, 1955 in the Kandalaksha Sanctuary on the White Sea coast of the USSR, north of Archangel, and was captured alive by a fisherman 8 miles south of Fremantle, Western Australia, May 16, 1956.

Highest-Flying

The celebrated example of a skein of 17 Egyptian geese (*Alopochen aegyptiacus*), photographed by an astronomer from Dehra Dun, India, Sept 17, 1919 as they crossed the sun at a height estimated at between 11 and 12 miles (58,080–63,360 ft), has been discredited by experts. The highest acceptable altitude recorded for a bird is 27,000 ft for 30 whooper swans (*Cygnus c. cygnus*) flying in from Iceland to the UK. They were spotted by an airline pilot over the Outer Hebrides on Dec 9, 1967, and the height was also confirmed by air traffic control in Northern Ireland after the skein had been picked up on radar.

Highest g Force in Bird World

Recent American scientific experiments have revealed that the beak of the red-headed woodpecker (*Melanerpes erythrocephalus*) hits the bark of a tree with an impact velocity of 1,300 mph. This means that when the head snaps back the brain is subject to a deceleration of about 1,000 g.

Most Airborne Birds

The most airborne of all land birds is the common swift (*Apus apus*) which remains aloft for at least nine months of the year, but the sooty tern (*Sterna fuscata*) remains continuously aloft for three or four years after leaving the nesting grounds before it returns to the breeding grounds.

Birds with Most Acute Vision

Birds of prey (Falconiformes) have the keenest eyesight in the avian

LARGEST AND SMALLEST EGGS
(left): The ostrich egg at about 3¾ lb
weighs 352 times as much as the
Helena's hummingbird's egg. BIRD
WATCHER (above): Stuart Keith has
sighted over 5,457 birds or 63% of the
known species in the world.

world. Their visual acuity is at least 8–10 times stronger than that of
human vision. The golden eagle (*Aquila chrysaetos*) can detect an 18-in-
long hare at a range of 2,150 yd (possibly even 2 miles), in good light and
against a contrasting background, and a peregrine falcon (*Falco peregrinus*) can detect a pigeon at a range of over 3,500 ft.

Largest Bird Eggs

Of living birds, the one producing the largest egg is the ostrich
(*Struthio camelus*). The average egg weighs 3.63–3.88 lb, measures 6–8 in
in length, 4–6 in in diameter and requires about 40 min for boiling. The
shell, though 1/16th in thick, can support the weight of a 280-lb man.

Smallest Bird Eggs

The smallest egg laid by any bird is that of Helena's hummingbird
(*Mellisuga helenae*), the world's smallest bird. One measuring 0.45 in
long and 0.32 in wide is now in the US National Museum, Washington,
DC. This egg, which weighs 0.176 oz, was collected at Boyate, Santiago
de Cuba, May 8, 1906.

Incubation

The longest incubation period is that of the wandering albatross (*Diomedea exulans*), with a normal range of 75–82 days. There is one case of
an egg of the mallee fowl (*Leipoa ocellata*) of Australia taking 90 days to
hatch. Its normal incubation period is 62 days. The shortest incubation
period is the 10 days of the great spotted woodpecker (*Dendrocopus
major*) and the black-billed cuckoo (*Coccyzus erythropthalmus*). The
idlest of cock birds are hummingbirds (family Trochilidae), eider ducks
(*Somateria mollissima*) and golden pheasants (*Chrysolophus pictus*),
among whom the hen bird does 100% of the incubation, whereas the female common kiwi (*Apteryx australis*) leaves this entirely to the male for
75–80 days.

Largest Nests

The largest bird's nest on record is one 9½ ft wide and 20 ft deep built by bald eagles (*Haliaeetus leucocephalus*) near St Petersburg, Fla, reported in 1963 and estimated to weigh more than 2 tons. The incubation mounds built by scrubfowl (family Megapodidae) have, however, been measured up to 50 ft in diameter and 20 ft in height.

Longest Feathers

The longest feathers grown by any bird are those of the cock long-tailed fowls, or onagadori (a strain of *Gallus gallus*), which have been bred in southwestern Japan since the mid-17th century. In 1973 a tail covert measuring 34 ft 9½ in was reported by Masasha Kubota of Kochi, Shikoku.

The tail feathers of the flying Reeve's pheasant (*Syrmaticus reevesi*) of north and west China can exceed 8 ft.

Most Feathers

In a series of "feather counts" on various species of birds, a whistling swan (*Cygnus columbianus*) was found to have 25,216 feathers. A ruby-throated hummingbird (*Archilochus colubris*) had only 940, although hummingbirds have more feathers per area of body surface than any other living bird.

Champion Bird-Watcher

The world's leading bird-watcher is G. Stuart Keith, an Englishman who works at the American Museum of Natural History, New York City. In the 33 years to March 1980, his score is 5,457 species of the 8,650 known species.

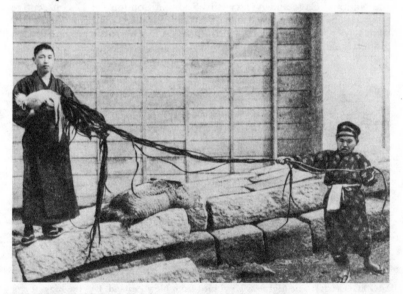

LONGEST FEATHERS: Tail feathers on the cock birds of the onagadori have been known to measure more than 34 ft long.

DOMESTICATED BIRDS

Heaviest Turkey

The greatest dressed weight recorded for a turkey (*Meleagris gallopavo*) is 77 lb ¼ oz for a 53-week-old stag reared by Leacroft Turkeys, Ltd of Barrwell, England. It won the annual heaviest turkey competition held in London Dec 9, 1979.

Most Expensive Turkey

The highest price reached at auction (auctioneer William Rushton) for a turkey was £1,800 ($4,000) paid by Tom Granby, a Liverpool wholesale poultry merchant for the 77-lb stag (see above) at the Waldorf Hotel, London, on Dec 7, 1979.

Heaviest Chicken

The heaviest breed of chicken is one called the white sully developed by Grant Sullens of West Point, Calif, over a period of 7 years. One monstrous rooster named "Weirdo" reportedly weighed 22 lb in Jan 1973, and was so ferocious that he crippled a dog which came too close and killed two cats.

The record flight by a chicken is 302 ft 8 in by "Lola B" at the 8th annual International Chicken Flying Association meet at Rio Grande, Ohio, in June 1979.

Most Talkative Bird

The world's most talkative bird is a male African gray parrot (*Psittacus erythacus*) named "Prudle," owned by Mrs Lyn Logue of Golders Green, London, England, which won the "best talking parrot-like bird" title at the National Cage and Aviary Bird Show in London for 12 consecutive years (1965–76) before retiring undefeated. Prudle, who has a vocabulary of nearly 1,000 words, was taken from a nest in a tree about to be felled at Jinja, Uganda, in 1958.

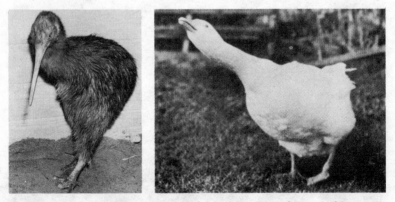

BIG EGG (left): The flightless Kiwi bird from New Zealand, lays the biggest egg in proportion to its size. OLDEST BIRD (right): "George," a gander lived almost 50 years.

RECORD FLIGHT for a chicken was 302 ft 8 in by "Lola B" in a meet in Ohio in June 1979.

Longest-Lived Domestic Birds

The longest-lived domesticated bird (excluding the ostrich) is the domestic goose which normally lives about 25 years. A gander named "George," owned by Mrs Florence Hull of Lancashire, England, died on Dec 16, 1976, aged 49 years 8 months. He was hatched in Apr 1927. The longest-lived small cage bird is the canary (*Serinus canaria*). The oldest example on record was a 34-year-old cock bird named "Joey," owned by Mrs K. Ross of Hull, England. The bird was purchased in Calabar, Nigeria, in 1941, and died Apr 8, 1975.

The oldest budgerigar (*Melopsittacus undulatus*) (also called parakeet) on record was a hen bird named "Charlie," owned by Miss J. Dinsey of Stonebridge, London, England, which lived for 29 years 2 months, and died June 20, 1977.

3. REPTILES (*REPTILIA*)

(Crocodiles, snakes, turtles, tortoises and lizards)

Largest and Heaviest Reptiles

The largest reptile in the world is the estuarine or salt-water crocodile (*Crocodylus porosus*) of Southeast Asia, northern Australia, New Guinea, the Philippines and the Solomon Islands. Adult bulls average 12–14 ft in length and scale about 1,100 lb. In 1823 a notorious man-eater 27 ft in length and weighing an estimated 4,400 lb was shot at Jala Jala on Luzon Island in the Philippines after terrorizing the neighborhood for many years. Its skull, the largest on record (if we exclude fossil remains) is now preserved in the Museum of Comparative Zoology at Harvard University, Cambridge, Mass. Another outsized example with a reputed length of 33 ft and a maximum bodily girth of 13 ft 8 in was shot in the Bay of Bengal, India, in 1840, but the dimensions of its skull (preserved in the British Museum of Natural History, London) suggest that it must have come from a crocodile measuring about 24 ft.

The holder of the "official" record is a 20-ft-2-in bull harpooned by Keith Adams in the MacArthur River near Borroloola in northern Australia June 26, 1960.

In July 1957 an unconfirmed length of 28 ft 4 in was reported for an estuarine crocodile shot by Mrs Kris Pawlowski on MacArthur Bank in the Norman River, northwestern Queensland, Australia.

Largest Lizards

The largest of all lizards is the Komodo monitor or Ora (*Varanus komodoensis*), a dragon-like reptile found on the Indonesian islands of Komodo, Rintja, Padar and Flores. Adult males average 8 ft in length and weigh 175–200 lb. Lengths up to 23 ft (*sic*) have been quoted for this species, but the largest specimen to be accurately measured was a male presented to an American zoologist in 1928 by the Sultan of Bima which taped 10 ft 0.8 in. In 1937 this animal was put on display in the St Louis Zoological Gardens for a short period. It then measured 10 ft 2 in in length and weighed 365 lb.

The longest lizard in the world is the slender Salvadori dragon (*Varanus salvadori*) of New Guinea. One of 18 ft was reported by "Operation Drake" in Dec 1979.

Oldest Lizard

The greatest age recorded for a lizard is more than 54 years for a male slow worm (*Anguis fragilis*) kept in the Zoological Museum in Copenhagen, Denmark, from 1892 until 1946.

Largest Chelonians

The largest of all chelonians is the Pacific leatherback turtle (*Dermochelys coriacea schlegelii*). The average adult measures 6–7 ft in overall length (length of carapace 4–5 ft) and weighs between 660 and 800 lb. The greatest weight reliably recorded is 1,908 lb for a specimen captured off Monterey, Calif on Aug 29, 1961. Its length was 8 ft 4 in overall.

The largest living tortoise is *Geochelone* (*Testudo*) *gigantea* of the Indian Ocean islands of Aldabra, Mauritius, Réunion and Seychelles (introduced 1874). Adult males sometimes exceed 350 lb in weight, and a specimen weighing 900 lb was allegedly collected in Aldabra in 1847. The largest desert tortoise is the protected *Gopherus agassizi* of the southwestern US, which normally weighs about 10–12 lb when fully grown. In Jan 1976 a weight of 23 lb 14 oz was recorded for a huge male with a shell 15 in long, found in the Mojave Desert, Calif.

Longest-Lived Chelonians

Tortoises are the longest-lived of all vertebrates. Reliable records over 100 years include a common box tortoise (*Testudo carolina*) of 138 years and a European pond tortoise (*Emys orbicularis*) of 120+ years. The greatest proven age of a continuously observed tortoise is 116+ years for a Mediterranean spur-thighed tortoise (*Testudo graeca*) which died in Paignton Zoo, Devon, England, in 1957.

Slowest-Moving Chelonians

In a recent "speed" test carried out in the Seychelles, in the Indian Ocean, a male giant tortoise (*Geochelone gigantea*) could only cover 5 yd in 43.5 sec (0.23 mph) despite the enticement of a female tortoise. The National Tortoise Championship held at Tickhill, South Yorkshire, England, has the animals going up a 1:12 grade and the meet record is 18 ft in 43.7 sec by "Charlie."

Smallest Reptiles

The smallest known species of reptile is believed to be *Sphaerodactylus*

LARGEST CHELONIAN: This giant tortoise from Aldabra Island in the Indian Ocean provides transportation for a smaller relative.

parthenopion, a tiny gecko found only on the island of Virgin Gorda, one of the British Virgin Islands in the Caribbean. It is known only from 15 specimens, including some gravid females, found between Aug 10 and 16, 1964. The three largest females measured 0.71 in from snout to vent, with a tail of approximately the same length.

It is possible that another gecko, *Sphaerodactylus elasmorhynchus,* may be even smaller. The only specimen ever discovered was an apparently mature female, with a snout-vent length of 0.67 in and a tail of the same length, found March 15, 1966 among the roots of a tree in the western part of the Massif de la Hotte in Haiti.

A species of dwarf chameleon, *Evoluticauda tuberculata,* found in Madagascar, and known only from a single specimen, has a snout-vent length of 0.71 in and a tail length of 0.55 in. Chameleons, however, are more bulky than geckos, and it is not yet known if this specimen was fully grown.

Shortest Snakes

The shortest known snake is the thread snake *Leptotyphlops bilineata,* found on the Caribbean islands of Martinique, Barbados and St. Lucia. It has a maximum recorded length of 4.7 in.

The shortest venomous snake is the striped dwarf garter snake (*Elaps dorsalis*) of South Africa. Adults average 6 in in length.

Heaviest Snakes

The heaviest snake is the anaconda (*Eunectes murinus*), which is nearly

PYTHONS (above): 22-ft-long skins are hung up to dry in a London warehouse. (Left) "Susie", a 22-ft-long python alive and well in India.

SNAKE EATING: This reticulated python has just swallowed a large bush pig.

FASTEST?: The black mamba (above) sustained a speed of 7 mph, and the race runner (left) hit 18 mph in a spurt when chased by a car.

twice as heavy as a reticulated python of the same length. The specimen shot in Brazil *c.* 1960 (see below) was not weighed, but based on its maximum bodily girth of 44 in, it must have weighed nearly 500 lb.

The heaviest venomous snake is the eastern diamondback rattlesnake (*Crotalus adamanteus*), found in the southeastern US. One specimen measuring 7 ft 9 in in length weighed 34 lb. Less reliable weights up to 40 lb and lengths up to 8 ft 9 in have been reported.

A posthumous weight of 28 lb was reported for a king cobra (*Ophiophagus hannah*) 14 ft 5 in long at the New York Zoological Park (Bronx Zoo) in Feb 1973.

Longest Snakes

The longest of all snakes (average adult length) is the reticulated python (*Python reticulatus*) of Southeast Asia, Indonesia and the Philippines, which regularly exceeds 20 ft. In 1912 a specimen measuring exactly 32 ft 9½ in was shot near a mining camp on the north coast of Celebes in the Malay archipelago.

Lengths of 37½ ft, 42 ft and even 45 ft have been claimed for the anaconda (*Eunectes murinus*) of tropical South America, but these extreme measurements were probably based on stretched skins. The greatest authenticated length recorded for an anaconda is 27 ft 9 in for a female killed in Brazil *c.* 1960.

The longest snake living in captivity today is probably a female reticulated python named "Cassius" owned by Adrian Nyoka of Knaresborough Zoo, North Yorkshire, England, which measures 25 ft and weighs 240 lb. It was collected in Malaysia in 1972.

The longest venomous snake in the world is the king cobra (*Ophiophagus hannah*), also called the hamadryad, of Southeast Asia and the Philippines. A specimen collected near Port Dickson in Malaya in April 1937 grew to 18 ft 9 in in the London Zoo. It was destroyed at the outbreak of war in 1939.

Oldest Snake

The greatest irrefutable age recorded for a snake is 40 years 3 months and 14 days in the case of a common Boa (*Boa constrictor constrictor*) at Philadelphia Zoological Gardens. Named "Popeye," he was purchased from a London dealer in Dec 1936, and he was euthanased (his life was humanely ended) on Apr 15, 1977 because of medical problems associated with advanced age.

Fastest-Moving Land Snake

The fastest-moving land snake is probably the slender black mamba (*Dendroaspis polylepis*). On Apr 23, 1906 an angry black mamba was timed at a speed of 7 mph over a measured distance of 47 yd near Mbuyuni on the Serengeti Plains, Tanzania. Stories that black mambas can overtake galloping horses (maximum speed 43.26 mph) are wild exaggerations, though a speed of 15 mph may be possible for short bursts over level ground.

The highest speed measured for any reptile on land is 18 mph by a six-lined race runner (*Cnemidophorus sexlineatus*) pursued by a car near McCormick, SC, in 1941. The highest speed claimed for any reptile in

LONGEST VENOMOUS SNAKE: The king cobra, 18 ft 9 in in length.

water is 22 mph by a frightened Pacific leatherback turtle (see *Largest Chelonians*).

Most Venomous Snakes

The most venomous snake is the sea snake (*Hydrophis belcheri*) which has a venom 100 times as toxic as that of the Australian taipan (*Oxyuranus scutellatus*). The snake abounds around Ashmore Reef in the Timor Sea, off the coast of northwestern Australia.

The most venomous land snake is the small scaled or fierce snake (*Parademansia microlepidotus*) of southwestern Queensland and northeastern South Australia and Tasmania. One specimen yielded 0.00385 oz of venom after milking, a quantity sufficient to kill at least 125,000 mice. Until 1976, this 6–ft–6–in–long snake was regarded as a western form of the taipan, but its venom differs significantly from the latter.

It is estimated that between 30,000 and 40,000 people (excluding Chinese and Russians) die from snakebite each year, 75% of them in densely populated India. Burma has the highest mortality rate with 15.4 deaths per 100,000 population per annum.

Longest Fangs

The longest fangs of any snake are those of the Gaboon viper (*Bitis gabonica*), of tropical Africa. In a 6-ft-long specimen, the fangs measured 1.96 in. A Gaboon viper bit itself to death on Feb 12, 1963 in the Philadelphia Zoological Gardens. Keepers found the dead snake with its fangs deeply embedded in its own back.

4. AMPHIBIANS (*AMPHIBIA*)

(Salamanders, toads, frogs, newts, caecilians, etc.)

Largest Amphibian

The largest species of amphibian is the Chinese giant salamander (*Megalobatrachus davidianus*), which lives in the cold mountain streams and marshy areas of northeastern, central and southern China. The average adult measures 39 in in total length and weighs 24 to 28 lb. One huge individual collected in Kweichow (Guizhou) Province in southern China in the early 1920's measured 5 ft in total length and weighed nearly 100 lb. The Japanese giant salamander (*Megalobatrachus japonicus*) is slightly smaller, but one captive specimen weighed 88 lb when alive and 100 lb after death, the body having absorbed water from the aquarium.

Largest Newt

The largest newt is the pleurodele or ribbed newt (*Pleurodeles waltl*), found in Morocco and on the Iberian Peninsula. Specimens measuring up to 15.74 in in total length and weighing over 1 lb have been reliably reported.

Largest Frog

The largest known frog is the rare Goliath frog (*Rana goliath*) of Cameroon and Equatorial Guinea. A female weighing 7 lb 4.5 oz was caught in the rapids of the River Mbia, Equatorial Guinea, on Aug 23, 1960. It had a snout-vent length of 13.38 in and measured 32.08 in overall with legs extended. In Dec 1960 another giant frog known locally as "agak" or "carn-pnag" and said to measure 12–15 in snout to vent and to weigh over 6 lb was reportedly discovered in central New Guinea, but further information is lacking. In 1969 a new species of giant frog was discovered in Sumatra.

LARGEST FROG (left): The Goliath frog of West Africa (shown with a falcon for size comparison) can be over 32 in long and weigh up to 7¼ lb. LARGEST AMPHIBIAN (right): The Chinese giant salamander, which lives in cold mountain streams, can grow to a length of 5 ft and weight 100 lb.

LARGEST AND SMALLEST TOADS: The So. American marine toad (left) can weigh up to 2 lb 11¼ oz. The tiniest (above) measure less than one inch.

Largest Tree Frog

The largest species of tree frog is *Hyla vasta,* found only on the island of Hispaniola (Haiti and the Dominican Republic) in the West Indies. The average snout-vent length is about 3.54 in but a female collected from the San Juan River, Dominican Republic, in March 1928 measured 5.63 in.

Largest Toad

The largest toad is probably the marine toad (*Bufo marinus*) of tropical South America. An enormous female collected on Nov 24, 1965 at Miraflores Vaupes, Colombia, and later exhibited in the reptile house at the Bronx Zoo, New York City, had a snout-vent length of 9.37 in and weighed 2 lb 11¼ oz at the time of its death in 1967.

Smallest Amphibian

The smallest species of amphibian is believed to be the arrow-poison frog *Sminthillus limbatus,* found only in Cuba. Fully-grown specimens have a snout-vent length of 0.44–0.48 in.

Smallest Newt ·

The smallest newt is believed to be the striped newt (*Notophthalmus perstriatus*) of the southeastern US. Adult specimens average 2.01 in in total length.

Smallest Tree Frog

The smallest tree frog is the least tree frog (*Hyla ocularis*), found in the southeastern US. It has a maximum snout-vent length of 0.62 in.

Smallest Toad

The smallest toad is the sub-species *Bufo taitanus beiranus,* first discovered *c.* 1906 near Beira, Mozambique, East Africa. Adult specimens have a maximum recorded snout-vent length of 0.94 in.

Smallest Salamander

The smallest species of salamander is the pygmy salamander (*Desmognathus wrighti*), which is found only in Tenn, NC, and Va. Adult specimens measure 1.45–2.0 in in total length.

Longest-Lived Amphibian

The greatest authentic age recorded for an amphibian is about 55 years for a male Japanese giant salamander (*Megalobatrachus japonicus*) which died in the aquarium at Amsterdam Zoological Gardens June 3, 1881. It was brought to Holland in 1829, at which time it was estimated to be 3 years old.

Highest and Lowest

The greatest altitude at which an amphibian has been found is 26,246 ft in the Himalayas for a common toad (*Bufo vulgaris*). This species has also been found at a depth of 1,115 ft in a coal mine.

Most Poisonous Venom

The most active known venom is the batrachotoxin derived from the skin secretions of the kokoi (*Phyllobates latinasus*), an arrow-poison frog of northwestern Colombia, South America. Only about 1/100,000th gram (0.0000004 oz) is enough to kill a man.

Longest Frog Jump

The record for three consecutive leaps is 33 ft 5½ in by a female South African sharp-nosed frog (*Rana oxyrhyncha*) named "Santjie" at a frog derby held at Lurula Natal Spa, Paulpietersburg, Natal, Africa May 21, 1977.

At the annual Calaveras County Jumping Frog Jubilee at Angels Camp, Calif, in 1975, another specimen "Ex Lax" made a *single* leap of 17 ft 6¾ in for its owner Bill Moniz.

5. FISHES (*PISCES, BRADYODONTI, SELACHII AND MARSIPOLI*)

Largest Fresh-Water Fishes

The largest fish which spends its whole life in fresh or brackish water is the rare Pa Beuk or Pla Buk (*Pangasianodon gigas*), a giant catfish found in the Mekong River of Laos and Thailand. Adult males average 8 ft in length and weigh about 360 lb. This size was exceeded by the European catfish or wels (*Silurus glanis*). In the 19th century lengths of up to 15 ft and weights up to 720 lb were reported for Russian specimens, but today anything over 6 ft and 200 lb is considered large. The arapaima (*Arapaima glanis*), also called the pirarucu, found in the Amazon and other South American rivers and often claimed to be the largest fresh-water fish, averages 6½ ft and 150 lb. The largest "authentically recorded" measured 8 ft 1½ in and weighed 325 lb. It was caught in the Rio Negro,

Brazil, in 1836. In Sept 1978 a Nile perch (*Lates niloticus*) weighing 416 lb was netted in the eastern part of Lake Victoria, Kenya.

Largest Sea Fishes

The largest fish is the rare, plankton-feeding whale shark (*Rhiniodon typus*) which is found in the warmer areas of the Atlantic, Pacific and Indian Oceans. It is not, however, the largest marine animal, since it is smaller than the larger species of whales (mammals). A whale shark measuring 60 ft 9 in long and weighing an estimated 90,000 lb was caught in a bamboo fish-trap at Koh Chik, in the Gulf of Siam, in 1919.

The largest carnivorous fish (excluding plankton-eaters) is the great white shark (*Carcharodon carcharias*), also called "the man-eater," which ranges from the tropics to temperate zone waters. In June 1930 a specimen measuring 37 ft in length was reportedly trapped in a herring weir at the White Head Island, New Brunswick, Canada, but may have been a wrongly identified basking shark (*Cetorhinus maximus*). In May 1948 a great white shark measuring 21 ft in length was captured after a fierce battle by fishermen off Havana, Cuba. It weighed 7,302 lb.

The longest of the bony or "true" fishes (Pisces) is the Russian sturgeon (*Acipenser huso*), also called the Beluga, which is found in the temperate areas of the Adriatic, Black and Caspian Seas, but enters large rivers like the Volga and the Danube for spawning. Lengths up to 26 ft 3 in have been reliably reported, and a gravid female taken in the estuary of the Volga in 1827 weighed 3,250 lb.

The heaviest bony fish in the world is the ocean sunfish (*Mola mola*), which is found in all tropical, sub-tropical and temperate waters. On Sept 18, 1908 a huge specimen was accidentally struck by the SS *Fiona* off

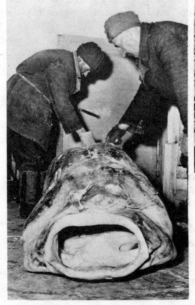

LARGEST FRESH-WATER FISH (left): This European catfish, or wels, measured 11 ft long and weighed 565 lb. Russians have reported wels of 15 ft. LARGEST FISH (above): The whale shark (not a mammal) grows up to 60 ft long, can weigh 90,000 lb, and lays the largest eggs of any living creature.

LARGEST CARNIVOROUS FISH: The terrifying jaws of the great white shark called "the maneater," have become a popular nightmare in recent years, after movies popularized the species.

Bird Island about 40 miles from Sydney, NSW, Australia, and towed to Port Jackson. It measured 14 ft between the anal and dorsal fins and weighed 5,017 lb.

Smallest Sea Fishes

The smallest recorded marine fishes are the Marshall Islands goby (*Eviota zonura*), measuring 0.47–0.63 in, and *Schindleria praematurus* from Samoa, measuring 0.47–0.74 in, both in the Pacific Ocean. Mature specimens of the latter, largely transparent and first identified in 1940, have been known to weigh only 2 mg, equivalent to 17,750 to the oz—the lightest of all vertebrates and the smallest catch possible for any fisherman.

The smallest known shark is the long-faced dwarf shark (*Squaliolus laticaudus*) of the western Pacific. Adult specimens measure about 4.33 in long.

Smallest Fresh-Water Fish

The shortest known fish and the shortest of all vertebrates is the dwarf pygmy goby (*Pandaka pygmaea*), a colorless and nearly transparent fish found in streams and lakes on Luzon, the Philippines. Adult males measure only 0.28–0.38 in long and weigh only 4–5 mg (0.00014–0.00017 oz).

Fastest Fishes

The cosmopolitan sailfish (*Istiophorus platypterus*) is generally considered to be the fastest species of fish, although the practical difficulties of measurement make data extremely difficult to secure. A figure of 68.1 mph (100 yd in 3 sec) has been cited for one off Fla. The swordfish (*Xiphias gladius*) has also been credited with very high speeds, but the evidence is based mainly on bills that have been found deeply embedded in ships' timbers. A speed of 50 knots (57.6 mph) has been calculated from a penetration of 22 in by a bill into a piece of timber, but 30–35 knots (35–40 mph) is the most conceded by some experts. Speeds in excess of 35 knots (40 mph) have also been attributed to the marlin (*Tetrapturus sp.*), the wahoo (*Acanthocybium solandri*), the great blue shark (*Prionace glauca*), and the bonefish (*Albula vulpes*); and the bluefin tuna (*Thunnus thynnus*) has been scientifically clocked at 43.4 mph in a 20-sec dash. The four-winged flying fish (*Cypselurus heterururs*) may also exceed 40 mph during its rapid rush to the surface before take-off (the average speed in the air is about 35 mph). Record flights of 90 sec, 36 ft in altitude and 3,-640 ft in length have been recorded in the tropical Atlantic.

Longest-Lived Fishes

Aquaria are of too recent origin to be able to establish with certainty which species of fish can fairly be regarded as the longest-lived. Early indications are that it is the lake sturgeon (*Acipenser fulvescens*) of North America. In one study of the growth rings (annuli) of 966 specimens caught in the Lake Winnebago, Wis region, 1951–54, the oldest sturgeon was found to be a male, 6 ft 7 in long, which gave a reading of 82 years and was still growing. In July 1974 a figure of 228 years (*sic*) was attributed by growth ring count to a female Koi fish, a form of fancy carp named "Hanako" living in a pond in Higashi Shirakawa, Gifu Prefecture, Japan, but the greatest authoritatively accepted age for this species is "more than 50 years."

The death of an 88-year-old female European eel (*Anguilla anguilla*) named "Putte" in the aquarium at Halsingborn Museum, Sweden was reported in 1948. She was allegedly born in the Sargasso Sea of the North Atlantic in 1860, and was caught in a river as a 3-year-old elver (young eel).

Oldest Goldfish

Goldfish (*Carassius auratus*) have been reported to live for over 40 years in China. A specimen named "Ted," owned by A. R. Wilson of Worthing, Sussex, England, was still alive in April 1980, aged 41 years.

Shortest-Lived Fishes

The shortest-lived fishes are probably certain species of the sub-order Cyprinodontei (killifish) found in Africa and South America which normally live about 8 months in the wild.

Most Abundant Fish

The most abundant species is the herring (*Clupea harengus*) which has been estimated by marine biologists to number at least 1 million million in the Atlantic Ocean.

Deepest Fish

The greatest depth from which a fish has been recovered is 27,230 ft in the Puerto Rico Trough (27,488 ft) in the Atlantic by Dr Gilbert L. Voss of the US research vessel *John Elliott*. The fish was a 6½-in-long *Bassogigas profundissimus* taken in Apr 1970 and was only the fifth such brotulid ever caught.

Dr Jacques Piccard and Lieutenant Don Walsh, US Navy, reported they saw a sole-like fish about 1 ft long (tentatively identified as *Cha-*

FASTEST FISH: Some experts believe the swordfish is capable of speeds nearing 60 mph, because swordfish bills have been found deeply embedded in ships' timbers.

scanopsetta lugubris) from the bathyscaphe *Trieste* at a depth of 35,802 ft in the Challenger Deep (Marianas Trench) in the western Pacific Jan 24, 1960. This sighting, however, has been questioned by some authorities, who still regard the brotulids of the genus *Bassogigas* as the deepest-living vertebrates.

Most Venomous Fish

The most venomous fish is the stonefish (family Synanceidae) of the tropical waters of the Indo-Pacific. Direct contact with the spines of its fins, which contain a strong neurotoxic poison, often proves fatal.

Most and Least Fish Eggs

The ocean sunfish (*Mola mola*) produces up to 300 million eggs, each of them measuring about 0.05 in diameter. The egg yield of the tooth carp *Jordanella floridae* of Florida is only about 20 over a period of several days.

Most Electric Fish

The most powerful electric fish is the electric eel (*Electrophorus electricus*), which is found in the rivers of Brazil, Colombia, Venezuela and Peru. An average-sized specimen can discharge 400 volts at 1 ampere, but measurements up to 650 volts have been recorded.

WALKING CATFISH: Not only can some species walk but others (from Africa) carry an electric discharge of about 350 volts at 1 amp.

FIVE-ARMED STARFISHES:
The one on the left was found
by a Russian expedition in
1970 in the flooded crater of a
volcano in the Kurile Islands
of Siberia just north of Japan.
It weighed less than the
heaviest starfish (above), the
appropriately named
rhinoceros starfish, which
tipped the scales at 13 lb.

6. STARFISHES (*ASTEROIDEA*)

Largest and Heaviest Starfishes

The largest of the 1,600 known species of starfish in terms of total arm span is the very fragile brisingid (*Midgardia xandaros*). A specimen collected by the Texas A & M University research vessel *Alaminos* in the southern part of the Gulf of Mexico in the late summer of 1968 measured 54.33 in from tip to tip but the diameter of its disc was only 1.02 in. Its dry weight was only 2.46 oz. The heaviest species of starfish is the five-armed *Thromidia catalai* of the Western Pacific. One specimen, collected off Ilot Amedee, New Caledonia, Sept 14, 1969, and later deposited in the Noumea Aquarium, weighed an estimated 13.2 lb with a total arm span of 24.8 in.

Smallest Starfish

The smallest known starfish is *Marginaster capreensis* found deep in the Mediterranean, which is not known to exceed a diameter of 0.78 in.

Deepest Starfish

The greatest depth from which a starfish has been recovered is 24,881 for a specimen of *Porcellanaster ivanovi,* collected by the Russian research ship *Vityaz* in the Marianas Trench, in the Western Pacific in about 1962.

7. ARACHNIDS (*ARACHNIDA*)

Largest and Heaviest Spiders

The largest known spider is the "bird-eating" spider (*Theraphosa blondi*) of northern South America. A male specimen with a body 3½ in long and a leg span of 10 in, when fully extended, was collected in Apr 1925 at Montagne la Gabrielle, French Guiana. It weighed nearly 2 oz.

The heaviest spider ever recorded was a female "tarantula" of the long-haired species, *Lasiodora klugi,* collected at Manaos, Brazil, in 1945. It measured 9½ in across the legs and weighed almost 3 oz.

Smallest Spider

The smallest known spider is *Patu marplesi* (family Symphytognathidae) of Western Samoa. The type specimen (a male found in moss at *c.* 2,000-ft altitude near Malolelei, Upolu, in Jan 1956) measures 0.016 in overall—half the size of a printed period (.).

Largest and Smallest Webs

The largest webs are the aerial ones spun by the tropical orb weavers of the genus *Nephila,* which have been measured up to 18 ft 9¾ in in circumference.

The smallest webs are spun by spiders like *Glyphesis cottonae,* etc. which are about the size of a small postage stamp.

Most Venomous Spiders

The most venomous spider is probably *Latrodectus mactans* of the Americas, which is better known as the "black widow." Females of this species, measuring up to 2½ in overall, have a bite capable of killing a human being, but deaths are rare. The funnel web spider (*Atrax robustus*) of Australia, the jockey spider (*Latrodectus hasseltii*) of Australia and New Zealand, the button spider (*Latrodectus indistinctus*) of South Africa, the podadora (*Glyptocranium gasteracanthoides*) of Argentina and the brown recluse spider (*Loxosceles reclusa*) of the central and southern US have been credited with fatalities.

Rarest Spider

The most elusive of all spiders are the primitive atypical tarantulas of the genus *Liphistius* found in Southeast Asia.

LARGEST KNOWN SPIDER: The fearsome-looking "bird-eating" spider has only a 3½-inch-long body but a leg span of 10 in.

Fastest Spider

The highest speed measured for a spider on a level surface is 1.73 ft per sec (1.17 mph) in the case of a specimen of *Tegenaria atrica*. This is 33 times its body length per sec (compare with the human record of 5½ times its body length per sec).

Longest-Lived Spider

The longest-lived of all spiders are the primitive *Mygalomorphae* (tarantulas and allied species). One mature female tarantula, collected at Mazatlan, Mexico, in 1935 and estimated to be 12 years old at the time, was kept in a laboratory for 16 years, making a total of 28 years.

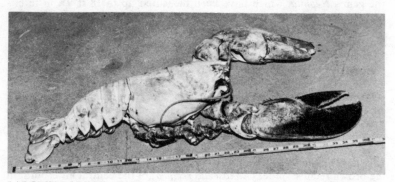

LARGEST LOBSTER: When caught off Nova Scotia, this mammoth crustacean weighed 44 lb and measured 42 in, but when it was cooked in a Bayville, NY restaurant it shrank to 36 in.

8. CRUSTACEANS

(Crabs, lobsters, shrimps, prawns, crayfish, barnacles, water fleas, fish lice, wood lice, sand hoppers and krill, etc.)

Largest Crustacean

The largest of all crustaceans (although not the heaviest) is the giant spider crab (*Macrocheira kaempferi*), also called the stilt crab, which is found in deep waters off the southeastern coast of Japan. Mature specimens usually have a 12–14-in-wide body and a claw span of 8–9 ft, but unconfirmed measurements up to 19 ft have been reported. A specimen with a claw span of 12 ft 1½ in weighed 41 lb.

Largest Lobster

The largest species of lobster, and the heaviest of all crustaceans, is the American or North Atlantic lobster (*Homarus americanus*). The largest lobster, a specimen weighing 44 lb 6 oz measuring 3 ft 6 in from the end of the tail-fan to the tip of the largest claw, was caught off Nova Scotia, Canada, on Feb 11, 1977. It was later sold to Steve Karathanos, owner of a Bayville, NY restaurant.

Smallest Crustaceans

The smallest known crustaceans are water fleas of the genus *Alonella,* which may measure less than 0.0098 in long. They are widely distributed.

The smallest known lobster is the Cape lobster (*Homarus capensis*) of South Africa which measures 3.9–4.7 in in total length.

The smallest crabs in the world are the aptly named pea crabs (family Pinnotheridae). Some species have a shell diameter of only 0.25 in, including *Pinnotheres pisum.*

Longest-Lived Crustacean

The longest-lived of all crustaceans is the American lobster (*Homarus americanus*). Very large specimens may be as much as 50 years old.

Deepest Crustacean

The greatest depth from which a crustacean has been recovered is 32,119 ft for an amphipod (order Amphipoda) collected by the Galathea Deep Sea Expedition in the Philippine Trench in 1951. The marine crab *Ethusina abyssicola* has been taken at a depth of 14,000 ft. Amphipods have also been collected in the Ecuadorean Andes at a height of 13,300 ft.

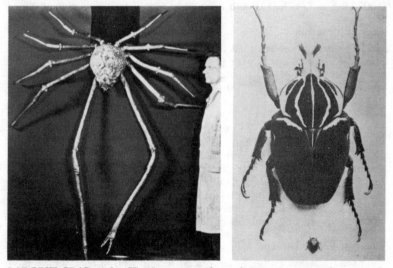

LARGEST CRAB (left): The Japanese spider crab has a leg span of over 12 ft. LARGEST INSECT: The Goliath beetle (right, next to a lady bug) weighs as much as 3½ oz and measures 4¾ in.

9. INSECTS

Heaviest Insects

The heaviest insects are the Goliath beetles (family Scarabaeidae) of equatorial Africa. The largest member of the group is *Goliathus goliathus.* In one group of fully-grown males the weight ranged from 2.5–3.5 oz.

Longest Insect

The longest insect in the world is the tropical stick-insect *Pharnacia serratipes*, females of which have been measured up to 12.99 in in body length. The longest beetle known (excluding antennae) is the Hercules beetle (*Dynastes hercules*) of Central and South America, which has been measured up to 7.08 in, but almost half of this length is accounted for by the "prong" from the thorax. The long-horn beetle *Batocera wallacei* of New Guinea has been measured up to 10.5 in, but 7.5 in of this was antenna.

Smallest Insects

The smallest insects recorded so far are the "hairy-winged" beetles of the family Ptiliidae (= Trichopterygidae) and the "battledore-wing fairy flies" (parasitic wasps) of the family Myrmaridae. They measure only 0.008 in in length, and the fairy flies have a wing span of only 0.04 in. This makes them smaller than some of the protozoa (single-celled animals).

The male bloodsucking banded louse (*Enderleinellus zonatus*), ungorged, and the parasitic wasp *Caraphractus cinctus* may each weigh as little as 0.005 mg, or 1/567,000th oz. The eggs of the latter each weigh 0.0002 mg or 1/141,750,000th oz.

Commonest Insect

The most numerous of all insects are the springtails (order Collembola), which have a very wide geographical range. It has been calculated that the top 9 in of soil in one acre of grassland contains 230 million springtails or more than 5,000 per sq ft.

Fastest-Flying Insects

Experiments have proved that a widely publicized claim by an American entomologist in 1926 that the deer bot-fly (*Cephenemyia pratti*) could attain a speed of 818 mph was wildly exaggerated. If true, it would have generated a supersonic "pop." Acceptable modern experiments have now established that the highest maintainable air speed of any insect, including the deer bot-fly, is 24 mph, rising to a maximum of 36 mph for short bursts. A relay of bees (maximum speed 11 mph) would use only a gallon of nectar in cruising 4 million miles at 7 mph.

Longest-Lived Insects

The longest-lived insects are queen termites (*Isoptera*), which have been known to lay eggs for up to 50 years.

Loudest Insects

The loudest of all insects is the male cicada (family Cicadidae). At 7,-400 pulses per min its tymbal (sound) organs produce a noise (officially described by the US Dept of Agriculture as "Tsh-ee-EEEE-e-ou") detectable over a quarter of a mile distance.

Southernmost Insect

The farthest south at which any insect has been found is 77 °S. (900 miles from the South Pole) in the case of a springtail (order Collembola).

LOCUST SWARM: The largest contained 250,000 million insects and covered 2,000 sq mi. Inset shows a 9-in-long desert locust.

Largest Locust Swarm

The greatest swarm of desert locusts (*Schistocera gregaria*) ever recorded was one covering an estimated 2,000 sq mi, observed crossing the Red Sea in 1889. Such a swarm must have contained about 250,000 million insects weighing about 550,000 tons.

Fastest Wing Beat

The fastest wing beat per min of any insect under natural conditions is 62,760 by a tiny midge of the genus *Forcipomyia*. In experiments with truncated wings at a temperature of 98.6 °F, the rate increased to 133,080 beats per min. The muscular contraction-expansion cycle in 0.00045 or 1/2,218th sec represents the fastest muscle movement ever measured.

Slowest Wing Beat

The slowest wing beat of any insect is 300 per min by the swallowtail butterfly (*Papilio machaon*). Most butterflies beat their wings at a rate of 460–636 per min.

Honey from a Hive

The greatest amount of wild honey ever extracted from a single hive is 404 lb, recorded by Ormond R. Aebi of Santa Cruz, Calif, Aug 29, 1974.

Largest Grasshopper

The bush-cricket with the largest wing span is the New Guinean grasshopper *Siliquofera grandis* with some females measuring more than 10 in. The *Pseudophyllanax imperialis,* found on the island of New Caledonia, in the southwestern Pacific Ocean, has antennae measuring up to 8 in.

MAMMOTH MOTH: This rare great owlet moth reputedly had a wing expanse of over 14 in, but the specimen was somehow mislaid.

Largest Dragonfly

The largest dragonfly is *Megaloprepes ceruleata* of Central and South America, which has been measured up to 7.52 in across the wings and 4.72 in in body length.

Largest Flea

The largest known flea is *Hystrichopsylla schefferi schefferi,* which was described from a single specimen taken from the nest of a mountain beaver (*Aplondontia rufa*) at Puyallup, Wash, in 1913. Females measure up to 0.31 in in length, which is the diameter of a pencil.

Flea Jumps

The champion jumper among fleas is the common flea (*Pulex irritans*). In one American experiment carried out in 1910 a specimen allowed to leap at will performed a long jump of 13 in and a high jump of 7¾ in. In jumping 130 times its own height a flea subjects itself to a force of 200 g. Siphonapterologists recognize 1,830 varieties.

Largest Butterflies and Moths (Order Lepidoptera)

The largest known butterfly is the Queen Alexandra birdwing (*Ornithoptera alexandrae*) of New Guinea. Females may have a wing span exceeding 11.02 in and weigh over 0.176 oz.

The largest moth (though not the heaviest) is the Hercules moth (*Coscinoscera hercules*) of tropical Australia and New Guinea. A wing area of up to 40.8 sq in and a wing span of 11 in have been recorded. In 1948 an unconfirmed measurement of 14.17 in was reported for a female captured near the post office at the coastal town of Innisfail, Queensland, Australia. The rare owlet moth (*Thysania agrippina*) of Brazil has been measured up to 11.81 in in wing span, and the Philippine atlas moth (*Attacus crameri caesar*) up to 11.02 in, but both these species are lighter than *C. hercules*.

Smallest Butterfly

The smallest of the estimated 140,000 known species of Lepidoptera are the moths *Johanssonia acetosae* (*Stainton*), found in Great Britain, and *Stigmella ridiculosa* from the Canary Islands, which have a wing span of 0.08 in and a similar body length. The smallest known butterfly is the dwarf blue (*Brephidium barberae*) from South Africa. It is 0.55 in from wing tip to wing tip.

Greatest Butterfly Collectors

There are only 400 species of butterflies absent from the collection of 62,000 owned by John F. Glick of Brentwood, Calif.

10. CENTIPEDES (*CHILOPODA*)

Longest and Shortest

The longest recorded species of centipede is a large variant of the widely distributed *Scolopendra morsitans,* found on the Andaman Islands, Bay of Bengal, India. Specimens have been measured up to 13 in in length and 1½ in in breadth. The shortest recorded centipede is an unidentified species which measures only 0.19 in.

Most Legs

The centipede with the greatest number of legs is *Himantarum gabrielis* of southern Europe which has 171–177 pairs when adult.

Fastest

The fastest centipede is probably *Scutigera coleoptrata* of southern Europe which can travel at a rate of 19.68 in per sec or 1.1 mph.

11. MILLIPEDES (*DIPLOPODA*)

Longest and Shortest

The longest species of millipede known are the *Graphidostreptus gigas* of Africa and *Scaphistostreptus seychellarum* of the Seychelles Islands in the Indian Ocean, both of which have been measured up to 11.02 in in length and 0.78 in diameter. The shortest millipede in the world is the British species *Polyxenus lagurus,* which measures 0.082–0.15 in in length.

Most Legs

The greatest number of legs reported for a millipede is 355 pairs (710 legs) for an unidentified South African species.

12. SEGMENTED WORMS (*ANNELIDA*)

Longest and Shortest Earthworms

The longest known species of giant earthworm is *Microchaetus rappi* (= *M. microchaetus*) of South Africa. An average-sized specimen measures 4 ft 6 in in length (25½ in when contracted), but much larger examples have been reliably reported. In *c.* 1937 a giant earthworm measuring 22 ft in length when naturally extended and 0.78 in in diameter was collected in the Transvaal, and in Nov 1967 another specimen measuring 11 ft in length and 21 ft when naturally extended was found reaching over the national road (width 19 ft 8½ in) near Debe Nek, eastern Cape Province, South Africa.

The shortest segmented worm known is *Chaetogaster annandalei,* which measures less than 0.019 in in length.

13. MOLLUSKS
(Squids, octopuses, snails, shellfish, etc.)

Largest Mollusk

In Nov 1896 the remains of an unknown marine animal weighing an estimated 6–7 tons were found on a beach near St Augustine, Fla. Tissue samples were later sent to the US National Museum in Washington, DC, and in 1970 they were *positively* identified as belonging to a giant form of octopus. It is estimated that this creature had a tentacular span of 200 ft.

Largest Squid

The largest squid (Architeuthis) ever recorded was one measuring 55 ft in total length (head and body 20 ft, tentacles 35 ft), captured on Nov 2, 1878 after it had run aground in Thimble Tickle Bay, Newfoundland. Its eyes were 9 in in diameter. The total weight was estimated to be 4,480 lb.

A giant squid *Architeuthis longimanus* measuring 57 ft but with tentacles of 49 ft, was washed ashore in Lyall Bay, New Zealand, in Oct 1887.

Most Ancient Mollusk

The longest existing living creature is *Neopilina galatheae,* a deep-sea worm-snail which had been believed extinct for about 320 million years, but which was found at a depth of 11,400 ft off Costa Rica by the Danish research vessel *Galathea* in 1952. Fossils found in NY State, in Newfoundland, and in Sweden show that this mollusk was also living about 500 million years ago.

Longest-Lived Mollusk

The longest-lived mollusk is the Quahog (*Venus mercenaria*), a thick-shelled clam found in the North Atlantic. Recent research in America involving the study of microscopic rings laid down annually on the tooth holding the shells together indicates that this species sometimes lives for 150 years.

Largest Bivalve Shells

The largest of all existing bivalve shells is the marine giant clam (*Tridacna gigas*), found on the Indo-Pacific coral reefs. A specimen measuring 43 in by 29 in and weighing 579½ lb was collected from the Great Barrier Reef of Australia in 1917, and is now preserved in the American Museum of Natural History, NYC. Another lighter specimen was measured at 53.9 in overall.

Smallest Shell

Probably the smallest bivalve shell is the coin shell (*Neolepton sykesi*), known only from a few specimens collected off Guernsey, Channel Islands and west Ireland, which measures 0.047 in long.

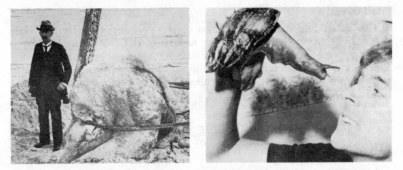

GIANT OCTOPUS (left): Half-buried remains of this monster, washed up at St Augustine, Fla in 1896 were first thought to be a whale but Dr DeWitt Webb made the final identification. Its arm span must have been 75–100 ft. LARGEST SNAIL (right): From Sierra Leone, Africa, came "Gee-Geronimo," 15½ in long.

Largest Gastropod Shells

The largest known gastropod is the trumpet or Baler conch (*Syrinx aruanus*) of Australia. One huge specimen collected at Bunbury, Western Australia, in 1974 and now owned by Morton Hahn of Randolph, NJ, weighed 35 lb when alive. Its shell is 28.1 in long and has a maximum girth of 38 in.

The largest known land gastropod is the African giant snail (*Achatina sp.*). A huge specimen which measured 15½ in from snout to tail (shell length 10¾ in) and weighed exactly 2 lb in Dec 1978 was collected by Christopher Hudson of Hove, East Sussex, England in June 1976 in Sierra Leone. He named the snail "Gee-Geronimo." Shell lengths of up to 14 in have been reliably reported in Sierra Leone.

Rarest Shell

A second example of the species *Tibia serrata* (Perry), first found in 1811 and believed lost, was reported in Aug 1977, from Bandar Abbas, Iran, by Franco Perantoni of Italy. It is gray-cream and golden-yellow and 5.1 in in length. A sum of $10,000 was refused by Philip Clover of Glen Ellen, Calif for a cone shell *Conus servus* in 1978.

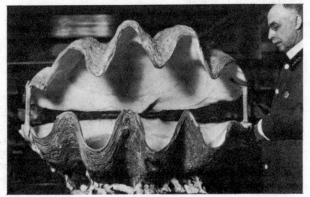

LARGEST SHELL: At 579½ lb, this marine giant clam holds the record. It is today preserved in the American Museum of Natural History, NYC.

Snail Speed

The fastest-moving species of land snail is probably the common garden snail (*Helix aspersa*). According to tests carried out in the US absolute top speed for this snail is 0.0313 mph (or 55 yd per hour) while some species are at full stretch at 0.00036 mph (or 23 in per hour). The snail-racing equivalent of the 4-minute mile is 24 in in 3 min, which would result in a 7,920-min or 5½-day mile.

14. RIBBON WORMS (*NEMERTINA OR RHYNCHOPODS*)

Longest Worm

The longest of the 550 recorded species of ribbon worms, also called nemertines (or nemerteans), is the "boot-lace worm" (*Lineus longissimus*), found in the shallow waters of the North Sea. A specimen washed ashore at St Andrews, Fife, Scotland, in 1864, after a severe storm, measured more than 180 ft in length, making it easily the longest recorded worm of any variety.

15. JELLYFISHES (*SCYPHOZOA OR SCYPHOMEDUSIA*)

Largest and Smallest

The longest jellyfish is *Cyanea arctica* of the North Atlantic with tentacles of up to 120 ft, 7½ ft in diameter.

Some true jellyfishes have a bell diameter of less than 0.78 of an inch.

Most Venomous

The most venomous coelenterates are the box jellies *Chironex fleekerei* of the Indo-Pacific region, which carry a neurotoxic venom similar in strength to that found in the Asiatic cobra. These jellyfish have caused the deaths of at least 66 people (1880–1979) off the coast of Queensland, Australia. Victims die within 1–3 min. A most effective defense is ladies' panty hose, outsize versions of which are now worn by Queensland life savers at surf carnivals.

16. SPONGES (*PARAZOA, PORIFERA OR SPONGIDA*)

Largest and Smallest

The largest sponge is the barrel-shaped loggerhead sponge (*Spheciospongia vesparium*), found off the islands of the West Indies and off Fla. Single individuals measure up to 3½ ft high and 3 ft in diameter. Neptune's cup or goblet (*Poterion patera*) of Indonesia grows up to 4 ft in height, but it is a less bulky animal. In 1909, a wool sponge (*Hippospongia canaliculatta*) measuring 6 ft in circumference was collected off the Bahama Islands. When first taken from the water it weighed between 80 and 90 lb, but after it had been dried and relieved of all excrescences it scaled 12 lb. (This sponge is now preserved in the US National Museum, Washington, DC.)

The smallest known sponge is the widely distributed *Leucosolenia blanca,* which measures 0.11 in in height when fully grown.

Deepest Sponges

Sponges have been taken from depths of up to 18,500 ft.

17. EXTINCT ANIMALS

Heaviest and Longest Animal

In the summer of 1972 the remains of an enormous sauropod, new to science, were discovered in a flood-plain bonejam on the Uncompahgre Plateau, Colo by an expedition, led by Dr James Jensen, from Brigham Young University, Provo, Utah. Excavations are still continuing, but a study of the incomplete series of cervical vertebrae indicates that this dinosaur must have had a neck length of approximately 39 ft (*cf.* 22 ft for Diplodocus). If the rest of "Ultrasaurus" (as it has been nicknamed) is built on brachiosaurid lines—the matching shoulder blades measure 8 ft in length—this presupposes an over-all length of *c.* 130 ft, a shoulder height of 37 ft, a raised head measurement of 75 ft, and a weight of at least 224 tons, making it the largest animal that has ever existed. In 1979 Dr Jensen discovered another shoulder blade in the same area which measured 8 ft 10 in.

DINOSAUR LEG (left): The immense size is demonstrated by a Russian boy with a giant fossil rhinoceros.
LONGEST DINOSAUR?: Researchers believe that this 8-ft-long scapula, shown alongside its discoverer, Dr James Jensen, may have belonged to a sauropod 130 ft long.

Largest Land Predator

The largest of the carnosaurs (family Megalosauridae) was probably *Tyrannosaurus rex,* which stalked about 75 million years ago over what are now Montana and Wyoming. No complete skeleton has ever been discovered, but composite remains indicate that it measured up to 35 ft in overall length, had a bipedal height of 18½ ft, and weighed 8 tons. In a recent reinterpretation of the Tyrannosaurus remains, 12 ft were chopped off the tail length to produce a more symmetrical animal.

The body of a huge Allosaurus, with a body much more massive in proportion to its height than Tyrannosaurus, was excavated near Kenton, Okla in 1934. This carnosaur had a bipedal height of 16 ft and measured 42 ft in overall length.

Most Brainless

The *Stegosaurus* ("plated reptile"), which measured up to 30 ft in length, had a walnut-sized brain weighing only 2½ oz. It represented 0.004 of 1% of its body weight of 1¾ tons compared with 0.074 of 1% for an elephant and 1.88% for a human. It roamed widely across the Northern Hemisphere about 150 million years ago.

Largest Dinosaur Eggs

The largest dinosaur eggs are those of *Hypselosaurus priscus sauropod* which lived about 80 million years ago. Some specimens found in Oct 1961 in the valley of the Durance, near Aix-en-Provence, southern France, would have had, uncrushed, a length of 12 in and a diameter of 10 in.

Largest Flying Creature

The largest flying creature was a winged reptile of the new order Quetzalcoatlus which glided over what is now Texas about 70 million years ago. Partial remains (four wings, a neck, hind legs, and mandibles) of three specimens recently discovered in Big Bend National Park, Tex, indicate that this reptile must have had a wing span of at least 36 ft and that the maximum expanse may have been as great as 68.89 ft. *Pteranodon ingens,* the previous title-holder, had a maximum expanse of 27 ft.

Largest Bird

The largest prehistoric bird was *Dromornis stirtoni,* a huge emu-like creature which lived in central Australia about 10–11 million years ago. Fossil leg bones found near Alice Springs in 1974 indicate that the bird must have stood 9–10 ft in height and weighed at least 1,100 lb. The flightless moa *Dinornis giganteus* of North Island, New Zealand, was taller, attaining a height of over 13 ft, but probably only weighed about 500 lb.

The largest prehistoric bird actually to fly was probably the condor-like *Teratornis incredibilis,* which lived in North America about 100 million years ago. Fossil remains of one of this species, discovered in Smith Creek Cave, Nev, in 1952, indicate a wing span of 16 ft 4¾ in, and weight of nearly 50 lb. A wing span measurement of 16 ft 4¾ in has also been reported for another flying bird named *Ornithodesmus latidens,* which flew over what is now Hampshire and the Isle of Wight, England, about 90 million years ago. Another gigantic flying bird named *Osteodontornis*

LARGEST CHELONIAN (left): A 6-ft-2-in man stands beside the shell of the largest known prehistoric turtle. TALLEST PREHISTORIC BIRD (right): A reconstruction of the flightless moa of New Zealand, over 13 ft tall.

orri, which lived in what is now Calif, about 20 million years ago, had a wing span of 16 ft and was probably even heavier. It was related to the pelicans and storks. The albatross-like *Gigantornis eaglesomei* has been credited with a wing span of 20 ft on the evidence of a single fossilized breastbone. It flew over what is now Nigeria between 34 and 58 million years ago.

Largest Marine Reptile

The largest marine reptile ever recorded was the short-necked pliosaur *Kronosaurus queenslandicus,* which swam in the seas around what is now Australia about 100 million years ago. It measured up to 55 ft in length, with a skull 11½ ft long. *Stretosaurus macromerus,* another short-necked pliosaur, was of comparable size. A mandible found in Cumnor, Oxfordshire, England, must have belonged to a reptile measuring at least 50 ft in length.

Largest Crocodile

The largest known crocodile was *Deinosuchus riograndensis,* which lived in the lakes and swamps of what is now Texas about 75 million years ago. Fragmentary remains discovered in Big Bend National Park, West Texas, indicate it must have measured at least 50 ft in total length. The less bulky gavial *Rhamphosuchus,* which lived in northern India about 7 million years ago, also reached a length of 50 ft.

Largest Chelonians

The largest prehistoric chelonian was the possibly marine pelomedusid turtle *Stupendemys geographicus,* which lived about 80 million years ago. Fossil remains discovered by a Harvard University paleontological expedition in northern Venezuela in 1972 indicate that this turtle had a carapace (shell) measuring 7½–8 ft in mid-line length and probably at least 12 ft in overall length. It had a computed weight of 6,000 lb.

The largest prehistoric tortoise was probably *Geochelone* (= *Colossochelys*) *atlas,* which lived in what is now northern India, Burma, Java, the Celebes and Timor between 1 and 2½ million years ago. The fossil remains of a specimen with a carapace 5 ft 5 in long (7 ft 4 in over the curve) and 2 ft 11 in high was discovered in 1923 near Chandigarh in the Siwalik Hills, India. This animal had an overall length of 8 ft and is computed to have weighed about 2,100 lb when it was alive. Fossil remains of similarly sized tortoises have been found recently in Fla and Tex.

Largest Fish

No prehistoric fish has yet been discovered that is larger than living species.

Longest Snake

The longest prehistoric snake was the python-like *Gigantophis garstini,* which inhabited what is now Egypt about 50 million years ago. Parts of a spinal column and a small piece of jaw discovered at El Faiyum indicate a length of about 33 ft, which is comparable with the longest constrictors living today.

Largest Amphibian

The largest amphibian ever recorded was the gavial-like *Prinosuchus plummeri* which lived 230 million years ago. In 1972 the fragmented remains of a specimen measuring an estimated 29.5 ft in life were discovered in northern Brazil.

Largest Insect

The largest prehistoric insect was *Meganeura monyi,* a dragonfly that lived about 280 million years ago. Fossil remains (impression of wings) discovered at Commentry, France, indicate that it had a wing span reaching 27½ in.

PLANT KINGDOM (*PLANTAE*)

Earliest Flower

The oldest fossil of a flowering plant with palm-like imprints was found in Colo in 1953 and dated about 65 million years old.

Largest Forest

The largest afforested areas are the vast coniferous forests of the northern USSR, lying mainly between latitude 55 °N. and the Arctic Circle. The total wooded areas amount to 2,700 million acres (25% of the world's forests), of which 38% is Siberian larch. The USSR is 34% afforested.

Rarest Plants

Plants thought to be extinct are rediscovered each year and there are thus many plants of which specimens are known in but a single locality. The small pink blossoms of *Presidio manzanita* survive in a single specimen reported in June 1978 at an undisclosed site in Calif.

Largest Blooms

The mottled orange-brown and white parasitic stinking corpse lily (*Rafflesia arnoldi*) has the largest of all blooms. These attach themselves to the cissus vines of the jungle in southeast Asia. They measure up to 3 ft across and ¾ in thick, and attain a weight of 15 lb.

The largest known inflorescence is that of *Puya raimondii,* a rare Bolivian plant with an erect panicle (diameter 8 ft) which emerges to a height of 35 ft. Each of these bears up to 8,000 white blooms. In 1974 the flower-spike of an agave in Berkeley, Calif was measured to be 52 ft long. (See also *Slowest-Flowering Plant.*)

The largest blossoming plant is the giant Chinese wisteria at Sierra Madre, Calif. It was planted in 1892 and now has branches 500 ft long. It covers nearly an acre, weighs 252 tons and has an estimated 1,500,000 blossoms during its blossoming period of five weeks, when up to 30,000 people pay admission to visit. In Nov 1974 it was reported that a passion plant, owned by Dennis and Patti Carlson of Blaine, Minn, and fed with a hormone, had grown to a length of 600 ft.

LARGEST BLOOM (left): The stinking corpse lily of Southeast Asia bears blooms up to 3 ft across which weigh up to 15 lb. SMALLEST FLOWERING PLANTS (right): The size of the newly discovered "Pilea microphylla" can be judged by comparing it with the point of a needle (on the right).

Smallest Flowering Plant

Many formerly unsuspected minute flowers have been discovered since 1972 by Mr and Mrs Robert Gilbreath of Calif. The smallest is the *Pilea microphylla* of western India, measuring 1/72 in diameter. The floating flowering aquatic duckweed *Wolffia punctata* has fronds only 1/35 in length.

Rarest Flower

The $20,000 prize offered by the Burpee Co. in 1924 for producing the first all-white marigold was won in 1945 by Alice Vonk of Sully, Iowa.

Plants at Highest Altitude

The *Stellaria decumbens* is the flowering plant found at the highest verified altitude—20,130 ft up in the Himalayas. A claimed height of 23,000 ft in the Himalayas for *Christolea crassifolia* remains inconclusive. A non-flowering plant of *Androsace microphylla* was recorded by A. Zimmermann at 20,333 ft on the 1952 Swiss Everest expedition.

Deepest and Densest Roots

The greatest reported depth to which roots have penetrated is a calculated 400 ft in the case of a wild fig tree at Echo Caves, near Ohrigstad, East Transvaal, South Africa. A single winter rye plant (*Secale cereale*) has been shown to produce 387 miles of roots in 1.83 cu ft of earth.

Fastest Growth

The case of a *Liliacea hesperogucca whipplei* growing 12 ft in 14 days was reported from Treco Abbey, Isles of Scilly, England, in July 1978.

Slowest-Flowering Plant

The slowest-flowering of all plants is the rare *Puya raimondii,* the largest of all herbs, discovered in Bolivia in 1870. The panicle emerges after about 150 years of the plant's life. It then dies. (See also above under *Largest Blooms.*)

Some agaves, erroneously called century plants, first flower after 40 years.

Largest Leaves

The largest leaves of any plant belong to the raffia palm (*Raphia ruffia*) of the Mascarene Islands in the Indian Ocean, and the Amazonian bamboo palm (*R. toedigera*) of South America, whose leaf blades may measure up to 65 ft in length with petioles up to 13 ft.

The largest undivided leaf is that of *Alocasia macrorrhiza,* found in Sabah, East Malaysia. One found in 1966 measured 9 ft 11 in long and 6 ft 3½ in wide, and had an area of 34.2 sq ft on one side.

FRUITS & VEGETABLES
World records set in the US reported by
Grace's Gardens, Hackettstown, NJ 07840.

Most and Least Nutritive Fruits

An analysis of the 38 commonly eaten raw (as opposed to dried) fruits shows that the one with the highest calorific value is the avocado (*Persea americana*) with 741 calories per edible lb. That with the lowest value is cucumber with 73 calories per lb. Avocados probably originated in Central and South America and also contain vitamins A, C, and E and 2.2% protein.

Biggest Apple

An apple weighing 3 lb 1 oz was reported by V. Loveridge of Ross-on-Wye, England in 1965.

Largest Artichoke

An 8-lb artichoke was grown in 1964 at Tollerton, N. Yorkshire England, by A. R. Lawson.

Largest Broccoli

A head of broccoli weighing 28 lb 14¾ oz was grown in 1964 by J. T. Cooke of Huntington, W. Sussex, England.

Largest Cabbage

In 1865 William Collingwood of The Stalwell, County Durham, England, grew a red cabbage with a circumference of 259 in. It reputedly weighed 123 lb.

Largest Carrot

A carrot weighing 11 lb was grown by Bob McEwan of Beeac, Vic, Australia, in Sept 1967.

Largest Cauliflower

A record cauliflower weighing 52 lb 11½ oz was also grown by Mr Cooke (see *Broccoli*) in 1966.

Largest Celery

A 35-lb bunch was reported grown by C. Bowcock of Willaston, England in 1973.

Largest Cucumber

A 13-lb example was grown by George J. Kucera of Mexia, Tex, in July 1978. A Vietnamese variety 6 ft long was reported by L. Szabo of Debrecen, Hungary in Sept 1976.

Longest Gourd

A gourd 82 in long was grown by Mark and Randy Ohlin of Poland, Ohio, in 1979. A gourd weighing 196 lb was reported from J. Leathes of Herringfleet Hall, Suffolk, England in 1846.

LONGEST GOURD (left): An 82-in-long gourd grown by two Ohio young men. LARGEST LEMON (below): Mrs. Knutzen of Whittier, Calif exhibits her record 6 lb 4 oz lemon.

Largest Kohlrabi

A kohlrabi weighing 36 lb was grown in 1979 by Emil Krejci of Mt Clemens, Mich.

Largest Lemon

Mrs D. G. Knutzen of Whittier, Calif, reported in Jan 1977 a lemon with a circumference of 28¾ in, weighing 6 lb 4 oz.

Largest Lettuce

A head of 25 lb was grown by C. Bowcock of Willaston, England in 1974.

Largest Lima Bean

One bean pod measuring 14 in in length was grown by Norma McCoy of Hubert, NC, in 1979.

Largest Melons

A watermelon weighing 200 lb was reported in Apr 1980. The growers were Ivan and Lloyd Bright of Hope, Ark. The largest cantaloupe reported was one of 41 lb 2 oz grown by Vernon Dulaney of Belle Rive, Ill.

Largest Mushrooms

A common mushroom with a 75-in circumference was found near the Lualaba River, Zaïre, in 1920. A mushroom weighing 18 lb 10 oz was reported from Whidbey Island, Wash, in Sept 1968.

Largest Okra Stalk

An okra stalk 17 ft tall was grown in 1979 by P. C. Cain of Kosciusko, Miss.

Largest Onion

An onion of 6 lb 3 oz was reported grown by T. Fenton of Preston, England in 1977.

Largest Orange

The heaviest orange is one weighing 3 lb 11 oz grown by Bill Calendine of Tucson, Ariz, in 1977.

Largest Parsnip

A parsnip 60 in long was reported by M. Zaninovich of Waneroo, Western Australia. The heaviest was 5 lb 15½ oz grown by Ray Kelley of Mabton, Wash, in 1979.

Largest Peanut

Ed Weeks of Tarboro, NC, grew a peanut 3½ in long in 1978.

Largest Pear

A pear weighing 3.09 lb was harvested on May 10, 1979 at K. and R. Yeomans, Armidale, NSW, Australia.

LARGEST PEANUT (left): Ed Weeks compares his prize 3½-in peanut with a more modest goober. LONGEST PEPPER: This 13½-inch chili pepper grown in NM is reportedly "medium hot."

Longest Pepper

A NuMex Big Jim pepper 13½ in long was grown by June Rutherford of Hatch, NM, in 1975. A sweet pepper plant owned by Ralph Savarese of Pascagoula, Miss grew to be 56 in tall, yielding 53 peppers, in 1978.

Largest Pineapple

A pineapple weighing 17 lb was picked by H. Retief in Malindi, Kenya, in Dec 1978.

Largest Potato

A potato weighing 18 lb 4 oz was reported dug up by Thomas Seddal in his garden in Chester, England, on Feb 17, 1795. A yield was reported of 515 lb from a 2½-lb parent seed by C. Bowcock of Willaston, England, planted in Apr 1977.

Largest Radishes

Radishes weighing 25 lb have been grown by Glen Tucker of Stanbury, South Australia, in Aug, 1974, and by Herbert Breslow of Ruskin, Fla, in 1977.

Largest Squash

A squash weighing 513 lb was grown by Harold Fulp, Jr., at Ninevah, Ind, in 1977. Mike Jovanovich of LaPonte, Ind grew 1,851 lb of squash from one seed in 1979.

Biggest Strawberry

One berry weighing 2⅜ oz was grown by Lester Slate of Dover-Foxcroft, Maine. A plant weighing 7¼ oz was reported by E. Oxley of Walton-on-the-Naze, England, in 1972.

LARGEST CANTELOUPE (left): This 41 lb 2 oz melon was grown in Illinois by Vernon Dulaney. LARGEST SQUASH (right): The Harold Fulp family of Nine-vah, Ind display their 513 lb Hungarian Mammoth squash.

Largest Sugar Beet

A 45½ lb sugar beet was grown by the Bob Meyer Farms in Brawley, Calif, in 1974.

Largest Sweet Potato

A 22½-lb specimen grown by George Wynn of Gibsonton, Fla in 1977 was reported.

Largest Tomato

A 6 lb 8 oz tomato was grown by Clarence Dailey of Monona, Wis, in Aug 1976. A 31-ft 6-in plant was grown in 1980 at the Chosen Hill School in Gloucester, England. A cherry tomato plant owned by James Groh-man of Temple, Pa, produced 107 tomatoes in 1978.

Largest Turnip

A turnip weighing 73 lb was reported in Dec 1768. In modern times the record is 35 lb 4 oz for a turnip grown by C. W. Butler of Nafferton, Humberside, England. A purple top turnip of 30 lb was grown by Den-verd Fleming of Phil Campbell, Ala, in 1979.

Largest Zucchini

A zucchini weighing 19.14 lb was grown in 1979 by Douglas Andre of Millington, Mich.

Largest Vines

The largest recorded grape vine was one planted in 1842 at Carpin-teria, Calif. By 1900 it was yielding more than 9 tons of grapes in some years, and averaging 7 tons per year. It died in 1920.

GARDEN FLOWERS & PLANTS

Largest Aspidistra

The aspidistra (*Aspidistra elatior*) was introduced as a parlor palm to Britain from Japan and China in 1822. The biggest aspidistra in the world is one 51¾ in tall, grown by Cliff W. Evans at Kiora, Moruya, NSW, Australia, and measured in Dec 1977.

Largest Begonia

A begonia plant 3 ft 8 in tall was grown by Ellen Cassidy of Richmond, British Columbia, Canada in 1979.

Fourteen-Leafed Clover

A fourteen-leafed white clover (*Trifolium repens*) grown on one petiole was found by Randy Farland near Sioux Falls, SD, June 16, 1975.

Largest Dahlia

A 9-ft-10¾-in dahlia was grown by H. W. Deem of Victoria, Australia, in 1977.

Largest Gladiolus

A 7-ft-10½-in gladiolus was grown in 1977 by W. Wilson of Dunfermline, Fife, Scotland.

Tallest Hollyhock

The tallest reported hollyhock (*Althaea rosea*) is one of 24 ft 3 in grown by W. P. Walshe of Eastbourne, E. Sussex, England in 1961.

LARGEST BEGONIA (below): Ellen Cassidy of British Columbia proudly displays her 3-ft-8-in-tall huge flowering plant. TALLEST SUNFLOWER: Frank Killand of Exeter, England grew these gigantic sunflowers, the tallest 23 ft 6½ in.

Largest Philodendron

A philodendron 300 ft long now grows in the La Carreta Restaurant in San Jacinto, Calif.

Largest Poinsettia Tree

Frank Trojanowski and his students in Trumbull, Conn, grew a 7-ft-6-in-tall poinsettia tree in 1978.

Largest Rhododendron

The largest species of rhododendron is the scarlet *Rhododendron arboreum,* examples of which reach a height of 60 ft at Mangalbaré, Nepal. The cross section of the trunk of a *Rhododendron giganteum,* from Yunnan, China, reputedly 90 ft high, is preserved at Inverewe Garden, Highland, Scotland.

Largest Rose Tree

A "Lady Banks" rose tree at Tombstone, Ariz, has a trunk 40 in thick, stands 9 ft high and covers an area of 5,380 sq ft, supported by 68 posts and several thousand feet of iron piping. This enables 150 people to be seated under the arbor. The original cutting came from Scotland in 1884.

Largest Sunflower

The record height of 23 ft 6½ in was reached by a sunflower grown by Frank Killand of Exeter, England in 1976.

Worst Weeds

The most intransigent weed is the mat-forming water weed *Salvinia auriculata,* found in Africa. It was detected on the filling of Kariba Lake, in May 1959 and within 11 months had choked an area of 77 sq mi, rising by 1963 to 387 sq mi. The worst land weeds are regarded as purple nut sedge, Bermuda grass, barnyard grass, jungle rice, goose grass, Johnson grass, Guinea grass, cogon grass and lantana.

Tallest Hedges

The world's tallest hedge is the Meikleour beech hedge in Perthshire, Scotland. It was planted in 1746 and has now attained a trimmed height of 85 ft. It is 600 yd long, and some of its trees now exceed 100 ft.

The tallest yew hedge in the world is in Earl Bathurst's Park, Gloucestershire, England. It was planted in 1720, runs for 170 yd, reaches 36 ft in height and 15 ft in thickness, and takes 20 man-days to trim.

The tallest box hedge, 35 ft in height, is at Birr Castle, Offaly, Ireland, and dates from the 18th century.

Largest Cactus

The largest of all cacti is the saguaro (*Cereus giganteus* or *Carnegiea gigantea*), found in Ariz, southeastern Calif, and Sonora, Mexico. The

REMOTEST TREE (above): This lonely tree stood in the middle of the Ténéré Desert in Africa with no other trees within 31 miles. Yet it was rammed in 1960 by a truck being backed up, and survived, but it has now been transplanted to a museum in the Niger. LARGEST CACTUS (right): This saguaro grew to a height of 52 ft, about 10 times as high as the woman standing beneath it.

green fluted column is surmounted by candelabra-like branches rising to a height of 52 ft 5¾ in in the case of a specimen measured on the boundary of the Saguaro National Monument, Ariz. They have waxy white blooms which are followed by edible crimson fruit. An armless cactus 78 ft in height was measured in Apr 1978 by Hube Yates in Cave Creek, Ariz.

Longest Seaweed

Claims made that seaweed off Tierra del Fuego, South America, grows to 600 and even 1,000 ft in length have gained currency. More recent and more reliable records indicate that the longest species of seaweed is the Pacific giant kelp (*Macrocystis pyrifera*), which does not exceed 196 ft in length. It can grow 17¾ in in a day. The Japanese seaweed *Sargassum muticum* introduced *c.* 1970 can grow to 30 ft.

Most Spreading Plant

The greatest area covered by a single clonal growth is that of the wild box huckleberry (*Gaylussacia brachyera*), a mat-forming evergreen shrub first reported in 1796. A colony covering 8 acres was discovered in 1845 near New Bloomfield, Pa. Another colony, covering about 100 acres, was "discovered" on July 18, 1920, near the Juniata River in Pennsylvania. It has been estimated that this colony began 13,000 years ago.

Largest Wreath

The largest wreath was constructed by the Interflora Australian Unit Ltd, District 4 at Mt Lawley, West Australia. It measured 43.8 ft in diameter.

TREES

Oldest Tree

The oldest recorded tree was a bristlecone pine (*Pinus longaeva*) designated WPN-114, which grew at 10,750 ft above sea level on the northeast face of the Wheeler Ridge of the Sierra Nevadas, Calif. During studies in 1963 and 1964 it was found to be about 4,900 years old, but was cut down with a chain saw. The oldest known *living* tree is the bristlecone pine named *Methuselah* at 10,000 ft on the Calif side of the White Mts, with a confirmed age of 4,600 years. In March 1974 it was reported that this tree produced 48 live seedlings. Dendrochronologists estimate the *potential* life span of a bristlecone pine at nearly 5,500 years, but that of a "big tree" (*Sequoiadendron giganteum*) at perhaps 6,000 years. A report in March 1976, stated that some enormous specimens of Japanese cedar (*Cryptomeria japonica*) had been dated by carbon-14 to 5200 BC. The great ages attributed to the Canary Islands dragon tree (*Dracaena draco*) are discounted by botanists.

Earliest Species of Tree

The earliest species of tree still surviving is the maidenhair tree (*Ginkgo biloba*) of China, which first appeared about 160 million years ago, during the Jurassic era. It was "re-discovered" by Kaempfer (Netherlands) in 1690, and reached England *c.* 1754. It has been grown in Japan since *c.* 1100 where it was known as *ginkyo* (silver apricot) and is now known as *icho*.

Most Massive Tree

The most massive living thing on earth is a California "big tree" (*Sequoiadendron giganteum*) named the "General Sherman," standing 272 ft 4 in tall, in Sequoia National Park, Calif. It has a true girth of 79.1 ft (at 5 ft above the ground). The "General Sherman" has been estimated to contain the equivalent of 600,120 board ft of timber, sufficient to make 5,000 million matches. The foliage is blue-green, and the red-brown tan bark may be up to 24 in thick in parts. In 1968 the official published figure for its estimated weight was 2,145 tons.

The seed of a "big tree" weighs only 1/6,000th oz. Its growth to maturity may therefore represent an increase in weight of over 250,000 million fold.

Tallest Trees

The tallest known species of tree is the coast redwood (*Sequoia sempervirens*), growing indigenously near the coast of Calif north of Monterey to the Oreg border. The tallest measured example is the Howard Libbey Tree in Redwood Creek Grove, Humboldt County, Calif, discovered by Dr Paul A. Zahl in 1963 to be 367.8 ft with an apparently dead top and re-estimated at 366.2 ft in 1970. It has a girth of 44 ft. The nearby tree announced to a Senate Committee by Dr Rudolf W. Becking June 18, 1966, to be 385 ft, proved on re-measurement to be no more than 311.3 ft tall.

The tallest non-sequoia is a Douglas fir at Quinault Lake Park Trail, Wash, of *c.* 310 ft. The tallest broadleaf tree is a *Eucalyptus regnans* measured in Western Australia at 338 ft.

The identity of the tallest tree of all time has never been satisfactorily

LONGEST-SURVIVING SPECIES (above):
The maidenhair tree first appeared 160 million
years ago. TALLEST TREE (right): The
Howard Libbey redwood in Calif's Redwood
Creek set a height record at 366.2 ft in 1970.

resolved. A claim as high as 525 ft has been made (subsequently reduced
on re-measurement, in May 1889 to 220 ft). The now accepted view is
that the maximum height recorded by a qualified surveyor was 375 ft for
the Cornthwaite Tree (*Eucalyptus regnans* formerly *E. Amygdalina*) in
Thorpdale, Gippsland, Victoria, Australia, measured in 1880. Claims for
a Douglas fir (*Pseudotsuga taxifolia*) felled by George Carey in 1895 in
British Columbia with a height of 417 ft and a 77-ft circumference have
been obscured, though not necessarily invalidated by a falsified photograph.

Trees of Greatest Girth

The Santa Maria del Tule tree, in the state of Oaxaca, in Mexico, is a
Montezuma cypress (*Taxodium mucronatum*) which had a girth of
112–113 ft at a height of 5 ft above the ground in 1949. A figure of 167 ft
in circumference was reported for the pollarded European chestnut
(*Castanea sativa*) known as the "Tree of the 100 Horses" on the edge of
Mt Etna, Sicily, Italy, in 1972.

OLDEST LIVING THINGS: The bristlecone pines (above) in Calif have been known to exist for 4,900 years. TALLEST CHRISTMAS TREE (right): Measuring 221 ft in height, this Douglas fir adorned a Seattle shopping center in 1950.

Tallest Christmas Tree

The tallest cut Christmas tree was a 221-ft Douglas fir erected at Northgate Shopping Center, Seattle, Wash, in Dec 1950.

Remotest Tree

The tree most distant from any other is believed to be one at an oasis in the Ténéré Desert, Niger Republic. There were no other trees within 31 miles. In Feb 1960 it survived being rammed by a truck being backed up by a French driver. The tree was transplanted and is now in the Museum of Niamey, Niger.

Fastest-Growing Tree

Discounting bamboo, which is not botanically classified as a tree, but as woody grass, the fastest rate of growth recorded is 35 ft 3 in in 13 months by an *Albizzia falcata* planted on June 17, 1974, in Sabah, Malaysia. The youngest recorded age for a tree to reach 100 ft is 5¾ years for a Camarere (*Eucalyptus deglupta*) in Baku Forest Reserve near Madang, Papua, New Guinea.

Slowest-Growing Trees

The speed of growth of trees depends largely upon conditions, although some species, such as box and yew, are always slow-growing. The extreme is represented by a specimen of Sitka spruce which required 98 years to grow to 11 in tall, with a diameter of less than 1 in, on the Arctic tree-line. The growing of miniature trees or *bonsai* is an Oriental cult mentioned as early as *c.* 1320.

Most Leaves

Little work has been done on the laborious task of establishing which species has the most leaves. A large oak has perhaps 250,000, but a cypress may have some 45–50 million leaf scales.

Most Expensive Tree

The highest price ever paid for a tree is $51,000 for a single Starkspur golden delicious apple tree from near Yakima, Wash, bought by a nursery in Missouri in 1959.

Heaviest and Lightest Woods

The heaviest of all woods is black ironwood (*Olea laurifolia*), also called South African ironwood, with a specific gravity of up to 1.49, and weighing up to 93 lb per cu ft.

The lightest wood is *Aeschynomene hispida,* found in Cuba, which has a specific gravity of 0.044 and a weight of only 2¾ lb per cu ft. The wood of the balsa tree (*Ochroma pyramidale*) is of very variable density—between 2½ and 24 lb per cu ft. The density of cork is 15 lb per cu ft.

Seeds

The largest seed is that of the double coconut or Coco de Mer (*Lodoicea seychellarum*), the single-seeded fruit of which may weigh 40 lb. This grows only in the Seychelles Islands in the Indian Ocean. The smallest seeds are those of epiphytic orchids, at 35 million to the oz (*cf.* grass pollens at up to 6,000 million grains per oz). A single plant of the American ragweed can generate 8,000 million pollen grains in 5 hours.

The most protracted claim for the viability of seeds is that made for the Arctic lupin (*Lupinus arcticus*) found in frozen silt at Miller Creek in the Yukon, Canada, in July 1954 by Harold Schmidt. The seeds were germinated in 1966 and dated by the radio-carbon method of associated material to at least 8,000 BC and more probably to 13,000 BC.

LARGEST SEED: The Coco de Mer seed may weigh 40 lb. It grows only in the Seychelles Islands in the Indian Ocean.

Mosses

The smallest of mosses is the pygmy moss (*Ephemerum*), and the longest is the brook moss (*Fontinalis*), which forms streamers up to 3 ft long in flowing water.

Tallest and Fastest-Growing Bamboo

The tallest recorded bamboo was a thorny bamboo culm (*Bambusa arundinacea*) felled at Pattazhi, Travancore, India, in Nov 1904, which measured 121½ ft. Some species of the 45 genera of bamboo have attained growth rates of up to 36 in per day (0.00002 mph), on their way to reaching a height of 100 ft in less than 3 months.

Largest and Smallest Ferns

The largest of all the more than 6,000 species of fern is the tree-fern (*Alsophila excelsa*) of Norfolk Island, in the South Pacific, which attains a height of up to 60 ft. The smallest are *Hecistopteris pumila,* found in Central America, and *Azolla caroliniana,* which is native to the US.

Grasses

The world's commonest grass is *Cynodon ductylon* or Bermuda grass. The "Callie" hybrid, selected in 1966, grows as much as 6 in a day and stolons reach 18 ft in length.

Largest Orchids

The largest of all orchids is *Grammatophyllum speciosum,* native to Malaysia. Specimens up to 25 ft high have been recorded. The largest orchid flower is that of *Phragmipedium caudatum,* found in tropical areas of America. Its petals grow up to 18 in long, giving it a maximum outstretched diameter of 3 ft. The flower is, however, much less bulky than that of the stinking corpse lily (see *Largest Blooms*).

Tallest and Smallest Orchids

The tallest free-standing orchid is *Grammatophyllum speciosum* (see above). *Galeola foliata* may attain 45 ft on decaying rainforest trees in Queensland, Australia. The smallest orchid is *Bulbophyllum minutissimum,* found in Australia. Claims have also been made for *Notylia norae,* found in Venezuela. The smallest orchid flowers are less than 0.04 in long, borne by *Stella graminea.*

Highest-Priced Orchid

The highest price ever paid for an orchid is £1,207.50 (then $6,000), paid by Baron Schröder to Sanders of St Albans for an *Odontoglossum crispum* (variety *pittianum*) at an auction by Protheroe & Morris of Bow Lane, London, England, on March 22, 1906. A cymbidium orchid called "Rosanna Pinkie" was sold in the US for $4,500 in 1952.

KINGDOM PROTISTA

Protista were first discovered in 1676 by Anton van Leeuwenhoek (1632–1723), a Dutch microscopist. Among Protista are characteristics common to both plants and animals. The more plant-like are termed Protophyta (protophytes), including unicellular algae, and the more animal-like are placed in the phylum Protozoa (protozoans) which includes amoebas and flagellates.

The largest protozoans which are known to have existed were the now extinct Nummulites, which each had a diameter of 0.95 in. The largest existing protozoan is *Pelomyxa palustris*, which may attain a length of up to 0.6 in. The smallest of all protophytes is *Micromonas pusilla*, with a diameter of less than 2 microns or 0.00008 in.

The protozoan *Monas stigmatica* has been measured to move a distance equivalent to 40 times its own length in a sec. No human can cover even seven times his own length in a sec.

The protozoan *Glaucoma*, which reproduces by binary fission, divides as frequently as every 3 hours. Thus in the course of a day it could become a "six greats grandparent" and the progenitor of 510 descendants.

KINGDOM FUNGI

The largest recorded specimen of the giant puff ball (*Lycoperdon gigantea*) was one 62 in in diameter and 18 in high found at Mellor, Derbyshire, England, in 1971. A flatter specimen 64 in in diameter was recorded in NY State in 1877.

A 72-lb example of the edible mushroom *Polyporus frondosus* was reported by Joseph Opple near Solon, Ohio, in Sept 1976.

The largest officially recorded tree fungus was a specimen of *Oxyporus* (*Fomes*) *nobilissimus,* measuring 56 in by 37 in and weighing at least 300 lb found by J. Hisey in Wash State in 1946.

Most Poisonous Toadstool

The yellowish-olive death cup (*Amanita phalloides*) is regarded as the world's most poisonous fungus. From 6 to 15 hours after tasting, the effects are vomiting, delirium, collapse and death. Among its victims was Cardinal Giulio de' Medici, Pope Clement VII (1478–1534).

KINGDOM PROCARYOTA

Earliest Life Form

Traces of yeast-like cells, *Isuasphaera,* from cherty lagers of quartzite from southwest Greenland dated to 3,800 million years ago were announced on Aug 9, 1979.

Spherical microfossils, unicellular and physically similar to the blue-green algae *Aphanocapsa,* were reported by Dr Elso S. Barghoorn of Harvard University and Dr Andrew H. Knoll in Oct 1977. Discovered in chert (flintlike rock) datable to 3,400 million years ago located 12 miles southwest of Barbertown, South Africa, their average diameter is 2.5 microns. There is some evidence that life forms were first existent even 500 million years earlier.

Largest and Smallest Bacteria

Anton van Leeuwenhoek (1632–1723) was the first to observe bacteria, in 1675. The largest of the bacteria is the sulphur bacterium *Beggiatoa mirabilis,* which is from 16 to 45 microns in width and which may form filaments several millimeters long.

The smallest of all free-living organisms are the pleuro-pneumonia-like organisms (P.P.L.O.) of the *Mycoplasma.* One of these, *Mycoplasma laidlawii,* first discovered in sewage in 1936, has a diameter during the early part of its life of only 100 millimicrons, or 0.000004 in. Examples of the strain known as H.39 have a maximum diameter of 300 millimicrons and weigh an estimated 1.0×10^{-16} of a gram. A blue whale would weigh 1.77×10^{23} or 177,000 quintillion times as much.

Longest-Lived Bacteria

The oldest deposits from which living bacteria are claimed to have been extracted are salt layers near Irkutsk, USSR, dating from about 600 million years ago. The discovery was not accepted internationally. The US Dry Valley Drilling Project in Antarctica claimed resuscitated rod-shaped bacteria from caves up to a million years old.

Toughest Bacteria

The bacterium *Micrococcus radiodurans* can withstand atomic radiation of 6,500,000 röntgens or 10,000 times greater than radiation that is fatal to the average man.

Largest and Smallest Viruses

Viruses were discovered in 1892 by Dmitriy Ivanovsky (1864–1920). The largest true viruses are the brick-shaped pox viruses (e.g. smallpox, vaccinia, orf, etc.), measuring *c.* 250 × 300 nanometers (1 nanometer equals .000000001 of a meter).

Of more than 1,000 identified viruses, the smallest is the sheep scrapie virus with a diameter of 14 nanometers or 14 millionths of a millimeter. Some 40 times smaller still is the nanovariant WS1 RNA, with a length of 91 nucleotides, described by Dr Walter Schaffner of the University of Zurich in 1977.

PARKS, ZOOS, AQUARIA AND OCEANARIA

Largest Park

The largest park is the Wood Buffalo National Park in Alberta, Canada (established 1922), which has an area of 11,172,000 acres (17,560 sq mi).

Largest Zoo

It has been estimated that throughout the world there are some 500 zoos with an estimated annual attendance of 330 million. The largest zoological preserve in the world is the Etosha Reserve, Namibia (South-West Africa), with an area which has grown since 1907 to 38,427 sq mi. (It is thus larger than Ireland.)

Oldest Zoo

The oldest known zoo is that at Schönbrunn, Vienna, Austria, built in 1752 by the Holy Roman Emperor Francis I for his wife Maria Theresa. The oldest privately owned zoo in the world is that of the Zoological Society of London, founded in 1826. Its collection is housed partly in Regent's Park, London (36 acres), and partly at Whipsnade Park, Bedfordshire (541 acres, opened 1931). At the stocktaking on Jan 1, 1980, it was found to house 11,495 specimens—2,153 mammals, 2,037 birds, 587 reptiles and amphibians, an estimated 2,896 fish, and an estimated total of 3,822 invertebrates. Locusts, bees and ants are excluded from this figure.

The earliest known collection of animals (not a public zoo) was that set up by Shulgi, a 3rd dynasty ruler of Ur in 2094–2407 BC at Puzurish in southeast Iraq.

Largest Aquarium

The largest, as opposed to fish farm, is the John G. Shedd Aquarium, 12th St and Lake Shore Drive, Chicago, completed in Nov 1929 at a cost of $3,250,000. The total capacity of its display tanks is 450,000 gallons, with reservoir tanks holding 2 million gallons. Exhibited are 5,500 specimens from 350 species. Most of these specimens are collected by the Aquarium collecting boat based in Miami, Fla, and are shipped by air to Chicago. The record attendances are 78,658 in a day on May 21, 1931, and 4,689,730 visitors in the single year of 1931.

Oceanaria

The first oceanarium, opened in 1938, is Marineland of Florida located 18 miles south of St Augustine. Up to 7 million gallons of sea water are pumped daily through two major tanks, one rectangular (100 ft long by 40 ft wide by 18 ft deep) containing 450,000 gallons and one circular (233 ft in circumference and 12 ft deep) containing 400,000 gallons. The tanks are seascaped, including coral reefs and even a shipwreck.

The largest salt water tank is that at Hanna-Barbera's Marineland of the Pacific located on the Palos Verdes Peninsula, Calif. It is 251½ ft in circumference and 22 ft deep, with a capacity of 640,000 gallons. The total capacity of the whole oceanarium is 2,500,000 gallons. Their killer whale "Orky" at 14,000 lb is the largest in captivity.

Chapter 3
The Natural World

1. NATURAL PHENOMENA
EARTHQUAKES

It is estimated that each year there are some 500,000 detectable seismic or micro-seismic disturbances of which 100,000 can be felt and 1,000 cause damage. (Note: Seismologists record all earthquake dates with the year first, based *not* on local time but on Greenwich Mean Time.)

Greatest Earthquake

Using the new Seismic moment magnitudes (defined in 1977), the strongest assessable earthquake has been the cataclysmic Lebu shock, south of Concepción, Chile, on 1960 May 22, assessed at 9.5.

Worst Death Toll

The greatest loss of life occurred in the earthquake in the Shensi, Shansi and Honan provinces of China, of 1556 Feb 2 (New Style) (Jan 23 Old Style), when an estimated 830,000 people were killed. The highest death toll in modern times has been in the Tangshan earthquake (magnitude 8.2) in eastern China on 1976 July 27 (local time was 3:00 a.m. on July 28). A first figure published Jan 4, 1977 revealed 655,237 killed, later adjusted to 750,000. The greatest material damage was in the earthquake on the Kwanto plain, Japan, at 11:58 a.m. of 1923 Sept 1 (magnitude 8.2, epicenter in Latitude 35°15′N., Longitude 139°30′E.). In Sagami Bay, the sea bottom in one area sank 1,310 ft. The official total of persons killed and missing in this earthquake, called the *Shinsai* or Great 'Quake, and the resultant fires was 142,807. In Tokyo and Yokohama 575,000 dwellings were destroyed. The cost of the damage was estimated at $2,800 million.

VOLCANOES

The total number of known active volcanoes is 455 with an estimated 80 more that are submarine. The greatest concentration is in Indonesia, where 77 of its 167 volcanoes have erupted within historic times. The name "volcano" was first applied to the now dormant Vulcano Island in the Aeolian group in the Mediterranean, and that name derives from Vulcan, Roman god of destructive fire.

Highest Volcanoes

The highest extinct volcano in the world is Cerro Aconcagua (Stone Sentinel), 22,834 ft high, on the Argentine side of the Andes. It was first climbed on Jan 14, 1897 by Mathias Zurbriggen, and was the highest mountain climbed anywhere until June 12, 1907.

The highest dormant volcano is Volcán Llullaillaco (22,057 ft), on the frontier between Chile and Argentina.

The highest volcano regarded as active is Volcán Antofalla (21,162 ft) in Argentina, though a more definite claim is made for Volcán Guayatiri or Guallatiri (19,882 ft), in Chile, which erupted in 1959.

Longest Lava Flow

The longest lava flow, known as *pahoehoe* (twisted cord-like solidifications), is that from the eruption of Laki in southeast Iceland, which flowed 40½–43½ miles. The largest known prehistoric flow is the Roza basalt flow in North America, *c.* 15 million years ago, which had an unsurpassed length (300 miles), area (15,400 sq mi) and volume (300 cu mi).

Largest Crater

The world's largest *caldera* or volcano crater is that of Mt Aso (5,223 ft) in Kyushu, Japan, which measures 17 miles north to south, 10 miles east to west and 71 miles in circumference.

Greatest Eruption

The total volume of matter discharged in the eruption of Tambora, a volcano on the island of Sumbawa, in Indonesia, Apr 5–7, 1815, has been estimated as 36.4 cu mi. The energy of this eruption, which lowered the height of the island from 13,450 ft to 9,350 ft, was 8.4×10^{26} ergs. The

HIGHEST EXTINCT VOLCANO (above): Cerro Aconcagua in Argentina at 22,834 ft is also the tallest mountain in the Americas. LARGEST CRATER (right): Mt Aso in Japan has a crater measuring 71 miles in circumference.

volcano thus lost 4,100 feet in height and a crater 7 miles in diameter was formed. This compares with a probable 15 cu mi ejected by Santorini and 4.3 cu mi ejected by Krakatoa (see *Greatest Explosion*). The internal pressure causing the Tambora eruption has been estimated at 46,500,000 lb per sq in.

Greatest Explosion

The greatest explosion (possibly since Santorini in the Aegean Sea *c.* 1470 B.C.) occurred *c.* 10:00 a.m. (local time), or 3:00 a.m. G.M.T., on Aug 27, 1883 with an eruption of Krakatoa, an island (then 18 sq mi) in the Sunda Strait between Sumatra and Java, in Indonesia. A total of 163 villages were wiped out, and 36,380 people killed by the wave it caused. Rocks were thrown 34 miles high, and dust fell 10 days later at a distance of 3,313 miles. The explosion was recorded 4 hours later on the island of Rodrigues, 2,968 miles away, as "the roar of heavy guns" and was heard over 1/13th part of the surface of the globe. This explosion has been estimated to have had about 26 times the power of the greatest H-bomb test detonation, but was still only a fifth of the size of the Santorini cataclysm.

GEYSERS: Waimangu in New Zealand (left) peaked at 1,500 ft in 1904 for a record. The name "geyser" comes from the Icelandic spout (right).

GEYSERS

Tallest Geyser

The Waimangu geyser, in New Zealand, erupted to a height in excess of 1,500 ft in 1904, but has not been active since it erupted violently at 6:20 a.m. Apr 1, 1917, killing 4 people.

Currently the world's tallest active geyser is the US National Park Service Steamboat Geyser, in Yellowstone National Park, Wyo, which erupted at intervals ranging from 5 days to 10 months between 1962 and 1969 to a height of 250–380 ft. The *Geysir* ("gusher") near Mt Hekla in south-central Iceland, from which all others have been named, spurts, on occasion, to 180 ft, while the adjacent Strokkur, reactivated by drilling in 1963, spurts at 10–15 min intervals.

Greatest Geyser Discharge

The greatest measured water discharge from a geyser is 990,000 gallons by the Giant Geyser in Yellowstone National Park, Wyo.

2. STRUCTURE AND DIMENSIONS

The earth is not a true sphere, but flattened at the poles and hence an ellipsoid. The polar diameter of the earth (7,899.809 miles) is 26.576 miles less than the equatorial diameter (7,926.385 miles). The earth also has a slight ellipticity of the equator since its long axis (about Longitude 37° W.) is 174 yd greater than the short axis. The greatest departures from the reference ellipsoid are a protuberance of 244 ft in the area of Papua, New Guinea, and a depression of 354 ft south of Sri Lanka (Ceylon) in the Indian Ocean.

The greatest circumference of the earth—at the equator—is 24,901.47 miles, compared with 24,859.75 miles at the meridian. The area of the surface is estimated to be 196,937,600 sq mi. The period of axial rotation, *i.e.* the true sidereal day, is 23 hours 56 min 4.0996 sec, mean time.

Earth's Structure

The mass of the earth is 6,585,600,000,000,000,000,000 tons and its density is 5.515 times that of water. The volume is an estimated 259,875,-620,000 cu mi. The earth picks up cosmic dust but estimates vary widely with 30,000 metric tons a day being the upper limit. Modern theory is that the earth has an outer shell or lithosphere about 25 miles thick, then an outer and inner rock layer or mantle extending 1,800 miles deep, beneath which there is an iron-nickel core at an estimated temperature of 3,700°C and at a pressure of 22,000 metric tons per sq in or 3,400 kilobars. If the iron-nickel core theory is correct, iron must be by far the most abundant element in the earth.

OCEANS

Largest Ocean

The area of the earth covered by the sea is estimated to be 139,670,000 sq mi, or 70.92% of the total surface. The mean depth of the hydrosphere was at one time estimated to be 12,450 ft, but recent surveys suggest a lower estimate of 11,660 ft. The total weight of the water is estimated as 1.45×10^{18} tons, or 0.022% of the earth's total weight. The volume of the oceans is estimated to be 308,400,000 cu mi, compared with 8,400,000 cu mi of fresh water.

The largest ocean is the Pacific. Excluding adjacent seas, it represents

45.8% of the world's oceans and is about 63,800,000 sq mi in area. From Guayaquil, Ecuador, on the east, to Bangkok, Thailand, on the west, the Pacific could be said to stretch 10,905 miles in the shortest straight navigable line.

Longest Voyage Possible

The longest possible great circle sea voyage is one of 19,860 miles from a point 150 miles west of Karachi, Pakistan, to a point 200 miles north of Uka Kamchatka, USSR, via the Mozambique Channel, Drake Passage, and Bering Sea.

Deepest Depths in the Ocean

The deepest part of the ocean was first discovered in 1951 by the British survey ship *Challenger* in the Marianas Trench in the Pacific Ocean. The depth was measured by sounding and by echo-sounder and published as 5,960 fathoms (35,760 ft). Subsequent visits to the Challenger Deep have resulted in claims by echo-sounder only, culminating in one of 36,198 ft or 6.85 mi by the USSR's research ship *Vityaz* in March 1959. On Jan 23, 1960 the US Navy bathyscaphe *Trieste* descended to 35,820 ft. A metal object, say a pound-ball of steel, dropped into water above this trench would take nearly 63 minutes to fall to the sea bed 6.85 miles below.

The average depth of the Pacific Ocean is 14,000 ft.

Remotest Spot in the Ocean

The world's most distant point from land is a spot in the South Pacific, approximately 48°30'S., 125°30'W., which is about 1,660 miles from the nearest points of land, namely Pitcairn Island, Ducie Island and Cape Dart, Antarctica. Centered on this spot, therefore, is a circle of water with an area of about 8,657,000 sq mi—about 7,000 sq mi larger than the USSR, the world's largest country (see Chapter 10).

Sea Temperature

The temperature of the water at the surface of the sea varies from −2°C (28.5°F) in the White Sea to 35.6°C (96°F) in the shallow areas of the Persian Gulf in summer. A freak geothermal temperature of 56°C (132.8°F) was recorded in Feb 1965 by the survey ship *Atlantis II,* near the bottom of Discovery Deep (7,200 ft) in the Red Sea. The normal sea temperature in the area is 22°C (71.6°F). Ice-focused solar rays have been known to heat lake water to nearly 26.8°C (80°F).

Largest Sea

The largest of the seas (as opposed to oceans) is the South China Sea, with an area of 1,148,500 sq mi. The Malayan Sea comprising the waters between the Indian Ocean and the South Pacific, south of the Chinese mainland, covering 3,144,000 sq mi, is not now an entity accepted by the International Hydrographic Bureau.

Largest Gulf

The largest gulf in the world is the Gulf of Mexico, with an area of 580,000 sq mi and a shoreline of 3,100 miles from Cape Sable, Fla, to Cabo Catoche, Mexico.

Largest Bay

The largest bay measured by shoreline length is Hudson Bay in northern Canada with a shoreline of 7,623 miles and an area of 317,500 sq mi.

Highest Sea-Mountain

The highest known submarine mountain or sea-mountain was one discovered in 1953 near the Tonga Trench between Samoa and New Zealand. It rises 28,500 ft from the sea bed, with its summit 1,200 ft below the surface.

GREATEST TIDES: A ship docked in the Bay of Fundy rises and falls about 50 ft between high and low tides.

Greatest Tides

The greatest tides in the world occur in the Bay of Fundy, which separates the peninsula of Nova Scotia from Maine and the Canadian province of New Brunswick. Burncoat Head in the Minas Basin, Nova Scotia, has the greatest mean spring range with 47.5 ft, and an extreme range of 53.5 ft.

Extreme tides are due to lunar and solar gravitational forces affected by their perigee, perihelion, and conjunctions. Barometric and wind effects can superimpose an added "surge" element. Coastal and sea-floor configurations can accentuate these forces.

Greatest and Strongest Currents

The greatest current in the oceans of the world is the Antarctic Circumpolar Current or West Wind Drift Current, which was measured in 1969 in the Drake Passage between South America and Antarctica, to be flowing at a rate of 9,500 million cu ft per sec—nearly three times that of the Gulf Stream. Its width ranges from 185 to 1,240 miles and has a proven surface flow rate of 4/10ths of a knot.

The world's strongest currents are the Nakwakto Rapids, Slingsby Channel, British Columbia, Canada (Lat. 51°05′N., Long. 127°30′W.) where the flow rate may reach 16.0 knots (18.4 mph).

Highest Waves

The highest officially recorded sea wave was measured from the USS *Ramapo* proceeding from Manila, Philippines, to San Diego, Calif, on the night of Feb 6–7, 1933 during a 68-knot (78.3 mph) hurricane. The wave was computed to be 112 ft from trough to crest.

The highest instrumentally measured wave was one calculated to be exactly 86 ft high, recorded by the British ship *Weather Reporter* in the North Atlantic on Dec 30, 1972 in Lat. 59°N., Long. 19°W.

It has been calculated on the statistics of the Stationary Random Theory that one wave in more than 300,000 may exceed the average by a factor of 4.

On July 9, 1958 a landslip caused a wave to wash 1,740 ft high along the fjord-like shore of Lituya Bay, Alaska.

"Tidal" Wave

The highest recorded seismic sea wave, or *tsunami*, was one of an estimated 278 ft, which appeared off Ishigaki Island, Ryukyu Chain, Apr 24, 1971. It tossed an 850-ton block of coral more than 1.3 miles. *Tsunami* (a Japanese word which is singular and plural) have been observed to travel at 490 mph. Between 479 BC and 1977 there were at least 500 instances of *tsunami*, of which 270 were destructive.

Icebergs

The largest iceberg on record was an Antarctic tabular iceberg of over 12,000 sq mi (208 miles long and 60 miles wide) sighted 150 miles west of Scott Island, in the South Pacific Ocean, by the USS *Glacier* Nov 12, 1956. This iceberg was thus larger than Belgium.

The 200-ft-thick Arctic ice island T.1 (140 sq mi), discovered in 1946, took 17 years to be plotted.

The tallest iceberg measured was one of 550 ft reported off western Greenland by the USCG icebreaker *East Wind* in 1958.

The most southerly Arctic iceberg was sighted in the Atlantic by a USN weather patrol at Lat. 28°44'N., Long. 48°42'W., in Apr 1935.

The most northerly Antarctic iceberg was a remnant sighted in the Atlantic by the ship *Dochra* at Lat. 26°30'S., Long. 25°40'W., Apr 30, 1894.

Straits

The longest straits in the world are the Tatarskiy Proliv or Tartar Straits between Sakhalin Island and the USSR mainland, running 497 miles from the Sea of Japan to Sakhalinsky Zaliv. This distance is marginally longer than the Malacca Straits, which extend 485 miles.

The broadest named straits are the Davis Straits between Greenland and Baffin Island, which at one point narrow to 210 miles. The Drake Passage between the Diego Ramírez Islands, Chile, and the South Shetland Islands, is 710 miles across.

The narrowest navigable straits are those between the Aegean island of Euboea and the mainland of Greece. The gap is only 45 yd wide at Khalkis. The Seil Sound, Strathclyde, Scotland, narrows to a point only 20 ft wide where a bridge joins the island of Seil to the mainland and is thus said to span the Atlantic.

NARROWEST STRAIT: The mainland of Greece is separated from the Aegean Island of Euboea by only 45 yd.

TALLEST ICEBERG (left): Sighted off Greenland was this gigantic 550-ft-high ice float. HIGHEST WAVE (above): A landslide off this shore caused a wave to wash 1,740 ft up the mountain at Lituya Bay, Alaska, killing all the shrubbery.

LAND

There is satisfactory evidence that at one time the earth's land surface comprised a single primeval continent of 80 million sq mi, now termed Pangaea, and that this split about 190 million years ago, during the Jurassic period, into two super-continents, termed Laurasia (Eurasia, Greenland and North America) and Gondwanaland (comprising Africa, Arabia, India, South America, Oceania and Antarctica), named after Gondwana, India, which itself split 120 million years ago. The South Pole was apparently in the area of the Sahara as recently as the Ordovician period of *c.* 450 million years ago.

Rocks

The age of the earth is generally considered to be within the range 4,600 ± 100 million years, by analogy with directly measured ages of meteorites and of the moon. However, no rocks of this great age have yet been found on the earth, since geological processes have presumably destroyed the earliest record.

The greatest reported age for any scientifically dated rock is 3,800 ± 100 million years for granite gneiss rock found near Granite Falls in the Minnesota River valley, as measured by the lead-isotope and rubidium-uranium methods by the US Geological Survey, and announced on Jan 26, 1975. These metamorphic samples compare with the Amitsoq gneiss from Godthaab, Greenland, which is unreservedly accepted to be between 3,700 and 3,750 million years old.

The largest exposed rocky outcrop is the 1,237-ft-high Mt Augustus (3,627 ft above sea level), discovered June 3, 1858 about 200 miles east of Carnarvon, Western Australia. It is an up-faulted monoclinal gritty conglomerate 5 miles long and 2 miles across and thus twice the size of the celebrated monolithic arkose Ayer's Rock (1,100 ft), 250 miles southwest of Alice Springs, in Northern Territory, Australia.

Largest and Smallest Continents

Only 29.08%, or an estimated 57,270,000 sq mi, of the earth's surface is land, with a mean height of 2,480 ft above sea level. The Eurasian land mass is the largest with an area (including islands) of 21,053,000 sq mi.

The smallest is the Australian mainland, with an area of about 2,940,000 sq mi, which, together with Tasmania, New Zealand, New Guinea and the Pacific Islands, is described as Oceania. The total area of Oceania is about 3,450,000 sq mi, including West Irian (formerly West New Guinea) which is politically in Asia.

Land Remotest from the Sea

There is an unpinpointed spot in the Dzoosotoyn Elisen (desert), northern Sinkiang, China, that is more than 1,500 miles from the open sea in any direction. The nearest large town to this point is Wulumuchi (Urumchi) to its south.

Largest Peninsula

The world's largest peninsula is Arabia, with an area of about 1,250,000 sq mi.

Largest Islands

Discounting Australia, which is usually regarded as a continental land mass, the largest island is Greenland (part of the Kingdom of Denmark), with an area of about 840,000 sq mi. There is some evidence that Greenland is in fact several islands overlaid by an ice-cap in which case it would have an area of 650,000 sq mi.

The largest island surrounded by fresh water is the Ilha de Marajó (13,500 sq mi), in the mouth of the Amazon River, Brazil.

The largest island in a lake is Manitoulin Island (1,068 sq mi) in the Canadian (Ontario) section of Lake Huron. The island itself has a lake of 41.09 sq mi on it, called Manitou Lake, and in that lake are a number of islands. The largest inland island (*i.e.* land surrounded by rivers) is Ilha do Bananal, Brazil, with 7,000 sq mi.

Remotest Islands

The remotest island in the world is Bouvet Øya (formerly Liverpool Island), discovered in the South Atlantic by J. B. C. Bouvet de Lozier Jan 1, 1739 and first landed on by Capt George Norris on Dec 16, 1825. Its position is 54°26'S., 3°24'E. This uninhabited Norwegian dependency is about 1,050 miles from the nearest land—the uninhabited Queen Maud Land coast of eastern Antarctica.

The remotest inhabited island in the world is Tristan da Cunha, discovered in the South Atlantic by Tristão da Cunha, a Portuguese admiral, in March 1506. It has an area of 38 sq mi (habitable area 12 sq mi) and was annexed by the United Kingdom Aug 14, 1816. After evacuation in 1961 (due to volcanic activity), 198 islanders returned in Nov 1963. The nearest inhabited land is the island of St. Helena, 1,320 miles to the northeast. The nearest continent, Africa, is 1,700 miles away.

Largest Atolls

The largest atoll is Kwajalein in the Marshall Islands, in the central Pacific. Its slender 176-mile-long coral reef encloses a lagoon of 1,100 sq mi.

LARGEST ATOLL: Kwajalein in the Marshall Islands has a coral reef 176 miles around, enclosing a lagoon of 1,100 sq mi.

The atoll with the largest land area is Christmas Atoll, in the Line Islands, in the central Pacific Ocean. It has an area of 184 sq mi. Its two principal settlements, London and Paris, are 4 miles apart.

Highest Rock Pinnacle

The highest rock pinnacle is Ball's Pyramid near Lord Howe Island in the Pacific, which is 1,843 ft high, but has a base axis of only 218 yd. It was first scaled in 1965.

Longest Reef

The longest reef is the Great Barrier Reef off Queensland, northeastern Australia, which is 1,260 statute miles in length. Between 1959 and 1971 a large section between Cooktown and Townsville was destroyed by the proliferation of the Crown of Thorns starfish (*Acanthaster planci*).

Greatest Archipelago

The greatest archipelago is the 3,500-mile-long crescent of over 13,000 islands which forms Indonesia.

Highest Mountains

An eastern Himalayan peak of 29,028 ft above sea level on the Tibet-Nepal border (in an area first designated Chu-mu-lang-ma on a map of 1717) was discovered to be the world's highest mountain in 1852 by the Survey Department of the Government of India, from theodolite readings taken in 1849 and 1850. In 1860 its height was computed to be 29,002 ft. On July 25, 1973, the Chinese announced a height of 8,848.1 m or 29,029 ft 3 in. In practice the altitude can only be justified as 29,028 ± 25 ft. The 5½-mile-high peak was named Mt Everest after Sir George Everest (1790–1866), formerly Surveyor-General of India. Other names for Everest are Sagarmatha (Nepalese), Qomolongma (Chinese) and Mi-ti Gu-ti Cha-pu Long-na (Tibetan). After a total loss of 11 lives since the first reconnaissance in 1921, Everest was finally conquered at 11:30 a.m. May 29, 1953. (For details of ascents, see Mountaineering in Ch. 12.)

The mountain whose summit is farthest from the earth's center is the Andean peak of Chimborazo (20,561 ft), 98 miles south of the equator in Ecuador. Its summit is 7,057 ft further from the earth's center than the summit of Mt Everest. The highest mountain on the equator is Volcán Cayambe (19,285 ft), Ecuador, at Longitude 77° 58′ W.

The highest insular mountain in the world is the unsurveyed Ngga Pula, formerly Mt Sukarno, formerly Carstensz Pyramide, in Irian Jaya, Indonesia. According to cross-checked altimeter estimates, it is 16,500 ft high.

The highest separate unclimbed mountain in the world is now only the 31st highest—Zemu Gap Peak (25,526 ft) in the Sikkim Himalayas.

The world's tallest mountain measured from its submarine base (3,280 fathoms) in the Hawaiian Trough to peak is Mauna Kea (Mountain White) on the island of Hawaii, with a combined height of 33,476 ft, of which 13,796 ft are above sea level. Another mountain whose dimensions, but not height, exceed those of Mt Everest is the Hawaiian peak of Mauna Loa (Mountain Long) at 13,680 ft. The axes of its elliptical base, 16,322 ft below sea level, have been estimated at 74 mi and 53 mi. It should be noted that Cerro Aconcagua (22,834 ft) is more than 38,800 ft above the 16,000-ft-deep Pacific abyssal plain or 42,834 ft above the Peru-Chile Trench, which is 180 mi distant in the South Pacific.

Greatest Mountain Ranges

The greatest land mountain range is the Himalaya-Karakoram, which contains 96 of the world's 109 peaks of over 24,000 ft. The greatest of all mountain ranges is, however, the submarine Indian-East Pacific Oceans Cordillera, extending 19,200 miles from the Gulf of Aden to the Gulf of California by way of the seabed between Australia and Antarctica, with an average height of 8,000 ft above the base ocean depth.

Longest Line of Sight

Alaska's Mt McKinley (20,320 ft) has been sighted from Mt Sanford (16,237 ft) 230 mi away. Hvannadalshnukur (6,952 ft) on the eastern coast of Iceland, has been sighted from the Faeroe Islands 340 mi distant across the Norwegian Sea.

Greatest Plateau

The most extensive high plateau is the Tibetan Plateau in Central Asia. The average altitude is 16,000 ft and the area is 77,000 sq mi.

Sheerest Wall

The 3,200-ft-wide northwest face of Half Dome, Yosemite, Calif, is 2,200 ft high, but nowhere departs more than 7° from the vertical. It was first climbed (Class VI) in 5 days in July 1957 by Royal Robbins, Jerry Gallwas, and Mike Sherrick.

Highest Halites

Along the northern shores of the Gulf of Mexico for 725 miles there exist 330 subterranean "mountains" of salt, some of which rise more than 60,000 ft from bedrock and appear as the low salt domes first discovered in 1862.

Sand Dunes

The highest measured sand dunes are those in the Saharan sand sea of Isaouane-n-Tifernine of east central Algeria at Lat. 26° 42′ N., Long. 6° 43′ E. They have a wave-length of nearly 3 miles and attain a height of 1,410 ft.

HIGHEST MOUNTAIN (left): A team of Chinese scientists braves the intense cold and steep slope of Mt Everest in a 1975 expedition. GREATEST PLATEAU (above): Raising horses on a 16,000-ft-high plateau is what some Tibetans are doing.

Deepest and Largest Depressions

The deepest depression so far discovered is beneath the Hollick-Kenyon Plateau in Marie Byrd Land, Antarctica, where, at a point 5,900 ft above sea level, the ice depth is 14,000 ft, hence indicating a bedrock depression 8,100 ft below sea level.

The deepest exposed depression on land is the shore surrounding the Dead Sea, 1,291 ft below sea level. The deepest point on the bed of this lake is 2,600 ft below the Mediterranean. The deepest part of the bed of Lake Baykal in Siberia, USSR, is 4,872 ft below sea level.

The greatest submarine depression is a large area of the floor of the northwest Pacific which has an average depth of 15,000 ft.

The largest exposed depression in the world is the Caspian Sea basin in the Azerbaydzhani, Russian, Kazakh, and Turkmen republics of the USSR and northern Iran. It is more than 200,000 sq mi, of which 143,550 sq mi is lake area. The preponderant land area of the depression is the Prikaspiyskaya Nizmennost', lying around the northern third of the lake and stretching inland for a distance of up to 280 miles.

Longest and Shortest Rivers

The two longest rivers are the Amazon (*Amazonas*), flowing into the South Atlantic, and the Nile (*Bahr-el-Nil*) flowing into the Mediterranean. Which is the longer is more a matter of definition than of measurement.

The true source of the Amazon was discovered in 1953 to be a stream named Huarco, rising near the summit of Cerro Huagra (17,188 ft) in Peru. This stream progressively becomes the Toro, then the Santiago, then the Apurímac, which in turn is known as the Ene, and then the Tambo before its confluence with the Amazon prime tributary, the Ucayali. The length of the Amazon from this source to the South Atlantic *via* the Canal do Norte was measured in 1969 to be 4,007 miles (usually quoted to the rounded-off figure of 4,000 miles).

If, however, a vessel navigating downriver turns to the south of Ilha de Marajó through the straits of Breves and Boiuci into the Pará, the total length of the waterway becomes 4,195 miles. The Pará is not, however, a tributary of the Amazon, being hydrologically part of the basin of the Tocantins.

The length of the Nile watercourse, as surveyed by M Devroey (Belgium) before the loss of a few miles of meanders due to the formation of Lake Nasser, behind the Aswan High Dam, was 4,145 miles. This course is the hydrologically acceptable one from the source in Burundi of the Luvironza branch of the Kagera feeder of the Victoria Nyanza via the White Nile (*Bahr-el-Jebel*) to the delta.

> The world's shortest named river is the D River, Lincoln City, Ore, which connects Devil's Lake to the Pacific Ocean and is 440 ft long at low tide.

Greatest Flow

The greatest flow of any river is that of the Amazon, which discharges an average of 4,200,000 cu ft of water per sec into the Atlantic Ocean, rising to more than 7 million "cusecs" in full flood. The lowest 900 miles of the Amazon average 300 ft in depth.

Largest Basin and Longest Tributaries

The largest river basin is that drained by the Amazon (4,007 miles). It covers about 2,720,000 sq mi, has about 15,000 tributaries and sub-tributaries, of which four are more than 1,000 miles long. This includes the longest of all tributaries, the Madeira with a length of 2,100 miles, which is surpassed by only 14 rivers in the whole world.

The longest sub-tributary is the Pilcomayo (1,000 miles long) in South America. It is a tributary of the Paraguay River (1,500 miles long), which is itself a tributary of the Paraná (2,500 miles).

Submarine and Subterranean Rivers

In 1952 a submarine river 250 miles wide, known as the Cromwell Current, was discovered flowing eastward 300 ft below the surface of the Pacific for 3,500 miles along the equator. Its volume is 1,000 times that of the Mississippi.

In Aug 1958 a crypto-river was tracked by radio-isotopes flowing under the Nile, with a mean annual flow six times greater—500,000 million cu meters (20 million million cu ft).

Greatest River Bores

The bore on the Ch'ient'ang'kian (Hang-chou-fe) in eastern China is the most remarkable in the world. At spring tides, the wave attains a height of up to 25 ft and a speed of 13 knots. It is heard advancing at a range of 14 miles.

The bore on the Hooghly branch of the Ganges travels for 70 miles at more than 15 knots. The annual downstream flood wave on the Mekong River of Southeast Asia sometimes reaches a height of 46 ft. The greatest volume of any tidal bore is that of the Canal do Norte (10 miles wide) in the mouth of the Amazon.

LARGEST AND DEEPEST LAKE: Baykal (left) in central Siberia is the fresh-water lake with the greatest volume—it is 6,365 ft deep. HIGHEST LAKE is Titi-caca (right) in South America at 12,506 ft above sea level. Balsa boats float on this lake.

Longest Estuary

The longest estuary is that of the often-frozen Ob', in the northern USSR, at 550 miles. It is up to 50 miles wide.

Largest Delta

The largest delta is that created by the Ganga (Ganges) and Brahma-putra in Bangladesh (formerly East Pakistan) and West Bengal, India. It covers an area of 30,000 sq mi.

Largest Lakes

The largest inland sea or lake is the Kaspiskoye More (Caspian Sea) between southern USSR and Iran. It is 760 miles long and its total area is 143,550 sq mi. Of the total area, 55,280 sq mi (38.6%) are in Iran, where the lake is named the Darya-ye-Khazar. Its maximum depth is 3,215 ft and its surface is 92 ft below sea level. Since 1930 it has diminished 15,-000 sq mi in area with a fall of 62 ft, while the shoreline has retreated more than 10 miles in some places. The USSR government plans to re-verse the flow of the upper Pechora River from flowing north to the Barents Sea by blasting a 70-mile-long canal with nuclear explosives into the south-flowing Kolva River so that *via* the Kama and Volga rivers the Caspian will be replenished.

The fresh-water lake with the greatest surface area is Lake Superior, one of the Great Lakes. The total area is about 31,800 sq mi, of which 20,700 sq mi are in the US (Minn, Wis and Mich) and 11,100 sq mi in Ontario, Canada. It is 600 ft above sea level. The fresh-water lake with the greatest volume is Baykal (see page 146) with an estimated volume of 5,520 cu mi.

Highest Lake

The highest steam-navigated lake is Lago Titicaca (maximum depth 1,214 ft), with an area of about 3,200 sq mi (1,850 sq mi in Peru, 1,350 sq mi in Bolivia), in South America. It is 130 miles long and is situated at 12,506 ft above sea level.

There is an unnamed glacial lake near Mt Everest at 19,300 ft. Tibet's largest lake, Nam Tso (772 sq mi), lies at an elevation of 15,000 ft.

Deepest Lake

The deepest lake is Ozero (Lake) Baykal in central Siberia, USSR. It is 385 miles long and between 20 and 46 miles wide. In 1957 the lake's Olkhon Crevice was measured to be 6,365 ft deep and hence 4,872 ft below sea level.

Largest Lagoon

The largest lagoon in the world is Lagoa dos Patos in southernmost Brazil. It is 158 miles long and extends over 4,110 sq mi.

Underground Lake

Reputedly the largest underground lake is the Lost Sea, which lies 300 ft underground in the Craighead Caverns, Sweetwater, Tenn. Discovered in 1905, it covers an area of 4½ acres.

Highest Waterfall

The highest waterfall (as opposed to a vaporized "Bridal Veil") is the Salto Angel (Angel Falls), in Venezuela, on a branch of the Carrao River, an upper tributary of the Caroní, with a total drop of 3,212 ft and the longest single drop 2,648 ft. It was re-discovered in 1935 by a US pilot named Jimmy Angel (d Dec 8, 1956). He later crashed nearby on Oct 9, 1937. The fall, known by the Indians as Cherun-Meru, was first reported by Ernesto Sanchez La Cruz in 1910.

Greatest Waterfall Flow

On the basis of the average annual flow, the greatest waterfall is the Guairá (374 ft high), known also as the Salto dos Sete Quedas, on the Alto Paraná River between Brazil and Paraguay. Although attaining an average height of only 110 ft, its estimated annual average flow over the lip (5,300 yd wide) is 470,000 cu ft per sec. It has a peak flow of 1,750,000 cu ft per sec. The amount of water this represents can be imagined by supposing it was pouring into the dome of the Capitol in Washington, DC— it would fill it completely in 3/5ths of a sec.

The seven cataracts of Boyoma (formerly Stanley) Falls in the Congo (Zaïre) have an average annual flow of 600,000 cu ft per sec.

It has been calculated that, when some 5½ million years ago the Mediterranean basins began to be filled from the Atlantic through the Straits of Gibraltar, a waterfall was formed 26 times greater than the Guairá and perhaps 2,625 ft high.

Widest Waterfalls

The widest waterfalls are Khône Falls (50–70 ft high) in Laos, with a width of 6.7 miles and a flood flow of 1,500,000 cu ft per sec.

Longest Fjords

The longest "fjord" is the Nordvest Fjord arm of the Scoresby Sund in eastern Greenland, which extends inland 195 miles from the sea. The

HIGHEST WATERFALL: Angel Falls in Venezuela has a single drop of 2,648 ft, and a total fall of 3,212 ft. Note the airplane passing in front of the Falls.

longest of Norwegian fjords is the Sogne Fjord, which extends 113.7 miles inland from Sygnefest to the head of the Lusterfjord arm at Skjolden. It averages barely 3 miles in width and has a deepest point of 4,085 ft. If measured from Huglo along the Bømlafjord to the head of the Sørfjord arm at Odda, the Hardangerfjorden can also be said to extend 113.7 miles. The longest Danish fjord is Limfjorden (100 miles long).

Longest and Fastest-Moving Glaciers

It is estimated that 6,020,000 sq mi, or about 10.4% of the earth's land surface, is permanently glaciated. The longest known glacier is the Lambert Glacier, discovered by an Australian aircraft crew in Australian Antarctic Territory in 1956–57. It is up to 40 miles wide and, with its upper section known as the Mellor Glacier, it measures at least 250 miles in length. With the Fisher Glacier limb, the Lambert forms a continuous ice passage about 320 miles long. The longest Himalayan glacier is the

Siachen (47 miles) in the Karakoram range, though the Hispar and Biafo combine to form an ice passage 76 miles long.

The fastest-moving glacier is the Quarayaq in Greenland which flows 65–80 ft per day.

Greatest Avalanches

The greatest avalanches, though rarely observed, occur in the Himalayas, but no estimate of their volume has been published. It was estimated that 3½ million cu meters (120 million cu ft) of snow fell in an avalanche in the Italian Alps in 1885. (See also *Disasters*.)

Natural Bridge (Arch)

The longest natural bridge in the world is the Landscape Arch in the Arches National Park 25 miles north of Moab, Utah. This natural sandstone arch spans 291 ft and is set about 100 ft above the canyon floor. In one place erosion has narrowed its section to 6 ft.

Larger in mass, however, is the Rainbow Bridge, Utah, discovered on Aug 14, 1909, with a span of 278 ft but over 22 ft wide.

The highest natural arch is the sandstone arch 25 miles west-northwest of K'ashih, Sinkiang, China, estimated in 1947 to be nearly 1,000 ft tall, with a span of about 150 ft.

Largest Desert

Nearly an eighth of the world's land surface is arid with an annual rainfall of less than 9.8 in. The Sahara Desert in North Africa is the largest in the world. At its greatest length, it is 3,200 miles from east to west. From north to south it is between 800 and 1,400 miles. The area covered by the desert is about 3,250,000 sq mi. The land level varies from 436 ft below sea level in the Qattara Depression, Egypt, to the mountain Emi Koussi (11,204 ft) in Chad. The diurnal temperature range in the western Sahara may be more than 80 °F.

Largest Swamp

The largest tract of swamp is in the basin of the Pripet or Pripyat River—a tributary of the Dnieper in the USSR. These swamps cover an estimated area of 18,125 sq mi.

LONGEST NATURAL BRIDGE: This Landscape Arch near Moab, Utah spans 291 ft. Its size can by judged by the man near the left side.

TALLEST CAVE COLUMN: The 106-ft-tall Bicentennial column in Ogle Cave in Carlsbad Cavern, NM, overshadows the visitor at its foot.

Longest and Largest Cave and Cavern

The most extensive cave system is under the Mammoth Cave National Park, Ky, first discovered in 1799. On Sept 9, 1972 an exploration group led by Dr John P. Wilcox completed a connection, pioneered by Mrs Patricia Crowther, on Aug 30, between the Flint Ridge Cave system and the Mammoth Cave system, so making a combined system with a total mapped passageway length of 211.8 miles.

The Big Room of Carlsbad Caverns, NM, covers 14 acres with a ceiling height ranging from 80 to 255 ft. The longest axis is 1,800 ft.

DEEPEST CAVES BY COUNTRIES

These depths are subject to continuous revisions.

Depth in Ft

4,600	Gouffre Jean Bernard	France
3,645	Schneeloch, Salzburg area	Austria
3,602	Sima G E S, Malaga	Spain
3,162	Kilsi (Kievskaya)	USSR
3,117	Antro di Corchia	Italy
2,940	Sistema Purificacion	Mexico
2,713	Hölloch, Muotathal	Switzerland
2,569	Jaskini Snieznej Tatras	Poland
2,464	Ghar Parau, Zagros Mts	Iran
2,296	Kef Toghobeit	Morocco
2,247	Poloska Jama	Yugoslavia

Tallest Stalagmite

The tallest known stalagmite is La Grande Stalagmite in the Aven Armand cave, Lozère, France, which has attained a height of 98 ft from the cave floor. It was found in Sept 1897.

The tallest cave column is the 106-ft-tall Bicentennial Column in Ogle Cave in Carlsbad Cavern National Park, NM.

LARGEST GORGE: The Grand Canyon on the Colorado River in Arizona extends over 217 miles, is as much as 13 miles wide, and up to 7,000 ft deep. An awesome sight, it keeps changing color all day long as the shadows change.

Longest Stalactite

The longest known stalactite is a wall-supported column extending 195 ft from roof to floor in the Cueva de Nerja, near Málaga, Spain. Probably the longest free-hanging stalactite is one of 38 ft in the Poll an Ionain cave in County Clare, Ireland.

Largest and Deepest Gorges

The largest land gorge is the Grand Canyon on the Colorado River in north-central Ariz. It extends from Marble Gorge to the Grand Wash Cliffs, over a distance of 217 miles, varies in width from 4 to 13 miles and is up to 7,000 ft deep.

The submarine Labrador basin canyon is *c.* 2,150 miles long.

The deepest canyon in low relief territory is Hell's Canyon, dividing Oregon and Idaho. It plunges 7,900 ft from the Devil Mountain down to the Snake River.

A stretch of the Kali River in central Nepal flows 18,000 ft below its flanking summits of the Dhaulagiri and Annapurna groups.

The deepest submarine canyon yet discovered is one 25 miles south of Esperance, Western Australia, which is 6,000 ft deep and 20 miles wide.

Sea Cliffs

The highest sea cliffs yet pinpointed anywhere in the world are those on the north coast of east Molokai, Hawaii, near Umilehi Point, which descend 3,300 ft to the sea at an average gradient of more than 55°.

3. WEATHER*

The meteorological records given here necessarily relate largely to the last 130 to 150 years, since data before that time are both sparse and unreliable. Reliable registering thermometers were introduced as recently as *c.* 1820.

The longest continuous observations have been maintained at the Radcliffe Observatory, Oxford, England, since 1815.

Upper Atmosphere

The lowest temperature ever recorded in the atmosphere is −225.4°F at an altitude of about 50 to 60 miles, during noctilucent cloud research above Kronogård, Sweden, July 27–Aug 7, 1963.

A jet stream moving at 408 mph at 154,200 ft (29.2 miles) was recorded by Skua rocket above South Uist, Outer Hebrides, Scotland, on Dec 13, 1967.

Most Equable Temperature

The location with the most equable recorded temperature over a short period is Garapan, on Saipan, in the Mariana Islands, Pacific Ocean. During the nine years 1927–35, inclusive, the lowest temperature recorded was 67.3°F Jan 30, 1934, and the highest was 88.5°F Sept 9, 1931, giving an extreme range of 21.2°F. Between 1911–66 the Brazilian offshore island of Fernando de Noronha had a minimum temperature of 65.5°F Nov 17, 1913, and a maximum of 89.6°F March 2, 1965, an extreme range of 24.1°F.

Greatest Temperature Ranges

The highest *shade* temperature ever recorded was 136.4°F at Al' Aziziyah (El Azizia), Libya, on Sept 13, 1922. This information from the National Geographical Society is not officially recognized by the Libyan Ministry of Communications. A reading of 140°F at Delta, Mexico in Aug 1953 is not now accepted because of over-exposure to roof radiation. The official Mexican record of 136.4° at San Luis, Sonora, on Aug 11, 1933 is not internationally accepted. A freak heat flash from Coimbra, Portugal, in Sept 1933, said to have caused the temperature to rise to 158°F for 120 sec is apocryphal.

The lowest *screen* temperature ever recorded was −126.9°F at Vostok (11,220 ft above sea level), Antarctica on Aug 24, 1960. The coldest permanently inhabited place is the Siberian village of Oymyakon in the USSR, where the temperature reached −96°F in 1964.

---

* For more specialized weather records, see "Weather Facts and Feats," a Guinness Superlatives Book, published in 1980 by Sterling.

Reading top to bottom: HOTTEST
PLACE ON EARTH: Dallol,
Ethiopia averaged 94° F over a 6-
year period. COLDEST PLACE:
Soviet researchers chose this
Antarctic "inaccessibility station" to
conduct experiments where the
thermometer averages 72° F below
zero. LARGEST HAILSTONE: This
1.67-lb monster fell in Coffeyville,
Kans, in 1979. WINDIEST PLACE:
Gales reach 200 mph here at
Commonwealth Bay, George V
Coast, Antarctica.

The greatest temperature variation recorded in a day is 100 °F (a fall from 44 °F to −56 °F) at Browning, Mont, Jan 23–24, 1916. The most freakish rise was 49 °F in 2 min at Spearfish, SD, from −4 °F at 7:30 a.m. to 45 °F at 7:32 a.m. Jan 22, 1943.

The greatest recorded temperature ranges in the world are around the Siberian "cold pole" in the eastern USSR. Verkhoyansk (67°33′N., 133°23′E.) has ranged 192 °F from −94 °F (unofficial) to 98 °F.

Deepest Permafrost

The greatest recorded depth of permafrost is 4,920 ft, reported in Apr 1968 in the basin of the Lena River, Siberia, USSR.

Humidity and Discomfort

Human discomfort depends not merely on temperature but on the combination of temperature, humidity, radiation and wind speed. The US Weather Service uses a Temperature-Humidity Index, which equals two-fifths of the sum of the dry and wet bulb thermometer readings plus 15. When the THI in still air reaches 75, at least half of the people will be uncomfortable while at 79 few, if any, will be comfortable. A THI reading of 98.2 has been recorded twice in Death Valley, Calif—on July 27, 1966 (119 °F, 31% humidity) and on Aug 12, 1970 (117 °F, 37% humidity). A person driving at 45 mph in a car without a windshield in a temperature of −45 °F would, by the chill factor, experience the equivalent of −125 °F, which is within 2 °F of the world record.

Most Intense Rainfall

Difficulties attend rainfall readings for very short periods but the figure of 1.50 in in 1 min at Barst, Guadeloupe, Nov 26, 1970, is regarded as the most intense recorded in modern times. The cloudburst of "near two foot in less than a quarter of half an hour" at Oxford, England, on the afternoon of May 31 (Old Style), 1682, is regarded as unacademically recorded.

Cloud Extremes

The highest standard cloud form is cirrus, averaging 27,000 ft and above, but the rare nacreous or mother-of-pearl formation sometimes reaches nearly 80,000 ft. The lowest is stratus, below 3,500 ft. The cloud form with the greatest vertical range is cumulonimbus, which has been observed to reach a height of nearly 68,000 ft in the tropics.

Mirages

The largest mirage on record was that sighted in the Arctic at 83 ° N., 103 ° W. by Donald B. MacMillan in 1913. This type of mirage, known as the Fata Morgana, appeared as the same "hills, valleys, snow-capped peaks extending through at least 120 degrees of the horizon" that Peary had named Crocker Land 6 years earlier.

On July 17, 1939, a mirage of Snaefell Jokull glacier (4,715 ft) on Iceland was seen from the sea when 335–350 miles distant.

Longest-Lasting Rainbow

A rainbow lasting for at least 3 hours was reported from North Wales Aug 14, 1979.

Lightning

The visible length of lightning strokes varies greatly. In mountainous regions, when clouds are very low, the flash may be less than 300 ft long. In flat country with very high clouds, a cloud-to-earth flash sometimes measures 4 miles, though in extreme cases such flashes have been measured at 20 miles. The intensely bright central core of the lightning channel is extremely narrow. Some authorities suggest that its diameter is as little as half an inch. This core is surrounded by a "corona envelope" (glow discharge) which may measure 10 to 20 ft in diameter.

The speed of a lightning discharge varies from 100 to 1,000 miles per sec for the downward leader track, and reaches up to 87,000 miles per sec (nearly half the speed of light) for the powerful return stroke.

Every few million strokes there is a giant discharge, in which the cloud-to-earth and the return lightning strokes flash from the top of the thunder clouds. In these "positive giants" energy of up to 3,000 million joules (3×10^{16} ergs) is sometimes recorded. The temperature reaches about 30,000 °C (54,000 °F), which is more than five times greater than that of the surface of the sun. A theory that lightning was triggered by cosmic rays was published in 1977.

Waterspouts

The highest waterspout of which there is reliable record was one observed May 16, 1898, off Eden, NSW Australia. A theodolite reading from the shore gave its height as 5,014 ft. It was about 10 ft in diameter.

OTHER WEATHER RECORDS

Hottest Place (Annual mean): Dallol, Ethiopia, 94 °F, 1960–66.
In Death Valley, Calif, 120 °F or more reported 43 consecutive days.

Coldest Place (Annual mean): Pole of Cold (78 °S., 96 °E.), Antarctica, −72 °F (16 °F lower than Pole).

Greatest Rainfall (24 hours): 73.62 in, Cilaos, La Réunion, Indian Ocean, March 15–16, 1952. (Calendar month): 366.14 in, Cherrapunji, Meghalaya, India, July, 1861. (12 months): 1,041.78 in, Cherrapunji, Meghalaya, Aug 1, 1860–July 31, 1861.

Greatest Snowfall (24 hours): 76 in, Silver Lake, Colo, Apr 14–15, 1921. (12 months): 1,224.5 in, Paradise, Mt Rainier, Wash, Feb 19, 1971–Feb 18, 1972. (Single): 189 in, Mt Shasta Ski Bowl, Calif. (Greatest depth): 25 ft 5 in at Paradise, Mt Rainier, Wash, Apr 17, 1972.

Maximum Sunshine (Year): 97%+ (over 4,300 hours), eastern Sahara. 768 days, Feb 9, 1967–March 17, 1969, St. Petersburg, Fla.

Minimum Sunshine: Nil at North Pole—for winter stretches of 186 days.

Barometric Pressure (Highest): 1,083.8 mb. (32 in), Agata, Siberia, USSR, Dec 31, 1968. (Lowest): 870 mb. (25.69 in), at 16.44 ° N., 137.46 ° E., in the Philippine Sea, Oct 12, 1979.

Highest Surface Wind-speed: 231 mph, Mt Washington (6,288 ft), NH, Apr 12, 1934. 280 mph in a tornado at Wichita Falls, Tex, Apr 2, 1958.

Thunder Days (Year): 322 days, Bogor (formerly Buitenzorg), Java, Indonesia (average, 1916–19).

Wettest Place (Annual mean): Mt Waialeale (5,148 ft), Kauai, Hawaii, 451 in (average, 1920–72). In 1948, max 621 in.

Driest Place (Annual mean): Calama, in the Desierto de Atacama, Chile. None.

Longest Drought: c. 400 years to 1971, Desierto de Atacama, Chile.

Most Rainy Days (Year): Mt Waialeale, Kauai, Hawaii, up to 350 days per year.

Largest Hailstones: 1.67 lb (7½ in diameter, 17½ in circumference), Coffeyville, Kans, Sept 3, 1970. An ice block of coalesced hailstones 35–70 oz reported at Manchester, Eng, Apr 2, 1973.

Longest Sea Level Fogs (Visibility less than 1,000 yd): Fogs persist for weeks on the Grand Banks, Newfoundland, Canada, and the average is more than 120 days per year.

Windiest Place: The Commonwealth Bay, George V Coast, Antarctica, where gales reach 200 mph.

LIGHTNING: A giant discharge like this occurs only once in a few million strokes.

Chapter 4

The Universe & Space

"Astronomy Facts and Feats" by Patrick Moore, a Guinness Superlatives Book (Sterling), contains more information on the subjects covered in this chapter.

Light-Year

That distance traveled by light (speed 186,282.397 miles per sec, or 670,616,629.4 mph, *in vacuo*) in one tropical (or solar) year (365.24219878 mean solar days at Jan 0, 12 hours Ephemeris time in 1900 AD) and is 5,878,499,814,000 miles. The unit was first used in March 1888.

Magnitude

A measure of stellar brightness such that the light of a star of any magnitude bears a ratio of 2.511886 to that of a star of the next magnitude. Thus a fifth magnitude star is 2.511886 times as bright, while one of the first magnitude is exactly 100 (or 2.511886^5) times as bright, as a sixth magnitude star. In the case of such exceptionally bright bodies as Sirius, Venus, the moon (magnitude -11.2) or the sun (magnitude -26.7), the magnitude is expressed as a minus quantity.

Proper Motion

That component of a star's motion in space which, at right angles to the line of sight, constitutes an apparent change of position of the star in the celestial sphere.

The universe is the entirety of space, matter and antimatter. An appreciation of its magnitude is best grasped by working outward from the earth, through the solar system and our own Milky Way galaxy, to the remotest extra-galactic nebulae and quasars.

Meteor Shower

Meteoroids are mostly of cometary or asteroidal origin. A meteor is the light phenomenon caused by entry of a meteoroid into earth's atmosphere. The greatest meteor "shower" on record occurred on the night of Nov 16–17, 1966, when the Leonid meteors (which recur every 33¼ years) were visible over North America. It was calculated that meteors passed over Arizona at a rate of 2,300 per min for a period of 20 min from 5 a.m. Nov 17, 1966.

LARGEST METEORITE
(above): The "Tent"
meteorite weighing over 34
tons is on display at the
Hayden Planetarium in NYC.
**LARGEST PIECE OF
STONY METEORITE**
(right): This 3,902-lb chunk
of stone fell in a shower on
Kirin, China in 1976.

Oldest and Largest Meteorites

It was reported in Aug 1978 that dust grains in the Murchison meteorite which fell in Australia in Sept 1969 predate the formation of the solar system.

When a meteoroid penetrates to the earth's surface, the remnant is described as a meteorite. This occurs about 150 times per year over the whole land surface of the earth. The largest known meteorite is one found in 1920 at Hoba West, near Grootfontein in southwest Africa. This is a block of about 9 ft long by 8 ft broad, weighing 132,000 lb.

The largest meteorite exhibited by any museum is the "Tent" meteorite, weighing 68,085 lb, found in 1897 near Cape York, on the west coast of Greenland, by the expedition of Commander (later Rear-Admiral) Robert Edwin Peary (1856–1920). It was known to the Eskimos as the Abnighito and is now exhibited in the Hayden Planetarium in New York City.

The largest piece of stony meteorite recovered is a piece of 3,902 lb which was part of a shower that struck Kirin, Kaoshan Province, China, March 8, 1976. The oldest dated meteorites are from the Allende fall over Chihuahua, Mexico, Feb 8, 1969, dating back 4,610 million years.

There was a mysterious explosion of 12½ megatons at Lat. 60° 55′ N., Long. 101° 57′ E., in the basin of the Podkamennaya Tunguska River, 40 miles north of Vanavar, in Siberia, USSR at 00 hrs 17 min 11 sec UT June 30, 1908. The cause was variously atributed to a meteorite (1927), a comet (1930), a nuclear explosion (1961) and to antimatter (1965). This devastated an area of about 1,500 sq mi, and the shock was felt more than 600 miles away. The theory is now favored that this was the terminal flare of stony debris from a comet, possibly Encke's Comet, at an altitude of less than 20,000 ft. A similar event may have occurred over the Isle of Axeholm, Lincolnshire, England, a few thousand years before.

LARGEST PROVEN CRATER (in northern Arizona) was gouged out in about 25,000 BC. It is 575 ft deep, almost a mile wide.

Largest Craters

It has been estimated that some 2,000 asteroid-earth collisions have occurred in the last 600 million years. A total of 96 collision sites or astroblemes have been recognized. A crater 150 miles across and a half mile deep has been postulated in Wilkes Land, Antarctica, since 1962. It would have been caused by a 14,560 million-ton meteorite striking at 44,000 mph. In Dec 1970 USSR scientists reported an astrobleme in the basin of the Popigai River with a 60-mile diameter and a maximum depth of 1,300 ft. There is a possible crater-like formation or astrobleme 275 miles in diameter on the eastern shore of Hudson Bay, where the Nastapoka Islands are just off the coast.

Evidence was published in 1963 discounting a meteoric origin for the crypto-volcanic Vredefort Ring (diameter 26 miles) to the southwest of Johannesburg, South Africa, but this claim has now been reasserted.

The largest proven crater is the Coon Butte or Barringer Crater, discovered in 1891 near Winslow, northern Ariz. It is 4,150 ft in diameter and now about 575 ft deep, with a parapet rising 130–155 ft above the surrounding plain. It has been estimated that an iron-nickel mass with a diameter of 200–260 ft, and weighing about 2,240,000 tons, gouged this crater c. 25,000 BC.

The New Quebec (formerly the Chubb) "Crater," first sighted June 20, 1943, in northern Ungava, Canada, is 1,325 ft deep and measures 6.8 miles around its rim.

Fireball

The brightest fireball ever recorded photographically was one observed over Sumava, Czechoslovakia, Dec 4, 1974, by Dr Zdeněk Ceplecha, which had a momentary magnitude of −22, or 10,000 times brighter than a full moon.

Tektites

The largest tektite of which details have been published was one of 7.04 lb found in 1932 at Muong Nong, Saravane Province, Laos, and now in the Paris Museum.

Aurorae

Polar lights, known since 1560 as Aurora Borealis or Northern Lights in the northern hemisphere and since 1773 as Aurora Australis in the southern hemisphere, are caused by electrical solar discharges in the upper atmosphere and occur most frequently in high latitudes. Aurorae are visible at some time on *every* clear dark night in the polar areas within 20° latitude of the magnetic poles.

Reliable figures exist only from 1952. Extreme cases of displays in very low latitudes were those reported at Cuzco, Peru (Aug 2, 1744); Honolulu, Hawaii (Sept 1, 1859); and, questionably, Singapore (Sept 25, 1909).

The extreme height of aurorae has been measured at 620 miles, while the lowest may descend to 45 miles.

THE MOON

The earth's closest neighbor in space and only natural satellite is the moon, at a mean distance of 238,855 statute miles center to center or 233,812 miles surface to surface. Its closest approach (perigee) and most extreme distance away (apogee) measured surface to surface are 216,420 and 247,667 miles respectively. It has a diameter of 2,159.3 miles and has a mass of 7.23×10^{19} long tons with a mean density of 3.34. The average orbital speed is 2,287 mph.

FAR SIDE OF THE MOON (top left): Never seen on earth, the hidden side was first photographed by a Soviet space probe in 1959. FOOTSTEP (above) IN THE MOON'S DUST: A US astronaut made this. LUNAR SURFACE (right): Rocks taken from the moon's surface have been analyzed to be 4,720 million years old.

The first direct hit on the moon was achieved at 2 min 24 sec after midnight (Moscow time) Sept 14, 1959, by the Soviet space probe *Lunik II* near the *Mare Serenitatis.* The first photographic images of the hidden side were collected by the USSR's *Lunik III* from 6:30 a.m. Oct 7, 1959, from a range of up to 43,750 miles, and transmitted to the earth from a distance of 292,000 miles. The first "soft" landing was made by the USSR's *Luna IX* in the area of the Ocean of Storms Feb 3, 1966.

Largest and Deepest Craters

Only 59% of the moon's surface is directly visible from the earth because it is in "captured rotation," *i.e.,* the period of rotation is equal to the period of orbit. The largest wholly visible crater is the walled plain Bailly, toward the moon's South Pole, which is 183 miles across, with walls rising to 14,000 ft. Partly on the averted side, the Orientale Basin measures more than 600 miles in diameter.

The deepest crater is the moon's Newton crater, with a floor estimated to be between 23,000 and 29,000 ft below its rim and 14,000 ft below the level of the plain outside. The brightest directly visible spot on the moon is *Aristarchus.*

Highest Moon Mountains

As there is no sea level on the moon, the heights of lunar mountains can be measured only in relation to a reference sphere with a radius of 1,079.943 miles. Thus the greatest elevation attained by any of the 12 US astronauts has been 25,688 ft, on the Descartes Highlands, by Capt John Walter Young, USN, and Major Charles M. Duke, Jr, Apr 27, 1972.

Temperature Extremes on the Moon

When the sun is overhead, the temperature on the lunar equator reaches 243 °F (31 °F above the boiling point of water). By sunset the temperature is 58 °F, but after nightfall it sinks to −261 °F.

"Blue Moon"

Owing to sulphur particles in the upper atmosphere from a forest fire covering 250,000 acres between Mile 103 and Mile 119 on the Alaska Highway in northern British Columbia, Canada, the moon took on a bluish color, as seen from Great Britain, on the night of Sept 26, 1950. The moon appeared green after the Krakatoa eruption of Aug 27, 1883 (see *Volcanoes*) and in Stockholm for 3 min Jan 17, 1884.

THE SUN

The earth's 66,620 mph orbit of 584,017,800 miles around the sun is elliptical, hence our distance from the sun varies. The orbital speed varies between 65,520 mph (minimum) and 67,750 mph. The average distance of the sun is 1.000000230 astronomical units or 92,955,829 miles. The closest approach (perihelion) is 91,402,000 miles, and the farthest departure (aphelion) is 94,510,000 miles. The solar system is revolving around the center of the Milky Way once in each 225 million years at a speed of 481,000 mph and has a velocity of 42,500 mph relative to stars in our immediate region such as Vega, toward which it is moving.

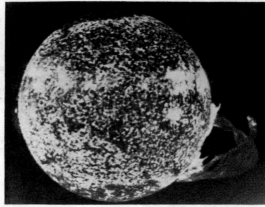

TOTAL ECLIPSE
(above): The sun
covered by the
moon is the most
spectacular natural
phenomenon.
SOLAR
ERUPTION
(right): This flare
spanned more than 365,000 miles.

Sun's Temperature and Dimensions

The sun has an internal temperature of about 16,000,000 °K (K stands for the Kelvin absolute scale of temperatures), a core pressure of 560 million tons per sq in and uses up nearly 4½ million tons of hydrogen per sec, thus providing a luminosity of 3×10^{27} candlepower, or 1½ million candlepower per sq in. The sun has the stellar classification of a "yellow dwarf" and, although its density is only 1.407 times that of water, its mass is 332,946 times as much as that of the earth. It has a mean diameter of 865,270 miles. The sun with a mass of $2,096 \times 10^{27}$ tons represents more than 99% of the total mass of the solar system.

Largest and Most Frequent Sunspots

To be visible to the *protected* naked eye, a sunspot must cover about one two-thousandth part of the sun's disc and thus have an area of about 500 million sq mi. The largest recorded sunspot occurred in the sun's southern hemisphere on Apr 8, 1947. Its area was about 7,000 million sq mi, with an extreme longitude of 187,000 miles and an extreme latitude of 90,000 miles. Sunspots appear darker because they are more than 1,500 °C cooler than the rest of the sun's surface temperature of 5,525 °C. The largest observed solar prominence was one protruding 365,000 miles, photographed on Dec 19, 1973 during the third and final Skylab mission.

In Oct 1957 a smoothed sunspot count showed 263, the highest recorded index since records started in 1755 (*cf.* previous record of 239 in May 1778). In 1943 a sunspot lasted for 200 days from June to Dec.

Earliest Recorded Eclipses

The earliest extrapolated eclipses that have been identified are 1361 BC (lunar) and Oct 2136 BC (solar). For the Middle East only, lunar eclipses have been extrapolated to 3450 BC and solar ones to 4200 BC.

Longest Eclipse Duration

The maximum possible duration of an eclipse of the sun is 7 min 31 sec. The longest actually *measured* was June 20, 1955 (7 min 8 sec), seen from the Philippines. That of July 16, 2186 in the mid-Atlantic should

HALLEY'S COMET (left): Due to be sighted from earth in Dec 1984, this comet has been traced back to 467 BC. Halley correctly predicted its appearance on Christmas Day 1758. CRAB NEBULA (lower left): The explosion of this super-nova occurred in about 3000 BC, but it was not visible on earth until the year 1054 AD. It is still expanding at the rate of 800 miles per sec. REMOTEST CELESTIAL BODY VISIBLE to the naked eye is the Great Galaxy in Andromeda (below), 2,200,000 light-years away.

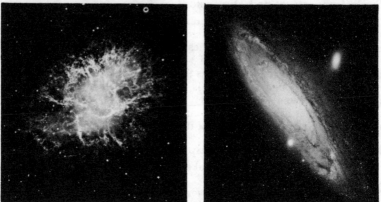

last 7 min 29 sec. This will be the longest for 1,469 years. Durations can be extended by observers being airborne, as on June 30, 1973 when an eclipse was "extended" to 72 min for observers aboard a *Concorde* jet. An annular eclipse may last for 12 min 24 sec. The longest totality of any lunar eclipse is 104 min. This has occurred many times.

Most and Least Frequent Eclipses

The highest number of eclipses possible in a year is seven, as in 1935, when there were five solar and two lunar eclipses; or four solar and three lunar eclipses, as will occur in 1982. The lowest possible number in a year is two, both of which must be solar, as in 1944 and 1969.

Earliest Recorded Comets

The earliest records of comets date from the 7th century BC. The speeds of the estimated 2,000,000 comets vary from 700 mph in outer space to 1,250,000 mph when near the sun.

The successive appearances of Halley's Comet have been traced back to 467 BC. It was first depicted in the Nuremberg Chronicle of 684 AD.

The first prediction of its return by Edmund Halley (1656–1742) proved true on Christmas Day, 1758, 16 years after his death. Its next perihelion should be at 9:30 p.m. Greenwich Mean Time Feb 9, 1986, exactly 75.81 years after the last, which was Apr 19, 1910. The 33rd sighting may occur as early as Dec 1984.

Closest Comet Approach

On July 1, 1770 Lexell's Comet, traveling at a speed of 23.9 miles per sec (relative to the sun), came within 745,000 miles of the earth. However, the earth is believed to have passed through the tail of Halley's Comet, most recently on May 19, 1910.

Largest Comets

Comets are so tenuous that it has been estimated that even the head of one rarely contains solid matter much greater than 0.6 mile in diameter. The tails, as in the case of the brightest of all, the Great Comet of 1843, may trail for 205 million miles. The head of Holmes Comet of 1892 once measured 1½ million miles in diameter.

Comet Bennett which appeared in Jan 1970 was found to be enveloped in a hydrogen cloud measuring some 8 million miles long.

Shortest and Longest Comet Period

Of all the recorded periodic comets (these are members of the solar system), the one which most frequently returns is Encke's Comet, first identified in 1786. Its period of 1,206 days (3.3 years) is the shortest established. Not one of its 51 returns (to the end of 1977) has been missed by astronomers. Now increasingly faint, it is expected to "die" by Feb 1994. The most frequently observed comets are Schwassmann-Wachmann I, Kopff and Oterma, which can be observed every year between Mars and Jupiter.

The path of Delavan's Comet of 1914 has not been accurately determined but it is not expected to return for perhaps 24 million years.

PLANETS
Planets (including the earth) are bodies within the solar system which revolve around the sun in definite orbits.

Largest, Fastest and Hottest Planets

Jupiter, with an equatorial diameter of 88,780 miles and a polar diameter of 82,980 miles, is the largest of the nine major planets, with a mass 317.83 times and a volume 1,318 times that of the earth. It also has the shortest period of rotation, with a "day" of only 9 hours 50 min 30.003 sec in its equatorial zone.

Mercury, which orbits the sun at an average distance of 35,983,100 miles, has a period of revolution of 87.9686 days, so giving the highest average speed in orbit of 107,030 mph.

A surface temperature of c. 896 °F has been estimated from measurements made from Venus by the USSR probes *Venera 7* and *Venera 8* in 1970 and 1972.

Smallest and Coldest Planets

The smallest and coldest planet is Pluto, which has an estimated surface temperature of −360°F (100°F above absolute zero). Its mean distance from the sun is 3,674,488,000 miles and its period of revolution is 248.54 years. Its diameter is about 1,880 miles and it has a mass about 1/500th that of the earth. Pluto was first recorded by Clyde William Tombaugh (b Feb 4, 1906) at Lowell Observatory, Flagstaff, Ariz Feb 18, 1930 from photographs taken on Jan 23 and 29, and announced on March 13. Because of its orbital eccentricity, Pluto will be closer to the sun than Neptune between Jan 23, 1979 and March 15, 1999.

Nearest Planet to Earth

The fellow planet closest to the earth is Venus, which is, at times, about 25,700,000 miles inside the earth's orbit, compared with Mars' closest approach of 34,600,000 miles outside the earth's orbit. Mars, known since 1965 to be cratered, has temperatures ranging from 85°F to −190°F.

Planet Features

By far the highest and most spectacular surface feature is Olympus Mons (formerly Nix Olympica) in the Tharsis region of Mars, with a diameter of 310–370 miles and a height of 75,450–95,150 ft above the surrounding plain.

Viewed from earth, by far the brightest of the five planets visible to the naked eye is Venus, with a maximum magnitude of −4.4. The faintest is Pluto, with a magnitude of 14. Uranus at magnitude 5.7 is only marginally visible.

Earth is the densest planet with an average figure of 5.515 times that of water, while Saturn has an average density only about one-eighth of this value or 0.705 times that of water.

The planet with the longest "day" or period of rotation is Venus, which spins on its axis once every 243.16 days, so its "day" is longer than its "year" (224.7007 days). The shortest "day" is that of Jupiter (see *Largest Planet*).

The most dramatic recorded conjunction (coming together) of the seven principal members of the solar system besides the earth (sun, moon, Mercury, Venus, Mars, Jupiter and Saturn) occurred on Feb 5, 1962, when 16° covered all seven during an eclipse. It is possible that the seven-fold conjunction of Sept 1186 spanned only 12°. The next notable conjunction will take place May 5, 2000.

Largest Asteroids

In the belt which lies between Mars and Jupiter, there are some 45,000 (only 2,200 numbered as of Jan 1980) minor planets or asteroids which are, for the most part, too small to yield to diameter measurement. The largest and first discovered (by Piazzi at Palermo, Sicily, Jan 1, 1801) of these is *Ceres,* with a diameter of 634 miles. The only one visible to the naked eye is *Vesta* (diameter 341 miles), discovered March 29, 1807 by Dr Heinrich Wilhelm Olbers, a German amateur astronomer. The closest measured approach to the earth by an asteroid was 485,000 miles, in the case of *Hermes* on Oct 30, 1937.

The most distant detected is Object Kowal found between Saturn and Uranus Oct 18–19, 1977, by Charles Kowal from the Hale Observatory, Calif, and tentatively named *Chiron.*

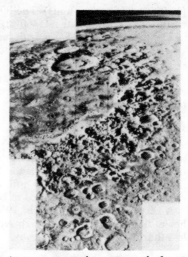

FASTEST PLANET (left): Mercury orbits the sun every 88 days at a speed of more than 100,000 mph. SURFACE OF MARS (right): Sightings by Mariner IX proved the existence of many craters but no canals.

Most Satellites

Of the nine major planets, all but Venus and Mercury have known natural satellites. The planet with the most is Jupiter, with four large and ten small moons. The earth and Pluto are the only planets with a single satellite. The distance of the solar system's known satellites from their parent planets varies from the 5,827 miles of *Phobos* from the center of Mars to the 14,730,000 miles of Jupiter's outer satellite *Sinope* (Jupiter IX). The solar system has, excluding the moonlets which are in Saturn's "E" ring, but including Pluto's probable moon *Charon* (announced in July 1978), a total of 34 satellites.

Largest and Smallest Satellites

The largest satellite is *Titan* (Saturn VI) with a diameter of not less than 3,400 miles and a possible atmospheric thickness of 90 miles. The heaviest satellite known is *Ganymede* (Jupiter III) which is 2.02 times heavier than our moon.

The smallest satellite is *Leda* (Jupiter XIII) with a diameter of less than 9 miles.

STARS

Largest and Most Massive Stars

The fainter component of Plaskett's Star, discovered by J. S. Plaskett from the Dominion Astrophysical Observatory, Victoria, British Columbia, Canada, in 1922, is the most massive star known, with a mass *c.* 55 times that of the sun. Betelgeux (at top left in the constellation Orion) has a diameter of more than 250 million miles, and in 1978 was found to be surrounded by a tenuous "shell" of potassium of 1.6 million million miles

(11,000 astronomical units). The light from Betelgeux which reaches the earth today left the star in 1460 AD.

The diameter of IRS 5 is believed to be 9,500 million miles.

Smallest Stars

The least massive stars known are the two components of the binary star *Wolf 424,* a faint star in the constellation Virgo. Each of the two stars has only 0.06 solar masses.

Farthest Star

The solar system, with its sun, nine principal planets, 33 satellites, asteroids and comets, was estimated in 1921 to be about 32,000 light-years from the center of the lens-shaped Milky Way galaxy (diameter 100,000 light-years) of about 100,000 million stars. The most distant star in our galaxy was therefore estimated to be about 80,000 light-years distant.

A recalibration published in 1980 however indicates that our galaxy has a diameter of *c.* 70,000 light-years only, with the most distant stars less than 60,000 light-years away.

Nearest Stars

Excepting the special case of our own sun, the nearest star is the very faint *Proxima Centauri,* which is 4.22 light-years (24,800,000 million miles) away. The nearest star visible to the naked eye is the southern hemisphere star *Alpha Centauri,* or *Rigel Kentaurus* (4.35 light-years), with a magnitude of −0.29. By 11,800 AD, the nearest star will be Barnard's Star (see *Stellar Planets*) at a distance of 3.75 light-years.

Brightest Star

Sirius A (*Alpha Canis Majoris*), also known as the Dog Star, is apparently the brightest star of the 5,776 stars visible in the heavens, with an apparent magnitude of −1.46. It is in the constellation *Canis Major* and is visible in the winter months of the northern hemisphere, being due south at midnight on the last day of the year. The Sirius system is 8.64 light-years distant and has a luminosity 26 times as much as that of the sun. It has a diameter of 1,450,000 miles and a mass of 4,704,000,000,-000,000,000,000,000,000 tons. The faint white dwarf companion star Sirius B has a diameter of only 6,000 miles but is 350,000 times heavier than the earth.

Most and Least Luminous Stars

If all stars could be viewed at the same distance, the most luminous would be the apparently faint variable *S. Doradûs,* in the Greater Magellanic Cloud (*Nebecula Major*), which can be nearly one million times brighter than the sun, and has an absolute magnitude of −8.9. The variable η *Carinae* in *c.* 1840 was perhaps 4 million times more luminous than the sun. The faintest star detected visually is a very red star, known as LP 425–140, which is 23.5 light-years distant, with about one-millionth of the sun's brightness.

Longest Name for a Star

The longest name for any star is *Shurnarkabtishashutu,* which is Arabic for "under the southern horn of the bull."

THIS TELESCOPE, which measures stellar distances at the Royal Greenwich Laboratory in England, uses the parallax measurement procedure.

Constellations

The largest of the 89 constellations is *Hydra* (the Sea Serpent) which covers 1,302.844 sq degrees or 6.3% of the hemisphere and contains at least 68 stars visible to the naked eye (to 5.5 mag.). The constellation *Centaurus* (Centaur), ranking ninth in area, embraces, however, at least 94 such stars. The smallest constellation is *Crux Australis* (Southern Cross) with an area of 68.477 sq degrees compared with the 41,252.96 sq degrees of the whole sky.

Brightest Super-Nova

Super-novae, or temporary "stars" which flare and then fade, occur perhaps five times in 1,000 years in our galaxy. The brightest "star" ever seen by historic man is believed to be the super-nova SN 1006 in Apr 1006 near *Lupus β* which flared for 2 years and attained a magnitude of −9 to −10. It is now believed to be the radio source G.327.6 + 14.5, nearly 3,000 light-years distant.

Stellar Planets

Planetary companions, with a mass of less than 7% of their parent star, have been reported for 61 *Cygni* (1942), *Lalande 21185* (1960), *Krüger 60, Ci 2354, BD + 20° 2465* and one of the two components of 70 *Ophiuchi*.

A planet with 6 times the mass of Jupiter, 750 million miles from *Epsilon Eridani* (see below), was reported by Peter van de Kamp in Jan 1973.

In Aug 1975, van de Kamp reported that Barnard's Star (Munich 15040) possibly had two planets equivalent in mass to Jupiter and Saturn.

Listening operations ("Project Ozma") on *Tau Ceti* and *Epsilon Eridani* were maintained from Apr 4, 1960 to March 1961, using an 85-ft radio telescope at Deer Creek Valley, Green Bank, W Va. The apparatus was probably insufficiently sensitive for any signal from a distance of 10.7 light-years to be received. Monitoring has been conducted from Gorkiy, USSR, since 1969.

Black Holes

The first tentative identification of a Black Hole was announced in Dec 1972 in the binary-star X-ray source Cygnus X-1. This is a small, dark companion of some 10 solar masses, from which the escape velocity tends to c (the velocity of light). The critical size has been estimated to be as low as a diameter of 3.67 miles. In early 1978 supermassive Black Holes were suggested with a mass of 100 million suns—2×10^{35} metric tons.

THE UNIVERSE

Outside the Milky Way galaxy, which possibly moves around the center of the local super-cluster of 2,500 neighboring galaxies at a speed of 1,350,000 mph, there exist 10,000 million other galaxies. These range in size up to the largest known object in the universe, the radio galaxy 3C–345, announced from Effelsberg, near Bonn, West Germany in March 1980, which is 78 million light-years across. It is estimated to be 5,000 million light-years distant.

Farthest Visible Object

The remotest heavenly body visible to the naked eye is the Great Galaxy in *Andromeda* (Mag. 3.47) known as Messier 31. This is a rotating nebula of spiral form, its distance from the earth about 2,200,000 light-years, or about 13,000,000,000,000,000,000 miles, and it is moving toward us.

It is just possible, however, that, under ideal seeing conditions, Messier 33, the Spiral in Triangulum (Mag. 5.79), can be glimpsed by the naked eye of keen-sighted people at a distance of 2,300,000 light-years.

"Quasars"

In Nov 1962 the existence of quasi-stellar radio sources ("quasars" or QSO's) was established. No satisfactory model has yet been constructed to account for the immensely high luminosity of bodies apparently so distant and of such small diameter. In Apr 1975 it was announced that 3C–279 had a measured luminosity of 2.75×10^{14} times that of the sun.

"Pulsars"

The earliest observation of a pulsating radio source of "pulsar" CP 1919 by Dr Jocelyn Bell Burnell was announced from the Mullard Radio Astronomy Observatory, Cambridgeshire, England, on Feb 29, 1968. The 100th was announced from Jodrell Bank, England in June 1973. The fastest so far discovered is NP 0532 in the Crab Nebula with a pulse period of 33 milliseconds. It is now accepted that pulsars are rotating neutron stars with an inner core density of 74,400 million metric tons per cu in.

Remotest Object

The interpretation of very large red-shifts exhibited by quasars is controversial. The record value of $Z = 3.53$ for Quasar OQ172 has been interpreted in Aug 1978 as between 13,500 and 15,500 million light-years. On some assessments published in 1979 and 1980 such a recession speed

ROCKETRY: (Left above) The earliest flight into space was the Soviet's Vostok I. (Center) The most powerful rocket today is the Saturn V, which stands 363 ft tall. Note the man in the circle. Today's rockets are a far cry from Dr Goddard's 1926 invention (right) which used liquid fuel and climbed 41 ft.

would be consistent with distances of no more than 10,000 light-years. The 3° background radiation or primordial hiss discovered in 1965 by Arno Penzias and Robert Wilson of Bell Laboratories appears to be moving at a velocity of 99.9998% of the speed of light.

Age of the Universe

Estimates of the age of the universe are dependent upon the value ascribed to Hubble's ratio. Values ranging between 40 and 110 km/s/Mpc yield estimates between 8,000 and 25,000 million years. The most comprehensive survey, published in Aug 1978, gave a value of 14½ ± 1 eon (an eon being 1,000 million years) consistent with a value of 60 km/s/Mpc and is known as the Schramm model.

ROCKETRY AND MISSILES

War rockets, propelled by a charcoal-saltpeter-sulphur gunpowder, were described by Tsen Kung Liang of China in 1042. These early rockets became known in Europe by 1258.

The first launching of a liquid-fueled rocket (patented July 14, 1914) was by Dr Robert Hutchings Goddard (1882–1945) (US) at Auburn, Mass March 16, 1926, when his rocket reached an altitude of 41 ft and traveled a distance of 184 ft. The USSR's earliest rocket was the semi-liquid-fueled GIRD-IX tested Aug 17, 1933.

Longest Ranges

On March 16, 1962 Nikita Khrushchev, then Prime Minister of the USSR, claimed in Moscow that the USSR possessed a "global rocket" with a range of 19,000 miles (more than half the earth's circumference), capable of hitting any target in the world from either direction.

Most Powerful Rocket

It has been suggested that the USSR lunar booster which blew up at Tyura Tam in the summer (July ?) of 1969 had a thrust of 10–14 million lb. There is some evidence of a launch of a USSR "G" class lunar booster, larger than *Saturn V*, May 11, 1973.

The most powerful rocket that has been publicized is the *Saturn V*, used for the Project Apollo and Skylab programs, on which development began in Jan 1962 at the John F. Kennedy Space Center, Merritt Island, Fla. The rocket is 363 ft 8 in tall, with a payload of over 82 tons in the case of *Skylab 1*, and gulps 15 tons of propellant per sec for 2½ min. Stage I (S-IC) is 138 ft tall and powered by five Rocketdyne F-1 engines, using liquid oxygen (LOX) and kerosene, each delivering 1,514,000 lb thrust. Stage II (S-II) is powered by 5 LOX and liquid hydrogen Rocketdyne J-2 engines with a total thrust of 1,141,453 lb, while Stage III (designated S-IVB) is powered by a single 228,290-lb-thrust J-2 engine. The whole assembly generates 175,600,000 hp and weighs up to 7,600,000 lb when fully loaded, as in the case of *Apollo XVII*. *Saturn V* was first launched Nov 9, 1967 from Cape Canaveral (then Kennedy), Fla.

Highest Velocity Space Vehicles

The first space vehicle to achieve the Third Cosmic velocity sufficient to break out of the solar system was *Pioneer 10*. The Atlas SLV-3C launcher with a modified Centaur D second stage and a Thiokol Te-364-4 third stage left the earth at an unprecedented 32,114 mph March 2, 1972. The highest recorded velocity of any space vehicle has been 149,125 mph by the US-German solar probe *Helios B* launched Jan 15, 1976. By May 10, 1979 *Pioneer 10* was 1,800 million miles distant.

Highest Payload

Skylab I launched May 14, 1973 fell on its 34,981st orbit of the earth over the Western Australian coast on July 11, 1979, thus leaving *Salyut 6* as the heaviest object in space. Large pieces of *Skylab I* were found 7.45 miles south of Rawlinna and sold to a Hong Kong syndicate.

Ion Rockets

Speeds of up to 100,000 mph are envisaged for rockets powered by an ion discharge. An ion thruster has been maintained for 9,715 hours (404 days 19 hours) at the Lewis Research Center in Cleveland, Ohio. Ion rockets were first used in flight by NASA's SERT I rocket, July 20, 1964.

Space Flight

See Chapter 11 for human achievements in space.

The dynamics of artificial satellites were first propounded by Sir Isaac Newton (1642–1727) in his *Philosophiae Naturalis Principia Mathematica* ("Mathematical Principles of Natural Philosophy"), begun in March 1686 and first published in the summer of 1687.

The first artificial satellite was successfully put into orbit at an altitude of 142/588 miles and a velocity of more than 17,750 mph from Tyura Tam, a site located 170 miles east of the Aral Sea, on the night of Oct 4, 1957. This spherical satellite, *Sputnik* ("Fellow Traveler") *1*, officially designated "Satellite 1957 Alpha 2," weighed 184.3 lb, with a diameter of 22.8 in, and its lifetime is believed to have been 92 days, ending on Jan 4, 1958. It was designed under the direction of Dr Sergey Pavlovich Korolyov (1907–66).

By Jan 1978 it was estimated that there were 4,470 discrete pieces of hardware in earth orbit. By Oct 1977 it was estimated that 40% of all launches were from Plesetsk, USSR.

Largest Space Object

The heaviest object orbited is the *Apollo 15* (spacecraft plus third stage) which, prior to translunar injection in parking orbit, weighed 155.9 tons. The 442-lb US R.A.E. (radio astronomy explorer) B, or Explorer 49, launched on June 10, 1973, has antennae 1,500 ft from tip to tip.

Earliest Successful Manned Satellites

The first successful manned space flight began at 9:07 a.m. (Moscow time), or 6:07 a.m. G.M.T., Apr 12, 1961. Flight Major (later Colonel) Yuriy Alekseyevich Gagarin (b March 9, 1934) completed a single orbit of the earth in 89.34 min in the USSR's space vehicle *Vostok* ("East") *I* (10,416 lb). The take-off was from Tyura Tam in Kazakhstan, and the landing was 108 min later near the village of Smelovka, near Engels, in the Saratov region of the USSR. The maximum speed was 17,560 mph and the maximum altitude 203.2 miles in a flight of 25,394.5 miles. Major Gagarin, invested a Hero of the Soviet Union and awarded the Order of Lenin and the Gold Star Medal, was killed in a jet plane crash near Moscow on March 27, 1968.

First Fatality in Space Flight

Col. Vladimir Mikhailovich Komarov (b March 16, 1927) was launched in *Soyuz* ("Union") *I* at 00:35 a.m. G.M.T. Apr 23, 1967. The spacecraft was in orbit for about 25½ hours before crashing on the final descent due to parachute failure. Komarov was thus the first man indisputably known to have died during space flight.

First Extra-Terrestrial Vehicles

The first wheeled vehicle landed on the moon was the Soviet *Lunokhod I* which began its earth-controlled travels on Nov 17, 1970. It moved a total of 6.54 miles on gradients up to 30° in the Mare Imbrium and did not become non-functioning until Oct 4, 1971.

The lunar speed and distance record was set by the *Apollo XVI* Rover with 11.2 mph and 22.4 miles.

Most Expensive Project

The total cost of the US manned space program up to and including the lunar mission of *Apollo XVII* has been estimated at $25,541,400,000. The cost of the USSR space program from 1958 to Sept 1973 has been estimated to have cost $45,000 million.

Closest Approach to the Sun

The research spacecraft *Helios B* approached within 27 million miles of the sun on Apr 16, 1976. It was carrying both US and West German instrumentation.

Chapter 5

The Scientific World

ELEMENTS

For table of the 107 elements, chemical compounds and atomic tables, see the *Guinness Book of Essential Facts* (Sterling, 1979).

All known matter in the solar system is made up of chemical elements. The total of naturally occurring elements so far detected is 94, comprising, at ordinary temperature, 2 liquids, 11 gases and 81 solids. The so-called "fourth state" of matter is plasma, when negatively charged electrons and positively charged ions are in flux.

Lightest and Heaviest Sub-Nuclear Particles

By Jan 1979 the existence of 23 "stable particles, 37 meson resonance triplets and 56 baryon resonance multiplets" was accepted, representing the possible eventual discovery of 221 particles and an equal number of anti-particles. Of SU(3) particles, the one with the highest mass is the omega minus, announced Feb 24, 1964 from the Brookhaven National Laboratory, near Upton, Long Island, NY. It has a mass state of 1672.2 MeV. Sub-atomic concepts require that the masses of the graviton, photon, and neutrino should all be zero. Based on the sensitivities of various cosmological theories, upper limits for the masses of these particles are 7.6×10^{-67}g. for the graviton; 3.0×10^{-53}g. for the photon and 1.4×10^{-32}g. for the neutrino (*cf.* 9.10953×10^{-28}g. for the mass of an electron).

Most and Least Stable Particles

The proton was measured in 1974 to be stable against decay for a lifetime in excess of 2×10^{30} years.

The least stable or shortest-lived nuclear particles discovered are the rho prime meson (definite proof of existence announced on Jan 29, 1973), and the four baryon resonances N (2650), N (3030), Δ (2850), and Δ (3230), all lasting 1.6×10^{-24} second.

Finest Powder

Particulate matter of 25 to 40 Å was reportedly produced by an electron beam evaporation process at the Atomic Energy Establishment, Harwell, England, in Oct 1972. The paper was published by Dr P. RamaKrishnan.

Most Absorbent Substance

The US Dept of Agriculture Research Service announced on Aug 18, 1974 that "H-span" or Super Slurper, composed of one half starch derivative and one fourth each of acrylamide and acrylic acid, can, when treated with iron, retain water 1,300 times its own weight.

Smelliest Substance

The most evil-smelling substance, of the 17,000 smells so far classified, must be a matter of opinion, but ethyl mercaptan (C_2H_5SH) and butyl seleno-mercaptan (C_4H_9SeH) are powerful claimants, each with a smell reminiscent of a combination of rotting cabbage, garlic, onions and sewer gas.

Most Expensive Perfume

The retail prices of the most expensive perfumes tend to be fixed at public relations rather than economic levels. The most expensive ingredient in perfume is pure French middle note jasmine essence at £2,900 ($6,960) per kilogram or £82.20 ($197) per oz. The most expensive perfume in the world is *De Berens No. 1* retailing at $150 per ⅓ oz.

Most Potent Poison

The rickettsial disease, Q-fever, can be instituted by a *single* organism but is only fatal in 1 in 1,000 cases. About 10 organisms of *Francisella tularenesis* (formerly known as *Pasteurella tularenesis*) can institute tularemia, variously called alkali disease, Francis disease or deerfly fever, and this is fatal in upwards of 10 cases in 1,000.

Most Powerful Nerve Gas

In the early 1950's, substances known as V-agents, notably VX, 300 times more toxic than phosgene ($COCl_2$) used in World War I, were developed at the Chemical Defence Experimental Establishment, Porton Down, Wiltshire, England, which are lethal at 1 milligram per man. Patents were applied for in 1962 and published in Feb 1974.

Most Powerful Drugs

The most powerful commonly available drug is d-Lysergic Acid Diethylamide tartrate (LSD-25, $C_{20}H_{25}N_3O$) first produced in 1938 for

SWEETEST SUBSTANCE: Seeds from Katemfe, the plants that exude a taste 5,600 times as sweet as sugar.

common cold research and as a hallucinogen by Dr Albert Hoffmann (Swiss) Apr 16–19, 1943.

The most potent analgesic drug is Etorphine or M-99, announced in June 1963 by Dr K. W. Bentley (b 1923) and D. G. Hardy of Reckitt & Sons Ltd in Hull, England. The drug has almost 10,000 times the potency of morphine.

Most Prescribed Drug

The benzodiazepine group tranquilizing drug Valium, discovered by Hoffmann—La Roche, is the world's most widely used drug. In 1979 more than 40 million prescriptions were filled in the US alone.

LIQUOR: A commercial grain alcohol (left) of 190 proof. (Above) A claret that sold for $28,000 at a rare wine auction in 1979.

DRINK

Most Alcoholic Liquor

The strength of liquor is gauged by degrees proof. In the US, proof spirit is that mixture of ethyl alcohol (C_2H_5OH) and water which contains one half its volume of alcohol of a specific gravity of 0.7939 at 60 °F, referred to water at 60 °F as unity. Pure or absolute alcohol is thus 200 proof. A "hangover" is due to toxic congenerics such as amyl alcohol ($C_5H_{11}OH$).

During independence (1918–40) the Estonian Liquor Monopoly marketed 196 proof potato alcohol. In 31 US states *Everclear* (190 proof or 95% alcohol) is marketed by the American Distilling Co, "primarily as a base for homemade cordials." Royal Navy (UK) rum, introduced in 1692, was 79.8% before 1948, but was reduced to 46.3% alcohol by weight before its abolition on July 31, 1970.

Strongest and Weakest Beer

The strongest and most expensive beer is EKU Kulminator Urtyp Hell from Kulmbach, W Germany, which retails for up to $1.70 for a ½-pint bottle. It is 13.2% alcohol by volume at 20 °C with an original gravity of 1117.6 °.

The weakest liquid ever marketed as beer was a sweet ersatz beer which was brewed in Germany by Sunner, Colne-Kalk, in 1918. It had an original gravity of 1000.96 °, with less than 0.2% alcohol.

Liqueurs

The most expensive liqueur in France is *Eau de vie de poire avec poire,* sold for 150 francs ($33.75) a bottle at Fauchon in Paris.

The most expensive bottle of spirits sold at auction was a magnum of *Grande Armée Fine Champagne Cognac* 1811 at Christie's of London on Nov 13, 1978, for £780 ($1,560). *Cognac Delamain* (1875) retails for 3300 francs ($745) a bottle at Fauchon in Paris.

Oldest Vintage Wine

The oldest datable wine has been an amphora salvaged and drunk by Capt Jacques Cousteau from the wreck of a Greek trader sunk in the Mediterranean *c.* 230 BC. Wine jars recovered from the Pompeii eruption of 79 AD were found labelled VESUVINUM—the oldest known trade mark. A bottle of 1748 Rudesheimer Rosewein was auctioned at Christie's of London, for £200 ($450) Dec 6, 1979.

Most Expensive Wine

The highest price paid for a bottle of wine of any size is $28,000 for a bottle of 1806 Château Lafite claret purchased at Heublein's 11th annual National Auction of Rare Wines on May 24, 1979 by Charles F. Maras. There is allegedly only one other bottle surviving.

Greatest Wine Auction and Tasting

The largest single sale of wine was conducted by Christie's of London, July 10–11, 1974 at Quaglino's Ballroom when 2,325 lots containing 432,000 bottles realized £962,190 (then $2,309,256).

The largest wine tasting ever was held for 1,737 people at Nederburg, South Africa March 4, 1978 with 15 openers, 93 pourers and 2,012 bottles.

Largest and Smallest Bottles

The largest bottles normally used in the wine and spirit trade are the jeroboam (equal to 4 bottles of champagne or, rarely, of brandy, and from 5 to 6½ bottles of claret, depending on whether the bottle was blown or molded) and the double magnum (equal, since *c.* 1934, to 4 bottles of claret or, more rarely, red burgundy). A complete set of champagne bottles would consist of the ¼ bottle, ½ bottle, bottle, magnum, Jeroboam, Rehoboam, Methuselah, Salmanazer, Balthazar and the Nebuchadnezzar, which has a capacity of 16 liters (33.8 pints), and is equivalent to 20 bottles.

In May 1958 a 5-ft-tall sherry bottle with a capacity of 20½ Imperial gallons (24.6 US gallons) was blown in Stoke-on-Trent, Staffordshire, England. This bottle, with the capacity of 131 normal bottles, was named an "Adelaide."

The smallest bottles of liquor ever sold have been the 24-minim bottles of Scotch whisky marketed by the Cumbrae Supply Co. of Scotland. They contained 1/20 of a fluid oz.

Champagne Cork Flight

The longest distance for a champagne cork to fly from an untreated and unheated bottle 4 ft from level ground is 103 ft 8 in by Ronald Rose at Idlewild Park, Reno, Nev on July 4, 1979.

Miniature Bottles

The largest reported collection of unduplicated miniature bottles is one of 6,506 as of May, 1980, by David Maund of Eastleigh, England.

TELESCOPES

Earliest Telescope

Although there is evidence that early Arabian scientists understood something of the magnifying power of lenses, the first use of lenses to form a telescope has been attributed to Roger Bacon (c. 1214–92) in England. The prototype of modern refracting telescopes was completed by Johannes Lippershey for the Netherlands government on Oct 2, 1608.

Largest Reflector

The largest telescope in the world is the 236.2-inch telescope sited on Mt Semirodriki, near Zelenchukskaya in the Caucasus Mts, USSR, at an altitude of 6,830 ft. Work on the mirror, weighing 78 tons, was not completed until the summer of 1974. Regular observations were begun on Feb 7, 1976, after 16 years' work. The weight of the 138-ft-high assembly is 946 tons. Being the most powerful of all telescopes, its range, which includes the location of objects down to the 25th magnitude, represents the limits of the observable universe. Its light-gathering power would enable it to detect the light from a candle at a distance of 15,000 miles.

A design for a 400-in reflector comprising 60 independently controlled fitting hexagonal mirrors was adopted in Nov 1979. If sited on Mauna Kea, Hawaii it would be expected to cost $50 million and be completed by 1989. The design of a 984-in composite hexagonal reflector was announced by the USSR in Aug 1979.

Largest Refractor

The largest refracting (i.e. magnification by lenses) telescope in the world is the 62-ft-long, 40-in telescope completed in 1897 at the Yerkes Observatory, Williams Bay, Wis, belonging to the University of Chicago. In 1900, a 49.2-in refractor 180 ft in length was built for the Paris Exposition, but its optical performance was too poor to justify attempts to use it.

Solar Telescope

The world's largest solar telescope is the 480-ft-long McMath telescope at Kitt Peak National Observatory near Tucson, Ariz. It has a focal length of 300 ft and an 80-in heliostat mirror. It was completed in 1962 and produces an image measuring 33 in in diameter.

OBSERVATORIES AND TELESCOPES: (reading clockwise from top left): OLDEST EXTANT: This observatory is in South Korea, built in 632 AD. HIGHEST: Atop Mt Evans, Colo, this observatory is 14,100 ft high. LARGESTS: The Russian reflector (below) of 236.2 in diameter is in the Caucasus Mts. The McMath solar telescope (left) is in an Indian reservation in Arizona.

Earliest and Highest Observatories

The oldest astronomical observatory building extant is the Chomsong-dae in Kyongju, South Korea, which was built in 632 AD.

The highest-altitude observatory in the world is the University of Denver's High Altitude Observatory at an altitude of 14,100 ft, opened in 1973, on Mt Evans, Colo. The principal instrument is a 24-in Ealing Beck reflecting telescope.

Precious Stone Records

The carat was standardized at 205 mg (.007054) oz. in 1877. The metric carat of 200 mg was introduced in 1914.

Largest
Diamond (pure crystallized carbon) 3,106 metric carats (over 1¼ lb)—*The Cullinan*, found by Capt M. F. Wells, Jan 26, 1905, in the Premier Mine, Pretoria, South Africa

Largest Cut Stone
530.2 metric carats. 74 facets. Cleaved from *The Cullinan* in 1908 in Amsterdam by Jak Asscher and polished by Henri Koe. Known as *The Star of Africa* No. 1 and now in the British Royal Sceptre

Other Records
The rarest color for diamond is blood red. The largest example is a flawless 5.05-carat stone from South Africa now in a private collection in the US. The smallest brilliant cut diamond was one of 57 facets exhibited by Chrest of Paris in 1979. It weighed 0.0015 of a carat and had a diameter of less than 1/50 of an inch. The 137.02-carat Premier Rose diamond was bought by Goldberg-Weiss in Dec 1978, for a reputed $11,500,000. The 353.9-carat rough stone from which it was found in the Premier Mine in Apr 1978, was auctioned by De Beers for $5,170,000 in May to a Mouw-Goldberg-Weiss syndicate. The record price for a diamond ring is "nearly" $3 million for the 69.42-carat ring of Elizabeth Taylor bought in June 1979 by the dealer Henry L. Lambert of NYC and subsequently sold at an undisclosed price exceeding that.

An 18.35-carat ring was sold for $520,000 at Sotheby Parke Bernet, NYC, in Apr 1977. The Swiss customs at Geneva confirmed on Apr 16, 1972 the existence of a hexagonal emerald of about 20,000 carats, thus possibly worth more than $100 million.

Emerald (green beryl) $[Be_3Al_2(SiO_3)_6]$

11,130-carat crystal from Strentensk, Ural Mts, USSR in 1834. Now in the Mineralogical Museum, Moscow.

Note: The sapphire head and bust and are in the custody of the Kazanjian Foundation of Los Angeles. Auction record for a single stone was set by a step-cut sapphire of 66.03 carats at £579,300 (about $1,332,400) from the Rockefeller Collection at Sotheby's Zurich on May 9, 1980.

Sapphire (corundum, any color but red) (Al_2O_3) 2,302-carat stone found at Anakie, Queensland, Australia, in c. 1935, now a 1,318-carat head of President Abraham Lincoln (1809–65)

1,444-carat black star stone carved from a 2,097-carat stone in 1953–55 into a bust of Gen Dwight David Eisenhower (1890–1969)

Ruby (red corundum (Al_2O_3) 3,421-carat broken stone reported found in July 1961 (largest piece 750 carats)

1,184 carat natural gem stone of Burmese origin. The largest star ruby is the 138.72-carat Rosser Reeves stone on display at the Smithsonian in Washington, DC

A world record carat price of $100,639 was set at Christie's sale in Geneva in Nov 1979 for a 4.12-carat cabochon-shaped ruby.

Largest Radio-Telescope

The largest radio-telescope installation is the US National Science Foundation VLA (Very Large Array). It is Y-shaped with each arm 13 miles long with 27 mobile antennae (each 82 ft in diameter) on rails. It is 50 miles west of Socorro in the Plains of San Augustin, NM and the completion date will be in Jan 1981 at an estimated total cost of $78 million.

Largest Dish Telescopes

Radio waves of extraterrestrial origin were first detected by Karl Jansky of Bell Telephone Laboratories, Holmdel, NJ, using a 100-ft-long shortwave rotatable antenna in 1932. The largest trainable dish-type radio-telescope is the 328-ft-diameter, 3,360-ton assembly at the Max Planck Institute for Radio Astronomy of Bonn in the Effelsberger Valley, W Germany; it became operative in May 1971. The cost of the installation, begun in Nov 1967, was DM36,920,000 ($14,760,000).

The world's largest dish-type radio-telescope is the partially-steerable ionospheric assembly built over a natural bowl at Arecibo, Puerto Rico, completed in Nov 1963 at a cost of about $9 million. It has a diameter of 1,000 ft and the dish covers 18½ acres. Its sensitivity was raised by a factor of 1,000 and its range to the edge of the observable universe at some 15,000 million light-years by the fitting of new aluminum plates at a cost of $8,800,000. Rededication was on Nov 16, 1974.

The RATAN-600 radio-telescope being built in the northern Caucasus, USSR, will have mirror dishes on a 1,968.5-ft perimeter.

Planetaria

The ancestor of the planetarium is the rotatable Gottorp Globe, built by Andreas Busch in Denmark between 1654 and 1664 to the orders of Olearius, court mathematician to Duke Frederick III of Holstein. It is 34.6 ft in circumference, weighs 4 tons and is now preserved in Leningrad, USSR. The stars were painted on the inside.

The earliest optical installation was not until 1923 in the Deutsches Museum, Munich, by Zeiss of Jena, Germany.

The world's largest planetarium, with a diameter of 82½ ft, is in Moscow.

RECORD CHUNK OF JADEITE: Karl Ebner stands beside the jade boulder he discovered in 1977 at Watson Lake, British Columbia, Canada. It weighs 63,307 lb.

Records for Other Precious Materials

Largest	Where Found	Notes on Present Location, etc.
Pearl (Molluscan consecretion 14 lb 1 oz 9½ in long × 5½ in in diameter—*Pearl of Lao-tze*)	At Palawan, Philippines, May 7, 1934, in shell of giant clam	The property since 1936 of Wilburn Dowell Cobb, valued at $4,080,000 in July 1971, sold in 1980 by his estate for $200,000 to a Beverly Hills, Calif jeweler
Opal (SiO_2 NH_2O) 220 troy oz (yellow-orange)	Andamooka, South Australia, Jan 1970	The Andamooka specimen (34,215 carats) which was unearthed by a bulldozer, is in two filling pieces, making a block 11 × 10 × 5 in. Owned by the Palgrave Corp since Sept 1969, displayed in Sydney and valued in excess of $1 million
Rock Crystal (Quartz) (SiO_2) Ball: 106¾ lb 12⅞ in in diameter, the *Warner* sphere	Burma (originally a 1,000-lb piece)	US National Museum, Washington, DC
Topaz $Al_2SiO_4(F, OH)_2$ "Brazilian Princess" 21,327 carats, 221 facets (light blue)	Light blue, from Brazil	Exhibited by Smithsonian Institution, Nov 1978. Valued at $1,066,350, or $50 a carat. Cut from a 79-lb crystal. World's largest faceted stone.
Amber (coniferous fossil resin) 33 lb 10 oz	Reputedly from Burma, acquired in 1860	Bought by John Charles Bowing (d 1893) for £300 in Canton China. Natural History Museum, London, since 1940
Turquoise monolith $[CuAl_6(PO_4)_4(OH)_8 \cdot 4H_2O]$ 218 lb	Riverside County, Calif Jan 17, 1975	Found by Chester Jastromb and Kenneth Casper. Original weight was probably c. 250 lb
Nephrite Jade $Ca_2(Mgte)_5(Si_8O_{11})_2(OH)_2$ Boulder of 143 tons (315,315 lb)	Reported in China, Sept 17, 1978	Jadeite can be virtually any color except red or blue
Marble (Metamorphosed $CaCO_3$) 100.8 tons (single slab)	Quarried at Yule, Colo	A piece of over 50 tons was dressed from this slab for the coping stone of the Tomb of the Unknown Soldier in Arlington National Cemetery, Va
Nuggets—Gold (Au) 7,560 oz (472½ lb) (reef gold) *Holtermann Nugget*	Beyers & Holtermann Star of Hope Gold Mining Co, Hill End, NSW, Australia Oct 19, 1872	The purest large nugget was the *Welcome Stranger*, found at Moliagul, Victoria, Australia, which yielded 2,248 troy oz of pure gold from 2,280¼ oz
Silver (Ag) 2,750 lb troy	Sonora, Mexico	Appropriated by the Spanish Government before 1821

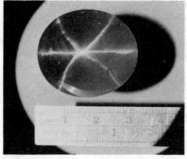

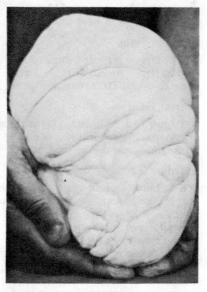

RUBY (above): The Rosser Reeves
Ruby, the largest star ruby ever
discovered, weighs 138.72 carats and
is on exhibit at the Smithsonian
Institution, Wash, DC. PEARL
(right): This baroque giant, weighing
14 lb 1 oz, was valued at more than
$4 million but sold in 1980 for
$200,000. DIAMONDS (below):
The Hope, the largest blue diamond
at 44.4 carats, also in the
Smithsonian, carries a legendary
curse, while the British Royal Sceptre features the Star of Africa No 1 with
74 facets, cut from the famous Cullinan diamond.

GEMS
Most Precious Gems

From 1955, the value of rubies rose, due to a drying up of supplies
from Ceylon and Burma. A flawless natural ruby of good color was carat
for carat more valuable than emerald, diamond or sapphire and, in the
case of a 6-carat ruby, now brings $60,000. The ability to produce very

large corundum prisms of 12 in or over in length in the laboratory for use in lasers seems to have little bearing on the market for natural gems.

Largest Gems

The largest recorded stone of gem quality was a 520,000-carat (229-lb) aquamarine ($Al_2Be_3[Si_6O_{18}]$) found near Marambaia, Brazil in 1910. It yielded over 200,000 carats of gem quality cut stones.

Rarest Gems

Painite ($Ca_4Al_{20}BSiO_{36}$) is the rarest. It was discovered by A.C.D. Pain in Moyok, Burma, in 1951, and a red crystal of 1.7 grams is in the British Museum, Natural History, London.

Hardest Gems

The hardest of all gems, and hardest known naturally occurring substance, is diamond, which is, chemically, pure carbon. Diamond is 90 times as hard as the next hardest mineral corundum (Al_2O_3), and those from Borneo, in Indonesia, and New South Wales, Australia, have a particular reputation for hardness. Hardnesses are compared on Mohs' scale, on which talc is 1, a fingernail is 2½, window glass 5, topaz 8, corundum 9, and diamond 10. Diamonds average 7,000 on the Knoop scale, with a peak value of 8,400. This index represents a micro-indentation index based on kilograms per one hundredth of a square millimeter ($kg/(mm^2)^{-2}$).

Densest Gem Mineral

The densest of all gem minerals is stibiotantalite [$(SbO)_2 (Ta,Nb)_2O_6$], a rare brownish-yellow mineral found in San Diego County, Calif with a density of 7.46 grams per cc. The alloy platiniridium has a density of more than 22.0.

PHOTOGRAPHY

Earliest Cameras

The earliest photograph was taken in the summer of 1826 by Joseph Nicéphore Niepce (1765–1833), a French physician and scientist. It showed the courtyard of his country house at Gras, near St Loup-de-Varennes. It probably took 8 hours to expose and was taken on a bitumen-coated polished pewter plate measuring 7¾ in by 6½ in.

One of the earliest photographs taken was one of a diamond-paned window in Lacock Abbey, Wiltshire, England, taken in Aug 1835 by William Henry Fox Talbot (1800–1877), the inventor of the negative-positive process.

Largest and Smallest Cameras

The largest camera ever built is the 30¼-ton Rolls-Royce camera built for Product Support (Graphics) Ltd of Derby, England, completed in 1959. It measures 8 ft 10 in high, 8 ft 3 in wide and 35 ft long. The lens is a 63″ f/15 Cooke Apochromatic. Its value after improvements in 1971 was in excess of $240,000.

Apart from cameras built for intra-cardiac surgery and espionage, the smallest camera that has been marketed is the circular Japanese "Petal" camera with a diameter of 1.14 in and a thickness of 0.65 in. It has a focal length of 0.47 in. The BBC-TV program *Record Breakers* showed prints from this camera Dec 3, 1974.

Most Expensive Camera

The most expensive complete range of camera equipment is that of Nikon of Tokyo, Japan who marketed a range of 20 cameras with 63 lenses and 336 accessories in 1980. The total cost of the range would exceed $147,000.

The highest auction price for an antique camera was £21,000 ($42,000) for a J. B. Dancer stereo camera patented in 1856 and sold at Christie's, London, on Oct. 12, 1977.

Fastest Camera

In 1972, Prof Basor of the USSR Academy of Sciences published a paper describing an experimental camera with a time resolution of 5×10^{-13} of a second or ½ a picosecond. The fastest production camera in the world is the Imacon 600 manufactured by John Hadland (P.I.) Ltd of Bovingdon, England, which is capable of 600 million pictures per sec. Uses include laser, ballistic, detonic, plasma and corona research.

First Aerial Photography

The earliest aerial photograph was taken in 1858 by Gaspard Félix Tournachon (1820–1910), *alias* Nadar, from a balloon near Villacoublay, on the outskirts of Paris, France.

MOST EXPENSIVE CAMERA EQUIPMENT: The 1980 Nikon system now includes 20 camera models, 63 lenses and 336 accessories.

FASTEST
CAMERA (above)
is the Imacon,
which can take 600
million pictures in
one second.
LARGEST
CAMERA (right):
Almost 9 ft high,
the 30¼-ton Rolls
Royce is 35 ft long.

NUMERATION

In dealing with large numbers, scientists use the notation of 10 raised to various powers, to eliminate a profusion of zeros. For example, 19,160,000,000,000 miles would be written 1.916×10^{13} miles. Similarly, a very small number, for example, 0.0000154324 of a gram, would be written 1.54324×10^{-5} gram (g.). Of the prefixes used before numbers the smallest is "atto-," from the Danish *atten* for 18, indicating a million million millionth part (10^{18}) of the unit, and the highest is "exa-" (Greek, *hexa*=six), symbol E, indicating 10^{18} or six groups of 3 zeros meaning a quintillion fold.

Prime Numbers

A prime number is any positive integer (excluding 1) having no integral factors other than itself and unity, *e.g.* 2, 3, 5, 7, or 11. The lowest prime number is 2. The highest known prime number is $2^{44497}-1$ (a number of 13,395 digits), announced on May 30, 1979, after a 2-month-long run on a Cray One Computer at the Univeristy of Calif's Lawrence Livermore Laboratory by Harry Nelson, 47, and David Slowinski, 25.

Perfect Numbers

A number is said to be perfect if it is equal to the sum of its divisors other than itself, *e.g.* 1+2+4+7+14=28. The lowest perfect number is 6 (1+2+3). The highest known, and the 25th so far discovered, is $(2^{21701}-1) \times 2^{21700}$. It is a consequence of the highest known prime (see above).

Highest Numbers

The highest lexicographically accepted named number in the system of successive powers of ten is the centillion, which is 10 raised to the power 600 or 10^{303} in the US system. The highest named number outside the decimal notation is the Buddhist *asankhyeya,* which is equal to 10^{140} or 100 quinto-quadragintillions.

The number 10^{100} (10 duotrigintillion) is designated a Googol, a term devised by Dr Edward Kasner of the US (d 1955). Ten raised to the power of a Googol is described as a Googolplex. Some conception of the magnitude of such numbers can be gained when it is said that the number of atoms in some models of the observable universe probably does not exceed 10^{85}.

The highest number ever used in a mathematical proof is a bounding value published in 1977 and known as Graham's number. It concerns bichromatic hypercubes and is inexpressible without the special "arrow" notation, devised by Knuth in 1976, extended to 64 layers.

Earliest Measures

The earliest known measure of weight is the *beqa* of the Amratian period of Egyptian civilization *c.* 3800 BC found at Naqada, Egypt. The weights are cylindrical with rounded ends from 188.7 to 211.2 grams (6.65–7.45 oz). The unit of length used by the megalithic tomb-builders in Britain *c.* 2200 BC appears to have been 2.72 ± 0.003 ft. This was deduced by Prof Alexander Thom.

Smallest Linear Unit

The shortest unit of length is the atto-meter, which is 1.0×10^{-16} of a centimeter.

Most Accurate and Inaccurate Versions of "Pi"

The greatest number of decimal places to which *pi* (π) has been calculated is 1 million by the French mathematicians Jean Guilloud and Mlle Martine Bouyer, achieved May 24, 1973 on a CDC 7600 computer, but not verified until Sept 3, 1973. The published value to a million places was 3.141592653589793 ... (omitting the next 999,975 places) ... 5779458151. The publication of this has been described as the world's most boring 400-page book.

In 1897, the General Assembly of Indiana enacted in House Bill No. 246 that *pi* was *de jure* 4, for the most inaccurate version.

Longest Roman Numeral

The date requiring the most Roman tellers is 1888, with 13, namely MDCCCLXXXVIII. It was used on the entrance to the High Court of New South Wales (Australia) completed in that year, so drawing the comment that the building would become equally famous for the length of its sentences.

Longest Slide Rule

The longest slide rule is one 323 ft 9.5 ins in length completed on Nov 11, 1979 by Greg Maggs and Robert Kolstad at the University of Illinois College of Law Building in Champaign, Ill.

Longest and Shortest Time Measure

The longest measure of time is the *kalpa* in Hindu chronology. It is equivalent to 4,320 million years. In astronomy a cosmic year is the period of rotation of the sun around the center of the Milky Way galaxy, *i.e.* about 225,000,000 years. In the Late Cretaceous Period of *c.* 85 million years ago, the earth rotated faster so resulting in 370.3 days per year, while in Cambrian times, some 600 million years ago, there is evidence that the year contained 425 days.

Owing to variations in the length of a day, which is estimated to be increasing irregularly at the average rate of about 2 milliseconds per century, due to the moon's tidal drag, the second has been redefined. Instead of being 1/86,400th part of a mean solar day, it is now reckoned as 1/31,556,925.9747th part of the solar (or tropical) year at 1900 AD, Jan 0 at 12 hours, Ephemeris time. In 1958 the second of Ephemeris time was computed to be equivalent to 9,192,631,770 ± 20 cycles of the radiation corresponding to the transition of a cesium 133 atom when unperturbed by exterior fields. The greatest diurnal change recorded has been 10 milliseconds on Aug 8, 1972, due to the most violent solar storm recorded in 370 years of observation. The shortest blip of light is one of 0.2 of a picosecond (0.2×10^{-12} of a sec) produced by the Center of Laser Studies, University of Southern Calif, in Aug 1978. Light travels 0.0023 in in that period of time.

PHYSICAL EXTREMES (TERRESTRIAL)

Highest Temperatures

The highest man-made temperatures yet attained are those produced in the center of a thermonuclear fusion bomb, which are of the order of 300 million-400 million °C. Of controllable temperatures, the highest effective laboratory figure reported is 67 million °C at the University of Rochester's Laser Energetics Laboratory on May 22, 1979. Prior to 1963, a figure of 3,000 million °C was reportedly achieved in the USSR with Ogra injection-mirror equipment.

Lowest Temperatures

The lowest temperature reached is 5×10^8 Kelvins above absolute zero attained in a 2-stage nuclear demagnetization cryostat at the Helsinki University of Technology, Otaniema, Finland by the team of Prof Olli V. Lounasmaa (b 1920) and announced in March 1979. Absolute or thermodynamic temperatures are defined in terms of ratios rather than as differences reckoned from the unattainable absolute zero, which on the Kelvin scale is −273.15 °C or −459.67 °F.

The lowest equilibrium temperature ever attained is 0.0003 °K by nuclear refrigeration in a 3-lb copper specimen by Prof Lounasmaa and his team at the Helsinki University of Technology (see above), Apr 17, 1974.

Highest Pressures

The highest sustained laboratory pressures yet reported are of 1.7 megabars (12,300 tons force per sq in) achieved in the giant hydraulic diamond-faced press at the Carnegie Institution's Geophysical Laboratory in Washington, DC, reported in June 1978. This laboratory announced solid hydrogen achieved at 57 kilobars pressure on March 2, 1979. If created, metallic hydrogen is expected to be silvery white but soft, with a density of 1.1 g/cc. The pressure required for this transition is estimated by H. K. Mao and P. M. Bell to be 1 megabar at 25 °C. Using dynamic methods and impact speeds of up to 18,000 mph, momentary pressures of 75 million atmospheres (548,000 tons per sq in) were reported from the US in 1958.

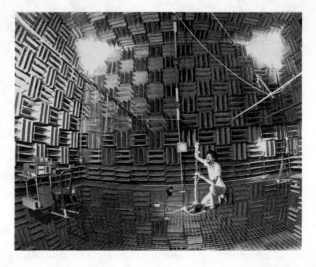

SILENCE! This room in the Bell Telephone Lab absorbs sounds so completely you can't even hear a pin drop.

Highest Vacuum

The highest or "hardest" vacuums obtained in scientific research are of the order of 10^{-14} torr, achieved at the IBM Thomas J. Watson Research Center, Yorktown Heights, NY in Oct 1976 in a cryogenic system with temperatures down to $-269\,°C$ ($-452\,°F$). This is equivalent to depopulating baseball-sized molecules from 1 yard apart to 50 miles apart.

Fastest Centrifuge

The highest man-made rotary speed ever achieved and the fastest speed of any earth-bound object is 4,500 mph by a swirling tapered 6-in carbon fiber rod in a vacuum at Birmingham University, England, reported Jan 24, 1975.

Loudest Noise

The loudest noise created in a laboratory is 210 decibels or 400,000 acoustic watts reported by NASA in Oct 1965. The noise came from a 48-ft steel and concrete horn at Huntsville, Ala. Holes can be bored in solid material by this means.

Quietest Place

The "dead room," measuring 35 ft by 28 ft, in the Bell Telephone System Laboratory at Murray Hill, NJ is the most anechoic room in the world, eliminating 99.98% of reflected sound.

Highest Note

The highest note yet attained is one of 60,000 megahertz (60 GHz) (60,000 million vibrations per sec), generated by a "laser" beam striking a sapphire crystal at MIT, Cambridge, Mass, in Sept 1964.

Highest Measured Frequency

The US National Bureau of Standards announced in May 1979 that D.

A. Jennings, F. R. Peterson and K. M. Evenson had attained a frequency of 2.6010328×10^{14} Hz (260 terahertz) with a helium-neon laser emission at Boulder, Colo.

Hottest Flame

The hottest flame that can be produced is from carbon subnitride (C_4N_2) which at one atmosphere pressure is calculated to reach 5261 K.

Finest Balance

The most accurate balance is the Sartorius Model 4108, manufactured in Göttingen, W Germany, which can weigh objects of up to 0.5 grams (about .018 oz) to an accuracy of 0.01 μg or 0.00000001 g, which is equivalent to little more than one-sixtieth of the weight of ink on this period dot (.).

Lowest Viscosity

The California Institute of Technology announced on Dec 1, 1957, that there was no measurable viscosity, *i.e.* perfect flow, in liquid helium II, which exists only at temperatures close to absolute zero (-273.15 °C or -459.67 °F).

Lowest Friction

The lowest coefficient of static and dynamic friction of any solid is 0.02, in the case of polytetrafluoroethylene ($[C_2F_4]_n$), called PTFE—equivalent to wet ice on wet ice. It was first manufactured in quantity by E. I. du Pont de Nemours & Co Inc in 1943, and is marketed as Teflon.

In the centrifuge at the University of Virginia a 30-lb rotor magnetically supported has been spun at 1,000 revolutions per sec in a vacuum of 10^{-6} mm of mercury pressure. It loses only one revolution per sec per day, thus spinning for years.

Most Powerful Electric Current

The most powerful electric current generated is that from the Zeus capacitor at the Los Alamos Scientific Laboratory, NM. If fired simultaneously the 4,032 capacitors would produce for a few microseconds twice as much current as that generated elsewhere on earth.

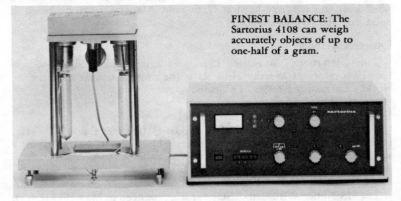

FINEST BALANCE: The Sartorius 4108 can weigh accurately objects of up to one-half of a gram.

Strongest and Weakest Magnetic Fields

The strongest magnetic field strength achieved has been one of 301 kilogauss at the Francis Bitter National Magnet Laboratory at MIT, Cambridge, Mass, announced in July 1977. The outer magnet is of superconducting niobium-titanium.

The weakest magnetic field measured is one of 8×10^{-11} gauss in the heavily shielded room at the same laboratory. It is used for research by Dr David Cohen into the very weak magnetic fields generated in the heart and brain.

Heaviest Magnet

The heaviest magnet is one measuring 196 ft in diameter, with a weight of 40,000 tons, for the 10 GeV synchrophasotron in the Joint Institute for Nuclear Research at Dubna, near Moscow. Intermagnetics General Corporation announced in 1975 plans for a 180 kG vanadium-gallium magnet.

Most Powerful Microscope

The most powerful microscope was announced by Dr Lawrence Bartell and Charles Ritz of the University of Michigan in July 1974 with an image magnification of 260 million fold. It uses an optical laser to decode holograms produced with 40 Kev radiation and has produced photographs of electron clouds of atoms of neon and argon.

Finest Cut

Biological specimens embedded in epoxy resin can be sectioned by a glass knife microtome to a thickness of 1/875,000th in or 2.9×10^{-5} mm under ideal conditions.

Sharpest Objects

The University of California Medical Center, San Francisco, announced in July 1974 the ultimate in sharpness—glass electrodes more than 200 times slimmer than a diamond phonograph stylus. These can be used for exploring the cells in the eye. The points are 0.05 μm.

Most Durable Light

The average bulb lasts for 750 to 1,000 hours. There is some evidence that a carbon filament bulb burning in the Fire Department, Livermore, south Alameda County, Calif has been burning since 1901.

Brightest Light

The brightest steady artificial light sources are "laser" beams, with an intensity exceeding the sun's 1,500,000 candles per sq in by a factor of well in excess of 1,000.

In May 1969 the USSR Academy of Sciences announced blast waves traveling through a luminous plasma of inert gases heated to 90,000 K. The flare-up for up to 3 microseconds shone at 50,000 times the brightness of the sun, viz. 75 billion candles per sq in. Of continuously burning sources, the most powerful is a 200-kilowatt high pressure xenon arc lamp of 600,000 candle-power, reported from the USSR in 1965.

LASER BEAMS travel in straight lines. This model demonstrator in the Bell Telephone Laboratories, where the maser and laser were devised and developed, shows how cohesive light is amplified by reflection.

The synchrotron radiation from a 4 in × ½ in slit in the SPEAR high energy physics plant at the end of the 2-mile-long Stanford Linear Accelerator, Calif has been described as the world's most powerful light beam.

The most powerful search light ever developed was one produced during the 1939–45 war by the General Electric Company Ltd at the Hirst Research Centre in Wembley, Greater London, England. It had a consumption of 600 kw and gave an arc luminance of 300,000 candles per sq in and a maximum beam intensity of 2,700 million candles from its parabolic mirror (diameter 10 ft).

Most Powerful "Laser" Beams

The first illumination of another celestial body was achieved May 9, 1962, when a beam of light was successfully reflected from the moon by the use of an optical "maser" (microwave amplification by stimulated emission of radiation) or "laser" (light amplification by stimulated emission of radiation) attached to a 48-in telescope at MIT, Cambridge, Mass. The spot was estimated to be 4 miles in diameter on the moon. The device was propounded in 1958 by Dr Charles Hard Townes (b US 1915) of Bell Telephone Laboratories. A "maser" light flash is focused into a liquid nitrogen-cooled ruby crystal. Its chromium atoms are excited into a high-energy state in which they emit a red light which is allowed to escape only in the direction desired. Such a flash for 1/5,000th sec can bore a hole through a diamond by vaporization at 10,000 °C., produced by 2×10^{23} photons.

The "Shiva" laser was reported at the Lawrence Livermore Laboratory, Calif to be concentrating 2.6×10^{13} watts into a pinhead-sized target for 9.5×10^{-11} sec in a test on May 18, 1978.

Most Powerful Particle Accelerator

The 1.24-mile diameter proton synchrotron at the Fermi National Accelerator Laboratory at Batavia, Ill, is the highest-energy "atom-smasher" in the world. An energy of 500 billion (5×10^{11}) electron volts was attained by June 1976. Plans to double the energy to nearly 1 Tera electron volts have begun. This involves 1,000 superconducting magnets maintained at a temperature of −452 °F by means of the world's largest 1170-gallon-per-hour helium liquefying plant, which began operating Apr 18, 1980.

The $76,800,000 CERN intersecting storage rings (ISR) project near Geneva, Switzerland, started on Jan 27, 1971, using two 28 GeV proton beams and is designed to yield the equivalent of 1,700 GeV or 1.7 TeV (1.7 million million electron volts) in its center of mass experiments.

Plans for a 12-nation 6.36-mile diameter ring costing $1,000 million, probably in Switzerland, reached design stage in March 1979.

Wind Tunnels

The largest wind tunnel is a low-speed tunnel with a closed test section measuring 40 × 80 ft, built in 1944, at Ames Research Center, Moffett Field, Calif. The tunnel encloses 900 tons of air and cost approximately $7 million. The maximum volume of air that can be moved is 60 million cu ft per min. On July 30, 1974, NASA announced an intention to increase it in size to 80 × 120 ft for 345-mph speeds with a 135,000 hp system.

The most powerful is the 216,000-hp installation at the Arnold Engineering Test Center at Tullahoma, Tenn. The highest Mach number attained with air is Mach 27 at the plant of the Boeing Company, Seattle, Wash. For periods of microseconds, shock Mach numbers of the order of 30 (22,830 mph) have been attained in impulse tubes at Cornell University, Ithaca, NY.

Largest Bubble Chamber

The largest bubble chamber is the $7 million installation completed in Oct 1973, at Weston, Ill. It is 15 ft in diameter and contains 7,259 gallons of liquid hydrogen at a temperature of −247 °C (−412.6 °F) with a superconducting magnet of 30,000 gauss.

LARGEST ATOM SMASHER: The Fermi National Accelerator Laboratory in Batavia, Ill has a 1.24-mile diameter and cost $250 million.

Smallest Hole

Inco Nickel Company was reported to have produced a hole with a diameter of a ten millionth of an inch (0.000004 mm), or one thousand times smaller than the width of a human hair.

A hole of 40 Å was shown visually using a JEM 100C electron microscope and quantel Electronics devices at the Dept of Metallurgy, Oxford, England on Oct 28, 1979. To find such a hole is equivalent to finding a pinhead in a haystack measuring 1.2 miles × 1.2 miles.

LONGEST SLIDE RULE: This gigantic device is 323 ft 9½ in in length—longer than a football field.

Chapter 6

The Arts & Entertainment

1. PAINTING*

Earliest Art

Pieces of ochre with ground facets found at Lake Mungo, NSW, Australia, reported in 1973 to be dated *ante* 30,000 BC *may* have been used as cave art pigments. If confirmed, these would antedate even the earliest cave art found in southern France.

Largest Paintings

Panorama of the Mississippi, completed by John Banvard (1815–91) in 1846, showing the river scene for 1,200 miles in a strip probably 5,000 ft long and 12 ft wide, was the largest painting in the world, with an area of more than 1.3 acres. The painting is believed to have been destroyed when the rolls of canvas, stored in a barn at Cold Spring Harbor, NY, caught fire shortly before Banvard's death May 16, 1891.

The largest painting now in existence is probably *The Battle of Gettysburg,* completed in 1883, after 2½ years of work, by Paul Philippoteaux (France) and 16 assistants. The painting is 410 ft long, 70 ft high and weighs 11,792 lb. It depicts the climax of the Battle of Gettysburg, in south-central Pa, July 3, 1863. In 1964, the painting was bought by Joe King of Winston-Salem, NC, after being stored by E. W. McConnell in a Chicago warehouse since 1933.

The largest "Old Master" is *Il Paradiso,* painted between 1587 and 1590 by Jacopo Robusti, *alias* Tintoretto (1518–94), and his son Domenico on Wall "E" of the Sala del Maggior Consiglio in the Palazzo Ducale (Doge's Palace) in Venice, Italy. The work is 72 ft 2 in long and 22 ft 11½ in high and contains more than 100 human figures.

Largest Poster

A poster 800 ft long and 10 ft high was painted by 480 artists for the British Safety Council at South Bank, London, July 26–29, 1979.

Most Valuable Painting

The "Mona Lisa" (*La Gioconda*) by Leonardo da Vinci (1452–1519) in the Louvre, Paris, was assessed for insurance purposes at the highest fig-

---

* For further details on art, see "Art Facts and Feats" A Guinness Superlatives Book (Sterling)

ure ever at $100 million for its move for exhibition in Washington, DC and NY City from Dec 14, 1962, to March 12, 1963. However, insurance was not concluded because the cost of the closest security precautions was less than that of the premiums. It was painted in *c.* 1503–07 and measures 30.5 × 20.9 in. It is believed to portray Mona (short for Madonna) Lisa Gherardini, the wife of Francesco del Giocondo of Florence. The husband is said to have disliked it and refused to pay for it. Francis I, King of France, in 1517 bought the painting for his bathroom for 4,000 gold florins or 492 oz of gold (in mid-1980 equivalent to $250,000).

Highest Auction Prices

The highest price ever bid in a public auction for any painting was $6,400,000 for J. M. W. Turner's *Juliet and Her Nurse,* painted in Venice in 1836, and sold May 29, 1980 at Sotheby Parke Bernet, NYC, on behalf of 82-year-old owner Flora Whitney Miller who said, "I'm staggered." With the 10% Sotheby buyer's fee, the total amounted to $7,040,000. The 3 ft × 4 ft canvas had been in Mrs Miller's family since 1901 and had not been on public view until 1966.

The highest price ever paid for a painting by a female artist is $150,000 at Parke Bernet NY, March 3, 1971, for *Summertime* by Mary Cassatt (US) (b Pittsburgh 1844–d 1926). She worked mainly in Paris.

HIGHEST PRICED PAINTINGS—PROGRESSIVE RECORDS

Price	Painter, title, sold by and sold to	Date
$32,500	Antonio Correggio's *The Magdalen Reading* (in fact spurious) to Elector Friedrich Augustus II of Saxony.	1746
$42,500	Raphael's *The Sistine Madonna* to Elector Friedrich Augustus II of Saxony.	1759
$80,000	Van Eycks' *Adoration of the Lamb,* 6 outer panels of Ghent altarpiece by Edward Solby to the Government of Prussia.	1821
$123,000*	Murillo's *The Immaculate Conception* by estate of Marshall Soult to the Louvre (against Czar Nicholas I) in Paris.	1852
$350,000	Raphael's *Ansidei Madonna* by the 8th Duke of Marlborough to the National Gallery, London.	1885
$500,000	Raphael's *The Colonna Altarpiece* by Sedelmeyer to J. Pierpont Morgan.	1901
$514,400	Van Dyck's *Elena Grimaldi-Cattaneo* (portrait) by Knoedler to Peter Widener (1834–1915).	1906
$514,400	Rembrandt's *The Mill* by 6th Marquess of Lansdowne to Peter Widener.	1911
$582,500	Raphael's smaller *Panshanger Madonna* by Joseph (later Baron) Duveen (1869–1939) to Peter Widener.	1913
$1,572,000	Leonardo da Vinci's *Benois Madonna* to Czar Nicholas II in Paris.	1914
$2,300,000*	Rembrandt's *Aristotle Contemplating Bust of Homer* by Mr/Mrs Alfred Erickson to Metropolitan Museum of Art.	1961
$5,000,000– $6,000,000	Leonardo da Vinci's *Ginevra de' Benci* by Prince Franz Josef II of Liechtenstein to National Gallery, Washington.	1967
$5,544,000*	Velázquez's *Portrait of Juan de Pareja,* sometimes known as *The Slave of Velázquez* by the Earl of Radnor (UK) to Wildenstein Gallery, NY.	1970
$6,400,000*	Turner's *Juliet and Her Nurse* by Flora Whitney Miller to an anonymous buyer.	1980

* Indicates price at auction, otherwise prices were by private treaty.

Miniature Portrait

The highest price ever paid for a portrait miniature is $172,500 by an anonymous buyer at a sale held by Sotheby's, London, Mar 24, 1980, for

HIGHEST-PRICED PAINTING: Sold at auction for $6,400,000, Turner's "Juliet and Her Nurse" in 1980 beat the record set 10 years before by almost $1 million.

a miniature of Jane Broughton, age 21, painted on vellum by Nicholas Hilliard (1547–1619) in 1574. The painted surface measures 1.65 in in diameter.

Modern Painting

The highest price paid for a modern painting is $2 million paid in 1973 by the National Gallery, Canberra, Australia, for *Blue Poles* painted in 1953 by Jackson Pollock (US) (1912–56).

Living Artist

The highest price paid for paintings in the lifetime of the artist is $1,950,000 paid for the two canvases *Two Brothers* (1905) and *Seated Harlequin* (1922) by Pablo Diego José Francisco de Paula Juan Nepomuceno Crispin Crispiano de la Santisima Trinidad Ruiz y Picasso (1881–1973), born in Spain. This was paid by the Basle City government to the Staechelin Foundation to enable the Basle Museum of Arts to retain the painting after an offer of $2,560,000 had been received from the US in Dec 1967.

Highest Price Drawing

The highest price ever attached to any drawing was £804,361 ($2,252,210) for the cartoon *The Virgin and Child with St John the Baptist and St Anne,* measuring 54½ in × 39¼ in, drawn in Milan, probably in 1499–1500, by Leonardo da Vinci (1452–1519). The National Gallery (London) retained possession in 1962, after three US bids of over $4 million were reputedly made for the cartoon.

Youngest Exhibitor

Lewis Melville "Gène" Lyons (b Apr 30, 1962) painted his *Trees and Monkeys* on June 4, 1965, submitted it to the Royal Academy of Arts, England, on March 17, 1967, for its Annual Summer Exhibition, and it was exhibited on Apr 29, 1967.

Most Repetitious Painter

Antonio Bin of Paris has painted the *Mona Lisa* on some 300 occasions. These copies sell for up to $2,250 each.

Most Prolific Painter

Picasso was the most prolific of all painters. In a career that lasted 78 years, it has been estimated that he produced about 13,500 paintings, 100,000 prints, 34,000 book illustrations, plus drawings, tapestries, sculptures and ceramics. His lifetime work has been valued at well over $1 billion. At his death Picasso left 1,885 paintings, 1,228 sculptures, 7,089 drawings, 3,222 ceramic works, 17,411 prints and 11 tapestries. The Museum of Modern Art in NY gave over its entire museum to a one-man show of Picasso's work, May–Sept 1980.

Morris Katz (b 1932) of Greenwich Village, NYC, was reported at around noon June 29, 1979, to have "knocked off" his 82,000th saleable painting. Described as the "King of Shlock Art," he sells his paintings "cheap and often."

Most Prolific Portrait Painter

John A. Wismont, Jr (b NYC, Sept 20, 1941), formerly of Disneyland, Anaheim, California, painted 45,423 watercolor paintings in his career (up to 1978) including 9,853 in 1976.

Finest Brush

The finest standard brush sold is the 000 in Series 7 by Winsor and Newton, known as the "triple goose." It is made of 150–200 Kolinsky sable hairs weighing 0.000529 oz.

Oldest and Largest Museums

The oldest museum in the world is the Ashmolean Museum in Oxford, England, built in 1679.

The largest museum is the American Museum of Natural History between 77th and 81st Sts on Central Park West, NYC. Founded in 1874, it comprises 19 interconnected buildings with 23 acres of floor space.

Largest Galleries

The world's largest art gallery is the Winter Palace and the neighboring Hermitage in Leningrad, USSR. One has to walk 15 miles to visit each of the 322 galleries, which house nearly 3 million works of art and archeological remains.

OLDEST MUSEUM: The Ashmolean in Oxford, England was built in 1679.

MOST PROLIFIC PAINTER: Pablo Picasso became famous for his cubistic painting of which "Femme Assise" (left above) is a prime example. LARGEST ART
GALLERY: The Hermitage and Winter Palace in Leningrad (right) with 322 galleries together display nearly 3 million art objects.

The largest modern art museum is the Georges Pompidou National
Center for Art and Culture opened in Paris in 1977 with a floor space of
183,000 sq ft.

Earliest Mural

The earliest known murals on man-made walls are those at Çatal
Hüyük in southern Anatolia, Turkey, dating from c. 5850 BC.

Largest Mural

The largest logo and mural painting is the American Revolution Bicentennial symbol on the curved roof of the Arizona Veterans Memorial
Coliseum, Phoenix, Ariz. It occupies 110,000 sq ft, or more than 2½ acres.
It was painted over in 1977. After being outlined with the aid of a computer, it took 45 man-days, under the supervision of its designer John M.
Glitsos, to apply the necessary 870 gallons of patriotic red, white and
blue paint Aug 18–26, 1973.

A ground mural, measuring 1,400 ft long by 100 ft wide, named *Yellow
Brick Road—Leisure Time,* painted on a disused runway near the Ta-
miami Stadium, South Dade, Fla, was completed March 18, 1976.

Largest Mosaic

The largest mosaic is on the walls of the central library of the Univer-
sidad Nacional Autónoma de México, Mexico City. There are four walls,
the two largest measuring 12,949 sq ft each representing the pre-Hispanic
past.

Largest Cartoon

The largest cartoon ever exhibited was one covering five stories (50 ft
× 150 ft) of a University of Arizona building, drawn by Dr Peter A.
Kesling for Mom 'n' Dad's Day, 1954.

LARGEST GROUND FIGURES: Seen as art only from the air, these lines in the Nazca Desert of Peru are one of the world's greatest mysteries.

2. SCULPTURES

Earliest Sculptures

The earliest known examples of sculpture are the so-called Venus figurines from Aurignacian sites, dating to *c.* 25,000–22,000 BC, *e.g.* the famous Venus of Willendorf from Austria and the Venus of Brassempouy (Landes, France). A piece of ox rib found in 1973 at Pech de l'Aze, Dordogne, France, in an early Middle Paleolithic layer of the Riss glaciation *c.* 105,000 BC appears to have several intentionally engraved lines on one side. The earliest authenticated and dated art are engravings of female genitals and animals from La Terrasie in Perigord, France, dated to *c.* 25,000 BC from the early Aurignacian period.

Largest Sculptures

The largest sculptures are the mounted figures of Jefferson Davis (1808–89), Gen Robert Edward Lee (1807–70) and Gen Thomas Jonathan ("Stonewall") Jackson (1824–63), covering 1.33 acres on the face of Stone Mountain, near Atlanta, Ga. They are 90 ft high. Roy Faulkner was on the mountain face for 8 years 174 days with a thermo-jet torch, working with the sculptor Walker Kirtland Hancock and other helpers from Sept 12, 1963 to March 3, 1972.

When completed the world's largest sculpture will be that of the Indian chief Tashunca-Uitco (*c.* 1849–77) known as Crazy Horse, of the Oglala tribe of the Dakota or Nadowessioux (Sioux) group. The sculpture was begun on June 3, 1948 near Mount Rushmore, SD. A projected 561 ft high and 641 ft long, it has required blasting 6,500,000 tons of stone and is the life work of one man, Korczak Ziolkowski.

Most Expensive Sculptures

The highest price ever paid for a sculpture is $3,900,000 paid by private treaty in London in early 1977 by J. Paul Getty's Museum in California for the 4th-century BC bronze statue of a youth attributed to the school of Lysippus. It was found by fishermen on the seabed off Faro, Italy in 1963. The $46-million museum with 38 galleries, opened in Malibu in Jan 1974, has a $1,400 million endowment.

The highest price paid for the work of a living sculptor is $260,000 given at Sotheby Parke Bernet Galleries, NYC, March 1, 1972, by Fischer Fine Arts of London, England, for the 75-in wooden carving *Reclining Figure* by Henry Moore (b Castleford, W Yorkshire, England, July 30, 1898), sold by Cranbrook Academy, Bloomfield Hills, Mich.

Ground and Hill Figures

In the Nazca Desert south of Lima, Peru there are straight lines (one more than 7 miles long), geometric shapes and plants and animals drawn on the ground sometime between 100 BC and 700 AD for an uncertain but probably religious or astronomical purpose by a still unknown civilization. They were first detected from the air *c.* 1928 and can only be recognized as artwork from the air.

In Aug 1968 a 330-ft-tall figure was found on a hill above Tarapacá, Chile.

Most Massive Mobile

The most massive recorded mobile is *Quest* by Jerome Kirk, installed at TRW Inc., Redondo Beach, Calif in Sept 1968. It is a 32-ft-long pivotal mobile weighing 5.98 tons. The term "mobile" was coined to contrast with "stabile" sculpture by Marcel Duchamp (1887–1968) in 1932.

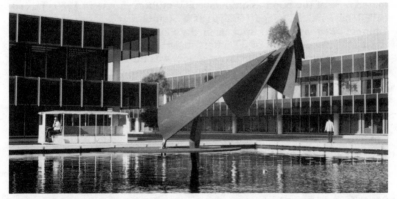

LARGEST MOBILE: This 6-ton sculpture in California, called "Quest," composed of 7 triangular metal "wings," required 6 men and a 25-ton crane to install it.

3. LANGUAGE AND LITERATURE

Earliest Language

Anthropologists have evidence that the truncated pharynx of Neanderthal man precluded his speaking anything akin to a modern language any more than an ape or a modern baby. Cro-Magnon man of 40,000 BC had however developed an efficient vocal tract. Clay tablets of the neolithic Danubian culture discovered in Dec, 1966, at Tartaria, Moros River, Rumania have been dated to the fifth or fourth millennium BC. The tablets bear symbols of bows and arrows, gates and combs. Writing tablets bearing an early form of the Elamite language dating from 3,500 BC were found in southeastern Iran in 1970. Tokens or tallies from Tepe Asiab and Ganji-I-Dareh Tepe in Iran have however been dated to 8,500 BC.

Oldest Language

The written language with the longest continuous history is Egyptian from the earliest hieroglyphic inscriptions on the palette of Narmer, dated to *c.* 3100 BC to Coptic used in churches at the present day, more than 5,000 years later. Hieroglyphs were used until 394 AD, and thus may be overtaken by Chinese characters as the most durable script in the 21st century.

Oldest Words in English

Some as yet unpublished research indicates some words of a pre-Indo-European substrate survive in English, including apple (apal), bad (bad), gold (gol), and tin (tin).

Commonest Language

Today's world total of languages and dialects still spoken is about 5,000 of which some 845 come from India. The language spoken by more people than any other is Northern Chinese, or Mandarin, by an estimated 68% of the population, hence 660 million people in 1980. The so-called national language (*Guóyŭ*) is a standardized form of Northern Chinese (*Běifanghuà*) as spoken in the Peking area. This was alphabetized into *zhùyīn fùhào* of 37 letters in 1918. In 1958 the *pinyin* system, which is a phonetic pronunciation guide, was introduced. The next most commonly spoken language and the most widespread is English, by an estimated 395 million in mid-1980. English is spoken by 10% or more of the population in 37 sovereign countries.

Rarest Language

There are believed to be 20 or more languages, including 6 North American Indian languages, in which no one can converse, because there is only one speaker left alive. Eyak is still spoken in southeastern Alaska by 2 aged sisters if they meet.

Most Complex Language

The following extremes of complexity have been noted: Chippewa, the North American Indian language of Minnesota, has the most verb forms with up to 6,000; Tillamook, the North American Indian language of Oregon, has the most prefixes with 30; Tabassaran, a language in Daghestan, USSR, uses the most noun cases with 35; the Eskimo language uses 63 forms of the present tense and simple nouns have as many as 252 inflections.

In Chinese, the 40-volume *Chung-wen Ta Tz'u-tien* Dictionary lists 49,905 characters. The fourth tone of "i" has 84 meanings, varying as widely as "dress," "hiccough" and "licentious." The written language provides 92 different characters for "i⁴." The most complex written character in Chinese is that representing *xie* which has 64 strokes and means "talkative." The most complex in current use is *yu*, which consists of 32 strokes and means to urge or implore.

Rarest and Commonest Sounds

The rarest speech sound is probably the sound written ř in Czech which occurs in very few languages and is the last sound mastered by Czech children. In the southern Bushman language !xo, there is a click, articulated with both lips, which is written ⊙. The l sound in the Arabic word *Allah,* in some contexts, is pronounced uniquely in that language. The commonest sound is the vowel *a* (as in English "father"); no language is known to be without it.

Most and Least Irregular Verbs

Esperanto was first published by Dr Ludwig Zamenhof (1859–1917), of Warsaw, in 1887 without irregular verbs and is now estimated from textbook sales to have a million speakers. The even earlier language Volapuk, invented by Johann Martin Schleyer (1831–1912) also has absolutely regular configuration. Swahili has a strict 6-class pattern of verbs and no verbs which are irregular to this pattern. According to more daunting grammars published in W Germany, English has 194 irregular verbs, though there are arguably 214.

Largest Vocabulary

The English language contains about 490,000 words, plus another 300,000 technical terms, the most in any language, but it is doubtful if any individual uses more than 60,000.

Smallest Literature

Of written languages, that with the smallest literature is Tyrrhenian, also known as Lemnian, once spoken on the island of Lemnon and believed to be related to Etruscan. The only surviving fragment is a 10-line inscription from the 6th century BC.

Greatest Linguist

If the yardstick of ability to speak with fluency and reasonable accuracy is adhered to, it is doubtful whether any human could maintain fluency in more than 20–25 languages concurrently or achieve fluency in more than 40 in a lifetime.

The most multilingual living person in the world is Georges Henri Schmidt (b Strasbourg, France, Dec 28, 1914), who served as Chief of the UN Terminology Section 1965–71. In the 1975 edition of *Who's Who in the United Nations* he listed "only" 19 languages because he was then unable to find the time to "revive" his former fluency in 12 others.

Historically, the greatest linguists have been proclaimed as Cardinal Mezzofanti (fluent in 26 or 27), Prof Rask (1787–1832), Sir John Bowering (1792–1872), and Dr Harold Williams of New Zealand (1876–1928), who was fluent in 28 languages.

Oldest Alphabet

The development of the use of an alphabet in place of pictograms occurred in the Sinaitic world between 1700 and 1500 BC. This western Semitic language developed the consonantal system based on phonetic and syllabic principles.

The oldest letter is "O," unchanged in shape since its adoption in the Phoenician alphabet *c.* 1300 BC. The newest letters in the English alphabet are "j" and "v," which are of post-Shakespearean use, *c.* 1630. There are now some 65 alphabets in use.

Longest and Shortest Alphabets

The language with most letters is Cambodian with 72 (including useless ones). Rotokas, spoken in the center of Bougainville Island in the South Pacific, has least with 11 (just a, b, e, g, i, k, o, p, ř, t and u). Amharic has 231 formations from 33 basic syllabic forms, each of which has seven modifications, so this Ethiopian language cannot be described as alphabetic.

Most and Least Consonants and Vowels

The language with most consonantal sounds is the Caucasian language Ubyx, with 80, and that with the least is Rotokas with only 6 consonants. The language with the most vowels is Sedang, a central Vietnamese language with 55 distinguishable vowel sounds. The language with the least (2 vowels) is the Caucasian language Abkhazian. The English record for consecutive vowels is 6 in the musical term *euouae*. The Estonian word Jäääärne, meaning "the edge of the ice," has the same 4 consecutively. Voiauai, a language in Pará state, Brazil, consists solely of 7 vowels. The English word "latchstring" has 6 consecutive consonants, but the German word Angstschweiss has 8.

Largest Letter

The largest permanent letters in the world are the giant 600-ft letters spelling READYMIX on the ground in the Nullarbor near East Balladonia, W Australia. This was constructed in Dec 1971.

Longest Words

The longest word ever to appear in literature occurs in *The Ecclesiazusae,* a comedy by Aristophanes (448–380 BC). In the Greek it is 170 letters long but transliterates into 182 letters in English, thus: lopadotemachoselachogaleokranioleipsanodrimhypotrimmatosilphioparaomelitokatakechymenokichlepikossyphophattoperisteralektryonoptekephalliokigklopeleiolagoiosiraiobaphetraganopterygon. The term describes a fricassee of 17 sweet and sour ingredients, including mullet, brains, honey, vinegar, pickles, marrow (the vegetable) and ouzo (a Greek drink laced with anisette).

The longest word in the Oxford English Dictionary is floccipaucinihilipilification (alternatively spelt in hyphenated form with "n" in seventh place), with 29 letters, meaning "the action of estimating as worthless," first used in 1741, and later by Sir Walter Scott (1771–1832). Webster's Third International Dictionary lists among its 450,000 entries pneumonoultramicroscopicsilicovolcanoconiosis (45 letters), the name of a miner's lung disease.

The nonce word used by Dr Edward Strother (1675–1737) to describe the spa waters at Bristol was aequeosalinocalcalinoceraceoaluminosocupreovitriolic (52 letters).

The longest regularly formed English word is praetertranssubstantiationalistically (37 letters), used by Mark McShane in his novel *Untimely Ripped,* published in 1963. The medical term hepaticocholangiocholecystenterostomies (39 letters) refers to the surgical creations of new communications between gall bladders and hepatic ducts and between intestines and gall bladders. The longest in common use are disproportionableness and incomprehensibilities (21 letters). Interdenominationalism (22 letters) is found in Webster's and hence perhaps interdenominationalistically (28 letters) is permissible.

Longest Palindromic Words

The longest known palindromic word (same spelling backwards as forwards) is *saippuakivikauppias* (19 letters), the Finnish word for a dealer in lye. The longest in the English language is *redivider* (9 letters). The 9-letter word, *Malayalam,* is a proper noun given to the language of the Malayali people in Kerala, southern India, while *Kanakanak* near Dellingham, Alaska, is a 9-letter palandromic place name. The 9-letter word *ROTAVATOR* is a registered trademark belonging to Howard Machinery Ltd, of England. The contrived chemical term *detartrated* has 11 letters. In American English the word *releveler* is also a 9-letter palindrome, though in England the word is spelled *releveller* and hence is not palindromic.

Some baptismal fonts in Greece and Turkey bear the circular 25-letter inscription NIΨON ANOMHMATA MH MONAN OΨIN meaning "wash (my) sins not only (my) face."

Most Meanings

The most overworked word in English is the word "set" which has 58 noun uses, 126 verbal uses and 10 as a participial adjective.

Commonest Words and Letters

In written English, the most frequently used words are in order: the, of, and, to, a, in, that, is, I, it, for *and* as. The most used in conversation is I. The commonest letter is "e" and the commonest initial letter is "T."

Most Homophones

The most homophonous sounds in English are *air* and *sol* which, according to the researches of Dora Newhouse of Los Angeles, both have 38 homophones. The homophone with the most variant spellings is *air*, with aire, are, ayr, e'er, eir, ere, err, erre, eyre, heir, eire, eyr *and* ore.

Most Accents

Accents were introduced in French in the reign of Louis XIII (1601–43). The word with most accents is *hétérogénéité*, meaning heterogeneity. An atoll in the Pacific Ocean 320 miles east southeast of Tahiti is named Héréhérétué.

Shortest Holoalphabetic Sentence

The contrived headline describing the reaction of despicable vandals from the valley thwarted by finding a block of quartz with carvings (already) upon it—"Quartz glyph job vex'd cwm finks"—represents the ultimate in containing all (but only) 26 letters. This was devised by Jeff Grant of Hastings, New Zealand.

Worst Tongue-Twisters

The most difficult tongue-twister is deemed by Ken Parkin of Teesside, England, to be "The sixth sick sheik's sixth sheep's sick"—especially when spoken quickly.

Longest Abbreviation

The longest known abbreviation is S.K.O.M.K.H.P.K.J.C.D.P.W.B., the initials of the Syarikat Kerjasama Orang-orang Melayu Kerajaan Hilir Perak Kerana Jimat Cermat Dan Pinjaman Wang Berhad. This is the Malay name for the Lower Perak Malay Government Servants' Co-operative Thrift and Loan Society Limited, in Teluk Anson, Perak, West Malaysia (formerly called Malaya). The abbreviation for this abbreviation is Skomk.

The 55-letter full name of Los Angeles (El Pueblo de Nuestra Señora la Reina de los Angeles de Porciuncula) is abbreviated to LA, or 3.63% of its length.

Longest Acronym

The longest acronym is NIIOMTPIABOPARMBETZHELBE-TRABSBOMONIMONIMONKONOTDTEKHSTROMONT with 56 letters (54 in Cyrillic) in the *Concise Dictionary of Soviet Terminology* meaning: The laboratory for shuttering, reinforcement, concrete and ferro-concrete operations for composite-monolithic and monolithic constructions of the Department of the Technology of Building—assembly operations of the Scientific Research Institute of the Organization for building mechanization and technical aid of the Academy of Building and Architecture of the USSR.

Longest Anagrams

The longest non-scientific English words which can form anagrams are the 18-letter transpositions "conservationalists" and "conversationalists." The longest scientific transposals are cholecystoduodenostomy/duodenocholecystostomy and hydropneumopericardium/pneumohydropericardium, each of 22 letters.

Longest Sentence in Literature

A sentence of 1,300 words appears in *Absalom, Absalom!* by William Faulkner, and one of 3,153 words with 86 semi-colons and 390 commas occurs in the *History of the Church of God* by Sylvester Hassell of Wilson, NC, *c.* 1884. Some authors such as James Joyce (1882–1941) eschew punctuation altogether. The first 40,000 words of the *Gates of Paradise* by George Andrzeyevski appear to lack any punctuation.

The longest sentence recorded ever to have gotten past the editor of a major newspaper is one of 1,030 words in the TV column by Clarence G. Peterson, which appeared in the Aug 19, 1970 edition of the *Chicago Tribune.*

The Report of the President of Columbia University, 1942–43, contained a sentence of 4,284 words.

Longest Place Names

The official name for Bangkok, capital of Thailand, is Krungthep Mahanakhon. The full name is however: Krungthep Mahanakhon Bovorn Ratanakosin Mahintharayutthaya Mahadilok pop Noparatratchathani Burirom Udomratchanivetmahasathan Amornpiman Avatarnsathit Sakkathattiyavisnukarmprasit (167 letters) which, in the most scholarly transliteration, emerges with 175 letters.

The longest place name now in use is Taumatawhakatangihangakoauauotamatea (turipukakapikimaungahoronuku) pokaiwhenuakitanatahu, the unofficial 85-letter version of the name of a hill (1,002 ft above sea level) in the Southern Hawke's Bay district of North Island, New Zealand. This Maori name means "the hill whereon was played the flute of Tamatea, circumnavigator of lands, for his lady love." The official version has 57 letters (1 to 36 and 65 to 85).

Ijouaououene, Morocco, has 8 consecutive vowels.

Shortest Place Names

The shortest place names in the world are the French village of Y (population 143), so named since 1241, the Danish village Å on the island Fyn, the Norwegian village of Å (pronounced "Aw"), the Swedish place Å in Vikholandet, U in the Caroline Islands of the Pacific, and the Japanese town of Sosei which is alternatively called Aioi or O. There was

LONGEST PLACE NAME IN USE: A 57-letter Maori name for a hill in New Zealand. In 1959 the first letter in the third line was changed from "A" to "O".

once a 6 in West Virginia. Today in the US, there are 7 two-lettered place names, including Ed and Uz, both in Kentucky.

Earliest and Longest Personal Names

The earliest personal name which has survived is seemingly that of a predynastic King of Upper Egypt *ante* 3050 BC, who is indicated by the hieroglyphic sign for a scorpion. It has been suggested that the name should be read as Sekhen. The earliest English name is Divitiacus, King of the Suessiones, the Gaulish ruler of the Kent area *c.* 75 BC under the name Prydhain.

The longest name used by anyone is Adolph Blaine Charles David Earl Frederick Gerald Hubert Irvin John Kenneth Lloyd Martin Nero Oliver Paul Quincy Randolph Sherman Thomas Uncas Victor William Xerxes Yancy Zeus Wolfeschlegelsteinhausenbergerdorff, Senior, who was born at Bergedorf, near Hamburg, Germany, Feb 29, 1904. On printed forms, he uses only his eighth and second Christian names and his shortened surname, which actually has 550 more letters. He lives in Philadelphia, and has recently shortened his surname to Wolfe+585, Senior.

The longest Christian or given name on record is Napua-mohala-on-aona-a-me-ka-wehiwehi-o-na-kuahiwi-a-me-na-awawa-ke-hoomaka-ke-hoaala-ke-ea-o-na-aina-nani-akea-o-hawaii-i-ka-wanaao (102 letters), in the case of Miss Dawne E. Lee of Honolulu, so named in Feb 1967. The name means "the abundant, beautiful blossoms of the mountains and valleys begin to fill the air with their fragrance throughout the length and breadth of Hawaii."

Shortest Personal Name

The single-letter surname O, of which 28 examples appear in Belgian telephone directories, besides being the commonest single-letter name, is the one obviously causing the most distress to those concerned with the prevention of cruelty to computers. There are two one-letter Burmese names: E (calm), pronounced "aye," and U (egg), pronounced "oo." U used before the name means "uncle."

Most Christian Names

The great-great-grandson of Carlos III of Spain, Don Alfonso de Borbón y Borbón (1866–1934), had 89 Christian names, of which several were lengthened by hyphenation.

Commonest Family Names

The commonest family name in the world is the Chinese name Chang which is borne, according to estimates, by between 9.7% and 12.1% of the Chinese population, so indicating even on the lower estimate that there are at least some 75 million Changs—more than the entire population of all but 7 of the 164 other sovereign countries of the world.

The commonest surname in the English-speaking world is Smith. There are 659,050 nationally insured Smiths in Great Britain, of whom 10,102 are plain John Smith, and another 19,502 are John plus one or more given-name Smiths. Including uninsured persons, there are over 800,000 Smiths in England and Wales alone. There were an estimated 2,382,509 Smiths in the US in 1973.

HIS NAME UP IN LIGHTS: Mr. Wolfe + 585, Senior, of Philadelphia watches as a New York City electrical sign misspells his 590-letter surname.

There are, however, estimated to be 1,600,000 persons in Britain with M', Mc or Mac (Gaelic "son of") as part of their surnames. The commonest of these is Macdonald which accounts for about 55,000 of the Scottish population.

Commonest Christian Names

In the UK, the most favored first name for boys is Mark with the narrowest of leads over Paul and Stephen/Steven, while in the US, David is tops over Michael and Bruce. In the UK it is Sara for girls over Claire, and in the US it is a close race with Barbara probably winning out over Carol and Joy/Joyce.

Most Contrived Name

In the US, the determination to derive commercial or other benefit from being the last listing in the local telephone book has resulted in self-given names starting with six z's—the extreme example being Mr Zachary Zzzzzzzzzzzra in the San Francisco book. Last in the book for Madison, Wis, however, is Mr Hero Zzyzzx (pronounced Ziz-icks) whose name, he claims, is for real.

Oldest Text

The oldest known written text is the pictographic expression of Sumerian speech, dating from *c.* 3500 BC. The Samarian papyri, written in Aramaic, found 8½ miles north of Jericho, are dated 375–335 BC.

Oldest Printed Work

The oldest surviving printed work is a Korean scroll or *sutra,* printed from wooden blocks found in the foundations of the Pulguk Sa pagoda, Kyongju, Korea, Oct 14, 1966. It has been dated no later than 704 AD. It was claimed in Nov 1973 that a 28-page book of Tang dynasty poems at Yonsei University, Korea, was printed from metal type *c.* 1160.

Oldest Mechanically Printed Book

It is generally accepted that the earliest mechanically printed full-length book was a "42-line" Gutenberg Bible, printed at Mainz, Germany, *c.* 1454 by Johann Henne zum Gensfleisch zur Laden, called "zu Gutenberg" (*c.* 1398–*c.* 1468). Work on watermarks published in 1967 indicates a copy of a surviving printed "Donatus" Latin grammar was made from paper made in *c.* 1450. The earliest exactly dated printed work is the Psalter completed Aug 14, 1457, by Johann Fust (*c.* 1400–1466) and Peter Schöffer (1425–1502), who had been Gutenberg's chief assistant. The earliest printing by William Caxton, though undated, would appear to be *The Recuyel of the Historyes of Troye* in late 1473 to spring 1474.

Manuscripts

The highest price ever paid is £280,000 (then $490,000) paid at Christie's, London, on Nov 17, 1976, for a single leaf of *The Death of Zahhak* from the 258-page Persian *Shahnamel,* commissioned by Shah Ismai'l in 1522 and sold by Arthur J. Houghton of NYC. The splitting of this manuscript has been greatly criticized. It has been estimated that the total value of this manuscript, acquired by Mr Houghton in 1959, may be as high as $60 million.

Largest Publication

The largest publication in the world is the 1,112-volume set of *British Parliamentary Papers* of 1800–1900 published by the Irish University Press in 1968–1972. A complete set weighs 3.64 tons, costs $65,000 and would take 6 years to read at 10 hours per day. The production and binding involved the death of 34,000 Indian goats and $39,000 worth of gold ingots. The total print run was 500 sets.

Smallest Book

The smallest marketed bound printed book with cursive material is one of 15 pages measuring 1/12 × 1/12 × 1/32 of an inch comprising *Three Blind Mice* and produced by Glenniffer Press of Paisley, Scotland, in 1978. The song is thought to be the earliest secular song ever printed (1609).

SMALLEST BOOK (below): "Three Blind Mice" is the title of this miniature volume printed in Scotland.

TOP-SELLING POST CARD (right): Created by Donald McGill in 1904, this greeting card sold more than 350 million copies by 1962.

" Do you like Kipling ? "

" I don't know, you naughty boy, I've never kippled ! "

Most Expensive Book

The highest price ever paid for a printed book is $2,400,000 for one of the only 21 known complete copies of the Gutenberg Bible, printed in Mainz, (West) Germany, in *c.* 1454. It was bought from the Carl and Lily Pforzheimer Foundation by Texas University in a sale arranged by Quaritch of London in NYC, June 9, 1978.

Post Cards

The top-selling post card of all time was said to be a drawing by Donald McGill (1875–1962 with the caption: He: "Do you like Kipling?" She: "I don't know, you naughty boy, I've never kippled." It sold about 6 million. Between 1904 and his death McGill sold more than 350 million cards to users and deltiologists (picture post card collectors).

The world's first post cards were issued in Vienna on Oct 1, 1869. Pin-up girls came into vogue in 1914 having been pioneered in 1900 by Raphaël Kirchner (1876–1917). The most expensive on record were ones made in ivory for an Indian prince which involved the killing of 60 elephants.

Highest-Priced Printed Document

The highest price ever paid for a broadsheet was $404,000 for one of the 16 known copies of *The Declaration of Independence,* printed in Philadelphia in 1776 by Samuel T. Freeman & Co., and sold to a Texan in May 1969.

Highest-Priced Atlas

The highest price paid for an atlas is $697,000 for a 16th century Mercator atlas of Europe sold at Sotheby's, London, March 13, 1979.

Longest Novel

The longest important novel ever published is *Les hommes de bonne volonté* by Louis Henri Jean Farigoule (b Aug 26, 1885), *alias* Jules Romains, of France, in 27 volumes in 1932–46. The English version, *Men of Good Will,* was published in 14 volumes in 1933–46 as a "novel-cycle." The 4,959-page edition published by Peter Davies Ltd. has an estimated 2,070,000 words, excluding a 100-page index. The novel *Tokuga-Wa Ieyasu* by Sohachi Yamaoka has been serialized in Japanese daily newspapers since 1951. Now completed, it will require nearly 40 volumes in book form.

Earliest and Largest Encyclopaediae

The earliest known encyclopaedia was compiled in Athens by Speusippus (*post* 408–*c.* 338 BC) in *c.* 370 BC. He was a nephew of Plato. The largest encyclopaedia ever compiled was the *Great Standard Encyclopaedia* of Yung-lo ta tien of 22,937 manuscript books (370 still survive); written by 2,000 Chinese scholars in 1403–08.

Most Comprehensive Encyclopaedia

The most comprehensive academic encyclopaedia is the *Encyclopaedia Britannica,* first published in Edinburgh, Scotland, in Dec, 1768–1771. A group of booksellers in the US acquired reprint rights in 1898 and complete ownership in 1899. In 1943, the *Britannica* was given to the University of Chicago. The current 30-volume 15th edition contains 33,141 pages and 43 million words from 4,277 contributors. It is now edited in Chicago and in London.

Longest Index

The Ninth Collective Index of *Chemical Abstracts,* completed on Aug 23, 1978, contains 20,550,000 entries in 95,882 pages in 57 volumes, and weighs 251 lb.

Largest Dictionary

The largest dictionary now published is the 12-volume Royal quarto *The Oxford English Dictionary* of 15,487 pages published between 1884 and 1928 with a first supplement of 963 pages in 1933 and a further 4-volume supplement, edited by R. W. Burchfield, in which the third and fourth volumes, have yet to appear. The work contains 414,825 word listings, 1,827,306 illustrative quotations and reputedly 227,779,589 letters and figures, 63.8 times more than the Bible. The greatest outside contributor has been Margharita Laski with 175,000 since 1958.

Oldest Bible

Biblical texts in Hebrew are known to have become stabilized as early as 70 AD. The oldest leather and papyrus Dead Sea Scrolls date from *c.* 250 BC. The oldest known Bible is the *Codex Vaticanus,* written in Greek *ante-*350 AD, and preserved in the Vatican Museum, Rome.

The earliest complete Bible printed in English was edited by Miles Coverdale (*c.* 1488–1569), while living in Antwerp, and printed in 1535. The New Testament in English, had, however, been printed by William Tyndale in Cologne and in Worms, Germany, in 1525.

Most Prolific Writers

The most prolific writer for whom a word count has been published was Charles Hamilton, *alias* Frank Richards (1875–1961), the Englishman who created Billy Bunter. At the height of his career in 1908 he wrote the whole of the boys' comics *Gem* (founded 1907) and *Magnet* (1908–1940) and most of two others, totaling 80,000 words a week. His lifetime output has been put at 100 million words. He enjoyed the advantages of electric light rather than candlelight, and of being unmarried.

The champion of the goose-quill era was Józef Ignacy Kraszewski (1812–1887) of Poland, who produced more than 600 volumes of novels and historical works.

The greatest number of novels published by any author is 904 by Kathleen Lindsay (Mrs Mary Faulkner) (1903–1973) of Somerset West, Cape Province, South Africa. She wrote under six pen names, two of them masculine. The most prolific living novelist is Lauran Paine of California, who has had some 850 works published under 70 pen names.

After receiving a probable record 743 rejection slips the British novelist, John Creasey (1908–73), under his own name and 13 *noms de plume* had 564 books totaling more than 40 million words published from 1932 to his death on June 9, 1973.

Enid Mary Blyton (Mrs Darrell Waters) (1898–1968) (UK), completed

600 titles of children's stories, many of them brief, with 59 in the single year 1955. They have been translated into a record 128 languages.

Oldest Authoress

The oldest authoress was Mrs Alice Pollock (*née* Wykeham-Martin) (1868–1971) of Haslemere, Surrey, England, whose book *Portrait of My Victorian Youth* (Johnson Publications) was published in March 1971 when she was aged 102 years 8 months.

Youngest Author

The youngest recorded commercially published author is Dorothy Straight (b May 25, 1958) of Washington, DC, who wrote *How the World Began* in 1962, aged 4. It was published in Aug 1964 by Pantheon Books.

Highest-Paid Writer

In 1958, a Mrs Deborah Schneider of Minneapolis wrote 25 words to complete a sentence in a competition for the best blurb for Plymouth cars. She won from about 1,400,000 entrants the prize of $500 every month for life. On normal life expectations she would collect $12,000 per word. No known anthology includes Mrs Schneider's deathless prose.

By way of comparison, a modern author of a very highly successful 100,000-word filmed novel might expect to earn $17.50 per word.

Greatest Advance

The greatest advance paid for any book is $3,203,875 by Bantam Books for *Princess Daisy* by Judith Krantz in a publishers' auction in NYC, Sept 5, 1979.

Most Rejections

The greatest recorded number of publishers' rejections for a manuscript is 109 for the 130,000-word manuscript "World Government Crusade" by Gilbert Young (b 1906) since 1958. His public meeting in Bath, England, in support of his parliamentary candidacy as a World Government Candidate, however, drew a crowd of one.

Highest Printings

The world's most widely distributed book is the Bible, portions of which have been translated into 1,659 languages. This compares with 222 languages for Lenin. It has been estimated that between 1815 and 1975 some 2,500 million Bibles were printed, of which 1,500 million were handled by Bible Societies. The total distribution of Bibles by the United Bible Societies (covering 150 countries) in the year 1979 was 9,088,578.

It has been reported that 800 million copies of the red-covered booklet *Quotations from the Works of Mao Tse-tung* were sold or distributed between June 1966, when possession became virtually mandatory in China, and Sept 1971, when their promoter, Marshal Lin Piao, was killed.

The total disposal through non-commercial channels by Jehovah's Witnesses of the 192-page hardbound book *The Truth That Leads to Eternal Life,* published by the Watchtower Bible and Tract Society of Brooklyn, NY, reached 97 million in 116 languages by Apr 1, 1980.

Some 75 million copies of *The American Spelling Book* by Noah Webster were distributed with Federal funds.

Top-Selling Authors

The all-time sales estimate of books by Erle Stanley Gardner (1889–1970) (US) to Jan 1, 1980, is 311,803,986 copies in 37 languages. The top-selling woman writer has been Dame Agatha Christie (*née* Agatha Mary Clarissa Miller), later Lady Mallowan (formerly Mrs Archibald Christie) (1890–1976). Her 87 crime novels have sold an estimated 300 million copies in 103 languages. *Sleeping Murder* was published posthumously in 1977.

Currently the top-selling authoress is Barbara Cartland (Mrs McCorquodale) with global sales exceeding 100 million copies for 242 novels in 18 languages.

It was announced on March 13, 1953, that 672,058,000 copies of the works of Marshal Iosif Vissarionovich Dzhugashvili, *alias* Stalin (1879–1953), had been sold or distributed in 101 languages.

Best Sellers

It is believed that the 1879 edition of *The McGuffey Reader,* compiled by Henry Vail and published for school distribution in the US by Van Antwerp Bragg and Co sold 60 million copies in the pre-copyright era.

For a long time, the world's best selling copyrighted book, the annual reference work *The World Almanac & Book of Facts,* first published in 1868 and currently edited by George E. Delury, has now been surpassed. Its cumulative sale to Jan 1980 is estimated at more than 39 million copies, increasing by 1,100,000 each year.

The authors who have written what is now the all-time copyrighted best seller as well as the world's fastest-selling title are Norris Dewar McWhirter (b Aug 12, 1925) and his twin brother Alan Ross McWhirter (killed Nov 27, 1975), editors and compilers of the *Guinness Book of World Records,* first published from 107 Fleet Street, London, England, in Oct 1955. In May 1980 global sales in 23 languages had passed 40 million copies.

The novel with the highest sales has been *Valley of the Dolls* (first published March 1966) by Jacqueline Susann (Mrs Irving Mansfield) (1921–74) with a world-wide total of 22,042,000 to Apr 24, 1980. In the first 6 months Bantam sold 6.8 million.

Slowest Seller

The accolade for the world's slowest-selling book (known in publishing as slooow-sellers) probably belongs to David Wilkins' Translation of the New Testament from Coptic into Latin, published by Oxford University Press in 1716 with 500 copies. Selling an average of one each 139 days it was in print for 191 years.

Shortest Review

The Calgary-Herald book critic Brian Brennan, after years of frustra-

TOP-SELLING WOMAN WRITER (left): Agatha Christie, whose 87 crime novels have sold 300 million copies in 103 languages. She also wrote "The Mousetrap," the longest-running play—28 years. YOUNGEST AUTHORESS (right): Dorothy Straight, at the age of 4 in 1964 had her book published commercially.

AUTHOR OF TOP-SELLING NOVEL (left): Jacqueline Susann holds the record for the best-selling novel "Valley of the Dolls," with more than 20 million copies sold. LEAST SUCCESSFUL AUTHOR (right): William A. Gold, after 18 years of unceasing labor, involving 3 million words in 8 full-length books and 7 novels, finally struck pay dirt with a 50-cent sale to a newspaper in Canberra, Australia.

tion as a would-be record-breaker, finally submitted a 3-letter review on the 1980 US edition of *Guinness* used on the TV serial *Soap*. It was published on Dec 1, 1979 and merely said "Wow!"

Longest Literary Gestation

The standard German dictionary *Deutsches Wörterbuch,* begun by the brothers Grimm in 1854, was finished in 1971. *Acta Sanctorum,* begun by Jean Bolland in 1643, arranged according to saints' days, reached the month of Nov in 1925, and an introduction for Dec was published in 1940.

Fastest Publishing

The fastest time in which a book has been published is 46½ hours from receipt of manuscript to finished copies in the case of *Miracle on Ice* by the staff of *The New York Times* on Feb 27–28–29 1980. The 96-page story of the US Olympic gold medal ice hockey team was published by Bantam Books Inc.

Largest Printers

The largest printers in the world are R. R. Donnelley & Co of Chicago. The company, founded in 1864, has plants in 15 main centers, and has turned out $957 million worth of work per year. More than 67,000 tons of inks and 1,100,000 tons of paper and board are consumed every year.

The largest printer under one roof is the US Government Printing Office in Washington, DC, founded in 1860. The Superintendent of Documents Division dispatches items worth more than $44 million every year. The inventory is numbered at 24,500 titles in print.

Largest Print Order

The initial print order for the 51st Automobile Association (England) Members' Handbook (1980–81) was 4,800,000 copies. The total print run since 1908 has been 77,200,000.

Longest-Lived Comic Strip

The most durable newspaper comic strip has been the Katzenjammer Kids (Hans and Fritz) created by Rudolph Dirks, first published in the *New York Journal* on Dec 12, 1897, and carried on by his son, John.

The earliest strip was *The Yellow Kid* which first appeared in the *New York Journal* on Oct 18, 1896. The most widely syndicated is *Blondie,* which appears in 1,800 newspapers in 58 countries, and in 33 languages.

Most Widely Syndicated Cartoonist

Ranan R. Lurie (b May 26, 1932) is the most widely syndicated cartoonist in the world. His work is published in 45 countries.

Earliest Autographs

The earliest surviving signature known is of "El Cid" or Rodrigo Diaz of Spain (1043-99) dated *c.* 1070. The earliest English sovereign whose handwriting is known to have survived is Edward III (1327–1377). The earliest full signature to have survived is that of Richard II (dated July

MOST SUCCESSFUL SLOGAN (above): Jack Gasnick sold 50 million of these buttons. MOST AUTOGRAPHS: Artist Dong Kingman (right) signed 120,000 of his lithographs in 12 days.

26, 1386). The Magna Carta does not bear even the mark of King John (reigned 1199–1216), but carries only his seal. An attested cross of King Canute (1016–1035) has survived.

Most Expensive Autographs

The highest price ever paid on the open market for a single letter is $100,000 paid on Oct 18, 1979 at a Charles Hamilton Auction in NYC for a brief receipt signed by Button Gwinnett (1732–77), one of the three men from Georgia and the 56 signatories to the Declaration of Independence on July 4, 1776.

An expense account by Paul Revere, dated Jan 3, 1774 and signed by John Hancock, was auctioned for $70,000 at Sotheby Parke Bernet, NYC, April 26, 1978.

The highest price paid for a signed autograph letter of a living person is $6,250 at the Hamilton Galleries for a letter from ex-President Richard M. Nixon to a Brigadier General dated Dec 14, 1971.

Most Autographs

Dong Kingman, well-known Chinese-American watercolor artist, signed personally 10,000 each of 12 of his lithographed paintings (making 120,000 in all) in Hong Kong in 12 days of continuous sitting, May 8–19, 1980, for Rocky Aoki's Benihana Collection.

Bond Signing

The greatest feat of autographing was performed by L. E. Chittenden (d 1902), the Registrar of the US Treasury. In 48 hours (Mar 20–22, 1863), he signed 12,500 bonds worth $10 million, which had to catch a steam packet to England. He suffered years of pain thereafter and the bonds were never used.

Poets Laureate

The youngest Poet Laureate was Laurence Eusden (1688–1730), who at the age of 30 years 3 months on Dec 24, 1718, was appointed. The greatest age at which a poet has succeeded is 73 in the case of William Wordsworth (1770–1850) on Apr 6, 1843. The longest-lived Laureate was John Masefield, who died on May 12, 1967, aged 88 years 345 days. The longest which any poet has worn the laurel is 41 years 322 days, in the case of Alfred (later the 1st Lord) Tennyson (1809–92), who was appointed Nov 19, 1850, and died in office Oct 6, 1892.

Longest Poem

The lengthiest poem ever published has been the Kirghiz folk epic *Manas,* which appeared in printed form in 1958, but which has never been translated into English. It runs to "more than 500,000 lines." Short translated passages appear in *The Elek Book of Oriental Verse.*

The longest poem ever written in the English language appears to be one on the life of King Alfred by John Fitchett (1766–1838) of Liverpool, England, which ran to 129,807 lines and took 40 years to write. His editor, Robert Riscoe, added the concluding 2,585 lines.

Most Successful Poem

The most translated poem is believed to be "If" by Joseph Rudyard Kipling (1865–1936), first published in 1910. It has appeared in 27 languages and according to Kipling was "anthologized to weariness."

Longest Letter

The longest handwritten personal letter based on word count is one of 1,113,747 words written in 8 months ending in May 1976 by Jacqueline Jones of Lindale, Texas, to her sister Mrs Jean Stewart of Springfield, Me.

Letters to the Editor

The longest recorded letter to an editor was one of 13,000 words (a third of a modern novel) written to the editor of the *Fishing Gazette* by A.R.I.E.L. and published in 7-point type spread over two issues in 1884.

The shortest literary correspondence on record was that between Victor Marie Hugo (1802–85) and his publisher, Hurst and Blackett, in 1862. The author was on holiday and anxious to know how his new novel *Les Misérables* was selling. He wrote "?". The reply was "!".

Most Durable Pen Pals

The longest sustained correspondence on record is one of 72 years between Mrs E. Darlington of Marple, Cheshire, England and Mrs Gertrude Walker of Hawthorn, South Australia, which started Jan 5, 1906.

Most Personal Mail

The highest confirmed count of letters received by any private citizen in a year is 900,000 letters by baseball star Henry Aaron, reported by the

US Postal Department in June 1974 the year that he surpassed Babe Ruth's career home run record.

Longest Diary

The diary of Edward Robb Ellis (b 1911) of NYC, begun in 1927 after 52 years is estimated to run to 15 million words.

Earliest and Largest Crossword Puzzles

The earliest crossword was one with 32 clues invented by Arthur Wynne (b Liverpool, England) and published in the *New York World* on Dec 21, 1913.

The largest crossword ever published is one compiled by Stephen Robinson of Coventry, England, published by Onsworld Ltd of Stamford, England, on Oct 22, 1979. It contains 6,257 clues across and 6,051 down and covers 18½ sq ft.

The largest crosswords regularly published are "Mammoth" crosswords based on grids of 73 by 73 (5,329 total) squares with up to 828 clues by First Features Ltd, Hastings, England, since May 1, 1970.

Fastest and Slowest Solutions

The fastest recorded time for completing *The Times* (London) crossword under test conditions is 3 min 45.0 sec by Roy Dean, 43, of Bromley, Greater London, in the BBC "Today" radio studio on Dec 19, 1970.

In May 1966, *The Times* of London received an announcement from a Fijian woman that she had just succeeded in completing their crossword No. 673 from the issue of Apr 4, 1932.

Christmas Cards

The first Christmas card was designed by J. C. Horsley in London in 1843. It was suggested by, and sent to, the artist's friend, Henry Cole. The Cole-Horsley cards sold for one shilling.

The greatest number of personal Christmas cards sent out is believed to be 62,824 by Werner Erhard of San Francisco, founder of est, in Dec 1975.

FIRST CHRISTMAS CARD: The tradition of sending Christmas cards began in 1843, when J. C. Horsley sent this one to his friend, Henry Cole.

Birthday Cards

The most parsimonious recorded use of a birthday card is that between Mrs Amelia Finch (b Apr 18, 1912) of Lakehurst, NJ, and Mr Paul E. Warburgh (b Feb 1, 1902) of Huntington, NY, who have exchanged the same birthday card since Feb 1, 1927.

Oldest Map

The oldest known map of any kind is a clay tablet depicting the Euphrates River flowing through northern Mesopotamia (Iraq), dated *c.* 3800 BC. The earliest printed map in the world dates from Isodore of Sevillés *Etymologiarum* of 1472.

Largest Libraries

The largest library is the Library of Congress (founded Apr 24, 1800), on Capitol Hill, Washington, DC. By 1979, it contained 75,685,055 items, including 18,930,905 books and pamphlets. With the James Madison Memorial Extension, which was dedicated in Apr 1980, the buildings contain 35 acres of floor space and 50 miles of book shelves.

The largest non-statutory library is the New York Public Library (founded 1895) on Fifth Avenue, NYC, with a floor area of 525,276 sq ft and 80 miles of shelving. Including 83 branch libraries, its collection embraces 10,018,241 volumes, 11,370,919 manuscripts, and 441,663 maps.

Overdue Books

The most overdue book taken out by a known borrower was a book on febrile diseases (London, 1805, by Dr J. Currie) checked out in 1823 from the University of Cincinnati Medical Library and reported returned Dec 7, 1968, by the borrower's great-grandson Richard Dodd. The fine was calculated as $2,264, but waived.

Most Newspapers

The US had 1,756 English-language daily newspapers on Oct 1, 1978. They had a combined net paid circulation of 62,200,000 copies per day as of Sept 30, 1978. The peak year for US newspapers was 1910, when there were 2,202. The leading newspaper readers in the world are the people of Sweden, where 564 newspapers were sold for each 1,000 of the population.

Oldest Newspaper

The oldest existing newspaper is the Swedish official journal *Post och Inrikes Tidningar,* founded in 1645. It is published by the Royal Swedish Academy of Letters. The oldest existing commercial newspaper is the *Haarlems Dagblad/Oprechte Haarlemsche Courant,* published in Haarlem, in the Netherlands. The *Courant* was first issued as the *Weeckelycke Courante van Europa* on Jan 8, 1656, and a copy of issue No. 1 survives.

Largest and Smallest Issues

The most massive single issue of a newspaper was *The New York Times* of Sunday, Oct 17, 1965. It comprised 15 sections with a total of 946 pages, including about 1,200,000 lines of advertising. Each copy weighed 7½ lb and sold for 50 cents locally.

The largest page size ever used has been 51 in × 35 in for *The Constellation,* printed in 1859 by George Roberts as part of the Fourth of July celebrations in NYC.

The smallest recorded page size has been 3 in × 3¾ in, as used in the *Daily Banner* of Roseburg, Oregon (25 cents per month), issues of which, dated Feb 1 and 2, 1876, survive.

Highest Newspaper Circulation

The first newspaper to achieve a circulation of one million was *Le Petit Journal,* published in Paris, which reached this figure in 1886, when selling at 5 centimes (fractionally more than one cent) per copy.

The highest circulation for any newspaper is that for the *Yomiuri Shimbun* (founded 1874) of Japan which attained a figure of 13,782,158 copies on Apr 1, 1980. This has been achieved by totaling the figures for editions published in various centers with a morning figure of 8,687,519 and an evening figure of 5,094,639.

Most Read Newspaper

The newspaper which achieves the closest to a saturation circulation is *The Sunday Post,* established in Glasgow, Scotland, in 1914. In 1979, its total estimated readership of 2,828,000 represented more than 71% of Scotland's entire population aged 15 and over.

Largest Circulation Periodicals

The largest circulation of any weekly periodical is that of *TV Guide,* which, in 1974, became the first magazine in history to sell 1,000 million copies in a year. The weekly average for July to Dec 1979, was 19,043,358.

In its 39 international editions the *Reader's Digest* (established Feb 1922) circulates 29,973,000 copies monthly, in 15 languages, including a US edition of more than 17,750,000 copies.

Parade, the syndicated Sunday newspaper color magazine supplement, is distributed with 130 newspapers every Sunday, yielding a circulation of 21,123,793 as of May 1980.

Oldest Periodical

The oldest continuing periodical in the world is the *Philosophical Transactions of the Royal Society,* which first appeared March 6, 1665.

Advertising Rates

The highest price ever for a single page of advertising is $152,475 for a four-color back cover of *Parade* (circulation more than 21 million per week).

The highest expenditure ever incurred on a single advertisement in a periodical is $3,200,000 by Gulf and Western Industries for insertions in the Feb 5, 1979 *Time* magazine (US and selected overseas editions).

The world's highest newspaper advertising rate is 30,262,500 yen ($129,000) for a full page in the morning edition and 23,944,500 yen ($102,000) for the evening edition of the *Asahi Shimbun* of Tokyo (Apr 1980), at the rate of 235 yen to the dollar.

4. MUSIC*

Oldest Instruments

The oldest surviving musical notation dates from *c.* 1800 BC. A heptonic scale deciphered from a clay tablet by Dr Duchesne-Guillemin in 1966–67 was found at a site in Nippur, Sumer, now Iraq. Also dated *c.* 1800 BC is an Assyrian love song to a Ugarit god, reconstructed for an 11-string lyre from a tablet of notation and lyric at the University of California, Berkeley, March 6, 1974. Musical history is, however, able to be traced back to the 3rd millennium BC when the yellow bell (*huang chung*) had a recognized standard musical tone in Chinese temple music. Whistles and flutes made from perforated phalange bones have been found at Upper Paleolithic sites of the Aurignacian Period (*c.* 25,000–22,000 BC), *e.g.* at Istallóskö, Hungary, and in Molodova, USSR.

Earliest Piano

The earliest pianoforte in existence is one built in Florence, Italy, in 1720, by Bartolommeo Cristofori (1655–1731) of Padua, and now preserved in the Metropolitan Museum of Art, NY.

Grandest Piano

The grandest grand piano built was one of 1⅓ tons, 11 ft 8 in long, made by Chas. H. Challen & Son Ltd of London in 1935. The longest bass string measured 9 ft 11 in and the tensile stress on the 726-lb frame was 33.6 tons.

Most Expensive Piano

The highest price ever paid for a piano is $390,000 for a Steinway grand of *c.* 1888 sold at Sotheby Parke Bernet, NYC on March 26, 1980 for the Martin Beck Theatre and bought by a non-pianist.

Organs

The largest and loudest musical instrument ever constructed and now only partly functional is the Auditorium Organ in Atlantic City, NJ. Completed in 1930, this heroic instrument has two consoles (one with seven manuals and another movable one with five), 1,477 stop controls and 33,112 pipes ranging in tone from 3/16 in to the 64-ft tone. It is powered with blower motors of 365 horse-power, cost $500,000 and has the volume of 25 brass bands, with a range of 7 octaves.

The largest church organ is in Passau Cathedral, Germany. It was completed in 1928 by D. F. Steinmeyer & Co. It has 16,000 pipes and five manuals.

The most versatile electric organ is the 8-manual Kawai T50 built in Japan in 1977 to mark the company's golden jubilee.

The grand organ at John Wanamaker's department store in Philadelphia, installed in 1911, was enlarged until by 1930 it had six manuals and 30,067 pipes including a 64-ft tone Gravissima.

The loudest organ stop in the world is the Ophicleide stop of the

---

* "Music Facts and Feats," A Guinness Superlatives Book (Sterling) can be referred to for a more detailed treatment of musical facts and records.

OLDEST MUSICAL NOTATION: Clay tablet that dates from 1800 BC has been deciphered as the earliest musical scale preserved from ancient times.

Grand Great in the Solo Organ in the Atlantic City Auditorium (see above). It is operated by a pressure of 100 in of water (3½ lb per sq in) and has a pure trumpet note of earsplitting volume, more than 6 times the volume of the loudest locomotive whistles.

Most Durable Organist

The longest recorded career as an organist is 81 years in the case of Charles Bridgeman (1779–1873) of All Saints Parish Church, Hertford, England, who was appointed in 1792, and who was still playing in 1873. The year in which he reached his crescendo was not recorded.

Largest Double Bass

The largest double bass ever constructed was 14 ft tall, built in 1924 in Ironia, NJ by Arthur K. Ferris, allegedly on orders from the Archangel Gabriel. It weighed 1,300 lb with a sound box 8 ft across, and had leathern strings totaling 104 ft. Its low notes could be felt rather than heard.

Most Valuable Cello

The highest price paid at auction for a violoncello is $290,000 at Sotheby's, London on Nov 8, 1978 for a Stradivari made in Cremona, Italy in 1710.

Most Valuable Violin

The highest price ever paid at auction for a violin is $297,250 for one of the "Hubermann" *ex* Kreisler Stradivari dated 1733 at Sotheby's, London, on May 3, 1979. Some 700 of the 1,116 violins by Stradivarius (1644–1737) have survived. His inlaid "Hellier" violin was sold by private treaty in the US in March 1979, for a reported $400,000.

Underwater Violinist

The only violinist to surmount the problems of playing the violin under water has been Mark Gottlieb. Submerged in the Evergreen State

College swimming pool in Olympia, Wash, in March 1975, he gave his first submarine rendition of Handel's "Water Music." He is still working on the problems of bow speed and *détaché*. He joined with his sister, Karen, on the organ to perform the world's first underwater duet, a stirring rendition of "The Blue Danube," for the first "Guinness Spectacular" TV Show on ABC television in May 1979.

Most Durable Fiddler

Otto E. Funk, 62, walked 4,165 miles from NYC to San Francisco, playing his Hopf violin every step of the way westward. He arrived June 16, 1929, after 183 days on the road. Rolland S. Tapley retired as a violinist from the Boston Symphony Orchestra after playing for a reputedly unrivaled 58 years from Feb 1920 to Aug 27, 1978.

Stringed Instrument

The largest moveable stringed instrument ever constructed was a pantaleon with 270 strings stretched over 50 sq ft, used by George Noel in 1767. The greatest number of musicians required to operate a single instrument was the 6 needed to play the gigantic orchestrion, known as the Appolonican built in 1816 and played until 1840.

Largest and Most Expensive Guitars

The largest and presumably also the loudest playable guitar is an electric guitar 9 ft 10 in tall, weighing 380 lb, built by the Odessey Guitar Company of Vancouver, British Columbia, Canada. An example can be seen in the Guinness Museum in Niagara Falls, Ontario, Canada.

The most expensive standard-sized guitar is the German chittara battente, built by Jacob Stadler (dated 1624), which sold for £10,500 ($25,200) at Christie's, London, June 12, 1974.

The largest non-electric guitar was made by the Harmony Co of Chicago and stands 8 ft 10 in tall, weighs 80 lb and has a volume of 16,000 cu in (*cf,* the standard 1,024 cu in). Examples are exhibited in the Guinness Museums in NYC and San Francisco.

Brass Instruments

The largest recorded brass instrument is a tuba standing 7½ ft tall, with 39 ft of tubing and a bell 3 ft 4 in across. This contrabass tuba was constructed for a world tour by the band of John Philip Sousa (1854–1932), the "march king," *c.* 1896–98, and is still in use. This instrument is now owned by a circus promoter in South Africa.

Longest Alphorn

The longest alphorn is 43 ft 11½ in long, built from a spruce log by Herr Stocker in Switzerland in 1976. It weighs 70½ lb.

Largest Drum

The largest drum is the Disneyland Big Bass Drum with a diameter of 10 ft 6 in and a weight of 450 lb. It was built in 1961 by Remo, Inc of North Hollywood, Calif, is mounted on wheels and towed by a tractor.

MUSICAL INSTRUMENTS (reading clockwise from top left): LARGEST TUBA—7½ ft tall, it uses 39 ft of tubing. LARGEST GUITAR—8 ft 10 in tall, this is for two musicians to play together. It is on exhibit in the Guinness Museum. LARGEST ALPHORN—nearly 44 ft long, built in Switzerland in 1976. SMALLEST VIOLIN: Fully functional and only 2 in long, made by Morris Samskin of Brooklyn. Also in the Guinness Museum. LARGEST HARMONICA: Stan Harper is playing the Hohner 48-chord which has 354 separate holes. LARGEST ELECTRIC GUITAR: 9 ft 10 in tall, it weighs 380 lb.

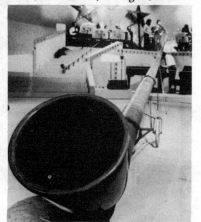

Easiest and Most Difficult Instruments

The American Music Conference announced in Sept 1977, that the easiest instrument is the ukelele and the most difficult are the French horn and the oboe. The latter has been described as "the ill woodwind that no one blows good."

Largest Orchestras

The most massive orchestra ever assembled was one of 20,100 at the Ullevaal Stadium, Oslo, June 28, 1964, made up of Norges Musikkorps Forbund bands from all over Norway.

On June 17, 1872, Johann Strauss the Younger (1825–99) conducted an orchestra of 987 instruments supported by a choir of 20,000, at the World Peace Jubilee in Boston, Mass. The number of first violinists was 400.

Largest Marching Band

The largest on record was one of 1,976 musicians and 54 drill majors, flag bearers and directors who marched 2 miles down Pennsylvania Ave, Washington, DC, in President Nixon's Second Inaugural Parade, Jan 20, 1973.

Greatest Classical Concert Attendance

The greatest attendance at any classical concert was an estimated 400,000 for a presentation by the Boston Pops Orchestra, conducted by Arthur Fiedler (b Dec 17, 1894, d July 10, 1979) at the Hatch Memorial Shell, Boston, Mass on July 4, 1977. At the 1978 concert the 83-year-old conductor was presented with a testimonial bearing a record 500,000 signatures.

Pop Festival Attendance

The greatest claimed attendance was 600,000 for a rock festival ("Summer Jam") at Watkins Glen, NY July 29, 1973. Of those attending, about 150,000 actually paid for admission. There were 12 "sound towers."

The highest recorded paid attendance for a single pop recording group in concert is 76,229 for an appearance by the British group Led Zeppelin, at the Silver Dome, Pontiac, Mich, April 30, 1977. The gross for this performance was a record $792,361.

One-Man Concert Attendance

The largest live audience ever attracted by a solo performer is an estimated 175,000 in the Maracaña Stadium, Rio de Janeiro, Brazil to hear Frank Sinatra (b 1917) sing on Jan 26, 1980.

Highest and Lowest Notes

The extremes of orchestral instruments (excluding the organ) range between a handbell tuned to g''''' or 6,272 cycles per sec, and the sub-contrabass clarinet, which can reach C,, or 16.4 cycles per sec. The highest note on a standard pianoforte is C''''', 4,186 cycles per sec, which is also the violinist's limit. In 1873, a sub double bassoon able to reach B,,,# or 14.6 cycles per sec was constructed, but no surviving specimen is

LARGEST PLANET: Jupiter, with an equatorial diameter of 88,780 miles and a volume 1,318 times that of the earth, is the largest planet in the solar system. Visible at the lower right is Ganymede, the heaviest satellite in the solar system and the largest of Jupiter's 14 moons. This photo was taken by Voyager 1 on Jan 24, 1979, from more than 25 million miles away.

FIRE-EATING: "Stromboli" demonstrates the art of the fire-eater in which he has ignited 136 flames from a single whisky glass of fuel.

A

LARGEST INDEX: The Ninth Collective Index of *Chemical Abstracts,* completed Aug 23, 1978, contains over 95,882 pages and 20,550,000 entries to form a 251-lb stack nearly 10 ft high, leaving the researcher with the choice of "looking it up" or "looking up to it."

HEAVIEST WATERMELON: Richard and Jason Bright have found a large plaything in this 200-lb watermelon grown by Ivan and Lloyd Bright in Hope, Ark, and reported to Grace's Gardens in Apr 1980.

CROOKEDEST STREET: Lombard Street in San Francisco between Hyde and Leavenworth has 5 consecutive hairpin turns as it descends steeply one way.

GREATEST EXPLOSION: The island of Santorini, off Greece in the Aegean Sea, was the scene of history's mightiest known eruption. The explosion which occurred about 1470 BC was 5 times greater than the explosion of Krakatoa, which has been estimated at 26 times greater than the greatest H-bomb ever detonated. Inset shows the crater vent.

D

LONGEST FALL WITHOUT A PARACHUTE: This is a recent photo of Vesna Vulovic, a Jugoslavenski Aerotransport hostess, who survived when her DC-9 blew up at 33,330 ft over Czechoslovakia in 1972 when she was 23 years old. She fell inside a section of the tail unit and was hospitalized for 16 months after emerging from a 27-day coma.

LARGEST ROPE: Consisting of 4 strands (each of 3,780 yarns), this coir fiber launching rope, made in 1858 by John and Edwin Wright for the British liner Great Eastern, measures nearly 4 ft in circumference.

E

BIG TOYS: This 27-ft-long Raggedy Ann doll (© Bobbs Merrill) (left) was made at Macy's "Clowning Around Day" in Aug 1979 and is on display at the Guinness Exhibit Hall in the Empire State Building, NYC. Tom Kuhn's 256-lb Custom Yo-Yo (below) was test-launched from a 100-ft crane in San Francisco in Oct 1979.

F

WINNING WOMEN: Golfer Nancy Lopez-Melton (left) won nearly $200,000 in prize money in 1979 to break the women's yearly earnings record that she had set the year before. Grete Waitz (#5, right) set the women's marathon record in the NYC Marathon in 1979 by breaking her own record, set on the same course one year earlier, by nearly 5 min.

ALPINE ACE: Sweden's Ingemar Stenmark has won 51 individual events in World Cup competition, the most by any man. His streak of 15 consecutive victories in the World Cup giant slalom is unmatched. He satisfied another career ambition by winning two Olympic gold medals in Lake Placid in 1980.

GREATEST CONCERT ATTENDANCE: The largest live audience ever attracted by a solo performer is an estimated 175,000 who crowded into the Maracaña Stadium (the world's largest soccer stadium), Rio de Janeiro, Brazil to hear Frank Sinatra sing on Jan 26, 1980.

H

known. The extremes for the organ are g′′′′′′ (the sixth G above middle C) (12,544 cycles per sec) and C₋ (8.12 cycles per sec) obtainable from ¾-in and 64-ft pipes, respectively.

Most Prolific Composers

The most prolific composer of all time was probably Georg Philipp Telemann (1681–1767) of Germany. He composed 12 complete sets of services (one cantata every Sunday) for a year, 78 services for special occasions, 40 operas, 600 to 700 orchestral suites, 44 Passions, plus concertos and chamber music.

The most prolific symphonist was Johann Melchior Molter (c. 1695–1765) of Germany, who wrote 165. Joseph Haydn (1732–1809) of Austria wrote 104 numbered symphonies, some of which are regularly played today.

Most Rapid Composer

Among classical composers the most rapid was Wolfgang Amadeus Mozart (1756–91) of Austria, who wrote c. 1,000 operas, operettas, symphonies, violin sonatas, divertimenti, serenades, motets, concertos for piano and many other instruments, string quartets, other chamber music, masses and litanies, of which only 70 were published before he died, aged 35. His opera *The Clemency of Titus* (1791) was written in 18 days and three symphonic masterpieces, *Symphony No. 39 in E flat major, Symphony in G minor* and the *"Jupiter" Symphony in C,* were reputedly written in the space of 42 days in 1788. His overture to *Don Giovanni* was written in full score at one sitting in Prague in 1787 and finished on the day of its opening performance.

Longest Silence

The most protracted silence in modern sheet music is one entitled *4 minutes 33 seconds* in a totally silent *opus* by John Cage (US). Commenting on this trend among young composers, Igor Fyodorovich Stravinsky (1882–1971) said that he looked forward to their subsequent compositions being "works of major length." The longest subsequently submitted, though not marketed, by a serious composer has been a modest 12¾ min "composed" on June 30, 1979.

Longest Symphony

The longest of all single classical symphonies is the orchestral *Symphony No. 3 in D minor* by Gustav Mahler (1860–1911) of Austria. This work, composed in 1896, requires a contralto, a women's and a boys' choir, in addition to a full orchestra. A full performance requires 1 hour 34 min, of which the first movement alone takes 32 min.

The *Symphony No. 2* (the Gothic, now renumbered as *No. 1*), composed in 1919–22 by Havergal Brian (1876–1972) was played by over 800 performers (4 brass bands) in the Victoria Hall, Hanley, Staffordshire, England on May 21, 1978, conducted by Trevor Stokes. Brian wrote an even vaster work based on Shelley's *Prometheus Unbound* lasting 4 hours 11 min but the full score has been missing since 1961.

The symphony *Victory at Sea* written by Richard Rodgers and arranged by Robert Russell Bennett for NBC-TV in 1952 lasted 13 hours.

Longest Piano Composition

The longest non-repetitious piece for piano ever composed was the Opus Clavicembalisticum by Kaikhosru Shapurji Sorabji (b 1892). The composer himself gave it its only public performance on Dec 1, 1930 in Glasgow, Scotland. The work is in 12 movements with a theme and 44 variations and a Passacaglia with 81 and a playing time of 2¾ hours.

Highest-Paid Pianist

The highest-paid classical concert pianist was Ignace Jan Paderewski (1860–1941), Prime Minister of Poland (1919–21) who accumulated a fortune estimated at $5 million of which $500,000 was earned in a single season in 1922–23. The *nouveau riche* wife of a US industrialist once required him to play behind a curtain.

Liberace (b May 16, 1917 West Allis, Wis) earns more than $2 million for each 26-week season with a peak of $138,000 for a single night's performance at Madison Square Garden, NYC, in 1954. His full name is Wladziu Valentino Liberace.

Pianist Sergei Vassilievitch Rachmaninov (1873–1943) had a span of 12 white notes and could play a left-hand chord of C, E flat, G, C, G.

Highest-Paid Violinist

The Austrian-born Fritz Kreisler (1875–1962) is reputed to have received more than $2 million during his career.

Highest-Paid Singers

Of great fortunes earned by singers, the highest on record are those of Enrico Caruso (1873–1921), the Italian tenor, whose estate was about $9 million, and the Italian-Spanish coloratura soprano Amelita Galli-Curci (1889–1963), who received about $3 million. In 1850, up to $653 was paid for a single seat at the concerts given in the US by Johanna ("Jenny") Maria Lind (1820–87), later Mrs Otto Goldschmidt, the "Swedish Nightingale." She had a range of nearly three octaves, of which the middle register is still regarded as unrivaled.

The tenor "Count" John Francis McCormack (1884–1945) of Ireland gave up to 10 concerts to capacity audiences in a single season in Carnegie Hall, NYC.

While no agreement exists as to the identity of history's greatest singer, there is unanimity on the worst. The excursions of the soprano Florence Foster Jenkins (1868–1944) into lieder and even high coloratura culminated on Oct 25, 1944 in her sell-out concert at Carnegie Hall, NYC. The diva's (already high) high F was said to have been made higher in 1943 by a crash in a taxi. It is one of the tragedies of musicology that Madame Jenkins' *Clavelitos,* accompanied by Cosme McMoon, was never recorded for posterity. Eight of her other "renderings" were, however.

Longest Opera

The longest of commonly performed operas is *Die Meistersinger von Nürnberg* by Wilhelm Richard Wagner (1813–83) of Germany. A normal uncut performance of this opera as performed by the Sadler's Wells com-

HIGHEST-PAID IN THEIR FIELDS: Liberace (left), the pianist, earns more than $2 million each season with a high of $138,000 for a single night. Enrico Caruso (right) left an estate of $9 million in 1921 after an operatic career, when taxes were low and the dollar worth more than today. In this photo he is dressed for the role of Pagliacci. His record of "Vesti la Giubba" was the first disc to sell one million.

pany between Aug 24 and Sept 19, 1968 entailed 5 hours 15 min of music. *The Heretics* by Gabriel von Wayditch, a Hungarian-American, is orchestrated for 110 pieces and lasts 8½ hours.

Shortest Opera

The shortest opera written was *The Deliverance of Theseus* by Darius Milhaud (b Sept 1892), first performed in 1928, which lasts for 7 min 27 sec.

Longest Aria

The longest single aria, in the sense of an operatic solo, is Brünnhilde's immolation scene in Wagner's *Götterdämmerung*. A well-known recording has been precisely timed at 14 min 46 sec.

Opera Houses

The largest is the Metropolitan Opera House, Lincoln Center, NYC, completed in Sept 1966, at a cost of $45,700,000. It has a capacity of 3,800 seats in an auditorium 451 ft deep. The stage is 234 ft in width and 146 ft deep.

The tallest opera house is one housed in a 42-story building on Wacker Drive in Chicago.

The Teatro della Scala (La Scala) in Milan, Italy, shares with the Bolshoi Theatre in Moscow, the distinction of having the greatest number of tiers. Each has 6 with the topmost being nicknamed the *Galiorka* by Russians.

Youngest and Oldest Opera Singers

The youngest opera singer in the world has been Jeanette Gloria (Ginetta) La Bianca, (b Buffalo, NY May 12, 1934) who made her official debut as Rosina in *The Barber of Seville* at the Teatro dell'Opera, Rome, May 8, 1950, aged 15 years 361 days, but who appeared as Gilda in *Rigoletto* at Velletri, Italy, 45 days earlier. Miss La Bianca was taught by Lucia Carlino and managed by Angelo Carlino.

The tenor Giovanni Martinelli sang Emperor Altoum in *Turandot* in Seattle, Wash Feb 4, 1967, when aged 81.

Longest Operatic Encore

The longest listed in the *Concise Oxford Dictionary of Opera* was of the entire opera of Cimarosa's called *Il Matrimonio Segreto* at its premiere in 1792. This was at the request of Austro-Hungarian Emperor Leopold II (1790–92).

Oldest Bell

The oldest bell is the tintinabulum found in the Babylonian Palace of Nimrod in 1849 by Mr (later Sir) Austen Henry Layard (1817–94). It dates from *c.* 1000 BC. The oldest known tower bell is one in Pisa, Italy dated MCXVII (1107).

Largest Carillon

The largest carillon (minimum of 23 bells) is the Laura Spelman Rockefeller Memorial carillon in Riverside Church, NYC. It has 74 bells weighing 112 tons. The bourdon weighs 40,926 lb. This bell, cast in England, with a diameter of 10 ft 2 in, is the largest *tuned* bell in the world.

Heaviest Bell

The heaviest bell is the Tsar Kolokol, cast on Nov 25, 1735 in Moscow. It weighs 216 tons, measures 19 ft 4¼ in in diameter, is 19 ft 3 in high, and its greatest thickness is 24 in. The bell is cracked, and a fragment, weighing about 12 tons, is broken from it. The bell has stood on a platform in the Kremlin, in Moscow, since 1836.

The heaviest bell in use is the Mingun bell, weighing 101.4 tons, in Mandalay, Burma, which is struck by a teak boom from the outside. It has a diameter of 16 ft 8½ in at the lip.

The heaviest swinging bell in the world is the Petersglocke in the southwest tower of Cologne Cathedral, Germany, cast in 1923, with a diameter of 11 ft 1¾ in, weighing 28.4 tons.

Bell Ringing

Eight bells have been rung to their full "extent" (40,320 unrepeated changes of Plain Bob Major) only once without relays. This took place in a bell foundry at Loughborough, Leicestershire, England, beginning at 6:52 a.m. on July 27, 1963 and ending at 12:50 a.m. on July 28, after 17 hours 58 min. The peal was composed by Kenneth Lewis of Altrincham, Cheshire, and the 8 ringers were conducted by Robert B. Smith, aged 25, of Marple, Cheshire. Theoretically it would take 37 years 355 days to ring 12 bells (maximus) to their full extent of 479,001,600 changes.

Oldest Song

The oldest is the *shaduf* chant, which has been sung since time immemorial by irrigation workers on the man-powered pivot-rod bucket raisers of the Nile water mills (or *saqiyas*) in Egypt. The oldest known harmonized music performed today is the English song *Sumer is icumen in* which dates from *c.* 1240.

HEAVIEST BELL (above): In the Kremlin in Moscow since 1836, this bell weighs 216 tons, is cracked, with a 12-ton fragment lost.

MOST SUCCESSFUL SONG WRITER: Paul McCartney, once of the Beatles, now of Wings, shows his collection of awards for his records.

Top Songs of All Time

The most frequently sung songs in English are *Happy Birthday to You* (based on the original *Good Morning to All,* by Mildred and Patty S. Hill of New York, published in 1935 and in copyright until 2010); *For He's a Jolly Good Fellow* (originally the French *Malbrouk*), known at least as early as 1781, and *Auld Lang Syne* (originally the Strathspey *I fee'd a Lad at Michaelmas*), some words of which were written by Robert Burns (1759–96). *Happy Birthday* was sung in space by the Apollo IX astronauts March 8, 1969.

Top Selling Sheet Music

Sales of three non-copyright pieces are known to have exceeded 20 million copies, namely *The Old Folks at Home* by Stephen Foster (1855), *Listen to the Mocking Bird* (1855) and *The Blue Danube* (1867). Of copyright material, the two top-sellers are *Let Me Call You Sweetheart* (1910, by Whitson and Friedman) and *Till We Meet Again* (1918, by Egan and Whiting), each with some 6 million by 1967. Other huge sellers have been *St Louis Blues, Stardust* and *Tea for Two.*

Most Successful Song Writer

In terms of sales of single records, the most successful of all song writers has been Paul McCartney, formerly of the Beatles and now of Wings. Between 1962 and Jan 1, 1978 he wrote jointly or solo 43 songs which sold one million or more records.

National Anthems

The oldest national anthem is the *Kimigayo* of Japan, in which the words date from the 9th century. The anthem of Greece constitutes the first four verses of the Solomos poem, which has 158 verses. The shortest anthems are those of Japan, Jordan and San Marino, each with only four lines. Of the 23 wordless national anthems, the oldest is that of Spain, dating from 1770.

Longest Rendering of an Anthem

"God Save the King" was played non-stop 16 or 17 times by a German military band on the platform of Rathenau Railway Station, Brandenburg, on the morning of Feb 9, 1909. The reason was that King Edward VII was struggling inside the train to get into his German Field-Marshal uniform before he could emerge.

Earliest Hymns

More than 950,000 Christian hymns are in existence. The earliest exactly datable hymn is the Heyr Rimna Smiour (Hear, the maker of heaven) from 1208 by the Icelandic bard and chieftain Kolbeinn Tumason (1173–1208). The music and parts of the text of a hymn in the *Oxyrhynchus Papyri* from the 2nd century are the earliest known hymnody.

Longest and Shortest Hymns

The longest hymn is *Hora novissima tempora pessima sunt; vigilemus* by Bernard of Cluny (12th century), which runs to 2,966 lines. In English the longest is *The Sands of Time are Sinking* by Mrs Anne Ross Cousin, *née* Cundell (1824–1906), which is in full 152 lines, though only 32 lines in the Methodist Hymn Book. The shortest hymn is the single verse in Long Metre *Be Present at our Table, Lord,* anonymous but attributed to "J. Leland."

Most Prolific Hymnists

Mrs Frances Jane Van Alstyne, *née* Crosby (US) (1820–1915), wrote more than 8,500 hymns although she had been blinded at the age of 6 weeks. She is reputed to have knocked off one hymn in 15 minutes. Charles Wesley (1707–88) wrote about 6,000 hymns. In the seventh (1950) edition of *Hymns Ancient and Modern* the works of John Mason Neale (1818–66) appear 56 times.

5. THEATRE

Theatre as we know it has its origins in Greek drama performed in honor of a god, usually Dionysus. The earliest amphitheatres date from the 5th century BC. The largest of all known is one at Megalopolis in central Greece, where the auditorium reached a height of 75 ft and had a capacity of 17,000. The first stone-built theatre in Rome (erected in 55 BC) could accommodate 40,000 spectators.

Oldest Theatre

The oldest indoor theatre is the Teatro Olimpico in Vicenza, Italy. Designed in the Roman style by Andrea di Pietro, *alias* Palladio (1508–80), it was begun three months before his death and finished in 1582 by his

LARGEST ALL-PURPOSE THEATRE: The Perth Entertainment Centre in Western Australia seats 8,003 people and boasts a stage area of 12,000 sq ft.

pupil Vincenzo Scamozzi (1552–1616). It is preserved today in its original form.

Largest and Smallest Theatres

The largest building used for theatre is the National People's Congress Building (*Ren min da hui tang*) on the west side of Tian an men Square, Peking, China. It was completed in 1959 and covers an area of 12.9 acres. The theatre seats 10,000 and is only occasionally used as such, as in 1964 for the play "The East Is Red."

The highest capacity purpose-built theatre is the Perth Entertainment Centre in Western Australia, completed at a cost in Australian dollars of $8.3 million in Nov 1976, with a capacity of 8,003 seats. The stage area is 12,000 sq ft.

The smallest regularly operated professional theatre is the Mull Little Theatre, near Dervaig, Isle of Mull, Scotland, with a capacity of 36 seats.

Largest Amphitheatre

The largest amphitheatre ever built is the Flavian amphitheatre or Colosseum of Rome, Italy, completed in 80 AD. Covering 5 acres and with a capacity of 87,000, it has a maximum length of 612 ft and maximum width of 515 ft.

Largest Stage

The largest stage is in the Ziegfeld Room, Reno, Nev with a 176-ft passenelle, 3 main elevators capable of lifting 1,200 show girls, two 62½ ft circumference turntables and 800 spotlights.

Longest Runs

The longest continuous run of any show is of *The Mousetrap* by Agatha Christie (Lady Mallowan) (1890–1976). This thriller opened at the Ambassadors Theatre (capacity 453), London, Nov 25, 1952 and moved after 8,862 performances "down the road" to St. Martin's The-

LONGEST RUNNING "BROADWAY" SHOW: Kenneth Waissman, producer of "Grease," accepts a certificate presented by Geri Martin of the Guinness staff during a celebration held on the stage of the Royale Theatre, NYC, as the record 3,243rd performance takes place. Almost all the actors who had performed in the show gathered for the party.

atre, London, March 25, 1974. The Silver Jubilee performance on Nov 25, 1977 was No. 10,390, and the 11,500th was on July 22, 1980.

The greatest number of performances of any theatrical presentation is 45,140 (to April 27, 1980) in the case of *The Golden Horseshoe Revue*—a show staged at Disneyland Park, Anaheim, Calif. The show was first put on on July 17, 1955. The three main performers, Wally Boag, Fulton Burley, and Betty Taylor, play as many as five houses a day in a routine lasting 45 min.

The long-run record for any "Broadway" show was set on Dec 8, 1979 when *Grease* was performed for the 3,243rd time, beating the record of *Fiddler on the Roof.* After opening at the Eden Theatre on Feb 14, 1972, *Grease* moved to the Royale Theatre on Nov 27, 1972, where it finally closed on Apr 13, 1980, after a total of 3,388 performances. The book, music and lyrics were written by Jim Jacobs (b Chicago, 1942) and Warren Casey (b Yonkers, NY, 1935). Profits of $4 million have accrued to the producers Kenneth Waissman and his wife Maxine Fox from the gross $70 million in the US alone including motion picture profits.

The off-Broadway musical show *The Fantasticks* by Tom Jones and Harvey Schmidt achieved its 8,318th performance as it entered its 21st year at the Sullivan Street Playhouse, Greenwich Village, NYC May 3, 1980. It has been played in a record 3,788 productions in 55 countries.

One-Man Shows

The longest run of one-man shows is 849 by Victor Borge in his *Comedy in Music* from Oct 2, 1953, to Jan 21, 1956, at the Golden Theater, NYC.

The world aggregate record for one-man shows is 1,700 performances of *Brief Lives* by Roy Dotrice (b Guernsey, England, May 5, 1923) including 400 straight at the Mayfair Theatre, London, ending July 20, 1974. He was on stage for more than 2½ hours per performance of this 17th century monologue, and required 3 hours for makeup and 1 hour for removal, thus aggregating 40 weeks in the chair as well.

Youngest Broadway Producer

Margo Feiden (Margo Eden) (b NY, Dec 2, 1944) produced the musical *Peter Pan,* which opened Apr 3, 1961, when she was 16 years 5 months old. She wrote *Out Brief Candle,* which opened Aug 18, 1962, and is now a leading art dealer.

Longest Play

The longest recorded theatrical production has been *The Warp* by Neil Oram, directed by Ken Campbell, a 10-part play cycle played at the Institute of Contemporary Art, the Mall, London, Jan 18–20, 1979. Russell Denton was on stage for all but 5 min of the 18 hours 5 min. The three intermissions totaled 3 hours 10 min.

Most Durable Actor

Richard Hearne (b Norwich, England, Jan 30, 1909, d 1979) played a baby at the age of 6 weeks and performed continuously through childhood in circus, pantomime and musical comedy. On Christmas 1977, he was in *Cinderella* at the London Palladium.

Most Durable Leading Actress

Dame Anna Neagle (b Oct 20, 1904) played the lead in *Charlie Girl* at the Adelphi Theatre, London, England, for 2,062 of 2,202 performances between Dec 15, 1965 and March 27, 1971. She played the same rôle a further 327 times in 327 performances in Australasia.

Most Ardent Theatregoers

The highest precisely recorded number of paid theatre attendances is 3,400 shows in 27 years from March 28, 1953 to March 28, 1980, by John Iles of Salisbury, Wiltshire, England. He estimates that he has traveled 140,181 miles and seen 149,091 performers, spending 8,814 hours (over 52 weeks) inside theatres.

It has been estimated by the press that H. Howard Hughes (b 1904) of Fort Worth, Tex, had seen 4,160 shows in the period 1956–1976.

Edward Sutro (1900–78) in England saw 3,000 first-night productions from 1916 to 1956, and possibly more than 5,000 in his 60 years of theatre-going.

Shakespeare

The first all-amateur company to have staged all 37 of Shakespeare's

---

Shortest Runs

The shortest run on record was that of *The Intimate Revue* at the Duchess Theatre, London, March 11, 1930. Anything which could go wrong did. With scene changes taking up to 20 minutes apiece, the management scrapped seven scenes to get the finale on before midnight. The run was described as "half a performance."

A number of Broadway productions open and close the same night. There were 11 such "turkeys" in the 1978–79 season.

The largest loss from a short run was $2 million poured down the drain by *Ballroom* in 1979.

MAN OF 1,000 DISGUISES: Jan Leighton of NYC has played 1,632 historical roles on television, on the stage and for advertising. Left to right are Leighton as (top row) Sherlock Holmes, Popeye, Groucho Marx; (bottom row) Albert Einstein, Napoleon and Leighton himself, undisguised.

plays was The Southsea Shakespeare Actors, Hampshire, England, when in Oct 1966, they presented *Cymbeline*. The amateur director throughout was K. Edmonds Gateloy.

Ten members of the English Speaking Theatre, Amsterdam, completed a dramatic reading of all 37 plays, 154 sonnets and five narrative poems in 30 hours exactly, Apr 26–27, 1980. (*This category has now been retired.*)

The longest play is *Hamlet,* with 4,042 lines and 29,551 words, 1,242 words longer than *Richard III.* Of Shakespeare's 1,277 speaking parts, the longest is the title role in *Hamlet* with 11,610 words.

Most Roles

The greatest recorded number of theatrical, film and television rôles is 1,632 from 1951 to Apr 1980 by Jan Leighton (US).

Ice Shows

Holiday on Ice Productions Inc, founded by Morris Chalfen in 1945, stages the world's most costly live entertainment with its seven productions playing simultaneously in several of 75 countries drawing 20 million spectators paying $40 million in a year. The total number of skaters and other personnel exceeds 900.

Shortest Criticism

The shortest dramatic criticism in theatrical history was that attributed to Wolcott Gibbs (1902–58), writing about the farce *Wham!* He wrote the single word "Ouch!"

Cabaret

The highest night-club fee in history was $100,000 collected by Liza Minnelli (b March 12, 1946) for the New Year's Eve show at The Colonie Hill Club, Long Island, NY, Jan 1, 1975. Patrons paid $150 per seat.

Longest Chorus Line

The longest permanent chorus line is formed by the Rockettes in the Radio City Music Hall, NYC, which opened in Dec 1932. The 36 girls dance precision routines across the 144-ft-wide stage.

MOST MEDIA AWARDS FOR AN ACTRESS (right, below): Rita Moreno, seen here talking to her friend, Kermit, has won an Oscar, a Tony, a Grammy and an Emmy for her performance in movies, theatre, on records and on television.

LONGEST RUN FOR ONE-MAN SHOWS: Victor Borge (above) played 849 times in 27 months.

LONGEST CHORUS LINE: Stretching across the 144-ft-wide stage at Radio City Music Hall in NYC, the Rockettes are 36 girls strong.

Professional Wrestling

Kanji Antonio Inoki of Japan received $2 million for the wrestler vs boxer bout against Muhammad Ali (draw) in Tokyo, June 26, 1976. Lou Thesz (still active) has won 7 of the world's many "world" titles. "Fabulous" Moolah has won major US women's alliance titles every year since 1956. The heaviest wrestler ever has been William J. Cobb of Macon, Ga (b 1926), who was billed in 1962 as the 802-lb "Happy" Humphrey. Ed "Strangler" Lewis (1890–1966), *né* Robert H. Friedrich, fought 6,200 bouts in 44 years, losing only 33 matches. He won world titles in 1921, 1922, 1928 and 1931–32.

6. RADIO BROADCASTING

The earliest description of a radio transmission system was written by Dr Mahlon Loomis (b Fulton County, NY, July 21, 1826, d 1886) on July 21, 1864, and demonstrated between two kites at Bear's Den, Loudoun County, Va, in Oct 1866. He received US Patent No. 129971, entitled Improvement in Telegraphing, on July 20, 1872.

Earliest Patent

The first patent for a system of communication by means of electromagnetic waves, numbered No. 12039, was granted June 2, 1896, to the Italian-Irish Marchese, Guglielmo Marconi (1874–1937). A public demonstration of wireless transmission of speech was given in the town square of Murray, Ky, in 1892 by Nathan B. Stubblefield. He died, destitute, March 28, 1928. The first permanent wireless installation was at The Needles on the Isle of Wight, Hampshire, England, by Marconi's Wireless Telegraph Co, Ltd, in Nov 1896.

Earliest Broadcast

The first advertised broadcast was made on Dec 24, 1906, by Canadian-born Prof Reginald Aubrey Fessenden (1868–1932) from the 420-ft mast of the National Electric Signaling Company at Brant Rock, Mass. The transmission included Handel's *Largo*. Fessenden had achieved the broadcast of speech as early as Nov 1900, but this was highly distorted.

Transatlantic Transmissions

The earliest transatlantic wireless signals (the letter S in Morse Code) were received by Marconi, George Stephen Kemp and Percy Paget from a 10-kilowatt station at Poldhu, Cornwall, England, at Signal Hill, St John's, Newfoundland, Canada, at 12:30 p.m. Dec 12, 1901. Human speech was first heard across the Atlantic in Nov 1915, when a transmission from the US Navy station at Arlington, Va, was received by US radio-telephone engineers up on the Eiffel Tower, Paris.

Earliest Radio-Microphone

The first radio-microphone, which was in essence also the first "bug," was devised by Reg Moores (GB) in 1947, and first used on 76 MHz in the ice show *Aladdin* at Brighton Sports Stadium, England, in Sept 1949.

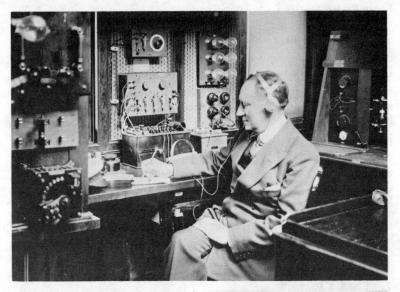

INVENTORS: Radio was first patented by Guglielmo Marconi (above) on June 2, 1896. John Logie Baird (right), seated here before one of his early transmitters, gave the earliest public demonstration of television, using a mechanical scanning system. Thomas Alva Edison (below), one of the most versatile inventors, not only developed electric light, but created the first practical phonograph. He is seen here in his study with a cylinder machine.

Most Radio Stations

The country with the greatest number of radio broadcasting stations is the US. In 1978, there were 8,608 authorized, of which 4,547 were AM and 4,061 FM.

Longest Radio Broadcast

The longest continuous radio broadcast (excluding disc-jockeying) has been one of 336 hours by Bill Tinsley of WATN radio, Watertown, NY, March 17–31, 1979.

Highest Radio Listener Response

The highest recorded response to a radio show occurred Nov 27, 1974, when on a 5-hour talk show on WCAU, Philadelphia, Howard Sheldon, the astrologist, registered a total of 388,299 calls on the "Bill Corsair Show."

BBC Radio set a 30 million adult listener record on June 6, 1950 for a boxing match between Lee Savold (US) and Bruce Woodcock (GB).

7. TELEVISION

The invention of television, the instantaneous viewing of distant objects, was not an act but a process of successive and interdependent discoveries. The first commercial cathode ray tube was introduced in 1897 by Karl Ferdinand Braun (1850–1918), but was not linked to "electric vision" until 1907 by Boris Rosing of Russia in St Petersburg (now Leningrad). A. A. Campbell Swinton (GB 1863–1930) published the fundament of television transmission on June 18, 1908 in a brief letter to *Nature* entitled "Distant Electric Vision." The earliest public demonstration of television was given on Jan 27, 1926, by John Logie Baird (1888–1946) of Scotland, using a development of the mechanical scanning system suggested by Paul Nipkov in 1884. He had achieved the transmission of a Maltese Cross over 10 ft in Hastings, East Sussex, England, in Feb 1924, and the first facial image (of William Taynton, 15) on Oct 30, 1925. Taynton had to be bribed with 2 shillings sixpence. A patent application for the Iconoscope had been filed Dec 29, 1923, by Dr Vladimir Kosma Zworykin (born in Russia 1889, became a US citizen in 1924), though not issued until Dec 20, 1938. The patent application filed on Jan 7, 1927, by Philo Taylor Farnsworth (US) was, however, granted on Aug 26, 1930. Farnsworth succeeded with a low-definition image at 202 Green Street, Los Angeles, in Nov 1927.

Video Tape Recording

Alexander M. Poniatoff first demonstrated video tape recording, known as Ampex (his initials plus "ex" for excellence) in 1956.

Earliest Service

The first high-definition television broadcasting service was opened from Alexandra Palace, London, Nov 2, 1936, when there were about 100 sets in the UK. A television station in Berlin, Germany, began low-definition (180 line) transmission March 22, 1935. The transmitter burned out in Aug 1935.

Most Transmitters and Sets

In 1977, the total estimated number of television transmitters in use or under construction was 20,000 serving 384 million sets (90 per 1,000 people worldwide).

In the US, where 98% of the population was reached by 1976, the number of homes with color sets was 60,395,000 by mid-1979.

Television Viewing

In July 1978 it was estimated that the *average* American child, by his or her 18th birthday, has watched the equivalent of 710 solid days (17,040 hours) of TV, seen more than 350,000 commercials and more than 15,000 TV murders. There are 571 TV sets per 1,000 people in the US compared with 348 in Sweden and 330 in Britain.

Iceland has a TV-free day on Thursday to reduce disruption of family life. Otherwise transmissions are normally limited to between 8 and 11 p.m. Upper Volta had only one set for each 1,000 inhabitants by 1974.

Smallest Set

The smallest TV set is the 26-oz Sinclair "Microvision" with overall dimensions of 7 × 2 × 3½ in and a screen measuring 2 in diagonally, manufactured by Sinclair Radionics Ltd of Cambridgeshire, England.

SMALLEST TV: With a screen that measures 2 in diagonally, this set is easily portable.

Transatlantic Transmissions

The earliest transatlantic transmission by satellite was achieved at 1 a.m. July 11, 1962, *via* the active satellite *Telstar I* from Andover, Me, to Pleumeur Bodou, France. The picture was of Frederick R. Kappell, chairman of the American Telephone and Telegraph Company, which owned the satellite. The first "live" broadcast was made July 23, 1962, and the first woman to appear was the *haute couturière* Ginette Spanier, directrice of Balmain, Paris, the next day. On Feb 9, 1928, the image of John Logie Baird (see above) and a Mrs Howe was transmitted from Station 2KZ at Coulsdon, Surrey, England, to Station 2CVJ, Hartsdale, NY.

Greatest TV Audience

The greatest number of viewers for a televised event is an estimated 1,000 million for the live and recorded transmissions of the XXth and XXIst Olympic Games in Munich and Montreal in 1972 and 1976. The estimate for the papal visit to Ireland by Pope John Paul II on Sept 29, 1979 was also 1,000 million.

The program which attracted the highest viewership was the episode of *Roots* first transmitted by ABC on Jan 30, 1977 to an estimated 36,380,000 households in the US.

Largest TV Prizes

The greatest amount won by an individual in TV prizes was $264,000 by Teddy Nadler (b 1910) of St Louis on quiz programs in the US up to Sept 1958. He reportedly had to pay $155,000 in federal and state taxes, and has been unemployed since.

On July 24, 1975, WABC-TV, NYC transmitted the first televised Grand Tier draw of the State Lottery in which the winner took the grand prize of $1 million. This was, of course, taxable.

Don Chu of Forrest City, Ark, won $128,000 on a quiz show aired by KTVE-TV June 18, 1977. Barbara Anne Eddy of Vancouver, British Columbia, won the same amount on this show taped Feb 1, 1978, but a Canadian pays no tax.

Largest Contracts

The largest TV contract ever signed was one for $34 million in a three-year no-option contract between Dean Martin (b Dino Paul Crocetti, June 7, 1917) and NBC in 1968.

Currently, television's highest-paid performer is Johnny Carson, the host of the *Tonight* show. His current five-year NBC contract reportedly calls for annual payments of some $2,500,000 for a 125-day working year, with perhaps double that in percentages on commercial fees. His revised contract will call for a shorter working year.

The highest-paid current affairs or news performer is Barbara Walters, who signed a 5-year contract with ABC in Apr 1976 for about $1 million per year.

Mary Tyler Moore (b Dec 29, 1937), as head of her own production company, reputedly earned some $2,250,000 for the last series of episodes of the show in which she starred, which ended in 1977.

Peter Falk (b Sept 16, 1927) was paid from $300,000 to $350,000 per single episode (six total) for his series *Columbo,* so totaling $1,950,000 in 1976.

Commercial Payments

In 1977, James Coburn of Beverly Hills, Calif was reputedly paid $500,000 for uttering two words on a series of Schlitz beer commercials. The words "Schlitz Light" were thus priced at a quarter of a million dollars per syllable.

Brooke Shields (b May 31, 1965) was reportedly paid $250,000 for one minute of film by a Japanese TV commercial film maker in 1979.

Faye Dunaway was reported in May 1979 to have been paid $900,000 for uttering 6 words for a Japanese department store TV commercial.

The same Brooke Bond chimpanzee commercial first transmitted on Nov 21, 1921 in England has been repeated 1,687 more times up to Oct 1979.

TOPS IN TV PAY: No one has surpassed the record $34 million contract that NBC paid Dean Martin (left) in 1968. Nor has any TV commentator topped the $1 million per year that Barbara Walters (center) gets from ABC. Johnny Carson (right) may work less and get the same $2½ million a year from NBC in the future.

Most Takes for a TV Commercial

The highest number of "takes" for a TV commercial was 28 by Pat Coombs, the comedienne, who in 1973 supported Dick Emery on BBC-TV. Her explanation was: "Every time we came to the punch line I just could not remember the name of the product."

Largest Production

The BBC production of the 37 plays of Shakespeare in 1978–84 will cost a minimum of $14 million. The series was conceived by its producer, Cedric Messina.

Longest Program

The longest pre-scheduled telecast on record was one of 163 hours 18 min by GTV 9 of Melbourne, Australia, covering the Apollo XI moon mission July 19–26, 1969. The longest continuous TV transmission under a single director was the Avro Television Production *Open Het Dorpe* transmitted in the Netherlands Nov 26–27, 1962 for 23 hours 20 min under the direction of Theo Ordaman.

Most Durable TV Show

The most durable is NBC's *Meet the Press,* first transmitted Nov 6, 1947 and weekly since Sept 12, 1948. It was originated by Lawrence E. Spivak, who until 1975 appeared weekly as either moderator or panel member.

Greatest Sale

The greatest number of episodes of any TV program ever sold was 1,144 episodes of *Coronation Street* to CBKST, Saskatoon, Saskatchewan, Canada, by Granada Television, May 31, 1971. This constituted 20 days 15 hours 44 min of continuous viewing.

Most Successful Telethons

The most successful TV appeals are those transmitted in New Zealand. The telethon appeal on South Pacific TV, Auckland, in 1978 for the Arthritis and Rheumatism Foundation raised $3,002,750 from an audience of 2,550,000 people, for the per capita record.

Most Prolific Scriptwriter

The most prolific television writer is the Rt. Hon. Lord Willis (b Jan 13, 1918), who in the period 1949–79 has created 24 series, 25 stage plays, and 22 feature films. His total output since 1945 can be estimated at 15,500,000 words.

Highest TV Advertising Rates

The highest TV advertising rate was reportedly $468,000 per minute for CBS network prime time during the transmission of Super Bowl XIV, Jan 20, 1980.

8. MOTION PICTURES*

The greatest impetus in the development of cinematography came from the inventiveness of Etienne Jules Marey (1830–1903) of France in the 1870's.

The earliest demonstration of a celluloid cinematograph film on a screen was given at 44 Rue de Rennes, Paris, France, March 22, 1895, by Auguste Marie Louis Nicolas Lumière (1862–1954) and Louis Jean Lumière (1864–1948), French brothers. The film was entitled *La Sortie des Ouvriers de l'Usine Lumière,* taken probably in Aug or Sept 1894, outside the factory gates at Lyons. Louis Aimé Augustin Le Prince, according to evidence in *The Shell Book of Firsts,* achieved dim moving outlines on a white-washed wall at the Institute for the Deaf, Washington Heights, NYC, as early as 1885.

Earliest Sound Movie

The earliest sound-on-film motion picture was achieved by Eugene Augustin Lauste (b Paris, Jan 17, 1857) who patented his process Aug 11, 1906 and produced a workable system using a string galvanometer in 1910 in London. The event is more usually attributed to Dr Lee de Forest (1873–1961) in NYC, March 13, 1923. The first all-talking picture was *Lights of New York,* shown at the Strand Theatre, NYC, July 6, 1928.

Movie-Going

The people of Taiwan go to the movies more often than those of any other country in the world, with an average of 66 attendances per person per year according to the latest data. The Soviet Union claims to have the most movie theatres in the world, with 163,400 in 1974, but this includes buildings equipped with 16-mm projectors. The US has some 16,000 actual movie theatres.

Largest Movie Theatre

The largest is the Radio City Music Hall, NYC, opened on Dec 27, 1932, with 5,945 seats (now 5,882). The Roxy, opened in NYC on March 11, 1927, had 6,214 seats but was closed March 29, 1960.

---

* For more records and greater details on this subject, see *Movie Facts and Feats, A Guinness Record Book* by Patrick Robertson (1980, Sterling).

Movie Theatre Seats

The Falkland Islands (off South America) and the Cook Islands (in the South Pacific) have more seats for watching films per total population than any other country, with 250 for each 1,000 inhabitants. The least number are in the Central African Empire which has 8 theatres.

The world's largest drive-in cinema is at Newington, Conn, with a capacity for 4,000 cars.

Oldest Movie Theatre

The earliest structure designed and exclusively used for exhibiting projected films is believed to be one erected at the Atlanta Show, Ga in Oct 1895, to exhibit C. F. Jenkins' phantoscope.

Biggest Screen

The permanently installed cinema screen with the largest area is one 70 ft tall × 96 ft wide, installed in the Pictorium Theater at Marriott's Great America Entertainment Center, Santa Clara, Calif, May 16, 1978. It was made by Harkness Screens Ltd of Hertfordshire, England.

A temporary screen 297×33 ft was used at the 1937 Paris Exposition.

Most and Least Expensive Films

The most expensive film ever completed has been *Star Trek* which received its world premiere in Washington, DC on Dec 6, 1979. Paramount stated that the cost of this space epic directed by Gene Roddenberry, was $46 million. *War and Peace,* the USSR government adaptation of the masterpiece of Tolstoy directed by Sergei Bondarchuk (b 1921) over the period 1962–67, is said to have cost more than $96 million. More than 165,000 uniforms had to be made. The re-creation of the Battle of Borodino involved 120,000 Red Army "extras" at 3 rubles ($3.30) per month. The film runs for 6 hours 13 min.

The least expensive film was Cecil Hepworth's highly successful release of *Rescued by Rover* in 1905 in England which cost $37.40.

Film Rights

The highest price ever paid for film rights is $9,500,000 announced on Jan 20, 1978 by Columbia for *Annie,* the Broadway musical by Charles Strouse starring Andrea McArdle, Dorothy Loudon and Reid Shelton based on the comic strip *Little Orphan Annie,* which opened at the Alvin Theater in NYC on Apr 21, 1977.

Highest Box Office Gross

The film with the highest world gross earnings is *Star Wars,* written and produced by Gary Kurtz and directed by George Lucas, which from May 25, 1977 to Jan 1, 1979 grossed $267 million worldwide.

Longest Film

Out One: Noli me tangere directed by Jacques Rivette (b Rouen, March 1, 1928) lasted 12 hours 40 min, but was only shown once at Le Havre, France, Sept 9–10, 1971.

The longest film ever released was * * * * by Andy Warhol (b Andrew Warhola in Cleveland, Ohio, 1931), which lasted 24 hours. It proved, not surprisingly, except reportedly to its creator, a commercial failure, and was withdrawn and re-released in 90-minute form as *The Loves of Ondine.*

Highest Earnings by an Actor

The highest rate of pay in cinema history is being contested between Marlon Brando (b Apr 3, 1924) for his brief part in *Superman* and Steve McQueen (b 1930) for his role in *Tai Pan*. Each received in excess of $2,500,000, but the final amount will depend on box office percentages.

Dar Robinson was paid $100,000 for the 1,100-ft-high leap he made from the CN Tower in Toronto in Nov 1979 for *High Point*. His parachute opened at only 300 ft above the ground.

Largest Studios

The largest complex of film studios are those of Universal Studios at Universal City, Los Angeles. The back lot contains 561 buildings. There are 34 sound stages.

Most Oscars

Walter (Walt) Elias Disney (1901–66) won more "Oscars"—the awards of the Academy of Motion Picture Arts and Sciences, instituted on May 16, 1929, for 1927–28—than any other person. The physical count comprises 20 statuettes and nine other plaques and certificates, including posthumous awards.

The films with most awards have been *Ben Hur* (1959) with 11, followed by *Gone with the Wind* (1939) and *West Side Story* (1961), both with 10. The film with the highest number of nominations was *All About Eve* (1950) with 14. It won 6.

The only performer to win three Oscars for her starring rôles has been Katharine Hepburn (b Nov 9, 1909), in *Morning Glory* (1933), *Guess Who's Coming to Dinner* (1967) and *The Lion in Winter* (1968). She was nominated 11 times. All three Oscars are on display at the Guinness World Records Exhibit Hall in the Empire State Building in NYC.

Only 4 actors have won 2 Oscars in starring roles—Fredric March in 1932, 1946; Spencer Tracy in 1937–38, Gary Cooper in 1941–1952; and Marlon Brando in 1954–1972.

The youngest person ever to win an Oscar was Shirley Temple with her 1934 award at age 6, and the oldest is George Burns at age 80 for *The Sunshine Boys* in 1976.

Oscars are named after Oscar Pierce of Texas. When the figurines were first delivered to the executive offices of the Academy of Motion Picture Arts and Sciences, the Executive Secretary exclaimed, "Why, they look just like my Uncle Oscar." And the name stuck.

CINEMA WINNERS:
Walt Disney (above) with
his 29 Academy Awards.
(Right) Katharine
Hepburn won 3 Oscars for
starring roles. (Below,
left) Marlon Brando, the
highest-paid actor played
in "The Godfather" with
Al Pacino. (Below, right)
"Star Wars" is the biggest
money-making movie, and
here are two of the robot
stars.

9. PHONOGRAPH

The phonograph was first *conceived* by Charles Cros (1842–88), a French poet and scientist who described his idea in sealed papers deposited in the French Academy of Sciences Apr 30, 1877. The first practical device was realized by Thomas Alva Edison (1847–1931), who gained his first patent Feb 19, 1878 for a machine constructed by his mechanic, John Kruesi. It was first demonstrated on Dec 7, 1877.

The first practical hand-cranked, wax-coated-cylinder phonograph was manufactured in the US by Chichester Bell and Charles Sumner Tainter in 1886. The forerunner of the modern disc phonograph was patented in 1887 by Emile Berliner (1851–1929), a German immigrant to the US. Although a toy machine based on his principle was produced in Germany in 1889, the gramophone was not a serious commercial competitor to the cylinder phonograph until 1896.

Pre-recorded tapes were first marketed by Recording Associates in NYC in 1950.

The country with the greatest number of record players is the US with an estimated 75,300,000 by Dec 1976. A total of more than half a billion dollars is spent annually on 500,000 juke boxes in the US.

Sales in the US of discs and tapes reached $2,740 million in 1976, which includes sales of 273 million stereo LP's, 190 million singles and 127.8 million stereo tapes.

Oldest Records

The oldest record in the BBC library is an Edison solid-wax cylinder, recorded in Edison's laboratory and dated June 26, 1888. The BBC library, the world's largest, contains over 750,000 records, including 5,250 with no known matrix. The library also contains a collection of early Berliner discs. Their disc, *Sweet Marie,* sung by George Gaskin, was most probably made in 1895.

The earliest jazz record made was *Indiana* and *The Dark Town Strutters Ball,* recorded for the Columbia label in NYC on or about Jan 30, 1917 by the Original Dixieland Jazz Band, led by Dominick (Nick) James La Rocca (1889–1961). This was released May 31, 1917. The first jazz record to be released was the ODJB's *Livery Stable Blues* (recorded Feb 24), backed by *The Dixie Jass Band One-Step* (recorded Feb 26), released by Victor on March 7, 1917.

Smallest Record

The smallest functional record is one 1⅜ inches in diameter of *God Save the King* of which 250 were made by HMV Record Co in 1924.

Most Successful Recording Artists

On June 9, 1960 the Hollywood Chamber of Commerce presented Harry Lillis (*alias* Bing) Crosby, Jr (1904–77) with a platinum disc to commemorate the alleged sale of 200 million from 2,600 singles and 125 albums he had recorded. On Sept 15, 1970 he received a second platinum disc when Decca Records claimed a sale of 300,650,000 discs.

Crosby's first commercial recording was *I've Got the Girl* recorded on Oct 18, 1926 (master number W142785 [Take 3] issued on the Columbia

TOP-SELLING SINGERS: Bing Crosby (left) received a platinum record in 1960 to commemorate his 200-millionth record sale. Elvis Presley (right) earned a record 38 golden discs.

label), and his first million-seller was *Sweet Leilani* in 1937. No independently audited figures of his global lifetime sales from his royalty reports have ever been published, and experts regard figures so high as this, before the industry became highly developed, as exaggerated.

Similarly no independently audited figures have been published for Elvis Aaron Presley (b Tupelo, Miss, 1935, d 1977). In view of Presley's 150 major hits on singles and 70 best-selling albums from 1956 and continuing after his death, it may be assumed that it was he who succeeded Crosby as the top-selling solo artist of his time.

Most Successful Group

The singers with the greatest sales of any group have been The Beatles. This group from Liverpool, England, comprised George Harrison (b Feb 25, 1943), John Ono (formerly John Winston) Lennon (b Oct 9, 1940), James Paul McCartney (b June 18, 1942) and Richard Starkey, *alias* Ringo Starr (b July 7, 1940).

The all-time Beatles sales by the end of 1978 have been estimated at 100 million singles and 100 million albums—a total unmatched by any other recording act.

Earliest Golden Disc

The first recorded piece to sell a million copies and become a "golden disc" were performances by Enrico Caruso (b Naples, Italy, 1873, d 1921) of the aria *Vesti la giubba* (*On with the Motley*) from the opera *I Pagliacci* by Ruggiero Leoncavallo (1858–1919), the earliest version of which was recorded on Nov 12, 1902.

The first single recording to surpass the million mark was Alma Gluck's rendition of *Carry Me Back to Old Virginny* on the Red Seal Victor label on a 12-in single-faced (later backed) record (No. 74420).

The first actual golden disc was one sprayed by RCA Victor for presentation to Glenn Miller (1904–44) for his *Chattanooga Choo Choo* on Feb 10, 1942.

Most Golden Discs

The only *audited* measure of million-selling singles and 500,000-selling albums within the US is certification by the Recording Industry Association of America introduced March 14, 1958. Out of the 2,644 RIAA gold-record awards made to May 1, 1980, the most have gone to The Beatles with 42 (plus one with Billy Preston) as a group. Paul McCartney has an additional 20 awards outside the group with Wings.

The most awards to an individual is 38 to Elvis Presley, spanning 1958 to Jan 1, 1979. Globally, however, Presley's total of million-selling singles has been authoritatively put at "approaching 80." Presley's biggest earning year of 1965 ($4.7 million) was almost surpassed by his estate's earnings of $4,993,897 in the 12 months following his death. His twin brother had died at birth.

Most-Recorded Songs

Two songs have each been recorded over 1,000 times—*Yesterday* by Paul McCartney and John Lennon, with 1,186 versions between 1965 and Jan 1, 1973, and *Tie a Yellow Ribbon Round the Old Oak Tree,* written by Irwin Levine and L. Russell Brown, with more than 1,000 versions recorded from 1973 to Jan 1, 1979.

Biggest Sellers

The greatest seller of any record to date is *White Christmas* by Irving Berlin (b Israel Bailin, at Tyumen, Russia, May 11, 1888), with 25 million for the Crosby single (recorded May 29, 1942) and more than 100 million in other versions.

The highest claim for any "pop" record is an unaudited 25 million for *Rock Around the Clock,* copyrighted in 1953 by the late Max Friedman and James E. Myers, under the name of Jimmy De Knight, and recorded Apr 12, 1954 by Bill Haley and the Comets.

The best-selling album of all time is the double album (4 sides) of the soundtrack of the film *Saturday Night Fever,* with 25 million copies sold worldwide by May 1, 1979. The majority of the songs were written by the Bee Gees, comprising the three Gibb brothers, Barry Alan (b Isle of Man, Sept 1, 1947) and the twins Robin and Maurice (b Dec 22, 1949).

The first classical long-player to sell a million was a performance featuring the pianist Harvey Lavan (Van) Cliburn, Jr (b Kilgore, Tex, July 12, 1934) of the *Piano Concerto No. 1* by Pyotr Ilyich Tchaikovsky (1840–93) of Russia. This recording was made in 1958 and sales reached 1 million by 1961, 2 million by 1965 and about 2,500,000 by Jan 1970.

Fastest Seller

The fastest-selling record of all time is *John Fitzgerald Kennedy—A Memorial Album* (Premium Albums), an LP recorded on Nov 22, 1963, the day of Mr Kennedy's assassination, which sold 4 million copies at 99 cents in six days (Dec 7–12, 1963), thus ironically beating the previous speed record set by the humorous LP *The First Family* about the Kennedys in 1962–63.

Best-Seller Chart Records

Singles record charts were first published by *Billboard* on July 20, 1940, when the No. 1 record was *I'll Never Smile Again* by Tommy Dorsey (b Nov 19, 1905, d Nov 26, 1956). Three discs have stayed at the top for a record 13 consecutive weeks—*Frenesi* by Artie Shaw from Dec

1940; *I've Heard that Song Before* by Harry James from Feb 1943; and *Goodnight Irene* by Gordon Jenkins and the Weavers from Aug 1950. *I Go Crazy* by Paul Davis stayed on the chart for 40 consecutive weeks from Aug 1977. The Beatles have had the most No. 1 records (20) and Elvis Presley has had the most hit singles on the *Billboard Hot 100*—97 from 1956 to May 1978.

Billboard first published an album chart on March 15, 1945, when the No. 1 record was *King Cole Trio* featuring Nat "King" Cole (b March 17, 1919, d Feb 15, 1965). *South Pacific* was No. 1 for 69 weeks (non-consecutive) from May 1949. *Johnny's Greatest Hits* by Johnny Mathis stayed on the chart for 490 weeks (over 9 years) from Apr 1958. The Beatles had the most No. 1 recordings (15) and Presley the most hit albums (75 from 1956 to May 1979).

Advance Sales

The greatest advance sale was 2,100,000 for *Can't Buy Me Love* by The Beatles, released in the US on March 16, 1964.

Most Recordings

Miss Lata Mangeshker (b 1928) has reportedly recorded between 1948 and 1974 not less than 25,000 solo, duet and chorus-backed songs in 20 Indian languages. She frequently has 5 sessions in a day and has "backed" 1,800 films to 1974.

Loudest Pop Group

The amplification for *The Who* concert at Charlton Athletic Football Ground, London, England, May 31, 1976, provided by a Tasco PA system, had a total power of 76,000 watts from eighty 800 W Crown DC 300 A amplifiers and twenty 600 W Phase Linear 200's. The readings at 50 m (164 ft) from the front of the sound system were 120 decibels. Exposure to such noise levels causes PSH—Permanent Shift of Hearing or partial deafness.

Chapter 7
The World's Structures

EARLIEST STRUCTURES

The earliest known human structure is a rough circle of loosely piled lava blocks found in 1960 on the lowest cultural level at the Lower Paleolithic site at Olduvai Gorge in Tanzania. The structure was associated with artifacts and bones and may represent a work-floor, dating to *circa* 1,750,000 BC.

The earliest evidence of *buildings* yet discovered is that of 21 huts with hearths of pebble-lined pits and delimited by stake holes, found in Oct 1965 at the Terra Amata site in Nice, France thought to belong to the Acheulián culture of 120,000 years ago. Excavation carried out between June 28 and July 5, 1966 revealed one hut with palisaded walls having axes of 49 and 20 ft.

The oldest free-standing structures are now believed to be the megalithic temples at Mgarr and Skarba in Malta and Ggantija in Gozo, dating from *c.* 3250 BC.

The remains of a stone tower 20 ft high built into the walls of Jericho have been excavated, and dated to 5000 BC.

1. BUILDINGS FOR WORKING

Largest Commercial Buildings

The greatest ground area covered by any building is that by the Ford Parts Redistribution Center, Pennsylvania Ave., Brownstown Township, Mich. It encloses a floor area 3,100,000 sq ft or 71.16 acres. Opened on May 20, 1971, it employs 1,400 people. The fire-control system comprises 70 miles of pipelines with 37,000 sprinklers.

The building with the largest cubic capacity is the Boeing Company's main assembly plant at Everett, Wash, completed in 1968. The building, constructed for the manufacture of Boeing 747 jet airliners, has a maximum height of 115 ft and has a capacity of 200 million cu ft.

Largest Scientific Building

The most capacious scientific building is the Vehicle Assembly Building (VAB) at Complex 39, the selected site for the final assembly and launching of the Apollo moon spacecraft on the Saturn V rocket, at the John F. Kennedy Space Center (KSC) on Merritt Island near Cape Canaveral, Fla. It is a steel-framed building measuring 716 ft in length, 518 ft in width and 525 ft in height. The building contains four bays, each with its own door 460 ft high. Construction began in Apr 1963 by the Ursum

Consortium. Its floor area is 343,500 sq ft (7.87 acres) and its capacity is 129,482,000 cu ft. The building was "topped out" on Apr 14, 1965 at a cost of $108,700,000.

Largest Administrative Building

The largest ground area covered by any office building is that of the Pentagon, in Arlington, Va. Built to house the US Defense Department's offices, it was completed Jan 15, 1943 and cost about $83 million. Each of the outermost sides of the Pentagon is 921 ft long and the perimeter of the building is about 1,500 yd. The 5 stories of the building enclose a floor area of 6½ million sq ft. During the day 29,000 people work in the building. The telephone system of the building has more than 44,000 telephones connected by 160,000 miles of cable and its 220 staff members handle 280,000 calls a day. Two restaurants, 6 cafeterias and 10 snack bars and a staff of 675 form the catering department of the building. The corridors measure 17 miles in length and there are 7,748 windows to be cleaned.

Largest Office Building

The largest office buildings are the twin towers comprising the World Trade Center in NYC, with a total of 4,370,000 sq ft (100.32 acres) of rentable space in each. The taller tower (Tower B) is 1,362 ft high.

LARGEST BUILDING BY AREA: The Pentagon in Arlington, Va.

LARGEST OFFICE BUILDING: World Trade Center (left) in NYC has twin towers and more than 4 million sq ft. Sears Tower (right) in Chicago is taller, with 110 stories and a height of 1,454 ft.

Tallest Buildings

The *tallest* office building is the Sears Tower, the national headquarters of Sears Roebuck & Co on Wacker Drive, Chicago, with 110 stories, rising to 1,454 ft and completed in 1974. Its *gross* area is 4,400,000 sq ft (101.0 acres). It was topped out on May 4, 1973, surpassing the World Trade Center in New York in height, at 2:35 p.m. March 6, 1973 with the first steel column reaching to the 104th story. The addition of two TV antennae brought the total height to 1,559 ft. The building's population is 16,700, served by 103 elevators and 18 escalators. It has 16,000 windows.

In Asia, where buildings must be constructed to be earthquake-proof, the tallest building is the 60-story "Sunshine 60" in Ikebukuro, Tokyo, Japan, completed in 1978 to a height of 787.4 ft. It has the world's fastest elevators, which go 2,000 ft/min.

England may soon have a 139-story office building to be 1,825 ft tall. The Merseyside County Council unveiled highly tentative plans on Nov 9, 1979 for a £50 million ($115 million) project.

Largest Embassy

The largest embassy is the USSR embassy on Bei Xiao Jie, Peking, China, in the northeastern corner of the walled city. The whole 45-acre area of the old Orthodox Church mission (established 1728), now known as the *Bei guan,* was handed over to the USSR in 1949.

Largest Garage

The largest garage (as opposed to parking lot) is at O'Hare Airport, Chicago, with 6 levels and a capacity for 9,250 cars. It is operated by Allright Auto Parks, Inc, the world's largest parking company.

The largest private garage ever built was one for 100 cars at the Long Island, NY, mansion of William Kissam Vanderbilt (1849–1920).

The largest parking lot is believed to be that at the National Exhibition Centre in Birmingham, England, with a capacity of 15,000 cars. The parking lots at Disneyland, Anaheim, Calif cover 110 acres.

Largest Hangars

The largest hangar is the Goodyear Airship hangar at Akron, O, which measures 1,175 ft long, 325 ft wide and 200 ft high. It covers 364,000 sq ft (8.35 acres) and has a capacity of 55 million cu ft.

The largest single fixed-wing aircraft hangar is the Lockheed-Georgia engineering test center at Marietta, Ga measuring 630 ft × 480 ft (6.94 acres) completed in 1967. The maintenance hangar at Frankfurt/Main

LARGEST HANGAR: In Akron, Ohio, Goodyear has this gigantic building to house zeppelins of the US Navy. It is 200 ft high.

Airport, W Germany, covers slightly less area but has a frontage of 902 ft. The cable-supported roof has a span of 426.5 ft.

Delta Air Lines' jet base, on a 140-acre site at Hartsfield International Airport, Atlanta, Ga has 36 acres under its roof.

Tallest Chimneys and Cooling Towers

The tallest chimney is the $5½ million International Nickel Company's stack, 1,245 ft 8 in tall, at Copper Cliff, Sudbury, Ontario, Canada, completed in 1970. It was built by Canadian Kellogg Ltd and the diameter tapers from 116.4 ft at the base to 51.8 ft at the top. It weighs 42,998 tons and became operational in 1971.

The world's most massive chimney is one of 1,148 ft at Puentes, Spain, built by M. W. Kellogg Co. It contains 20,600 cu yd of concrete and 2,900,000 lb of steel and has an internal volume of 6,700,000 cu ft.

The largest cooling tower is adjacent to the nuclear power plant at Uentrop, W Germany, completed in 1976, which is 590 ft tall.

Largest Sewage Works

The largest single sewage works is the West-Southwest Treatment Plant, opened in 1940 on a site of 501 acres in Chicago. It serves an area containing 2,940,000 people. It treated an average of more than 835 million gallons of wastes per day in 1973. The capacity of its sedimentation and aeration tanks is 1,600,000 cu yd.

Largest Glass Greenhouse

The largest glasshouse is one covering 7.34 acres owned by Van Heyningen Bros, at Holland Nurseries, Littlehampton, West Sussex, England.

Grain Elevator

The largest single-unit grain elevator is that operated by the C-G-F Grain Company at Wichita, Kans. Consisting of a triple row of storage tanks, 123 on each side of the central loading tower or "head house," the unit is 2,717 ft long and 100 ft wide. Each tank is 120 ft high, with an inside diameter of 30 ft, giving a total storage capacity of 20 million bushels of wheat. The largest collection of elevators is at Thunder Bay, Ontario, Canada, on Lake Superior, with a total capacity of 103.9 million bushels.

Wooden Buildings

The oldest extant wooden buildings are those comprising the Pagoda, Chumanar Gate, and the Temple of Horyu (Horyu-ji), built at Nara, Japan, in 670 AD. The nearby Daibutsuden, built in 1704–11, once measured 285.4 ft long, 167.3 ft wide and 153.3 ft tall. The present dimensions are 188 ft × 165.3 ft × 159.4 ft.

The largest timber buildings are the two US Navy airship hangars built in 1942–43 at Tillamook, Ore. Now used as a saw mill by the Louisiana-Pacific Corporation, they measure 1,000 ft long, 170 ft high at the crown and 296 ft wide at the base. They are worth $6 million.

Air-Supported Structure

The largest air-supported roof is the roof of the 80,600-capacity octagonal Pontiac Silverdome Stadium, Mich measuring 522 ft wide and 722 ft

LARGEST AIR-SUPPORTED ROOF: The octagonal Pontiac Silverdome Stadium in Mich has its roof held up by 5 lb of air pressure per sq in.

long. The air pressure is 5 lb per sq in, supporting the 10-acre translucent fiberglass roofing. The structural engineers were Geiger-Berger Associates of NYC. The largest standard-size air hall is one in Lima, Ohio, which is 860 ft long, 140 ft wide and 65 ft high made by Irvin Industries of Stamford, Conn.

2. BUILDINGS FOR LIVING

Castles and Forts

Fortifications existed in all the great early civilizations, including that of ancient Egypt from 3000 BC. Fortified castles in the more accepted sense only existed much later. The oldest in the world is that at Gomdan, Yemen, which originally had 20 stories and dates from before 100 AD.

The largest inhabited castle is the British Royal residence of Windsor Castle, Berkshire. It is primarily of 12th-century construction and is in the form of a waisted parallelogram, 1,890 ft × 540 ft. The total area of Dover Castle (England), however, covers 34 acres with a width of 1,100 ft and a curtain wall of 1,800 ft, or, if underground works are taken in, 2,300 ft.

The largest ancient castle is Prague Castle, Czechoslovakia, originating in the 9th century. It is a very oblong, irregular polygon with an axis of 1,870 ft and an average traverse diameter of 420 ft, with a surface area of 18 acres.

The walls of Babylon, north of Al Hillah, Iraq, built in 600 BC were up to 85 ft in thickness.

Largest Palaces

The largest palace is the Imperial Palace (*Gu gong*) in the center of Peking (*Bei jing*, the northern capital), China, which covers a rectangle 1,050 yd × 820 yd, an area of 177.9 acres. The outline survives from the construction of the third Ming emperor Yung-lo of 1402–24, but due to constant rearrangements most of the intramural buildings are 18th century. These consist of 5 halls and 17 palaces of which the last occupied by the last Empress was the Palace of Accumulated Elegance (*Chu xia gong*) until 1924.

The largest residential palace is the Vatican Palace, in the Vatican City, an enclave in Rome, Italy. Covering an area of 13½ acres, it has 1,400 rooms, chapels and halls, of which the oldest date from the 15th century.

The largest palace in royal use is Buckingham Palace, London, so named after its site, bought in 1703 by John Sheffield, the 1st Duke of Buckingham and Normandy (1648–1721). Buckingham House was reconstructed in the Palladian style between 1835 and 1836, following the design of John Nash (1752–1835). The 610-ft-long East Front was built in 1846 and refaced in 1912. The Palace which stands in 39 acres of garden, has 600 rooms including a ballroom 111 ft long.

The world's largest moats are those which surround the Imperial Palace in Peking. From plans drawn by French sources they appear to measure 54 yd wide and have a total length of 3,600 yd. The city's moats total 23½ miles in all.

Tallest Apartments

The tallest block of apartments in the world is Lake Point Towers of 70 stories, 645 ft high in Chicago.

Largest Hotels

The hotel with the most rooms is the Hotel Rossiya in Moscow, with 3,200 rooms providing accommodation for 5,350 guests, opened in 1967. It would thus require more than 8½ years to spend one night in each room. In addition, there is a 21-story "Presidential" tower in the central courtyard. The hotel employs about 3,000 people and has 93 elevators. The ballroom is reputed to be the world's largest. Muscovites are not permitted as residents while foreigners are charged 16 times more than the very low rate charged to officials of the USSR.

The largest commercial hotel building in the world is the Waldorf-Astoria, opened on Oct 1, 1931 on Park Avenue, between 49th and 50th Streets, NYC. It occupies a complete block of 81,337 sq ft (1.87 acres) and reaches a maximum height of 625 ft 7 in. The Waldorf-Astoria has

LARGEST PALACE: The "Forbidden City" in Peking, now a museum but formerly the Imperial Palace, includes within its walls 17 actual palaces and 5 halls.

47 stories and 1,852 guest rooms, maintains the largest hotel radio receiving system in the world and has an electricity bill of about $2 million a year. The Waldorf can accommodate 10,000 people at one time, with a staff of 1,700. Its restaurants have catered for parties up to 6,000 at a time. The coffee-makers' daily output reaches 1,000 gallons. The hotel has housed six heads of state simultaneously.

Tallest Hotels

The tallest hotel, measured from the street level of its main entrance to the top, is the 723-ft-tall 70-story Peachtree Center Plaza Hotel in Atlanta, Ga opened in Jan 1976. The $50 million, 1,100-room hotel was designed by architect John Portman, is operated by Western International Hotels, and owned by Portman Properties. Their Detroit Plaza Hotel in Detroit is taller when measured from its back entrance to the top. This hotel, opened in early 1977, is 748 ft tall starting from its lower street level. Designed by the same architect as the Peachtree, it is operated also by Western International Hotels, and contains 1,400 rooms.

Ground was broken in June 1980 for the building of a $235 million Raffles City hotel project in Singapore, which will be 70 stories and 754 ft high at its central tower.

Most Expensive Hotel Room

The costliest hotel accommodation is the Celestial Suite on the ninth floor of the Astro Village Hotel, Houston, Texas, which is rented for $2,500 a day. This compares with the official NYC Presidential Suite in the Waldorf-Astoria at $1,500 a day.

Spas

The largest spa measured by number of available hotel rooms is Vichy, Allier, France, with 14,000 rooms. Spas are named after the watering place called Spa in the Liège province of Belgium where hydropathy was developed from 1626. The highest French spa is Baréges, Hautes-Pyrénées, at 4,068 ft above sea level.

Barracks

The oldest purpose-built barracks are believed to be Collins Barracks, formerly the Royal Barracks, Dublin, Ireland, completed in 1704 and still in use.

Largest House

The largest private house in the world is 250-room Biltmore House in Asheville, NC. It is owned by George and William Cecil, grandsons of George Washington Vanderbilt II (1862–1914). The house was built between 1890 and 1895 on an estate of 119,000 acres, at a cost of $4,100,000, and is now valued at $55 million with 12,000 acres.

The most expensive private house ever built is The Hearst Ranch at San Simeon, Calif. It was built 1922–39 for William Randolph Hearst (1863–1951), at a total cost of more than $30 million. It has more than 100 rooms, a 104-ft-long heated swimming pool, an 83-ft-long assembly hall and a garage for 25 limousines. The house would require 60 servants to maintain it.

HOTELS: The Detroit Plaza (above) is about the same height as its sister hotel, The Peachtree in Atlanta—tallest in the world at 70 stories. The Rossiya in Moscow (right) has the most rooms—3,200. The Celestial Suite of the Astro Village Hotel in Houston (bathroom, below) is the most expensive at $2,500 per day.

LARGEST PRIVATE HOUSE: Biltmore House in Asheville, NC, has 250 rooms. It cost $4,100,000 to build in the 1890's, but today it is valued at $55,000,000.

The highest asking price for a privately furnished house has been £3,800,000 ($6,460,000) by Mr Ravi Tikkoo for Kenstead Hall, London. The buyer by private treaty on Apr 6, 1977 was Crown Prince Fahd of Saudi Arabia. The adjacent $1 million Risinghurst was bought for servants, and extensions and renovations were uncompleted by mid-1980 but had cost more than $16 million.

The most expensive penthouse apartment is a 4-story penthouse at the top of Galleria International on East 57th Street, NYC. With 4 main bedrooms, a 22-ft swimming pool, library, sauna and several solariums, it was on the market in March 1976 for $3,500,000.

3. BUILDINGS FOR ENTERTAINMENT

Largest Circus

The largest permanent circus is Circus Circus, Las Vegas, Nev, opened Oct 18, 1968 at a cost of $15 million. It covers an area of 129,000 sq ft capped by a 90-ft-high tent-shaped flexiglass roof. (Circus Stunt records are in Chapter 11.)

The largest traveling circus is the Circus Vargas in the US which can accommodate 5,000 people under its Big Top.

Largest Stadiums

The largest stadium is the Strahov Stadium in Praha (Prague), Czechoslovakia. It was completed in 1934 and can easily accommodate 240,000 spectators for mass displays of up to 40,000 Sokol gymnasts.

The largest football stadium is the Maracaña Municipal Stadium in Rio de Janeiro, Brazil, which has a normal capacity of 205,000, of whom 155,000 may be seated. A crowd of 199,854 was accommodated for the World Cup soccer final between Brazil and Uruguay on July 16, 1950. A dry moat, 7 ft wide and over 5 ft deep, protects players from spectators and *vice versa*. The stadium also has facilities for indoor sports, such as boxing, and these provide accommodation for an additional 32,000 spectators.

The largest covered stadium in the world is the Azteca Stadium, Mexico City, opened in 1968, which has a capacity of 107,000, of whom nearly all are under cover.

Largest One-Piece Roof

The transparent acrylic glass "tent" roof over the Munich Olympic Stadium, W Germany, measures 914,940 sq ft in area. It rests on a steel net supported by masts. The roof of longest span is the 680-ft diameter of the Louisiana Superdome (see photo). The major axis of the elliptical Texas Stadium, Irving, Tex, completed in 1971 is, however, 784 ft 4 in.

Largest Indoor Arena

The largest indoor stadium is the 13-acre $173 million 273-ft-tall Superdome in New Orleans, La, completed in May 1975. Its maximum seating capacity for conventions is 95,427 or 76,791 for football. Box suites rent for $35,000, excluding the price of admission. A gondola with six 312-in TV screens produces instant replay.

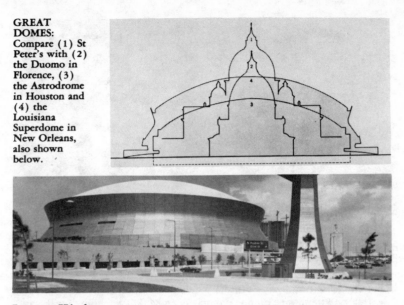

GREAT DOMES: Compare (1) St Peter's with (2) the Duomo in Florence, (3) the Astrodrome in Houston and (4) the Louisiana Superdome in New Orleans, also shown below.

Largest Kitchen

The largest kitchen ever set up has been the Indian Government field kitchen set up in April 1973 at Ahmadnagar, Maharashtra, in the famine area, which daily provided 1.2 million subsistence meals.

Night Clubs

The oldest night club (*boîte de nuit*) is "Le Bal des Anglais" at 6 Rue des Anglais, Paris 5, France. It was founded in 1843 but closed *c.* 1960.

The largest night club in the world is Gilley's Club (formerly Shelly's) built in 1955 and extended in 1971 on Spencer Highway, Pasadena, Tex. It has a seating capacity of more than 3,000 and a total capacity of 5,500.

In the more classical sense the largest night club is "The Mikado" in the Akasaka district of Tokyo, Japan, with a seating capcaity of 2,000. It is "manned" by 1,250 hostesses. Binoculars are essential to an appreciation of the floor show.

> The lowest night club is the "Minus 206" in Tiberias, Israel, on the shores of the Sea of Galilee. It is 676 ft below sea level. An alternative candidate is "Outer Limits," opposite the Cow Palace, San Francisco, which was raided for the 151st time on Aug 1, 1971. It has been called both "The Most Busted Joint" and "The Slowest to Get the Message."

Largest Amusement Park

The largest amusement resort is Disney World on 27,443 acres of Orange and Osceola Counties, 20 miles southwest of Orlando in central Florida. It was opened on Oct 1, 1971. This $400 million investment attracted 10,700,000 visitors in its first year.

The most attended resort in the world is Disneyland, Anaheim, Calif

AMUSEMENTS: Largest Ferris Wheel (left) is the one built in London in 1897 for the Earl's Court Exhibition with 40 cars and a 300-ft diameter. The Highest and Fastest Roller Coaster is "The Beast" at King's Island near Cincinnati, with a 141-ft-high drop and a speed of almost 65 mph.

where the total number of visitors reached 197 million by Oct 1, 1979. The greatest attendance on one day has been 84,000, spending on the average $15, indicating a gross of over $1¼ million in a day.

Fairs

The earliest major international fair was the Great Exhibition of 1851 in the Crystal Palace, Hyde Park, London, which in 141 days attracted 6,039,195 admissions.

The largest International Fair site was that for the St Louis Louisiana Purchase Exposition, which covered 1,271.76 acres. It also staged the 1904 Olympic Games and drew an attandance of 19,694,855.

The record attendance for any fair was 64,218,770 for Expo '70 held on an 815-acre site at Osaka, Japan, from March to Sept 13, 1970. It made a profit of 19,439,402,017 yen (over $45 million).

Ferris Wheel

The original Ferris Wheel, named after its constructor, George W. Ferris (1859–96), was erected in 1893 at the Midway, Chicago, at a cost of $385,000. The wheel was 250 ft in diameter, 790 ft in circumference, weighed 1,198 tons, and carried 36 cars each seating 60 people, making a total of 2,160 passengers. The structure was removed in 1904 to St Louis, and was eventually sold as scrap for $1,800. In 1897, a Ferris Wheel with a diameter of 300 ft was erected for the Earl's Court Exhibition, London. It had 10 1st-class and 30 2nd-class cars. The largest wheel now operating is the Riesenrad in Prater Park, Vienna, Austria, with a diameter of 197 ft. It was built in 1896 and carried 15 million people in its first 75 years to June 13, 1971.

Longest and Fastest Roller Coaster

The maximum speeds claimed for roller coasters have in the past been exaggerated for commercial reasons. The highest and hence fastest and also the longest roller coaster in the world is *The Beast* at King's Island near Cincinnati, Ohio. Scientific tests at the base of its 141-ft-high drop returned a speed of 64.77 mph on Apr 5, 1980. The total track length of 7,400 ft incorporates 800 ft of tunnels, a 540-degree helix and a second drop of 135 ft.

Longest Slide

The longest slide in the world is at Bad Tölz, W Germany. This has a length of 0.76 mile and a vertical drop of 721 ft.

Largest Pleasure Beach

The largest pleasure beach is Virginia Beach, Va. It has 28 miles of beach front on the Atlantic and 10 miles of estuary frontage. The area embraces 255 sq mi and contains 134 hotels and motels.

Longest Pleasure Pier

The longest pleasure pier is Southend Pier at Southend-on-Sea in Essex, England. It is 1.34 miles in length, and was first opened in Aug 1889, with final extensions made in 1929. In 1949–50, the pier had 5,750,000 visitors. The resort with the most piers is Atlantic City, NJ with 6 pre-war and 5 currently.

Bars

The largest beer-selling establishment is the Mathäser, Bayerstrasse 5, Munich, W Germany, where the daily sale reaches 100,800 pints. It was established in 1829, was demolished in World War II, rebuilt by 1955, and now seats 5,500 people. Consumption at the Dube beer halls in the Bantu township of Soweto, Johannesburg, South Africa, may, however, be higher on some Saturdays when the average of 7,160 gallons (57,280 pints) is far exceeded.

The longest bar with beer pumps was built in 1938 at the Working Men's Club, Mildura, Victoria, Australia. It has a counter 298 ft in length, served by 27 pumps. Temporary bars have been erected of greater length. The Falstaff Brewing Corp put up a temporary bar 336 ft 5 in in length of Wharf St., St Louis, on June 22, 1970.

The bar at Erickson's on Burnside Street, Portland, Ore in its heyday (1883–1920) ran continuously around and across the main saloon, measuring 684 ft. The chief bouncer, Edward "Spider" Johnson, had a chief assistant named "Jumbo" Reilly who weighed 322 pounds and was said to resemble "an ill-natured orangutan." Beer was 5 cents for 16 fluid ounces.

LONGEST SLIDE: This one in West Germany is ¾ mile long and drops 721 ft.

LARGEST WINE CELLAR: Almaden's Cienega Cellar near San Jose, Calif, contains 37,229 small (50-gallon) barrels of fine aging table wines, reportedly the largest number of barrels under one roof.

Wine Cellar

The largest wine cellars are at Paarl, those of the Ko-operative Wijn-bouwers Vereeniging (K.W.V.), near Capetown, in the center of the wine district of South Africa. They cover an area of 25 acres and have a capacity of 36 million gallons. Their largest blending vats have a capacity of 54,880 gallons, and are 17 ft high and 26 ft in diameter.

Beer Garden

The largest beer garden is the Augustiner Biergarten in Munich, W Germany, founded in 1901 with space for 5,200 people. It has sold as much as 2,640 gallons in a single day.

4. TOWERS AND MASTS

Tallest Structure

The tallest structure is the guyed Warszawa Radio mast at Konstan-tynow near Gabin and Plock in Poland, which is 2,120 ft 8 in tall, or more than four-tenths of a mile. The mast was completed July 18, 1974 and put into operation July 22, 1974. Work began on the tubular steel construction, with its 15 steel guy ropes, in 1970. It was designed by Jan Polak and weighs 615 tons. The mast is so high that anyone falling off the top would reach terminal velocity, and hence cease to be accelerating, before hitting the ground. It recaptured for Europe a record held in the US since the Chrysler Building surpassed the Eiffel Tower in 1929.

Tallest Tower

The tallest self-supporting tower (as opposed to a guyed mast) is the $44 million CN Tower in Metro Centre, Toronto, Canada. It rises to 1,822 ft 1 in. Excavation began Feb 12, 1973, for the 145,000-ton structure of reinforced, lost-tensioned concrete, and it was topped out on Apr 2, 1975. A 416-seat restaurant revolves in the 7-floor Sky Pod at 1,140 ft, from which the visibility extends to hills 74½ miles distant. Lightning strikes the top about 200 times (in 30 storms) each year.

The tallest tower built before the era of television masts is the Tour Eiffel (Eiffel Tower), in Paris, designed by Alexandre Gustave Eiffel (1832–1923) for the Paris exhibition and completed on March 31, 1889. It

EIFFEL TOWER (left) built in 1889, once carried the world's largest advertising sign. With TV antenna now, it is 1,052 ft tall. LONGEST SUSPENSION BRIDGE (above): The Humber Estuary Bridge, just short of a mile long between towers, is the new record holder for suspension bridges, beating NY's Verrazano.

was 985 ft 11 in tall, now extended by a TV antenna to 1,052 ft 4 in, and weighs 8,091 tons. The maximum sway in high winds is 5 in. The whole iron edifice, which has 1,792 steps, took 2 years, 2 months, and 2 days to build and cost 7,799,401 francs 31 centimes.

5. BRIDGES

Arch construction was understood by the Sumerians as early as 320 BC and a reference exists to a Nile bridge in 2650 BC. The oldest surviving datable bridge in the world is the slab stone single-arch bridge over the River Meles in Smyrna (now Izmir), Turkey, which dates from *c.* 850 BC.

Longest Suspension Bridge

The longest bridge span is the main span of the £67 million ($135 million) Humber Estuary Bridge in England, at 4,626 ft, due to open in Oct 1980. Work began on July 27, 1972. The towers are 533 ft 1⅛ in tall from datum and are 1⅜ inches out of parallel, to allow for the curvature of the earth. Including the Hessle and Barton side spans, the bridge stretches 1.37 miles. On March 22, 1980 an accident occurred with the slinging of the decking. Further delays due to industrial disruption makes the target date of 1980 for completion most unlikely.

The Mackinac Straits Bridge between Mackinaw City and St Ignace, Mich is the longest suspension bridge measured between anchorages (1.58 miles) and has an overall length, including viaducts of the bridge proper measured between abutment faces, of 3.63 miles. It was opened in Nov 1957 (dedicated June 28, 1958) at a cost of $100 million and has a main span of 3,800 ft.

The double-deck road-railroad Akashi-Kaikyo suspension bridge linking Honshu and Shikoku, Japan, is planned to be completed in 1988. The main span will be 5,840 ft in length with an overall suspended length with side spans totaling 11,680 ft. Work began in Oct 1978, and the eventual cost is expented to exceed 1 trillion yen ($4,500 million).

Plans for a Messina Bridge linking Sicily with the Italian mainland are dependent on Common Market budgets. One preliminary study calls for towers 1,000 ft high and a span exceeding 6,070 ft. The total cost has been estimated to exceed $4,000 million.

Longest Cantilever Bridge

The Québec Bridge (Pont de Québec) over the St Lawrence River in Canada has the longest cantilever span—1,800 ft between the piers and 3,239 ft overall. It carries a railroad track and two roadways. Begun in 1899, it was finally opened to traffic Dec 3, 1917, at a cost of Can. $22,500,000 and 87 lives.

Longest Steel Arch Bridge

The longest steel arch bridge is the New River Gorge bridge near Fayetteville, W Va, completed in 1977, with a span of 1,700 ft.

Railroad Bridge

The longest railroad bridge in the world is the Huey P. Long Bridge, Metairie, La, with a railroad section 22,996 ft (4.35 miles) long. It was completed Dec 16, 1935, with a longest span of 790 ft.

The Yangtse River Bridge completed in 1968 in Nanking, China, is the longest combined highway and railroad bridge. The rail deck is 4.20 miles and the road deck an additional 2.85 miles.

Floating Bridge

The longest floating bridge is the Second Lake Washington Bridge in Seattle, Wash. Its total length is 12,596 ft and its floating section measures 7,518 ft (1.42 miles). It was built at a cost of $15 million, and completed in Aug 1963.

Widest Bridge

The bridge with the widest roadway is the Crawford Street Bridge in Providence, RI, with a width of 1,147 ft.

The widest long-span bridge is the 1,650-ft-span Sydney Harbour Bridge, Australia, which is 160 ft wide. It carries 2 electric overhead railroad tracks, 8 lanes of roadway and a cycleway and footway. It was officially opened March 19, 1932.

The River Roch in England is bridged for a distance of 1,460 ft where the culvert passes through the center of Rochdale, Greater Manchester, and this is sometimes claimed as a breadth.

Highest Bridge

The highest bridge is the suspension bridge over the Royal Gorge of the Arkansas River in Colorado. It is 1,053 ft above the water level. It has a main span of 880 ft and was constructed in 6 months, ending on Dec 6,

BRIDGES: The Québec
Bridge over the St. Lawrence
River in Canada is the longest
cantilever span at 1,800 ft.
The highest bridge (right) is
up 1,053 ft above the Royal
Gorge of the Arkansas River
in Colorado. This great
Roman aqueduct (below) was
built near Nimes, France in 19
AD and has triple tiers. The
widest long-span bridge is the
Sydney Harbour Bridge in
Australia (bottom) which is
160 ft wide and carries 2
electric overhead railroad
tracks, 8 lanes of roadway and
a cycleway and footway.

1929. The highest railroad bridge in the world is at Fades, outside Clermont-Ferrand, France. It was built in 1901–09 with a span of 472 ft and is 435 ft above the River Sioule.

Covered Bridge

The longest covered bridge is that at Hartland, New Brunswick, Canada, measuring 1,282 ft overall, completed in 1899.

Longest Bridging

The world's longest bridging is the Second Lake Pontchartrain Causeway, opened March 23, 1969, joining Lewisburg and Metairie, La. Its length is 126,055 ft (23.87 miles). It cost $29,900,000 and is 228 ft longer than the adjoining First Causeway completed in 1956.

The longest railroad viaduct in the world is the rock-filled Great Salt Lake railroad trestle, carrying the Southern Pacific Railroad 11.85 miles across the Great Salt Lake, Utah. It was opened as a pile and trestle bridge March 8, 1904, and converted to rock fill in 1955–1960.

The longest stone arch bridging in the world is the 3,810-ft-long Rockville Bridge north of Harrisburg, Pa with 48 spans containing 219,520 tons of stone and completed in 1901.

Longest Aqueduct

The greatest of ancient aqueducts was the Aqueduct of Carthage in Tunisia, which ran 87.6 miles from the springs of Zaghouan to Djebel Djougar. It was built by the Romans during the reign of Publius Aelius Hadrianus (117–138 AD). By 1895, 344 arches still survived. Its original capacity has been calculated at 8,400,000 gallons per day. The triple-tiered aqueduct Pont du Gard, built in 19 AD near Nîmes, France, is 160 ft high. The tallest of the 14 arches of the Aguas Livres Aqueduct, built in Lisbon, Portugal, in 1784, is 213 ft 3 in.

The longest aqueduct, in the modern sense of a water conduit as opposed to an irrigation canal, is the California State Water Project aqueduct, completed in 1974 to a length of 826 miles, of which 385 miles is canalized.

LONGEST BRIDGE SPANS IN THE WORLD—BY TYPE

	feet		opening
Suspension	4,626	Humber Estuary, England	?1980
Cantilever	1,800	Québec Railway, Québec, Canada	1917
Steel arch	1,700	New River Gorge, Fayetteville, W. Virginia	1977
Covered bridge	1,282	Hartland, New Brunswick, Canada	1899
Continuous truss	1,232	Astoria, Columbia River, Oregon	1966
Cable-stayed	1,500	Second Hooghly, Calcutta, India	1977
Chain suspension	1,114	Hercilio Luz, Florianopolis, Brazil	1926
Concrete arch	1,000	Gladesville, Sydney, Australia	1964
Plate and box girder	984	Rio Niterói, Rio de Janeiro, Brazil	1974

6. CANALS

Relics of the oldest canals in the world, dated by archeologists to *c.* 4000 BC were discovered near Mandali, Iraq, early in 1968.

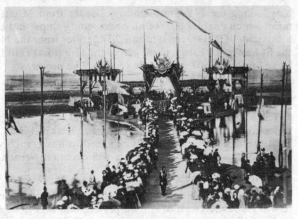

LONGEST BIG SHIP CANAL: The Suez, shown here at its opening in 1869, is 100.6 miles long, still the record holder.

Longest Canals

The longest canalized system is the Volga-Baltic Canal opened in Apr 1965. It runs 1,850 miles from Astrakhan up the Volga, *via* Kuybyshev, Gorkiy and Lake Ladoga, to Leningrad, USSR. The longest canal of the ancient world was the Grand Canal of China from Peking to Hangchow. It was begun in 540 BC and not completed until 1327 by which time it extended for 1,107 miles. The estimated work force *c.* 600 AD reached 5 million on the Pien section. By 1950 the silt had piled up to the point that it was, in no place, more than 6 ft deep. It is now, however, opened up and plied by ships of up to 2,240 tons.

The Beloye More (White Sea) Baltic Canal from Belomorsk to Povenets in the USSR is 141 miles long with 19 locks. It was completed with the use of forced labor in 1933 and cannot accommodate ships of more than 16 ft in draft.

The longest big ship canal is the Suez Canal, linking the Red and Mediterranean Seas, opened Nov 16, 1869, but inoperative from June 1967 to June 1975. The canal was planned by the French diplomat Ferdinand de Lesseps (1805–1894) and work began Apr 25, 1859. It is 100.6 miles in length from Port Said lighthouse to Suez Roads, 197 ft wide. The work force was 8,213 men and 368 camels. The largest vessel to transit has been S.S. *British Progress,* a VLCC (Very Large Crude Carrier) of 228,569 tons dwt (length 1,081.5 ft; beam 159.7 ft at a maximum draft 84 ft). This was southbound in ballast on July 5, 1976.

Busiest Canal

The busiest big ship canal is the Panama, first transited on Aug 15, 1914. In 1974, there were a record 14,304 ocean-going transits. The largest liner to transit is *Queen Elizabeth 2* (66,851 gross tons) in Jan 1980, for a toll of $89,154.62. The ships with the greatest beam to transit have been the *Acadia Forest* and the *Atlantic Forest,* each of 106.9 ft. The lowest toll was 36 cents for the swimmer Richard Halliburton in 1928. The fastest transit has been 2 hours 41 min by the US Navy hydrofoil *Pegasus* on June 20, 1979.

Seaway

The longest artificial seaway is the St Lawrence Seaway (189 miles long) along the NY State-Ontario border from Montreal to Lake Ontario, which enables 80% of all ocean-going ships, and bulk carriers with a capacity of 29,000 tons, to sail 2,342 miles from the North Atlantic, up the St Lawrence Estuary and across the Great Lakes to Duluth, Minn, on Lake Superior (602 ft above sea level). The project cost $470 million and was opened Apr 25, 1959.

Irrigation Canal

The longest irrigation canal is the Karakumskiy Kanal, stretching 528 miles from Haun-Khan to Ashkhabad, Turkmenistan, USSR. In Sept 1971 the navigable length was reported to have reached 280 miles. The length of the $925 million project will eventually reach 930 miles.

Largest and Deepest Locks

The largest single lock connects the Schelde with the Kanaaldok system at Zandvliet, west of Antwerp, Belgium. It is 1,640 ft long and 187 ft wide and is an entrance to an impounded sheet of water 11.2 miles long.

The deepest lock is the John Day Dam lock on the Columbia River, Ore and Wash, completed in 1963. It can raise or lower barges 113 ft and is served by a 1,100-ton gate.

Highest Lock Elevator

The highest lock elevator overcomes a head of 225 ft at Ronquieres on the Charleroi-Brussels Canal, Belgium. The two 236-wheeled caissons, each able to carry 1,510 tons, take 22 minutes to cover the 4,698-ft-long ramp.

Largest Canal Cut

The Gaillard Cut (known as the "Ditch") on the Panama Canal is 270 ft deep between Gold Hill and Contractor's Hill with a bottom width of 500 ft. In one day in 1911 as many as 333 dirt trains each carrying 400 tons left this site. The total amount of earth excavated for the whole Panama Canal was 666,194,450 sq yd to Oct 1, 1979. This total will be raised by the further widening of the Gaillard Cut.

7. DAMS

The earliest known dams were those uncovered by the British School of Archeology in Jerusalem in 1974 at Jawa in Jordan. These stone-faced earth dams are dated to c. 3200 BC.

Most Massive Dam

Measured by volume, the largest dam is the 98-ft-high New Cornelia Tailings earthfill dam near Ajo, Ariz with a volume of 274,026,000 cu yd, completed in 1973 to a length of 6.74 miles. The Guri dam across the Caroni River in Venezuela will eventually have a volume of 363,394,000 sq yd.

Largest Concrete Dam

The largest concrete dam, and the largest concrete structure, is the

HIGHEST DAM: The Grand Dixence on the Dixence River in Valais, Switzerland, reaches a height of 935 ft.

Grand Coulee Dam on the Columbia River, Wash. Work was begun in 1933, it began operating on March 22, 1941, and was completed in 1942, at a cost of $56 million. It has a crest length of 4,173 ft and is 550 ft high. It contains 10,585,000 cu yd of concrete, and weighs about 21,600,000 tons. The hydroelectric power plant (now being extended) will have a capacity of 9,780,000 kw.

Highest Dam

The highest dam is the Grand Dixence in Switzerland, completed in Sept 1961 at a cost of $372 million. It is 935 ft from base to rim, 2,296 ft long and the total volume of concrete in the dam is 7,792,000 cu yd.

The Rogunsky earthfill dam in the USSR is expected to have a final height of 1,066 ft when completed.

The damming of the Vakhsh River at Tadjikistan, USSR with a rock-fill was due for completion after 20 years of work in 1980. The final height will be 986 ft. Many microseisms have caused the rate of filling to be slowed down.

Longest River Dam and Sea Dam

The longest river dam is the 62-ft-high Kiev dam on the Dnieper River, USSR, which was completed in 1964 to a length of 33.6 miles. In the early 17th century, an impounding dam of moderate height was built in Lake Hungtze, Kiangsu, China, to a reputed length of 62 miles.

The longest sea dam is the Afsluitdijk stretching 20.195 miles across the mouth of the Zuider Zee in two sections of 1.553 miles (mainland of North Holland to the Isle of Wieringen) and 18.641 miles (Wieringen to Friesland). It has a sea-level width of 293 ft and a height of 24 ft 7 in.

Strongest Structure

The world's strongest structure will be the Sayano-Shusenskaya dam on the Yenisey River, USSR. Under construction, it is designed to bear a load of 20,160,000 tons from a fully-filled reservoir.

Largest Reservoirs and Man-Made Lake

The most voluminous man-made reservoir is Bratsk reservoir on the Angara River, USSR, with a volume of 137,214,000 acre-ft. The dam was completed in 1964.

The largest artificial lake measured by surface area is Lake Volta, Ghana, formed by the Akosombo dam, completed in 1965. By 1969, the lake had filled an area of 3,275 sq mi with a shoreline 4,500 miles in length.

The completion in 1954 of the Owen Falls Dam near Jinja, Uganda, across the northern exit of the White Nile River from the lake Victoria Nyanza, marginally raised the level of that *natural* lake by adding 166 million acre-feet, and technically turned it into a reservoir with a surface area of 17,169,920 acres (26,828 sq mi).

Largest Polder

The largest of the five great polders in the old Zuider Zee, Netherlands, will be the 149,000-acre (232.8-sq-mi) Markerwaard. Work on the 66-mile-long surrounding dyke was begun in 1957. The water area remaining after the erection of the 1927–32 dam (20 miles in length) is called IJssel Meer, which will have a final area of 487.5 sq mi.

Largest Levees

The most massive levees ever carried out are the Mississippi levees begun in 1717 and vastly augmented by the US Government after the disastrous floods of 1927. These extend for 1,732 miles along the main river from Cape Girardeau, Mo, to the Gulf of Mexico and comprise more than 1,000 million cu yd of earthworks. Levees on the tributaries comprise an additional 2,000 miles. The 650-mile segment from Pine Bluff, Ark, to Venice, La, is continuous.

8. TUNNELS

Longest Tunnel

The longest tunnel of any kind is the NYC-W Delaware water supply tunnel begun in 1937 and completed in 1944. It has a diameter of 13 ft 6 in and runs for 105 miles from the Rondout Reservoir in the Catskill Mountains into the Hillview Reservoir, on the border line of NYC and Yonkers.

Bridge-Tunnel

The longest bridge-tunnel system is the Chesapeake Bay Bridge-Tunnel, extending 17.65 miles from eastern shore of Virginia to Virginia Beach, Va. It cost $200 million, took 42 months to complete, and opened on Apr 15, 1964. The longest bridged section is Trestle C (4.56 miles long) and the longest tunnel is the Thimble Shoal Channel Tunnel (1.09 miles).

Canal-Tunnel

The longest canal-tunnel is that on the Rove Canal between the port of Marseilles, France and the Rhône River, built in 1912–27. It is 4.53 miles long, 72 ft wide and 50 ft high, involving 2,250,000 cu yd of excavation.

Subway Tunnel

The longest continuous vehicular tunnel is the London Transport Board underground railway line from Morden to East Finchley, *via* Bank, in London. In use since 1939, it is 17 miles 528 yd long. The diameter of the tunnel is 12 ft and the station tunnels 22.2 ft.

Railroad Tunnel

The longest main-line rail tunnel is the 13-mile 1,397-yd Oshimizu Tunnel on the Tokyo-Niigata Joetsu line in central Honshu, Japan, under the Tanigawa Mt, which was holed through on Jan 25, 1979. The cost of the whole project will by March 1981 reach $6,300 million. There have been 13 fatalities in 7 years.

LONGEST MAIN-LINE RAILROAD TUNNEL: The Oshimizu Tunnel in Japan will extend over 13 miles by March 1981.

Sub-aqueous Tunnel

The longest sub-aqueous railroad tunnel will be the Seikan Rail Tunnel (33.49 miles), 328 feet beneath the sea bed of the Tsugaru Strait between Tappi Saki, Honshu, and Fukushima, Hokkaido, Japan. Once due to be completed by March 1979 at a cost of $552 million, major flooding on May 6, 1976, has put back completion beyond 1982. Tests started on the sub-aqueous section (14.5 miles) in 1963 and construction in June 1972. The tunnel will be 787 ft below sea level.

Currently the world's longest sub-aqueous rail tunnel is the Shin Kanmon Tunnel, completed in May 1974 which runs 11.61 miles from Honshu to Kyushu, Japan.

Road Tunnel

The longest road tunnel is the 8.7-mile-long Arlberg Road Tunnel from St. Anton and Langen in western Austria, opened to traffic Dec 9, 1978.

The largest diameter road tunnel was blasted through Yerba Buena Island in San Francisco Bay. It is 76 ft wide, 58 ft high and 540 ft long. More than 35 million vehicles pass through on its two decks every year.

Irrigation Tunnel

The longest irrigation tunnel is the 51.5-mile-long Orange-Fish Rivers Tunnel, South Africa, begun in 1967, at an estimated cost of $150 million. The boring was completed in Apr 1973. The lining to a minimum thickness of 9 in will give a completed diameter of 17 ft 6 in. The total work force at times exceeded 5,000 men. Some of the access shafts in the 8 sections descend more than 1,000 ft.

Tunneling

The record for rapid tunneling was set in 1967 in the 5-mile-long Oso Irrigation Tunnel in Colo, when the "mole" (giant boring machine) was advanced 419 ft on the 57-sq-ft tunnel face in one day.

9. SPECIALIZED STRUCTURES

Seven Wonders of the World

The Seven Wonders of the World were first designated by Antipater of Sidon in the 2nd century BC. They included the Pyramids of Giza, built by three Fourth Dynasty Egyptian Pharaohs, Khwfw (Khufu or Cheops), Kha-f-Ra (Khafre, Khefren or Chephren) and Menkaure (Mycerinus) near El Giza (El Gizeh), southwest of El Qahira (Cairo) in Egypt. The Great Pyramid ("Horizon of Khufu") was finished c. 2580 BC. Its original height was 480 ft 11 in (now, since loss of its topmost stones and the pyramidion, reduced to 449 ft 6 in) with a base line of 756 ft and thus covering slightly more than 13 acres. It has been estimated that a permanent work force of 4,000 required 30 years to maneuver into position the 2,300,000 limestone blocks averaging 2¾ tons each, totaling about 7,225,000 tons and a volume of 90,700,000 cu ft. A cost estimate published in Dec 1974 indicates that today it would require 405 men working 6 years at a cost of $1,130 million.

Of the other 6 wonders, only fragments remain of the Temple of Artemis (Diana) of the Ephesians, built c. 350 BC at Ephesus, Turkey (destroyed by the Goths in 262 AD), and of the Tomb of King Mausolus of Caria, built at Halicarnassus, now Bodrum, Turkey, c. 325 BC. No trace remains of the Hanging Gardens of Semiramis, at Babylon, Iraq (c. 600 BC); the 40-ft-tall marble, gold and ivory statue of Zeus (Jupiter) by Phidias (5th century BC) at Olympia, Greece (lost in a fire at Istanbul); the 117-ft-tall statue by Chares of Lindus of the figure of the god Helios (Apollo), called the Colossus of Rhodes (sculptured 292–280 BC, destroyed by an earthquake in 224 BC); or the 400-ft-tall lighthouse built by Sostratus of Cnidus c. 270 BC as a pyramid-shaped tower of white marble (destroyed by an earthquake in 1375 AD) on the island of Pharos (Greek, *pharos*=lighthouse), off the coast of El Iskandarya (Alexandria), Egypt.

Tallest Statue

The tallest free-standing statue is that of the "Motherland," an enormous prestressed concrete female figure on Mamayev Hill, outside Volgograd, USSR, designed in 1967 by Yevgenyi Vuchetich, to commemorate victory in the Battle of Stalingrad (1942–43). The statue from its base to the tip of a sword clenched in her right hand measures 270 ft.

The US sculptor Felix de Welton has announced a plan to replicate the Colossus of Rhodes to a height of 308 ft.

Near Bamiyan, Afghanistan, there are the remains of the recumbent Sakya Buddha, built of plastered rubble, which was "about 1,000 ft long" and is believed to date from the 3rd or 4th century AD.

TALLEST FREE-STANDING STATUE (left): This mammoth female figure called "Motherland" stands outside Volgograd, USSR. It is 270 ft tall to the top of her sword. TALLEST MONUMENT (right): The Gateway Arch at the Mississippi River in St. Louis is 630 ft high.

Tallest Monuments

The tallest monument is the stainless steel Gateway to the West Arch in St Louis, completed Oct 28, 1965, to commemorate the westward expansion after the Louisiana Purchase of 1803. It is a sweeping arch, spanning 630 ft and rising to a height of 630 ft, which cost $29 million. It was designed in 1947 by Eero Saarinen (d 1961).

The tallest monumental column commemorates the battle of San Jacinto (Apr 21, 1836), on the bank of the San Jacinto River near Houston, Tex. General Sam Houston (1793–1863) and his force of 743 Texan troops killed 630 Mexicans (out of a total force of 1,600) and captured 700 others, with the loss of 9 men killed and 30 wounded. Constructed in 1936–39, at a cost of $1½ million, the tapering column is 570 ft tall, 47 ft square at the base, and 30 ft square at the observation tower, which is surmounted by a star weighing 220 tons. It is built of concrete, faced with buff limestone, and weighs 35,150 tons.

Largest Prehistoric Monuments

The largest megalithic prehistoric monuments are the 28½-acre earthworks and stone circles of Avebury, Wiltshire, England rediscovered in 1646. The earliest calibrated date in the area of this neolithic site is *c.* 4200 BC. The whole work is 1,200 ft in diameter with a 40-ft ditch around the perimeter and required an estimated 15 million man-hours of work. The largest trilithons exist at Stonehenge, to the south of Salisbury Plain,

Wiltshire, with single sarsen blocks weighing over 50 tons and requiring over 550 men to drag them up a 9° gradient. The earliest stage in the construction of the ditch has been dated to 2180 BC ± 105. Whether Stonehenge was a lunar calendar, a temple, or an eclipse-predictor remains debatable.

Tallest Columns

The tallest columns are the 36 fluted pillars of Vermont marble in the colonnade of the Education Building, Albany, NY. Each one measures 90 ft tall and 6½ ft in base diameter.

The tallest load-bearing stone columns are those measuring 69 ft in the Hall of Columns of the Temple of Amun at Karnak, opposite Thebes on the Nile, the ancient capital of Upper Egypt. They were built in the 19th dynasty in the reign of Rameses II in *c.* 1270 BC.

Largest and Oldest Pyramids

The largest pyramid, and the largest monument ever constructed, is the Quetzalcóatl at Cholula de Rivadabia, 63 miles southeast of Mexico City. It is 177 ft tall and its base covers an area of nearly 45 acres. Its total volume has been estimated at 4.3 million cu yd, compared with 3,360,000 cu yd for the Pyramid of Cheops (see above). The pyramid-building era here was between the 2nd and 6th centuries AD.

The oldest known pyramid is the Djoser step pyramid at Saqqâra, Egypt, constructed to a height of 204 ft, originally with a Tura limestone casing, *c.* 2650 BC. The oldest New World pyramid is that on the island of La Venta in southeastern Mexico built by the Olmec people *c.* 800 BC. It is 100 ft tall with a base diameter of 420 ft.

Tallest Totem Pole

The tallest totem pole is 173 ft tall raised on June 6, 1973 at Alert Bay, British Columbia, Canada. It tells the story of the Kwakiutl and took 36 man-weeks to carve.

PYRAMIDS: The Djoser (left) of Egypt, built in 2650 BC, is the oldest, while the Quetzalcóatl (below) near Mexico City is the largest monument ever, covering nearly 45 acres.

Tallest Flagpole

The tallest flagpole ever erected was outside the Oregon Building at the 1915 Panama-Pacific International Exposition in San Francisco. Trimmed from a Douglas fir, it stood 299 ft 7 in in height. The tallest unsupported flagpole is a 170-ft-tall (plus 10 ft below ground) metal pole weighing 28,000 lb, erected in 1943 at the US Merchant Marine Academy in King's Point, NY. The pole, built by Kearney-National Inc, tapers from 24 in to 5½ in at the jack.

Obelisks

The longest an obelisk has remained *in situ* is that at Heliopolis, near Aswan, Egypt, erected by Senusret I *c.* 1750 BC.

The largest standing obelisk is that in the Piazza of St John in Lateran, Rome, erected in 1588. It came originally from the Circus Maximus (erected 357 AD) and before that from Heliopolis, Egypt (erected *c.* 1450 BC). It is 110 ft in height and weighs 504 tons.

Largest Earthworks and Mound

The largest earthworks carried out prior to the mechanical era were the Linear Earth Boundaries of the Benin Empire in the Bendel state of Nigeria. These were first reported in 1900 and partially surveyed in 1967. In Apr 1973 it was estimated that the total length of the earthworks was probably between 4,000 and 8,000 miles with a total of from 500 million to 600 million cu yd of earth moved.

The largest artificial mound is the gravel mound built as a memorial to the Seleucid King Antiochus I (reigned 69–34 BC). Located on the summit of Nemud Dagi (8,205 ft high) southeast of Malatya, eastern Turkey, the mound measures 197 ft tall and covers 7.5 acres.

Largest Tomb

The largest tomb is that of Emperor Nintoku (d *c.* 428 AD) south of Osaka, Japan. It measures 1,594 ft long × 1,000 ft wide × 150 ft high.

Ziggurat (Stage or Temple Tower)

The largest surviving ziggurat (from the verb *zaqaru,* Babylonian, to build high) is the Ziggurat of Ur (now Muqqayr, Iraq) with a base 200 ft × 150 ft built to at least 3 stories of which only the first and part of the second now survive to a height of 60 ft. It has been variously dated between *c.* 2050 BC and *c.* 2800 BC.

Largest Dome

The world's largest dome is the Louisiana Superdome in New Orleans. It has an outside diameter of 680 ft. (For more details, see *Largest Indoor Arena.*)

The largest dome of ancient architecture is that of the Pantheon, built in Rome in 112 AD, with a diameter of 142½ ft.

Largest Drydock

The largest drydock is that at Koyagi, Nagaṣaki, Japan completed in 1972. It measures 3,248 ft × 328 ft with a maximum shipbuilding capacity of 1 million tons deadweight.

LONGEST WALL: It has been estimated that it took 300,000 laborers over a decade to build the Great Wall of China.

Largest Dock Gate

The largest dock gate is that at Nigg Bay, Cromarty Firth, Scotland, first operated in March 1974. It measures 408 ft long, 50 ft high, with a 4-ft-thick base, and is made of reinforced concrete. With its sill, quoins and roundheads, it weighs a total of 17,882 tons.

Longest Jetty

The longest deep-water jetty is the Quai Hermann du Pasquier at Le Havre, France with a length of 5,000 ft. Part of an enclosed basin, it has a constant depth of water of 32 ft on both sides.

Longest Pier

The longest pier is the Dammam Pier in El Hasa, Saudi Arabia, on the Persian Gulf. A rock-filled causeway 4.84 miles long joins the steel trestle pier 1.80 miles long, which joins the Main Pier (744 ft long), giving an overall length of 6.79 miles. The work was begun in July 1948 and completed March 15, 1950.

Longest Breakwater

The longest breakwater protects the port of Galveston, Texas. The granite south breakwater is 6.74 miles long.

Lighthouses

The lighthouse with the most powerful light is Créac'h d'Ouessant lighthouse, established in 1638 and last altered in 1939 on l'Île d'Ouessant, Finistère, Brittany, France. It is 163 ft tall and, in times of fog, has a luminous intensity of up to 500 million candelas.

The lights with the greatest visible range are those 1,092 ft above the ground on the Empire State Building, NYC. Each of the four-arc mercury bulbs has a rated candlepower of 450 million, visible 80 miles away on the ground and 300 miles away from aircraft. They were switched on on March 31, 1956.

The tallest lighthouse is the steel tower 348 ft tall near Yamashita Park in Yokohama, Japan. It has a power of 600,000 candles and a visibility range of 20 miles.

Waterwheel

The largest waterwheel is the Mohammadieh Noria wheel at Hama, Syria, with a diameter of 131 ft. It dates from Roman times.

Water Flume

The first of the now nearly 250 water flumes was built in Newport Beach, Calif in 1971.

Longest Stairs

The longest is the service staircase for the Niesenbahn funicular which rises to 7,759 ft near Spiez, Switzerland. It has 11,674 steps and a banister. The T'ai Chan temple stairs of 6,600 stone-cut steps in the Shantung Mts, China, ascend 4,700 ft in 5 miles.

Longest Wall

The Great Wall of China, completed during the Ch'in dynasty, reign of Shih Huang-ti (246–210 BC), has a main-line length of 2,150 miles with a further 1,780 miles of branches and spurs, with a height of from 15 to 39 ft and up to 32 ft thick. It runs from Shanhaikuan, on the Gulf of Pohai, to Yümên-kuan and Yang-kuan and was kept in repair up to the 16th century. Some 32 miles of the Wall have been destroyed since 1966. Part of the Wall was blown up to make way for a dam in July 1979.

Longest Fence

The longest fence is the dingo-proof fence enclosing the main sheep areas of Queensland, Australia. The wire fence is 6 ft high, goes 1 ft underground, and stretches for 3,437 miles, more than the distance from Seattle to NY.

Largest Windows

The largest sheet of glass ever manufactured was one of 538.2 sq ft, or 65 ft 7 inches × 8 ft 2½ inches, exhibited by the Saint Gobain Company in France at the *Journées Internationales de Miroiterie* in March 1958. The largest single windows are those in the Palace of Industry and Technology at Rondpoint de la Défense, Paris, with an extreme width of 715.2 ft and a maximum height of 164 ft.

Doors

The largest doors are the 4 in the Vehicle Assembly Building near Cape Canaveral, Fla with a height of 460 ft. (See *Largest Scientific Buildings*)

The world's thickest door is the 48.5-ton shield made by Ray Proof Inc for the RTNS-II source at Lawrence Livermore Laboratory, Calif, which is 8 ft thick.

Largest Maze

The largest maze is at Longleat, near Warminster, Wiltshire, England, with 1.61 miles of paths flanked by 16,180 yew trees. It was opened on June 6, 1978.

Cemetery

The world's largest cemetery is one in Leningrad, USSR, which contains over 500,000 of the 1,300,000 victims of the German army's siege of 1941–42.

The largest crematorium is at the Nikolo-Arkhangelskoye Cemetery, East Moscow, completed in March 1972. It has 7 twin furnaces and several Halls of Farewell for atheists.

Largest Garbage Dump

Reclamation Plant No. 1, Fresh Kills, Staten Island, NY, opened in March 1974, is the world's largest sanitary landfill. In its first 4 months, 500,000 tons of refuse from NYC was dumped on the site by 700 barges.

Largest Revolving Globe

The largest revolving globe is the 24-ton sphere (27 ft 11 in in diameter) in the Coleman Map Building, Wellesley, Mass completed at a cost of $200,000 in 1956.

Largest Marquee (Canopy or Field Tent)

A marquee 310 ft long × 480 ft wide and consisting of 18¾ miles of 36-in wide canvas covered a ground area of 148,800 sq ft at the Royal Horticultural Society's Annual show in 1951 on the grounds of the Royal Hospital, Kensington and Chelsea, Greater London.

Advertising Signs

The largest advertising sign ever erected was the electric Citroën sign on the Eiffel Tower, Paris. It was switched on on July 4, 1925 and could be seen 24 miles away. It was in six colors with 250,000 lamps and 56 miles of electric cables. The letter "N" which terminated the name "Citroën" between the second and third levels measured 68 ft 5 in in height. The whole apparatus was taken down after 11 years in 1936.

The largest neon advertising sign was owned by the Atlantic Coast Line Railroad Co at Port Tampa, Fla. It measured 387 ft 6 in long and 76 ft high, weighed 196 tons and contained about 4,200 ft of red neon tubing. It was demolished on Feb 19, 1970.

Broadway's largest current billboard is 11,426 sq ft in area—equivalent to 107 ft × 107 ft. Broadway's largest working sign in Times Square, NYC, in 1966, showed two 42½-ft-tall "bottles" of Haig Scotch Whisky and an 80-ft-long "bottle" of Gordon's Gin being "poured" into a frosted glass.

The most massive working sign today is reputed to be outside the Circus Circus Hotel, Reno, Nev, named Topsy the Clown. It is 127 ft tall and weighs over 40 tons with 1.4 miles of neon tubing. The clown's smile measures 14 ft across.

The highest advertising signs are the four Bank of Montreal logos atop the 72-story 935-ft-tall First Canadian Place building in Toronto. Each

LARGEST REVOLVING GLOBE: This massive decoration has gone to Wellesley.

LARGEST FOUNTAIN (above): This 560-ft-high column in Fountain Hills, Ariz, uses 7,000 gals a min.

sign, built by Claude Neon Industries Ltd measures 20 ft × 22 ft, and was lifted into place by helicopter.

Largest Bonfire

A bonfire 120 ft high was built at Whitehaven, Cumbria, England, in 1902 in celebration of the Coronation of Edward VII. It used 672 tons of wood and 2,400 gallons of petroleum.

Largest Building Demolished by Explosives

The largest was the 21-story Traymore Hotel, Atlantic City, NJ on May 26, 1972. The 600-room hotel had a cubic capacity of 6,495,500 cu ft. Controlled Demolition Inc of Towson, Md did the job.

The tallest chimney ever demolished was the American Smelting and Refining Co chimney at Crockett, Calif on June 14, 1973. It stood 605 ft 5 in and was brought down by the same company.

Tallest Fountain

The tallest fountain is at Fountain Hills, Ariz built at a cost of $1½ million for McCulloch Properties Inc. At full pressure of 375 lb/sq in and at a rate of 7,000 gallons/min, the 560-ft column of water weighs more than 9 tons. The nozzle speed achieved by the three 600 hp pumps is 46.7 mph.

Tallest Scaffolding

The greatest scaffolding structure ever erected was one 486 ft high, using 152 miles of tubing, for the reconstruction of Guy's Hospital, London, in 1971.

Largest Vat

The largest vat is named "Strongbow," used by H. P. Bulmer Ltd, a cider company in Hereford, England. It measures 64½ ft in height, 75½ ft in diameter, and has a capacity of 1,956,000 gallons.

Naturist Resorts

The oldest naturist resort (the term "nudist camp" is deplored by naturists) is Der Freilichtpark, Klingberg, W Germany, established in 1903. The largest is the Centre Helio-Marin, Montalivet, near Bordeaux, France. Extending over 1¼ miles of coast and covering 420 acres, it has 1,200 chalets and 50,000 visitors per year. However, 100,000 people visit the smaller Centre Helio-Marin at Cap d'Agde, southern France, which covers 222 acres.

10. BORINGS AND MINES

Man's deepest penetration into the earth's crust is under Rig No. 32 gas well at No. 1 Bertha Rogers Field, Washita County, Okla. After 503 days of drilling, the Loffland Brothers Drilling Co. reached 31,441 ft (5.95 miles) on Apr 3, 1974. The hole temperature at the bottom was 475°F. A conception of the depth of this hole can be gained by the realization that it was sufficient in depth to lower the Sears Building of Chicago (the world's tallest) down it more than 21 times.

In May 1976 drilling was begun at Saatly, Azerbaijan, USSR in an attempt to reach the Mohorovicic discontinuity, a target depth of 49,212 ft.

A drilling 31,911 ft deep on the Kola Peninsula, USSR, was announced in July, 1979. The intention is to persist to 34,450 ft.

The deepest recorded drilling into the sea bed by the *Glomar Challenger* of the US Deep Sea Drilling Project is one of 5,709 ft, and the deepest site is one 20,483 ft below sea level.

Oil Fields

The largest oil field is the Ghawar Field, Saudi Arabia, developed by ARAMCO, which measures 150 miles by 22 miles. The Groningen gas field in the Netherlands, exploited since 1965, has reserves of 100 trillion (100×10^{12}) cu ft. This may be matched by the Dome find of 1972 off Qatar.

Greatest Gusher

The most prolific wildcat recorded is the 1,160-ft-deep Lucas No. 1, at Spindletop, about 3 miles south of Beaumont, Tex, on Jan 10, 1901. The gusher was heard more than a mile away and yielded 800,000 barrels during the 9 days it was uncapped. The surrounding ground subsequently yielded 142 million barrels.

Greatest Oil Spill

The worst oil spill in history was 260,000 tons of oil from the supertankers *Atlantic Empress* and *Aegean Captain* when they collided off Tobago on July 19, 1979.

GREATEST GUSHER (left): In Jan 1901, this well near Beaumont, Tex lost 800,000 barrels of oil during the 9 days it was uncapped after exploding. DEEPEST PENETRATION (right): The Loffland rig drilled almost 6 miles down.

The slick from the Mexican marine blow-out beneath the drilling rig *Ixtoc I* in the Bay of Campeche, Gulf of Mexico on June 3, 1979 reached 400 miles by Aug 5, 1979.

Greatest Flare

The greatest gas fire ever burnt was at Gassi Touil in the Algerian Sahara from noon on Nov 13, 1961 at 9:30 a.m. on Apr 28, 1962. The pillar of flame rose 450 ft and the smoke 600 ft. It was eventually extinguished by Paul Neal ("Red") Adair, aged 47, of Austin, Tex, using 550 lb of dynamite. His fee was understood to be about $1 million.

Oil Platforms

The deepest fixed leg oil platform sits in 1,025 ft of water 100 miles southeast of New Orleans, La. The overall height of the structure in this $275 million enterprise is 1,265 ft. Experiments have been proceeding with FTL's (Floating Tension Leg) structures for production platforms at even greater depths.

The world's most massive oil platform is the Central Ninian production and storage platform built at Loch Kishorn, Highland, Scotland. When towed out to the North Sea site on May 5, 1978 it was the heaviest object ever moved—661,500 tons ballasted weight. She was towed by 8 tugs with a combined strength of 92,000 ihp. The height of the concrete structure is 509 ft and the overall height 820 ft. The tallest fixed leg platform in the North Sea is one 750 ft in height built by Redpath Dorman Long for Shell-Esso at Methil, Fife and moved to the Brent Field in April 1976.

The production platform in the deepest water is BNOC's Thistle A platform in 530 ft of water.

Largest Gas Tank

The largest gas holder or tank is that at Fontaine l'Eveque, Belgium, where disused mines have been adapted to store up to 17,650 million cu ft of gas at ordinary pressure. Probably the largest conventional gas tank is that at Wien-Semmering, Vienna, Austria, completed in 1968, with a height of 274 ft 8 in and a capacity of 10.59 million cu ft.

Wells

The deepest water well is the Stensvad Water Well 11-W1 7,320 ft deep drilled by the Great Northern Drilling Co Inc in Rosebud County, Mont in Oct–Nov 1961.

The Thermal Power Co geothermal steam well begun in Sonoma County, Calif in 1955 is now down to 9,029 ft.

The highest recorded flow rate of any artesian well is 20,000 gallons/min, certified in 1973 for a well 20 miles northwest of Orlando, Fla by the Wekiva River.

Mines

The earliest known mining operations were in the Ngwenya Hills of the Hhohho District of northwestern Swaziland where hematite (iron ore) was mined for body paint c. 41,000 BC. The earliest known copper mines were reported in Feb 1977, in the Timna Valley, north of Elath, Israel, tentatively dated *ante* 3000 BC.

The deepest mine is the Western Deep Levels Mine at Carletonville, South Africa. The deepest penetration attained is 11,752 ft in the No. 2 Shaft. At such extreme depths where the rock temperatures reach 131°F, refrigerated ventilation is necessary. Rock bursts due to the pressures on the 2,500-million-year-old rock are a continuous hazard.

Gold Mines

The largest gold-mining area is the Witwatersrand gold field extending 30 miles east and west of Johannesburg, South Africa. Gold was discovered there in 1886 by George Harrison and by 1944 more than 45% of the world's gold was mined there by 320,000 Bantu and 44,000 Europeans. In 1979 50% of the world's supply came from this area whose production reached a peak of 1,103 tons in 1970.

The largest gold mine in area is East Rand Proprietary Mines of South Africa, whose 8,785 claims cover 12,100 acres. The largest, by volume extracted, is Randfontein Estates Gold Mine Co Ltd with 170 million cu yd—enough to cover Manhattan Island to a depth of 8 ft. The main tunnels if placed end to end would stretch a distance of 2,600 miles.

The world's most productive gold mine is Maruntan, USSR, with an estimated 88 tons per year.

The richest gold mine historically has been Crown Mines with nearly 49.4 million oz. The richest in yield in 1977 was W Driefontein with 0.75 oz per ton milled, but Vaal Reefs produced the most with 73.8 tons in 1978.

Iron Mines

The largest iron mine is at Lebedinsky, USSR, in the Kursk Magnetic Anomaly which has altogether an estimated 22,400 million tons of rich (45–65%) ore and 11,200,000 million tons of poorer ore in seams up to 2,000 ft thick. The world's greatest reserves are, however, those of Brazil, estimated to total 65,000 million tons, or 35% of the world's total surface stock.

Copper Mines

Historically the world's most productive copper mine has been the Bingham Canyon Mine, Utah, belonging to the Kennecott Copper Corp with over 9 million tons in the 65 years 1904–68. Currently the most productive is the Chuquicamata mine of the Anaconda Company 150 miles north of Antofagasta, Chile, with more than 330,000 tons.

The largest underground copper mine is the San Manuel Copper Mine in Arizona, owned by the Magma Copper Co with 355.8 miles of underground workings, and an average annual extraction of over 193 million tons of ore.

Silver, Lead and Zinc Mines

The largest lead, zinc and silver mine is the Kidd Creek Mine of Texasgulf Canada Ltd, located at Timmins, Ontario, Canada.

Since 1970, the leading lead mine has been the Vibernum Trend in southeast Missouri with 489,397 tons in 1972, from which is extracted some 10% of the world's output of lead.

The largest zinc smelter is the Cominco Ltd plant at Trail, British Columbia, Canada, which has an annual capacity of 295,000 tons of zinc and 900 tons of cadmium.

Tungsten Mine

The largest tungsten mine with published output figures is the Union Carbide mine in Mount Morgan, near Bishop, Calif. Opened in 1937, it has a capacity of 2,200 tons per day and a work force of 420.

Tin Mining

The most productive dredging for tin ever recorded was 882.9 tons of concentrate (76.8% pure tin) by Ayer Hitam No. 2 Dredge at Puchong, Malaysia in the 30 days of Nov 1976 at 237 ft below surface level in a pond lowered 70 ft by pumping.

Platinum

The largest platinum refinery is the Impala plant at Springs Mine,

South Africa. Largest producer is the Rustenburg Group, with more than 1 million oz per year.

Uranium

The largest uranium mine, located at Rossing in Namibia (South-West Africa) went into full production in 1978.

Production is expected to start in 1984 on the greater find of at least 275,000 tons of high grade uranium oxide, some 7,875 ft under Mid-west Lake in northern Saskatchewan, Canada.

Largest Quarry

The largest excavation is the Bingham Canyon Copper Mine, 30 miles south of Salt Lake City, Utah. From 1906 to mid-1976 the total excavation has been 3,700 million tons over an area of 2.81 sq miles to a depth of 2,540 ft. This is seven times the amount of material moved to build the Panama Canal. Three shifts of 900 men work around the clock with 39 electric shovels, 67 locomotives, 113 dump trucks and 17 drilling machines for the 31.3 tons of explosive used daily. The record extraction in one 24-hour day is 504,167 tons on Oct 13, 1974.

The deepest open pit of the premechanical, pick-and-shovel era is the Kimberley Open Mine in South Africa, which took 43 years (1871 to 1914) to dig to a depth of nearly 1,200 ft, with a diameter of about 1,500 ft and a circumference of nearly a mile, covering an area of 36 acres. Over 3 tons (14,504,566 carats) of diamonds have been extracted from the 23,500,000 tons of earth dug out. The inflow of water has now risen to a depth of 845 ft.

Largest Stone

The largest mined slab of quarried stone on record is one of 2,016 tons of slate from Spoutcrag Quarry, Langdale Valley, Cumbria, England, in May 1969.

Spoil Dump

The largest artificial spoil dump is the New Cornelia Tailings at Ten Mile Wash, Ariz, with a volume of 274,026,000 cu yd.

LARGEST QUARRY (left) is the Bingham Canyon Copper Mine in Utah. DEEPEST OPEN PIT DUG BY MAN is the Kimberley diamond mine in So Africa.

Chapter 8

The Mechanical World

1. SHIPS

Evidence of seafaring between the Greek mainland and the island of Melos to trade obsidian *c.* 7250 BC was published in 1971. Oars found in bogs at Magle Mose, Sjaelland, Denmark, and Star Carr, North Yorkshire, England, have been dated to the 8th millennium BC.

The oldest surviving boat is the 142-ft-long 40-ton Nile boat buried near the Great Pyramid of Khufu, Egypt, *c.* 2515 BC, and now reassembled.

The oldest shipwreck ever found is one of a Cycladic trading vessel.located off the islet of Dhokos, near the Greek island of Hydra reported in May 1975 and dated to 2450 BC ± 250.

Earliest Power Vessels

Propulsion by steam engine was first achieved when in 1783 the Marquis Jouffroy d'Abbans ascended a reach of the Saône River near Lyons, France in the 180-ton paddle steamer *Pyroscaphe.*

The tug *Charlotte Dundas* was the first successful power-driven vessel. She was a paddlewheel steamer built in Scotland in 1801–02 by William Symington (1763–1831), using a double-acting condensing engine constructed by James Watt (1736–1819).

The earliest regular steam run was by the *Clermont,* built by Robert Fulton (1765–1815), a US engineer, which maintained a service from NYC to Albany (150 miles in 32 hours) from Aug 17, 1807.

Oldest Vessels Afloat

The oldest active steam ship is the *Skibladner,* which has plied Lake Mjøsa, Norway, since 1856. Originally built in Motala, Sweden, she has had two major refittings.

OLDEST STEAMSHIP IN USE: The "Skibladner" has been plying a lake in Norway since 1856, after only two major refittings.

The oldest mechanically propelled boat of certain date is the 48-ton Brestal steam-driven dredger or drag-boat *Bertha* of 50 ft, designed by I. K. Brunel in 1844 and afloat at the Exeter Maritime Museum, Devon, England.

G. H. Pattinson's 40-ft steam launch *Dolly,* raised after 67 years from Ullswater, England in 1962, and now on Lake Windermere, also probably dates from the 1840's.

Earliest Turbine

The first turbine ship was the *Turbinia,* built in 1894, at Wallsend-on-Tyne, England, to the design of Charles Algernon Parsons (1854–1931). The *Turbinia* was 100 ft long and of 44½ tons displacement with machinery consisting of three steam turbines totaling about 2,000 shaft hp. At her first public demonstration in 1897 she reached a speed of 34.5 knots (39.7 mph).

Earliest Atlantic Crossings

The earliest crossing of the Atlantic by a power vessel, as opposed to an auxiliary-engined sailing ship, was a 22-day voyage, begun in Apr 1827, from Rotterdam, Netherlands to the West Indies by the *Curaçao.* She was a 127-ft wooden paddle boat of 438 tons, built as the *Calpe* in Dover, England in 1826, and purchased by the Dutch Government for the West Indian mail service. The earliest Atlantic crossing entirely under steam (with intervals for desalting the boilers) was by HMS *Rhadamanthus* from Plymouth, England to Barbados in 1832. The earliest crossing of the Atlantic under continuous steam power was by the condenser-fitted packet ship *Sirius* (703 tons) from Queenstown (now Cobh), Ireland to Sandy Hook, NJ in 18 days 10 hours Apr 4–22, 1838.

Wooden Ships

The heaviest wooden ship ever built was the *Richelieu,* 333 ft 8 in long, of 8,534 tons launched in Toulon, France on Dec 3, 1873.

> The longest modern wooden ship ever built was the NY-built *Rochambeau* (1867–72) formerly the *Dunderberg,* which measured 377 ft 4 in overall. It should be noted that the biblical length of Noah's Ark was 300 cubits or, at 18 in to a cubit, 450 ft.

Longest Dug-out Canoe

The longest canoe is the 117-ft-long, 20-ton Kauri wood Maori war canoe *Nga Toki Matawhaorua,* built with adzes at Kerikeri Inlet, New Zealand in 1940 to hold a crew of 70 or more.

Largest Sailing Ships

The largest sailing vessel ever built was the *France II* (5,806 gross tons), launched at Bordeaux in 1911. The *France II* was a steel-hulled, 5-masted barque (square-rigged on 4 masts and fore and aft rigged on the aftermost mast). Her hull measured 418 ft overall. Although principally designed as a sailing vessel with a stump topgallant rig, she was also fitted with two steam engines. She was wrecked in 1922.

The only 7-masted sailing vessel ever built was the 375.6-ft-long *Thomas W. Lawson* (5,218 gross tons), built at Quincy, Mass in 1902. She was lost in the English Channel on Dec 15, 1907.

Largest Junks

The largest junk on record was the seagoing *Cheng Ho* of *c.* 1420, flagship of Admiral Cheng Ho's 62 treasure ships, with a displacement of 3,100 tons and a length variously estimated up to 538 ft and believed to have had 9 masts.

A river junk 361 ft long, with treadmill-operated paddlewheels, was recorded in 1161 AD. In *c.* 280 AD a floating fortress 600 ft square, built by Wang Chün on the Yangtze, took part in the Chin-Wu river war. Present-day junks do not, even in the case of the Chiangsu traders, exceed 170 ft in length.

Longest Day's Run Under Sail

The longest day's run claimed by any sailing ship was one of 465 nautical miles (535.45 statute miles) in 23 hours 17 min by the *Champion of the Seas* (2,722 registered tons) of the Liverpool Black Ball Line, running before a northwesterly gale in the south Indian Ocean under Capt Alex. Newlands. The elapsed time between the fixes was 23 hours 17 min, giving an average of 19.97 knots.

Largest Sails

The largest spars ever carried were those in the British Royal Navy battleship *Temeraire,* completed at Chatham, Kent, on Aug 31, 1877. The fore and main yards measured 115 ft in length. The mainsail contained 5,100 sq ft of canvas, weighing 2 tons, and the total sail area was 25,000 sq ft.

Fastest Atlantic Crossing

The fastest Atlantic crossing was made by the *United States* (then 51,988, later 38,216, gross tons), former flagship of the United States Lines. On her maiden voyage between July 3 and 7, 1952, from NYC to Le Havre, France and Southampton, England she averaged 35.59 knots, or 40.98 mph, for 3 days 10 hours 40 min (6:36 p.m. GMT July 3, to 5:16 a.m. July 7) on a route of 2,949 nautical miles from the Ambrose Light Vessel, NJ to the Bishop Rock Light, Isles of Scilly, Cornwall, England. During this run, July 6–7, 1952, she steamed the greatest distance ever covered by any ship in a day's run (24 hours)—868 nautical miles, hence

LONGEST DUGOUT CANOE: This 20-ton Kauri wood Maori war canoe, built at Kerikeri, New Zealand in 1940, is 117 ft long and seats more than 70 paddlers.

averaging 36.17 knots (41.65 mph). The maximum speed attained from her 240,000 shaft hp engines was 38.32 knots (44.12 mph) in trials June 9–10, 1952.

Fastest Pacific Crossing

The fastest crossing of the Pacific Ocean (4,840 nautical miles) was 6 days 1 hour 27 min by the containership *Sea-Land Commerce* (50,315 tons) from Yokohama, Japan to Long Beach, Calif in 1973, at an average speed of 33.27 knots (38.31 mph).

Southernmost Sail

The farthest south ever reached by a ship was achieved on Feb 15, 1912, when the *Fram* reached latitude 78° 41′ S, off the Antarctic coast.

Largest Passenger Liner

The largest liner afloat and longest liner ever built is the *Norway* of 63,379 tons and 1,035 ft in length. She was built as the *France* in 1961 and renamed after purchase in June 1979 by Knut Kloster of Norway. Her second maiden voyage was from Southampton on May 7, 1980.

The *Queen Elizabeth 2* set a "turn-around" record of 8 hours 3 min in NYC on May 17, 1972. In her 1980 World Cruise, the price of her major suites was $212,700 each.

The original *Queen Elizabeth,* no longer afloat, was the largest ever built with 83,673 gross tons but a length of 1,031 ft, 4 ft shorter than the *Norway.*

Largest Battleships

The largest battleship now is the USS *New Jersey,* with a full-load displacement of 59,000 tons and an overall length of 888 ft. She was the last fire support ship on active service and was decommissioned on Dec 17, 1969.

The Japanese battleships *Yamato* (completed on Dec 16, 1941 and sunk southwest of Kyushu by US planes on Apr 7, 1945) and *Musashi* (sunk in the Philippine Sea by 11 bombs and 16 torpedoes on Oct 24, 1944) were the largest battleships ever commissioned, each with a full-load displacement of 72,809 tons. With an overall length of 863 ft, a beam of 127 ft and a full-load draught of 35½ ft, they mounted nine 18.1-in guns in three triple turrets. Each gun weighed 181 tons and was 75 ft in length, firing a 3,200-lb projectile.

Largest Aircraft Carrier

The warships with the largest full-load displacement in the world are the US Navy aircraft carriers USS *Nimitz* and *Dwight D. Eisenhower* at 91,400 tons. They are 1,092 ft in length overall and have a speed well in excess of 30 knots with their nuclear-powered 280,000 shaft hp reactors. They have to be refuelled after about 900,000 miles steaming. Their complement is 6,100. The total cost of the *Eisenhower,* commissioned on Oct 18, 1977 exceeded $2 billion excluding the more than 90-plus aircraft carried. The USS *Enterprise* is, however, 1,102 ft long and thus still the longest warship ever built.

Fastest Destroyer

The highest speed attained by a destroyer was 45.02 knots (51.84 mph) by the 3,120-ton French destroyer *Le Terrible* in 1935. She was built in Blainville and powered by four Yarrow small-tube boilers and two Rateau geared turbines giving 100,000 shaft hp. She was removed from the active list at the end of 1957.

Longest, Fastest and Deepest Submarines

The $1,250 million nuclear-powered submarine USS *Ohio* was due to go into operational service in late 1980, with 24 Trident I missiles of 4,600-mile range and a submerged displacement of 18,700 tons. She is 560 ft in length. The USSR Delta II class submarines, first reported in Nov 1973 with 16 SSN 8 missiles may be even larger. Four or five were in service by Jan 1977, although larger submarines were reported under construction.

The fastest submarines are the US Navy's tear-drop hulled nuclear vessels of the *Los Angeles* class. They have been listed officially as capable of a speed of "30 plus knots" but the true figure is believed to be dramatically higher. The first 4 were commissioned in 1975–76, with an additional 19 in 1979–80.

The two US Navy vessels able to descend 12,000 ft are the 3-man *Trieste II* (DSV 1) of 303 tons, recommissioned in Nov 1973 and the DSV 2 (deep submergence vessel) USS *Alvin*. The *Trieste II* was reconstructed from the record-breaking bathyscaphe *Trieste,* but without the Krupp-built sphere, which enabled it to descend to 35,820 ft.

Largest Barges

Two RoRo (roll-on roll-off) barges of 16,700 tons and 580-ft length each, owned and operated by the Crowley Maritime Corp of San Francisco are currently the largest. They carry up to 376 trailer trucks each with tri-level loading, between Florida and Puerto Rico. The company has on the drawing board plans for 700-ft long barges for 1982.

LARGEST BARGE: This roll-on roll-off barge is one of the two that can carry 376 trailer trucks.

Largest Tanker

The largest tanker and ship of any kind is the French *Pierre Guillaumat* of 555,031 tons deadweight (274,838 grt), completed for Compagnie Nationale de Navigation on Nov 9, 1977. She is 1,359 ft long with a beam of 206.9 ft, has a draught of 93.8 ft, and is powered by 4 turbines delivering 65,000 shp. She can maintain a speed of 18.4 mph. *Bellamya* (completed for Société Maritime Shell on Dec 31, 1976) is 275,276 grt but 553,662 dwt.

Largest Cargo Vessel

The largest vessel capable of carrying dry cargo is the Liberian ore/oil carrier *World Gala* of 282,450 dwt with a length of 1,109 ft and beam of 179 ft, owned by Liberian Trident Transports Inc, completed in 1973.

Most Powerful Tugs

The largest and most powerful tugs are the *Wolraad Waltemade* and her sister ship *John Ross* (2,822 grt) rated at 19,200 hp and with a bollard pull of 172.7 tons at 90% of full power. They have an overall length of 310 ft 5 in and a beam of 49 ft 10 in. They were built to handle the largest tankers, and were completed respectively in Apr 1976 (Leith, Scotland) and in Oct 1976 (Durban, South Africa).

Largest Car Ferry

The largest car and passenger ferry is the 30.5-knot, 24,600 grt GTS *Finnjet* which entered service across the Baltic between Helsinki and Travemünde, W Germany May 13, 1977. She can carry 350 cars and 1,532 passengers.

Largest Hydrofoil

The largest naval hydrofoil is the 212-ft-long *Plainview* (310 tons full load), launched by Lockheed Shipbuilding and Construction Company at Seattle, Wash June 28, 1965. She has a service speed of 50 knots (57 mph).

Three 165-ton Supramar PTS 150 Mk. III hydrofoils, carrying 250 passengers at 40 knots, ply the Malmö-Copenhagen crossing between Swe-

LARGEST FERRY: The GTS "Finnjet" can attain a speed of 30.5 knots as it crosses the Baltic Sea, carrying up to 350 cars and 1,532 passengers.

MOST POWERFUL ICEBREAKER: "Arktika," the USSR's atomic-powered ship can break through 13-ft-thick ice at 4.6 mph.

den and Denmark. They were built by Westermoen Hydrofoil Ltd of Mandal, Norway.

A 500-ton wing ground effect vehicle capable of carrying 900 tons has been reported in the USSR.

Most Powerful Dredger

The most powerful dredger is the 468.4-ft-long *Prins der Nederlanden* of 10,586 grt. Using two suction tubes, she can dredge 22,400 tons of sand from a depth of 115 ft in less than one hour.

Most Powerful Icebreaker

The most powerful icebreaker is the USSR's 25,000-ton atomic-powered icebreaker *Arktika,* able to smash through ice up to nearly 13 ft thick. On Aug 9, 1977 she sailed from Murmansk and reached the North Pole at 2 a.m. GMT on Aug 17.

The largest *converted* icebreaker is the 1,007-ft-long SS *Manhattan* (43,000 shp), which was converted by the Humble Oil Co into a 150,000-ton icebreaker with an armored prow 69 ft 2 in long. She made a double voyage through the Northwest Passage in arctic Canada from Aug 24 to Nov 12, 1969. The Northwest Passage was first navigated by Roald Amundsen (Norway) in the sailing sloop *Gjöa* on July 11, 1906.

Most Expensive Yacht

King Khalid's Saudi Arabian 212-ft $10-million royal yacht was upstaged as the most expensive in 1979 by a five-deck 282-footer built by the Benetti Shipyard, Viaveggio, Italy for a reputed $24 million to the order of Adnan Khashoggi. It has a helicopter and 5 speed boats.

Largest Collision

The closest approach to an irresistible force striking an immovable object occurred on Dec 16, 1977, 22 miles off the coast of southern Africa, when the tanker *Venoil* (330,954 dwt) struck her sister ship *Venpet* (330,869 dwt).

Largest Whale Factory

The largest whale factory ship is the USSR's *Sovietskaya Ukraina* (32,034 gross tons), with a summer dwt of 46,000 tons, completed in Oct 1959. She is 713.6 ft in length and has a 94 ft-3 in-beam.

Deepest Anchorage

The deepest anchorage ever achieved is one of 24,600 ft in the mid-Atlantic Romanche Trench by Capt Jacques-Yves Cousteau's research vessel *Calypso,* with a 5½-mile-long nylon cable, on July 29, 1956.

Largest Wreck

The largest ship ever wrecked has been the 312,186-dwt VLCC (Very Large Crude Carrier) *Energy Determination* which blew up and broke in two in the Straits of Hormuz on Dec 12, 1979. Her full value was $58 million.

Greatest Roll

The ultimate in rolling was recorded in heavy seas off Coos Bay, Ore, Nov 13, 1971 when the US Coast Guard motor lifeboat *Intrepid* made a 360-degree roll.

2. ROAD VEHICLES*

Before the widespread use of tarred road surfaces from 1845 coach-riding was slow and hazardous. The zenith in speed was reached on July 13, 1888, when J. Selby, Esq, drove the "Old Times" coach 108 miles from London to Brighton and back with 8 teams and 14 changes in 7 hours 50 min to average 13.79 mph. Four-horse carriages could maintain a speed of 21⅓ mph for nearly an hour.

CARS

Most Cars

In 1978 it was estimated that in the US 138 million drivers drove 147 million vehicles 1,480,000 million miles, or 206.2 miles per week per driver.

Earliest Automobiles

The earliest car of which there is record is a 2-ft-long steam-powered model, constructed by Ferdinand Verbiest (d 1687), a Belgian Jesuit priest, which he described in his *Astronomia Europaea.* His 1668 model was possibly inspired either by Giovanni Branca's description of a steam

---

* Automotive records in greater detail may be found in *Car Facts and Feats*, one of the Guinness Family of Books (Sterling).

turbine published in 1629, or by writings on "fire carts" during the Chu dynasty (*c.* 800 BC) in the library of the Emperor K'ang-hsi of China, to whom he was an astronomer during the period *c.* 1665–80.

The earliest mechanically-propelled passenger vehicle was the first of two military steam tractors completed at the Paris Arsenal in 1769 by Nicolas-Joseph Cugnot (1725–1804). This reached about 2¼ mph. His second, larger tractor, completed in 1771, today survives in the *Conservatoire national des arts et métiers* in Paris.

The first true internal-combustion-engined vehicle was built by a Londoner, Samuel Brown (patented Apr 25, 1826) whose 4-hp 2-cylinder atmospheric gas 88 liter engined carriage climbed Shooters Hill, Blackheath, Kent, England in May 1826.

Earliest Gasoline-Driven Cars

The first successful gasoline-driven car, the Motorwagen, built by Karl-Friedrich Benz (1844–1929) of Karlsruhe, ran at Mannheim, Germany in late 1885. It was a 560-lb 3-wheeler reaching 8–10 mph. Its single-cylinder 4-stroke chain-drive engine (bore 91.4 mm, stroke 160 mm) delivered 0.85 hp at 200 rpm. It was patented on Jan 29, 1886. Its first 1-km road test was reported in the local newspaper, the *Neue Badische Landeszeitung,* of June 4, 1886, under the heading "Miscellaneous." Two were built in 1885 of which one has been preserved in "running order" at the Deutsches Museum, Munich.

Earliest Registrations

The world's first plates were probably introduced by the Parisian police in France in 1893. The first American plates were in 1901 in NY. Registration plates were introduced in Britain in 1903. The original A1 plate was secured by the 2nd Earl Russell (1865–1931) for his 12-hp Napier. This plate, willed to Trevor Laker of Leicester, was sold in Aug 1959, for £2,500 (then $7,000) in aid of charity. It was reported in Apr 1973 that a "cherished" number plate changed hands in a private sale for

HIGH-PRICED PLATE: This "A 1" license plate sold for $7,000 in 1959—more than the cost of many cars.

£14,000 (then $35,000). Sir Run Run Shaw, the movie producer, on Dec 9, 1978 bid HK $330,000 (about $66,000) for a "Good Fortune" number plate at a Hong Kong Government charity auction.

Fastest Cars

The highest speed attained by any wheeled land vehicle is 739.666 mph or Mach 1.0106 in a one-way stretch by the ròcket-engined *Budweiser Rocket,* designed by William Fredrick, and driven by Stan Barrett at Edwards Air Force Base, Calif on Dec 17, 1979. The vehicle, owned by Hal Needham, has a 48,000-hp rocket engine with 6,000 lb of extra thrust from a sidewinder missile. The rear wheels (100 lb solid discs) lifted 10 in off the ground above Mach 0.95 acting as 7,500 rpm gyroscopes.

The highest speed attained by any jet-engined car is 613.995 mph over a flying 666.386 yd by the 34-ft-7-in-long, 9,000-lb *Spirit of America— Sonic I,* driven by Norman Craig Breedlove (b Los Angeles, March 23, 1938) on Bonneville Salt Flats, Utah, on Nov 15, 1965. The car was powered by a General Electric J79 GE-3 jet engine, developing 15,000 lb static thrust at sea level.

The highest speed attained by a wheel-driven car is 429.311 mph over a flying 666.386 yd by Donald Malcolm Campbell (1921–67), a British engineer, in the 30-ft-long *Bluebird,* weighing 9,600 lb, on the salt flats at Lake Eyre, South Australia, on July 17, 1964. The car was powered by a Bristol-Siddeley Proteus 705 gas-turbine engine developing 4,500 shp. Its *peak* speed was *c.* 445 mph. It was rebuilt in 1962, after a crash at about 360 mph on Sept 16, 1960.

The highest speed attained by a piston-engined car is 418.504 mph over a flying 666.386 yd by Robert Sherman Summers (b Omaha, Neb Apr 4, 1937) in *Goldenrod* at Bonneville Salt Flats, Utah, on Nov 12, 1965. The car, measuring 32 ft long and weighing 5,500 lb was powered by four fuel-injected Chrysler Hemi engines (total capacity 27,924 cc) developing 2,400 bhp.

The diesel-engined prototype 230-hp 3-liter Mercedes C 111/3 attained 203.3 mph in tests on the Nardo Circuit, Italy, Oct 5–15, 1978.

Fastest Racing Car

The fastest racing car yet produced was the Porsche 917/30 Can-Am car powered by a 5,374-cc flat 12 turbo-charged engine developing 1,100 bhp. On the Paul Ricard circuit near Toulon, France in Aug 1973 Mark Donohue (US) reached a speed of 257 mph. The two models built took 2.2 sec to go from 0 to 60 mph, 4.3 sec from 0 to 100 mph, and 12.6 sec from 0 to 200 mph. In 1973, the UOP Shadow Can-Am car's 8.1-liter turbo-charged Chevrolet V8 engine developed 1,240 bhp.

Fastest Production Road Model

Various detuned track cars have been licensed for road use but are not purchasable production models. Manufacturers of very fast and very expensive models are understandably reluctant to allow maximum speed tests to be carried out. The fastest manufacturer's *claim* (as opposed to independent road-tests) for a production road car, is 195.7 mph for the Lamborghini Countach P400. The 5.3 liter V8 Aston Martin Lagonda *Bulldog* announced on Apr 15, 1980 has a claimed top speed of 190 mph and a 0–60 mph acceleration of "just over 5 sec."

FASTEST CARS: (Top) The "Budweiser Rocket"—739.666 mph. (Right) The Aston-Martin "Bulldog," a road car—190 mph. (Below) Breedlove's "Spirit of America," jet propelled—613.995 mph—and the Porsche 917/30 Can Am (leftmost car in the photo) a track racer—257 mph.

The highest road-tested acceleration reported is 0–60 mph in 5.3 sec and 0–100 mph in 12.3 sec by *Motor* (May 19, 1979 issue) for a Porsche 3,299 cc Turbo at Ehra-Lessien, W Germany. The engine yielded 300 bhp (DIN) at 5500 rpm.

Most Durable Car

The highest recorded mileage for a car is 1,184,880 authenticated miles by Aug 1978 for a 1957 Mercedes 180D owned by Robert O'Reilly of Olympia, Wash.

Longest in Production

The longest any car has been in production is 42 years (1938 to date), including wartime interruptions, in the case of the West German Volkswagen "Beetle" series, originally designed by Ferdinand Porsche. It ceased production on Jan 19, 1978, with 19,200,000 cars produced. Residual production continues in South America.

Largest Cars

Of cars produced for private road use, the largest has been the Bugatti "Royale" Type 41, known as the "Golden Bugatti," of which only 6 (not 7) were made at Molsheim, France by the Italian, Ettore Bugatti, and some survive. First built in 1927, this car has an 8-cylinder engine of 12.7 liter capacity, and measures over 22 ft in length. The hood is over 7 ft long.

A special $100,000 "stretched" 1976 Fleetwood Cadillac built for Joel D. Nelson of Bakersfield, Calif exhibited in Apr 1979, measures 29 ft 6 in long. It is fitted inside with 2 color TV sets, an 8-speaker stereo system, a sink, refrigerator, bar, videotape recorder and camera, 4 telephones and a safe.

The longest limousine is the 9-door 1968 6-wheeled Oldsmobile Toronado which measures 28 ft overall.

(For cars not intended for private use, see *Largest Engines.*)

Most Expensive Used Cars

The greatest price paid for a used car is $421,040 for a 1936 Mercedes-Benz Roadster from the M. L. Cohn collection by a telephone bidder in

LARGEST PRODUCTION CAR: This 1931 Type 41 "Royale" Bugatti, called the "Golden Bugatti," was over 22 ft long, but was not the longest. Six were made.

LONGEST CAR (top and left above): This spacious Cadillac is 29½ ft long, with a 1976 Fleetwood body specially extended for Joel Nelson of Bakersfield, Calif. Inside it is equipped with such necessities as a bar, sink and refrigerator, 4 telephones and a safe, and as accessories an 8-speaker stereo system with a videotape recorder and camera. It is said to have cost $100,000. MOST INEXPENSIVE CAR (Right, above): The 1922 Red Bug Buckboard listed at $150, even $125. It weighed 245 lb. MOST EXPENSIVE USED CAR (below): This 1936 Mercedes-Benz Roadster brought $421,040 from a telephone bidder from Monaco in 1979 at a Los Angeles auction. The car is from the M. L. Cohn Collection.

Monaco at Christie's sale Feb 25, 1979 at the Los Angeles Convention Center.

The greatest collection of vintage cars is the William F. Harrah Collection of 1,700, estimated to be worth more than $4 million in Reno, Nev. Mr Harrah was still looking for a Chalmers-Detroit 1909 Tourabout, an Owen car of 1910–12, and a Nevada Truck of 1915 when he died in 1978.

Most Expensive Special Cars

The most expensive car ever built is the Presidential 1969 Lincoln Continental Executive delivered to the US Secret Service on Oct 14, 1968. It has an overall length of 21 ft 6.3 in with a 13-ft-4-in wheelbase and, with the addition of 2 tons of armor plate, weighs 12,000 lb. The cost for research, development and manufacture was estimated at $500,000, but it is rented for a mere $5,000 per annum. Even if all four tires were to be shot out it can travel at 50 mph on inner rubber-edged steel discs.

Carriage House Motor Cars Ltd of NYC in March 1978 completed 4 years' work on converting a 1973 Rolls-Royce, including lengthening it by 30 in. The price tag was $500,000.

Most Inexpensive

The cheapest car of all-time was the 1922 Red Bug Buckboard, built by Briggs and Stratton Co of Milwaukee, Wis listed at $150–$125. It had a 62-in wheel base and weighed 245 lb. The early models of the King Midget cars were sold in kit form for self-assembly for as little as $100 as late as 1948.

Largest Engines

The most powerful piston-engine car is "Quad A1." It was designed and built in 1964 by Jim Lytle and was first shown in May 1965 at the Los Angeles Sports Arena. The car features 4 Allison V–12 aircraft engines with a total of 6,840 cu in (112,087 cc) displacement and 12,000 hp. The car has 4-wheel drive, 8 wheels and tires, and dual 6-disc clutch assemblies. The wheelbase is 160 in. It weighs 5,860 lb and has 96 spark plugs and 96 exhaust pipes.

The largest car ever used was the "White Triplex," sponsored by J. H. White of Philadelphia. Completed early in 1928, after 2 years' work, the car weighed about 4½ tons and was powered by three Liberty V12 aircraft engines with a total capacity of 81,188 cc developing 1,500 bhp at 2,000 rpm. It was used to break the world speed record, but crashed at Daytona, Fla on March 13, 1929.

Currently, the most powerful car on the road is the 6-wheeled Jameson-Merlin powered by a 27,000-cc 1,760-hp Rolls-Royce V12 Merlin aero-engine, governed down to a maximum speed of 185 mph. It has a range of 300 miles with tanks of 72-gallon capacity. The vehicle weighs 2.96 tons overall.

The highest engine capacity of a production car was 13½ liters (824 cu in), in the case of the Pierce-Arrow 6-66 Raceabout of 1912–18, the Peerless 6-60 of 1912–14 and the Fageol of 1918. The largest currently available is the V-8 engine of 500.1 cu in (8,195 cc), developing 235 bhp net, used in the 1972 Cadillac Fleetwood Eldorado.

FASTEST
ROUND-THE-WORLD
(above): The National Car
drivers stopped to rest and
snap camels in Turkey in
1976. LARGEST DRAG
RACER (right): The "Quad
A 1" is powered by 4 aircraft
engines.

Fastest Round-the-World Driving

The fastest circumnavigation embracing more than an equator's length of driving (26,514.23 road miles) through 28 countries was one of 102 days 18 hours 26 min 54.7 sec by Johnnie Parsons in the US Bicentennial Global Record Run, July 4–Oct 15, 1976 in a Pontiac Grand Prix from National Car Rental. He averaged 47.22 mph.

Paula Murphy (*née* Mulhauser) drove the same race in a Pontiac Sunbird, finishing on Oct 17, 1976, with 26,412.20 miles in 105 days 2 hours 29 min 25.0 sec.

Gasoline Consumption

The world record for fuel economy on a closed circuit course (one of 14.076 miles) was set by Ben Visser (US) in a highly modified 90.8 cu in 1959 Opel CarAvan Station Wagon in the annual Shell Research Laboratory contest at Wood River, Ill, driven by Ben and Carolyn Visser on Oct 2, 1973 with 451.90 ton-miles per gallon and 376.59 miles on one gallon of gasoline. The tire pressure was 200 lb/sq in and the maximum speed was 12 mph.

In Oct 1979 at the International Fuel Saving Competition for cars and special vehicles in Switzerland a 200-cc diesel-engined 3-wheeler driven by Franz Maier of Stuttgart, W Germany covered 1284.13 km on 1 liter of fuel—equivalent to 3020.28 miles to the gallon.

Gas Station Pumping

The highest gallonage sold through a single pump is claimed by Mornington Motors Ltd, Dunedin, New Zealand, for dispensing 7,813.77 Imperial gallons (9,376.5 US gallons) in 24 hours on June 25, 1977.

LONGEST BUS (above): View toward the rear of the 76-ft-long articulated Wayne bus that carries 187 passengers. LARGEST TIRES (right): These 11½-ft-diameter tires made by Goodyear in Topeka, Kans weigh 12,500 lb each and cost $50,000 each. They are used on the world's LARGEST DUMP TRUCK (shown loaded, below), the Terex Titan, 56 ft high, made by a branch of General Motors.

Most Massive Vehicles and Largest Windshield Wipers

The most massive vehicle ever constructed is the Marion 8-caterpillar crawler used for conveying *Saturn V* rockets to their launching pads at the John F. Kennedy Space Center, Cape Canaveral, Fla. It measures 131 ft 4 in by 114 ft and two of them built at the same time cost $12,300,000. The loaded train weight is 9,000 tons. Its windshield wipers with 42-in blades are the world's largest.

The most massive automotive land vehicle is "Big Muskie," the 10,700-ton mechanical shovel built by Bucyrus Erie for the Musk mine. It is 487 ft long, 151 ft wide and 222 ft high with a grab capacity of 325 tons.

Buses

The first municipal motor bus service was inaugurated on Apr 12, 1903, between the Eastbourne railway station and Meads, East Sussex, in England. A steam-powered bus named *Royal Patent* ran between Gloucester and Cheltenham, England, for 4 months in 1831.

The longest regularly scheduled bus route is Greyhound's "Super-cruiser" Miami-to-San Francisco route over 3,240 miles in 81 hours 50 min (average speed of travel 39.59 mph). The total Greyhound fleet numbers 5,500 buses.

The longest buses are the 12-ton, 76-ft-long articulated buses, with 121 passenger seats and room for an additional 66 "strap-hangers," built by the Wayne Corporation of Richmond, Ind for use in the Middle East.

Largest Dump Truck

The largest dump truck is the Terex Titan 33-19 manufactured by the Terex Division of the General Motors Corp. It has a loaded weight of 604.7 tons and a capacity of 350 tons. When unloading, its height is 56 ft. The 16-cylinder engine delivers 3,300 hp and the fuel tank holds 1,560 gallons. It went into service in Nov 1974.

Most Powerful Fire Engine

The most powerful fire appliance is the 860-hp 8-wheel Oshkosh fire truck used for aircraft fires. It can discharge 49,920 gallons of foam through 2 turrets in just 150 sec. It weighs 66 tons.

Most Powerful Wrecker

The most powerful wrecker is the Vance Corp 28-ton 30-ft-long Monster No. 2 stationed at Hammond, Ind. It can lift in excess of 179 tons on its short boom.

Largest Earth Mover

The Balderson "Double Dude" plow harnessed to a Caterpillar SXS D9H 820 flywheel hp tractor can cast 14,185 cu yd of earth per hour.

Largest Tractor

The largest tractor is the $325,000, 65-ton Northern Manufacturing Co 8-wheeled 16V-747. It is 14 ft tall and 20 ft 7 in wide with an 848.6-gallon tank. It was launched in Oct 1978.

Longest Motor Trip

The longest continuous trailer tour is one of 143,716 miles by Harry B. Coleman and Peggy Larson in a Volkswagen Camper from Aug 20, 1976 to Apr 20, 1978 through 113 countries. Saburo Ouchi (b Feb 7, 1942) of Tokyo, Japan, drove 167,770 miles in 91 countries from Dec 2, 1969 to Feb 10, 1978. He said Queensland, Australia has the worst roads in the world for his Volkswagen "Kombi."

Largest Road Load

The world's record road load is one of 830 tons when a nuclear reactor vessel was moved from Seneca to Marseilles, Ill on a 384-wheel Schearele trailer by the Reliance Truck Co, on Feb 12, 1977.

The greatest weight moved on wheels was a 2,399-ton module for the Claymore field North Sea oil platform measuring 200 × 50 × 28 ft on a 640-wheeled Magnaload platform at Willington Quay, Wallsend, England in Aug 1976.

Largest Tires

The largest tires are manufactured in Topeka, Kans by the Goodyear Co for giant dump trucks. They are 11 ft 6 in in diameter, weigh 12,500 lb and cost more than $50,000. A tire 17 ft in diameter is believed to be the practical upper limit.

ROUND THE WORLD by land and sea; the "Half-Safe" being loaded in London.

Amphibious Vehicle

The only transatlantic crossing by an amphibious vehicle was achieved by Ben Carlin (Australia) in an amphibious jeep called "Half-Safe." Mr Carlin completed the last leg of the Atlantic crossing (across the English Channel) on May 8, 1958, having completed a circumnavigation of 39,000 miles over land and 9,600 miles by river and sea.

Snowmobiling

The longest snowmobile journey to date was the cross-country trip from Westport, Wash to Lubec, Maine, a distance of 5,004.5 miles, completed by driver Fritz Sprandel of Schnecksville, Pa, on his Scorpion 440 Whip snowmobile, in 62 days from Dec 4, 1977 to Feb 4, 1978.

LONGEST TAXI RIDE: Mrs Ann Drache and Mrs Nesta Sgro hired cabby Jack Keator from Hoboken, NJ to drive them 6,752 miles around 15 of the US states in Sept 1976. The fare was $2,500.

Largest Taxi Fleet

The largest taxi fleet was that of NYC, which amounted to 29,000 cabs in Oct 1929, compared with the present figure of 12,500, plus an equal number of "gypsy" cabs.

Longest Skid Marks

The longest recorded skid marks on a public road were 950 ft long, left by a Jaguar car involved in an accident on the M.1 near Luton, Bedfordshire, England June 30, 1960. Evidence given in the High Court case *Hurlock v. Inglis and others* indicated a speed "in excess of 100 mph" before the application of the brakes.

The skid marks made by the jet-powered *Spirit of America,* driven by Craig Breedlove, after the car went out of control at Bonneville Salt Flats, Utah Oct 15, 1964 were nearly 6 miles long.

Driving in Reverse

Charles Creighton (1908–70) and James Hargis of Maplewood, Mo drove their Ford Model A 1929 roadster in reverse from NYC to Los Angeles (3,340 miles), July 26–Aug 13, 1930 *without* stopping the engine once. They arrived back in NY on Sept 5, again in reverse, thus completing 7,180 miles in 42 days.

The highest average speed attained in any non-stop reverse drive exceeding 500 miles was achieved by Gerald Hoagland, who drove a 1969 Chevrolet Impala 501 miles non-stop in 17 hours 38 min at Chemung Speed Drome, NY July 9–10, 1976 to average 28.41 mph.

Most Successful Mechanic

Leopold Alfonso Villa (1899–1979) was a racing mechanic, or chief engineer, for Malcolm and Donald Campbell when they set 21 world speed records (10 land, 11 water) from 1924 to 1964.

Longest Tow

The longest tow on record was one of 4,759 miles from Halifax, Nova Scotia to Canada's Pacific coast, when Frank J. Elliott and George A. Scott of Amherst, Nova Scotia persuaded 168 passing motorists in 89 days to tow their Model T Ford (in fact, engineless) to win a $1,000 bet on Oct 15, 1927.

Lawn Mowers

The widest gang mower on record is the 5.6-ton 60-ft-wide 27-unit Big Green Machine, used by the sod farmer Jay Edgar Frick of Monroe, Ohio. It mows an acre in 60 sec.

From March 28 to Apr 1, 1959 a Ransome *Matador* motorized mower was driven for 99 hours non-stop over 375 miles from Edinburgh to London.

MOTORCYCLES*

Earliest

The earliest internal-combustion-engined motorized bicycle was a wooden-framed machine built during Oct-Nov 1885 by Gottlieb Daimler (1834–1900) of Germany at Bad Cannstett and first ridden by Wilhelm Maybach (1846–1929). It had a top speed of 12 mph and developed one-half of one hp from its single cylinder 264-cc 4-stroke engine at 700 rpm. Known as the "Einspur," it was lost in a fire in 1903. The earliest factory which made motorcycles in quantity was opened in 1894 by Heinrich and Wilhelm Hildebrand and Alois Wolfmüller at Munich, Germany. In its first 2 years this factory produced over 1,000 machines, each having a water-cooled 1,488-cc twin-cylinder 4-stroke engine developing about 2.5 bhp at 600 rpm—the highest capacity motorcycle engine ever put into production.

Fastest Road Motorcycle

The highest speed returned in an independent road test for a catalogued road machine is 154.2 mph for a Dunstall Suzuki GS 1000 CS.

Fastest Track Motorcycle

There is no satisfactory answer to the identity of the fastest track machine, other than to say that the current Kawasaki, Suzuki and Yamaha machines have all been geared to attain speeds marginally in excess of 186 mph under race conditions.

Most on One Machine

Sgt. John Patrick Toothey, with 18 other policemen on his machine with him, drove a Kawasaki 1,000-cc motorcycle a distance of 880 yd on May 18, 1979 at the Brisbane Show Grounds, Australia. The total weight was 4,641 lb.

---

* For more details on this subject see *Motorcycling Facts and Feats,* a Guinness Superlatives Book (Sterling).

WIDEST LAWN MOWER: The 27 units that make up the Big Green Machine can cut a swath 60 ft wide and mow an acre of grass in only one minute.

Duration

The longest time a solo motorcycle has been kept in non-stop motion is 500 hours by Owen Fitzgerald, Richard Kennett and Don Mitchell who covered 8,432 miles in Western Australia July 10–31, 1977.

Circumnavigation by Motorcycle

Ernest O'Gaffney, 41, departed from NYC on his Kawasaki KZ 1000 "Spirit of America" on Nov 27, 1978, and arrived back 79 days later on Feb 15, 1979, having traversed 25 countries in a 35,000-mile circumnavigation of the earth.

BICYCLES AND UNICYCLES

The first design for a machine propelled by cranks and pedals, with connecting rods, has been attributed to Leonardo da Vinci (1452–1519) or one of his pupils, dated *c.* 1493. The earliest such design actually built was in 1839–40 by Kirkpatrick Macmillan (1810–78) of Dumfries, Scotland. It is now in the Science Museum, London.

Longest Bicycle

The longest tandem bycycle ever built is the 1½-ton Vestergaard multipede built at Koege, Denmark in Apr 1976. It seats 35, measures 72 ft in length, and has an additional stabilizing wheel.

Fastest Cycle Riding

The speed records for human-powered vehicles are 49.38 mph (single rider) by Ralph Therrio in 1977, and 54.43 mph (multiple riders) by Jan Russell and Butch Stanton aboard "White Lightning," their supine-supine recumbent streamlined tricycle, at the Ontario Speedway, Calif, May 7, 1978.

Unicycle Records

Robert Neil "Bob" McGuinness (b 1951) unicycled 3,976 miles across Canada from Halifax to Vancouver in 79 days, June 6–Aug 24, 1978.

Stephen Gordon of Tujunga, Calif set a speed record for 100 miles in 11 hours 50 min, May 3–4, 1980.

The tallest unicycle ever mastered is one 65 ft 7¼ in tall ridden (with a safety belt or mechanic) by Carlho Sem Abrahams (b Paramaribo, Surinam, Dec 3, 1962) in Tokyo, Japan for 23 ft 8½ in in March 1980 for a Guinness TV show.

The sprint record from a standing start over 100 meters is 14.89 sec by Floyd Crandall (US) in Tokyo, Japan in March 1980.

Largest Bicycle

A classic ordinary bicycle with a 64-in-diameter front wheel and a 20-in diameter back wheel was built c. 1886 by the Pope Manufacturing Co of Mass. It is now owned by Paul Niquette of Connecticut.

Smallest Bicycle

The world's smallest wheeled *rideable* bicycle is one with 2⅛-in wheels, weighing 2 lb, built and ridden by Charlie Charles at Circus Circus Hotel, Las Vegas, Nev.

3. RAILROADS*

Railed trucks were used for mining as early as 1550 at Leberthal, Alsace, near the French-German border, and at the Broseley Colliery, Shropshire, England in Oct 1605, but the first self-propelled locomotive ever to run on rails was built by Richard Trevithick (1771–1833) for the 3-ft-gauge plateway at Coalbrookdale, Shropshire, in 1803.

The earliest established railway to have a steam-powered locomotive was the Middleton Colliery Railway, set up by an Act of June 9, 1758, running between Middleton Colliery and Leeds Bridge, Yorkshire, England. This line was converted to the use of steam locomotives built by Matthew Murray (1765–1826) in 1812. The Stockton and Darlington Railway, Cleveland, England, which ran from Shildon through Darlington to Stockton, opened Sept 27, 1825. The 7.8-ton *Locomotion* could pull 54 tons at a speed of 15 mph. It was designed and driven by George Stephenson (1781–1848).

The first regular steam passenger run was inaugurated over a one-mile section on the 6¼-mile track from Canterbury to Whitstable, Kent, England, on May 3, 1830, hauled by the engine *Invicta.*

The first electric railway was Werner von Siemen's 600-yd-long Berlin electric track opened for the Berlin Trades Exhibition May 31, 1879.

Steam Locomotive Speed

The highest speed ever ratified for a steam locomotive was 126 mph over 440 yd by the London & North Eastern Railway 4–6–2 No. 4468 *Mallard,* which hauled 7 coaches weighing 268.8 tons gross on July 3, 1938. The engine suffered severe damage. On June 12, 1905, a speed of 127.06 mph was claimed for the "Pennsylvania Special" near Ada, Ohio, but this has never been accepted by leading experts.

---

* For much greater detail and more records, see *Rail Facts and Feats,* a Guinness Superlatives Book (Sterling).

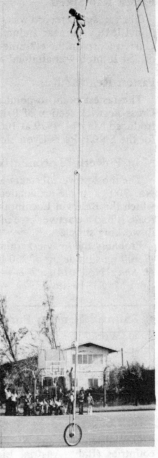

LARGEST BIKE (top left): Paul Niquette rides his 1886 model with a 64-in front wheel and a 20-in back wheel. TALLEST UNICYCLE (above): Carlho Abrahams went on a 65-ft-7¼-in unicycle his father and he built for a ride of more than 23 ft for Japanese TV in March 1980. That unicycle was 20 ft higher than his previous one pictured here. SMALLEST BICYCLE (left): Charlie Charles of Las Vegas points to the bike he made and rides in his act. It has 2⅛-in wheels and weighs 2 lb.

Fastest Rail Speed

The rail speed record was set by the US Federal Railroad Administration LIMRV (Linear Induction Motor Research Vehicle), built by the Garrett Corp on the 6.2-mile-long Pueblo, Colo test track, when a speed of 254.76 mph was attained on Aug 14, 1974.

Fastest Regular Run

The fastest point-to-point schedule in the world is that of the Kings Cross-Berwick section of British Rail's Eastern Region HST Service introduced May 14, 1979 at 106.25 mph. Speeds of 186.4 mph are planned for the SNCF Paris-Lyon electrified line by 1982.

Most Powerful Locomotive

The most powerful steam locomotive, measured by tractive effort, was No. 700, a triple-articulated or triplex 2-8-8-8-4 6-cylinder engine which the Baldwin Locomotive Co built in 1916 for the Virginian Railroad. It had a tractive force of 166,300 lb working compound and 199,560 lb working simple.

Probably the heaviest train ever hauled by a single engine was one of 17,100 tons made up of 250 freight cars stretching 1.6 miles by the *Matt H. Shay* (No. 5014), a 2-8-8-8-2 engine which ran on the Erie Railroad from May 1914 until 1929.

Railroad Handcar Pumping

"World" Championships pumped over a 220-yd shuttle course sponsored by the Jaycees of Jacksonville, Ill on Sept 12, 1976, produced best times of 62.177 sec for men (Jerry Johnson and Tom Sheehan) and 81.123 sec for women (Chris Ruyle and Jeanne McCulloch).

Most Countries in 24 Hours

C. W. Blenmink and A. C. M. Ligtenberg traveled by rail in a record 9 countries (Italy, Austria, Liechtenstein, Switzerland, France, Luxembourg, Belgium, W Germany and home to the Netherlands) on March 23-24, 1980, covering 729.4 miles in 21 hours 53 min.

Longest Rail Journey

The longest train journey is the 9-day-2-hour "odyssey" from Lisbon, Portugal to Khabarovsk in eastern USSR via Omsk.

Steepest Grade

The steepest standard gauge gradient by adhesion is 1:11 between Chedde and Servoz on the meter gauge electric SNCF Chamonix line, France.

Highest Track

The highest standard gauge (4 ft 8½ in) track is on the Peruvian State Railways at La Cima, on the Morocoha Branch at 15,806 ft above sea level. The highest point on the main line is 15,688 ft in the Galera tunnel.

LONGEST LINE: The Trans-Siberian railroad between Moscow and the Soviet Far East takes more than 8 days to make 97 stops. A short cut to save 310 miles is being built. The line will then traverse only 3,700 bridges.

Longest Line

The longest run is one of 5,864½ miles on the Trans-Siberian Line between Moscow and Nakhodka in the Soviet Far East. There are 97 stops on the journey, which takes 8 days 4 hours 25 min. The Baykal-Amur Magistral (BAM) northern line, begun with forced labor in 1938, is expected to be open in 1983, and will cut 310 miles off the route around the southern end of Lake Baykal. A total of 10,000 million cu ft of earth must be removed and 3,700 bridges built in this $14,400 million project.

Longest Straight Length

The longest straight is on the Commonwealth Railways Trans-Australian line over the Nullarbor Plain from Mile 496 between Nurina and Loongana, Western Australia, to Mile 793 between Ooldea and Watson, South Australia, 297 miles dead straight although not level.

Widest and Narrowest Gauges

The widest gauge in standard use is 5 ft 6 in. This width is used in Spain, India, Pakistan, Bangladesh, Sri Lanka, Argentina and Chile. In 1885, there was a lumber railway in Oregon with a gauge of 8 ft.

The narrowest gauge in use on public rail lines is 1 ft 3 in on the Ravenglass & Eskdale Railway, Cumbria, England (7 miles), and the Romney, Hythe & Dymchurch line in Kent, England (14 miles).

Busiest Rail System

The most crowded rail system is the Japanese National Railways, which by 1979 carried 19,660,000 passengers daily. Professional pushers are employed in the Tokyo service to squeeze in passengers before the doors can be closed. Among articles reported lost in the crush in 1979 were 498,446 umbrellas, 214,691 eyeglasses and hats, 353,501 clothing items and also a person's ashes and 15 Buddhist memorial tablets.

Longest Freight Train

The longest and heaviest freight train on record was one about 4 miles in length, consisting of 500 coal cars with three 3,600-hp diesels pulling, with 3 more pushing on the Iaeger, West Virginia to Portsmouth, Ohio stretch of 157 miles on the Norfolk and Western Railway on Nov 15, 1967. The total weight was more than 47,000 tons.

Greatest Load

The heaviest single pieces of freight ever conveyed by rail are limited by the capacity of the rolling stock. The only rail carrier with a capacity of 937 tons is a 36-axle "Schnabel," 283 ft 1½ in long, built for a US railway by Krupp, W Germany in 1978.

The heaviest load ever moved on rails was the Church of the Virgin Mary built in 1548 at Most, Czechoslovakia, weighing nearly 12,000 tons, moved in Oct-Nov 1975 because it was in the way of mining for coal deposits. It was moved 800 yd at 0.0013 mph over a period of 4 weeks at a cost of $15,300,000.

Largest and Highest Stations

The biggest railroad station is Grand Central Terminal, NYC, built 1903–13. It covers 48 acres on 2 levels with 41 tracks on the upper level and 26 on the lower. On average, more than 550 trains and 180,000 people per day use it, with a peak of 252,288 on July 3, 1947.

The highest station is Condor, Bolivia, at 15,705 ft on the meter-gauge Rio Mulato-to-Potosí line.

Waiting Rooms

The largest waiting rooms are in Peking Station, Chang'an Boulevard, Peking, China, opened in Sept 1959, with a capacity of 14,000.

Longest Platform

The longest railroad platform is the Khargpur platform, West Bengal, India, which measures 2,733 ft in length. The State Street Center subway platform in "The Loop" in Chicago, measures 3,500 ft in length.

Subways

The earliest (first section opened Jan 10, 1863) and one of the most extensive underground railway or rapid transit systems is that of the London Transport Executive, with 260 miles of route, of which 81 miles is bored tunnel and 20 miles is "cut and cover." This whole system is operated by a staff of 12,100 serving 279 stations. The 500 trains comprising 4,228 cars carried 594 million passengers in 1979. The record for a day is 2,073,134 on VE Day, May 8, 1945. The greatest depth is 221 ft. The record for touring all of the 279 stations is 18 hours 22 min by 4 men on March 25, 1980.

The busiest subway is operated by the NYC Transit Authority (first section opened on Oct 27, 1904) with a total of 229.76 route miles of track and 1,018,833,642 passengers in 1978. The stations are close set and total 458. The record for traveling the whole system was 21 hours 8½ min by Mayer Wiesen and Charles Emerson on Oct 8, 1973, when the trains ran on a different schedule than they do today.

MODEL TRAIN
MARATHON:
On this circular
track Roy Catton
ran 6 cars and
an engine for
864½ hours
continuously,
covering 678
miles.

EXPERIMENTAL
MONORAIL
(right): The
Japanese National
Railway tried this
magnetically
levitated train
which reached a
speed of 321 mph
to set a monorail
record on their
test track.

Highest Speed Monorail

The highest speed ever attained on rails is 3,090 mph (Mach 4.1) by an unmanned rocket-powered sled on the 6.62-mile-long captive track at the US Air Force Missile Development Center at Holloman, NM, on Feb 19, 1959. The highest speed reached carrying a chimpanzee is 1,295 mph.

The highest speed attained by a tracked hovercraft is 255.3 mph by the jet-powered *L'Aérotrain 02,* invented by Jean Bertin.

An experimental, magnetically levitated Japanese National Railway train on a test track near Miyazaki reached 321 mph on Dec 21, 1979.

Model Railways

The non-stop duration record for a model train (locomotive plus 6 coaches) is 864 hours 30 min from June 1 to July 7, 1978, covering 678 miles, organized by Roy Catton at "Pastimes" Toy Store, Mexborough, S. Yorkshire, England.

The longest recorded run by a model steam locomotive is 144 miles in 27 hours 18 min by the 7¼-in gauge "Winifred" built in 1974 by Wilf Grove at Thames Ditton, Surrey, England on Sept 8–9, 1979. "Winifred" works on 80 lb/sq in pressure and is coal-fired with a 2⅛-in bore cylinder and a 3⅛-in stroke.

The longest train ever operated was one of 501 cars with 9 HO-scale engines by The Model Railroad Club of New Jersey at Union, NJ, July 22, 1978, when it traversed its own length.

4. AIRCRAFT*

Note.—The use of the Mach scale for aircraft speeds was introduced by Prof Ackeret of Zurich, Switzerland. The Mach number is the ratio of the velocity of a moving body to the local velocity of sound. This was first employed by Dr Ernst Mach (1838–1916) of Austria in 1887. Thus Mach 1.0 equals 760.98 mph at sea level at 15° C (59°F) and is assumed, for convenience, to fall to a constant 659.78 mph in the stratosphere, *i.e.* above 11,000 m (36,089 ft).

Earliest Flights

The first controlled and sustained power-driven flight occurred near Kill Devil Hill, Kitty Hawk, NC at 10:35 a.m. on Dec 17, 1903, when Orville Wright (1871–1948) flew the 12-hp chain-driven *Flyer I* at an airspeed of 30 mph, a ground speed of 6.8 mph and an altitude of 8–12 ft for 12 sec, watched by his brother Wilbur (1867–1912), 3 life-savers and 2 others. Both brothers, from Dayton, Ohio, were bachelors because, as Orville put it, they had not the means to "support a wife as well as an airplane." The *Flyer* is now in the National Air and Space Museum of the Smithsonian Institution, Washington, DC.

The first hop by a man-carrying airplane entirely under its own power was made when Clément Ader (1841–1925) of France flew in his *Eole* for about 164 ft at Armainvilliers, France, on Oct 9, 1890.

Richard William Pearce (1877–1953) flew for at least 50 yd along the Main Waitohi Road, South Canterbury, New Zealand, in a self-built petrol-engined monoplane, probably on March 31, 1903.

The earliest "rational design" for a flying machine (according to the British Royal Aeronautical Society) was published by Emanuel Swedenborg (1688–1772) in Sweden in 1717.

Cross-Channel Flight

The earliest flight across the English Channel by an airplane was made on Sunday, July 25, 1909, when Louis Blériot (1872–1936), of France, flew his *Blériot XI* monoplane, powered by a 23-hp Anzani engine, from Les Baraques, France to a meadow near Dover Castle, England in 36½ min after taking off at 4:41 a.m.

Transatlantic Flights

The first crossing of the North Atlantic by air was made by Lt-Cdr (later Rear Admiral) Albert C. Read (1887–1967) and his crew (Stone, Hinton, Rodd, Rhoads and Breese) in an 84-knot Curtiss flying boat NC-4 of the US Navy from Trepassy Harbour, Newfoundland, Canada *via* the Azores, to Lisbon, Portugal, May 16 to 27, 1919. The whole flight of 4,717 miles originating from Rockaway Air Station, Long Island, NY, on May 8, required 53 hours 58 min terminating at Plymouth, England on May 31. The Newfoundland-Azores leg (1,200 miles) took 15 hours 18 min at 81.7 knots.

The first non-stop transatlantic flight was achieved from 4:13 p.m. GMT on June 14, 1919 from Lester's Field, St John's, Newfoundland, 1,960 miles to Derrygimla bog near Clifden, County Galway, Ireland, at 8:40 a.m. GMT June 15, when the pilot Capt John William Alcock

---

* For more detail and more records see *Air Facts and Feats*, one of the Guinness Family of Books (Sterling).

FIRST CROSSING OF ATLANTIC BY AIRPLANE: Albert Read and his 5-man crew flew this Curtiss flying boat from Newfoundland to Portugal in May 1919.

(1892–1919), and Lt Arthur Whitten Brown (1886–1948) flew across in a Vickers *Vimy,* powered by two 360-hp Rolls-Royce *Eagle VII* engines. Both men were given knighthoods on June 21, 1919 when Alcock was 26 years 227 days old, and won a £10,000 (then $50,000) prize given by a London newspaper.

The 79th man to complete a transatlantic trip but the first to fly alone was Capt (later Col) Charles A. Lindbergh (1902–74), who took off in his 220-hp Ryan monoplane *Spirit of St Louis* at 12:52 p.m. GMT on May 20, 1927 from Roosevelt Field, Long Island, NY. He landed at 10:21 p.m. GMT on May 21, 1927 at Le Bourget airfield, Paris, France. His flight of 3,610 miles lasted 33 hours 29½ min and he won a prize of $25,000.

The record for the most transatlantic flights is held by Capt John M. Winston, a senior British Airways Flight Engineer, who flew 1,277 transatlantic flights from May 10, 1947 to Dec 14, 1978—a total of 20,100 hours.

The transatlantic flight speed record is 1 hour 54 min 56.4 sec by Maj James V. Sullivan, 37, and Maj Noel F. Widdifield, 33, flying a Lockheed SR-71A eastwards on Sept 1, 1974. The average speed, slowed by refueling by a KC-135 tanker aircraft, for the NY-London stage of 3,461.53 miles was 1,806.963 mph. The solo record (Gander to Gatwick) is 8 hours 47 min 32 sec by Capt John J. A. Smith in a Rockwell 685 on March 12, 1978.

FIRST FLIGHT ACROSS THE ENGLISH CHANNEL: In 1909, only 6 years after the Wright Brothers first flew, Louis Blériot flew this monoplane from France to England.

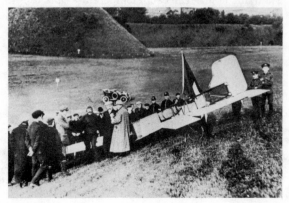

Transpacific Flight

The first non-stop Pacific flight was by Maj Clyde Pangborn and Hugh Herdon in the Bellanca cabin plane *Miss Veedol* from Sabishiro Beach, Japan, 4,558 miles to Wenatchee, Wash in 41 hours 13 min on Oct 3–5, 1931. (For earliest crossing see 1924 flight below.)

Circumnavigational Flights

A strict circumnavigation of the earth requires passing through two antipodal points and is thus a minimum distance of 24,859.75 miles. (The FAI permits flights which exceed the length of the Tropic of Cancer or Capricorn, namely 22,858.754 miles.)

The earliest such flight (26,345 miles) was made by two US Army Douglas DWC amphibians in 57 "hops." The *Chicago* was piloted by Lt Lowell H. Smith and Lt Leslie P. Arnold and the *New Orleans* was piloted by Lt Erik H. Nelson and Lt John Harding. The planes took off from Seattle, Wash on Apr 6, 1924 and landed back there on Sept 28, 1924.

The earliest solo claim was by Wiley Hardemann Post (1898–1935) (US) in the Lockheed Vega *Winnie Mae,* starting and finishing at Floyd Bennett Field, NYC July 15–22, 1933, in 10 "hops." His distance of 15,596 miles with a flying time of 115 hours 36 min was, however, at too high a latitude to qualify.

The fastest flight has been a non-stop eastabout flight of 45 hours 19 min by 3 USAF B-52's led by Maj-Gen Archie J. Old, Jr. They covered 24,325 miles on Jan 16–18, 1957, finishing at March Air Force Base, Riverside, Calif having averaged 525 mph with 4 in-flight refuelings by KC-97 aerial tankers.

The smallest aircraft to complete a circumnavigation is a 20-ft-11-in single-engined 180-hp Thorp T-18, built in his garage by its pilot Donald P. Taylor of Sage, Calif. His 26,190-mile flight in 37 stages took 176 flying hours, ending in Oshkosh, Wis on Sept 30, 1976.

Circum-Polar Flight

The first circum-polar flight was flown solo by Capt Elgen M. Long, 44, in a Piper Navajo, Nov 5 to Dec 3, 1971. He covered 38,896 miles in 215 flying hours. The cabin temperature sank to −40°F over Antarctica.

Jet-Engine Flight

Proposals for jet propulsion date back to Capt Marconnet (1909) of France and Henri Coanda (1886–1972) of Rumania, and to the turbojet proposals of Maxime Guillaume in 1921. The earliest testbed run was that of the British Power Jets Ltd's experimental WU (Whittle Unit) on Apr 12, 1937, invented by Flying Officer (now Air Commodore Sir) Frank Whittle (b Coventry, June 1, 1907), who had applied for a patent on jet propulsion in 1930.

The first flight by an airplane powered by a turbojet engine was made by the Heinkel He 178, piloted by Flugkapitän Erich Warsitz, at Marienehe, Germany Aug 27, 1939. It was powered by a Heinkel He S3b engine (834-lb st as installed with long tailpipe) designed by Dr Hans von Ohain and first tested in Aug 1937.

FIRST FLIGHTS AROUND THE WORLD: The "Chicago" and the "New Orleans" made aviation history with the first circumnavigational flights in 1924.

Supersonic Flight

The first supersonic flight was achieved Oct 14, 1947 by Capt (later Brigadier-General) Charles ("Chuck") Elwood Yeager, USAF retired (b Feb 13, 1923), over Edwards Air Force Base, Muroc, Calif in a US Bell XS-1 rocket plane (*Glamorous Glennis*), with Mach 1.015 (670 mph) at an altitude of 42,000 ft.

Largest and Smallest Planes

The aircraft with the largest wing span ever constructed was Howard R. Hughes' H.2 *Hercules* flying boat, which rose 70 ft into the air in a test run of 1,000 yd off Long Beach Harbor, Calif on Nov 2, 1947. The 8-engined 213-ton aircraft had a wing span of 320 ft and a length of 219 ft. It never flew again. The craft cost $40 million, and was piloted by Howard Hughes himself on its one run. It was not scrapped until Apr 1976.

The highest recorded gross takeoff weight of any aircraft has been 425 tons in the case of a Boeing 747-200B Jumbo plane during certification tests of its Pratt & Whitney JT9D-7Q engines on May 23, 1979.

The lightest mechanically-powered plane ever flown was the prototype Birdman TL-1, a single-seat monoplane designed and built by Emmet M. Tally III of Daytona Beach, Fla and first flown on Jan 25, 1975. As mar-

PLANE WITH LARGEST WINGS: Howard Hughes' mammoth flying boat, nicknamed the "Spruce Goose," with a wing span of 320 ft, flew only 1,000 yds when tested in 1947 and never flew again. It had 8 engines and weighed 213 tons.

LIGHTEST AIRPLANE (above): The Tally Birdman TL-1 weighs only 288 lb at takeoff. SMALLEST PLANE (left): Ray Stits, designer, stands next to his "Sky Baby" which measured only 9 ft 10 in long, but could fly at speeds up to 185 mph. HEAVIEST BOMBER (below): The B-52H Stratofortress can drop as many as 84 conventional bombs from its fuselage as well as carry 24 under its wings. This USAF giant can also carry 12 thermonuclear bombs instead. FASTEST AIRLINER (bottom) is the USSR's Tu-144, which can go 1,585 mph with 140 passengers.

keted in kit form it has a wing span of 34 ft, a weight of 122 lb empty, and a normal takeoff weight of 288 lb. It is powered by an 11.5 hp McCulloch MC-101 DT single-cylinder 2-stroke engine driving a pusher propeller, and has a maximum speed of 50 mph and a range of 168 miles on 4 gallons of fuel. The pilot sits on an exposed seat.

The lightest and smallest twin-engined airplane is the MC10 Cricri single-seat monoplane designed and built by Michel Colomban of Rueil-Malmaison, France, and first flown as a prototype on July 19, 1973 by 68-year-old Robert Buisson. It has a wing span of 16 ft ¾ in, an empty weight of 154 lb, a takeoff weight (including the pilot) of 375 lb. Two 10-hp Valmet SM 160J single-cylinder 2-stroke engines give it a maximum speed of 136 mph and a range of 496 miles. The Cricri is aerobatic.

The smallest airplane ever flown is the Stits Sky Baby biplane, designed and built by Ray Stits at Riverside, Calif and first flown by Robert H. Starr May 26, 1952. It was 9 ft 10 in long, with a wing span of 7 ft 2 in, and weighed 452 lb empty. Powered by an 85-hp Continental C85 engine, it reaches a top speed of 185 mph.

Heaviest and Fastest Bombers

The heaviest bomber is the 8-jet sweptwing Boeing B-52H *Stratofortress,* which has a maximum takeoff weight of 488,000 lb. It has a wing span of 185 ft and is 157 ft 6¾ in in length, with a speed of over 650 mph. The B-52 can carry 12 SRAM thermonuclear short-range attack missiles or 24 750-lb bombs under its wings and 8 more SRAMs or 84 500-lb bombs in the fuselage.

The 10-engined Convair B-36J, weighing 205 tons, had a greater wing span, at 230 ft, but is no longer in service. It had a top speed of 435 mph.

The fastest operational bombers are the French Dassault Mirage IV, which can fly at Mach 2.2 (1,450 mph) at 36,000 ft; the General Dynamics FB-111A, with a maximum speed of Mach 2.5; and the Soviet swing-wing Tupolev Tu-26 known to NATO as "Backfire," which has an estimated over-target speed of Mach 2.0 and a combat radius of 3,570 miles.

Airliners

The highest capacity jet airliner is the Boeing 747, "Jumbo Jet," first flown on Feb 9, 1969. It has a capacity of from 385 to 500 passengers with a maximum speed of 608 mph. Its wing span is 195.7 ft and its length, 231.3 ft. It entered service on Jan 22, 1970.

The fastest airliner is probably the USSR's Tu-144, which first flew on Dec 31, 1968, and began passenger operations between Moscow and Alma-Ata (2,190 miles) on Nov 1, 1977, offering an average speed of 1,245 mph (Mach 1.9). It has a capacity of 140 passengers and is able to attain 1,585 mph.

The supersonic BAC/Aerospatiale Concorde, first flown on March 2, 1969, with a capacity of 128 passengers, cruises at up to Mach 2.2 (1,450 mph). It flew at Mach 1.05 on Oct 10, 1969, exceeded Mach 2 for the first time on Nov 4, 1970, and became the first supersonic airliner used for passenger service on Jan 21, 1976, when Air France and British Airways opened service simultaneously between, respectively, Paris—Rio de Janeiro and London—Bahrain. Services between London/NY and Paris/NY began Nov 22, 1977. The NY-London record time is 2 hours 59 min 14 sec (average 1,166.031 mph) set Jan 20, 1980.

The most capacious airliner is the commercial adaptation of the USAF Lockheed C-5A Galaxy known as the Lockheed 500-3 with 51,707 cu ft of space. The wing span is 222.7 ft and the length is 245.9 ft.

Highest Speed

The official air speed record is 2,193.167 mph by Capt Eldon W. Joersz and Maj George T. Morgan, Jr, in a Lockheed SR-71A near Beale Air Force Base, Calif on July 28, 1976 over a 10–15-mi course.

The fastest fixed-wing aircraft was a North American Aviation X-15A-2, which flew for the first time (after modification from X-15A) on June 28, 1964, powered by a liquid oxygen and ammonia rocket propulsion system. Ablative materials on the airframe enabled a temperature of 3,000°F to be withstood. The landing speed was 210 knots (242 mph) momentarily. The highest speed attained was 4,534 mph (Mach 6.72) when piloted by Maj William J. Knight, USAF (b 1930) on Oct 3, 1967. An earlier version piloted by Joseph A. Walker (1920–66) reached 354,200 ft (67.08 miles) over Edwards Air Force Base, Calif on Aug 22, 1963. The program was suspended after the final flight of Oct 24, 1968.

PIGGY BACK ROCKET AND PLANE: The Space Shuttle Orbiter built for NASA by Rockwell International and Boeing.

Potentially the fastest aircraft ever flown is the Space Shuttle Orbiter built for NASA by Rockwell International, and first flown piggyback atop a converted Boeing 747 on Feb 18, 1977. When flown into space, from 1980, the Orbiter will take off like a rocket, operate in orbit like a spacecraft (at up to 17,600 mph) and land at speeds as high as 223 mph.

The OV-101 *Enterprise* made 5 unpowered free flights between Aug 12 and Oct 26, 1977.

Fastest Jet

The fastest jet aircraft is the USAF Lockheed SR-71 reconnaissance aircraft which first flew on Dec 22, 1964 and attained a speed of 2,193.167 mph July 1976 (see above). It is reportedly capable of attaining an altitude ceiling of close to 100,000 ft. The SR-71 has a span of 55.6 ft, a length of 107.4 ft and weighs 170,000 lb at takeoff. Its reported range is

FASTEST JET: The Lockheed SR71, which in 1964 flew at almost 2,200 mph, can climb to 100,000 ft in altitude.

2,982 miles at Mach 3 at 78,750 ft. At least 30 are believed to have been built.

The fastest combat aircraft in service is the USSR Mikoyan MIG-25 fighter (code name "Foxbat"). The reconnaissance "Foxbat-B" has been tracked by radar at about Mach 3.2 (2,110 mph). When armed with 4 large underwing air-to-air missiles known to NATO as "Acrid," the fighter "Foxbat-A" is limited to Mach 2.8 (1,845 mph). The single-seat "Foxbat-A" spans 45 ft 9 in, is 73 ft 2 in long, and has a maximum take-off weight of 79,800 lb.

Fastest Biplane

The fastest recorded biplane was the Italian Fiat C.R.42B, with a 1,010-hp Daimler-Benz DB601A engine, which attained 323 mph in 1941. Only one was built.

Fastest Piston-Engined Aircraft

The fastest speed at which a piston-engined plane has ever been measured was for a cut-down privately owned Hawker *Sea Fury* which attained 520 mph in level flight over Texas in Aug 1966, piloted by Mike Carroll (k 1969) of Los Angeles. The official record is 499.048 mph over Mud Lake, Tonopah, Nev by Steve Hinton in a modified North American P51D *Mustang* powered by a 3,800 hp Rolls-Royce Griffon, over a 1.86-mile course at restricted altitude Aug 14, 1979.

Fastest Propeller-Driven Aircraft

The Soviet Tu-114 turboprop transport is the fastest propeller-driven airplane. It recorded a speed of 545.76 mph carrying heavy payloads over measured circuits. It is developed from the Tupolev Tu-95 bomber, known in the West as the "Bear," and has four 14,795-hp engines. The turboprop powered Republic XF-84H prototype US Navy fighter which flew on July 22, 1955 had a top design speed of 670 mph, but was abandoned.

Largest Aircraft Propeller

The largest aircraft propeller ever used was the 22-ft-7½-in diameter

Garuda propeller, fitted to the Linke-Hofmann R II built in Wroclaw, Poland, which flew in 1919. It was driven by four 260-hp Mercedes engines and turned at only 545 rpm.

Greatest Altitude

The official altitude record by an aircraft taking off from the ground under its own power is 123,524 ft (23.39 miles) by Aleksandr Fedotov (USSR) in a Mikoyan E-266M (MIG-25) aircraft, powered by two 30,865-lb thrust turbojet engines on Aug 31, 1977.

The greatest recorded height by any pilot without a pressure cabin or even a pressure suit has been 49,500 ft by British Squadron Leader G. W. H. Reynolds, in a Spitfire Mark VC over Libya in 1942.

Flight Duration

The flight duration record is 64 days, 22 hours, 19 min and 5 sec, set by Robert Timm and John Cook in a Cessna 172 "Hacienda." They took off from McCarran Airfield, Las Vegas, Nev just before 3:53 p.m. local time on Dec 4, 1958 and landed at the same airfield just before 2:12 p.m. on Feb 7, 1959. They covered a distance equivalent to 6 times around the world with continued refueling without landing.

The record for duration without refueling is 84 hours 32 min, set by Walter E. Lees and Frederic A. Brossy in a Bellanca monoplane with a 225-hp Packard Diesel engine, at Jacksonville, Fla, May 25–28, 1931.

Longest and Shortest Scheduled Flights

The longest scheduled non-stop flight is the weekly Pan-Am Sydney-San Francisco non-stop Flight 816 (13 hours 25 min) in a Boeing 747 SP (Special Performance) opened in Dec 1976 over 7,475 statute miles. The longest delivery flight by a commercial jet is 8,936 nautical miles or 10,290 statute miles from Seattle, Wash to Capetown, South Africa by South African Airway's Boeing 747 SP *Matroosberg*. She made the 17-hour 22½-min flight loaded with 196.5 tons of pre-cooled fuel March 23–29, 1976.

The shortest scheduled flight is made by Loganair between the Orkney Islands (Scotland) of Westray and Papa Westray, which has been flown with twin-engined 10-seat Britten-Norman Islander transports since Sept 1967. Though scheduled for 2 minutes, in favorable wind conditions it is accomplished in 58 sec by Capt Andrew D. Alsop.

The flight from Jovhat to Lilabari in India costs $3.50 and is the cheapest listed in the ABC World Airways Guide in 1979.

Youngest and Oldest Pilots

The youngest age at which anyone has ever qualified as a military pilot is 15 years 5 months in the case of Sgt Thomas Dobney (b May 6, 1926) of the British Royal Air Force. He had lied about his age (14 years) on induction.

Betty Bennett took off, flew and landed solo at the age of 10 on Jan 4, 1952 in Cuba. Clark O. Pelaez (b May 4, 1957) flew a Piper Tri-Pacer solo at Cebu City, Philippines, on Apr 24, 1968, aged 10 years 11 months.

LARGEST AIRPORT: In Texas, Dallas/Fort Worth boasts of a landing field with 4 runways and 5 terminal buildings now, but it will be extended to serve 150 million passengers a year with 260 gates when completed.
YOUNGEST PILOT: Betty Bennett at age 10 took off and landed solo in Cuba in 1952.

The oldest pilot is Ed McCarty (b Sept 18, 1885) of Kimberly, Idaho who in 1979 was flying his rebuilt 30-year-old Ercoupe at the age of 94. Glenn E. Messer of Birmingham, Ala has been flying "steady" since May 13, 1911. Albert E. Savoy (b Feb 22, 1895) was issued his first private pilot's license on Nov 8, 1977, aged 82 years 8 months.

Most Flying Hours

Max Conrad (1903–1979) (US) logged 52,929 hours 40 min of flight time, a total of more than 6 years airborne, between 1928 and mid-1974. He completed 150 transatlantic crossings in light aircraft.

Most Takeoffs and Landings from Airports

Al Yates and Bob Phoenix of Texas made 193 takeoffs and daylight landings in 14 hours 57 min in a Piper Seminole on June 15, 1979.

Largest Airports

The largest airport is the Dallas/Fort Worth Airport, Tex which extends over 17,500 acres in the Grapevine area. Opened in Jan 1974 at an initial cost of nearly $800 million, the present 4 runways and 5 terminal buildings (with an automated shuttle train) are planned to be extended to 9 runways and 13 terminals with 260 gates with an ultimate capacity of 150 million passengers per year.

The total airport reserve area of Mirabel (Montreal's airport) is 88,960 acres, of which 17,300 acres are operational.

The planned area of the Jeddah airport, Saudi Arabia, due to be completed at a cost of $6,460 million by 1982, has been announced as 26,250 acres, but a still larger area—73,600 acres—has been set aside for the country's Riyadh airport reportedly due for opening in mid-1983.

Busiest Airport

The busiest airport is the Chicago International Airport, O'Hare Field, with a total of 735,524 movements in fiscal 1978 and 47,842,510 passengers in calendar 1979. This represents a takeoff or landing every 42.9 sec around the clock. Heathrow Airport outside London handles more *international* traffic than any other.

The busiest landing area ever has been Bien Hoa Air Base, South Vietnam, which handled more than one million takeoffs and landings in 1970. The largest "helipad" was An Khe, South Vietnam.

Airports Farthest and Nearest to City Centers

The airport farthest from the city center it allegedly serves is Viracopos, Brazil, which is 60 miles from São Paulo. The Gibraltar airport is 800 yd from the center.

Highest and Lowest Airports

The highest airport in the world is La Sa (Lhasa) Airport in Tibet at 14,315 ft. The highest landing ever made by a fixed-wing plane was at 19,947 ft on Dhaulagri in the Nepal Himalayas by a Pilatus Porter, named *Yeti,* supplying the 1960 Swiss Expedition. The lowest landing field is El Lisan on the east shore of the Dead Sea, 1,180 ft below sea level, but during World War II BOAC short C-class flying boats operated from the surface of the Dead Sea 1,292 ft below sea level. The lowest international airport is Schiphol, Amsterdam, Netherlands, at 13 ft below sea level.

Longest Runway

The longest runway is 7 miles in length (of which 15,000 ft is concreted) at Edwards Air Force Base on the bed of Rogers Dry Lake at Muroc, Calif. The whole test center airfield extends over 65 sq mi. In an emergency, an auxiliary 12-mile strip is available along the bed of the Dry Lake.

The longest civil airport runway is one of 16,076 ft (3.04 miles) at Upington, South Africa, constructed in 5 months, Aug 1975–Jan 1976.

Fastest Helicopters

A Bell YUH-1B Model 533 compound research helicopter, boosted by 2 auxiliary turbojet engines, attained an unofficial speed record of 316.1 mph over Arlington, Tex, in April 1969. The official world speed record for a pure helicopter is 228.9 mph set by Gourguen Karapetyan in a Mil A-10 on a 15–25 km course near Moscow, on Sept 21, 1978.

Largest and Smallest Helicopter

The largest helicopter is the Soviet Mil Mi-12 ("Homer"), also known as the V-12, which set an international record by lifting a payload of 88,636 lb to a height of 7,398 ft Aug 6, 1969. It is powered by four 6,500-hp turboshaft engines, and has a span of 219 ft 10 in over its rotor tips with a fuselage length of 121 ft 4½ in and weighs 115.7 tons.

FASTEST HELICOPTER (above):
The Bell YUH set a speed record of
316.1 mph over Texas in 1969 that
has never been exceeded.

AUTOGYROS preceded helicopters
in development. Kenneth Wallis
(right) set a distance record of
543.27 miles non-stop in his little
WA-116 in 1975.

The Aerospace General Co one-man rocket-assisted mini-copter
weighs about 160 lb and can cruise 250 miles at 85 mph.

Highest Helicopters

The altitude record for helicopters is 40,820 ft by an Aerospatiale SA
315 B Lama over France on June 21, 1972. The highest recorded landing
has been at 23,000 ft, below the southeast face of Everest, in a rescue sortie in May 1971. The World Trade Center Helipad is 1,385 ft above street
level in NYC, on the South Tower.

Autogyros

The autogyro or gyroplane, a rotorcraft with an unpowered rotor
turned by the airflow in flight, preceded the practical helicopter with en-
gine-driven rotor. Juan de la Cierva (Spain) made the first successful autogyro flight with his model C.4 (commercially named an *Autogiro*) at
Getafe, Spain, on Jan 9, 1923. On Dec 6, 1955, Dr Igor B. Bensen (US)
flew his very simple open-seat Gyro-Copter and then made his design
available in kit form to amateur builders and pilots.

Wing Cdr Kenneth H. Wallis (GB) holds the straight-line distance
record of 543.27 miles, set in his WA-116F autogyro on Sept 28, 1975
(non-stop from Lydd, Kent, England, to Wick, Highland, Scotland).
Wallis flew his WA-116 with a 72-hp McCulloch engine to a record altitude of 15,220 ft on May 11, 1968, and to a record speed of 111.2 mph
over a 3-km (1.86 mile) straight course on May 12, 1969.

Flying Boats

The fastest flying boat ever built has been the Martin XP6M-1 Seamaster, the US Navy 4-jet-engined minelayer, flown in 1955–59 with a top speed of 646 mph. In Sept 1946, the Martin JRM-2 Mars flying boat set a payload record of 68,327 lb.

The official flying-boat speed record is 566.69 mph, set by Nikolai Andrievsky and a crew of 2 in a Soviet Beriev M-10, powered by 2 AL-7 turbojets, over a 10–15 mile course on Aug 7, 1961. The M-10 holds all 12 records listed for jet-powered flying boats, including an altitude of 49,088 ft set by Georgiy Buryanov and crew over the Sea of Azov Sept 9, 1961.

Human-Powered Flight

The distance record for human-powered flight was set June 12, 1979 by Dr Paul MacCready's man-powered 70-lb aircraft *Gossamer Albatross* with a 96-ft wing span, piloted and pedaled by 136-lb Bryan Allen. The *Albatross* took off from Folkestone, England and landed at Cap Gris-Nez, France 2 hours 49 min later, a flight spanning 22.26 miles, winning the £100,000 ($230,000) prize offered by Henry Kremer for the first man-powered crossing of the English Channel.

Ballooning

The earliest recorded ascent was by a model hot-air balloon invented by Father Bartolomeu de Gusmão (*né* Lourenço) (b Santos, Brazil, 1685), which was flown indoors at the Casa da India, Terreiro do Paço, Portugal on Aug 8, 1709.

The record distance traveled by a balloon is 3,107.61 miles in 137 hours 5 min 50 sec by the American Yost HB-72 helium-filled balloon *Double Eagle II* Aug 12–17, 1978 from Sprague Farm, Presque Isle, Me to Coquerel Farm, Miserey, France. The crew on this first North Atlantic crossing consisted of Ben L. Abruzzo, 48, Maxie L. Anderson, 44, and Larry M. Newman, 31, from Albuquerque, NM.

For hot-air ballooning the distance record is 350.7 miles by Philip Charles Clark (GB), set on Jan 25, 1978, in the Cameron balloon *Sungas* from Bristol, England to Châlons-sur-Marne, France. The largest hot-air balloon ever built is the UK Cameron A-500 of 500,000 cu ft capacity *Gerard A. Heineken,* first flown on Aug 18, 1974. The altitude record is 52,400 ft by Chauncey Dunn in an open gondola over Indiana in the summer of 1979.

Highest Manned and Unmanned Balloons

The greatest altitude reached in a manned balloon is the unofficial 123,800 ft by Nicholas Piantanida (1933–66) of Bricktown, NJ from Sioux Falls, SD on Feb 1, 1966. He landed in a cornfield in Iowa but did not survive.

The official record is 113,740 ft by Cdr Malcolm D. Ross, USNR, and the late Lt-Cdr Victor E. Prather, USN, in an ascent from the deck of USS *Antietam* on May 4, 1961 over the Gulf of Mexico.

The record altitude in an open basket is 38,789 ft by Kingswood Sprott Jr over Lakeland, Fla on Sept 27, 1975.

The highest altitude attained by an unmanned balloon was 170,000 ft, by a Winzen Research balloon of 47,800,000 cu ft, launched at Chico, Calif, in Oct 1972.

HUMAN-POWERED FLIGHT: Bryan Allen, a 136-lb Englishman, pedaled his way across the English Channel in this appropriately named 70 lb "Gossamer Albatross" to win $230,000 in 1979.

Largest Balloon

The largest balloon built is one with an inflatable volume of 70 million cu ft, by Winzen Research Inc, Minnesota.

Airships

The earliest flight of an airship was by Henri Giffard from Paris in his coal-gas 88,300-cu ft 144-ft-long rigid airship Sept 24, 1852.

The largest non-rigid airship ever constructed was the US Navy ZPG 3-W. It had a capacity of 1,516,300 cu ft, was 403.4 ft long and 85.1 ft in diameter, with a crew of 21. It first flew on July 21, 1958, but crashed into the sea in June 1960.

The largest rigid airship was the 236-ton German *Graf Zeppelin II* (LZ130), with a length of 803.8 ft and a capacity of 7,062,100 cu ft. She made her maiden flight on Sept 14, 1938 and in May and August 1939 made radar spying missions in British air space. She was dismantled in April 1940. Her sister ship, the *Hindenburg,* was 5.6 ft longer.

The most people ever carried in an airship were 207 in the US Navy *Akron* in 1931. The transatlantic record is 117 by the German *Hindenburg* in 1937.

The FAI accredited distance record for airships is 3,967.1 miles, set by the German *Graf Zeppelin,* captained by Dr Hugo Eckener between Oct 29 and Nov 1, 1928.

The longest recorded flight by a non-rigid airship (without refueling) is 264 hours 12 min by a US Navy Goodyear-built ZPG-2 class ship (Cdr J. R. Hunt, USN) from the S Weymouth, Mass Naval Air Station March 4, 1957 and landing back at Key West, Fla March 15 after having flown 9,448 miles.

Hovercraft

The ACV (air-cushion vehicle) was first made practical by Sir Christopher S. Cockerell (b June 4, 1910), a British engineer who had the idea in 1954, published his Ripplecraft Report 1/55 on Oct 25, 1955 and patented it on Dec 12, 1955. The earliest patent relating to an air-cushion craft was taken out in 1877 by John I. Thornycroft (1843–1928) of Chiswick, London and the Finn Toivo Kaario developed the idea in 1935. The first flight by a hovercraft was made by the 4½-ton Saunders Roe SR-N1 at Cowes, Isle of Wight, on May 30, 1959. With a 1,500-lb thrust Viper turbojet engine, this craft reached 68 knots in June 1961. The first hovercraft public service was opened across the Dee Estuary, Great Britain by the 60-knot 24-passenger Vickers-Armstrong VA-3 in July 1962.

The world's largest hovercraft is the 342-ton British-built SRN 4 MK III with a capacity of 416 passengers and 60 cars. It is 186 ft in length, powered by 4 Siddeley Marine Proteus engines which give a maximum speed in excess of the permitted operating speed of 65 knots.

The fastest warship is the 78-ft 112-ton US Navy test vehicle SES-100B. She attained 91.9 knots (103.9 mph) on Jan 25, 1980 on the Chesapeake Bay Test Range, Md. A contract for a 3,360-ton Large Surface Effect Ship (LSES) was placed by the US Dept of Defense with Bell Aerospace in Sept 1977 for delivery in mid-1981.

The highest altitude at which a hovercraft is operating is on Lake Titicaca, Peru where, since 1975, an HM2 Hoverferry hovers 12,506 ft above sea level.

The longest hovercraft journey was one of 5,000 miles through 8 West African countries between Oct 15, 1969, and Jan 3, 1970, by the British Trans-African Hovercraft Expedition.

Model Aircraft

The record for altitude is 26,929 ft by Maynard L. Hill (US) on Sept 6, 1970, using a radio-controlled model. The speed record is 213.70 mph by V. Goukoune and V. Myakinin (both USSR) with a radio-controlled model at Klementyeva, USSR, on Sept 21, 1971. The record duration flight is one of 28 hours 28 min by B. Laging at Ballarat, Victoria, Australia, on Oct 1, 1978.

The first model helicopter to fly across the English Channel was an 11-lb model Bell 212 radio-controlled helicopter piloted by Dieter Ziegler for the 32 miles between Ashford, Kent, England and Ambleteuse, France on July 17, 1974.

Smallest

The smallest model aircraft to fly is one weighing 0.004 oz powered by attaching a horsefly and designed by Don Emmick of Seattle, Wash in June 1979. One flew for 5 min.

Paper Airplane

The flight duration record for a paper aircraft over level ground is 15.0 sec by William Harlan Pryor in the Municipal Auditorium, Nashville, Tenn March 26, 1975. A paper plane was reported and witnessed to have flown 1¼ miles after a throw by "Chick" C. O. Reinhart from a 10th-story office window at 60 Beaver Street, NYC across the East River to Brooklyn, NY in Aug, 1933. It was helped by a thermal updraft from a coffee-roasting plant.

An indoor distance record of 140 ft 2 in was recorded by Tony Felch in the Mary E. Sawyer Auditorium in LaCrosse, Wis on Aug 9, 1979.

5. POWER PRODUCERS

Earliest and Largest Windmills

The earliest recorded windmills are those used for grinding corn in Iran (Persia) in the 7th century AD. The oldest Dutch mill is the towermill at Zeddam, Gelderland, built *c.* 1450.

A 140-ft tall, $21 million windmill with 200-ft blades at Boone, NC began operating on July 11, 1979 for the US Dept of Energy. It generates 2,000 kW in 25-mph winds. A 2,500-kW turbine was under construction in 1980.

Oldest Steam Engine

The oldest steam engine in working order is the 1812 Boulton & Watt 26-hp 42-in bore beam engine on the Kennet & Avon Canal at Great Bedwyn, Wiltshire, England. It was restored by the Crofton Society in 1971.

Atomic Power

The first atomic pile was built in an abandoned squash court at the University of Chicago. It "went critical" at 3:25 p.m. on Dec 2, 1942. The largest atomic or nuclear power station is the Ontario Hydro's Pickering station which in 1973 attained full output of 2,160 MW.

Largest Power Plant

The largest power station is the USSR's hydro-electric station at Krasnoyarsk on the Yenisey River, Siberia, with a power of 6,096 MW. Its third generator turned in March 1968 and the twelfth became operative by Dec 1970. The turbine hall completed in June 1968 is 1,378 ft long.

LARGEST POWER STATION: The hydro-electric station at Krasnoyarsk can generate a total of 6,096,000 kW.

The reservoir backed up by the dam was reported in Nov 1972 to be 240 miles long.

The largest planned power plant is the Itaipu on the Paraná River on the Brazil-Paraguay border, with an ultimate power of 12,600,000 kW, from 18 turbines.

Largest Nuclear Reactor

The largest single nuclear reactor in the world is the 1,098 MW Brown's Ferry Unit 1 General Electric boiling-water-type reactor located on the Wheeler Reservoir near Decatur, Ala, which became operative in 1973. The Grand Gulf Nuclear Station at Port Gibson, Miss will have a capacity of 1,290 MW when complete.

Largest Generator

Generators in the 2,000,000 kW (or 2,000 MW) range are now in the planning stages both in the UK and the US. The largest under construction is one of 1,300 MW by the Brown Boveri Co of Switzerland for the Tennessee Valley Authority.

Biggest Blackout

The greatest power failure in history struck 7 northeastern US states and Ontario, Canada, Nov 9-10, 1965. About 30 million people in 80,000 sq mi were plunged into darkness. Only two people were killed. In NYC the power failed at 5:27 p.m. on Nov 9, and was not fully restored for 13½ hours. The total losses resulting from another NYC power failure, on July 13, 1977, which lasted as long as 25 hours in some areas, have been estimated at more than $1 billion, including losses due to looting.

Tidal Power Station

The first major tidal power station is the *Usine marèmotrice de la Rance,* officially opened on Nov 26, 1966 at the Rance estuary in the Golfe de St Malo, Brittany, France. Built in 5 years, at a cost of $75,600,000, it has a net annual output of 544 million kW/h. The 880-yd barrage contains 24 turbo-alternators. This harnessing of the tides has imperceptibly slowed the earth's rate of revolution.

Biggest Boiler

The largest boilers ever designed are those ordered in the US from the Babcock & Wilcox Co with a capacity of 1,330 MW, so involving the evaporation of 9,330,000 lb of steam per hour.

Largest Turbines

The largest turbines are those rated at 820,000 hp with an overload capacity of 1 million hp, 32 ft in diameter, with a 449-ton runner and a 350-ton shaft, for the Grand Coulee "Third Powerplant."

The largest integral reversible pump turbine was made by Allis-Chalmers for the $50 million Taum Sauk installation of the Union Electric Co in St Louis, Mo. It has a rating of 240,000 hp as a turbine and a capacity of 1,320,000 gallons per min as a pump. The Tehachapi Pumping Plant in Calif, completed in 1972, pumps 21,960,000 gallons per min over 1,700 ft up.

6. ENGINEERING

The earliest machinery still in use is the *dâlu*—a water-raising instrument known to have been in use in the Sumerian civilization which originated *c.* 3500 BC in Lower Iraq—even earlier than the *Saqiyas* of the Nile.

Largest Press

The two most powerful production machines are forging presses in the US. The Loewy closed-die forging press, in a plant leased from the US Air Force by the Wyman-Gordon Co at North Grafton, Mass weighs 10,600 tons and stands 114 ft 2 in high, of which 66 ft is sunk below the operating floor. It has a rated capacity of 50,000 tons, and went into operation in Oct 1955. The other similar press is at the plant of the Aluminum Company of America in Cleveland. There has been a report of a press in the USSR with a capacity of 82,500 tons, at Novo Kramatorsk.

The Bêché and Grohs counterblow forging hammers, manufactured in W Germany, are rated at 66,120 tons.

Largest Lathe

The largest lathe is the 72-ft-long 431-ton giant lathe built by the Dortmunder Rheinstahl firm of Wagner, in Germany, in 1962. The face plate is 15 ft in diameter and can exert a torque of 289,000 ft-lb when handling objects weighing up to 225 tons.

Largest Excavator

The largest excavator is the 14,325-ton bucket wheel excavator being assembled at the open cast lignite mine of Hambach, W Germany with a rating of 260,000 cu yd per 20-hour working day. It is 690 ft in length and 269 ft tall. The wheel is 222 ft in circumference with 6.5-cu-yd buckets.

Dragline Excavators

The Ural Engineering Works at Ordzhonikdze, USSR, completed in March 1962 has a dragline known as the ES-25(100) with a boom of 328 ft and a bucket with a capacity of 31.5 cu yd. The largest walking dragline is the Bucyrus-Erie 4250W with an all-up weight of 13,440 tons and a bucket capacity of 220 cu yd on a 310-ft boom. This, the largest mobile land machine, is now operating on the Central Ohio Coal Co's Muskingum site in Ohio.

Largest Blast Furnace

The largest blast furnace is one with an inner volume of 179,040 cu ft and a 48-ft 6½-in diameter hearth at the Oita Works, Kyushu, Japan, completed in Oct 1976, with an annual capacity of 4,905,600 tons.

Largest Forging

The largest forging on record is a generator shaft 55 ft long weighing 450,600 lb forged by Bethlehem Steel in Oct 1973 for Japan.

Longest Pipelines

The longest crude oil pipeline is the Interprovincial Pipe Line Co's installation from Edmonton, Alberta, Canada, to Buffalo, NY, a distance of 1,775 miles. Along the length of the pipe 13 pumping stations maintain a flow of 8,280,000 gallons of oil per day.

The eventual length of the Trans-Siberian Pipeline will be 2,319 miles, running from Tuimazy through Omsk and Novosibirsk to Irkutsk. The first 30-mile section was opened in July 1957.

The world's most expensive pipeline is the Alaska pipeline running 798 miles from Prudhoe Bay to Valdez. By completion of the first phase in 1977 it had cost at least $6,000 million. The pipe is 48 in in diameter and will eventually carry up to 2 million barrels of crude oil per day.

The longest submarine pipeline is the Ekofisk-Emden line stretching 260 miles under the North Sea, completed in July 1975.

The longest natural gas pipeline is the Trans-Canada Pipeline which by 1974 had 5,654 miles of pipe up to 42 in in diameter.

Largest Oil Tanks

The largest oil tanks ever constructed are the five Aramco 1½ million barrel storage tanks at Ju'aymah, Saudi Arabia. The tanks are 72 ft tall with a diameter of 386 ft and were completed in March 1980.

Largest Cat Cracker

The largest catalytic cracker is the Exxon Co's Bayway Refinery plant at Linden, NJ with a fresh feed rate of 5,040,000 gallons per day.

Largest Nuts

The largest nuts ever made weigh 5,264 lb each and have an outside diameter of 50½ in and a 31½-in thread. Known as Moorthrust, they are manufactured by Doncaster Moorside Ltd of Oldham, England, for securing propellers.

Largest Valve

The largest valve is the 32-ft diameter 190.4-ton butterfly valve designed by Boving & Co Ltd of London for use at the Arnold Air Force Base engine test facility in Tennessee.

LARGEST BUTTERFLY VALVE (left): Made in London, it is used in Tennessee. ELEVATOR MOTOR (above) for lifts in Japanese skyscraper that go 2,000 ft per min.

THE ALASKAN PIPELINE is one of the most extensive, and expensive, engineering projects in recent years.

Highest Aerial Ropeways and Cable Cars

The highest and longest aerial ropeway is the Teleférico Mérida (Mérida téléphérique) in Venezuela, from Mérida City (5,379 ft) to the summit of Pico Espejo (15,629 ft), a rise of 10,250 ft. The ropeway is in four sections, involving 3 car changes in the 8-mile ascent in one hour. The fourth span is 10,070 ft in length. The two cars work on the pendulum system—the carrier rope is locked and the cars are hauled by means of three pull ropes powered by a 230-hp motor. They have a maximum capacity of 45 persons and travel at 32 ft per sec (21.8 mph).

The longest single-span ropeway is the 13,500-ft-long span from the Coachella Valley to Mt San Jacinto (10,821 ft), Calif opened Sept 12, 1963.

Fastest Passenger Elevators

The fastest domestic passenger elevators are the express elevators to the 60th floor of the 787.4-ft-tall "Sunshine 60" building, Ikebukuro, Tokyo, Japan, completed Apr 5, 1978. They were built by Mitsubishi Corp and operate at a speed of 2,000 ft per min, or 22.72 mph.

Much higher speeds are achieved in the winding cages of mine shafts. A hoisting shaft 6,800 ft deep, owned by Western Deep Levels Ltd in South Africa, winds at speeds of up to 40.9 mph (3,595 ft per min). Otitis-media (popping of the ears) presents problems at speeds much above even 10 mph.

First and Longest Escalators

The name "escalator" was registered in the US on May 28, 1900, but the earliest "Inclined Elevator" was installed by Jesse W. Reno on the pier at Coney Island, NYC in 1896.

The longest escalators are on the Leningrad Underground, USSR, which have a vertical rise of 195 ft.

The longest "moving sidewalks" are those installed in 1970 in the Neue Messe Centre, Düsseldorf, W Germany, which measure 738 ft between comb plates.

Largest Transformer

The largest single-phase transformers are rated at 1,500,000 kV of which 8 are in service with the American Electric Power Service Corporation. Of these, 5 step down from 765 to 345 kV.

Longest Transmission Lines

The longest span between pylons of any power line is that across the Sogne Fjord, Norway, between Rabnaberg and Fatlaberg. Erected in 1955 by the Whitecross Co Ltd of Warrington, England as part of the high-tension power cable from Refsdal power station at Vik, it has a span of 16,040 ft and a weight of 13 tons. In 1967, two further high-tensile steel/aluminum lines 16,006 ft long, and weighing 37 tons, manufactured by Whitecross and British Insulated Callender's Cables Ltd, were erected here.

Highest Power Lines

The highest are those across the Straits of Messina, with towers of 675 ft (Sicily side) and 735 ft (Calabria) and 11,900 ft apart.

Highest Voltages

The highest voltages now carried are 1,330,000 volts on the DC Pacific Inter-tie in the US for a distance of 1,224 miles. The Ekibastuz DC transmission lines in Kazakhstan, USSR, are planned to be 1,490 miles long with a 1,500,000-volt capacity.

Longest Conveyor Belt

The longest single flight conveyor belt was started up on Aug 23, 1979 by the Utah Dept of Transportation over a distance of 13 miles between Antelope Island and a road construction site near Salt Lake City. It is powered by 42 250 hp electric motors.

The longest multi-flight conveyor is one of 62 miles between the phosphate mine near Bucraa and the Atlantic port of El Aaiun, Morocco, built by Krupp and completed in 1972. It has 11 flights of between 5.6 and 6.8 miles in length and is driven at 10.06 mph.

Smallest Monkeywrench

The smallest standard ratchet monkeywrench is the No. 0 model made by the precision engineers, Leytool Ltd of London E10, England, with a head outside diameter of ½ in and a width of ¼ in.

Fastest Typesetting Machine or Printer

The fastest printer is the Radiation Inc electro-sensitive system at the Lawrence Radiation Laboratory, Livermore, Calif. Recording of up to 30,000 lines per min each containing 120 alphanumeric characters is attained by controlling electronic pulses through chemically impregnated recording paper which is rapidly moving under closely spaced fixed styli. It can thus print the wordage of the whole Bible (773,692 words) in 65 sec—3,333 times as fast as the world's fastest human typist.

Smallest Tubing

The smallest tubing is made by Accles and Pollock Ltd of Warley, England. Made of pure nickel with an outside diameter of 0.0005 in, and an inside diameter of 0.00013 in, it was announced on Sept 9, 1963. The average human hair measures from 0.002 to 0.003 in in diameter. The tubing, which is stainless, can be used for the artificial insemination of bees and "feeding" nerves, and weighs only 5 oz per 100 miles.

Longest and Strongest Wire Rope

The longest wire rope is the stage winder at No. 9 shaft at Vaal Reefs Gold Mine, South Africa, which measures 9½ miles, installed in July 1979. Each of the two ropes weighs 130 tons.

The thickest ever made are spliced crane strops 11¼ in thick, made of 2,392 individual wires in March 1979 by British Ropes at Willington Quay, Tyneside, England.

Largest Radar Installations

The largest of the three installations in the US Ballistic Missile Early Warning System is the one near Thule, Greenland 931 miles from the North Pole, completed in 1960 at a cost of $500 million. Its sister stations are at Cape Clear, Alaska, completed in July 1961, and a $115 million installation at Fylingdales Moor, North Yorkshire, England completed in June 1963. The largest scientific radar installation is the 21-acre ground array at Jicamarca, Peru.

Most Powerful Cranes

The most powerful crane is the 60,000-ton 584-ft-long converted tanker *Odin,* owned by Heerema Engineering Service of The Hague, Netherlands. On May 26, 1976 she made a test lift of 3,360 tons at a radius maximum of 105 ft in the Calard Canal, Europoort, Holland.

The 92.3-ft-wide Rahco (R. A. Hanson Disc. Ltd.) gantry crane at the Grand Coulee Dam Third Powerplant was tested to lift a load of 2,500 tons in 1975. It successfully lowered a 3,944,000-lb generator rotor with an accuracy of 1/32 in.

The tallest mobile crane is the 890-ton Rosenkranz K10001 with a lifting capacity of 1,100 tons and a combined boom and jib height of 663 ft. It is carried on 10 trucks, each limited to 75 ft 8 in and an axle weight of 130 tons. It can lift 33.6 tons to a height of 525 ft.

Greatest Lift

The heaviest lifting operation in engineering history was of the 41,000-ton roof of the Velodrome in Montreal, Canada, in 1975. It was raised by jacks some 4 in to strike its centering.

Oldest Clocks

The earliest mechanical clock, that is, one with an escapement, was completed in China in 725 AD by I Hsing and Liang Ling-tsan.

MOST ACCURATE CLOCK (left): The Olsen clock in the Copenhagen Town Hall makes no more error than ½ sec in 300 years. LARGEST FOUR-FACED CLOCK (below) is this one in the Allen-Bradley Co building that has helped make Milwaukee famous.

The oldest surviving working clock is the faceless clock dating from 1386, or possibly earlier, at Salisbury Cathedral, Wiltshire, England, which was restored in 1956 having struck the hours for 498 years and ticked more than 500 million times. Earlier dates, ranging back to *c.* 1335, have been attributed to the weight-driven clock in Wells Cathedral, Somerset, England, but only the iron frame is original. A model of Giovanni de Dondi's heptagonal astronomical clock of 1348–64 was completed in 1962.

Largest Clock

The most massive clock is the Astronomical Clock in the Cathedral of St Pierre, Beauvais, France, constructed between 1865 and 1868. It contains 90,000 parts and measures 40 ft high, 20 ft wide and 9 ft deep. The Su Sung clock, built in China at K'aifeng in 1088–92, had a 22-ton bronze armillary sphere for 1⅔ tons of water. It was removed to Peking in 1126 and was last known to be working in its 40-ft-high tower in 1136.

Public Clocks

The largest four-faced clock is that on the building of the Allen-Bradley Co of Milwaukee, Wis. Each face has a diameter of 40 ft 3½ in with a minute hand 20 ft in overall length.

The tallest four-faced clock is that of the Williamsburgh Savings Bank, Brooklyn, NYC. It is 430 ft above street level.

Most Accurate Clock

The most accurate and complicated clock in the world is the Olsen clock, installed in the Copenhagen Town Hall, Denmark. The clock, which has more than 14,000 units, took 10 years to make and the mechanism of the clock functions in 570,000 different ways. The celestial pole motion of the clock will take 25,753 years to complete a full circle, the slowest moving designed mechanism in the world. The clock is accurate to 0.5 sec in 300 years—50 times more accurate than the previous record holder.

Most Accurate Time Measurer

The most accurate time-keeping devices are the twin atomic hydrogen masers installed in 1964 in the US Naval Research Laboratory, Washington, DC. They are based on the frequency of the hydrogen atom's transition period of 1,420,450,751,694 cycles per sec. This enables an accuracy to within one sec per 1,700,000 years.

Computers

The first electronic digital computer, called ENIAC, was completed by J. Presper Eckert Jr and John W. Mauchly at the Moore School of Electrical Engineering, University of Pennsylvania in 1946. Computers were then advanced by the invention of the point-contact transistor by John Bardeen and Walter Brattain announced in July 1948, and the junction transistor by R. L. Wallace, Morgan Sparks and Dr William Shockley in early 1951. The Microcomputer was invented in 1969–73 by M. E. Hoff Jr of Intel Corporation with the production of the microprocessor silicon chip "4004."

The computer planned to be the world's biggest by a factor of 40 is the $50 million NASF (Numerical Aerodynamic Simulation Facility) at NASA's Ames Research Center, Palo Alto, Calif. The tenders from CDC and Burroughs called for a capacity of 12.8 gigaflops (12,800 million complex calculations per sec).

Most Powerful and Fastest Computer

The world's most powerful and fastest computer is the CRAY-1, designed by Seymour R. Cray of Cray Research Inc, Minneapolis. The clock period is 12.5 nanoseconds and memory ranges up to 1,048,576 64-bit words, resulting in a capacity of 8,388,608 bytes of main memory. It attains speeds of 200 million floating point operations per sec. With 32 CRAY DD-19 disk storage units, it has a storage capacity of 7.7568×10^{10} bits. The cost of a mid-range system was quoted in mid-1979 at $8.8 million.

Oldest Watch

The oldest watch (portable clockwork timekeeper) is one made of iron by Peter Henlein in Nürnberg, Bavaria, Germany, c. 1504, and now in the Memorial Hall, Philadelphia. The earliest wristwatches were those of Jacquet-Droz and Leschot of Geneva, Switzerland, dating from 1790.

Smallest and Thinnest Watch

The smallest watches are produced by Jaeger Le Coultre of Switzerland. Equipped with a 15-jeweled movement, they measure just over ½ in in length and 3/16th in in width. The movement, with its case, weighs under ¼ oz.

The thinnest wristwatch is the Concord Delirium IV which measures .039 in (.98 mm) in thickness and retailed for $16,000 in June 1980 with a gold bracelet.

Most Expensive Watches

Excluding watches with jeweled cases, the most expensive standard men's pocket watch is the Swiss *Grande Complication* by Audemars-Piguet, which retailed for $94,000 in May 1980.

The heavily-jeweled *Kallista* watch by Vacheron et Constantin of Genoa, Italy was valued in Oct 1979 at $3,700,000.

The record price for an antique watch is $166,300 paid to Capt Peter Belin, USN by L. C. Mannheimer of Zurich at Sotheby Parke Bernet, NYC on Nov 29, 1979 for a gold studded case watch of *c.* 1810 made by William Anthony of London.

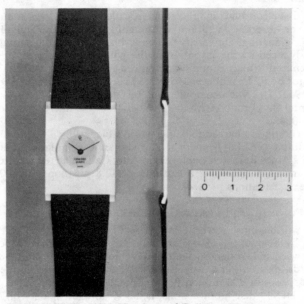

THINNEST WATCH: The Concord Delirium IV, at 0.98 mm or 0.039 in, is thinner than a dime. This product of Swiss technology claims to feature the world's smallest battery, motor, and quartz tuning fork.

Chapter 9

The Business World

In this chapter, the pound sterling has been converted, unless otherwise noted, at an average exchange rate of £1 = $2.20 for 1979, $2.30 for 1980, and at the prevailing rates for earlier dates.

1. COMMERCE

Oldest Industry

Agriculture is often described as "the oldest industry in the world," whereas in fact there is no evidence that it was practiced before *c.* 11,000 BC. The oldest known industry is flint knapping, involving the production of chopping tools and hand axes, dating from about 1,750,000 years ago. Salt panning could be of comparable antiquity.

Oldest Company

The oldest company is the Faversham Oyster Fishery Co of England, referred to in the Faversham Oyster Fishing Act of 1930 as existing "from time immemorial," *i.e.* in English law from before 1189.

Greatest Assets

The business with the greatest amount in physical assets is the Bell System, which comprises the American Telephone and Telegraph Co, with headquarters at 195 Broadway, NYC, and its subsidiaries. The Bell System's total assets on the consolidated balance sheet on Feb 29, 1980 were valued at $115,505,319,000. The plant involved included 139,100,000 telephones. The number of employees is 1,035,000. A total of 20,109 attended the annual meeting in Apr 1961, thereby setting a world record.

The first company to have assets in excess of $1 billion was the US Steel Corp with $1,400 million at the time of its creation by merger in 1900.

Greatest Sales and Capital

The first company to surpass the $1 billion mark in annual sales was the US Steel Corp in 1917. Now there are some 450 corporations with sales exceeding $2 billion (285 of which are in the US). The list is headed by the Exxon Corp of NY with sales of $79,106,471,000 in 1979.

Greatest Profit and Loss

The greatest net profit made by an industrial company in a year is $3,508 million by General Motors in 1978.

The greatest loss ever recorded by any enterprise in a year was $1,097 million by the Chrysler Corp in 1979.

Biggest Work Force

The greatest payroll of any single civilian organization is that of the USSR National Railway system with a total work force of 2,031,200 in 1976.

Largest Take-Over

The largest take-over in commercial history has been the bid of £438,000,000 ($1,051,200,000) by Grand Metropolitan Hotels Ltd, England, for the brewers Watney Mann on June 17, 1972. Watney Mann was then valued at £378,200,000 ($907,200,000).

Largest Write-Off

The largest reduction of assets in the history of private enterprise was the $800 million write-off of Tristar aircraft development costs by Lockheed announced Nov 23, 1974.

Greatest Bankruptcy

William G. Stern (b Hungary, 1936), a US citizen since 1957, who set up Welstar Group Holding Co in the London property market in 1971, was declared bankrupt for $229,480,345 in Feb 1979.

Advertising Agency

The largest advertising agency in 1979, as listed in *Advertising Age,* is Dentsu Inc of Japan with estimated total billings of $2,437 million.

Biggest Advertiser

The biggest advertiser is Sears Roebuck and Co with $491 million spent in 1979, excluding its catalogue.

Aircraft Manufacturer

The largest aircraft manufacturer is the Boeing Co of Seattle, Wash. The annual sales totaled $8,131 million in 1979, and it had 102,000 employees and assets valued at $3,625 million on Jan 1, 1980.

Cessna Aircraft Co of Wichita, Kans had total sales of $939 million in 1979. The company has produced more than 160,000 aircraft since Clyde Cessna's first was built in 1911.

Largest Airlines

The largest airline is the USSR State airline "Aeroflot," so named since 1932. This was instituted on Feb 9, 1923, with the title of Civil Air Fleet of the Council of Ministers of the USSR, abbreviated to "Dobrolet." It operates 1,300 aircraft over about 560,000 miles of routes, employs 400,000 people and carries 100 million passengers to over 80 countries.

The commercial airline carrying the greatest number of passengers

(Apr 1980) was Eastern Airlines (formed 1938) with 42,236,177 passengers. The company had 49,163 employees and a fleet of 252 jet planes.

Oldest Airline

The oldest existing national airline is Koninklijke-Luchtvaart-Maatschappij N.V. (KLM) of the Netherlands, which opened its first scheduled service (Amsterdam-London) on May 17, 1920, having been established Oct 7, 1919. One of the original constituents of B.O.A.C., Handley-Page Transport Ltd, was founded in May 1919, and merged into Imperial Airways in 1924. Delag (Deutsche Luftschiffahrt A.G.) was founded at Frankfurt am Main Nov 16, 1909, and started a scheduled airship service in June 1910. Chalk's International Airline has been flying amphibians between Miami, Fla and the Bahamas since July 1919. Albert "Pappy" Chalk flew from 1911 to 1975.

Aluminum Producer

The largest producer of primary aluminum is the Aluminum Company of America (Alcoa) of Pittsburgh, with its affiliated companies. The company had an output of 1,886,000 tons in 1979, with sales of $4,785,582,679.

The Aluminum Company of Canada Ltd owns the largest aluminum smelter in the western world, at Arvida, Quebec, with a capacity of 475,000 tons per year.

Art Auctioneering

The largest and oldest firm of art auctioneers is the Sotheby Parke Bernet Group of London and New York, founded in 1744. Their turnover in 1978–79 was $410,038,000. The highest total for any house sale auction was theirs on May 18–27, 1977, at the 6th Earl of Rosebery's home at Mentmore, Buckinghamshire, England, which reached £6,389,933 ($10,900,000). The government had turned down an offer of £2 million.

The highest total of any sale of fine art is $34,100,000 for a collection ranging from medieval art to impressionist paintings from the estate of Baron Robert von Hirsch, in a 7-day auction conducted by Sotheby's in London from June 19–27, 1978.

Bicycle Factory

The 64-acre plant of TI Raleigh Industries Ltd at Nottingham,

LARGEST BICYCLE FACTORY: This plant at Nottingham, England has the capacity to make 2 million bicycles.

England, is the largest factory producing complete bicycles, components and wheeled toys. The factory employs 10,000 and has the capacity to make more than 2 million bicycles and 850,000 wheeled toys per year.

Bookstores

The bookshop with the most titles and the longest shelving (30 miles of it) is W. & G. Foyle Ltd of London. First established in 1904 in a small shop in Islington, the company is now at 119–125 Charing Cross Road. On one site, the area is 75,825 sq ft.

The most capacious bookstores measured by square footage are those of Barnes & Noble Bookstores on Fifth Avenue at 18th Street, NYC. They cover 154,250 sq ft with 12.87 miles of shelving.

The largest second-hand booksellers are Richard Booth (Bookseller) Ltd, Hay-on-Wye, Powys, Wales, with 8.49 miles of shelving and a running stock of 900,000 to 1,100,000 in 30,091 sq ft of selling space.

Breweries

The oldest brewery is the Weihenstephan Brewery in Freising, near Munich, W Germany, founded in 1040.

The largest single brewer is Anheuser-Busch Inc of St Louis. In 1978 the company sold 41,600,000 barrels, the greatest annual volume ever produced by a brewing company. The company's St Louis plant covers 100 acres and after completion of current modernization projects will have an annual capacity in excess of 12 million barrels.

The largest brewery on a single site is Adolph Coors Co of Golden, Colo which sold 12,800,000 barrels in 1978.

Arthur Guinness, Son & Co Ltd, founded in 1759, is the largest exporter of beer, ale and stout in the world. Exports of Guinness from the Republic of Ireland in the 52 weeks ending March 15, 1980, were 920,719 bulk barrels (1 bulk barrel = 36 Imperial gallons) which is equivalent to 1,456,962 half-pint glasses per day. The main brewery extends over 57.22 acres at St James's Gate, Dublin, Ireland, the largest in Europe.

Brickworks

The largest brickworks is the London Brick Co plant at Stewartby, Bedfordshire, England. The works, established in 1898, now cover 221 acres and have a production capacity of 13 million bricks and brick equivalent every week.

Car Manufacturer

The largest car manufacturer is General Motors Corp of Detroit. During its peak year of 1979, worldwide sales totaled $63,311,200,000. Its assets on Dec 31, 1979, were valued at $32,215,800,000. Its total 1979 payroll was $18,851 million to an average of 853,000 employees. Dividends paid in 1979 were $1,533,200,000.

Largest Car Plant

The largest single automobile plant is the Volkswagenwerk, Wolfsburg, W Germany, with 56,400 employees and a capacity of over 4,100 vehicles daily. The surface area of the factory buildings is 363 acres and that of the whole plant, with 43.5 miles of rail sidings, is 4,895 acres.

LARGEST AUTO PLANT: On this "rear-end merry-go-round" at the Wolfsburg, W Germany factory, 5 Volkswagen workers can make 240 sections per hour.

Greatest Car Salesman

The all-time record for automobile salesmanship in individual units sold is 1,425 in 1973, by Joe Girard of Detroit, author of "How to Sell Anything to Anybody" and winner of the Number One Car Salesman title every year from 1966 to 1977. His lifetime total of one-at-a-time "belly to belly" selling was 13,001 units sold, all retail. He retired Jan 1, 1978 to teach others his art and to write books on selling.

Chocolate Factory

The largest chocolate factory is that built by Hershey Foods Corp of Hershey, Pa in 1903–05. It now has 2 million sq ft of floor space.

Computer Company

The largest computer firm is International Business Machines Corp (IBM) which has been resisting since 1969 the Justice Dept's largest anti-trust suit. In 1979, assets were $24,529,974,000, with sales of $22,862,776,000.

Department Stores

F. W. Woolworth, which celebrated its centenary year in 1979, now operates a total of 6,040 stores worldwide. Frank W. Woolworth opened his first Five and Ten Cent Store in Lancaster, Pa, on June 21, 1879. The 1979–80 earnings were a record $180 million.

LARGEST CHOCOLATE FACTORY: Even the streets of the town of Hershey, Pennsylvania have names like Chocolate Avenue.

FIRST "5&10": Woolworth's first store (above) in Lancaster, Pennsylvania gave birth to a chain that now numbers more than 6,000.

WORLD'S LARGEST SINGLE STORE (right, above): Macy's New York annually produces a Thanksgiving Day Parade which marches 2½ miles to their Herald Square store and is called "the longest running show on Broadway."

Largest Single Store

The largest store is R. H. Macy & Co Inc at Broadway and 34th St, NYC. It has a floor space of 50.5 acres, and 12,000 employees who handle 400,000 items. The sales of the company and its subsidiaries totaled $2,058,048,000 in 1979. Mr Rowland Hussey Macy's sales on his first day at his fancy goods store on 6th Avenue, Oct 27, 1858, were recorded as $11.06.

Fastest-Moving Merchandise

The department store with the fastest-moving stock is the Marble Arch premier store of Marks & Spencer Ltd at 458 Oxford Street, London. The figure of more than $1,275-worth of goods per sq ft of selling space (total 90,400 sq ft) per year is believed to be an understatement. The company has 251 branches in the UK and nearly 6 million sq ft of selling space. It now has stores in Continental Europe and Canada.

Distillery

The largest distilling company is The Seagram Company Ltd of Canada. Its sales in the year ending July 31, 1979, totaled $2,554,096,000, of which $2,150,339,000 were from sales by Joseph E. Seagram & Sons Inc in the US. The group employs about 15,000 people, including about 10,800 in the US.

The largest of all Scotch whisky distilleries is Carsebridge at Alloa, Central Region, Scotland, owned by Scottish Grain Distillers Ltd. This distillery is capable of producing more than 9 million gallons of alcohol per year. The largest establishment for blending and bottling Scotch whisky is owned by John Walker & Sons Ltd at Kilmarnock, Strathclyde, where over 3 million bottles are filled each week. "Johnnie

Walker" is the world's largest-selling brand of Scotch whisky. The largest malt Scotch whisky distillery is the Tomatin Distillery, Highland, Scotland, established at 1,028 ft above sea level in 1897, with an annual capacity of 5 million proof gallons. The world's largest-selling brand of gin is Gordon's.

Drug Store Chain

The largest chain is that of Boots The Chemists, which has 1,116 retail branches. The firm was founded in England by Jesse Boot (1850–1931), the 1st Baron Trent.

Fisheries

The highest recorded catch of fish was 72,434,000 tons in 1973. Peru had the largest ever national haul with 13,406,000 tons in 1970, comprising mostly anchoveta.

The largest net yet manufactured is one that can fish 8,800,000 cu yd per hour, announced in W Germany in March 1974.

General Merchandise at Retail

The largest general merchandising retailer is Sears Roebuck and Co of Chicago (founded by Richard Warren Sears in the North Redwood railroad station in Minnesota in 1886). The net sales were $17,514 million in the year ending Jan 31, 1980, when the corporation had 864 retail stores and 2,816 catalogue, retail and telephone sales offices and independent catalogue merchants in the US, and total assets valued at $16,421,972,000.

Grocery Store Chain

The largest grocery chain is Safeway Stores Inc of Oakland, Calif with sales in 1979 amounting to $13,717,861,000 and total current assets valued at $1,207,814,000 as of Dec 21, 1979. The company has 2,425 stores totaling 59,470,000 sq ft. The total payroll covers 148,876 people.

Hotels

The top revenue-earning hotel business is Holiday Inns Inc with the year's revenues on Dec 31, 1979 of $1,178 million from 1,741 inns (296,251 rooms) in 59 countries. The business was founded by Charles Kemmons Wilson with his first inn on Summer Avenue in Memphis, Tenn in 1952.

Insurance Companies and Losses

The company with the highest volume of insurance in force is the Prudential Insurance Co of America, Newark, NJ, with $367,284 million as of Dec 31, 1979. The admitted assets are $54,734 million.

It was estimated in 1978 that the total premiums paid in the US had surpassed $100 billion or $1,400 per household.

The largest single association is the Blue Cross, the medical insurance organization, with a membership of 83,187,312 on Jan 1, 1980. Benefits paid out in 1979 totaled $17,575,807,000.

The largest marine insurance loss ever was the 125,000 grt VLCC (Very Large Crude Carrier) *Olympic Bravery,* insured at Lloyd's of London and valued at £25 million ($50 million), which ran aground off Ushant, France, on Jan 24, 1976. The 83,000 grt LNG (Liquid Natural Gas) Carrier *Aquarius,* built in 1977 by General Dynamics Co is currently insured for $175 million. This vessel is owned by Wilmington Trust Co, Delaware, and chartered to the Burmah Oil Co Ltd.

Highest Life Insurance Pay-out

Linda Mullendore, wife of a murdered Oklahoma rancher, received some $18 million as of Nov 14, 1970, the largest pay-out on a single life. Her husband had paid $300,000 in premiums in 1969.

Mineral Water

The world's largest mineral water firm is Source Perrier near Nîmes, France with an annual production of more than 2,100 million bottles, of which 1,200 million now come from Perrier and Contrexéville. The French drink 50 liters (106 pints) of mineral water per person per year.

Soft Drinks

The world's top-selling soft drink is Coca-Cola with over 240 million sold per day by the end of 1979 in more than 135 countries. "Coke" was invented by Dr John S. Pemberton of Atlanta, Ga in 1886, the company was formed in 1892, and its famous bottle was patented in 1915.

Oil Company and Refinery

The world's largest oil company is the Exxon Corp (formerly Standard Oil Co), with 169,000 employees and assets valued at $49,489,964,000 on Jan 1, 1980. The world's largest refinery is the Amerada Hess refinery at St Croix, Virgin Islands, with an annual capacity of 37,475,200 tons.

Paper Mill

The largest paper mill is that established in 1936 by the Union Camp Corp at Savannah, Ga, with an all-time record output of 1,002,967 tons in 1974.

Pharmaceutical Company

The largest company marketing pharmaceuticals and the largest of all chemical companies is Hoechst of W Germany, with drug sales of $14,950 million in 1979.

Photographic Store

The photographic store with the largest selling area is Jessop of Leicester Ltd's Photo Centre, Hinckley Road, Leicester, England which opened in June 1979 with an area of 20,000 sq ft.

Popcorn Plant

The largest popcorn plant is The House of Clarks Ltd of Dagenham, Barking, England (instituted in 1933), which in 1978–79 produced 65 million packets of popcorn.

Public Relations

The largest public relations firm is Hill and Knowlton Inc of 633 Third

Avenue, NYC, and ten other US cities. The firm employs a full-time staff of over 700 and also maintains offices in 22 cities overseas.

The world's pioneer public relations publication is *Public Relations News,* founded by Mrs Denny Griswold in 1944. It now has readers in 86 countries.

Publishing

The publishing company generating most net revenue is Time Inc of NYC, with $2,504 million in 1979. The largest educational book publishing concern in the world is the Book Division of McGraw-Hill Inc of NYC, with sales of $335,209,000 in 1979. The company published 1,231 new titles and 143 reprints.

Restaurant Chain

The largest restaurant chain is McDonald's Corp in Oakbrook, Ill, started Apr 15, 1955, in Des Plaines, a suburb of Chicago, by Ray A. Kroc, BH (Bachelor of Hamburgerology). By Jan 1, 1980, the number of restaurants licensed and owned in 24 countries and 3 US territories reached 5,747 with an aggregate output of 30 billion 100% beef hamburgers. Sales systemwide in 1979 were $5,385 million.

The world's largest fish and chips shop is Harry Ramsdens, White Cross, Guiseley, West Yorkshire, England, with a staff of 180 serving 1,510,000 customers each year, who consumed 348 tons of fish and 504 tons of potatoes.

Shipbuilding

In 1979, there were 16,004,093 tons gross of ships, excluding sailing ships, barges, and vessels of less than 100 tons, completed throughout the world. The figures for the USSR and the People's Republic of China are incomplete. Japan completed 5,260,635 tons gross (32.87% of the world's total).

The leading shipbuilding firm in 1979 was the Mitsubishi Heavy Industries Co of Japan, which launched 39 merchant ships totaling 622,115 tons gross.

Shipping Line

The largest shipping owners and operators are the Royal Dutch/Shell Group of Companies, whose fleets of owned/managed and chartered ships comprised 206 oil tankers (totaling 26 million dwt), 12 gas carriers

1894   1899–1902   1900 ——— 1916   1915   1923   1937   1957   1961   1975

TOP-SELLING SOFT DRINK: The familiar Coca-Cola bottle has not always been the same.

(totaling 1,026,000 cu yd capacity) and 14 dry bulk carriers (900,000 dwt) as of Dec 31, 1979.

Shopping Center

The largest shopping center is the Lakewood Center, Calif, with a gross building area of 2,451,438 sq ft on a 168-acre site. There is parking for 12,500 cars.

The world's first shopping center was Roland Park Shopping Center in Baltimore, Md, built in 1896.

The world's largest wholesale merchandise market is the Dallas Market Center, located on Stemmons Freeway, Dallas, Tex, with more than 7 million sq ft in 6 buildings. The complex covers 135 acres with some 3,000 permanent showrooms displaying merchandise of more than 22,000 manufacturers. The center attracts 500,000 buyers each year to its 27 annual markets and trade shows.

Steel Company

The largest producer of steel has been Nippon Steel of Tokyo, which produced 37,609,600 tons of steel and steel products in 1978–79. The Fukuyama Works of Nippon Kokan has a capacity of almost 18 million tons per annum. Its Jan 1978 work force was 76,034.

Tobacco Company

The largest tobacco company is the British-American Tobacco Co Ltd (founded in London in 1902). The company's subsidiaries and affiliates operate 118 tobacco factories in 51 countries. Consolidated turnover in 1978–79 was $9,964 million and total assets were $4,490,850,000 on December 31, 1979. The Group's sales in 1979 topped 550,000 million cigarettes.

The largest cigarette plant is the $300 million Philip Morris plant at Richmond, Va, which opened in Oct 1974. It employs 5,200 people producing 500 million cigarettes a day.

Toy Manufacturer

The largest single toy manufacturer is Mattel Inc of Hawthorne, Calif, founded in 1945. Its total sales in the year ending Feb 2, 1980 were $805,064,000 for 6 divisions, of which Mattel Toys is the largest.

Toy Store

The biggest toy store is Hamley's of Regent Street Ltd, founded in London in 1760 in the Holborn area, and moved to Regent Street in 1901. It has selling space of 30,000 sq ft on 11 floors with over 300 employees during the Christmas season. It was taken over by Debenhams on May 12, 1976.

Wine Company

The oldest champagne firm is Ruinart Père et Fils, founded in 1729. The oldest cognac firm is Augier Frères & Cie, established in 1643.

LAND

The world's largest landowner is the United States Government, with a holding of 775,249,000 acres (1,210,000 sq mi), which is nearly the area of India, and 12.8 times larger than the UK. The world's largest private landowner is reputed to be International Paper Co, with 9 million acres.

Land Values

Currently the most expensive land is in central Tokyo. It is estimated that 1 sq m (about 1 sq yd) of the Tamagama Takashimaya shopping center is worth 12 million yen ($50,000 approx).

The price for a grave site in Hong Kong may cost HK $200,000 (US $40,000 approx) for a 4 × 10 ft plot.

The real estate value per square meter of the two topmost French vineyards, the Grande and Petite Cognac vineyards in Bordeaux, has not been recently estimated.

Greatest Land Auction

The greatest auction ever was that at Anchorage, Alaska, on Sept 11, 1969, for 179 tracts of 450,858 acres of the oil-bearing North Slope, Alaska. An all-time record bid of $72,277,133 for a 2,560-acre lease was made by the Amerada Hess Corporation-Getty Oil consortium. The bid indicated a price of $28,233 per acre.

Highest and Lowest Rent

The highest recorded rentals in the world are for shop premises in Hong Kong at US $20 per sq ft *per month.*

The rent for a 3-room apartment in the Fuggerei in Augsburg, W Germany, since it was built by Jacob Fugger in 1519, has been 1 Rhine guilder (now DM 1.72 or $1) per month. Fugger was the extremely wealthy philanthropist who pioneered social welfare.

STOCK EXCHANGES

The oldest Stock Exchange of the 138 listed in the world is that in Amsterdam, in the Netherlands, founded in 1602.

Highest Value Stock

The highest price quoted was for a share of F. Hoffmann-La Roche of Basel, Switzerland, worth 101,000 Swiss francs ($38,486) on Apr 23, 1976.

New York Stock Exchange Records

The highest index figure on the Dow Jones average (instituted Oct 1896) of selected industrial stocks at the close of a day's trading was 1,051.70 on Jan 11, 1973, when the average of the daily "highs" of the 30 component stocks was 1,067.20.

The old record trading volume in a day on the NY Stock Exchange of 16,410,030 shares on Oct 29, 1929, the "Black Tuesday" of the famous "crash," was not surpassed until the first 20-million-share day

(20,410,000) was achieved on Apr 10, 1968, when the ticker tape fell 47 minutes behind. Many more issues have been listed since 1929. The current record for a day's trading is 81,618,520 shares on Oct 10, 1979.

The Dow Jones industrial average, which had hit a low of 381.71 on Sept 3, 1929, plunged 30.57 points on Oct 29, 1929, on its way to the Depression's lowest point of 41.22 on July 8, 1932. The largest decline in one day, 38.33 points, occurred on Oct 28, 1929. The total lost in security values from Sept 1, 1929, to June 30, 1932 was $74,000 million.

The greatest paper loss in a year was $209,957 million in 1974.

The record-setting daily increase of 28.40 on Oct 30, 1929, was most recently bettered on Nov 1, 1978, when the Dow Jones index increased 35.34 points to 827.79.

The largest transaction on record "share-wise" was on March 14, 1972, for 5,245,000 shares of American Motors at $7.25 each.

The largest stock trade in the history of the NY Exchange was a 1,874,300-share block of Cutler-Hammer stock at $55 per share in a $103,086,500 transaction on June 12, 1978.

The highest price paid in a transaction for a seat on the NY Stock Exchange was $625,000 in 1929. The lowest 20th century price was $17,000 in 1942.

The value of stocks listed on the NYSE passed the $1 million million (trillion) mark on Jan 31, 1980 with $1,019,000 million as total value.

Largest New Issue

The largest security offering in history was one of $1,375 million in American Telephone and Telegraph Co stock in a rights offer on 27,500,000 shares of convertible preferred stock on June 2, 1971.

Largest Equity

The greatest aggregate market value of any corporation is $33,500 million, given the closing price of 206⅝ on Dec 31, 1975, for IBM, multiplied by the 149,533,813 shares outstanding.

Largest Investment House

The largest investment company in the US, and once the world's largest partnership (124 partners before becoming a corporation in 1959), is Merrill Lynch, Pierce, Fenner & Smith, Inc of NYC (founded Jan 6, 1914). Its parent company has 26,860 employees, 581 offices, and 1,930,000 separate accounts. The firm is referred to in stock exchange circles as "We" or "We, the people" or "The Thundering Herd."

Largest Bank

The International Bank for Reconstruction and Development (founded Dec 27, 1945), the UN "World Bank" at 1818 H Street NW, Wash, DC, has an authorized share capital of $34,000 million. There were 130 members with a subscribed capital of $25,903,100,000 on Dec 31, 1977. The International Monetary Fund in Wash, DC, had 140 members with total quotas of SDR39,011 million ($49,934 million) on March 31, 1980.

The private commercial bank with the greatest deposits is the Bank of America National Trust and Savings Association, of San Francisco, with

$84,984,746,000 on Dec 31, 1979. Its total assets on that date were $108,389,318,000.

The bank with the most branches is The State Bank of India with 7,557 on Jan 1, 1980, with assets of $16,144,509,799.

Largest Bank Building

The tallest bank building is the Bank of Montreal's First Bank Tower, Toronto, which has 72 stories and stands 935 ft high. The largest bank vault, measuring 350 × 100 × 8 ft and weighing 984 tons, is in the Chase Manhattan Building, New York City, completed in May 1961. Its six doors weigh up to 44.7 tons apiece, but each can be closed by the pressure of a forefinger.

Most Directorships

The record for directorships was set in 1961 by Hugh T. Nicholson, formerly senior partner of Harmood Banner & Co, London, who, as a liquidating chartered accountant, became a director of all 451 companies of the Jasper Group in 1961 and had 7 other directorships.

MANUFACTURED ARTICLES

Antique

The largest antique ever sold has been the London Bridge in March 1968. The sale was made by Ivan F. Luckin of the Court of Common Council of the Corporation of London to the McCulloch Oil Corp of Los Angeles for $2,460,000. Over 10,000 tons of facade stonework were re-assembled at a cost of $6,900,000 at Lake Havasu City, Ariz, and "re-dedicated" Oct 10, 1971.

LARGEST ANTIQUE: London Bridge was sold for almost $2½ million and moved to Lake Havasu City, Arizona. When it was all in place in 1971, an official balloon was launched for the celebration.

Armor

The highest price paid for a suit of armor is £25,000 (equivalent to $125,000 at that time) paid in 1924 for the Pembroke suit of armor, made in the 16th century for the 2nd Earl of Pembroke.

Art Nouveau

The highest auction price paid for any piece of art nouveau is $360,000 for a spider-web leaded glass mosaic and bronze table lamp made by L. C. Tiffany, sold at Christie's, NYC, Apr 8, 1980.

Artwork (other than a painting)

The highest price paid at auction for any work of art other than a painting is $2,422,000 for a mid 12th century AD copper gilt and *champlevé* enamel plaque 5¾ in in diameter depicting *Operatio* (The Angel of Charity). This plaque once formed part of the famous Stavelot Retable, presumed to have been broken up during the French Revolution. It formed part of the collection of Robert von Hirsch, sold at Sotheby's, London, June 22, 1978.

Beds

In Bruges, Belgium, Philip, Duke of Burgundy, had a bed 12½ ft wide and 19 ft long erected for the perfunctory *coucher officiel* ceremony with Princess Isabella of Portugal in 1430. The largest bed in existence is the Great Bed of Ware, dating from *c.* 1580, from the Crown Inn, Ware, Hertfordshire, England, now preserved in the Victoria and Albert Museum, London. It is 10 ft 8½ in wide, 11 ft 1 in long and 8 ft 9 in tall. The largest bed currently marketed is the Super Size Diplomat bed, 9 ft wide and 9 ft long, sold in England for £2,200 ($5,000 approx).

The heaviest bed is a waterbed 9 ft 7 in wide and 9 ft 10 in long, owned by Milan Vacek of Canyon Country, Calif, since 1977. The thermostatically-heated water alone weighs 4,205 lb.

Beer Cans and Coasters

Beer cans date from a test marketing by Krueger Beer of Richmond, Va, in 1935. The largest collection is claimed by John F. Ahrens of Mt Laurel, NJ, with over 13,000 *different* cans.

The largest collection of beer coasters is owned by Leo Pisker of Vienna, who had collected nearly 80,000 different coasters from 146 countries by Apr 1980.

Bird

The highest price ever paid for a stuffed bird is £9,000 ($23,400 at the time). This was on March 4, 1971 in the salesrooms of Sotheby's, London, by the Iceland Natural History Museum for a specimen of the Great Auk (*Alca impennis*) in summer plumage, which was taken in Iceland *c.* 1821. This particular specimen stood 22½ in high. The Great Auk was a flightless North Atlantic seabird, which was finally exterminated on Eldey, Iceland in 1844, becoming extinct through hunting.

Blanket

The largest blanket ever made measured 68 × 100 ft and weighed 600

LARGEST
CIGAR
(above):
Smokable, and
weighing 60 lb,
this Danish cigar
is obviously
more than 9 ft
long. LARGEST
BLANKET
(right): Made
from 20,160
squares knitted
by readers of an
English women's
magazine, it
weighed 600 lb
and covered
6,800 sq ft.

lb. It was knitted in 20,160 6-in squares in 10 months (Oct 1977–July 1978) by the English *Woman's Weekly* readers for Action Research for The Crippled Child.

Candle

A candle 80 ft high and 8½ ft in diameter was exhibited at the 1897 Stockholm Exhibition by the firm of Lindahls. The overall height was 127 ft.

Carpets and Rugs

The earliest carpet known (and still in existence) is a woolen pile-knotted carpet, red on a white ground, excavated at Pazyryk, USSR in 1947 and dated to the 5th century BC, and now preserved in Leningrad. Of ancient carpets the largest on record was the gold-enriched silk carpet of Hashim (dated 743 AD) of the Abbasid caliphate in Baghdad, Iraq. It is reputed to have measured 180 × 300 ft.

The largest carpet now consists of 88,000 sq ft (over 2 acres) of maroon carpeting in the Coliseum, Columbus Circle, NYC. This was first used for the International Automobile Show, Apr 28, 1956.

The most magnificent carpet ever made was the Spring carpet of Khusraw made for the audience hall of the Sassanian palace at Ctesiphon, Iraq. It was about 7,000 sq ft of silk and gold thread, encrusted with emeralds. It was cut up as booty by military looters in 635 AD and from the known realization value of the pieces must have had an original value of some $2,400 million.

In 1946 the Metropolitan Museum of Art, NYC privately paid $1 million for the 26.5 × 13.6 ft Anholt Medallion carpet made in Tabriz or Kashan, Persia, c. 1590. The highest price ever paid at auction for a carpet is $229,900 for a Mamluk carpet 12 ft 5 in × 7 ft 3 in, presumed woven in Cairo c. 1500 and sold at Sotheby's, London March 29, 1978.

The most finely woven carpet known is one with more than 2,490 knots per sq in from a fragment of an Imperial Mughal prayer carpet of the 17th century, now in the Altman collections in the Metropolitan Museum of Art, NYC.

Ceramics

The auction record price for any ceramic object is £420,000 ($1,008,000) for the 16¼-in Ming blue and white bottle dated 1403–24 acquired by Mrs Helen Glatz, a dealer, at Sotheby Parke Bernet, London, Apr 2, 1974.

Chair

The world's largest chair measures 29 ft 6¼ in tall, 13 ft 9¼ in wide, and has stood outside the Edsbyverken furniture factory in Edsbyn, Sweden since 1944.

The highest price ever paid for a single chair is $85,000 for the John Brown Chippendale mahogany corner chair attributed to John Goddard of Newport, RI, and made c. 1760. This piece was included in the Christie collection dispersed by Sotheby Parke Bernet, NYC, Oct 21, 1972.

Chandelier

The largest chandelier was built in Murano, Italy in 1953 for the Casino Knokke, Belgium. It measures 26 ft 3 in in circumference and 23 ft in height, and weighs 3.9 tons with 1,896 electric lights.

Cigars

The largest smokable cigar in existence is 9 ft 1½ in long, 12¾ in in circumference and weighs 60 lb 3 oz. It was made by J. P. Schmidt Jr, Fredericia, Denmark and exhibited in May 1979.

The largest standard brand of cigar is the 9¾-in-long "Partagas Visible Immensas." The Partagas factory in Havana, Cuba manufactures special gift cigars 19.7 in long, which retail in Europe for more than $13 each.

Russo's Restaurant, Union Street, San Francisco has the largest known collection of cigar bands with some 5,000, dating from 1860.

The most expensive standard cigar in the world is the Montecristo "A," which retails in Great Britain at a suggested £5.82 ($13.50).

The most voracious smoker is Paul Mears of the University of Winnipeg, Manitoba, Canada, who won a contest in 1975 by smoking 35 full-size cigars simultaneously.

Simon Argevitch of Oakland, Calif, retained his record for the more esoteric art of smoking 14 cigars while simultaneously whistling, Sept 23, 1973 in NYC.

Cigarettes

The heaviest smokers in the world are the people of the US where about 665,000 million cigarettes (an average of 3,900 per adult) were

LARGEST CIGARETTE COLLECTION (above): Dr Robert Kaufman of NYC has 7,495 different brands from 170 countries to show. SMOKER Scott Case (right) got 110 lit cigarettes in his mouth simultaneously for 30 sec in the 1974 Oddball Olympics in Los Angeles.

consumed at a cost of some $15,000 million in 1978. The people of China, however, were estimated to consume 725,000 million in 1977.

Scott Case smoked 110 cigarettes simultaneously for 30 seconds at the Oddball Olympics in Los Angeles in May 1974.

The world's largest collection of cigarettes is that of Robert E. Kaufman, MD, of NYC. In Apr 1980, he had 7,495 different brands of cigarettes with 43 kinds of tips made in 170 countries. The oldest brand represented is "Lone Jack," made in the US c. 1885. Both the longest and shortest (see below) are represented.

The world's most popular cigarette is "Marlboro," a filter cigarette made by Philip Morris, which sold 203,500 million units in 1979.

The longest cigarettes ever marketed were "Head Plays," each 11 in long and sold in packets of 5 in the US in about 1930, to save tax. The shortest were "Lilliput" cigarettes, each 1¼ in long and ⅛ in in diameter, made in Great Britain in 1956.

Cigarette Cards

The earliest known and most valuable tobacco card is "Vanity Fair," dated 1876, issued by Wm. S. Kimball & Co, Rochester, NY.

The largest known collection belongs to Edward Wharton-Tigar (b 1913) of London, with a collection of more than 1 million cigarette and trade cards in about 45,000 sets. The highest price paid for a set is $4,600 on Oct 11, 1975, for Taddy's "Clowns," purchased by Ian Graham of Leeds, England, at auction in London.

Cigarette Lighter

The most expensive pocket cigarette lighter is the 18-carat gold and platinum Dunhill lighter, featuring the British Union Jack comprising 73 precious stones (diamonds, rubies and sapphires) and selling for $20,000 at Dunhill's in NYC in 1979. The 18-carat lighthouse table lighter made by Alfred Dunhill Ltd of London, set on an island of amethyst, retails for a record £32,500 ($75,000).

Cigarette Pack

The earliest surviving cigarette pack is the Finnish "Petit Canon" packet for 25, made by Tollander & Klärich in 1860, from the Ventegodt Collection. The rarest is the Latvian 700-year anniversary (1201–1901) Riga packet, believed to be unique, from the same collection.

Cloth

The most expensive of all cloths is Shatoosh (or Shatusa), a brown-gray wool from the throat hair of Indian goats. It is more expensive than vicuña and was sold by Neiman-Marcus of Dallas at $1,000 per yard, but supplies have now dried up.

Credit Card Collection

The largest collection of valid credit cards, as of May 3, 1980, is one of 1,003, all different, by Walter Cavanagh (b 1943) of Santa Clara, Calif (known as "Mr Plastic Fantastic"). The cost of acquisition was nil, and he keeps them in the world's largest wallet, 250 ft long, weighing 31 lb, and worth more than $1,250,000 in credit.

Curtain

The largest curtain ever built was the bright orange-red 4½-ton 185-ft-high curtain suspended 1,350 ft above and across the Rifle Gap, Grand Hogback, Colo, by the Bulgarian-born sculptor Christo (né Javacheff), 36, on Aug 10, 1971. It blew apart in a 50-mph gust of wind 27 hours later. The total cost of displaying this work of art was $750,000.

The world's largest functional curtain is one 550 ft long × 65 ft high in the Brabazon Hangar at British Aerospace, Filton, Bristol, used to enclose aircraft in the paint-spraying bay. It is electrically drawn.

Dolls

The highest price paid at auction for dolls is £16,000 ($36,800) for a pair of William and Mary painted wooden dolls in original clothes 22 in high at Sotheby's, London, Apr 19, 1974. After an export license was refused, they were purchased, after a public subscription, by the Victoria and Albert Museum, London.

A rag doll 27 ft high was made at Macy's NY "Clowning Around Day" on Aug 26, 1979 and presented for exhibition to the Guinness Museum in the Empire State Building, NYC.

Dress

The dress with the highest price tag ever exhibited was one designed by Serge Lepage, and exhibited in the Schiaparelli spring/summer collection in Paris on Jan 23, 1977. Called "The Birth of Venus" and studded with 512 diamonds, it carried a record price tag of $1,500,000.

Emperor Jean-Bédel Bokassa's coronation robe, with a 39-ft-long train, was encrusted with 785,000 pearls and 1,220,000 crystal beads by Guiselin of Paris for $144,500 for use at Bangui, Central African Empire in Dec 1977.

A platinum bikini valued at $9,500 was made by Mappin and Webb Jewelers, London. It was worn by Miss United Kingdom in the 1977 Miss World beauty pageant.

CUCKOO CLOCK (top): In Wooster, Ohio visitors to Mrs Grossniklaus' cheese factory can see the figures dance around. HIGHEST PRICE HAT (above): Worth almost $30,000, this was worn by Napoleon. LARGEST FLOAT (right): 51 beauty queens rode this 150-ft-long float in the 1977 Orange Bowl Parade in Miami. LARGEST SOFA MARKETED TODAY: Eight people fit comfortably on this 12-ft-2-in couch made in Calif.

Fabrics

The oldest surviving fabric discovered from Level VI A at Çátal Hüyük, Turkey, has been radio-carbon dated to 5900 BC.

The most expensive fabric obtainable is an evening-wear fabric 37½ in wide, hand embroidered and sequinned on a pure silk ground in a classical flower pattern. It has 29,900 tiny sequins per sq yd, and is designed by Alan Hershman of London; it cost $667 per meter in Apr 1980.

Fireworks

The largest firework ever produced was *Fat Man II,* made by NY Pyrotechnic Products Inc, fired near Titusville, Fla, Oct 22, 1977. The 720-lb shell was 40½ in in diameter.

Flags

The crest in the center of the Austrian flag has its origins in the 11th century, while that of Malta dates from 1090. The origins of the Iranian flag, with its sword-carrying lion and sun, are obscure, but "go beyond the 12th century." The study of flags is known as vexillology.

The largest flag made, the "Stars and Stripes," was displayed in Evansville, Ind on March 22, 1980 measuring 410 × 210 ft, in readiness for being hoisted on the Verrazano-Narrows Bridge, NYC, on July 4, 1980. It is the brainchild of advertising man Len Silverfine. His previous attempt was a flag nearly as big which was torn apart after a few hours during a test hanging on June 28, 1976.

Floats

The longest float used in any street carnival is the 200-ft-long dragon *Sun Loon* used in Bendigo, Victoria, Australia. It has 65,000 mirror scales. Six men are needed to carry its head alone.

The largest float is the 150-ft-long, 22-ft-wide "Agree" Float, bearing 51 All-American Homecoming Queens, used at the Orange Bowl parade, Miami, Fla, Dec 29, 1977.

Furniture

The highest price ever paid for a single piece of furniture is 7,600,000 francs ($1,700,000) for a 10-ft-high marquetry and ormolu Louis XV corner cabinet made by Dubois, sold at Sotheby Parke Bernet, Monte Carlo, June 25, 1979. On May 18, 1977, a bureau *en pente* of *c.* 1735 by Bernard van Risen Burgh was sold at Mentmore Towers, England, for £280,000 ($476,000).

The largest item of furniture is the Long Sofa—a wooden bench for old seafarers—measuring 236 ft in length, at Oskarshamn, Sweden.

The largest marketed sofa is the King Talmage Sofa, 12 ft 2 in in length, made by Talmageville Furniture manufacturers in California.

Glass

The most priceless example of the art of glass-making is usually regarded as the Portland Vase which dates from late in the 1st century BC or 1st century AD. It was made in Italy and was in the possession of the Barberini family in Rome from at least 1642. It was eventually bought by the Duchess of Portland in 1792, but smashed while in the British Museum in 1847.

An auction record was set at Sotheby's, London, June 4, 1979, when a 4th century Roman cage cup measuring 7 in in diameter and 4 in in height was sold for £520,000 ($1,040,000).

Gold Plate

The highest auction price for a single piece of gold plate is £66,000 (then $122,100) for an English George III salver, known as "The Rutland Salver," made by Paul Storr of London in 1801, and sold by Sotheby Parke Bernet, London, on May 4, 1978. The salver, which is 12 in in diameter, is engraved with the arms of Manners, Duke of Rutland and of the 16 towns and cities, the gold Freedom boxes of which were melted down to make the salver.

The gold coffin of the 14th century BC Pharaoh Tutankhamun, discovered by Howard Carter on Feb 16, 1923, in Luxor, western Thebes, Egypt, weighed 2,448 lb.

Gun

The highest price ever paid for a single gun is £125,000 ($312,500) given by the London dealers, F. Partridge, for a French flintlock fowling piece made for Louis XIII, King of France, c. 1615 and attributed to Pierre le Bourgeoys (d 1627) of Lisieux, France. This piece was included in the collection of the late William Goodwin Renwick (US) sold by Sotheby's, London, Nov 21, 1972.

Hat

The highest price ever paid for a hat is 165,570 francs (including tax) ($29,471) by Moët et Chandon, a champagne house, at an auction by

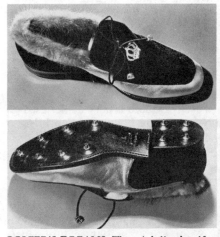

GOLFER'S DREAMS: The mink-lined golf shoes (above), with ruby-tipped gold spikes, and pearl-tipped laces, sell for $9,020 per pair. Samples are on display at the Guinness Museums and Exhibit Halls. The precious putter (right) is valued at $136,000.

Maîtres Liery, Rheims et Laurin, France on Apr 23, 1970, for one last worn by Emperor Napoleon I (1769–1821) on Jan 1, 1815.

Jade

The highest price ever paid for an item in jade is 1,250,000 Swiss francs ($390,625) for a necklace set with 31 graduated beads of Imperial green jade. This was sold by Christie's at the Hotel Richmond, Geneva, Switzerland May 9, 1973. The highest price paid for jade objects is HK $1.4 million ($297,000 US) for a pair of 19th century green jadeite table screens 17¼ in in height sold by Sotheby's in Hong Kong Nov 2, 1976.

Jig-Saw Puzzle

The largest jig-saw puzzle ever made is one 48 ft 1/16 in × 24 ft ⅛ in, built with 9,111 large pieces by the 75th Field Artillery Group, US Army, at Fort Sill, Okla, and exhibited on Nov 3, 1975. The *Festival of Britain* jig-saw by Efroc Ltd, now in Montserrat, though of much less area, contains an estimated 40,000 pieces.

Knife with Most Blades

The penknife with the greatest number of blades is the Year Knife made by the cutlers Joseph Rodgers & Sons Ltd, of Sheffield, England, whose trademark was granted in 1682. The knife was built in 1822 with 1,822 blades, and was designed to match the year of the Christian era until 2000 AD, but had to halt at 1,973 because there was no more space for blades.

Medal or Decoration

The highest price paid at auction for a single medal or decoration is $51,000 for the gold *Comitia Americana* awarded to Brig-Genl "Mad" Anthony Wayne (1745–96) of the US Army for his capture of Stony Point, NY on July 15, 1779. The medal was sold by a direct descendant of the general, Anthony Wayne Ridgeway, at Sotheby Parke Bernet, NYC on June 15, 1978.

Sheerest Nylon

The lowest denier nylon yarn ever produced is the 6 denier used for stockings exhibited at the Nylon Fair in London in Feb 1956. The sheerest stockings normally available are 9 denier. An indication of the thickness is that a hair from the average human head is about 50 denier.

Paperweight

The highest price ever paid for a glass paperweight is £48,000 ($96,000) at Christie's, London, July 10, 1979, for a St Louis 19th century paperweight.

Pencil

The longest pencil, 7 ft long, was made by the oldest pencil factory, Cumberland in England. It weighed 15¼ lb and its lead was 1 in thick.

MOST VALUABLE PIPE: This "flying horseman" shape was carved into meerschaum, a claylike mineral from Asia Minor that is particularly suitable for pipe smoking. It has been marketed in San Francisco for $10,000.

Pens

The most expensive writing pens are the 18-carat pair of pens (one fiber-tipped and one ballpoint) capped by diamonds of 3.88 carats sold by Alfred Dunhill Ltd, London, for £9,943 ($22,969) the pair (including taxes).

Most Expensive Pipe

A meerschaum pipe with a bowl fashioned in the shape of a "flying horseman" has been marketed in San Francisco for $10,000 since Aug 1978.

Pistols

The highest price paid for a pair of pistols at auction is the £78,000 ($178,400) given by the London dealer Howard Ricketts at Sotheby Parke Bernet, London on Dec 17, 1974, for a pair of English Royal flintlock holster pistols made *c.* 1690–1700 by Pierre Monlong. They were sent for sale by Anne, Duchess of Westminster.

Playing Cards

The rarest pack of playing cards is the 17th century "Lives of the Saints," published by the Bowles family and estimated to be worth $4,000. A 7 of diamonds signed by Edward Gibbon (who wrote *The Decline and Fall of the Roman Empire*) as an IOU in 1786 for £320 has been sold for $1,000.

Porcelain

The highest price ever paid for a single piece of English porcelain is £32,000 (about $77,000) for a Chelsea Boar's Head (of the red anchor period) sold at Sotheby's, London, Nov 13, 1973.

The record for English pottery is £15,015 ($30,030) for a Staffordshire 18th century salt-glaze pew group sold at Christie's, London, Dec 15, 1975.

The highest price paid at auction for a single piece of European porcelain is $213,675 for a 38½-in-high Meissen white porcelain figure of a Macaw modeled by Johann Joachim Kandler. This piece from the Robert von Hirsch collection was sold at Sotheby's, London on June 27, 1978.

Ropes

The largest rope ever made was a coir fiber launching rope with a circumference of 47 in made in 1858 for the British liner *Great Eastern* by John and Edwin Wright. It consisted of four strands, each of 3,780 yd.

The longest fiber rope ever made without a splice was one of 10,000 fathoms (11.36 miles) of 6½-in circumference manila by Frost Brothers (now British Ropes Ltd) in London in 1874.

Shoes

The most expensive standard shoes obtainable are the mink-lined golf shoes with 18-carat gold embellishments and ruby-tipped gold spikes by Stylo Matchmakers International Ltd of Northampton, England, which retail for $9,020 per pair.

The largest shoes ever sold, excluding those made for cases of elephantiasis, are a pair of size 42 built for the giant Harley Davidson of Avon Park, Fla. The largest shoes normally available are size 14.

The 1887 Jubilee Boot made for the Newark trades procession, Nottinghamshire, England, is 4 ft 3½ in long and weighs 81¾ lb. It is a size 141, and is owned by Clarks Shoe Museum, Somerset, England.

Silver

The highest price ever paid for silver was £612,500 ($1,163,750) for the Duke of Kingston tureens made in 1735 by Meissonier and sold by Christie's, Geneva, Nov 8, 1977.

Snuff Box

The highest price ever paid for a snuff box is $205,475 paid by Kenneth Snowman of Wartski's in a sale at Christie's, London, on June 26, 1974. This was for a gold and lapis lazuli example uniquely signed by Juste-Oreille Meissonier (d 1750), the French master goldsmith, and dated Paris 1728. It was made for Marie-Anne de Vaviere-Neubourg, the wife of Charles II of Spain, and measures 3¼ × 2¼ in.

Spoons

The highest price ever paid for a set of 12 spoons is £70,000 ($161,000) paid by Mrs How in a sale at Christie's, London, on June 26, 1974. They are Elizabethan silver-gilt spoons, made by Christopher Wace in 1592, and are known as the "Tichborne Celebrities."

Sword

The highest price recorded for a sword is $145,000 paid for the gold sword of honor presented by the Continental Congress of 1779 to Gen Marie Jean Joseph Lafayette, sold at Sotheby Parke Bernet, NYC, on Nov 20, 1976.

Table

A buffet table 2,606 ft long was set up by a hotelier in Marienheide, W Germany to feed 20,000 people attending a charitable fund-raising outdoor event in 1979.

MOST EXPENSIVE SWORD (left): Presented to Lafayette in 1779, it sold for $145,000 in 1976. LARGEST BOOT (right): Size 141, this Jubilee Boot of 1887 weighs 81¾ lb and is 4 ft 3½ in long. It can be seen in a shoe museum in England.

Tablecloth

The world's largest tablecloth is one 219 yd long × 2 yd wide double damask, made by John S. Brown & Sons Ltd of Belfast, N Ireland, and shipped to a royal palace in the Middle East. There was also an order for matching napkins for 450 places.

Tapestry

The earliest known examples of tapestry-woven linen are three pieces from the tomb of Thutmose IV, the Egyptian pharaoh, which date from 1483 to 1411 BC.

The highest price paid for a set of tapestries is £200,000 ($560,000) for four Louis XV pieces at Sotheby's, London, Dec 8, 1967.

The largest single piece of tapestry ever woven is "Christ in His Majesty," measuring 72 × 39 ft, designed by Graham Vivian Sutherland (b Aug 24, 1903), for an altar hanging in Coventry Cathedral, West Midlands, England. It cost $29,400, weighs 4/5 of a ton, and was delivered from Pinton Frères of Felletin, France on March 1, 1962.

The famous Bayeux *Telle du Conquest, dite tapisserie de la reine Mathilde,* a hanging 19½ in wide × 231 ft long depicts events of the period 1064–6 in 72 scenes and was probably worked in Canterbury, Kent, England *c.* 1086. It was "lost" for 2½ centuries from 1476 until 1724. The Overlord Embroidery of 34 panels each 8 × 3 ft, commissioned by Lord Dulverton (b 1915) from the Royal School of Needlework, London, was completed in 1979 after 100 man-years of work and is 41 ft longer than the Bayeux and has the largest area of any embroidery with 816 sq ft.

An uncompleted 8 in deep 1,130 ft embroidery of scenes from C. S. Lewis's Narnia children's stories has been worked by Mrs Margaret Pollard of Truro, Cornwall, England to the order of Michael Maine.

HIGHEST-PRICED SNUFF BOX (left): $205,475. LARGEST VASE: Made in Illinois in 1976, this stands 8 ft and weighs 650 lb.

Thimble

The record auction price for a thimble is £8,000 ($18,400) paid by the London dealer Winifred Williams at Christie's, Geneva on Dec 3, 1979 for a Meissen dentil-shaped porcelain piece of *c.* 1740.

Time Capsule

The largest time capsule is the Tropico Time Tunnel measuring 10,000 cu ft in a cave in Rosamond, Calif, sealed by the Kern Antelope Historical Society on Nov 20, 1966, and intended for opening in the year 2866.

Typewriters

The first patent for a typewriter was by Henry Mill in 1714, but the earliest known working machine was made by Pellegrine Turri (Italy) in 1808. The highest price paid for an antique machine is £1,200 ($2,640) for the 1902 Blickensderfer electric "golf-ball" machine now in the British Typewriter Museum, Bournemouth, Dorset, England.

Vase

The Chinese ceramic authority, Chingwah Lee of San Francisco, was reported in Aug 1978 to have appraised what is probably the most valuable vase, a unique 39-in K'ang Hsi 4-sided vase then in a bank vault in Phoenix, Ariz at $60 million.

The largest vase on record is one 8 ft high, weighing 650 lb, thrown by Sebastiano Maglio at Haeger Potteries of Dundee, Ill (founded 1872) during Aug 1976.

Wreaths

The most expensive wreath on record was that sent to the funeral of President Kennedy in Washington, DC on Nov 25, 1963, by the civic authority of Paris. It was handled by Interflora Inc and cost $1,200. The only rival was a floral tribute sent to the Mayor of Moscow in 1970 by Umberto Formichello, general manager of Interflora, which is never slow to scent an opportunity.

Writing Paper

The most expensive writing paper is that sold by Cartier, Inc, Fifth Avenue, NYC at $10,000 per 100 sheets with envelopes. It is of handmade paper from Finland with deckle edges and a "personalized" portrait watermark. Second thoughts and misspellings can be costly.

2. AGRICULTURE

It has been estimated that only 21% of the world's land surface is cultivatable and that only 7.6% is actually under cultivation. Evidence adduced in 1971 from Nok Nok Tha and Spirit Cave, Thailand, tends to confirm that plant cultivation and animal domestication was part of the Hoabinhian culture *c.* 11,000 BC. Reindeer may have been domesticated as early as *c.* 18,000 BC but definite evidence is lacking.

The earliest attested evidence for the cultivation of grain comes from the recently excavated site of Abu Hureyra, Syria on the Euphrates, associated with a Mesolithic Village dated *c.* 8500 BC. Cobs have been found in Tehuacán Valley caves, Mexico datable to *c.* 5020 BC. Goat was domesticated at Asiab, Iran by *c.* 8050 BC and dog at Star Carr, North Yorkshire, England by *c.* 7700 BC: the earliest definite date for sheep is *c.* 7200 BC at Argissa-Magula, Thessaly, Greece and for pig and cattle *c.* 7000 BC at the same site. The earliest date for horse is *c.* 4350 BC from Dereivka, Ukraine, USSR.

Farms

The largest farms are collective farms in the USSR. These have been reduced in number from 235,500 in 1940 to only 36,000 in 1969, and have been increased in size so that units of over 60,000 acres are not uncommon.

The pioneer farm of Laucidio Coelho near Campo Grande, Mato Grosso, Brazil, *c.* 1901 was 3,358 sq mi (2,150,000 acres) with 250,000 head of cattle at the time of his death in 1975.

Largest Wheat Field

The largest single fenced field sown with wheat was one of 35,000 acres, sown in 1951 near Lethbridge, Alberta, Canada.

Largest Hop Field

The largest hop field is one of 3,945 acres at Toppenish, Wash owned by John I. Haas, Inc, the world's largest hop growers, with hop farms in British Columbia (Canada), California, Idaho, Oregon and Washington, with a total net area of 37,650 acres.

Largest Vineyard

The largest vineyard extends over the Mediterranean façade between the Rhone and the Pyrenees in the départements (provinces) of Aude, Hérault, Gard and Pyrénées-Orientales. It has an area of 2,075,685 acres of which 52.3% is *monoculture viticole.*

Largest Cattle Station

The largest cattle station is Alexandria Station, Northern Territory, Australia, selected in 1873 by Robert Collins, who rode 1,600 miles to reach it. It now has 82 wells, a staff of 90 and originally extended over 7,207,608 acres. The present area is 6,500 sq mi which is stocked with 60,000 shorthorn cattle. Until 1915 the Victoria River Downs Station, Northern Territory, was over three times larger, with an area of 22,400,000 acres (35,000 sq mi).

Largest Sheep Station

The largest sheep station is Commonwealth Hill, in the northwest of South Australia. It grazes between 70,000 and 90,000 sheep, about 700 cattle and 54,000 uninvited kangaroos, in an area of 4,080 sq mi. The largest sheep move on record occurred when 27 horsemen moved a mob of 43,000 sheep 40 miles from Barcaldine to Beaconsfield Station, Queensland, Australia, in 1886.

Largest Rice Farm

The largest contiguous wild rice (*Zizania aquatica*) farm is Clearwater Rice Inc at Clearbrook, Minn with 2,000 acres. In 1972 it yielded 262,000 lb.

Largest Chicken Ranch

The largest chicken ranch is the 520-acre "Egg City," in Moorpark, Calif, established by Julius Goldman in 1961. Some 2 million eggs are laid daily by 3 million hens.

Egg-Laying

The highest authenticated rate of egg-laying is by "Princess Te Kawau," a Black Orpington, owned by Mrs D. M. Waddell, with 361 eggs in 364 days in an official test at Taranaki, New Zealand, ending on Mar 31, 1930.

Heaviest Egg

The heaviest egg *reported* is one of 16 oz with double yolk and double shell, laid by a white Leghorn at Vineland, NJ, Feb 25, 1956. The largest *recorded* was one of "nearly 12 oz" for a 5-yolked egg 12¼ in around the long axis and 9 in around the shorter axis laid by a Black Minorca at Mr Stafford's Damsteads Farm, Mellor, Lancashire, England in 1896.

Most Yolks

The highest claim for the number of yolks in a chicken's egg is 9 reported by Mrs Diane Hainsworth of Hainsworth Poultry Farms, Mt Morris, NY, in July 1971 and also from a hen in Kirghizia, USSR in Aug 1977.

Goose Egg

The white goose "Speckle" owned by Donny Brandenberg of Goshen, Ohio, on May 3, 1977 laid a 24-oz egg measuring 13½ × 9½ in circumferences.

Largest Turkey Farm

The largest turkey farm is that of Bernard Matthews Ltd, centered at Great Witchingham, Norfolk, England, with 1,076 workers tending 5,400,000 turkeys.

Largest Piggery

The largest piggery is at the Sljeme pig unit in Yugoslavia, which is able to process 300,000 pigs in a year. Even bigger units may exist in Rumania, but details are lacking.

Mushroom Farm

The largest mushroom farm is Butler County Mushroom Farm Inc, founded in 1937 in a disused limestone mine near West Winfield, Pa. It has over 1,000 employees working underground, in a maze of galleries 110 miles long, producing about 45 million lb of mushrooms per year.

Largest Community Garden

The largest recorded community garden project is that operated by the City Beautiful Council, and the Benjamin Wegerzyn Garden Center in Dayton, Ohio. It comprises 1,173 allotments, each of 812¼ sq ft.

Cheese

The most active cheese-eaters are the people of France, with an annual average in 1978 of 37.7 lb per person. The biggest producer is the US with a factory production of 3,739,014,720 lb in 1979.

The oldest and most primitive cheeses are the Arabian *kishk,* made of the dried curd of goat's milk. There are today 450 named cheeses of 18 major varieties, but many are merely named after different towns and differ only in shape or the method of packing. France has 240 varieties.

The most expensive cheese is La Baratte from the Loire Valley, France, at 140 francs per kg ($17.20 per lb) in 1979.

The largest cheese ever made was a cheddar of 34,591 lb, made in 43 hours, Jan 20–22, 1964, by the Wisconsin Cheese Foundation for exhibition at the NY World's Fair. It was transported in a specially designed 45-ft-long refrigerated tractor trailer "Cheese-Mobile."

Chicken Plucking

The record time for plucking chickens clean was set in the 1976 championship contest at Masaryktown, Fla, Oct 9, when a team of 4 women (Doreena Cary, Diane Grieb, Kathy Roads and Dorothy McCarthy) plucked 12 birds naked in 32.9 sec. Leaving a single feather produces the cry "Fowl!"

Ernest Hausen (1877–1955) of Fort Atkinson, Wisc, died undefeated after 33 years as a champion. On Jan 19, 1939 he was timed for one chicken at 4.4 sec, and reportedly twice did 3.5 sec a few years later.

Turkey Plucking

Vincent Pilkington of Cootehill, County Cavan, Ireland, killed and plucked 100 turkeys in 7 hours 32 min on Dec 15, 1978, including one in 2 min 44 sec.

Hand Milking

Andy Faust at Collinsville, Okla, in 1937, achieved 120 gallons in 12 hours.

Sheep Shearing

The highest recorded speed for sheep shearing in a working day was that of G. Phillips, who machine-sheared 694 lambs (average 77.1 per hour) in 9 hours at Tymawr Farms, Libanus, Powys, Wales, June 25, 1975. The hand-shearing (solo blade) record for a 9-hour day is 353 lambs by Peter Casserly of Christchurch, New Zealand, Feb 13, 1976.

In a shearing marathon, 4 men machine-sheared 1,649 sheep in 24 hours at Brecon, Powys, Wales, July 13–14, 1977.

Chapter 10

The Human World

1. POLITICAL AND SOCIAL

The land area of the earth is estimated at 57,560,000 sq mi (including inland waters), or 29.20% of the world's surface area.

Largest Political Division

The British Commonwealth of Nations, a free association of 41 sovereign independent states and 4 associated states, covers an area of 13,095,000 sq mi with a population which in 1979 just surpassed 1,000 million.

COUNTRIES

The total number of separately administered *de facto* territories in the world is 224, of which 165 were independent countries as of Aug 1, 1980. Of these, 39 sovereign and 42 non-sovereign are insular countries. Only 30 sovereign countries are entirely without a seaboard. The UN lists 4 *de jure* territories—Palestine (West Bank) and Gaza Strip, East Timor, and Western Sahara, but does not list Taiwan, Estonia, Latvia, Lithuania, Mayotte, the 4 Antarctic dependencies, Coral Island and Heard Island.

Largest Country

The country with the greatest area is the Union of Soviet Socialist Republics (the Soviet Union), comprising 15 Union (constituent) Republics with a total area of 8,649,500 sq mi, or 15% of the world's total land area, and a total coastline (including islands) of 66,090 miles. The country measures 5,580 miles from east to west and 2,790 miles from north to south.

Smallest Country

The smallest independent country is the State of the Vatican City, which was made an enclave within the city of Rome, Feb 11, 1929. The enclave has an area of 108.7 acres (0.17 sq mi).

The maritime country with the shortest coastline is Monaco with 3.49 miles excluding piers and breakwaters.

The world's smallest republic is Nauru, less than 1 degree south of the equator in the Western Pacific. It became independent on Jan 31, 1968,

SMALLEST INDEPENDENT COUNTRY: Vatican City, a 108.7-acre enclave within Rome, also has a zero birth rate.

has an area of 5,263 acres (8.2 sq mi) and a population of 8,000 (latest estimate, mid-1978). Tuvalu, a British dependency in Oceania, has an area of 6,080 acres (9.5 sq mi), but a population of only 6,000.

The smallest colony in the world is Gibraltar, with an area of 2½ sq mi. Pitcairn Island, the only inhabited (70 people in 1977) island of a group of 4 (total area 18½ sq mi), has an area of 1½ sq mi, or 960 acres.

The official residence, since 1834, of the Grand Master of the Order of the Knights of Malta totaling 3 acres and comprising the Villa del Priorato di Malta on the lowest of Rome's seven hills (the 151-ft Aventine) retains certain diplomatic privileges as does 68 Via Condotti. The order has accredited representatives to foreign governments. Hence, it is sometimes cited as the smallest "state" in the world.

Flattest and Most Elevated Countries

The country with the lowest highest point is the Republic of the Maldives, which attains 13 ft above sea level. The country with the highest lowest point is Lesotho. The egress of the Senqu (Orange) riverbed is 4,530 ft above sea level.

COUNTRY WITH THE SHORTEST COAST: Monaco on the Mediterranean has 3½ miles of coastline, and also has a population density of 37,280 people per sq mi.

Frontiers

The country with the most land frontiers is China, with 13—Mongolia, USSR, North Korea, Hong Kong, Macau, Vietnam, Laos, Burma, India, Bhutan, Nepal, Pakistan, and Afghanistan. France, if all her *Départements d'outre-mer* are included, may, if her territorial waters are extended, have 20 frontiers.

The longest *continuous* frontier is between Canada and the US, which (including the Great Lakes boundaries) extends for 3,987 miles (excluding 1,538 miles with Alaska).

The "frontier" of the Holy See in Rome measures 2.53 miles. The land frontier between Gibraltar and Spain at La Linea, closed since 1969, measures 1,672 yd. Zambia, Zimbabwe (formerly Rhodesia), Botswana and Namibia (South-West Africa) meet at a point.

Most Frequently Crossed Frontier

The frontier which is crossed most frequently is that between the US and Mexico. It extends for 1,933 miles and has more than 120 million crossings every year. The Sino-Soviet frontier, broken by the Sino-Mongolian border, extends for 4,500 miles with no reported figures of crossings.

Most Impenetrable Boundary

The 858-mile-long "Iron Curtain," dividing the Federal Republican (West) and the Democratic Republican (East) parts of Germany, utilizes 2,230,000 land mines and 50,000 miles of barbed wire, in addition to many watchtowers containing detection devices. The whole 270-yd-wide strip occupies 133 sq mi of East German territory.

CROWDED CITY: This part of Hong Kong (Victoria Island) is not as tightly packed as Kowloon Peninsula, which had 220,000 people per sq mi at one time. There are more than 4 million people crowded into 405 sq mi in Hong Kong.

POPULATIONS

Estimates of the human population of the world largely hinge on the accuracy of the component figure for the population of the People's Republic of China, which published no census between 1953 (582.6 million) and mid-1979 (958.05 million).

The daily increase in the world's population has been estimated at 214,000 per day or 148 per min. It was estimated that 286 were born and 114 died every minute in 1977–78. The world's population has doubled in the last 49 years and is now doubling at a rather faster rate.

WORLD POPULATION—PROGRESSIVE ESTIMATES

Date	Millions	Date	Millions
10000 BC	c. 5	1930	2,070
1 AD	c 200	1940	2,295
1000	c. 275	1950	2,533
1250	375	1960	3,049
1500	420	1970	3,704
1650	550–600	1975	4,033
1700	615	1976	4,107
1750	720	1977	4,182
1800	900	1978	4,258
1900	1,625	1980	4,410*
1920	1,862	2000	6,351**

* Provisional estimate for mid-year.
** Some demographers maintain that the figure will (or must) stabilize at 10–15,000 million, but above 8,000 million during the 21st century. The Tsui-Bogue estimate from the University of Chicago for 2000 AD is 5,800 million, compared with the US Bureau of the Census estimate of 6,351 million given.

It is estimated that 75,000 million humans have been born and died in the last 600,000 years.

Most Populous Country

The country with the largest population is China, which in *pinyin* is written Zhogguo. The mid-1979 UN estimate was 958,050,000. The rate of natural increase in the People's Republic of China is now estimated to have been reduced from 2.3% in 1971 to 1.2% in 1978, so the 1,000 million mark should not now be reached until April 1983.

Least Populous State

The independent state with the smallest population is the Vatican City or the Holy See (see *Smallest Country*), with 728 inhabitants in mid-1978, and a zero birth rate.

Most Densely Populated Places

The most densely populated territory is the Portuguese province of Macau (or Macao), on the southern coast of China. It has an estimated population of 276,000 (mid-1978) in an area of 6.2 sq mi, giving a density of 44,506 per sq mi.

Of territories with an area of more than 400 sq mi, Hong Kong (405 sq mi) contains 4,606,000 people (estimated mid-1978), giving the territory a density of 11,372 per sq mi. Hong Kong is now the most populous of all colonies. The name "Hong Kong" is the transcription of the local pronunciation of the Peking dialect version of Xiang gang (a port for incense). Kowloon, on the mainland, had a density which reached 219,559 per sq mi in 1961. On the Wah Fu estate, there are 55,000 people living on 24 acres, giving an unsurpassed spot density of more than 1,466,600 per sq mi. In 1959, at the peak of the housing crisis, it was reported that in one house designed for 12 people the number of occupants was 459, including 104 in one room and 4 living on the roof.

The Principality of Monaco, on the south coast of France, has a population of 26,000 (estimated June 30, 1978) in an area of 369.9 acres, giving a density of 37,230 per sq mi. This is being relieved by marine infilling which will increase the area to 447 acres.

Singapore has 2,334,000 (mid-1978 estimate) people in an inhabited area of 73 sq mi.

Of countries over 1,000 sq mi, the most densely populated is Bangladesh with a population of 84,655,000 (mid-1978 estimate) living in 55,126 sq mi at a density of 1,535 per sq mi.

The Indonesian island of Java (with an area of 48,763 sq mi) had a population of 69,037,000 (census of 1971), giving a density of 1,415 per sq mi.

Most Sparsely Populated Territory

Antarctica became permanently occupied by relays of scientists as of Oct 1956. The population varies seasonally and reaches 1,500 at times.

The least populated territory, apart from Antarctica, is Greenland, with a population of 51,000 (estimate of mid-1978) in an area of 840,000 sq mi, giving a density of one person to every 16.4 sq mi. Some 84.3% of the island comprises an ice-cap.

CITIES

Most Populous City

The most populous "urban agglomeration" in the world is the Tokyo-Yokohama Metropolitan Area, of 1,081 sq mi, containing an estimated 28,043,000 people in 1978. Of "cities proper," both Tokyo and Mexico City have populations exceeding 8½ million, while Greater Tokyo and Greater Mexico City have populations exceeding 11½ million.

Oldest City

The oldest known walled town is Jericho (Ariha), about 5 miles north of the Dead Sea. Radio-carbon dating on specimens from the lowest levels reached by archeologists indicate habitation there by perhaps 3,000 people as early as 7800 BC. The village of Zawi Chemi Shanidar, discovered in 1957 in northern Iraq, has been dated to 8910 BC. The oldest capital city in the world is Dimashq (Damascus), capital of Syria. It has been continuously inhabited since c. 2500 BC.

Elevations of Cities, Capitals and Dwellings

The highest capital city, before the domination of Tibet by China, was Lhasa, at an elevation of 12,087 ft above sea level.

La Paz, the administrative and *de facto* capital of Bolivia, stands at an altitude of 11,916 ft above sea level. The city was founded in 1548 by Capt Alonso de Mendoza on the site of an Indian village named Chu-

HIGHEST CAPITAL CITY (top left) La Paz, Bolivia sits high in the Andes at 11,916 ft above sea level. OLDEST CITY (top right): The walls of Jericho near the Dead Sea have been standing since 7800 BC and the city was inhabited by perhaps 3,000 people then. OLDEST CAPITAL: Damascus, Syria, has been inhabited continuously since 2500 BC.

quiapu. It was originally called Ciudad de Nuestra Señora de La Paz (City of Our Lady of Peace), but in 1825 was renamed La Paz de Ayacucho, its present official name. Sucre, the legal capital of Bolivia, stands at 9,301 ft above sea level.

The new town of Wenchuan, founded in 1955 on the Chinghai-Tibet road, north of the Tangla Range, is the highest at 16,732 ft above sea level. The highest dwellings in the world are those at Basisi, India, near the Tibetan border, at *c.* 19,700 ft.

The settlement of Ein Bokek, which has a synagogue, on the shores of the Dead Sea, is the lowest town in the world at 1,299 ft below sea level.

The northernmost capital is Reykjavik, Iceland, at 64° 08′ N. Its population was estimated to be 84,772 in 1974.

Largest Town in Area

The largest town in area is Mount Isa, Queensland, Australia. The area administered by the City Council is 15,822 sq mi.

Most Remote Town from Sea

The town most remote from the sea is Wulumuch'i (Urumchi) formerly Tihwa, Sinkiang, capital of the Uighur Autonomous Region of China, at a distance of about 1,400 miles from the nearest coastline. Its population was estimated to be 320,000 in 1974.

Emigration

More people emigrate from Mexico than from any other country. An estimated 800,000 emigrated illegally into the US in 1976 alone.

Immigration

The country which regularly receives the most legal immigrants is the US with 462,315 in 1977. It has been estimated that in the period 1820–1977, the US received 48,063,523 *official* immigrants. One person in every 24 in the US is, however, an *illegal* immigrant.

Birth Rate

The highest 1970–75 estimate by the UN is 51.0 per 1,000 for the Niger Republic. The rate for the whole world was 30.4 per 1,000 in 1975. A world-wide survey published in July 1979 showed only Nepal with a still rising birth rate. The lowest recorded rate is 7.5 for Monaco (1977).

Death Rate

The highest of the latest available recorded death rates is 26.3 deaths per 1,000 of the population in Yemen. The rate for the whole world was 12.3 per 1,000 in 1975. The lowest of the latest available recorded rates is 1.9 deaths per 1,000 in Tonga in 1976.

Natural Increase

The highest of the latest available recorded rates of natural increase is 29.1 (39.6 − 10.5) per 1,000 in Syria. The rate for the whole world was 30.4 − 12.3 = 18.1 in 1975.

The lowest rate of natural increase in any major independent country is W Germany with a negative figure of − 2.0 per 1,000 for 1977 (9.5 births and 11.5 deaths).

Marriage Ages

The country with the lowest average for marriage is India, with 20.0 years for males and 14.5 for females. At the other extreme is Ireland, with 31.4 for males and 26.5 for females. In the People's Republic of China, the *recommended* age for marriage for men has been 28 and for women 25.

Sex Ratio

There were estimated to be 1,003.5 men in the world for every 1,000 women (1975). The country with the largest recorded shortage of males is the USSR, with 1,143 females to every 1,000 males (1979 census). The country with the largest recorded woman shortage is Pakistan, with 885 to every 1,000 males in 1972. The figures are, however, probably under-enumerated due to *purdah,* a policy that keeps women from appearing in public.

Divorces

The country with the most divorces is the US with a total of 1,137,000 in 1978—a rate of 50.48% of the current annual total of marriages.

Infant Mortality

Based on deaths before one year of age, the lowest of the latest available recorded rates is 7.7 deaths per 1,000 live births in Sweden in 1978. The world rate in 1975 was 98.

The highest recorded infant mortality rate reported has been 195 to 300 per 1,000 live births for Burma in 1952, and 259 for Zaire in 1950.

In Ethiopia the infant mortality rate was unofficially estimated to be nearly 550 per 1,000 live births in 1969. Many countries have apparently ceased to make returns.

Life Expectation

There is evidence that life expectation in Britain in the 5th century AD was 33 years for males and 27 years for females. In the decade 1890–1900 the expectation of life among the population of India was 23.7 years.

Based on the latest available data, the highest recorded expectation of life at age 12 months is 73.0 years for males and 79.2 years for females in Iceland (1975–76).

The lowest recorded expectation of life at birth is 27 years for both sexes in the Vallée du Niger area of Mali in 1957 (sample survey, 1957–58). The figures for males in Gabon was 25 years in 1960–61, but 45 for females.

STANDARDS OF LIVING

National Incomes

The state with the highest income per native citizen in 1977 was Abu Dhabi, with some $70,000 each. In 1977, the US reached $9,430 per head.

Housing

For comparison, a dwelling unit is defined as a structurally separated room or rooms occupied by private households of one or more persons and having separate access or a common passageway to the street. The country with the greatest recorded number of private dwelling units is India, with 100,251,000 occupied in 1972.

Hospitals

The largest hospital is the Pilgrim State Hospital, a mental hospital at West Brentwood, LI, NY, with 3,816 beds. It formerly contained 14,200 beds.

The busiest maternity hospital in the world is the Mama Yemo Hospital in Kinshasha, Zaire, with 41,930 deliveries in 1976. The record "birthquake" occurred on one day in May 1976 with 175 babies born. It has 559 beds.

The longest stay in a hospital occurred when Martha Nelson was admitted to the Columbus State Institute for the Feeble-Minded in Ohio in 1875, and stayed until she died in Jan 1975, aged 103 years 6 months, in the Orient State Institution, Ohio, spending more than 99 years in institutions.

Physicians

The country with the most physicians is the USSR, with 831,300, or one to every 307 persons. China has more than one million para-medical personnel known as "barefoot doctors." The country with the lowest recorded proportion is Upper Volta, with 58 physicians (one for every 92,759 people) in 1970.

Eight sons of John Robertson of Dumbarton, Scotland, graduated as medical doctors between 1892 and 1914. The family of David L. Bernie of Dayton, Ohio, contains 27 members who are qualified MDs with 5 more in medical school.

The oldest doctor to continue practice was Frederick Walter Whitney Dawson (1876–1977). He was the first doctor to receive his license in the 20th century in London, England (Jan 1, 1901), and he was still practicing in Whangerai, New Zealand, in his 101st year.

Dentists

The country with the most dentists is the US, where 131,000 were registered members of the American Dental Association in 1978.

Psychiatrists and Psychologists

The country with the most psychiatrists is the US. The registered membership of the American Psychiatric Association was 22,000 in 1978. The membership of the American Psychological Association was 45,000 in 1978.

ROYALTY

Oldest Ruling House

The Emperor of Japan, Hirohito (b Apr 29, 1901), is the 124th in line from the first Emperor, Jimmu Tenno or Zinmu, whose reign was traditionally from 660 to 581 BC, but probably from c. 40 to c. 10 BC. He has been Emperor since Dec 25, 1926.

Longest Reigns

The longest recorded reign of any monarch is that of Pepi II, a Sixth Dynasty Pharaoh of ancient Egypt. His reign began in c. 2310 BC when he was aged 6, and lasted c. 94 years.

Currently the longest reigning monarch in the world is King Sobhuza II (b July 4, 1899), the *Ngwenyama* (Paramount Chief) of Swaziland, who began his reign at the age of 5 months. The country was placed under United Kingdom protection at that time, Dec 1899, and became independent on Sept 6, 1968. At the last published count in 1972, he had 112 wives.

The longest reign of any major European monarch was that of King Louis XIV of France, who ascended the throne May 14, 1643, aged 4 years 231 days, and reigned for 72 years 110 days until his death Sept 1, 1715, four days before his 77th birthday.

Grand Duke Karl Friedrich of Baden (1728–1811) ruled from May 12, 1738, for 73 years 29 days.

Musoma Kanijo, chief of the Nzega district of western Tanganyika

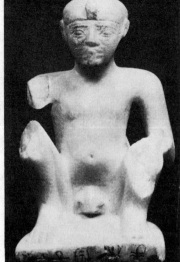

HEAVIEST MONARCH (above): King Taufa'ahau of Tonga weighed 462 lb. LONGEST REIGN (right): Pepi II of ancient Egypt was Pharaoh from age 6 to 100.

(now part of Tanzania), reputedly reigned for more than 98 years from 1864, when aged 8, until his death on Feb 2, 1963.

The 6th Japanese Emperor Koo-an traditionally reigned for 102 years (from 392 to 290 BC), but probably his actual reign was from about 110 AD to about 140 AD. The reign of the 11th Emperor Suinin was traditionally from 29 BC to 71 AD (99 years), but probably was from 259 to 291 AD.

Shortest Reign

King Vikramabahu II of the Kalinga Kshatriya dynasty of Ceylon (Sri Lanka) was assassinated a few hours after he was crowned at Polonnaruwa in 1196.

Youngest King and Queen

Of the world's 19 monarchies, the one with the youngest king is Bhutan (in the Himalayas) where King Jigme Singye Wangchuk (b Nov 11, 1955) succeeded to the throne on July 24, 1972, aged 16 years 8 months. The youngest queen is Margrethe II of Denmark (b Apr 16, 1940).

Heaviest Monarch

The heaviest monarch is the 6-ft 3-in-tall King Taufa'ahau of Tonga, who in Sept 1976, weighed 462 lb on the only adequate scale in the country (at the airport).

Most Prolific Royalty

The most prolific monogamous "royals" have been Prince Hartmann of Liechtenstein (1613–1686) who had 24 children, of whom 21 were live born, by Countess Elisabeth zu Salm-Reifterscheidt (1623–1688). HRH Duke Roberto I of Parma also had 24 children, but by two wives.

LEGISLATURES

Oldest Parliament

The earliest known legislative assembly was a bicameral one in Erech, Iraq, *c.* 2800 BC. The oldest legislative body is the *Alpingi* (Althing) of Iceland, founded in 930 AD. This body, which originally comprised 39 local chieftains was abolished in 1800, but restored by Denmark to a consultative status in 1843 and a legislative status in 1874. The legislative assembly with the oldest continuous history is the Tynwald Court of the Isle of Man, in the Irish Channel, which is believed to have originated more than 1,000 years ago.

Largest Legislature

The largest legislative assembly is the National People's Congress of the People's Republic of China. The Congress which was convened in 1979 had 3,471 members.

Smallest Quorum

The British House of Lords has the smallest quorum. To transact business there need be three peers present, including the Lord Chancellor or his deputy.

Highest-Paid Legislators

The most highly paid of all the world's legislators are US Congressmen, who receive a basic annual salary of $60,700 (since Oct 12, 1979). In addition, up to $1,021,167 per year is allowed for office help, with a salary limit of $49,941 for any one staff member per year (limited to 16). Besides, Senators are authorized up to $143,000 per year, depending on the state, for an Official Office Expense Account from which are paid official travel expenses, telegrams, long-distance telephone calls, air-mail postage, stationery, subscriptions to newspapers, and office expenses in the home state. When abroad they have access to "counterpart funds." They also are entitled to very low charges for filming, speech and radio transcriptions, and beauty treatments (females only).

Filibusters

The longest continuous speech in the history of the US Senate was that of Senator Wayne Morse of Oregon, Apr 24–25, 1953, when he spoke on the Tidelands Oil Bill for 22 hours 26 min without resuming his seat. Senator Strom Thurmond, Democrat (SC), spoke against the Civil Rights Bill for 24 hours 19 min, Aug 28–29, 1957, interrupted only briefly by the swearing-in of a new Senator.

The longest speech made in the UN was one of 4 hours 29 min by the president of Cuba, Fidel Castro Ruz (b Aug 13, 1927) in Aug 1960.

The record for a filibuster in any legislature is 43 hours by Texas State Senator Bill Meier from Euless, who spoke against nondisclosure of industrial accidents in May 1977.

Attendance Record

US Congressman William H. Natcher, a Democrat from Bowling Green, Ky, on Jan 6, 1980, completed his 26th year (1954–80) without

OLDEST PRIME MINISTER: Which was oldest? The Grand Vizier of Morocco (left) was reputed to be 112½ years old, but more accurately recorded was the life of Christopher Hornsrud of Norway who died at age 101.

missing a single vote (3,855 quorum calls and 7,873 roll-call votes to June 11, 1980).

State Representative Lucille H. McCollough was elected to the Michigan House of Representatives on Jan 1, 1955, and had a perfect attendance record into June 1980.

Oldest Prime Minister

The longest-lived prime minister of any country is believed to have been Christopher Hornsrud, who served as Prime Minister of Norway Jan 28 to Feb 15, 1928 (b Nov 15, 1859, d Dec 13, 1960), aged 101 years 28 days.

El Hadji Mohammed el Mokri, Grand Vizier of Morocco, died Sept 16, 1957, at a reputed age of 116 Muslim (*Hijri*) years, equivalent to 112.5 Gregorian years.

The oldest age of appointment has been 81 years in the case of Morarji Ranchhodji Desai of India (b Feb 29, 1896) in March 1977.

Longest Term of Office

Prof Dr António de Oliveira Salazar (1889–1970) was the President of the Council of Ministers (*i.e.* Prime Minister) of Portugal from July 5, 1932, for 36 years and 84 days until superseded on Sept 27, 1968, eleven days after going into a coma.

The longest-serving democratically elected premier was Tage Erlander of Sweden for 22 years 357 days, from Oct 10, 1946 to Oct 1, 1969.

Elections

The largest elections are those for the 529-seat Indian *Lok Sabha* (House of the People). The incoming Prime Minister, Mrs Indira Gandhi, was better known by her symbol (a cow) than by her name among the 335 million voters.

Longest Term

Members of Taiwan's National Assembly, elected in 1947, have been extended in office and include several hundred who celebrated their 32nd year in 1979.

Closest Elections

The ultimate in close general elections occurred in Zanzibar (now part of Tanzania) on Jan 18, 1961, when the Afro-Shirazi Party won by a single seat, after the seat of Chake-Chake on Pemba Island had been gained by a single vote.

The narrowest margin in an election for an office was in the Southern District of Mississippi on Aug 7, 1979, when Robert E. Joiner with 133,587 votes won by 5 votes for the post of highway commissioner.

Most One-Sided Election

North Korea recorded a 100% turn-out of electors and a 100% vote for the Workers' Party of Korea in the general election of Oct 8, 1962.

The highest personal majority by any politician has been 424,545 votes from a total electorate of 625,179 achieved by Ram Bilas Paswan, the Janata candidate for Hajipur in Bihar, India, in March 1977.

Most Rigged Election

In the 1928 presidential election of Liberia, the president, Charles D. B. King, was returned to office with an officially announced majority over his opponent of 234,000 votes. The total electorate at the time was less than 15,000.

Smallest Vote

Wideon Pyfrom (Free National Party), standing for the Rolleville constituency in the Bahamas, received no votes in the July 1977 elections.

Most Coups

Statisticians contend that Bolivia, since it became a sovereign country in 1825, has had 188 *coups d'état.*

Communist Parties

The largest national Communist party outside the USSR (which had 15 million members in 1975) and Communist states has been the Partito Communista Italiano (Italian Communist Party), with a membership of 2,300,000 in 1946. The total fell to 1,700,000 by 1976. The membership in mainland China was estimated to be 28 million in 1974.

Voting Ages

The eligibility extremes for voting are 15 years of age in the Philippines and 25 years in Andorra.

2. MILITARY AND DEFENSE

WAR

Longest War

The longest of history's countless wars was the "Hundred Years' War" between England and France, which lasted from 1338 to 1453 (115 years), although it may be said that the nine Crusades from the First (1096–1104) to the Ninth (1270–91), extending over 195 years, comprised a single Holy War.

Shortest War

The shortest war on record was that between the UK and Zanzibar (now part of Tanzania) from 9:02 to 9:40 a.m. on Aug 27, 1896. The UK battle fleet under Rear-Adm Harry Holdsworth Rawson (1843–1910) delivered an ultimatum to the self-appointed Sultan Sa'id Khalid to evacuate his palace and surrender. This was not forthcoming until after 38 min of bombardment. Admiral Rawson received the Brilliant Star of Zanzibar (first class) from the new Sultan Hamud ibn Muhammad. It was proposed at one time that elements of the local populace should be compelled to defray the cost of the ammunition used.

Bloodiest War

By far the most costly war in terms of human life was World War II (1939–45), in which the total number of fatalities, including battle deaths and civilians of all countries, is estimated to have been 54,800,000, assuming 25 million USSR fatalities and 7,800,000 Chinese civilians killed. The country which suffered most was Poland with 6,028,000 or 22.2% of her population of 27,007,000 killed. The total death toll from World War I was only 17.7% of that of World War II.

In the Paraguayan war of 1864–70 against Brazil, Argentina, and Uruguay, the Paraguayan population was reduced from 1,400,000 to 220,000, of whom only 30,000 were adult males.

Most Costly War

The material cost of World War II far transcended that of the rest of history's wars put together and has been estimated at $1.5 million million. In the case of the UK the cost was over five times as great as that of World War I. The total cost of World War II to the Soviet Union was estimated semi-officially in May 1959 at $280,000 million while a figure of $530,000 million has been estimated for the US.

Bloodiest Battle

The battle with the greatest recorded number of fatalities was the First Battle of the Somme in France, July 1–Nov 19, 1916, with more than 1,030,000—614,105 British and French and c. 420,000 (not 650,000) German. The gunfire was heard as far away as Hampstead Heath, London. The greatest battle of World War II and the greatest conflict ever of armor was the Battle of Kursk and Oryol which raged for 50 days, July 5–Aug 23, 1943, on the Eastern front, which involved 1,300,000 Red Army troops with 3,600 tanks, 20,000 guns and 3,130 aircraft in repelling a German Army Group which had 2,700 tanks. The final invasion of Berlin by the Red Army, Apr 6–May 2, 1945 is, however, said to have involved 3,500,000 men, 52,000 guns and mortars, 7,750 tanks and 11,000 aircraft on both sides.

Modern historians give no credence to the casualty figures attached to ancient battles, such as the 250,000 reputedly killed at Plataea (Greeks *vs.* Persians) in 479 BC or the 200,000 allegedly killed in a single day at Châlons-sur-Marne, France in 451 AD.

Greatest Seaborne Invasion

The greatest invasion in military history was the Allied land, air and sea operation against the Normandy coast of France on D-day, June 6, 1944. Thirty-eight convoys of 745 ships moved in on the first three days, supported by 4,066 landing craft, carrying 185,000 men and 20,000 vehicles, and 347 minesweepers. The air assault comprised 18,000 paratroopers from 1,087 aircraft. The 42 available divisions possessed an air support from 13,175 aircraft. Within a month 1,100,000 troops, 200,000 vehicles and 840,000 tons of stores were landed.

The Allied invasion of Sicily, July 10–12, 1943, involved the landing of 181,000 men in 3 days.

Greatest Airborne Invasion

The largest airborne invasion was the Anglo-American assault of three divisions (34,000) men, with 2,800 aircraft and 1,600 gliders, near Arnhem, Netherlands, Sept 17, 1944.

Greatest Evacuation

The greatest evacuation in military history was that carried out by 1,200 Allied naval and civil craft from the beachhead at Dunkerque (Dunkirk), France May 27–June 4, 1940. A total of 338,226 British and French troops were taken off.

WORST SIEGE: For 880 days from 1941 to 1944, Leningrad, USSR was isolated from the rest of the world by the German Army. Probably 1½ million people died during the siege.

GREATEST EVACUATION: The Allies in 1940 took 338,226 British and French troops off the beaches of Dunkerque, France when the Germans overran Europe in the early days of World War II.

Worst Sieges

The worst siege in history was the 880-day siege of Leningrad, USSR by the German Army, Aug 30, 1941–Jan 27, 1944. The best estimate is that between 1.3 and 1.5 million defenders and citizens died.

The longest recorded siege was that of Azotus (now Ashdod), Israel, which, according to Herodotus, was besieged by Psamtik I of Egypt for 29 years in the period 664–610 BC.

Largest Armed Forces

Numerically, the largest regular armed force is that of the People's Republic of China with 4,360,000. Her paramilitary forces of armed and unarmed militias have been estimated by the International Institute of Strategic Studies at between 90 and 115 million. Their mid-1979 estimates for the world's two principal military powers are 3,658,000 for the USSR and 2,022,000 for the US.

Defense

The estimated level of spending on armaments throughout the world in 1979 was $500,000 million. This represents $120 per person per year, or more than 6% of the world's total production of goods and services. It was estimated in 1979 that there were 22,750,000 full-time armed force regulars or conscripts.

The budgeted expenditure on defense by the US government in the year ending June 30, 1979, was $126,000 million or 6.9% of the country's GNP (gross national product).

The official Chinese estimate for 1978 was that the defense burden on the USSR's GNP was in excess of 15%, *i.e.* more than double that of the US.

NAVIES

Largest Navies

The largest navy in terms of manpower is the US Navy, with 524,200 sailors and 184,000 Marines in mid-1978. The active strength in 1979 included 13 aircraft carriers, 73 attack nuclear submarines and 7 diesel attack submarines, 41 strategic missile submarines, 73 guided missile warships (28 cruisers, 37 destroyers, and 7 frigates), and 65 amphibious warfare ships.

The USSR Navy has a larger submarine fleet of 338 boats, with 115 in reserve, and 90 of them carrying strategic atomic missiles, of which 71 are also nuclear powered. It has 2 aircraft carriers, 37 cruisers and 100 destroyers.

Greatest Naval Battles

The greatest number of ships and aircraft ever involved in a sea-air action was 231 ships and 1,996 aircraft in the Battle of Leyte Gulf, in the Philippines. It raged from Oct 22–27, 1944, with 166 Allied and 65 Japanese warships engaged, of which 26 Japanese and 6 US ships were sunk. In addition, 1,280 US and 716 Japanese aircraft were engaged.

ARMIES

Numerically, the largest army is the People's Republic of China's, with a total strength of some 3,600,000 in mid-1979. The total size of the USSR's army in mid-1979 was estimated by the International Institute of Strategic Studies at 1,825,000 men, believed to be organized into about 173 divisions. (See also *Largest Armed Forces,* above, which includes navies and air forces.)

Oldest Army

The oldest army is the 83-strong Swiss Guard in the Vatican City, with a regular foundation dating back to Jan 21, 1506. Its origins, however, extend back before 1400.

Oldest Old Soldier

The oldest age to which a veteran soldier has lived is 113 years 1 day by John B. Salling of the Army of the Confederate States of America and the last accepted survivor of the US Civil War (1861–65). He died in Kingsport, Tenn, March 16, 1959.

Youngest Soldier

President Francisco Macias Nguema of Equatorial Guinea decreed in March 1976 compulsory military service for all boys between 7 and 14. Any parent refusing to hand over his or her son "will be imprisoned or shot." Probably the youngest enlistment was by William Frederick Price (b June 1, 1891) who enlisted in the British Army at Aldershot, May 23, 1903, aged 11 years 356 days.

Tallest Soldier

The tallest soldier of all time was Väinö Myllyrinne (1909–63) who was inducted into the Finnish Army when he was 7 ft 3 in and later grew to 8 ft 1¼ in.

TANKS*

Earliest Tank

The first tank was "No. 1 Lincoln," modified to become "Little Willie," built by William Foster & Co Ltd of Lincoln, England. It first ran on Sept 8, 1915. Tanks were first taken into action by the Heavy Section Machine Gun Corps, which later became the Royal Tank Corps, at the battle of Flers-Courcelette, France on Sept 15, 1916. The Mark I Male, which was armed with a pair of 6-lb guns and 4 machine-guns, weighed 31.4 tons and was driven by a motor developing 105 hp, which gave it a maximum road speed of 3 to 4 mph.

Heaviest Tank

The heaviest tank ever constructed was the German Panzer Kampfwagen Maus II, which weighed 212 tons. By 1945 it had reached only the experimental stage and was not proceeded with.

The heaviest operational tank used by any army was the 91.3-ton 13-man French Char de Rupture 2C bis of 1923. It carried a 155-mm howitzer and had two 250-hp engines giving a maximum speed of 8 mph.

The world's fastest tank is the $1,800,000 XM-1, due for US Army service. The prototype reached 45 mph. The DM 3,600,000 ($1,900,000) German Leopard 2 has the greatest firepower with a 120-mm (4.72-in) gun.

FASTEST TANK: The prototype of this American XM-1 reached 45 mph.

---

* For further information see *Tank Facts and Feats* by Kenneth Macksey, a Guinness Superlatives Book (Sterling), which deals with all the aspects of the development and history of the tank and other armored fighting vehicles in detail.

Earliest Guns

Although it cannot be accepted as proved, the best opinion is that the earliest guns were constructed in North Africa, possibly by Arabs, c. 1250. The earliest representation of an English gun is contained in an illustrated manuscript dated 1326 at Oxford. The earliest anti-aircraft gun was an artillery piece on a high-angle mounting used in the Franco-Prussian War of 1870 by the Prussians against French balloons.

Largest Guns

The two most massive guns ever constructed were used by the Germans in the siege of Sevastapol on the Eastern Front in World War II. They were of a caliber of 800 mm (31.5 in) with barrels 94 ft long, and named Dore and Gustav. Their remains were discovered, one near Metzenhof, Bavaria in Aug 1945 and the other in the Soviet zone of Germany. They were built by Krupp as railway guns, carried on 24 cars, two of which had 40 wheels each. The whole assembly of the gun was 141 ft long and weighed 1482 tons, requiring a crew of 1,500 men. The range for a 9¼-ton projectile was 29 miles.

Greatest Range

The greatest range ever attained by a gun is by the HARP (High Altitude Research Project) gun consisting of two 16.5-in caliber barrels in tandem, 119.4 ft long and weighing 165 tons, at Yuma, Ariz. On Nov 19, 1966, a 185-lb projectile was fired to an altitude of 111.8 miles (590,550 ft). The static V3 underground firing tubes built by the Germans in 50° shafts at Mimoyecques, near Calais, France to bombard London were never operative, due to RAF bombing.

The famous long-range gun which shelled Paris in World War I in March 1918 was the *Kaiser Wilhelm Geschütz,* with a caliber of 220 mm (8.66 in), a designed range of 79.5 miles and an achieved range of 76 miles. The "Big Berthas" were mortars of 420-mm (16.53-in) caliber with a range of less than 9 miles.

Largest Cannon

The highest caliber cannon ever constructed is the *Tsar Puchka* (King of Cannons), now housed in the Kremlin, Moscow. It was built in the 16th century with a bore of 922 mm (36¼ in) and a barrel 10 ft 5 in long. It weighs 44 tons.

The Turks fired up to seven shots per day from a bombard 26 ft long, with an internal caliber of 42 in, against the walls of Constantinople (now Istanbul) Apr 12-May 29, 1453. It was dragged by 60 oxen and 200 men and fired a stone cannonball weighing 1,200 lb.

Mortars

The largest mortars ever constructed were Mallets mortar (Woolwich Arsenal, London, 1857), and the "Little David" of World War II, made in the US. Each had a caliber of 920 mm (36¼ in), but neither was ever used in action.

The heaviest mortar used was the tracked German 600-mm (23.6-in) siege piece known as "Karl" used against Stalingrad.

Military Engines

The largest military catapults, or onagers, were capable of throwing a missile weighing 60 lb a distance of 500 yd.

Longest March

The longest march in military history was the famous Long March by the Chinese Communists in 1934–35. In 368 days, of which 268 days were of movement, from Oct to Oct, their force of 90,000 covered 6,000 miles northward from Kiangsi to Yenan in Shensi *via* Yünnan. They crossed 18 mountain ranges and six major rivers and lost all but 22,000 of their force in continual rear-guard actions against Nationalist Kuo-min-tang (KMT) forces.

Most Rapid March

The most rapid recorded march by foot-soldiers was one of 42 miles covered in 11 hours 49 min in a night march by 9 soldiers in full battle dress carrying 40 lb from B Company, 4th Infantry Battalion of the Irish Army, Sept 12–13, 1944.

Largest Mutiny

In World War I, 56 French divisions, comprising some 650,000 men and their officers, refused orders in the Nivelle sector.

AIR FORCES

The earliest autonomous air force is the Royal Air Force of Great Britain, whose origin began with the Royal Flying Corps (created May 13, 1912); the Air Battalion of the Royal Engineers (Apr 1, 1911) and the Corps of Royal Engineers Balloon Section (1878) which was first operational in Bechuanaland (now Botswana) in 1884. The Prussian Army used a balloon near Strasbourg, France as early as Sept 24, 1870.

Largest Air Force

The greatest air force of all time was the US Army Air Force (now called the US Air Force), which had 79,908 aircraft in July 1944, and 2,411,294 personnel in March 1944. The US Air Force, including strategic air forces, had 563,000 personnel and 3,400 combat aircraft in mid-1979. The USSR Air Force, including Air Defense Forces with about 1,025,000 men in mid-1979, had 7,600 combat aircraft. In addition, the USSR's Offensive Strategic Rocket Forces had about 375,000 operational personnel in mid-1979.

Bombs

The heaviest conventional bomb ever used operationally was the British Royal Air Force's "Grand Slam," weighing 22,000 lb and measuring 25 ft 5 in long, dropped on Bielefeld railway viaduct, Germany, March 14, 1945. In 1949, the US Air Force tested a bomb weighing 42,000 lb at Muroc Dry Lake, Calif.

ATOM BOMB that dropped on Hiroshima: This is the "Little Boy" which had the explosive power of 20,000 tons of TNT.

Atomic Bombs

The two atom bombs dropped on Japan by the US in 1945 each had an explosive power equivalent to that of 20,000 tons (20 kilotons) of trinitrotoluene, called TNT. The one dropped on Hiroshima, known as "Little Boy," was 10 ft long and weighed 9,000 lb.

The most powerful thermonuclear device so far tested is one with a power equivalent to 57 million tons of TNT, or 57 megatons, detonated by the USSR in the Novaya Zemlya area at 8:33 a.m. GMT on Oct 30, 1961. The shock wave was detected to have circled the world three times, taking 36 hours 27 min for the first circuit. Some estimates put the power of this device at between 62 and 90 megatons. On Aug 9, 1961, Nikita Khrushchev, then the Chairman of the Council of Ministers of the USSR, declared that the Soviet Union was capable of constructing a 100-megaton bomb, and announced the possession of one in East Berlin, Germany, on Jan 16, 1963. It has been estimated that such a bomb would make a crater 19 miles in diameter and would cause serious fires at a range of from 36 to 40 miles.

Atom bomb theory began with Albert Einstein's publication of the $E = mc^2$ formula in *Annalen der Physik* in Leipzig on May 14, 1907. It became practical with the mesothorium experiments of Otto Hahn, Fritz Strassman, and Lise Meitner on Dec 17, 1938. Work started in the USSR on atomic bombs in June 1942, although the first chain reaction was not achieved until Dec 1945, by Dr Igor Vasilyevich Kurchatov.

The patent for the fusion or H-bomb was filed in the US on May 26, 1946, by Dr Janos (John) von Neumann (1903–57), a Hungarian-born mathematician, and Dr Klaus Julius Emil Fuchs (b Germany, 1911), the physicist who defected to Russia from England.

Largest Nuclear Arsenal

The most powerful ICBM's are the USSR's SS-18's, each with up to 10 one-megaton MIRV's (multiple independently targetable re-entry vehicles); thus each has power 50 times as great as the Hiroshima bomb. The US Minuteman III has 3 MIRV's, each of 335 kiloton force.

> No official estimate has been published of the potential power of the device known as Doomsday, but this far surpasses any tested weapon. If it were practicable to construct, it is speculated that a 50,000-megaton cobalt-salted device could wipe out the entire human race except people who were deep underground and did not emerge for more than five years.

Largest "Conventional" Explosion

The largest use of conventional explosive was for the demolition of the fortifications at Heligoland, Germany Apr 18, 1947. A charge of 4,476 tons was detonated by Commissioned Gunner E. C. Jellis of the Royal Navy aboard HMS *Lasso* lying 9 miles out to sea.

Most Bombed Country

The most heavily bombed country has been Laos. It has been estimated that between May 1964 and Feb 26, 1973 some 2½ million tons of bombs of all kinds were dropped along the North to South Ho Chi Minh Trail supply route to South Vietnam.

3. JUDICIAL

LEGISLATION AND LITIGATION

Oldest Statutes

The earliest known judicial code was that of King Ur-Nammu during the Third Dynasty of Ur, Iraq, *c.* 2145 BC.

Most Inexplicable Statute

Certain passages in several laws have always defied interpretation and the most inexplicable must be a matter of opinion. A judge of the Court of Session of Scotland has sent the editors of this book his candidate which reads, "In the Nuts (unground), (other than ground nuts) Order, the expression nuts shall have reference to such nuts, other than ground nuts, as would but for this amending Order not qualify as nuts (unground) (other than ground nuts) by reason of their being nuts (unground)."

Most Protracted Litigation

The longest contested lawsuit ever recorded ended in Poona, India, Apr 28, 1966, when Balasaheb Patloji Thorat received a favorable judgment on a suit filed by his ancestor Maloji Thorat 761 years earlier in 1205. The points at issue were rights of presiding over public functions and precedences at religious festivals.

Longest Impeachment

The British Parliament's impeachment of Gov Warren Hastings (1732–1818), for maladministration of India, began in 1788 and dragged on for 7 years, until his acquittal Apr 23, 1795. The trial itself lasted only 149 days.

Best-Attended Trial

The greatest attendance at any trial was at that of Major Jesús Sosa Blanco, aged 51, for an alleged 108 murders. At one point in the 12½-hour trial (5:30 p.m. to 6 a.m., Jan 22–23, 1959), 17,000 people were present in the Havana Sports Palace, Cuba.

Shortest Trial

On March 1, 1977, an ill-founded prosecution (under the 1974 British Air Navigation Order) brought against a pilot at Edinburgh airport was timed at No. 1 Sheriff Court, Edinburgh, Scotland, to have lasted 7 sec. Sheriff Skae uttered two words—"Not Guilty."

Highest Bail

The highest amount ever demanded as bail was $46,500,000 against Antonio De Angelis in a civil damages suit by the Harbor Tank Storage Co filed in the Superior Court, Jersey City, NJ, Jan 16, 1964, in the Salad Oil Swindle. He was released June 4, 1973.

Abul Hassen Ebtehaj, later Chairman of the Iranian Bank in Teheran, was granted bail in 1977 in excess of $50 million.

Greatest Damages

The highest damages ever actually paid have been $14,387,674 following the crash of a private aircraft at South Lake Tahoe, Calif, on Feb 21, 1967, to the sole survivor Ray Rosendin, 45, by the Santa Clara Superior Court on March 8, 1972. Rosendin received *inter alia* $1,069,374 for the loss of both legs and disabling arm injuries; $1,213,129 for the loss of his wife and $10,500,000 punitive damages against Avco-Lycoming Corp which allegedly violated Federal regulations when it rebuilt the aircraft engine owned by Rosendin Corp.

Personal Injury Damages

The greatest damages for personal injury ever awarded went to Janelle Lynn Stearns, 12, against Park Avenue Hospital Inc and Dr Howard K. Gifford, an anesthetist, in settlement for alleged medical malpractice resulting in severe brain damage following a tonsillectomy at Pomona, Calif in May 1973. If she lives to the average expectation of 63.9 additional years, the payments will total $26,541,832.

The largest single cash payment settlement for a single person has been $6,800,000 to John Coates, 42, a lawyer from Austin, Tex against Remington Arms Co Inc *et al,* on Oct 2, 1978. The case concerned severe injury from a defectively made hunting rifle.

Breach of Contract

The greatest damages ever awarded for a breach of contract were £610,392 ($1,709,000), awarded July 16, 1930, to the Bank of Portugal against the printers Waterlow & Sons Ltd of London, arising from their unauthorized printing of 580,000 five-hundred escudo notes in 1925. This award was upheld in the House of Lords on Apr 28, 1932. One of the perpetrators, Arthur Virgilio Alves Reis, served 16 years (1930–46) in jail.

Defamation Suit

A sum of $16,800,000 was awarded to Dr John J. Wild, 58, at the Hennepin District Court of Minnesota on Nov 30, 1972, against the Minnesota Foundation and others for defamation, bad-faith termination of a contract, and interference with professional business relationships, plus $10,800,000 in punitive damages. These amounts have not to date been appealed.

Greatest Compensation

On Aug 12, 1975, William De Palma (b 1938) of Whittier, Calif, agreed to a $750,000 settlement for 16 months' wrongful imprisonment in McNeil Island Federal Prison, Wash. He had been given a 15-year sentence for armed robbery in Buena Park, Calif, on forged fingerprint evidence in 1968.

Divorce Suits and Settlements

The highest alimony awarded by a court has been $2,261,000 against George Storer Sr, 74, in favor of his third wife Dorothy, 73, in Miami, Fla, on Oct 29, 1974. Mr Storer, a broadcasting executive, was also ordered to pay his ex-wife's attorney $200,000 in fees.

The greatest amount ever reported in a divorce settlement is half the estimated $100 million wealth of the publisher James Kent Cooke (b Canada, 1913) of Las Vegas, Nev, decreed by a Los Angeles court in March 1979, in favor of his wife, Mrs Jeannie Cooke (b 1917), after 42 years of marriage.

Mrs Soraya Khashoggi (*née* Sandra Jarvis Daley) filed the highest alimony claim ever of $2,500 million against her former husband, Adrian Khashoggi in Los Angeles on Aug 3, 1979. Her attorney, Marvin Mitchelson, explaining the size of the claim, alluded to Mr Khashoggi's wealth as including 13 homes, 3 private jumbo jets and a $44 million yacht, *Khalidia.*

Patent Case

The greatest settlement ever made in a patent-infringement suit is $9,250,000, paid in Apr 1952 by the Ford Motor Co to the Ferguson Tractor Co for a claim filed in Jan 1948.

Libel Suit

The largest libel settlement made has been one for $600,000 by the Hearst Corp, publishers of the *San Francisco Examiner,* in response to a $32-million suit brought by the Synanon Foundation Inc and its founder Charles E. Dederich on July 1, 1976, for adverse news articles.

Greatest Lien

The greatest lien ever imposed by a court is 40,000 million lire ($64,800,000) on Apr 9, 1974 in Milan, upon Vittorio and Ida Riva for back taxes allegedly due on a chain of cotton mills around Turin, Italy inherited by their brother Felice (who left for Beirut) in 1960.

Most Literal Legal Interpretation

Eugene Schneider of Carteret, NJ, allegedly cut his $80,000 home in half with a chain saw in July 1976 after his wife sued him for divorce, thus fulfilling in his eyes the equal division of property required by NJ law.

Largest Suit for Damages

The highest amount of damages ever sought is $675 million million (then equivalent to 10 times the US national wealth) in a suit by Mr I. Walton Bader brought in the US District Court, NYC, Apr 14, 1971, against General Motors and others for polluting all 50 States.

Shortest and Longest Wills

The shortest valid will in the world is "Vse zene," the Czech for "All to wife," written and dated Jan 19, 1967, by Herr Karl Tausch of Langen, Hesse, Germany. The shortest will contested but subsequently admitted to probate in English law was the case of *Thorn v. Dickens* in 1906. It consisted of the three words "All for Mother."

The longest will on record was that of Mrs Frederica Cook (US), in the early part of the century. It consisted of four bound volumes containing 95,940 words.

Most Durable Judge

The oldest recorded active judge was Judge Albert R. Alexander (b Nov 8, 1859) of Plattsburg, Mo, magistrate and probate judge of Clinton

COURT RECORDS: Judge Alexander of Plattsburg, Mo (left) served on the bench well into his 105th year. A fearsome example of American jurisprudence is Judge Hitchings of Norfolk, Va (right), whose verdicts stood in 96.5% of the traffic cases he tried.

County. He retired July 9, 1965, at the age of 105 years 8 months and died March 30, 1966. James Russell McElroy (b Oct 1, 1901) served 49 years 125 days (1927–1977) on the Circuit Court of Alabama. Judge Vernon D. Hitchings of Norfolk, Va, disposed of his millionth traffic case from Jan 1954 to Jan 19, 1977. Of these some 965,000 of his verdicts were unappealed or upheld on appeal.

Youngest Judge

No collated records on the ages of judicial appointments exist. However, Thomas J. Boynton (b Amherst, Ohio, Aug 31, 1838) is known to have been appointed Federal Judge at Key West, Fla, on Jan 20, 1864, aged 25 years 142 days. Judge Susan I. Broyles (b Alamosa, Colo, June 25, 1949) was appointed County Judge of Conejos County, Colo, on Jan 9, 1973, aged 23 years 198 days.

Most Successful Criminal Lawyer

Sir Lionel Luckhoo, senior partner of Luckhoo and Luckhoo, of Georgetown, Guyana, succeeded in getting his 225th successive murder charge acquittal by May 1979.

Deadliest Prosecutor

Joe Freeman Britt, District Attorney in the Sixteenth Judicial District in North Carolina, obtained 23 death verdicts in 28 months to mid-1976, when he had 13 defendants simultaneously on death row.

CRIME AND PUNISHMENT

Mass Killings

The greatest massacre ever imputed by the government of one sovereign nation against a government of another is that of 26,300,000 Chinese killed during the regime of Mao Tse-tung between 1949 and May 1965. This accusation was made by an agency of the USSR government in a radio broadcast Apr 7, 1969. In Apr 1971, the Executive *Yuan* or cabinet of the implacably hostile government of The Republic of China in Taipei, Taiwan announced its official estimate of the mainland death roll in the period 1949–69 as "at least 39,940,000." The Walker Report published by the US Senate Committee of the Judiciary in July 1971 placed the total death roll within China since 1949 between 32.25 and 61.7 million.

The death roll in the Great Purge, or *Yezhovshchina,* in the USSR, in 1936–38, has never been published, though evidence of its magnitude may be found in population statistics which show a deficiency of males from *before* the outbreak of the 1941–45 war. On Aug 17, 1942, Stalin indicated to Churchill in Moscow that 10 million *kulaks* (farmers with excessive wealth according to Communist standards) had been liquidated.

At the S.S. (*Schutzstaffel*) extermination camp known as Auschwitz-Birkenau (Oswiecim-Brzezinka), near Oswiecim, in southern Poland, where a minimum of 920,000 people (Soviet estimate is 4,000,000) were exterminated June 14, 1940–Jan 18, 1945, the greatest number killed in a day was 6,000.

Obersturmbannführer (Lt-Col) Karl Adolf Eichmann (b 1906) of the

S.S. was hanged in a small room inside Ramleh Prison, near Tel Aviv, Israel, at just before midnight (local time) on May 31, 1962, for his complicity in the deaths of an indeterminably massive number of Jews during World War II, under the instruction given in Apr 1941 by Adolf Hitler (1889–1945) for the "Final Solution" (*Endlösung*).

Forced Labor

No official figures have been published of the death roll in Corrective Labor Camps in the USSR, first established in 1918. The total number of such camps was known to be more than 200 in 1946, but in 1956 many were converted to less severe Corrective Labor Colonies. An estimate published in the Netherlands puts the death roll between 1921 and 1960 at 19 million. Solzhenitsyn's best estimate is an aggregate number of 66 million inmates. The study by S. Grossu, published 1975, stated there were then 2 million political prisoners in 96 camps.

In China, there are no published official figures on the numbers undergoing *Lao Fiao* (Education through Labor) or *Lao Dong Gai Zao* (Reform through Manual Labor). An estimate published by Bao Ruowang, who was released in 1964 because his father was a Corsican, was 16 million which then approached 3% of the population.

Genocide

In Cambodia, according to the Khmer Rouge foreign minister, Ieng Sarg, more than a third of the 8 million Khmers were killed between Apr 1975 and June 1979. Under the rule of Pol Pot, towns, money and property were abolished and execution by bayonet and club introduced for such offenses as falling asleep during the day, asking too many questions, playing non-Communist music, being old and feeble, being the offspring of an "undesirable" or being too well educated.

Largest Criminal Organization

The largest syndicate of organized crime is the Mafia (meaning "swank," from a Sicilian word) or La Cosa Nostra ("our thing") which is said to have infiltrated the executive, judiciary and legislative branches of the US Government. It consists of some 3,000 to 5,000 individuals in 24 "families" federated under "The Commission," with an estimated turnover in vice, gambling, protection rackets, cigarettes, bootlegging, hijacking, narcotics, loan-sharking, prostitution and some legitimate business estimated in May 1977 at $48,000 million per year, of which some $25,300 million is profit—9½ times more than Exxon's profit in 1979.

The biggest Mafia killing was Sept 11–13, 1931, when the topmost man, Salvatore Maranzano, *Il Capo di Tutti Capi,* and 40 allies were liquidated.

The Mafia is said to have got its start in the US from the lynching of 11 Mafiosi in New Orleans in 1890, for which a naive US government paid $30,000 compensation to the widows. This money was seized and used as the initial funding to prime the whole operation.

Murder Rates

The country with the highest recorded murder rate is Mexico with 46.3 registered homicides per 100,000 of the population in 1970. It has been estimated that the total number of murders in Colombia during *La Violencia* (1945–62) was about 300,000, giving a rate over a 17-year period of nearly 48 per day. A total of 592 deaths was attributed to one bandit leader, Teófilo ("Sparks") Rojas, aged 27, between 1948 and his death in an ambush near Armenia on Jan 22, 1963. Some sources attribute 3,500 slayings to him.

The highest homicide rates recorded in NYC have been 58 in a week in July 1972, and 13 in a day in Aug 1972. In 1973, the total for Detroit (population then 1,500,000) was 751.

The country with the lowest officially recorded rate in the world is Spain, with 39 murders (a rate of 1.23 per million population) in 1967, or one murder every 9 days. In the Indian protectorate of Sikkim, in the Himalayas, murder is, however, practically unknown, while in the Hunza area of Kashmir, in the Karakoram, only one definite case by a Hunzarwal has been recorded since 1900.

Most Prolific Murderers

It was established at the trial of Buhram, the Indian Thug, that he had strangled at least 931 victims with his yellow and white cloth *ruhmal* in the Oudh district between 1790 and 1840. It has been estimated that at least 2 million Indians were strangled by Thugs (*burtotes*) during the reign of the Thugee cult (pronounced "tugee") from 1550 until its final suppression by the British raj in 1853.

The greatest number of victims ascribed to a murderess has been 610 in the case of Countess Erszebet Bathory (1560–1614) of Hungary. At her trial which began Jan 2, 1611, a witness testified to seeing a list of her victims in her own handwriting totaling this number. All were alleged to be young girls from the neighborhood of her castle at Csejthe, where she died on Aug 21, 1614. She was walled up in her room for 3½ years, after being found guilty.

This century's top candidate for most prolific one-at-a-time murderer is the German, Bruno Lüdke (b 1909), who confessed to 85 murders of women between 1928 and Jan 29, 1943. He was executed by injection without trial in a hospital in Vienna, Apr 8, 1944.

Pedro Alonso López (b Colombia, 1949), known as the "Colombian Monster," was reported captured by the villagers of Ambato, Ecuador in early March 1980. He admitted to more than 300 murders of pre-teen girls in Colombia, Peru and Ecuador since 1973. The remains of 53 victims of the 110 admitted to in Ecuador were rapidly detected after his confessions.

John Wayne Gacy (b 1943) was sentenced to death by electrocution on March 13, 1980 for murdering 33 males in Chicago. The first of the 33 bodies was found on Dec 21, 1978 under his house in Northwood Township, Ill.

Gang Murders

During the period of open gang warfare in Chicago, the peak year was 1926, when there were 76 unsolved killings. The 1,000th gang murder in Chicago since 1919 occurred on Feb 1, 1967. Only 13 cases have ended in convictions.

Suicide

The estimated daily rate of suicides throughout the world surpassed 1,000 in 1965. The country with the highest recorded suicide rate is Hungary, with 42.6 per 100,000 of the population in 1977. The country with the lowest recorded rate is Jordan, with a single case in 1970 and hence a rate of 0.04 per 100,000.

The final total of the mass cyanide poisoning of the Peoples Temple cult near Port Kaituma, Guyana, Nov 18, 1978 was 910. The leader was the paranoid "Rev" Jim Jones of San Francisco, who had deposited millions of dollars overseas.

Last Guillotinings

The last person to be publicly guillotined in France was the murderer Eugen Weidmann before a large crowd at Versailles, near Paris, at 4:50 a.m. June 17, 1939.

Dr Joseph Ignace Guillotin (1738–1814) for whom the guillotine was named, died a natural death. He had not invented the machine but only advocated its use to the French constituent assembly. The machine was designed by Dr Antoine Louis.

Largest Hanging

The most people hanged from one gallows was 38 Sioux Indians by William J. Duly outside Mankato, Minn for the murder of unarmed citizens on Dec 26, 1862.

Most Hanging Attempts

In 1803 it was reported that Joseph Samuels was reprieved in Sydney, Australia after three unsuccessful attempts to hang him in which the rope broke twice.

Death Row

It was estimated that at mid-1980 some 600 prisoners in the US were on "death row."

Caryl Whittier Chessman, aged 38, convicted of 17 felonies, was executed on May 2, 1960, in the gas chamber at the California State Prison, San Quentin, Calif. In 11 years 10 months and one week on "death row," Chessman had won eight stays of execution.

Samanichi Hirasawa celebrated his 88th birthday on death row in Sendai Risan, northern Japan, on Feb 18, 1980.

Longest Prison Sentences

The longest recorded prison sentences were ones of 7,109 years awarded to two confidence tricksters by an Iranian court, June 15, 1969. The duration of sentences are proportional to the amount of the defalcations involved. A sentence of 384,912 years was *demanded* at the prosecution of Gabriel March Grandos, 22, at Palma de Mallorca, Spain March 11, 1972, for failing to deliver 42,768 letters, a sentence of 9 years per letter.

Juan Corona, a Mexican-American, was sentenced on Feb 5, 1973, at Fairfield, Calif, to 25 consecutive life terms for murdering 25 migrant

MOST SECURE PRISON: While Alcatraz Island in San Francisco Bay was a Federal prison (1934–63) no one ever escaped successfully.

farm workers he had hired, killed and buried in 1970–71 near Feather River, Yuba City, Calif. His 20th century record was surpassed in 1974 by Dean Corll, 27, of Houston, Tex, and in 1980 by John Wayne Gacy, 33.

Longest Time Served

Paul Geidel (b Apr 21, 1894) was convicted of 2nd degree murder on Sept 5, 1911 as a 17-year-old porter in a NYC hotel. He was released from the Fishkill Correctional Facility, Beacon, NY, aged 85, on May 7, 1980, having served 68 years 8 months 2 days—the longest recorded term in US history. He had first refused parole in 1974.

Penal Camps

The largest penal camp systems in the world were those near Karaganda and Kolyma, in the USSR, each with a population estimated in 1958 at between 1,200,000 and 1,500,000. The largest labor camp is now said to be the Dubrovlag Complex of 15 camps centered on Pot'ma, Mordovian Republic, USSR. The official NATO estimate for all Soviet camps was "more than one million" in March 1960 compared with a peak of probably 12 million during the Stalinist era.

Largest Prison

The largest prison in the world is Kharkov Prison, in the USSR, which has at times accommodated 40,000 prisoners.

Most Secure Prison

After it became a maximum security Federal prison in 1934, no convict was known to have lived to tell of a successful escape from the prison on Alcatraz Island in San Francisco Bay. A total of 23 men attempted it, but 12 were recaptured, 5 shot dead, one drowned and 5 presumed drowned. On Dec 16, 1962, three months before the prison was closed, one man reached the mainland alive, only to be recaptured on the spot. John Chase was imprisoned for a record 26 years on Alcatraz.

Most Expensive Prison

Spandau Prison, Berlin, built 100 years ago for 600 prisoners, is now used solely for the person widely and officially purported to be the Nazi war criminal Rudolf Hess (b Apr 26, 1894). The cost of maintenance of the staff of 105 has been estimated at $415,000 per year.

Longest Prison Escape

The longest recorded escape by a prisoner who was eventually recaptured was that of Leonard T. Fristoe, 77, who escaped from Nevada State Prison, on Dec 15, 1923, and was turned in by his son on Nov 15, 1969, at Compton, Calif. He had 46 years of freedom under the name Claude R. Willis. He had killed two sheriff's deputies in 1920.

Greatest Jail Break

In Feb 1979, US Army Col Arthur "Bull" Simons (ret) led a band of 14 to break into Gasre prison, Teheran, Iran, to rescue two fellow Americans. Some 11,000 other prisoners took advantage of this and the Islamic revolution followed in what became history's largest jail break.

In July 1971, Raoul Sendic and 105 other Tupamaro guerrillas escaped from a Uruguayan prison through a tunnel 298 ft long.

Most Parking Tickets

Henry Rabin, 40, of Skokie, Ill, was arrested in July 1975 for failing to pay 468 parking tickets in 2½ years. This top "scofflaw" was fined $5,000.

Most Appearances in Court

There are no collated records on the greatest number of convictions on an individual, but the highest recently reported is 1,433 for the gentlemanly but alcoholic Edward Eugene Ebzery, who died in Brisbane Jail, Queensland, Australia, Sept 23, 1967.

Lynchings

The worst year in the 20th century for lynchings in the US was 1901, with 130 lynchings (105 negroes, 25 whites), while the first year with no reported cases was 1952.

Robbery

The greatest robbery on record was of the Reichsbank following Germany's collapse in April and May 1945. The largest haul consisted of negotiable securities valued at $400 million. In Apr 1979, three men were convicted and sentenced to terms of imprisonment at Brantford, Ontario, Canada on a number of conspiracy charges connected with some of these bonds.

Gold bullion, foreign exchange and jewels worth $20 million (worth some $200 million today) were also stolen, allegedly by members of the German and American armies. None of this loot was ever recovered and none of the perpetrators were ever brought to trial.

Art Theft

The greatest recorded robbery by market valuation was the removal of 19 paintings, valued at $19,200,000, taken from Russborough House, Blessington, Ireland, the home of Sir Alfred and Lady Beit, by 4 men and a woman, Apr 26, 1974. They included the $6.9 million Vermeer *Lady*

LARGEST ART ROBBERY (left): Dr Rose Dugdale and her accomplices made off with 19 paintings, valued at almost $20 million. She was subsequently captured and convicted. YOUNGEST KIDNAP VICTIM (right): Carolyn Wharton of Beaumont, Texas was kidnapped when she was only 29 min old.

Writing a Letter with her Maid. The paintings were recovered May 4, 1974, near Glandore, Ireland. Dr Rose Bridgit Dugdale (b 1941) was subsequently convicted.

It is arguable that the value of the *Mona Lisa* at the time of its theft from the Louvre on Aug 21, 1911, was greater than this figure. It was recovered in Italy in 1913 when Vincenzo Perruggia was charged with its theft.

On Sept 1, 1964, antiquities reputedly worth $23 million were recovered from 3 warehouses near the Pyramids in Egypt.

Bank Robbery

During the extreme civil disorder prior to Jan 22, 1976, in Beirut, Lebanon, a guerrilla force blasted the vaults of the British Bank of the Middle East in Bab Idriss and cleared out safe deposit boxes with contents valued by former Finance Minister Lucien Dahadah at $50 million, and by another source at an "absolute minimum" of $20 million.

Jewel Robbery

The greatest recorded theft of jewels was from safe deposit boxes in the Palm Towers, Palm Beach, Fla, on Apr 14, 1976, estimated by police at about $6 million plus an additional $1 million in other items.

Jewels are believed to have constituted a major part of the Hotel Pierre, NYC, "heist" on Dec 31, 1971. An unofficial estimate ran as high as $5 million.

Train Robbery

The greatest recorded train robbery occurred between 3:03 a.m. and

3:27 a.m. on Aug 8, 1963, when a General Post Office mail train from Glasgow, Scotland was ambushed at Sears Crossing and robbed at Bridego Bridge near Mentmore, Buckinghamshire, England. The gang escaped with about 120 mailbags containing £2,631,784 ($6,053,103) worth of bank notes being taken to London for pulping. Only £343,448 ($961,654) was recovered.

Largest Object Ever Stolen by a Single Man

On a moonless night at dead calm high water on June 5, 1966, N. William Kennedy, armed with only a sharp axe, slashed free the mooring lines at Wolfe's Cove, St Lawrence Seaway, Quebec, Canada of the 10,639 dwt SS *Orient Trader* owned by Steel Factors Ltd of Ontario. The vessel drifted to a waiting blacked-out tug thus escaping a ban on any shipping movements during a violent wildcat waterfront strike. She sailed for Spain.

Greatest Kidnapping Ransom

Historically, the greatest ransom paid was that for their chief, Atahualpa, by the Incas to the Spanish conquistador Francisco Pizarro, in 1532–33 at Cajamarca, Peru, which included a hall full of gold and silver worth in modern money some $170 million.

The greatest ransom ever extorted is $60 million for the release of two businessmen, the brothers Jorge Born, 40, and Juan Born, 39, of Argentina, paid to the left-wing urban guerrilla group Montoneros in Buenos Aires, June 20, 1975.

The youngest person ever kidnapped has been Carolyn Wharton, who was born at 12:46 p.m., March 19, 1955, in the Baptist Hospital, Beaumont, Tex, and kidnapped by a woman disguised as a nurse at 1:15 p.m., when the baby was aged 29 min.

Greatest Hijack Ransom

The highest amount ever paid to hijackers has been $4,800,000 in small denomination notes by the W German government to Popular Front for the Liberation of Palestine representatives 30 miles outside Beirut, Lebanon, Feb 23, 1972. In return, a Lufthansa Boeing 747, which had been bound for Athens when it was hijacked an hour out of New Delhi and forced down at Aden, was released, along with its 14 crew members.

The longest air piracy has been one of 8,800 miles by three Filipino Moslem separatists from the southern Philippines in a BAC 111, changing to a DC8 at Bangkok, Thailand and arriving at Benghazi, Libya a week later on Apr 14, 1976.

Largest Narcotics Haul

The heaviest recorded haul of narcotics was made in the Bahamas on Aug 16, 1975, when 1,049 sacks of high-grade Colombian marijuana were discovered, with a weight of 86,280 lb, worth an estimated $24 million. The most valuable haul was of 937 lb of pure heroin worth $106¼ million retail seized aboard the 60-ton shrimp boat *Caprice des Temps* at Marseilles, France on Feb 28, 1972. The captain, Louis Boucan, 57, tried to commit suicide, but was sentenced to 15 years on Jan 5, 1973.

Thailand's Prime Minister Gen Kriangsak Chammanand personally ignited a 13 × 33-ft pit containing heroin (3,585 lb), marijuana (4,409 lb), amphetamines (2,679 lb) and 7,253 lb of other drugs in Bangkok on Jan 31, 1979. The street worth of the seizures, made in 1975–78, was put at "billions of dollars."

It was revealed on Apr 29, 1978 that 574 tons of marijuana were seized in raids on the Guajira peninsula, Colombia, on the two previous days. The wholesale value was estimated at $200 million.

It was revealed on Jan 31, 1973 that 398 lb of heroin and cocaine with a street value of $73 million had been stolen from safekeeping by the New York City Police Department—a record for any law enforcement agency.

The British Home Office disclosed on Dec 23, 1977, that 13 million LSD tablets with a street value approaching $170 million had been destroyed at the conclusion of "Operation Julie."

Largest Bribe

An alleged bribe of $84 million offered to Shaikh Zaid ibn Sultan of Abu Dhabi, United Arab Emirates, by a Saudi Arabian official in Aug 1955, is the highest on record. The affair concerned oil concessions in the disputed territory of Buraimi on the Persian Gulf.

Greatest Currency Forgery

The greatest recorded forgery was the German Third Reich government's forging operation, code name "Bernhard," engineered by S.S. *Sturmbannführer* Alfred Naujocks in 1940–41. It involved £150 million (now about $300 million) worth of Bank of England £5 notes.

Biggest Bank Fraud

The largest amount of money named in a defalcation case has been a gross £33 million ($75,900,000) at the Lugano, Switzerland, branch of Lloyd's Bank International Ltd Sept 2, 1974. Mark Colombo was arrested pending charges including falsification of foreign currency accounts and suppression of evidence.

Computer Fraud

Between 1964 and 1973, some 64,000 fake insurance policies were created on the computer of the Equity Funding Corporation involving $2,000 million.

Stanley Mark Rifkin (b 1966) was arrested in Carlsbad, Calif by the FBI on Nov 6, 1978, charged with defrauding a Los Angeles bank of $10.2 million by manipulation of a computer system. In June 1980 he was sentenced to 8 years.

Welfare Swindle

The greatest welfare swindle yet worked was that of the gypsy Anthony Moreno, on the French Social Security in Marseilles. By forging birth certificates and school registration forms, he invented 197 fictitious families and 3,000 children on which he claimed benefits from 1960 to mid-1968. Moreno, nicknamed "El Chorro" (the fountain), was later reported free of extradition worries and living in luxury in his native Spain having absquatulated with an estimated $6,440,000.

Passing Bad Checks

Mrs Ann Lorraine Ohlschlager, *alias* Ann Kosak, of Los Angeles was charged in Jan 1974 with writing $37 million in bad checks between Jan and Oct, 1973, netting a total of $463,000 from the United California Bank.

Fines

It was reported in Jan 1979 that Carlo Ponti, husband of Sophia Loren, was to be fined the equivalent of $26,400,000 by the Italian courts in connection with claims for taxes alleged to be unpaid.

4. ECONOMIC

MONETARY AND FINANCE

Largest Budget

The greatest annual expenditure budgeted by any country is $615,800 million by the US Government (federal expenditure) for the fiscal year ending Sept 30, 1981. The highest budgeted revenue in the US is $600,000 million for the fiscal year 1981.

In the US, the greatest surplus was $8,419,469,844 in 1947–48, and the greatest deficit was $61,800 million in 1978–79.

Foreign Aid

The total net foreign aid given by the US Government between July 1, 1945, and Jan 1, 1978, was $177,681 million.

The country which received most US aid in 1977 was Israel with $1,476 million. US foreign aid began with $50,000 to Venezuela for earthquake relief in 1812.

Highest Tax Rates

The country with the most confiscatory taxation is Norway where in Jan 1974 the Labor Party and Socialist Alliance abolished the 80% top limit; thus some 2,000 citizens were listed in the *Lignings Boka* as paying more than 100% of their taxable income. The shipping magnate Hilmer Reksten was assessed at 491%.

Least Taxed People

The lowest income tax is paid by the citizens of Bahrain, Kuwait, and Qatar, where the rate, regardless of income, is zero.

National Debt

The largest national debt is that of the US, where the gross Federal public debt surpassed the half-trillion dollar mark in 1975 and reached $826,800 million by Jan 1, 1980. This amount in dollar bills would make a pile 44,863 miles high, weighing 703,940 tons.

Biggest Savers

The world's top savers are the Swiss, with deposits averaging $11,225 per head.

National Wealth

The richest nation, measured by average income per capita of population, is the United Arab Emirates, with $14,000. The US, which took the lead in 1910, is now seventh behind Kuwait, Qatar, Switzerland ($11,000), Sweden and Denmark, in the 1977 figures.

It has been estimated that the value of all physical assets in the US in 1976 was $6.2 trillion, or $28,800 per person.

Poorest Country

The lowest published annual income of any country is Rwanda, with $70 per person.

Gross National Product

The estimated free world aggregate of GNP's in 1975 was about $10,200,000 million. The country with the largest GNP is the US, running at $2,456,900 million at Jan 1, 1980.

Gold Reserves

The country with the greatest monetary gold reserve is the US, whose Treasury had 264.6 million fine oz of the world's 927.02 million fine oz on hand in Jan 1980. Valued at $500 per fine oz, these amounts translate to $132,300 million and $463,510 million respectively. The US Bullion Depository at Fort Knox, 30 miles southwest of Louisville, Ky, is the principal depository of US gold. Gold is stored in standard mint bars of 400 troy oz (439 oz avoirdupois), measuring 7 × 3⅝ × 1⅝ in, and each worth more than $200,000 in the market (June 1980).

The greatest accumulation of the central banks' $50,000 million of gold bullion is now in the Federal Reserve Bank at 33 Liberty Street, NYC. Some $17,000 million or 14,000 tons is stored 85 ft below street level, in a vault 50 × 100 ft behind a steel door weighing nearly 100 tons.

GOLD! In the Federal Reserve Bank of NY, bars of gold are being transferred from one vault to another 85 ft below street level. This depository holds $17,000 million worth of the US's $50,000 million treasure of gold.

Worst Inflation

The world's worst inflation occurred in Hungary in June 1946, when the 1931 gold pengö was valued at 130 quintillion (1.3×10^{20}) paper pengös. Notes were issued for szazmillio billion (1 followed by 20 zeros or 10^{20}) pengös on June 3 and withdrawn on July 11, 1946. Notes for 1 sextillion or 10^{21} pengös were printed but not circulated.

In Germany, on Nov 6, 1923, the circulation of Reichsbank marks reached 400,338,326,350,700,000,000, a level of inflation 755,700 million times the 1913 levels.

Currency

Paper money is an invention of the Chinese, first tried in 910 AD and prevalent by 970 AD. The world's earliest bank notes (*banco-sedlar*) were issued in Stockholm, Sweden, in July 1661. The oldest surviving bank note is one for 5 dalers dated Dec 6, 1662.

The largest paper money ever issued was the one kwan note of the Chinese Ming dynasty issue of 1368–99, which measured 9×13 in. The smallest bank note ever issued was the 10 bani note of the Ministry of Finance of Rumania, issued in 1917. It measured (printed area) 1.09×1.49 in.

Highest and Lowest Denomination Currency

The highest denomination notes in circulation are US Federal Reserve Bank notes for $10,000. They bear the head of Salmon Portland Chase (1808–73), Secretary of the Treasury during Civil War days. None have been printed since July 1944 and the US Treasury announced in 1969 that no further notes higher than $100 would be issued. Only some 400 $10,000 bills remain in circulation.

The 1-cent Hong Kong note is worth one fifth of a US cent.

Largest Check

The greatest amount paid by a single check in the history of banking was one equivalent to $2,046,700,000, handed over by Daniel P. Moynihan, then the US Ambassador to India, in New Delhi, Feb 18, 1974. An internal US Treasury check for $4,176,969,623.57 was drawn on June 30, 1954.

COINS

Oldest Coins

The earliest certainly dated coins are the electrum (alloy of gold and silver) staters of Lydia, in Asia Minor (now Turkey), which were coined in the reign of King Gyges (*c.* 690–650 BC). Primitive uninscribed "spade" money of the Chou dynasty of China is now *believed* to date from *c.* 770 BC. A discovery at Tappeh Nush-i-jan, Iran, of silver ingot currency in 1972 has been dated to as early as 760 BC. The earliest dated coin is the Danish coin of the Bishop of Roskilde, dated MCCXXXIIII (1234), of which 6 are known.

CURRENCY:
The highest
denomination is
$10,000 (above)
and the least
value is one
Hong Kong cent
(right), worth
one fifth of a US
cent.

Smallest Coins

The smallest coins have been the Nepalese ¼ dam or Jawa, struck *c.* 1740 in silver in the reign of Jeya Prakash Malla. The Jawa, which weighed between 0.008 and 0.014 of a gram and measured about 2 × 2 mm, was sometimes cut into ½ and even ¼ Jawa, thus weighing 0.002 of a gram, or 14,000 to the oz.

Heaviest Coins

The Swedish copper 10 daler coin of 1644 attained a weight of 43 lb 7¼ oz. Of primitive exchange tokens, the most massive are the holed stone discs, or *Fé,* from the Yap Islands, in the western Pacific Ocean, with diameters of up to 12 ft, weighing up to 185 lb. A medium-sized one was worth one Yapese wife or an 18-ft canoe.

MOST MASSIVE
COINS: The larger of
these holed stone discs,
used for money in the
Yap Islands of the
western Pacific, can be
traded for one wife or
an 18-ft canoe.

HEAVIEST COIN (left): The Swedish 10 daler coin of 1644 weighed more than 43 lb. The HIGHEST DENOMINATION COIN is the $2,500 Bahamian containing 1 lb of 22-carat gold.

Coinless Countries

Laos is the only country presently without coins (paper money only). Cambodia abolished money under the Pol Pot regime in 1975, but reintroduced it in March 1980 with the riel as the monetary unit.

Highest and Lowest Denomination Coins

The 1654 Indian gold 200 mohur ($1,400) coin of the Mughul Emperor Khurram Shihab-ud-din Muhammad, Shah Jahan (reigned 1628–57), had the greatest intrinsic worth ever struck. It weighed 2,177 grams (70 troy oz) and hence has an intrinsic worth of $5,320. It had a diameter of 5¾ in. The only known example disappeared in Patna, Bihar, India, *c.* 1820, but a plaster cast of this coin exists in the British Museum, London.

Currently the highest denomination is the Bahamian $2,500 1977 gold coin, 72 mm (2.8 in) in diameter, struck by the Royal Canadian Mint, Ottawa. Each of the 250 examples struck contains 1 lb troy of 22 carat gold.

Lowest in face value today is the 5 aurar piece of Iceland issued in 1971. At today's currency rates, it would take 3,955 5-aurars to equal one US dollar.

Quarter farthings (sixteen to the British penny) were struck in copper at the Royal Mint, London in the Imperial coinage for use in Ceylon, in 1839 and 1851–53.

Most Expensive Coin

The highest price paid at auction for a single coin is $725,000 for the uncirculated Garrett specimen of the gold Brasher doubloon struck in NYC by Ephraim Brasher in 1787, of which only 7 are known. The bid was by lawyer Martin Monas for an undisclosed American collector at the St Moritz Hotel, NYC, Nov 29, 1979.

Rarest Coin

There are numerous coins of which only a single example is known. An example of a unique coin of threefold rarity (in alloy, denomination and reign) is one of the rare admixture of bronze with inlaid gold of Kaleb I of Axum (*c.* 500 AD). Only 700 Axumite coins of any sort are known.

Greatest Collection

The highest price paid for a coin collection has been $7,300,000 by Steven C. Markoff of A-Mark Coin Co Inc of Beverly Hills, Calif, for a hoard of 407,000 US silver dollars from the La Vere Redfield estate in a courtroom auction in Reno, Nev on Jan 27, 1976.

Largest Treasure Trove

The largest hoard ever found was one of about 80,000 aurei in Brescello near Modena, Italy in 1814, believed to have been deposited *c.* 37 BC.

The numerically largest hoard ever found was the Brussels hoard of 1908 containing *c.* 150,000 coins.

It is believed that the greatest undersea recovery of treasure will be made from the wreck of the 140-ft-long Spanish ship *Nuestra Señora de Concepción* which capsized off the north coast of the Dominican Republic in 1641. The first part of possibly $40 million of treasure was found by Seaquest International on Nov 30, 1978.

Largest Mint

The largest mint is the US Mint built in 1965–69 on Independence Mall, Philadelphia, covering 500,000 sq ft (11½ acres) with an annual capacity on a 3-shift 7-day-a-week production of 8,000 million coins. A single stamping machine can produce coins at a rate of 10,000 per hour.

TRADE UNIONS

The largest union is the Industrie-Gewerkschaft Metall (Metal Workers' Union) of W Germany, with a membership of 2,684,509 on Jan 1, 1980. The union with the longest name is probably the International Association of Marble, Slate and Stone Polishers, Rubbers and Sawyers, Tile and Marble Setters' Helpers and Marble Mosaic and Terrazzo Workers' Helpers (Wash DC).

Longest Working Week

Dr Adrian Caro of Norfolk and Norwich Hospital, England gave evidence in Nov 1971 that some housemen and registrars in hospitals were allowed only 4 hours 8½ min sleep per night, and had an active working week in extreme cases of 139 hours.

Labor Disputes

A labor dispute concerning monotony of diet and working conditions was recorded in 1153 BC in Thebes, Egypt. The earliest recorded strike was one by an orchestra leader from Greece named Aristos in Rome *c.* 309 BC. The cause was meal breaks.

The longest recorded strike ended on Jan 4, 1961, after 33 years. It concerned the employment of barbers' assistants in Copenhagen, Denmark. The longest recorded major strike was one at the plumbing fixtures factory of the Kohler Co in Sheboygan, Wis between Apr 1954 and Oct 1962. The strike is alleged to have cost the United Automobile Workers union about $12 million to sustain.

Lowest Unemployment

In Switzerland in Dec 1973 (population 6,600,000), the total number of unemployed was reported to be 81.

Working Careers

The longest working life has been 98 years by Mr Izumi of Japan (see Chapter 1, *Oldest Living Man*) who started work goading draft animals at a sugar mill at Isen, Tokanushima, Japan in 1872. He became a sugar cane farmer and retired in 1970.

The longest recorded working career in one job was that of Miss Polly Gadsby who started at the age of 9 and worked 86 years wrapping elastic for the same company in Leicester, England until she died in 1932 at the age of 95.

FOOD CONSUMPTION

Calories

Of all countries in the world, based on the latest available data, Belgium and Luxembourg have the largest available total of calories per person. The net supply averaged 3,645 per day in 1974. The lowest *reported* figure is 1,728 calories per day in Upper Volta in 1974. The highest calorific value of any foodstuff is that of pure animal fat, with 930 calories per 100 grams (3.5 oz). Pure alcohol provides 710 calories per 100 grams.

Protein

Australia and New Zealand have the highest recorded consumption of protein per person, an average of 106 grams (3.79 oz) per day in 1969.

Cereals

The greatest consumers of cereal products—flour, milled rice, etc.—are the people of Egypt, with an average of about 500 lb per person annually (600 grams per day) in 1966–67. Figures for 1977 from China suggest a possible consumption (including rice) of 890 grams (31.3 oz).

Starch

The greatest eaters of starchy food are the people of the US, who consumed 4.02 lb per person per day in 1972.

Sugar

The greatest consumers of sugars are the people of Bulgaria, with an average of 6.26 oz per person per day in 1977.

Meat

The greatest meat eaters in the world—figures include organs and poultry—are the people of the US, with an average consumption of 10.89 oz per person per day in 1977.

Soft Drinks

The people of the US undoubtedly consume more carbonated soft drinks than any other people—30.3 gallons per person in 1972, up from 16.8 gallons in 1962. Coffee consumption in the US in the same period dropped from 39.2 gallons to 35.6 gallons per person in 1972, but tea increased from 6.1 to 7.2 gallons. Cold juices (not included in the soft drink totals) reached 5 gallons per person in 1972.

ALCOHOLIC BEVERAGES

Beer

Of reporting countries, the nation with the highest beer consumption per person is W Germany, with 47.88 US gallons per person in 1978. In the Northern Territory of Australia, however, the annual intake has been estimated to be as high as 62.4 US gallons per person. A society for the prevention of alcoholism in Darwin had to disband in June 1966, for lack of support.

Wine

The greatest wine drinkers are the French, who consumed 32.16 US gallons per person for the year 1978.

Spirits

The greatest consumers of spirits are the people of Poland, who, in 1977, consumed an average of US 1.836 gallons per person per year.

Prohibition

The longest-lasting imposition of prohibition against consumption of alcoholic beverages has been 26 years in Iceland (1908–34). Other prohibitions have been in Russia, later the USSR (1914–24), and the US (1920–33). The Faroe Islands have had a public (as opposed to private licensed) prohibition since 1918.

Biggest Round of Drinks

The largest round of drinks ever recorded was one for 1,222 people stood by the *Sunday Sun* and shouted by Jack Amos in Newcastle upon Tyne, England, in Oct 1974, at the conclusion of the Jack o' Clubs road show.

Largest Dish

The largest single dish is roasted camel, prepared occasionally for Bedouin wedding feasts. Cooked eggs are stuffed in fish, the fish stuffed in cooked chickens, the chickens stuffed into a roasted sheep carcass and the sheep stuffed into a whole camel.

Largest Banquet

The greatest outdoor banquet ever staged was that by President Loubet, President of France, in the gardens of the Tuileries, Paris, Sept 22, 1900. He invited the mayors of France and their deputies, ending up with 22,295 guests. With the Gallic *penchant* for round numbers, the event has always been referred to as "le banquet des 100,000 maires." It was estimated that some 30,000 attended a military feast at Radewitz, Poland, on June 25, 1730, thrown by King August II (1709–1733).

The greatest number of people served indoors at a single sitting was 18,000 municipal leaders at the Palais de l'Industrie, Paris, on Aug 18, 1889.

The menu for the main 5½-hour banquet at the Imperial Iranian 2,500th anniversary gathering at Persepolis in Oct 1971 (see *Party Giving* in Chapter 11), was probably the most expensive ever compiled. It comprised quail eggs stuffed with Iranian caviar, a mousse of crayfish tails in Nantua sauce, stuffed rack of roast lamb, with a main course of roast peacock stuffed with *foie gras,* fig rings, and raspberry sweet champagne sherbet. Wines included *Château Lafite Rothschild* 1945 at $100 per bottle from the cellars of Maxim's, Paris.

Longest Bread

The longest one-piece loaf ever baked was one of 1,058 ft 10 in created by Franz Eichenauer and baked at the Peekskill Riverfront Green, NY, in an insulated aluminum pipe oven on Sept 16, 1979.

Most Expensive Food

The most expensive non-seasonal food is white truffle of Alba, Italy which sells according to its rarity for as high as $200 per lb on the US market. Truffles from oak roots in the Périgord district of France require drought between mid-July and mid-August. Only 7 of Europe's 70 species of this hypogeous mycorrhizal fungus are considered edible.

Largest Pies

The largest cherry pie weighed 7 tons and contained 4,950 lb of cherries. It measured 14 ft 4 in in diameter, 24 in in depth and was baked on the grounds of the Medusa Cement Corporation, Charlevoix, Mich, May 15, 1976, as part of the town's Bicentennial celebration.

The largest mince pie was one of 2,260 lb, measuring 20 × 5 ft, baked at Ashby-de-la-Zouch, Leicestershire, England, Oct 15, 1932.

The largest meat pie ever baked weighed 6.4 tons, measuring 18 × 6 ft and 18 in deep, in Denby Dale, W Yorkshire, England, baked on Sept 5, 1964. The first was in 1788, baked to celebrate King George III's return to sanity, but the fourth, for Queen Victoria's Jubilee in 1887, went a bit "off" and had to be buried in quicklime.

The largest apple pie ever baked was that in a 16-ft-8-in diameter dish at the Orleans County Fair, NY, Aug 2-3, 1977. Baking time of the 300 bushels of apples and 5,950 lb of sugar was 4 hours 40 min. The total weight was 21,210 lb.

Biggest Barbecue

The most monumental barbecue has been one for 5,829 people at the West Pasco Sertoma Club of New Port Richey, Fla, March 23, 1980, serving 4,036 lb of meat.

Largest Cakes

The largest cake ever assembled was the Baltimore City Bicentennial Cake of July 4, 1976, with ingredients weighing 69,860 lb. An estimated 10,000 dozen eggs, 21,600 lb of sugar, and a 415-lb pinch of salt were used.

The tallest recorded free-standing wedding cake was one of 39 tiers, 23 ft 7 in tall, baked and constructed by Mrs Rhoda Murray and Roy Butterworth Oct 20, 1978, in the Halifax Shopping Center, Halifax, Nova Scotia, Canada.

Largest Chocolate Easter Egg

The largest Easter egg ever made was one of 4,484 lb made in Melbourne, Australia March 2-16, 1978, by Red Tulip Chocolates Pty Ltd of Prahran, Victoria. It was 10 ft 2½ in high and 24 ft 9 in in circumference.

Longest Pastry

The longest cream slice (also known as *mille feuilles* invented in Florence in the 16th century) ever made was one 1,082 ft long, made by Fritz Strüben-Keller and the Bäckermeister Kegel Club in Liestal, Switzerland, June 10, 1979.

Largest Hamburger

The largest burger (made of beef) on record is one of 2,859 lb, 27½ ft in circumference, exhibited by Tip Top Butchers and Noonan's Bakery Pty Ltd at the Perth Royal Show, W Australia, Sept 24, 1975.

LONGEST BREAD: An audience in Peekskill, NY watches as Franz Eichenauer, General Foods research specialist, bakes a bread more than 1/5 of a mile long. Aerial view of the whole loaf on the right. He even made sandwiches out of it and sold 6,000.

LARGEST PIZZA: Measuring more than 80 ft across, this pie, baked in Glens Falls, NY, weighed 18,664 lb and was cut into 60,318 slices.

Largest Omelet

The largest omelet ever made was one produced with 12,440 eggs in a pan measuring 30 × 10 ft, cooked by students at Conestoga College, Kitchener, Ontario, Canada, June 29, 1979.

Largest Pizza

The largest pizza ever baked was one measuring 80 ft 1 in in diameter, 5,037 sq ft in area, and 18,664 lb in weight at the Oma Pizza Restaurant, Glens Falls, NY, owned by Lorenzo Amato, on Oct 8, 1978. It was cut into 60,318 slices.

Largest Popsicle®

The largest iced lollipop on a stick was one of 5,750 lb, constructed for the Westside Assembly of God Church, Davenport, Iowa, Sept 7, 1975.

Biggest Salami

The largest salami on record is one 18 ft 10 in long with a circumference of 28 in, weighing 457 lb, made by La Ron Meat Co, Cosby, Mo, Jan 29, 1978.

Longest Sausage

The longest sausage ever recorded was one of 2 miles made by Dewhurst's at Thamesmead, England, May 28, 1979, and cooked by Scouts at The Great Children's Party in Hyde Park, London, May 30–31, 1979. It was made with pork and seasoning and weighed 2,740 lb.

Largest Sundae

The most monstrous ice cream sundae ever concocted is one of 9,616 lb plus 90 lb of nuts, 250 lb of chocolate, 250 lb of strawberry topping and 65.6 lb of instant whip, constructed by the students of the Mark Twain Summer Institute, Clayton, Mo on Sept 2, 1979.

Longest Banana Split

The longest banana split ever made was one 7,005 ft long (1 mile 575 yd) embracing 11,400 bananas, 1,500 gallons of ice cream, 380 gallons of topping and 170 lb of nuts by the Alpha Phi Omega of Texas A&M University, Apr 26, 1980.

Spices

Prices for wild ginseng (root of *Panax quinquefolius*), from the Chan Pak Mt area of China, thought to have aphrodisiacal quality, were reported in Nov 1977 to be as high as $23,000 per oz in Hong Kong. Total shipments from Jilin province do not exceed 141 oz per year. The leading medical journal in the US has likened its effects to "corticosteroid poisoning."

The hottest of all spices is claimed to be Siling labuyo from the Philippines. The most prized condiment is Cà Cuong, a secretion recovered in minute amounts from beetles in N Vietnam. Owing to war conditions, the price rose to $100 per oz before supplies virtually ceased in 1975.

Candy

The top-selling candies are Life Savers, with 25,000 million rolls sold between 1913 and Nov 14, 1973. The aggregate depth of the "hole in the middle" exceeds 1 million miles. Paul Shirley, 21, of Sydney, Australia, made one last in his mouth for 4 hours 40 min on Feb 15, 1979, before the hole broke up.

Coffee

The world's greatest coffee drinkers are the people of Sweden, who consumed 17.34 lb of coffee per person per year in 1978.

The most expensive coffee is Jamaican High Blue Mountain Supreme, which retails for up to $16.80 per lb.

Tea

The world's greatest tea drinkers are the people of Ireland, who consumed 8.21 lb of tea per person per year in 1977.

The most expensive tea marketed is "Oolong Leaf Bud," specially imported by Fortnum and Mason of Piccadilly, London, where in May 1978, it retailed for $28.90 per lb. It is blended from very young Formosan leaves. Tea bags were invented by Thomas Sullivan of New York in 1904.

Fresh Water

The world's greatest consumers of fresh water are the people and industrial users of the US, whose average consumption was 1,855 gallons per person per day in 1974.

ENERGY

To express the various forms of available energy (coal, liquid fuels and water power, etc., but omitting vegetable fuels and peat), it is the practice to convert them all into terms of coal.

The highest consumption is in the US with an average of 25,312 lb per person. With only 5.3% of the world's population, the US consumes 28.6% of the world's gasoline and 32.9% of the world's electric power. For comparison, the UK average was 13,328 lb per person in 1977.

MASS COMMUNICATIONS AND TRANSPORTATION

Merchant Shipping

The world total of merchant shipping (excluding vessels of less than 100 tons gross, sailing vessels and barges) was 71,129 vessels of 413,021,426 tons gross on July 1, 1979. The largest merchant fleet as of mid-1979 was under the flag of Liberia with 2,466 ships of 81,528,175 tons gross.

Largest and Busiest Ports

Physically, the largest port is the Port of NY and NJ. The port has a navigable waterfront of 755 miles (460 miles in NY State and 295 miles in NJ) stretching over 92 sq mi. A total of 261 general cargo berths and 130 other piers give a total berthing capacity of 391 ships at one time. The total warehousing floor space is 18,400,000 sq ft (422.4 acres).

The world's busiest port and largest artificial harbor is the Rotterdam-Europoort in the Netherlands, which covers 38 sq mi. It handled 29,904 sea-going vessels carrying a total of 301 million metric tons of sea-going cargo, and about 200,000 barges, in 1979. It is able to handle 310 sea-going vessels simultaneously, of up to 318,000 metric tons and 68 ft draught.

Airlines

The country with the busiest airlines system is the US, where 226,781,368,000 revenue passenger miles were flown on scheduled domestic and local services in 1978. This was equivalent to an annual trip of 891.1 miles for every inhabitant of the US. It was estimated in 1978 that only 37% of adult Americans had never flown in their lives.

Railroads

The country with the greatest length of railroad is the US, with 213,835 miles of track on Jan 1, 1979.

Roads and Traffic

The country with the greatest length of road is the US (50 states), with 3,885,452 miles of graded roads on Jan 1, 1978.

The highest traffic volume of any point is at East Los Angeles, where there is an interchange of the Santa Ana, Pomona, Golden State, and Santa Monica Freeways with a 24-hour average on weekdays of 456,000 vehicles in 1979. The most heavily traveled stretch of road is between 43rd and 47th Sts on the Dan Ryan Expressway in Chicago, with an average daily volume of 254,700 vehicles.

Widest, Narrowest and Shortest Streets

The widest street is the Monumental Axis, running for 1½ miles from the Municipal Plaza to the Plaza of the Three Powers in Brasilia, the capital of Brazil. The 6-lane boulevard was opened in Apr 1960 and is 273.4 yd wide.

The Bay Bridge Toll Plaza has 23 lanes (17 westbound) serving San Francisco and Oakland.

The narrowest street is in Port Isaac, Cornwall, England where Temple

BUSIEST PORT: Rotterdam, Holland has canal barges mixing with ocean-going freighters, and can handle 310 big vessels at a time in its 38 sq miles. The Port of NY and NJ has 92 sq mi for berthing with 755 miles of waterfront, but is not as busy.

Bar, at its junction with Dolphin Street, is 19 5/16 in wide at its narrowest point. It is popularly known as "Squeeze-Belly Alley."

The title of "The Shortest Street in the World" has been claimed since 1907 by McKinley St in Bellefontaine, Ohio, which is built of vitrified brick and measures 30 ft in length.

The place with the highest traffic density is Hong Kong. By Jan 1, 1977, there were 191,146 motor vehicles on 678 miles of serviceable roads giving a density of 6.24 yd per vehicle.

Traffic Jam

The longest traffic jam ever reported was that of Feb 16, 1980 which stretched northward from Lyon, France 109.3 miles towards Paris.

Longest Highways

The longest motorable road is the Pan-American Highway, which will stretch 17,018 miles from northwest Alaska to southernmost Chile. There remains a gap of 250 miles, known as the Tapon del Darién in Panama, and the Atrato Swamp in Colombia. The first complete traverse was made by the 1972 British Trans-Americas Expedition led by Lt Col John Blashford-Snell, which emerged from the Atrato Swamp after 99 days. The Range Rover VXC 868 K which left Alaska on Dec 3, 1971, arrived in Tierra del Fuego on June 9, 1972.

The longest uninterrupted stretch of highway is the $3,500 million Interstate 75, which opened on Dec 21, 1977, and now runs 1,564 miles from Sault Ste Marie, Mich, to Tampa, Fla without a traffic light.

The longest designated street is Yonge Street, which runs north and west from Toronto, Canada. The first stretch, completed on Feb 16, 1796, ran 34½ miles. Its official length, now extended to Rainy River at the Manitoba-Minnesota border, is 1,178.3 miles.

Steepest and Crookedest Streets

The steepest streets are Filbert St, Russian Hill and 22nd St, Dolores Heights, San Francisco, with gradients of 31.5% or a rise of 1 ft for every 3.17 ft.

Lombard Street in San Francisco between Hyde and Leavenworth has 5 consecutive hairpin turns as it descends steeply one way.

Highest Trail

The highest trail is an 8-mile stretch of the Kang-ti-suu between Khaleb and Hsin-chi-fu, Tibet, which in two places exceeds 20,000 ft. The highest motor road is one 733.2 miles long between Tibet and southwestern Sinkiang, completed in Oct 1957, which includes passes of an altitude up to 18,480 ft above sea level.

Lowest Road

The lowest road is that along the Israeli shores of the Dead Sea, 1,290 ft below sea level. The lowest pass is the Rock Reef Pass in Everglades National Park, Fla, which is 3 ft above sea level.

Biggest Square

The Tien An Men (Gate of Heavenly Peace) Square in Peking, described as the navel of China, extends over 98 acres.

Drivers' Licenses

Regular drivers' licenses are issuable as young as 15 and without a driver education course only in Hawaii and Mississippi. Thirteen US states issue restricted juvenile licenses at 14.

LARGEST SQUARE: The Chairman Mao Memorial Hall stands in the middle of Tien An Men Square in Peking, China.

MOST DIFFICULT LEARNER:
Mrs Miriam Hargrave of England
(above) failed her driving test 39
times. FIRST PARKING
METERS (right) were installed
in Oklahoma City in 1935.

The easiest test for a driver's license is given in Egypt, where the ability to drive 6 meters (19.7 ft) forward and 6 meters in reverse has been deemed sufficient. In 1979 it was reported that accurate reversing between 2 rubber traffic cones had been added but this soon led to the substitution of white lines when the cones became damaged.

Oldest Driver

Roy M. Rawlins (b July 10, 1870) of Stockton, Calif was warned for driving at 95 mph in a 55-mph zone in June 1974. On Aug 25, 1974, he was awarded a Calif State license valid until 1978, but he died on July 9, 1975, one day short of his 105th birthday. Mrs Maude Tull of Inglewood, Calif, who began driving after her husband's death, when she was aged 91, was issued a renewal of her license on Feb 5, 1976, then aged 104.

Most Failures on Learner's Test

The record for persistence in taking and failing a test for a driver's license is held by Mrs Miriam Hargrave (b Apr 3, 1908) of Wakefield, Yorkshire, England, who failed her 39th driving test in 8 years on Apr 29, 1970, when she "crashed" through a set of red lights. She finally passed her 40th driving test on Aug 3, 1970. She spent $720 on 212 driving lessons and could no longer afford to buy a car. In 1978, she was reported to dislike right-hand turns.

Mrs Fannie Turner (b 1903) of Little Rock, Ark, passed her *written* test for a driver's license on her 104th attempt in Oct 1978.

Worst Driver

It was reported that a 75-year-old *male* driver received 10 traffic tickets, drove on the wrong side of the road four times, committed four hit-and-run offenses and caused six accidents, all within 20 minutes, in McKinney, Tex on Oct 15, 1966.

Earliest Traffic Lights

Semaphore-type traffic *signals* were set up in Parliament Square, London in 1868, with red and green gas lamps for night use. The first traffic light was installed in 1919 in Detroit.

Earliest Parking Meters

The earliest parking meters ever installed were those put in the business district of Oklahoma City, Okla, on July 19, 1935. They were the invention of Carl C. Magee (US).

Inland Waterways

The country with the greatest length of inland waterways is Finland. The total length of navigable lakes and rivers is about 31,000 miles.

The longest navigable natural waterway is the Amazon River, which sea-going vessels can ascend as far as Iquitos, in Peru, 2,236 miles from the Atlantic seaboard.

On a National Geographic Society expedition ending on March 10, 1969, Helen and Frank Schreider navigated downstream from San Francisco, Peru, 3,845 miles up the Amazon to Bélem.

Telephones

There were approximately 423,082,000 telephones in the world on Jan 1, 1979, it was estimated by the American Telephone and Telegraph Co. The country with the greatest number was the US with 162,076,000 instruments, equivalent to 744 for every 1,000 people or in 96 of every 100 households. The territory with fewest is Pitcairn Island with 32.

The country with the most telephones per head of population is Midway Islands, with 965 per 1,000 of the population on Jan 1, 1978. The countries with the fewest phones are Chad, Rwanda, Upper Volta and Nepal, each with less than 1 telephone per 100 people.

The greatest total of calls made in any country is in the US, with 221,482 million in 1977.

The city with most telephones is NYC, with 5,936,829 (808 per 1,000 people) as of Jan 1, 1978. In 1978, Washington, DC, reached the level of 1,495 telephones per 1,000 people, though in some small areas there are still higher densities, such as Beverly Hills, part of Los Angeles, with about 1,600 per 1,000.

Longest Telephone Cable

The longest submarine telephone cable is the Commonwealth Pacific Cable (COMPAC), which runs for more than 9,000 miles from Australia *via* Auckland, New Zealand, and Hawaii to Port Alberni, Canada. It cost about $98 million and was inaugurated on Dec 2, 1963.

Busiest Phone

The pay phone with the heaviest usage is one in the Greyhound bus terminal in Chicago, which averages 270 calls a day, and is thus used each 5 min 20 sec around the clock all year.

Largest Incorrect Telephone Bill

On Aug 18, 1975, the landlord of the Blue Bell Inn, Lichfield, Staffordshire, England received a telephone bill for $4,386,800,000. It was later admitted that this bill contained "an arithmetical error."

Postal Services

The country with the largest mail is the US, whose people posted nearly 97,000 million letters and packages in 1978. The US Postal Service then employed 665,567 people.

The US also takes first place in the average number of letters which each person mails during one year. The figure was 445 in 1978.

ERROR OF VALUE: When the Post Office makes a printing error, the sheet is usually destroyed, but some get out, as did this 1918 block of 4 with the Jenny airplane printed upside down. The block was sold in 1979 for half a million dollars.

POSTAGE STAMPS

Earliest Stamp

The earliest adhesive postage stamps ever issued were the "Penny Blacks" of Great Britain, bearing the head of Queen Victoria, placed on sale on May 1 for use on May 6, 1840. A total of 68,158,080 were printed. The British National Postal Museum possesses a unique full proof sheet of 240 stamps printed in Apr 1840 before the corner letters, plate numbers or marginal inscriptions were added.

Largest Stamp

The largest stamps ever issued were the special purpose 1913 Express Delivery stamps of China, which measured 9¾ × 2¾ in. The largest standard postage stamp is the Marshall Islands 75-cent stamp issued Oct 30, 1979, which measures 6.3 × 4.33 in.

Smallest Stamp

The smallest stamps ever issued were the 10 cents and 1 peso of the Colombian State of Bolívar 1863–66. They measured 0.31 × 0.37 in.

Highest and Lowest Denominations

The highest denomination stamp ever issued was a red and black stamp for £100 ($280) with head of George V issued in Kenya 1925–27. Although valid for postage, it was essentially for collection of revenue.

Owing to demonetization and inflation it is difficult to determine the lowest denomination stamp but it was probably the 1946 3000 pengö Hungarian stamp, worth at the time $1.6 × 10^{-14}$ parts of a cent.

EARLIEST STAMP (left): The Penny Black of 1840 featured Queen Victoria. Great Britain has never put its name on its stamps. HIGHEST DENOMINATION on a stamp is £100 for the Kenya 1925–27 issue (above) with the head of George V.

Highest Price Stamp

The highest price ever paid at auction for a stamp was $850,000 for one of the world's rarest stamps, a 1-cent black on magenta British Guiana provisional of 1856, postmarked Apr 4, 1856. It was sold by an Irwin R. Weinberg syndicate, which had bought it in 1970, to an anonymous collector at the Waldorf-Astoria Hotel, NYC on Apr 5, 1980.

High-Priced Error

$500,000 was paid for a 1918 US 24-cent airmail "Princeton" block of 4 of a Jenny biplane with the plane upside down by a Myron Kaller syndicate on July 19, 1979.

Rarest Stamps

Unique examples include the British Guiana of 1856 (see above), a Swedish 3-skilling banco yellow color error of 1855, a Gold Coast provisional of 1885, and US Postmaster stamps from Boscowen, New Haven and Lockport, NY.

Largest Philatelic Purchase

The Marc Haas collection of 3,000 postal and pre-postal covers to 1869 was sold for $11 million by Stanley Gibbons International Ltd of London in Aug 1979.

Telegrams

The country where most telegrams are sent is the USSR, whose population sent 492,631,000 telegrams in 1978.

5. EDUCATION

Illiteracy

Literacy is variously defined as "ability to read simple subjects" and "ability to read and write a simple letter." The looseness of definition and the scarcity of data for many countries preclude anything more than ap-

LARGEST UNIVERSITY BUILDING (left) is located on the Lenin Hills south of Moscow. Its 32 stories contain 40,000 rooms. OLDEST EDUCATIONAL INSTITUTION (above) is the University of Karueein, Fez, Morocco, founded 859 AD.

proximations, but the extent of illiteracy among adults (15 years old and over) is estimated to have been 34.7% in 1969.

The continent with the greatest proportion of illiterates is Africa, where 81.5% of adults were illiterate. The last published figure for Mali in 1960 showed 97.8% of people over 15 were unable to read.

Universities

Probably the oldest educational institution is the University of Karueein, founded in 859 AD in Fez, Morocco.

The university with the greatest enrollment in the world is the State University of New York, with 344,000 students enrolled in 1978. Its oldest college, at Albany, NY, was founded in 1844.

Bids for building the $3,400 million University of Riyadh, Saudi Arabia, were accepted in June 1978. The University will house 15,000 families and have its own mass transportation system.

The largest existing university building is the M. V. Lomonosov State University on the Lenin Hills, south of Moscow. It stands 787.4 ft tall, has 32 stories and contains 40,000 rooms. It was constructed in 1949–53.

The most northerly university is Inupiat University of the Arctic at Barrow, Alaska on Lat 71°16′N. Eskimo subjects are featured in the curriculum.

Professors

The youngest at which anybody has been elected to a chair (full professorship) in a university is 19, in the case of Colin MacLaurin (1698–1746), who was admitted to Marischal College, Aberdeen, Scotland as Professor of Mathematics on Sept 30, 1717. In 1725 he was made Professor of Mathematics at Edinburgh University on the recommendation of Sir Isaac Newton.

In July 1967, Dr Harvey Martin Friedman, PhD (b Sept 23, 1948) was appointed Assistant Professor of Mathematics at Stanford University, Calif, on Sept 1, 1967, just 3 weeks before his 19th birthday.

Most Durable Teachers

The longest period for which any professorship has been held is 63 years, in the case of Thomas Martyn (1735–1825), Professor of Botany at Cambridge University from 1762 until his death. His father, John Martyn (1699–1768), had occupied the chair from 1732 to 1762.

(Right) Thomas Martyn 63 years a teacher.

Dr Joel Hildebrand (b Nov 16, 1881), Professor Emeritus of Physical Chemistry at the University of California, Berkeley, first became an Assistant Professor in 1913, and was still researching in 1978.

David Rhys Davies (1835–1928) taught as a pupil teacher, teacher and, from 1879 to his death, as headmaster of Dame Anna Child's School, Whitton, Powys, England, for a total of 76 years 2 months.

Elsie Marguerite Touzel (b 1889) of Jersey, Channel Islands, began her teaching career aged 16 in 1905 and was still teaching at Les Alps School, Faldonet in 1979.

Col Ernest Achay Loftus (b Jan 11, 1884) served as a teacher over a span of 73 years, from Sept 1901 in York, England, until Feb 18, 1975 in Zambia, when he retired, aged 91 years 38 days.

Youngest Undergraduate

The most extreme recorded case of academic juvenility was that of William Thomson (1824–1907), later Lord Kelvin, who entered Glasgow University aged 10 years 4 months in Oct 1834, and matriculated on Nov 14, 1834.

Dr Merrill Kenneth Wolf (b Aug 28, 1931) of Cleveland, Ohio, took his B.A. in music from Yale University in Sept 1945, in the month of his 14th birthday.

Largest Schools

Enrollments have attained levels in excess of 430,000 in the Extension Course Institute of the US Dept of the Air Force, Gunter, Ala, which was founded May 1, 1950 and had over 8 million "graduates" by Jan 1, 1980.

At the time of its peak enrollment in 1934, De Witt Clinton High School in the Bronx, NYC had 12,000 students. It was founded in 1897 and now has an enrollment of 4,500.

Most Expensive

L'Institut "Le Rosey" at Rolle, Switzerland, charges annual fees of at least 25,000 Swiss francs (about $15,000).

Most Schools Attended

The documented record for the greatest number of schools attended by a pupil is 265 by Wilma Williams, now Mrs R. J. Horton, from 1933 to 1943 when her parents were in show business in the US.

Lecture Agency

The largest lecture agency is the American Program Bureau of Boston with 400 personalities on 40 major subject areas and a turnover of some $5 million. The top rate is $4,000 per hour commanded by Ralph Nader (b Winsted, Conn, Feb 27, 1934) equivalent to $66.66 per minute.

6. RELIGIONS

Oldest Religion

The oldest major formal religion is Hinduism. Its Vedic precursor was brought to India by Aryans *c.* 1500 BC. The Rig Veda Hindu hymnal was codified *c.* 900 BC or earlier.

Largest Religious Membership

Religious statistics are necessarily only approximate. The test of adherence to a religion varies widely in rigor, while many individuals, particularly in the East, belong to two or more religions.

Christianity is the leading religion, with some 1,070 million adherents in 1979. The Vatican statistics office reported that in 1979 there were 724,434,000 Roman Catholics including priests and nuns. The largest non-Christian religion is Islam (Muslim) with about 550 million followers.

Largest Clergy

The largest religious organization is the Roman Catholic Church, with 1,407,290 clergy (1979 estimate), including 404,306 priests and 950,379 nuns. The total number of cardinals, archbishops and bishops is 2,947. There are about 420,000 churches.

World Jewry

The total of world Jewry was estimated to be 14,300,000 in 1979. The highest concentration was in the US, with 5,800,000 of whom 2 million are in the NY area. The total in Israel is 3,060,000, in Britain 410,000 (of whom 280,000 are in Greater London and 13,000 in Glasgow). The total in Tokyo is less than 1,000.

Earliest Shrine

The earliest known shrine dates from the proto-neolithic Natufian culture in Jericho, where a site on virgin soil has been dated to the 9th millennium BC. A simple rectilinear red-plastered room with a niche housing a stone pillar, believed to be the shrine of a pre-pottery fertility cult dat-

LARGEST BUDDHIST TEMPLE: Built in the 8th century, this Indonesian-style structure is at Borobudur, near Jogjakarta.

LARGEST CATHEDRAL (above):
New York's St John the Divine
cathedral was begun in 1892 and is still
unfinished. LARGEST SYNAGOGUE:
Temple Emanu-El in NY can accommodate more than 6,000 worshippers.

ing from *c.* 6500 BC, was also uncovered in Jericho. The oldest surviving
Christian church is Qal'at es Salihiye in eastern Syria, dating from 232
AD.

Largest Temple

The largest religious building ever constructed is Angkor Wat (City
Temple), covering 402 acres, in Cambodia. It was built to the God
Vishnu by the Khmer King Suryavarman II in the period 1113–1150. Its
curtain wall measures 1,400 × 1,400 yd and its population, before it was
abandoned in 1432, was at times 80,000.

The largest Buddhist temple is Borobudur, near Jogjakarta, Indonesia,
built in the 8th century.

The largest Mormon temple is in Kensington, Md, dedicated in Nov
1974, with a floor area of 159,000 sq ft.

Largest Mosque

The largest mosque ever built was the now ruined al-Malawiya
mosque of al-Mutawakil in Samarra, Iraq, built in 842–852 AD and measuring 401,408 sq ft (9.21 acres) with dimensions of 784 × 512 ft.

The world's largest mosque in use is the Umayyad Mosque in Damascus, Syria, built on a 2,000-year-old religious site measuring 515 × 318 ft,
thus covering an area of 3.76 acres.

The largest mosque will be the Merdeka Mosque in Djakarta, Indonesia, which was begun in 1962. The cupola will be 147.6 ft in diameter and
the capacity in excess of 50,000 people.

Largest Synagogue

The largest synagogue is the Temple Emanu-El on Fifth Ave at 65th
St, NYC. The temple, completed in Sept 1929, has a frontage of 150 ft on
Fifth Ave and 253 ft on 65th St. The sanctuary proper can accommodate
2,500 people, and the adjoining Beth-El Chapel seats 350. When all the
facilities are in use, more than 6,000 people can be accommodated.

Largest Cathedral

The largest is the cathedral church of the Episcopalian Diocese of NY, St John the Divine, with a floor area of 121,000 sq ft and a volume of 16,822,000 cu ft. The cornerstone was laid on Dec 27, 1892, and work on the Gothic building was stopped in 1941, then restarted in earnest in July 1979. In NY it is referred to as "Saint John the Unfinished." The nave is the longest in the world, 601 ft in length, with a vaulting 124 ft in height.

The cathedral covering the largest area is that of Santa María de la Sede in Seville, Spain. It was built in Spanish Gothic style between 1402 and 1519 and is 414 ft long, 271 ft wide and 100 ft high to the vault of the nave.

Smallest Cathedral

The smallest cathedral is the Cathedral Chapel of St Francis of the American Catholic Church, built in 1933 at Laguna Beach, Calif with an area of 1,008 sq ft and seating for 42 people.

Largest Church

The largest church is the basilica of St Peter, built between 1492 and 1612 in Vatican City, Rome. Its length, measured from the apse, is 611 ft 4 in. Its area is 162,990 sq ft. The inner diameter of the famous dome is 137 ft 9 in and its center is 390 ft 5 in high. The external height is 457 ft 9 in.

The elliptical Basilique de St Pie X at Lourdes, France, completed in 1957 at a cost of $5,600,000, has a capacity of 20,000 under its giant span arches and a length of 656 ft.

The crypt of the underground Civil War Memorial Church in the Guadarrama Mountains, 28 miles from Madrid, Spain, is 853 ft in length. It took 21 years (1937–58) to build, at a reported cost of $392 million and is surmounted by a cross 492 ft tall.

Smallest Church

The smallest is the Union Church at Wiscasset, Maine with a floor area of 31½ sq ft (7 × 4½ ft). Les Vauxbelets Church in Guernsey, Channel Islands, has an area of 16 × 12 ft, room for one priest and a congregation of two.

Tallest Spires

The tallest *cathedral* spire is on the Protestant Cathedral of Ulm in Germany. The building is early Gothic and was begun in 1377. The tower, in the center of the west façade, was not finally completed until 1890 and is 528 ft high.

The tallest *church* spire is that of the Chicago Temple of the First Methodist Church on Clark St, Chicago. The building consists of a 22-story skyscraper (erected in 1924) surmounted by a parsonage at 330 ft, a "Sky Chapel" at 400 ft and a steeple cross at 568 ft above street level.

Minarets and Pagodas

The tallest minaret is one of 282 ft at the Sultan Hassan Mosque (founded 1356 AD) in Cairo, Egypt. The tallest free-standing stone tower is the Qutb Minar, south of New Delhi, India, built in 1194 to a height of 238 ft.

The tallest pagoda is the 326-ft-tall Shwe Dagon Pagoda in Rangoon, Burma, which was increased to its present height by Hsinbyushin, King of Ava (1763–1776).

The oldest pagoda in China is Sung-Yo Ssu in Honan, built with 15 12-sided stories in 523 AD.

Most Valuable Sacred Object

The sacred object of the highest intrinsic value is the 15th-century gold Buddha in the Temple of Three Friends in Bangkok, Thailand. It is 10 ft tall and weighs an estimated 6 tons. At $500 per fine ounce, its value has been calculated at $96 million for the gold alone.

Saints

There are 1,848 "registered" saints (including 60 St Johns), of whom 628 are Italians, 576 French and 271 from the British Isles. The first US-born saint is Mother Elizabeth Ann Bayley Seton (1774–1821) who was canonized Sept 14, 1975. The total includes 15 Popes.

The shortest interval that has elapsed between the death of a saint and his canonization was in the case of St Anthony of Padua, Italy, who died on June 13, 1231 and was canonized 352 days later on May 30, 1232.

The other extreme is represented by St Bernard of Tiron, for 20 years Prior of St Sabinus, who died in 1117 and was made a saint in 1861—744 years later.

Popes

The longest reign of any of the 264 Popes has been that of Pius IX (Giovanni Maria Mastai-Ferretti), who reigned for 31 years 236 days from June 16, 1846 until his death, aged 85, on Feb 7, 1878. Pope Stephen II was elected on March 24, 752, and died two days later.

Oldest Pope

It is recorded that Pope St Agatho (reigned 678–681) was elected at the age of 103 and lived to 106, but recent scholars have expressed doubts. The oldest of recent Pontiffs has been Pope Leo XIII (Gioacchino Pecci), who was born March 2, 1810, elected Pope at the third ballot on Feb 20, 1878, and died on July 20, 1903, aged 93 years 140 days.

Youngest Pope

The youngest of all Popes was Pope Benedict IX (d 1056) (Theophylact), who had three terms as Pope: in 1032–44; Apr to May, 1045; and Nov 8, 1047 to July 17, 1048. It would appear that he was aged only 11 or 12 in 1032, though the Catalogue of the Popes admits only to his "extreme youth."

Last Married Pope

The last married Pope was Adrian II (867–872). Rodrigo Borgia was the father of at least six children before being elected Pope Alexander VI in 1492. The first 37 Popes had no specific obligation to celibacy. Pope Hormisdas (514–523) was the father of Pope Silverius (536–537).

FIRST AMERICAN SAINT (left): Mother Elizabeth Ann Bayley Seton was canonized in Sept 1975. OLDEST STAINED GLASS WINDOW: In Augsburg Cathedral, Germany this window depicting the Prophets dates from about 1050.

Non-Italian Popes

The current Pope John Paul II, elected Oct 16, 1978 (b Karol Wojtyla, May 18, 1920, at Wadowice, near Krakow, Poland) is the first non-Italian Pope since Cardinal Adrian Florenz Boeyens (Pope Adrian VI) of the Netherlands, crowned on Aug 31, 1522.

Slowest and Fastest Election of a Pope

After 31 months without declaring "We have a Pope," the cardinals were subjected to a bread and water diet and the removal of the roof of their conclave by the Mayor of Viterbo before electing Teobaldo Visconti (c. 1210–76), the Archbishop of Liège, as Pope Gregory X at Viterbo, near Rome, on Sept 1, 1271. The papacy was, however, vacant for at least 3 years 214 days in 304–308.

The shortest conclave was that of Oct 21, 1503, for the election of Pope Julius II on the first ballot.

Church Attendance

The most extreme recorded case of perfect Sunday School Church attendance is that of Roland E. Daab, currently the Vice President of the Consistory of St Paul United Church of Christ, Columbia, Ill, who on March 23, 1980, attended service on his 3,200th consecutive Sunday, an unbroken period of more than 61 years.

Stained Glass

The oldest stained glass in the world represents the Prophets in a window of the cathedral of Augsburg, Bavaria, Germany, dating from c. 1050.

The largest stained glass window is the complete mural of The Resurrection Mausoleum, Justice, Ill, measuring 22,381 sq ft, in 2,448 panels completed in 1971.

Largest Crowd

The greatest recorded number of human beings assembled with a common purpose was an estimated 12,700,000 at the Hindu feast of Kumbh-Mela, which was held at the confluence of the Yamuna (formerly called the Jumna), the Ganges and the invisible "Sarasvati" at Allahabad, Uttar Pradesh, India, on Jan 19, 1977. The holiest time during this holiest day since 1833 was during the planetary alignment between 9:28 and 9:40 a.m., during which only 200,000 achieved immersion to wash away the sins of a lifetime.

Largest Funeral

The greatest attendance at any funeral is the estimated 4 million who thronged Cairo, Egypt, for the funeral of President Gamal Abdel Nasser (b Jan 15, 1918) on Oct 1, 1970.

Biggest Demonstrations

A figure of 2,700,000 was published from China for the demonstration against the USSR in Shanghai Apr 3–4, 1969, following border clashes, and one of 10 million for the May Day celebrations of 1963 in Peking.

WORST ACCIDENTS AND DISASTERS IN THE WORLD

	Deaths		
Pandemic	75,000,000	The Black Death (bubonic, pneumonic and septicaemic plague)	1347–51
	21,640,000	Influenza	Apr–Nov 1918
Famine	9,500,000[1]	Northern China	Feb 1877–Sept 1878
Flood	3,700,000	Yellow (Hwang-ho) River, China	Aug 1931
Circular Storm	1,000,000[2]	Ganges Delta isles, Bangladesh	Nov 12–13, 1970
Earthquake	830,000	Shensi Province, China (2 hours)	Jan 23, 1556
Landslide	180,000	Kansu Province, China	Dec 16, 1920
Atomic Bomb	141,000	Hiroshima, Japan	Aug 6, 1945
Conventional Bombing	c. 25,000[3]	Dresden, Germany	Feb 13–15, 1945
Snow avalanche	c. 25,000[4]	Yungay, Huascaran, Peru	May 31, 1970
Marine (single ship)	c. 7,700	*Wilhelm Gustloff* (25,484 tons) torpedoed off Danzig by USSR submarine S-13	Jan 30, 1945
Panic	c. 4,000[5]	Chungking, China (air raid shelter)	c. June 8, 1941
Dam Burst	2,209	Johnstown, Pa (South Fork Dam)	May 31, 1889
Explosion	1,963[6]	Halifax, Nova Scotia, Canada	Dec 6, 1917
Fire (single building)	1,670[7]	The Theatre, Canton, China	May 1845
Mining	1,572[8]	Honkeiko Colliery, China (coal dust explosion)	Apr 26, 1942
Riot	c. 1,200	NYC (anitconscription riots)	July 13–16, 1863
Crocodiles (disputed)	c. 900	Japanese soldiers, Ramree Island, Burma	Feb 19–20, 1945
Fireworks	>800	Dauphine's wedding, Seine, Paris	May 16, 1770
Tornado	689	South Central States, US (3 hours)	March 18, 1925
Aircraft (Civil)	582	KLM-Pan Am Boeing 747 Ground Crash, Tenerife, Canary Islands	March 27, 1977
Railroad	543[9]	Modane, France	Dec 12, 1917

Notes. 1.—In 1770 the great Indian famine carried away a proportion of the population estimated as high as one third, hence a figure of tens of millions. The figure for Bengal alone was probably about 10 million. It has been estimated that more than 5 million died in the post-World War I famine, in the USSR. The USSR government in July 1923 informed Mr (later President) Herbert Hoover that the ARA (American Relief Administration) had since Aug 1921 saved 20 million lives from famine and famine diseases.

2.—The figure published in 1972 for the E Pakistan disaster was from Dr Afzal, Principal Scientific Officer of the Atomic Energy Authority Centre, Dacca. One report asserted that less than half of the population of the 4 islands of Bhola, Charjabbar, Hatia and Ramagati (1961 Census 1.4 million) survived. The most damaging hurricane recorded was the billion dollar Betsy (name now retired) in 1965 with an estimated insurance pay-out of $750 million.

3.—The number of civilians killed by the bombing of Germany has been put variously as 593,000 and "over 635,000." A figure of c. 140,000 deaths in USAF fire raids on Tokyo of March 10, 1945 has been attributed. Total Japanese fatalities were 600,000 (conventional) and 220,000 (nuclear).

4.—A total of 10,000 Austrian and Italian troops is reported to have been lost in the Dolomite valley of Northern Italy on Dec 13, 1916 in more than 100 avalanches. The total is probably exaggerated though bodies were still being found in 1952.

5.—It was estimated that some 5,000 people were trampled to death in the stampede for free beer at the coronation celebration of Czar Nicholas II in Moscow in May 1896.

6.—Some sources maintain that the final death toll was over 3,000 on Dec 6–7.

7.—The worst-ever hotel fire killed 162 at the Hotel Taeyokake, Seoul, South Korea, Dec 25, 1971.

8.—The worst gold mining disaster in South Africa was 152 killed due to flooding in the Witwatersrand Gold Mining Co gold mine in 1909.

9.—Between 500 and 800 died in the Torro Tunnel, Léon, Spain, train disaster on Jan 3, 1944.

WORST ROAD DISASTER: 127 people died in 1973 when this bus plunged into an irrigation canal in Egypt.

Man-Eating Animal	436[10]	Champawat district, India, tigress shot by Col Jim Corbett	1907
Hail	246	Moradabad, Uttar Pradesh, India	Apr 20, 1888
Offshore Oil Plant	137	Alexander L., Kielland "Hotel," North Sea	March 27, 1980
Submarine	129	*Le Surcout* rammed in Caribbean	Feb 18, 1942
	129	USS *Thresher* off Cape Cod, Mass	Apr 10, 1963
Road (Single Vehicle)	127[11]	Bus plunged into irrigation canal, Sayyoum, Egypt	Aug 9, 1973
Helicopter	54	Israeli military "Sea Stallion," West Bank	May 10, 1977
Ski Lift (Cablecar)	42	Cavalese resort, Northern Italy	March 9, 1976
Mountaineering	40[12]	USSR Expedition on Mt Everest	Dec 1952
Lightning (Single Bolt)	21	Hut in Chinamasa Kraal near Umtali, Rhodesia	Dec 23, 1975
Yacht Racing	19	28th Fasnet Race 23 boats sank in Force II gale	Aug 13–15, 1979
Space	3	Apollo oxygen fire, Cape Kennedy, Fla	Jan 27, 1967
	3	*Soyuz* II re-entry over USSR	June 29, 1971

10.—In the period 1941–42 *c.* 1,500 Kenyans were killed by a pride of 22 man-eating lions, of which 18 were shot by a hunter named Rushby.

11.—The worst years ever for road deaths in the US have been 1969 (56,400). The world's highest death rate is said to be in Queensland, Australia. The US's 2 millionth victim since 1899 died in Jan 1973. The global total dead by Sept 1975 was put at 25 million.

12.—According to Polish sources, not confirmed by the USSR. On Mt Fuji, Japan 23 died in blizzard and avalanche on March 20, 1972.

Chapter 11

Human Achievements

1. ENDURANCE AND ENDEAVOR

Lunar Conquest

Neil Alden Armstrong (b Wapakoneta, Ohio, of Scottish-Irish-German ancestry, Aug 5, 1930), command pilot of the Apollo XI mission, became the first man to set foot on the moon on the Sea of Tranquillity at 02:56 and 15 sec a.m. GMT on July 21, 1969. He was followed out of the Lunar Module *Eagle* by Col Edwin Eugene Aldrin, Jr (b Glen Ridge, NJ, of Swedish, Dutch and British ancestry, Jan 20, 1930), while the Command Module *Columbia* piloted by Lt-Col Michael Collins (b Rome, Italy, of Irish and pre-Revolutionary American ancestry, Oct 31, 1930) orbited above.

LUNAR CONQUEST: The greatest human achievement of the 20th century was the landing of man on the moon in 1969. This is Col Edwin Aldrin stepping down from the lunar module, as photographed by Neil Armstrong, fellow astronaut and the first to land.

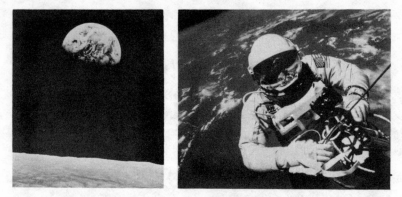

THE EARTH AS SEEN FROM THE MOON (left): The view seen by Apollo XI astronauts, the first to land on the moon. FIRST WALK IN SPACE (right): Ed White, tethered to his Gemini IV space vehicle, floats high over the earth.

Eagle landed at 20:17 and 42 sec GMT July 20 and blasted off at 17:54 GMT on July 21, after a stay of 21 hours 36 min. The *Apollo XI* had blasted off from Cape Kennedy, Fla at 13:32 GMT July 16 and was a culmination of the US space program, which, at its peak, employed 376,600 people and attained in the year 1966–67 a peak budget of $5,900 million.

There is evidence that Pavel Belgayev (USSR) was the cosmonaut selected by Russia for a manned lunar flight in *Zond 7* on Dec 9, 1968, but no launch took place.

First Woman in Space

The first and only woman to orbit the earth was Jr Lt (now Lt-Col) Valentina Vladimirovna Tereshkova-Nikolayev (b March 6, 1937), who was launched in *Vostok VI* from Tyura Tam, USSR, at 9:30 a.m. GMT June 16, 1963, and landed at 8:16 a.m. June 19, after a flight of 2 days 22 hours 42 min, during which she completed over 48 orbits (1,225,000 miles) and came to within 3 miles of *Vostok V*. She was formerly a textile worker. Her mission was variously reported to be punctuated with pleas to be brought back due to giddiness, or to be extended because of her excellent performance.

FIRST
WOMAN IN
SPACE:
Valentina
Nikolayev
(USSR) is also
the only woman
to orbit the
earth. She was in
space for almost
3 days and made
48 orbits in
1963, setting a
speed record of
17,470 mph.

First "Walk" in Space

The earliest undoubted instance of an astronaut floating free outside a space vehicle was by Astronaut Edward H. White II, for 21 minutes over Hawaii to the US Atlantic coast on June 3, 1965, from *Gemini IV*. Evidence for the earlier claim of Lt-Col Aleksey A. Leonov from *Voshkod 2* on March 18, 1965, is not internationally accepted.

Manned Flight

The greatest altitude attained by man was when the crew of the ill-fated *Apollo XIII* was at apocynthion (*i.e.* their furthest point behind the moon) 158 miles above its surface and 248,665 miles above the earth's surface at 6:21 a.m. EST on Apr 15, 1970. The crew consisted of Capt James Arthur Lovell, Jr, USN (b Cleveland, Ohio, March 25, 1928); John L. Swigert, Jr (b Denver, Colo, Aug 30, 1931); and Fred Wallace Haise, Jr (b Biloxi, Miss, Nov 14, 1933).

The greatest altitude attained by a woman in flight is 143.5 miles by Valentina Vladimirovna Tereshkova-Nikolayev (see above) during her 48-orbit flight in *Vostok VI* June 16–19, 1963. The record for a woman in an aircraft is 79,842 ft by Natalia Prokhanova (USSR) (b 1940) in an E-33 jet, May 22, 1965.

Longest Manned Space Flight

The longest time spent in space is 175 days, Feb 25–Aug 19, 1979 by Valeriy Ryumin, 40, and Vladimir Lyakhov, 38, on board the Salyut-Soyuz orbital research station. During this time they became the most traveled humans of all time with a mileage of more than 56 million miles. It was reported that on their return to Earth's gravity they had difficulty in relearning to walk and in picking up cups of tea. Additionally, in the mornings they tried to "swim" out of bed.

Oldest and Youngest Astronauts

The oldest of the 92 people in space has been Donald Kent ("Deke") Slayton (b Sparta, Wis, March 1, 1924) who was aged 51 years 146 days when launched on the *Apollo-Soyuz* mission on July 24, 1975. The youngest was Major (later Col) Gherman Stepanovich Titov (b Sept 11, 1935) who was 25 years 329 days old when he was launched in *Vostok II* on Aug 6, 1961.

Duration Record on the Moon

The crew of *Apollo XVII* collected a record 253 lb of rock and soil during their 22-hour-5-min "extra-vehicular activity." Astronauts Capt Eugene Andrew Cernan, USN (b Chicago, March 14, 1934) and Dr Harrison H. "Jack" Schmitt (b Santa Rosa, NM, July 3, 1935) were on the lunar surface for a record 74 hours 59½ min Dec 7–12, 1972. Schmitt was the 12th man on the moon. This longest of lunar missions took 12 days 13 hours 51 min.

Speed in Space

The fastest speed at which humans have traveled is 24,791 mph when the Command Module of *Apollo X* carrying Col (now Brig-Gen) Thomas Patten Stafford, USAF (b Weatherford, Okla, Sept 17, 1930),

OFFICIAL LAND SPEED RECORD HOLDER: Although Gary Gabelich in his "Blue Flame" went only 622.287 mph, his time was an average of a 2-way run, which eliminated wind advantage as a factor, and so is official.

Cdr (now Capt) Eugene Andrew Cernan and Cdr (now Capt) John Watts Young, USN (b San Francisco, Sept 24, 1930) reached their maximum speed on their trans-earth return flight at an altitude of 400,000 ft on May 26, 1969.

The highest speed ever attained by a woman is 17,470 mph by Valentina Vladimirovna Tereshkova-Nikolayev (see above), during her 48-orbit flight in *Vostok VI* June 16–19, 1963.

The highest speed ever achieved by a woman aircraft pilot is 1,669.89 mph by Svetlana Savitskaya (USSR), reported on June 2, 1975.

Speed on Land

The highest speed ever achieved on land is 739.666 mph or Mach 1.0106 in a one-way run by Stan Barrett (US) in the *Budweiser Rocket,* a rocket-engined 3-wheeled car at Edwards Air Force Base, Calif on Dec 17, 1979.

The official land speed record is 622.287 mph set by Gary Gabelich (b San Pedro, Calif, Aug 29, 1940) on Oct 23, 1970 on the Bonneville Salt Flats, Utah, in the rocket-powered *The Blue Flame,* built by Reaction Dynamics Inc of Milwaukee, Wis.

The highest land speed recorded by a woman is 524.016 mph by Mrs Kitty O'Neil Hambleton (US), in the 48,000-hp rocket-powered 3-wheeled S.M.1 *Motivator* over the Alvard Desert, Ore, on Dec 6, 1976. Her official 2-way record was 512.710 mph and she probably touched 600 mph momentarily.

Speed on Water

The highest speed ever achieved on water is an estimated 300 knots (345 mph) by Kenneth Peter Warby (b May 9, 1939) on the Blowering Dam Lake, NSW, Australia Nov 20, 1977, in his unlimited hydroplane *Spirit of Australia.* The official world water speed record is 319.627 mph, set Oct 8, 1978, by Warby on the Blowering Dam Lake.

The record for propeller-driven craft is 202.42 mph by Larry Hill in the supercharged hydroplane *Mr. Ed* at Long Beach, Calif, in Aug 1971. On a one-way run, the *Climax* reached a speed of 205.19 mph.

Sue Williams, 28, drove the unlimited hydroplane U-96 KYYX through a measured mile on Lake Washington, Seattle, at 163.043 mph July 26, 1978, for a women's world record.

Most Traveled Man

The man who visited more countries than anyone else was Jesse Hart Rosdail (1914–77) of Elmhurst, Ill. Of the 161 sovereign countries and 60 non-sovereign territories (221 in all) *then* listed by the *UN Population Report* of 1977, he visited 219, missing N Korea and French Antarctic Territories. He estimated his total mileage as 1,626,605 miles.

Though he has not visited so many currently existing countries, Mehmet S. Ersöz (b 1904, Turkey) has traveled much more widely within some 210 countries. His wife's total was 163 by mid-1978.

The most countries visited by a disabled person is 120 sovereign and 63 non-sovereign countries by Prof Daniel J. Crowley of Davis, Calif, who has been confined to a wheelchair since March 1946.

The Methodist preacher Francis Asbury of Birmingham, England, traveled 264,000 miles by horseback in N America from 1771 to 1815, preaching 16,000 sermons.

Most Isolated Human

The farthest any human has been removed from his nearest living fellow man is 2,233.2 miles in the case of the Command Service Module pilot Alfred M. Worden on the US *Apollo XV* lunar mission of July 30–Aug 1, 1971.

Fastest Round-the-World Trip

The fastest time for a round-the-world journey on scheduled flights for a circumnavigation is 44 hours 6 min by David J. Springbett, 41, of Taplow, England from Los Angeles eastward via London, Bahrain, Singapore, Bangkok, Manila, Tokyo and Honolulu Jan 8–10, 1980 over a 23,068-mile route.

The F.A.I. accepts any flight, taking off and landing at the same point, which is as long as the Tropic of Cancer (22,858.754 miles) as a circumnavigational flight.

FASTEST AROUND THE WORLD: David Springbett of England (left) made it in 44 hours 6 min on scheduled airlines in 1980. MOST TRAVELED MAN: J. Hart Rosdail (right) visited 219 countries and territories in his lifetime.

North Pole Conquests

The claims of both of the two US Arctic explorers, Dr Frederick Albert Cook (1865–1940) and Rear Adm Robert Edwin Peary, USN (1856–1920), in reaching the North Pole are subject to positive proof.

The earliest indisputable attainment of the North Pole over the sea ice was at 3 p.m. (CST) on Apr 19, 1968, by Ralph Plaisted (US) and three companions after a 42-day trek in four snowmobiles. Their arrival was independently verified 18 hours later by a US Air Force weather aircraft. The sea bed is 13,410 ft below the North Pole.

Naomi Uemara (b 1941), the Japanese explorer and mountaineer, became the first person to reach the North Pole in a solo trek across the Arctic ice cap at 04:45 GMT May 1, 1978. He had traveled 450 miles, setting out on March 7 from Cape Edward, Ellesmere Island, in northern Canada. He averaged over 8 miles per day with his sled "Aurora" drawn by 17 huskies (he had hoped to average 10.5 miles per day).

The first woman to set foot on the North Pole was Mrs Fran Phipps, wife of the Canadian bush pilot Weldy Phipps, Apr 5, 1971. Galina Aleksandrovna Lastovskaya (b 1941) and Lilia Vladislavovna Minina (b 1959) were crew members of the USSR atomic icebreaker *Arktika* which reached the pole on Aug 17, 1977.

Seven polar explorers from the USSR reached the North Pole across 900 miles of the ice cap from Henrietta Island on skis in 77 days, March 15–May 31, 1979.

Arctic Crossing

The first crossing of the Arctic sea ice was achieved by the British Trans-Arctic Expedition which left Point Barrow, Alaska, Feb 21, 1968, and arrived at the Seven Island Archipelago northeast of Spitzbergen 464 days later on May 29, 1969, after a haul of 2,920 statute miles and a drift of 700 miles, compared with a straight-line distance of 1,662 miles. The team was Wally Herbert (leader), 34, Maj Ken Hedges, 34, Allan Gill, 38, Dr Roy Koerner, 36 (glaciologist), and 40 huskies. This was the longest sustained (sled) journey ever made on polar pack ice and the first undisputed conquest of the North Pole by sled. Temperatures sank to −47° F during the trek.

South Pole Conquests

The first ships to cross the Antarctic circle (Lat 66° 30′ S) were the 193-crew *Resolution* (462 tons) under Capt James Cook (1728–79), the English navigator, and *Adventure* (336 tons) under Lt T. Furneaux, at 39° E, Jan 17, 1773.

The first person to sight the Antarctic *mainland*—on the best available evidence and against claims made for British and Russian explorers—was Nathaniel Brown Palmer (US) (1799–1877). On Nov 17, 1820, he sighted the Orleans Channel coast of the Palmer Peninsula from his 45-ton sloop *Hero*.

The South Pole (altitude 9,186 ft on ice and 336 ft bed rock) was first reached at 11 a.m. Dec 16, 1911, by a Norwegian party, led by Roald Engebreth Gravning Amundsen (1872–1928), after a 53-day march with dog sleds from the Bay of Whales, to which he had penetrated in the *Fram*. Subsequent calculations showed that Olav Olavson Bjaaland (the

CONQUEST OF NORTH POLE: Commander Robert E. Peary (above) took the picture (right, above) of his companions after they reached the North Pole Apr 6, 1909. CONQUEST OF SOUTH POLE: Helmer Hanssen (right) was one of the Norwegians led by Roald Amundsen in 1911. FIRST ARCTIC SEA CROSSING (below): This British expedition went by sled from Point Barrow, Alaska to near Spitzbergen, Norway in 464 days.

last survivor, dying in June 1961, aged 88) and Helmer **Hanssen** probably passed within 400–600 meters of the exact pole. The other two members of the party were Sverre H. Hassell and Oskar Wisting.

The first woman to set foot on Antarctica was Mrs Klarius Mikkelsen on Feb 20, 1935. No woman stood on the South Pole until Nov 11, 1969, when Lois Jones, Kay Lindsay, Eileen McSavenay, Jean Pearson, Tarry Lee Tickhall and Pam Young, all of the US, arrived by air.

Antarctic Crossing

The first surface crossing of the Antarctic continent was completed at 1:47 p.m. March 2, 1958, after a 2,158-mile trek lasting 99 days from Nov 24, 1957, from Shackleton Base to Scott Base via the Pole. The crossing party of 12 was led by Dr (now Sir) Vivian Ernest Fuchs (b Feb 11, 1908). The expedition used photographs from the first aerial trans-Antarctic crossing via the Pole made on Jan 13, 1956 by a US Navy Neptune P2 V bomber navigated by former Staff Sergeant (now Col) Robert C. Mount Spann.

Longest Sled Journey

The longest totally self-supporting polar sled journey ever made was one of 1,080 miles from west to east across Greenland, June 18–Sept 5, 1934 by Capt (now Sir) Martin Lindsay, Lt Arthur Godfrey, Andrew N. C. Croft and 49 dogs.

The same crossing was first made with man-hauled sledges by the Inter Services 1974 Trans-Greenland Expedition, led by Flt Lt D. R. Gleed, in 36 days.

First on Both North and South Poles

David S. Porter (b 1938) of Hope, NJ, visited the South Pole as a guest of the US Navy Dec 14, 1970 (temperature −38° F) and on Apr 9, 1979 he visited the North Pole where the temperature was −39° F.

Mountaineering

The conquest of the highest point on earth, Mt Everest (29,028 ft), was first achieved at 11:30 a.m. May 29, 1953, by Edmund Percival Hillary (New Zealand) and the Sherpa Tenzing Norgay.

The female record was set by Mrs Junko Tabei, 34, of Japan, on reaching Everest's summit May 16, 1975.

Deep Diving Records

The record depth for the extremely dangerous activity of breath-held diving is 282 ft by Jacques Mayol (France) off Elba, Italy on Nov 9, 1973. The pressure on Mayol's thorax was 136.5 lb of force per sq in, and his pulse fell to 36.

Enzo Maiorca (Italy) surfaced unconscious from his dive of 285 ft off Sorrento, Italy, on Sept 27, 1974.

The women's record is 147½ ft by Giuliana Treleani (Italy) off Cuba in Sept 1967.

The record dive with scuba (self-contained underwater breathing apparatus) is 437 ft by John J. Gruener and R. Neal Watson (US) off Freeport, Grand Bahama, on Oct 14, 1968.

DEEP SINKER: The US Navy manned bathyscaphe, "Trieste," reached the ocean floor 6.78 miles down in the deepest ocean descent ever, into the Marianas Trench near Guam in the Pacific in 1960.

The record dive utilizing gas mixtures is a simulated dive of 2,132 ft in a dry chamber by Delmar Shelton, 40; William Bell, 25; and Stephen Parker, 24, at the Duke University Medical Center, Durham, NC, 1980.

Some divers have survived free swimming for short intervals at 1,400 ft.

Underwater Rescue

The deepest underwater rescue achieved was of the *Pisces III* in which Roger R. Chapman, 28, and Roger Mallinson, 35, were trapped for 76 hours when it sank to 1,575 ft, 150 miles southeast of Cork, Ireland, Aug 29, 1973. She was hauled to the surface by the cable ship *John Cabot* after preliminary work by *Pisces V, Pisces II* and the remote control recovery vessel US CURV, on Sept 1, 1973.

The greatest depth of an actual escape without any equipment has been from 225 ft by Richard A. Slater from the rammed submersible *Nekton Beta* off Catalina Island, Calif on Sept 28, 1970.

Longest Search

For 68 years until 1972, Frank Jones of Lowestoft, Suffolk, England searched and failed to locate his missing brother Arthur Jones until he found him. Additionally he traced the existence of a second brother, William, and after a 71-year-long search he found that William had died.

Greatest Ocean Descent

The record ocean descent was achieved in the Challenger Deep of the Marianas Trench, 250 miles southwest of Guam, when the Swiss-built US Navy bathyscaphe *Trieste*, manned by Dr Jacques Piccard (b 1914) and Lt Donald Walsh, USN, reached the ocean bed 35,820 ft (6.78 miles) down, at 1:10 p.m. Jan 23, 1960. The pressure of the water was 16,883 lb per sq in (1,215.6 tons per sq ft), and the temperature 37.4° F. The descent required 4 hours 48 min and the ascent 3 hours 17 min.

MARINE CIRCUMNAVIGATION RECORDS (Compiled by Sq Ldr D. H. Clarke)

A true circumnavigation entails passing through two antipodal points (which are at least 12,429 statute miles apart).

CATEGORY*	VESSEL	NAME	START PLACE, DATE	FINISH DATE, DURATION
Earliest*	Vittoria Expedition of Fernao de Magalhaes (Magellan) (c. 1480–1521)	Juan Sebastion de Elcano or Del Cano (k 1526) and 17 crew	Seville, Spain Sept 20, 1519	San Lucar, Spain Sept 6, 1521, 30,700 miles
Earliest Woman	Etoile	Crypto-female valet of M de Commerson, named Baré	St Malo, 1766	1769
Earliest Fore-and-Aft Rigged Vessel	Union, 98 tons (Sloop)	John Boit Junior (US)	Newport, RI, 1794 (via Cape Horn westabout)	Newport, RI, 1796
Earliest Yacht	Sunbeam, 170-ft-5.8-in 3-mast topsail schooner	Lord and Lady Brassey (GB), passengers and crew	Cowes, Isle of Wight, 1876	Cowes, Isle of Wight, 1877
Earliest Solo	Spray, 36¾-ft gaff yawl	Capt Joshua Slocum, 51 (US) (a non-swimmer)	Newport, RI via Magellan Straits, Apr 24, 1895	July 3, 1898, 46,000 miles
Earliest Motorboat	Speejacks, 98 ft	Albert Y. Gowen (US), wife and crew	New York City, 1921	New York City, 1922
Earliest Woman Solo	Mazurek, 31-ft-2-in Bermuda sloop	Krystyna Chojnowska-Liskiewicz (Poland)	Las Palmas, Mar 28, 1976 Westward via Panama	Tied knot Mar 21, 1978
Earliest Woman Solo via Cape Horn	Express Crusader, 53-ft Bermuda sloop	Naomi James (NZ/GB)	Dartmouth, England, Sept 9, 1977 (Cape Horn, March 19, 1978)	Dartmouth, June 8, 1978 (266 days 19 hours)
Smallest Boat	Ahdori II, 20-ft-8-in Bermuda yawl	Hiroshi Aoki (Japan)	Osaka, Japan, June 13, 1972 (Cape Horn, Jan 12, 1973)	Osaka, July 29, 1974
Earliest Submarine	USS Triton	Capt Edward L. Beach, USN, plus 182 crew	New London, Conn, Feb 16, 1960	May 10, 1960, 30,708 miles
Fastest Solo (Multihull)	Manureva, 70-ft trimaran (ex Pen Duick IV)	Alain Colas (France)	St Malo via Sydney	March 29, 1974 (167 days)
Fastest Solo (Monohull)	Egregious, 37-ft Bermuda sloop	Webb Chiles (US)	San Diego, Oct 18, 1974 (Cape Horn, Dec 12, 1975)	San Diego, Oct 1, 1976 (202 days)
Fastest (Yacht)	Great Britain II, 72-ft ketch	1st Mike Gill (13 crew) 2nd R. Mullender (15 crew)	Thames, Aug 31, 1975 via Sydney (change crews)	67 days 5 hrs 19 min 66 days 22 hrs 31 min 196.6 mpd

* Eduard Roditi, author of *Magellan of the Pacific*, advances the view that Magellan's slave Enrique was the first circumnavigator. He had been purchased in Malacca, but knew the Filipino dialect, Vizayan, when he reached the Philippines from the east in 1521. The first to circumnavigate in both directions was Tobias Furneaux (GB) as 2nd lieutenant aboard the *Dolphin* from/to Plymouth, England east to west *via* the Magellan Straits, 1766–68, and as captain of the *Adventure* from/to Plymouth west to east *via* Cape Horn.

MARINE CIRCUMNAVIGATION RECORDS (continued)

Category	Vessel & Size	Captain	Start / Route	Finish / Duration
Fastest (Clipper)	*James Baines* 266 ft	Capt. C. McDonald (GB) and crew		Melbourne to Liverpool (69 days) 1855
Fastest (Yacht) (miles per day)	*Great Britain II,* 72-ft ketch	Rob James and crew	Plymouth, Aug 27, 1977 *via* Cape Town, Auckland, Rio de Janeiro	March 24, 1978, 134 days, 12 hrs, 26,815 miles, 199.4 mpd
Fastest Solo Westabout *via* Cape Horn	*Mermaid III,* 28-ft sloop	Kenichi Horie (Japan) (b 1939)	Osaka, Japan, Aug 1, 1973	May 5, 1974 (275 days 13 hrs)
Fastest Ever (Yacht) *via* Cape Horn	*Awahnee II,* 53 ft	Bob Griffith (US) and 5 crew	Bluff, NZ, 1970 (eastward)	Bluff, NZ, 1971 (84 days)
Fastest Ever (Clipper)	*Red Jacket* 260 ft	Capt S. Reid (GB) and crew	Liverpool to Melbourne (58 days) 1854 From/to Lat 26° 25′ W	62 days 22 hrs, 1854
Earliest Non-stop Solo (Port-to-Port)	*Suhaili,* 32.4-ft Bermuda ketch	Robin Knox-Johnston (GB) (b 1939)	Falmouth, England, June 14, 1968	Apr 22, 1969 (312 days) Longest alone at sea

TRANSATLANTIC MARINE RECORDS (Compiled by Sq Ldr D. H. Clarke)

CATEGORY	CAPTAIN	VESSEL & SIZE	START	FINISH	DURATION	
Earliest Canoe	"Finn-Man" (Eskimo)	Kayak, 11 ft 10 in	Greenland	Humber, England	Time not known	1613
Earliest Crossing (2 men)	C. R. Webb + 1 crew (US)	*Charter Oak,* 43 ft	New York	Liverpool	35 days	1857
Earliest Trimaran	John Mikes + 2 crew (US)	*Non Pareil,* 25 ft	New York (June 4)	Southampton, England	51 days	1868
Earliest Solo Sailing	Alfred Johnson (US)	*Centennial,* 20 ft	Gloucester, Mass	Wales	46 days	1876
Earliest Woman Sailing (with US husband)	Mrs Joanna Crapo (Scot)	*New Bedford,* 20 ft	Chatham, Mass	Newlyn, England	51 days	1877
Earliest Single-handed Race	J. W. Lawlor (US) (winner)	*Sea Serpent,* 15 ft	Boston (June 21)	Coverack, England	45 days	1891
Earliest Rowing (partial)	Six British deserters	Ship's boat, c. 20 ft	St Helena (June 10)	Belmonte, Brazil	28 days (83 mpd)	1799
Earliest Rowing by 2 Men (Northern)	George Harbo and Frank Samuelson (US)	*Richard K. Fox* 18⅓ ft	New York (June 6)	Isles of Scilly (Aug 1)	55 days (56 mpd)	1896
Fastest Solo Sailing West-East	J. V. T. McDonald (GB)	*Inverarity,* 38 ft	Nova Scotia	Ireland	16 days	1922

TRANSATLANTIC MARINE RECORDS (continued)

CATEGORY	CAPTAIN	VESSEL & SIZE	START	FINISH	DURATION	DATE
Earliest Canoe (with sail)	F. Romer (Germany)	Deutscher Sport, 21½ ft	Las Palmas (June 2)	St Thomas, VI	58 days (47 mpd)	1928
Earliest Woman Solo-Sailing West-East	Gladys Gradely (US)	Lugger, 18 ft	Nova Scotia	Hope Cove, Devon, England	60 days	1903
Earliest Woman Solo-Sailing East-West	Mrs Ann Davison (GB)	Felicity Ann, 23 ft	Las Palmas, November 20, 1952	Portsmouth, Dominica	65 days	1952–53
Fastest Woman Solo	Clare Francis (GB)	Robertson's Golly 37½ ft	Plymouth, Eng	Newport, RI	29 days 1 hr 52 min	1976
Fastest Crossing Sailing (multihull)	Eric Tabarly (France) + 2 crew	Pen Duick IV, 67 ft	Tenerife, Canary Is	Martinique	251.4 mpd (10 days 12 hrs)	1968
Fastest Crossing Sailing (monohull) East-West	Wilhelm Hirte and crew (Ger)	Kriter II, 80 ft	Canary Is	Barbados	13 days 8 hrs	1977
Fastest Crossing Yacht West-East	Wilson Marshall (US) and crew	Atlantic, 185 ft	Sandy Hook, NJ	Lizard, Cornwall, Eng (3,054 miles)	12 days 4 hrs (fastest noon to noon 341 miles)	1905
Fastest Crossing Sailing West-East	A. Eldridge (US) and crew	Red Jacket (Clipper) 260 ft	Sandy Hook	Liverpool Bar	12 days, 277.7 mpd	1854
Fastest Solo East-West (Northern) (monohull)	Jean-Yves Terlain (France)	Vendredi 13, 128 ft	Plymouth, Eng (June 13)	Newport, RI (July 8)	21 days 5¼ hrs	1972
Fastest Solo East-West (Northern) (multihull)	Prof Alain Colas (France)	Pen Duick IV, 70-ft trimaran	Plymouth, Eng (June 17)	Newport, RI (July 7)	20 days 13¾ hrs	1972
Fastest Solo East-West (Southern) (monohull)	Sir Francis Chichester (GB)	Gipsy Moth V, 57 ft	Portuguese Guinea	Nicaragua	179.1 mpd (22.4 days)	1970
Fastest Crossing Sail East-West	W. S. Johnson (US) and crew	Andrew Jackson (Clipper) 220 ft	Liverpool	New York	15 days 202 mpd	1860
Fastest Solo Rowing East-West	Sidney Genders, 51 (GB)	Khaggavisana, 19¾ ft	Penzance, Eng	Miami, Fla via Antigua	37.3 mpd 162 days 18 hrs	1970
Earliest Solo Rowing East-West	John Fairfax (GB)	Britannia, 22 ft	Las Palmas, Canary Is (Jan 20)	Ft Lauderdale, Fla (July 19)	180 days	1969
Earliest Solo Rowing West-East	Tom McClean (Ireland)	Super Silver, 20 ft	St John's, Newfoundland (May 17)	Black Sod Bay, Ireland (July 27)	70.7 days	1969

TRANSATLANTIC MARINE RECORDS (continued)

CATEGORY	CAPTAIN	VESSEL & SIZE	START	FINISH	DURATION	DATE
Smallest East-West (Southern)	Hugo S. Vihlen (US)	*The April Fool,* 5 ft 11⅞ in	Casablanca (Mar 29)	Ft Lauderdale, Fla (June 21)	85 days	1968
Smallest West-East	Gerry Spiess, 39 (US)	*Yankee Girl,* 10 ft	Norfolk, Va (June 1)	Falmouth, England (July 24)	54 days (3,800 miles)	1979
Smallest (across 2 oceans)	John Riding (GB)	*Sjo Ag,* 12 ft	Plymouth *via* Panama	New Zealand, 1973	Lost in Tasman Sea	1964/1974
Youngest Solo Sailing	David Sandeman, 17½ years	*Sea Raider,* 35 ft	Jersey, CI	Newport, RI	43 days	1976
Oldest Solo Sailing	Jean Gau, 72 years	*Atom,* 30 ft	New York	France (wrecked N Africa)	50 days	1975

TRANSPACIFIC MARINE RECORDS

CATEGORY	CAPTAIN	VESSEL & SIZE	START	FINISH	DURATION	DATE
Fastest (Trans Pac)	Bill Lee (US)	*Merlin* 67-ft sloop	Los Angeles	Honolulu	8 days 11 hrs 1 min	1977
Fastest Yacht (Australia-Horn)	O. K. Pennendreft (Fr) + 13 crew	*Kriter II* 80 ft	Sydney	Cape Horn	21 days (275 mpd)	1975/6
Fastest Clipper (Australia-Horn)	Capt J. N. Forbes (GB) and crew	*Lightning* 244 ft	Melbourne	Cape Horn	19 days 1 hr (315 mpd)	1854
Fastest Solo Monohull (Australia-Horn)	C. Baranowski (Poland)	*Polonez* 45 ft 3 in	Hobart	Cape Horn	45 days (135 mpd)	1973
Fastest Solo Multihull (Australia-Horn)	Alain Colas (Fr)	*Pen Duick IV* trimaran 70 ft	Sydney	Cape Horn	37 days (160 mpd)	1973/4
Earliest Solo (Woman)	Sharon Sites Adams (US)	*Sea Sharp II,* 31 ft	Yokohama	San Diego	75 days (5,911 miles)	
Earliest Rowing	John Fairfax (GB)	*Britannia II* 35 ft	San Francisco Apr 26, 1971	Hayman Is, Australia, Apr 22, 1972	362 days	1969 1971 /1972
	Sylvia Cook (GB)					
Earliest Rowing Solo	Anders Svedlund (Sweden)	*Waka Moana* 24 ft	Chile (June 2)	Samoa	118 days	1974

N.B.—The earliest single-handed Pacific crossings were achieved East-West by Bernard Gilboy (US) in 1882 in the 18-ft double-ender *Pacific* and West-East by Fred Rebel (Latvia) in the 18-ft *Elaine* (from Australia), and Edward Miles (US) in the 36¾-ft *Sturdy II* (from Japan), both in 1932.

Deepest Salvage

The greatest depth at which salvage has been achieved is 16,500 ft by the bathyscaphe *Trieste II* (Lt Cdr Mel Bartels, USN) to attach cables to an "electronics package" on the sea bed 400 miles north of Hawaii May 20, 1972.

Project Jennifer by USS *Glomar Explorer* in June–July 1974, to recover a Golfclass USSR submarine 750 miles northwest of Hawaii cost $550 million but was not successful.

Salvage by Divers

The deepest salvage by flexible dress divers was on the wreck of the SS *Niagara,* sunk by a mine in 1940, 438 ft down off Bream Head, Whangarei, North Island, New Zealand. All but 6% of the $6,300,000 of gold in her holds was recovered in 7 weeks. The record recovery was from the White Star Liner *Laurentic,* which struck a mine in 132 ft of water off Malin Head, Donegal, Ireland, in 1917, with $14 million of gold ingots in her Second Class baggage room. By 1924, 3,186 of the 3,211 gold bricks had been recovered with immense difficulty.

Mining Depths

Man's deepest penetration into the ground is in the Western Deep Levels Mine at Carletonville, Transvaal, South Africa, where a record depth of 11,752 ft had been attained. The rock temperature at this depth is 131° F.

The one-month (31-day) record is 1,251 ft for sinking a standard shaft 26 ft in diameter at Buffelsfontein Mine, Transvaal, South Africa, March 1962.

MARRIAGE AND DIVORCE

Longest Engagement

The longest engagement on record is one of 67 years between Octavio Guillen, 82, and Adriana Martinez, 82. They finally took the plunge in June 1969, in Mexico City.

Most Divorces and Marriages

The greatest number of marriages accumulated in the monogamous world is 21 by the former minister of religion Mr Glynn de Moss Wolfe (US) (b 1908) who in 1979 married for the 21st time since 1931 his 19th wife, Guadalupe Reyes Chavez, age 20. His total number of children is, he says, 40. He has long kept two wedding dresses (different sizes) in his closet for ready use. He has additionally suffered 16 mothers-in-law.

Mrs Beverly Nina Avery, then aged 48, a barmaid from Los Angeles, set a monogamous world record in Oct 1957 by obtaining her 16th divorce, this one from Gabriel Avery, her 14th husband. She alleged outside the court that 5 of the 14 had broken her nose.

The most often-marrying millionaire, Thomas F. Manville (1894–1967), contracted his 13th marriage to his 11th wife, Christine Erdlen Popa (1940–71), in NYC on Jan 11, 1960, when aged 65. His shortest marriage (to his seventh wife) effectively lasted only 7½ hours. His fortune of $20 million came from asbestos, which he unfortunately could not take with him.

MOST MARRIED MAN: Glynn de Moss Wolfe (right) tells (unmarried) David Frost (on television) why he has been married 21 times to 19 different women. His latest marriage was at age 71 to a young lady of 20.

Oldest Bride and Bridegroom

Dyura Avramovich, reportedly aged 101, married Yula Zhivich, admitting to 95, in Belgrade, Yugoslavia, in Nov 1963.

Longest Marriage

The longest recorded marriage is one of 86 years between Sir Temulji Bhicaji Nariman and Lady Nariman from 1853 to 1940 resulting from a cousin marriage when both were five. Sir Temulji (b Sept 3, 1848) died, aged 91 years 11 months, in Aug 1940 in Bombay.

The only reliable instance of an 83rd anniversary celebrated by a couple marrying at normal ages is that between the late Edd (105) and Margaret (99) Hollen (US) who celebrated their 83rd anniversary on May 7, 1972. They were married in Kentucky on May 7, 1889.

The most recent example of a marriage with both partners over the age of 100 was that of John and Harriet Orton, aged 102 and 100 respectively, of Great Gidding, Cambridgeshire, England, who celebrated their 79th anniversary on July 9, 1979.

Most Married Couple

Jack V. and Edna Moran of Seattle, Wash have married each other 40 times since the original and only really necessary occasion on July 27, 1937 in Seaside, Ore. Subsequent ceremonies have included those at Banff, Canada (1952), Cairo, Egypt (1966) and Westminster Abbey, London (1975).

Mass Wedding Ceremony

The largest mass wedding ceremony was one of 1,800 couples officiated over by Sun Myung Moon of the Holy Spirit Association for the Unification of World Christianity in Seoul, South Korea, Feb 14, 1975. The response to the question "Will you swear to love your spouse forever?" is "Ye."

Most Expensive Wedding

The most expensive private wedding is reputed to be that of Maria Niarchos, 20, to Alix Chevassus, 36, at her father's estate in Normandy,

France on June 16, 1979. Guests consumed an estimated 12,000 bottles of champagne and red wine, the supply of caviar outweighed the demand in four football-field-sized tents. The cost is conservatively estimated at $500,000.

Slowest Divorce

In March 1980 a divorce was reported in the Los Angeles Superior Court, Calif, between Bernardine and Leopold Delper in which both parties were 88 years old.

STUNTS AND MISCELLANEOUS ENDEAVORS

Accordion Playing. Rick Teegarten of San Pablo, Calif played an accordion for 80 hours, Feb 27–March 1, 1980.

Apple Peeling. The longest single unbroken apple peel on record is 172 ft 4 in peeled by Kathy Wafler, 17, of Wolcott, NY, in 11 hours 30 min at the Long Ridge Mall, Rochester, NY, Oct 16, 1976. The apple weighed 20 oz.

Apple Picking. The greatest recorded performance is 341 US bushels picked in 8 hours by Geoffrey Cash at Batlow, NSW, Australia, Apr 3, 1977.

Baby Carriage Pushing. The greatest distance covered in 24 hours in pushing a perambulator is 345.25 miles by Runner's Factory of Los Gatos, Calif with an all-star team of 57 California runners June 23–24, 1979. A team of 10 students from Sir Joseph Banks and East Hills High Schools with an adult "baby" covered 241.3 miles, Nov 16–17, 1979 at Chipping Norton, NSW, Australia.

Balancing on One Foot. The longest recorded duration for balancing on one foot is 33 hours by Kumar Anandan of Colombo, Sri Lanka, May 15–17, 1980. The disengaged foot may not be rested on the standing foot nor may any sticks be used for support or balance, but 5-minute rest breaks are allowed after each hour.

Balloon Blowing. In inflating with sheer lung power a standard meteorological balloon to a diameter of 8 ft, Noel Batten of Brisbane, Australia set an inaugural mark of 6 hours 6 min (gross) with a Totex 350-gram balloon Apr 13, 1979. (This category supplants *Hot Water Bottle Bursting* in this book.)

Balloon Flights. The longest reported toy balloon flight is one of 9,000 miles from Atherton, Calif (released by Jane Dorst) on May 21, 1972 and found on June 10 at Pietermaritzburg, South Africa.

Balloon Release. The largest balloon release on record was one of 130,000 helium balloons at Baltimore Memorial Stadium Oct 10, 1976.

Ball Punching. Kumar Anandan (see *Balancing on One Foot*) punched a ball 136 hours 28 min, Dec 26, 1979–Jan 1, 1980.

APPLE PEELING: Champion Kathy Wafler shows (left) how she starts the peeling and (right) the unbroken peel of 172 ft 4 in, a record.

Band, One-Man. The greatest number of instruments played in a single tune is 75 in 2 min 11.2 sec by Rory Blackwell at the EMI Bingo and Social Club, Derry's Cross, Plymouth, Devon, England Sept 6, 1977.

Don Davis of Hollywood, Calif was the first one-man band able to play 4 melody and 2 percussion instruments simultaneously without electronics, in 1974. For a rendition of the 4th movement of Beethoven's Fifth Symphony, he utilizes an 8-prong pendular perpendicular piano pounder and a semi-circular chromatic radially operated centrifugally sliding left-handed glockenspiel.

Mik Vallintine of New Romney, Kent, England, played his one-man band (at least 3 instruments played simultaneously) for 42 hours 29 min, June 16–18, 1980, for charity at East Cliff Pavilion, Folkestone, Kent, England.

A professor of music at the University of Connecticut certified on Aug 11, 1978, that James Blain played 8 instruments (4 melodic and 4 percussion) simultaneously.

ONE-MAN BAND: Don Davis of Hollywood, Calif, demonstrates his ability to play 4 melody and 2 percussion instruments at the same time, using a piano pounder and a glockenspiel.

BATON TWIRLERS: The Havant Hurricanes of England twirled a full 55 hours without a drop for a marathon record in Sept 1979.

Band Marathons. The longest recorded "blow-in" is 100 hours 2 min by the Du Val Senior High School band, Lanham, Md, directed by Lon Scarci, May 13–17, 1977.

Band, Pop. The playing duration record for a 4-man pop group is 144 hours by "Rocking Ricky and the Velvet Collars" at The Talardy Hotel, St Asaph, Wales Nov 12–18, 1976. The group at no time sank below a trio.

Barrel Jumping. The greatest reported distance achieved by a barrel-jumper on ice skates is 32 ft (over 13 barrels) by T. Karl Milne (b 1900) at Albany, NY Jan 13, 1930.

Barrel Rolling. The record for rolling a full 43.2-gallon metal beer barrel over a measured mile is 8 min 15 sec by a team of 6 from Tinwald Rugby Club, Ashburton, New Zealand, March 3, 1980.

Bathtub Racing. The record for the annual international 36-mile Nanaimo-to-Vancouver, British Columbia, bathtub race is 1 hour 29 min 40 sec by Gary Deathbridge, 25 (Australia) July 30, 1978. Tubs are limited to 75 in and 6-hp motors. The greatest distance for paddling a hand-propelled bathtub in 24 hours is 55 miles 425 yd by a team of 25 from Worcester Canoe Club, England Sept 28–29, 1979.

Baton Twirling. The Havant Hurricanes of Hayling Island, Hampshire, England twirled for 55 hours Apr 8–10, 1980.

Beard of Bees. The heaviest recorded "beard" of bees was an *estimated* 20,000 which swarmed on the bare chest and throat of Howard Davis of Bridgewater, Somerset, England in May 1952. He suffered not a single sting. A 17½-in deep beard of about 17,500 bees swarmed around a queen bee off the chin and down to the waist of Don Cooke of Ohio, on a Guinness Spectacular TV show, filmed in Los Angeles Apr 6, 1979. It was the 92nd time Cooke had performed this feat.

Bedmaking. The record time set under the rigorous rules of the Australian Bedmaking Championships is 28.2 sec by Wendy Wall, 34, of Sydney, NSW, Australia Nov 30, 1978.

Bed of Nails. The duration record for non-stop lying on a bed of nails (sharp 6-in nails 2 in apart) is 74 hours by Barry Walls at the Williams Furniture Futurestore, Birmingham, England Apr 30–May 3, 1980.

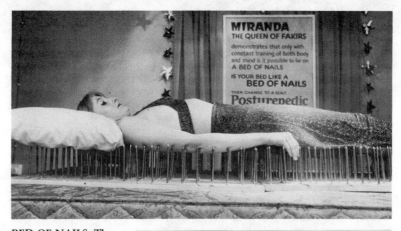

BED OF NAILS: The woman sleeping above holds the female endurance record of 30 hours without a rest! She is known as Miranda, Queen of the Fakirs. BEES (right): Don Cooke of Ohio is sporting a 17½-in-long beard with about 17,500 buzzing (and some biting) bees. It was his 92nd performance and was a record at the time.

Much longer durations are claimed by uninvigilated *fakirs*—the most extreme case being *Silki* who claimed 111 days in São Paulo, Brazil, ending on Aug 24, 1969.

The female endurance record is 30 hours non-stop set by Geraldine Williams (Miranda, Queen of the Fakirs) of Welwyn Garden City, Hertfordshire, England March 18–19, 1977.

Note that the category of "Iron Maiden" (lying between 2 beds of nails with added weight on top) has been retired with the ultimate record being set at 1642½ lb endured by Komar (Vernon E. Craig) of Wooster, Ohio at Old Chicago Towne March 6, 1977. No further claims for publication will be entertained or published.

Bed Pushing. The longest recorded push of a normally stationary object is 3,233 miles 1,150 yd in the case of a wheeled hospital bed by a team of 9, all employees of Bruntsfield Bedding Centre, Edinburgh, Scotland June 21–July 26, 1979.

Bed Racing. The record time for the annual Knaresborough **Bed Race** (established 1966) in North Yorkshire, England is 14 min 7.0 sec for the 1.96-mile course crossing the River Nidd, by the ICI Fibres Flying Fiasco team June 10, 1978.

Bell Ringing. The longest recorded handbell ringing recital has been one of 45 hours 5 min by the Wesley Bell Choir of the First United Methodist Church, Ypsilanti, Mich March 7–9, 1980.

Best Best Man. The world's champion "best man" is Wally Gant, a bachelor fishmonger from Wakefield, W Yorkshire, England, who officiated for the 50th time since 1931 in Dec 1964.

Bicycle Mounting. The most on a single cycle is 13, riding simultaneously, by the cyclist troupe from the Chinese Acrobatic Theatre of Shanghai which performs this trick regularly, but sometimes with only 12. (For other circus stunt records see page 450.)

Billiard Table Jumping. Joe Darby (1861–1937) cleared a 12-ft billiard table lengthwise, taking off from a running start, using only a 4-in-high solid wooden block, at Wolverhampton, England, Feb 5, 1892.

Bomb Defusing. The highest reported number of unexploded bombs defused by any individual is 8,000 by Werner Stephan in W Berlin, Germany, in the 12 years from 1945 to 1957. He was killed by a small grenade on the Grünewald blasting site on Aug 17, 1957.

Boomerang Throwing. The earliest mention of a word similar to "boomerang" is "wo-mur-rang" in Collins *Account N.S. Wales Vocabulary,* published in 1798. The earliest certain Australian account of a returning boomerang (term established in 1827) was in 1831 by Major (later Sir) Thomas Mitchell. Curved throwing sticks for hunting wild fowl were found in the tomb of Tutankhamen, dating from the mid-14th century BC.

World championships and codified rules were not established until 1970. Jeff Lewry won the world title in 1970-71-72-73, and the Australian title in 1974. The Boomerang Association of Australia's official record for distance reached before the boomerang returns is 289 ft 4 in (orbital path 885 ft) by Leo Meier (Switzerland) at Darlington Point, NSW, Australia, on Nov 6, 1976. The longest out-and-return on record is one of 370 ft by Al Gerhards at Old Westbury, LI, NY on Oct 20, 1979.

Brick Carrying. The record for carrying a brick (8 lb 15 oz) in a nominated ungloved hand with the arm extended in an uncradled downward pincer grip is 45 miles by David and Kym Barger of Lamar, Mo on May 21, 1977.

The feminine record of 19.2 miles was set by Cynthia Ann Smolko of Denville, NJ, on May 14, 1977, using a 9-lb-12-oz brick.

Brick Throwing. The greatest reported distance for throwing a standard 5 lb building brick is 146 ft 1 in by Geoffrey Capes at Braybrook School, Cambridgeshire, England, on July 19, 1978.

Bubble Gum Blowing. The largest bubble blown measured 19¼ in in diameter, created by Mrs Susan Montgomery Williams of Fresno, Calif,

BUBBLE GUM BLOWING (left): This doesn't even come close to the record 19¼-in bubble that Susan Montgomery Williams blew to win a Bubble-Yum contest in 1979, but it's the best she can do for the camera. CLAPPING (right): Sustaining an average of 140 claps per min for 42 hours 6 min is the record Pubudu Senanayaka of Sri Lanka set in 1980.

in a contest held in Jacksonville, Fla in 1979. Measurement was on a horizontal rather than a vertical basis, to eliminate any elongation due to gravity.

Camping Out. Two brothers Sven and Per and a sister Kari Heistad of Lebanon, NH have never slept indoors since March 1974. The coldest they have experienced is −35° F, which to them is a "three-bag night." Also remarkably the family has no television.

Canal Jumping. Douwe Bult (Netherlands) leapt 43 ft 8¾ in across water by swinging on a pole near Tokyo, Japan to win the event on the Japanese TV show "Challenge the Guinness '80."

Card Throwing. Kevin St Onge threw a standard playing card 185 ft 1 in on the Henry Ford Community College campus, Dearborn, Mich, June 12, 1979.

Catapulting. The greatest recorded distance for a catapult shot is 1,362 ft by James F. Pfotenhauer, using a patented 16½-ft "Monarch IV Supershot" and a 53-caliber lead shot on Ski Hill, Escanaba, Mich, on Sept 10, 1977.

Champagne Fountain. The tallest successfully filled column of champagne glasses is one 20 high, filled from the top by Carl Groves, Philip Keir, Keith Pepper and Bruce Ford at Foxey's Disco, Melbourne, Australia Jan 26, 1980.

Clapping. The duration record for continuous clapping (sustaining an average 140 claps per min audible at 100 yd) is 42 hours 6 min by Pubudu Senanayaka of Ananda College, Colombo, Sri Lanka Jan 18–19, 1980.

CIRCUS RECORDS

The following represent the greatest feats performed, either for the first time or, if marked with an asterisk, uniquely. A "mechanic" is a safety harness.

Category	Feat	Performer	Location	Year
Flying Trapeze	Earliest Act	Jules Leotard (France)	Circus Napoleon, Paris	1859
	Double back somersault	Eddie Silbon	Paris Hippodrome	1879
	Triple back somersault (female)	Lena Jordan (Latvia) to Lew Jordan (US)	Sydney, Australia	1897
	Triple back somersault (male)	Ernest Clarke to Charles Clarke	Publiones Circus, Cuba	1909
	Triple and a half back somersault	Tony Steel to Lee Strath Marilees	Durango, Mexico	1962
	Quadruple back somersault (in practice)	*Ernest Clarke to Charles Clarke	Orrin Bros Circus, Mexico City	1915
	Double Pass with back somersault	Buster and Anne Melzora with Paul Garee	Latrobe, Pa	1935
	Triple back somersault with 1½ twists	Terry Cavarette Lemus (b March 6, 1953)	Circus Circus, Las Vegas	1969
	Head to head stand on swinging bar	*Ed and Ira Millette (né Wolf)	Europe and US	1910–20
	Downward circles or "muscle grinding"	306 by Denise La Grassa (US)	Circus World Museum, Wis	1976
	Highest trapeze act		Calf-hang from helicopter	1978
	Single heel hang on swinging bar	Ryan Kelly (US)	Australia	1977
Horseback	Running leaps on and off	Angela Revelle (Angelique)	New York City	1915
	Three-high column without "mechanic"	*26 by "Poodles" Hanneford	Nouveau Cirque, Paris	1908
	Double back somersault mounted	*Willy, Beby and Rene Fredianis	Various	c. 1905
	Double back somersault from a 2-high to a trailing horse with "mechanic"	(John or Charles) Frederick Clarke		
		Aleksandr Sergey	Moscow Circus	1956
Fixed Bars	Triple flyaway to ground (male)	Phil Shevette, Andres Atayde	Woods Gymnasium, NYC-European tours	1925–27
	Triple flyaway to ground (female)	Phil Shevette	Folies Bergère, Paris	1896
Giant Springboard	Running forward triple back somersault	Loretto Twins, Ora and Pauline	Los Angeles	1914
Human Juggling	Back somersault feet to feet, a Risley	John Cornish Worland (1855–1933) of the US	St Louis, Mo	1874
Teeter Board	Quadruple back somersault to a chair	Richard Risley Carlisle (1814–74) and son	Theatre Royal, Edinburgh	1844
		Sylvester Mezzetti (voltigeur) to Butch Mezzetti (catcher)	Kehlavi Troupe at NY Hippodrome	1915–17
Aerialist	Five-high column	The Yacopis (Argentina)	Ringling Bros, Barnum & Bailey	1941
	Six-man-high perch pyramid	Emilia Ivanova (Bulgaria)	Inglewood, Calif	1976
Wire-Juggling	One-arm swings or planges (no net)	305 by Janet May Klemke (US)	Medina Shrine Circus, Chicago	1938
Low Wire (7 ft)	16 hoops (hands and feet)	Ala Naito (Japan) (female)	Madison Sq Garden, NYC	1937
	Feet to feet forward somersault	Con Colleano	Empire Theatre, Johannesburg	1923
High Wire (30–40 ft)	Four-high column (with mechanic)	Ala Naito (Japan) (female)	Madison Sq Garden, NYC	1937
	Three-layer, 7-man pyramid	*The Solokhin Brothers (USSR)	Moscow Circus	1962
Ground Acrobatics	Stationary double back somersault	Great Wallendas (Germany)	US	1961
Trampoline	Septuple twisting back somersault	François Gouleau (France)	St Petersburg, Fla	1905
	5 twisting back to shoulders	Marco Canestrelli (US)	Madison Sq Garden, NYC	1979
Flexible Pole	Double full-twisting somersault onto a 2-inch-diameter pole	Marco to Belmonte Canestrelli	Madison Sq Garden, NYC	1979
		The Robertos, Roberto Tabak (age 11)	Sarasota, Fla	1977
Human Pyramid (or Tuckle)	12 (3 high) (1,700 lb) supported by a single understander	Tahar Davis of the Hassani Troupe	Birmingham, Eng	1979

CIRCUS ACTS: Terry Lemus (top left) performs triple back somersault with 1½ twists. Solokhin Bros (top right) and Roberto Bros (below, right) show how they toss a somersaulter aloft and down on a 2-in-diameter pole. Tahar Davis (bottom left, hidden from camera) is the man who surpasseth all "understanders," by supporting 12 members of his troupe in a Human Pyramid.

BALANCING ACTS: The Chinese Acrobatic Theatre in Shanghai features 12 on a bike (above) and sometimes 13. The coin tower (right) with 130 coins perched on top of the edge of a silver dollar is the work of Alex Chervinsky who has been practicing coin balancing for 26 years.

Club Swinging. Bill Franks set a world record of 17,280 revolutions (4.8 per sec) in 60 min at Webb's Gymnasium, Newcastle, NSW, Australia Aug 2, 1934. M. Dobrilla swung continuously for 144 hours at Cobar, NSW, Australia, finishing on Sept 15, 1913.

Coal Bag Carrying. The greatest non-stop bag-carrying feat, carrying 1 cwt (112 lb) of household coal in an open bag, is 22.2 miles by Brian Newton, 29, from Leicester to Rearsby, England and back in 6 hours 7 min on Nov 12, 1976.

Coal Shoveling. The record for filling a 1,120-lb hopper with stove-size pieces of coal is 37 sec by Robert Taylor of Dobson, New Zealand Jan 5, 1980.

Coin Balancing. The greatest recorded feat of coin balancing is the stacking of 130 coins on top of a silver US dollar on edge by Alex Chervinsky of Lock Haven, Pa in 1974, after 26 years' practice.

Contest Winnings. The largest recorded individual prize won was $307,500 by Herbert J. Idle, 55, of Chicago in an encyclopedia contest run by Unicorn Press, Inc Aug 20, 1953.

Cow Chip Tossing. The record distance for throwing a dried cow chip depends on whether the projectile may or may not be "molded into a spherical shape." Purists do not permit "sphericalization." The greatest distance achieved under the "non-alteration" rule (established in 1970) is 219 ft 6 in by Robert D. Fleming of Taylorville, Ill on Aug 26, 1978.

Crawling. The longest continuous voluntary crawl (progression with one or the other knee in unbroken contact with the ground) on record is 14 miles by Kevin Tyerman at Hurlstone Agricultural High School, Glenfield, NSW, Australia, Nov 16, 1976.

The Baptist lay preacher Hans Mullikin, 39, arrived at the White House in Washington, DC on Nov 23, 1978, having crawled all but 8 of the 1,600 miles from Marshall, Tex.

Cucumber Slicing. Norman Johnson of the Blackpool College of Art and Technology, England sliced 12 in of a 1½-in-diameter cucumber at 20 slices to the inch (total 240 slices) in 24.2 sec on Sept 28, 1973.

Dancing. Marathon dancing must be distinguished from dancing mania, which is a pathological condition. The worst outbreak of dancing mania was at Aachen, Germany in July 1374, when hordes of men and women broke into a frenzied dance in the streets which lasted for hours till injury or complete exhaustion ensued.

The most severe marathon dance (staged as a public spectacle in the US) was one lasting 4,152½ hours (24 weeks 5 days). This was completed by Tony Alteriri and Vera Mikus (now Mrs Oglesby of Springfield, Pa) at Motor Square Garden, Pittsburgh, June 6–Nov 30, 1932. The rest allowance was progressively cut from 15 min per hour to 10, 7, 6, 5 and in

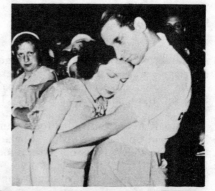

DANCE MARATHON (right): After almost 25 weeks contesting to win a prize of $1,000 in 1932, this is how Tony Alteriri and Vera Mikus looked.

LIMBO DANCING (below): Marlene Raymond, 15, slithered under a flaming bar 6⅛ in off the floor in 1973, without letting any part of her anatomy except her feet touch the floor.

the final weeks to only 3 min per hour until this Marathon Dance "Classic" was finally stopped by the authorities. The prize of $1,000 was equivalent to 24 cents per hour.

Largest Dance. The largest dance ever staged was that put on by the Houston Livestock Show at the Astro Hall, Houston, Tex Feb 8, 1969. The attendance was 16,500, with 4,000 turned away.

Dancing, Ballet. In the *entrechat* (a vertical spring from the fifth position with the legs extended criss-crossing at the lower calf), the starting and finishing position each count as one, such that in the *entrechat douze* there are *five* crossings and uncrossings. This was performed by Wayne Sleep for the BBC-TV *Record Breakers* program on Jan 7, 1973. He was in the air for 0.71 of a second.

The greatest number of spins called for in classical ballet choreography is the 32 *fouettés rond de jambe en tournant* in "Swan Lake" by Pyotr Ilyich Chaykovskiy (Tchaikovsky) (1840–93). Rowena Jackson (later Chatfield, b Invercargill, New Zealand 1925) achieved 121 such turns at her class in Melbourne, Australia in 1940.

The greatest recorded number of curtain calls ever received by ballet dancers is 89 by Dame Margaret Evelyn Arias, *née* Hookham (b Reigate, Surrey, England May 18, 1919), *alias* Margot Fonteyn, and Rudolf Hametovich Nureyev (born in a train near Irkutsk, USSR March 17, 1938), after a performance of "Swan Lake" at the Vienna Staatsoper, Austria in Oct 1964.

The largest number of ballet dancers used in a production has been 2,000 in the London Coster Ballet of 1962, directed by Lillian Romley at the Royal Albert Hall, London.

Dancing, Ballroom. The individual continuous record is 106 hours 5 min 10 sec by Carlos Sandrini in Buenos Aires, Argentina, in Sept 1955. Three girls worked shifts as his partner.

The most successful professional ballroom dancing champions have been Bill Irvine and Bobbie Irvine of London who won 13 world titles, 1960–72.

The oldest competitive ballroom dancer is Albert J. Sylvester (b Nov 24, 1889) of Corsham, Wiltshire, England, who on Apr 26, 1977, won the topmost amateur Alex Moore award for a 10-dance test with his partner, Paula Smith, in Bath, England. By 1979 he had won nearly 50 medals and trophies since he began dancing in 1974.

Dancing, Belly and Charleston. The longest recorded belly dance was one of 100 hours by Sabra Starr of Lansdowne, Pa at Teplitzki's Hotel, Atlantic City, NJ July 4–8, 1977. The Charleston duration record is 110 hours 58 min by the same Sabra Starr Jan 15–20, 1979.

Dancing, Conga. The longest recorded conga line was a "snake" of 8,128 people in Sidmouth, Devon, England Aug 25, 1978.

Dancing, Disco (including Jive, Twist and Go-Go). The longest recorded disco dancing marathon is one of 342 hours by George Thompson in Des Moines, Iowa, March 6–20, 1980.

DIVING SPECIALTIES: Acapulco divers fling themselves from a rock 118 ft high. Henri La Mothe (right), 76, dived from 28 ft up into 12⅜ in of water.

Dancing, Flamenco. The fastest flamenco dancer ever measured is Solero de Jerez, aged 17, who, in Brisbane, Australia in Sept 1967, in an electrifying routine attained 16 heel taps per sec or a rate of 1,000 per min.

Dancing, High Kicking. The record for high kicks is 8,491 in 4 hours 22 min by Doris Rogers, 26, at the Broom and Stone, Scarboro, Ont, Canada Feb 16, 1980.

Dancing, Limbo. The lowest height for a flaming bar under which a limbo dancer has passed is 6⅛ in off the floor at Port of Spain Pavilion, Toronto, on June 24, 1973, by Marlene Raymond, 15.
Strictly no part of the body other than the sole or side of the foot should touch the ground, though brushing the shoulder blade does not in practice usually result in disqualification.

Dancing, Tap. The fastest *rate* ever measured for any tap dancer has been 1,440 taps per min (24 per sec) by Roy Castle on the BBC-TV *Record Breakers* program on Jan 14, 1973. The greatest assemblage of tap dancers ever in a single routine is 1,801 organized by Beth Obermeyer for the TV show "Twin Cities Today" in Minneapolis Oct 15, 1979.

Dance Band. The most protracted session is one of 321 hours (13 days 9 hours) by the Black Brothers of Bonn, W Germany ending on Feb 2, 1968. Never less than a quartet were in action during the marathon.

Diving, Highest Shallow. Henri La Mothe (b 1904) set a record by diving 28 ft into 12⅜ inches of water in a child's wading pool on Apr 7, 1979 in Northridge, Calif for a Guinness TV program.

Diving, High. The highest regularly performed dive is that of professional divers from La Quebrada ("the break in the rocks") at Acapulco, Mexico, a height of 118 ft. The leader of the 27 divers in the exclusive Club de Clavadistas is Raul Garcia (b 1928) with more than 35,000 dives. The base rocks are 21 ft out from the takeoff, necessitating a leap 27 ft out. The water is only 12 ft deep.

Dana Kunze (US) dived 160 ft from a crane jib in Tokyo, Japan for Fuji TV on Sept 30, 1979.

On May 8, 1885, Sarah Ann Henley, aged 24, jumped from the Clifton Suspension Bridge across the Avon, England. Her 250-ft fall was slightly cushioned by her voluminous dress and petticoat acting as a parachute. She landed, bruised and bedraggled, in the mud on the Gloucestershire bank and was carried to a hospital by four policemen.

On Feb 11, 1968, Jeffrey Kramer, 24, leaped off the George Washington Bridge 250 ft above the Hudson River, NYC and survived. Of the 696 (to Jan 1, 1980) identified people who have made 240-ft suicide dives from the Golden Gate Bridge, San Francisco since 1937 only 12 survived, and the only one who managed to swim ashore unaided was Todd Sherratt, 17.

On July 10, 1921, a stuntman named William H. Bailey leapt from a seaplane into the Ohio River at Louisville. The alleged altitude was 310 ft.

Samuel Scott (US) is reputed to have made a dive of 497 ft at Pattison Falls (now Manitou Falls) Wis in 1840, but this would have entailed an entry speed of 86 mph. The actual height was probably 165 ft. Col Harry A. Froboess (Switzerland) jumped 360 ft into the Bodensee from the airship *Graf Hindenburg* June 22, 1936.

The greatest height reported for a dive into a flaming tank is 100 ft into 7½ ft of water by Bill McGuire, 48, at the Holiday Inn in Chicago City Center, Mich Aug 14, 1975.

Kitty O'Neil dived about 180 ft from a helicopter over Northridge, Calif onto an air cushion 30 × 60 ft on Sept 9, 1979 for a TV filmed stunt.

Domino Tumbling. The greatest number of dominoes set up single-handed and toppled in a row is 169,713 by Michael Cairney, 23, of London, England at the Mid-Hudson Civic Center, Poughkeepsie, NY June 9, 1979 under the auspices of the National Hemophilia Foundation. The dominoes, stretching 4.3 miles, fell at 2¼ mph, after taking Cairney 13 days to set up.

The record for a team (maximum of 4) setting up is 229,000 which fell consecutively but in groups in 1 min 46 sec in July 1979 in Auckland, New Zealand.

Drumming. The duration drumming record is 720 hours by Clifford Marshall Van Buren of Ridgefield, Conn Dec 26, 1977–Jan 25, 1978.

Ducks and Drakes. The best accepted ducks and drakes (stone-skipping) record is 24 skips (10 plinkers and 14 pitty-pats) by Warren Klope, 20, of Troy, Mich with 14 thin, flat, 4-in limestones, at the annual Mackinac Island, Mich stone-skipping tournament July 5, 1975. This was equaled by John S. Kolar of Birmingham, Mich and Glenn Loy Jr of Flint, Mich on July 4, 1977.

DOMINO TUMBLING: Michael Cairney (above), a 23-year-old civil engineer from London, set off a 169,713-domino topple in which he had the tiles walk up a 7-ft ramp, dial a phone and touch off a microswitch which took a Polaroid picture.

DUCKS AND DRAKES, also known as stone-skipping, is an event at which Warren Klope (left) excels. He holds the record for 10 plinkers and 14 pitty-pats, 24 skips in all.

Egg Dropping. The greatest height from which fresh eggs have been dropped to earth and landed intact is 600 ft from a helicopter by David S. Donoghue and John Cartwright Feb 8, 1974.

Egg Hunt. The greatest egg hunt on record involved 20,160 hard-boiled eggs hidden in the meadow of Stone Mt Park, Ga for a hunt on March 26, 1980 by 3,000 children aged 3 to 9.

Egg Shelling. Two kitchen hands, Harold Witcomb and Gerald Harding, shelled 1,050 dozen eggs in a 7¼-hour shift at Bowyers, Trowbridge, Wiltshire, England Apr 23, 1971. Both are blind.

Egg and Spoon Racing. Chris Riggio of San Francisco completed a 28½-mile fresh egg and dessert spoon marathon in 4 hours 34 min Oct 7, 1979.

Egg Throwing. The longest recorded distance for throwing a fresh hen's egg and catching it without breaking is 350 ft on their 58th try by William Cole and Jonathan Heller in Central Park, NYC March 17, 1979.

Escapology. The most renowned of all escape artists has been Ehrich Weiss, *alias* Harry Houdini (1874–1926), who pioneered underwater escapes from locked, roped and weighted containers while handcuffed and shackled with irons.

One of the major manufacturers of straitjackets acknowledges that an escapologist "skilled in the art of bone and muscle manipulation" could escape from a standard jacket in seconds. The fastest acknowledged claim is 1.68 seconds.

Records claimed for the highest escape from a helicopter or free-fall while handcuffed or hanging suspended upside down from a burning rope have been discontinued.

Feminine Beauty. Female pulchritude, being qualitative rather than quantitative, does not lend itself to records. It has been suggested that if the face of Helen of Troy (*c.* 1200 BC) was capable of launching 1,000 ships, then a unit of beauty sufficient to launch one ship should be called a millihelen.

The pioneer beauty contest was staged at Atlantic City, NJ in 1921, and was won by a blue-eyed blonde with a 30-in bust.

Ferris Wheel Riding. The endurance record for big wheel riding is 37 days by Rena Clark and Jeff Block at Frontier Village Amusement Park, San Jose, Calif July 1–Aug 7, 1978.

Fire Pumping. The greatest gallonage stirrup-pumped by a team of 8 in an 80-hour period is 8,995 US gallons by the Witney Brigade, Oxfordshire, England Aug 26–30, 1977.

Flute Marathon. The longest recorded time is 48 hours by flautist Joe Silmon on HMS *Grampus* in Gosport, Hampshire, England Feb 19–20, 1977.

Gladiatorial Combat. Emperor Trajan of Rome (98–117 AD) staged a display involving 4,941 pairs of gladiators over 117 days. Publius Ostorius, a freedman, survived 51 combats in Pompeii.

Gold Panning. The fastest time recorded for "panning" 8 planted gold nuggets with a 10-in-diameter pan is 13.4 sec by Dick Huber of Ahwahnee, Calif in the 20th World Gold Panning Championship at Tropico Gold Mine, Rosamond, Calif March 2, 1980. The record for women is 15.27 sec by Mrs. Carolyn Box, also of Ahwahnee at the 18th Championship March 4–5, 1978.

Golf Ball Balancing. Lang Martin of Charlotte, NC succeeded on Feb 9, 1980 in balancing 7 new golf balls vertically without using any adhesive, beating his own record of 6 in 1977.

Grape Catching. The longest recorded distance for catching a thrown grape in the mouth is 270 ft 4 in by Paul Tavilla of Arlington, Mass Aug 9, 1979. The grape thrower was Michael Weir.

HAND-TO-HAND BALANCING: From 1908 to 1917, Harry Berry and Nelson Soule (above) performed this act jumping from a 10-ft-tower onto a trampoline for takeoff. FOOT JUGGLING: Chester Cable (left) balances a 130-lb table on his feet, then twirls it side over side as many as 30 times in 1 min without stopping, using only his legs.

Grave Digging. It is recorded that Johann Heinrich Karl Thieme, sexton of Aldenburg, Germany dug 23,311 graves during a 50-year career. In 1826, his understudy dug *his* grave.

Ground Breaking. The highest number of participants in a ground-breaking ceremony is 5,714 for the Owens-Illinois headquarters building at SeaGate, Toledo, Ohio, May 22, 1979.

Guitar Playing. The longest recorded solo guitar-playing marathon is one of 200 hours 2 min by David Hathaway in Marion, Ind July 20–28, 1978.

Hairdressing. Gerry Stupple of Dover, Kent, England cut, set and styled hair continuously for 341 hours 58 min March 5–19, 1979.

Hair Splitting. The greatest reported achievement in hair splitting has been that of the former champion cyclist and craftsman Alfred West (b London, Apr 14, 1901) who succeeded in splitting a human hair 17 times into 18 parts on 8 occasions. Examples of his work are on permanent display in several Guinness World Records Museums.

Handshaking. The record for handshaking was set by President Theodore Roosevelt (1858–1919), who shook hands with 8,513 people at a New Year's Day White House presentation in Washington, DC Jan 1,

1907. Mayor Joseph Lazarow shook hands with 11,030 people on the Boardwalk, Atlantic City, NJ in 11 hours 5 min on July 3, 1977. Outside public life this record has become meaningless because aspirants either shake hands with anyone passing by or else shake the same hands repetitively.

Hand-to-Hand Balancing. The longest horizontal dive achieved in any hand-to-hand balancing act is 22 ft by Harry Berry (top mounter) and the late Nelson Soule (understander) of the Bell-Thazer Brothers from Kentucky, who played at state fairs and in vaudeville 1908–17. Berry used a 10-ft tower and trampoline for impetus. (For other circus stunt records, see page 450.)

Handwriting. The longest recorded handwritten letter-writing marathon was one of 505 hours and more than 3,998 letters and their envelopes by Raymond L. Cantwell of Oxford, England (trying to raise money for the Radcliffe Infirmary), Aug 25–Sept 16, 1978.

Hiking. The longest recorded hike is one of 18,500 miles through 14 countries from Singapore to London by David Kwan, aged 22, which occupied 81 weeks from May 4, 1957, or an average of 32 miles a day.

Hitchhiking. The title of world champion hitchhiker is claimed by Devon Smith who from 1947 to 1971 thumbed lifts totaling 291,000 miles.

Hoop Rolling. In 1968 it was reported that Zolilio Diaz (Spain) had rolled a hoop 600 miles from Mieres to Madrid and back in 18 days.

Hopscotch. The longest recorded hopscotch marathon is one of 70 hours by Carlton Palmer and Richard Jacobs of 1st Lion Farm Scout Pack, Smethwick, South Midlands, England Oct 24–27, 1979.

Hot Water Bottle Bursting. Contests involving the bursting of hot water bottles by sheer lung power are regarded as medically most inadvisable, and the category has been discontinued. (See *Balloon Blowing*.)

House of Cards. The greatest number of stories achieved in building free-standing houses of cards without creasing the cards or using any adhesives is 61 in the case of a tower using 3,650 cards by James Warnock at Cantley, Quebec, Canada, on Sept 8, 1978. The height was 11 ft 7 in.

Hula Hooping. The highest claim for sustaining gyrating hoops between shoulders and hips is 63 by Peter Hernandez at the "Olmec Olympics," Austin, Tex, Apr 1, 1979. Three complete gyrations are mandatory. The longest recorded marathon for a single hoop is 54 hours by Kym Coberly of Denton, Tex, Oct 7–9, 1978.

Human Cannonball. The record distance for firing a human from a cannon is 175 ft in the case of Emanuel Zacchini in the Ringling Bros and Barnum & Bailey Circus, in 1940. His muzzle velocity was estimated at 54 mph. On his retirement the management was fortunate in finding that his daughter, Florinda, was of the same caliber.

An experiment on Yorkshire TV in England on Aug 17, 1978, showed that when Sue Evans, 17, was fired from a cannon, she was ⅜ in shorter in height on landing.

In the Halifax explosion of Dec 6, 1917 (see *Worst Accidents*), A. B. William Becker (d 1969) was blown some 1,600 yd and found, still breathing, in a tree.

Human Chair (Unsupported Circle). The highest number recorded of people who have demonstrated the physical paradox of all being seated

HUMAN CANNON-BALLS: Emanuel Zacchini and his daughter Florinda (inset), being of the same caliber, were regularly shot from a cannon 175 ft across the arena in the 1930's and 1940's for the Ringling Bros Barnum & Bailey Circus.

without a chair is an unsupported circle of 5,147 (who held for 2 min 17 sec) by Girl Guides at State Jamboree in Sydney, Australia Oct 8, 1977.

Human Fly. The greatest climb achieved on the vertical face of a building occurred on May 26, 1977, when George Willig, 27, scaled the outside of the World Trade Center, NYC. He climbed 1,350 ft up in 3½ hours at the rate of 6.4 ft per min. He evaded police attempting to stop him as he climbed, but on descending by elevator from the 110th floor, he was led to a waiting police car, charged with criminal trespass and reckless endangerment. He was fined $1.10, one cent for each story he climbed.

The name of the masked "human fly" who rode at 240 mph atop a DC-8 jetliner in Apr 1977 has not been disclosed. It is, however, believed unlikely that he is a member of the jet set.

Joke Telling. Bob Carroll cracked jokes unremittingly for 24 hours 5 min at the Castillian Lounge, Clifton Park, NY Nov 19–20, 1979.

The duo duration record is 52 hours by Wayne Malton and Mike Hamilton at the Howard Johnson Motor Hotel, Toronto Airport, Canada, Nov 13–16, 1975.

Juggling. The only juggler in history able to juggle—as opposed to "shower"—10 balls or 8 plates was the Italian Enrico Rastelli, who was born in Samara, Russia, Dec 19, 1896, and died in Bergamo, Italy, on Dec 13, 1931.

Karate Chop. *Note: Claims for breaking bricks and wooden blocks are unsatisfactory because of the lack of any agreed standards of friability and the spacing of fulcrums upon which comparisons can be made.* Karatekas have been measured to exert a force of 3,000 newtons (675 lb of force) and can develop a downward chopping speed of 32.2 mph.

Kissing. The most prolonged osculatory marathon in cinematic history is one of 185 sec by Regis Toomey and Jane Wyman in *You're In the Army Now,* released in 1940.

In a Valentine's Day "Big Kiss-Off" for charity, Debbie Luray and Jim Schuyler kissed for 5 days 12 hours at the Ocean Mall, Singer Island, Fla Feb 14–19, 1980.

The most protracted kiss underwater was one of 2 min 18 sec by Toshiaki Shirai and Yukiko Nagata on Fuji TV in Tokyo, Japan on Apr 2, 1980.

James Whale, 27, of Metro Radio, Newcastle upon Tyne, England, kissed 4,049 girls in 8 hours in Tyneside, England, on Sept 22, 1978—a rate of one per 7.11 sec.

Kiss of Life. Five members of the Swansea St John Ambulance cadets maintained a "kiss of life" (mouth-to-mouth resuscitation) for 150 hours with 158,695 inflations, May 25–31, 1980. The "patient" was a dummy. A 168-hour "kiss of life" marathon was completed by 108 members of the Hawthorne Ambulance Service, Farmington, Maine, Sept 17–24, 1978.

Kite Flying. The single kite altitude record is 22,500 ft (minimum) to 28,000 ft (maximum) by Prof Phillip R. Kunz of the University of Wyo-

HUMAN FLY (left): George Willig scaled the face of the World Trade Center 110-story skyscraper in NYC while police followed him up. Then he came down, only to be fined $1.10 (Jerry Brooks took the photo.) HUMAN LIGHTNING ROD (right): Roy Sullivan of Va has been hit by lightning 7 times. He shows where it pierced his hat, but can't explain why he attracts lightning.

ming and Jay P. Kunz at Laramie, Wyo on Nov 21, 1967. A claim for a chain of kites reaching 37,908 ft was made by Steven W. Flack at Boonville-Oneida County Fairgrounds, NY on Sept 9, 1978.

The longest recorded flight is one of 169 hours by The Sunrise Inn team, Fort Lauderdale, Fla managed by Will Yolen, Apr 30–May 7, 1977.

The most kites flown on a single line is 4,128 by Kazuhiko Asaba, 55, at Kamakura, Japan Sept 21, 1978.

The largest kite ever flown was one with axes measuring 46 ft 3 in by 62 ft 6¾ in, launched by 500 people of the Tako Cassen Kyookai near Shirone City, Niigata, Japan, on March 20, 1980. It flew for over 13 min at an altitude of 393 ft and weighed an estimated 660 lb.

Knitting. The most prolific hand-knitter has been Mrs Gwen Matthewman (b 1927) of Featherstone, W Yorkshire, England, who in 1979 knitted 915 garments involving 11,012 oz of wool (equivalent to the fleece of 89 sheep). She has been timed to average 108 stitches per min in a 30-min test. Her technique has been filmed by the world's only Professor of Knitting—a Japanese.

Knot Tying. The fastest recorded time for tying the six Boy Scout Handbook knots (square knot, sheet bend, sheep shank, clove hitch, round turn and two half hitches and bowline) on individual ropes is 8.1 sec by Clinton R. Bailey Sr, 52, of Pacific City, Ore on Apr 13, 1977.

Leap Frogging. Fourteen students of Hanover High School, Hanover, NH, covered 555.25 miles in 148 hours, June 4–10, 1978.

Life Saving. In Nov 1974, the City of Galveston, Tex and the Noon Optimist Club unveiled a plaque to the deaf-mute lifeguard Leroy Colombo (1905–74), who saved 907 people from drowning in the waters around Galveston Island from 1917 to his death.

Lightning-Struck. The only living man in the world to be struck by lightning 7 times is former Shenandoah Park Ranger Roy C. Sullivan (US), the human lightning-conductor of Virginia. His attraction for lightning began in 1942 (lost big toenail) and was resumed in July 1969 (lost eyebrows), in July 1970 (left shoulder seared), on Apr 16, 1972 (hair set on fire) and, *finally*, he hoped, on Aug 7, 1973: as he was driving along a bolt came out of a small, low-lying cloud, hit him on the head through his hat, set his hair on fire again, knocked him 10 ft out of his car, went through both legs, and knocked his left shoe off. He had to pour a pail of water over his head to cool off. Then, on June 5, 1976, he was struck again for the sixth time, his ankle injured. When he was struck for the *seventh* time on June 25, 1977, while fishing, he was sent to Waynesboro Hospital with chest and stomach burns. He can offer no explanation for his magnetism, but he has donated his lightning-burnt Ranger hats to some of the Guinness World Records Exhibit Halls.

Lion Taming. The greatest number of lions mastered and fed in a cage simultaneously by an unaided lion-tamer was 40, by "Captain" Alfred Schneider in 1925.

Clyde (Raymond) Beatty (b Bainbridge, Ohio, June 10, 1903, d Ventura, Calif, July 19, 1965) likewise handled more than 40 "cats" (mixed lions and tigers) simultaneously. Beatty, top of the bill for 40 years, insisted on being called a lion-trainer. More than 20 lion-tamers have died of injuries since 1900.

Log Rolling. The record number of International Championships is 10 by Jubiel Wickheim (of Shawnigan Lake, BC, Canada) between 1956 and 1969. At Albany, Ore, on July 4, 1956, Wickheim rolled on a 14-in log against Chuck Harris of Kelso, Wash for 2 hours 40 min before losing.

Merry-Go-Round. The longest marathon ride on record is one of 312 hours 43 min by Gary Mandau, Chris Lyons and Dana Dover in Portland, Ore, Aug 20–Sept 2, 1976.

Message in a Bottle. The longest recorded interval between drop and pick-up is 64 years, between Aug 7, 1910 ("please write to Miss Gladys Potter") in Grand Lake, and Aug 1974 from Lake Huron. Miss Potter was traced and found to be Mrs Oliver Scheid, 76, of Columbus, Ohio.

A bottle apparently bearing a message written on Nov 19, 1899, by Capt Charles Weieerishen of the SS *Crown Princess Cecilia* off Varberg, Sweden, was reportedly picked up on the coast of Victoria, BC, Canada, on Dec 9, 1936.

Milk Bottle Balancing. The greatest distance walked by a person continuously balancing a full pint milk bottle on his head is 18 miles 880 yd by Willie Hollingsworth of Freeport, NY, March 24, 1979.

Modeling. The largest reported contract in the history of modeling is $1,500,000 for 5 years' rights to the face, eyes and lips of Cheryl Tiegs,

LION TAMING (above and right): Alfred Schneider could single-handedly control as many as 40 hungry lions at one time. MILK BOTTLE BALANCER: Willie Hollingsworth (left) of Freeport, NY, walked 18½ miles without dropping the full bottle from his head. MUSICAL CHAIRS (below): The game at Ohio State had 4,378 participants.

paid by the cosmetic group Noxell in Dec 1979. *Fortune* says her legs are still "up for grabs." Though God makes models, He makes very few.

Morse Code. The highest recorded speed at which anyone has received Morse code is 75.2 wpm—over 17 symbols per sec. This was achieved by Ted R. McElroy (US) in a tournament at Asheville, NC, July 2, 1939. The highest speed recorded for hand key transmitting is 175 symbols per min by Harry A. Turner of the US Signal Corps in 1942.

Musical Chairs. The largest game on record was one starting with 4,378 participants and ending with Lisa Springer on the last chair at Ohio State University in Columbus, Apr 27, 1980.

PARACHUTING RECORDS

Record	Holder	Detail	Place	Date
First from Tower	Louis-Sébastian Lenormand (1757–1839)	quasi-parachute	Montpellier, France	1783
First from Balloon	André-Jacques Garnerin (1769–1823)	2,230 ft	Monçeau Park, Paris	Oct 22, 1797
First from Aircraft (man)	Capt Albert Berry	US Army	St Louis	Mar 1, 1912
(woman)	Mrs Georgina "Tiny" Broadwick		Griffith Park, Los Angeles	June 21, 1913
First Free Fall	Mrs Georgina "Tiny" Broadwick	pilot, Glenn L. Martin	North Island, San Diego	Sept. 13, 1914
Lowest Escape	Squad Leader T. Spencer, RAF	30–40 ft	Wismar Bay, Baltic Sea	Apr 19, 1945
Longest Duration Fall	Lt Col Wm. H. Rankin, USMC	40 min, due to thermals	North Carolina	July 26, 1956
Highest Escape	Flt Lt J. de Salis and Fg Off P. Lowe, RAF	56,000 ft	Monyash, Derby, Eng	Apr 9, 1958
Longest Delayed Drop (man)	Capt Joseph W. Kittinger[1]	84,700 ft (16.04 miles) from balloon at 102,800 ft	Tularosa, NM	Aug 16, 1960
(woman)	O. Kommissarova (USSR)	46,250 ft	over USSR	Sept 21, 1965
(civilian)	R. W. K. Beckett (GB)	30,000 ft from 32,000 ft	D. F. Malan Airport, Capetown, S Africa	Nov 23, 1969
Most Southerly	Harry Ferguson (GB)	Operation Deep Freeze	South Pole	Nov 25, 1956
Most Northerly	Tech Sgt Richard J. Patton	$-39°$ F	$89°\ 39'$ N	Mar 31, 1969
Career Total (man)	Raymond Z. Munro (Canada)	8,000	over USSR	April 1978 to Nov 1973
(woman)	Anatolyi Osipov (USSR)	More than 1,000	Elsinore paracenter, Calif	May 1969
Highest Landing	Patty Wilson / Ten USSR parachutists[2]	23,405 ft	Lenina Peak	Jan 28, 1970
Heaviest Load	USAF C-130 Hercules	25.22 tons steel plates 6 parachutes	El Centro, Calif	Sept 7, 1970
Highest from Bridge	Donald R. Boyles	1,053 ft	Royal Gorge, Colo	Oct 4, 1970
Highest Tower Jump	Herbert Leo Schmidtz (US)	KTUL-TV Mast 1,984 ft	Tulsa, Okla	Julu 14, 1975
Biggest Star (Connected Free Fall)	32-member Enquirer team	Formation 5 sec (FAI rules)	Tahlequah, Okla	Oct 1978
Highest Column	8-member Enquirer team	170 ft	over Calif	July 26–
Most Traveled	Kevin Seaman from a Cessna Skylane (pilot, Charles Merritt)	12,186 miles	Jumps in all 50 US states	Oct 15, 1972
Oldest Man	Bob Broadbere (GB) (1892–1977)		Honiton, Devon, Eng	July 10, 1977
Oldest Woman	Mrs Ardeth Shuler Evitt (US)	85 years (broke glasses) first jump at 74 years 6 months	Mooresville, Ind	Aug 6, 1978
24-Hour Total	David Parchment (GB)	233 in 18 hours 7 min	Shobdon, Eng	June 19, 1979

[1] Maximum speed in rarefied air was 825.2 mph at 90,000 ft—marginally supersonic. [2] Four were killed.

OLDEST PARACHUTE JUMPER: (left) Mrs Evitt of Paris, Ill began her career at age 74 years 6 months. MOST NORTHERLY JUMP: Ray Munro (right) of Canada, a balloonist, parachuted in −39° F cold, within 1° of the North Pole.

Noodle Making. Stephen Yim (b Shanghai, China, 1949) made 256 noodle strips (exceeding 5 ft) in 63 sec on the BBC-TV *Record Breakers* program, Oct 21, 1973.

Omelet Making. Howard Helmer of NYC cooked 217 two-egg omelets in 30 min at Disneyland, Anaheim, Calif, on July 14, 1978.

Needle Threading. The record number of strands of cotton threaded through a number 13 needle (eye ½ × 1/16 in) in 2 hours is 3,795 by Brenda Robinson of the College of Further Education, Chippenham, Wiltshire, England, on March 20, 1971.

Onion Peeling. The record for onion peeling is 50 lb in 6 min 7 sec by Christine Espinoza in Rocky Ford, Colo on March 26, 1980.

Organ Marathons. The longest church organ recital ever sustained was one of 90 hours by Frank Hughes at Wesley College Chapel, Dublin, Ireland Oct 31–Nov 4, 1975.

The longest recorded electric organ marathon is 411 hours by Vince Bull at the Comet Hotel, Scunthorpe, England June 2–19, 1977.

Parachute, Longest Fall Without Parachute. The greatest altitude from which anyone has bailed out without a parachute and survived is 21,980 ft. This occurred in Jan 1942 when Lt (now Lt-Col) I. M. Chisov (USSR) fell from an Ilyushin 4 which had been severely damaged. He struck the ground a glancing blow on the edge of a snow-covered ravine and slid to the bottom. He suffered a fractured pelvis and severe spinal damage. It is estimated that the human body reaches 99% of its low-level terminal velocity after falling 1,880 ft, which takes 13–14 sec. This is 117–125 mph at normal atmospheric pressure in a random posture, but up to 185 mph in a head-down position.

Vesna Vulovic, 23, a Jugoslavenski Aerotransport hostess, survived when her DC-9 blew up at 33,330 ft over the Czechoslovak village of Ceska Kamenice on Jan 26, 1972. She fell inside a section of tail unit. She was hospitalized for 16 months after emerging from a 27-day coma, having broken many bones.

PLATE SPINNING: Shukuni Sasaki of Japan (above) kept 55 plates spinning at the same time on a TV show in 1980, bettering his own 1979 record. PENNY PYRAMID (left) Paul Jay Cohen of Philadelphia hides behind his mountain of 71,825 pennies which he piled 19 × 19 × 19 in high without any adhesive over a period of several months.

Party Giving. The most expensive private party ever thrown was that of Mr and Mrs Bradley Martin of Troy, NY. It was staged at the Waldorf-Astoria Hotel, NYC in Feb 1897. The cost to the host and hostess was estimated to be $369,200 in the days when dollars were made of gold.

Estimates as high as $600 million were made for the 49-nation Organization of African Unity summit conference staged in Libreville, Gabon in July 1977.

The "International Year of the Child" children's party in Hyde Park, London was attended by the Royal Family and 160,000 children, May 30–31, 1979.

The largest Christmas Party ever staged was that thrown by the Boeing Co in the 65,000-seat Kingdome, Seattle in two shows before an audience of 103,152 people on Dec 15, 1979. It was managed by general chairman John Mathiasen and produced by Greg Thompson with a cast of 2,506. The floor was decorated with 1,000 Christmas trees, each with 100 lights; 150,000 snow-white balloons and 3 ice ponds.

Piano Playing. The longest piano-playing marathon has been one of

1,172 hours 27 min (48 days 20 hours 27 min) playing 22 hours every day (with 5-min intervals each playing hour) from Jan 6 to Feb 24, 1978, by Roger Lavern at the Osborne Tavern, London.

The women's record is 133 hours non-stop (5 days 13 hours) by 280-lb Mrs Marie Ashton, aged 40, in a theatre at Blyth, Northumberland, England, Aug 18–23, 1958. Her last piece was "Five Minutes More." This category has since been discontinued.

Piano Tuning. The record time for pitch raising (one semi-tone or 100 cents) and then returning a piano to a musically acceptable quality is 4 min 20 sec by Steve Fairchild at the Piano Technicians Guild contest at the Dante Piano Co factory, NY, Feb 5, 1980.

Pipe Smoking. The duration record for keeping a pipe (0.1 oz of tobacco) continuously alight with only an initial match under IAPSC (International Association of Pipe Smokers Clubs) rules is 126 min 39 sec by 4-time champion William Vargo of Swartz Creek, Miss, at the 27th World Championships in 1975. The only other 4-time champion is Paul T. Spaniola (US). Longer durations have been recorded in less rigorously invigilated contests in which "tamping" and "gardening" were not unknown.

Plate Spinning. The greatest number of plates spun simultaneously is 55 by Shukuni Sasaki of Takamatsu, Japan on Jan 2, 1980.

Pogo Stick Jumping. The greatest number of jumps achieved on a pogo stick is 120,715 by Jeff Kane in 16 hours 12 min in Oak Lawn, Ill, June 9–10, 1980.

Pole Sitting. There being no international rules, the "standards of living" atop poles vary widely. The record squat is 399 days by Frank Perkins from June 1, 1975, to July 4, 1976, in an 8 × 8 ft box atop a 50-ft telegraph pole in San Jose, Calif.

Modern records do not, however, compare with that of St Simeon the Younger (*c.* 521–597 AD), called Stylites (Greek, *stylos* = pillar), a monk who spent his last 45 years on a stone pillar on the Hill of Wonders, Syria. This is probably the earliest example of record setting.

Potato Peeling. The peeling of 170 lb of potatoes to an institutional cookery standard by 5 teenagers (ages 14–16) with standard kitchen knives in 45 min was set in Sydney, Australia on June 11, 1977. The peelers were Julie Morris, Chris Hughes, Kerry White, Angus McKinnon and Julian Morgan.

Psychiatrist, Fastest. The world's fastest "psychiatrist" was Dr Albert L. Weiner of Erlton, NJ, who dealt with up to 50 patients a day in 4 treatment rooms. He relied heavily on narcoanalysis, muscle relaxants and electro-shock treatments. In Dec 1961, he was found guilty on 12 counts of manslaughter from using unsterilized needles. He had been trained in osteopathy, which includes all varieties of medicine, but had no specialization in psychiatry.

Quoit Throwing. The world's record for rope quoit throwing is an unbroken sequence of 4,002 pegs by Bill Irby, Sr of Australia in 1968.

Longest on a Raft. The longest recorded survival alone on a raft is 133 days (4½ months) by Second Steward Poon Lim (b Hong Kong) of the UK Merchant Navy, whose ship, the SS *Ben Lomond,* was torpedoed in the Atlantic 565 miles west of St Paul's Rocks at Lat 00° 30′ N and Long 38° 45′ W at 11:45 a.m. on Nov 23, 1942. He was picked up by a Brazilian fishing boat off Salinópolis, Brazil, Apr 5, 1943, and was able to walk ashore. In July 1943 he was awarded the British Empire Medal, and now lives in NYC.

Maurice and Maralyn Bailey survived 118⅓ days in an inflatable dinghy 4½ ft in diameter in the northeast Pacific from March 4 to June 30, 1973.

Ramp Jumping. The longest distance ever achieved for motorcycle long jumping is 212 ft by Alain Jean Prieur (b July 4, 1939) of France at Montlhéry near Paris, over 16 buses on Feb 6, 1977.

The pioneer of this form of exhibition—Evel Knievel (Robert Craig Knievel) (b Oct 17, 1938, in Butte, Mont) had suffered 433 bone fractures by his 1975 season.

The so-called T-bone dives or "dive bomber" crash by cars off ramps over and on to parked cars are often measured by the number of cars, but owing to their variable size and that their purpose is purely to cushion the shock, distance is more significant. The longest recorded distance is 176 ft by Dusty Russell in a 1963 Ford Falcon at Athens, Ga in Apr 1973.

The greatest endurance feat on a "wall of death" was 3 hours 33 min 35 sec by Hugo Dabbert, 40 at Göttingen, W Germany on July 17, 1979. He rode 4,567 laps on the 32.8 ft diameter wall on a Honda CM 185 averaging 25.72 mph for the 90.0 miles.

Riding in Armor. The longest recorded ride in full armor weighing 112 lb is one of 167 miles from Edinburgh to Dumfries, Scotland, in 3 days (riding time 28½ hours) by Dick Brown, 48, June 13–15, 1979.

Riveting. The record for riveting is 11,209 in 9 hours by J. Moir at the Workman Clark Ltd shipyard, Belfast, N Ireland in June 1918. His peak hour was his seventh with 1,409, an average of nearly 23½ per min.

Rocking Chair. The longest recorded duration of a "Rockathon" is 432 hours by Mrs Maureen Weston of Petreburgh Athletics Club, Peterborough, Cambridge, England Apr 14–May 2, 1977.

Roller Coasting. The endurance record for riding on a roller coaster is 168 hours by Jim King at Panama City, Fla, Aug 28–Sept 4, 1978. He covered a distance of 1,946.5 miles.

Rolling Pin. The record distance for a woman to throw a 2-lb rolling pin is 175 ft 5 in by Lorila Deane Adams, 21, at the Iowa State Fair, Aug 21, 1979.

Rummage Sale. The largest known rummage sale is that staged by the Winnetka Congregational Church in Illinois, which raised $91,890.17 in a one-day sale on May 9, 1980.

133 DAYS ON A RAFT (left): Poon Lim was shipwrecked and survived by making use of a flashlight which he pulled apart, and a piece of rope, to catch fish for food. **RIDING IN ARMOR** (right): Dick Brown rode 167 miles to regain his record.

RAMP JUMPING (above): Evel Knievel was the pioneer but has little in the way of records except 433 broken bones. ROLLER COASTER MARATHON (below): Jim King, disc jockey in Panama City, Fla wants to keep coasting longer than his current record of 168 hours.

See-Saw. The most protracted session for see-sawing indoors is one of 1,101 hours 40 min on an indoor suspension see-saw by George Partridge and Tamara Marquez of Auburn High School, Auburn, Wash, March 28–May 13, 1977.

Georgia Chaffin and Tammy Adams of Goodhope Junior High School, Cullman, Ala, completed 730½ hours outdoors, June 25–July 25, 1975.

Sermon. The longest sermon on record was delivered by the Rev Donald Thomas of Brooklyn, NY, for 93 hours, Sept 18–22, 1978.

From May 31 to June 10, 1969, the 14th Dalai Lama (b July 6, 1935, as Tenzin Gyalto), the exiled ruler of Tibet, preached a sermon on Tantric Buddhism for 5 to 7 hours per day to total 60 hours, in India.

Shaving. The fastest demon barber on record is Jerry Harley, who shaved 368 men in 60 min with a cut-throat razor at Command House, Chatham, Kent, England, Aug 20, 1979.

Sheaf Tossing. The best performance for tossing an 8-lb sheaf for height is 64.86 ft by Trond Ulleberg of Skolleborg, Norway, on Nov 11, 1978. Such pitchfork contests date from 1914.

Shoe Shining. In this category (limited to teams of 4 teenagers, an 8-hour time limit, and all shoes "on the hoof") the record is 6,334 pairs by the Bedford North (Newnham) Scout Group in England, July 16, 1977.

Shorthand, Fastest. The highest recorded speeds ever attained under championship conditions are: 300 words per minute (99.64% accuracy) for 5 minutes and 350 wpm (99.72% accuracy, that is, two insignificant errors) for 2 minutes by Nathan Behrin (US), in NYC in Dec 1922. Behrin (b 1887) used the Pitman system invented in 1837. Morris I. Kligman, official court reporter at the US Court House, NYC has taken 50,000 words in 5 hours (a sustained rate of 166.6 wpm). Rates are dependent upon the nature, complexity, and syllabic density of the material.

G. W. Bunbury of Dublin, Ireland, held the unique distinction of writing at 250 wpm for 10 minutes on Jan 23, 1894.

Showering. The most prolonged continuous shower bath on record is one of 336 hours by Arron Marshall of Rockingham Park, W Australia, July 29–Aug 12, 1978.

The feminine record is 120 hours 1 min by Penny Cresswell of Waikiki, W Australia, Sept 7–12, 1977.

Desquamation can be a positive danger.

Singing. The longest recorded solo singing marathon is one of 153 hours by Bob Anthony in Hayes, Middlesex, England, Sept 2–8, 1979. The marathon record for a choir is 72 hours 2 min by the combined choir of Girls High School and Prince Edward School, Salisbury, Zimbabwe, Sept 7–10, 1979.

Slinging. The greatest distance recorded for a slingshot is 1,147 ft 4 in using a 34-in-long sling and a 7½-oz stone by Melvyn Gaylor on the Newport Golf Course, Shide, Isle of Wight, England, Sept 25, 1970.

SOLO SINGER (left): Bob Anthony of Hayes, England sang continuously for 153 hours. SMOKE RINGER: 441 smoke rings from a cigar pull was the record set on Japanese TV, but was disallowed because Atsuhiro Nakamura tapped his cheeks. Next best was 355.

Smoke-Ring Blowing. The highest recorded number of smoke rings formed with the lips from a single pull of a cigarette with cheek tapping disallowed, is 355 by Jan van Deurs Formann of Copenhagen, Denmark, achieved in Switzerland in Aug 1979.

Snowshoe Travel. The fastest officially recorded time for covering a mile is 6 min 23.8 sec by Richard Lemay (Frontenac Club of Quebec) at Manchester, NH, in 1973.

Speech-Listening. The Guild of Professional Toastmasters (founded 1962) has only 12 members. Its founder, Ivor Spencer, listened to a speech in excess of 2 hours by the maudlin guest of honor of a retirement luncheon. The Guild also elects the most boring speaker of the year, but for professional reasons will not publicize the winners' names until a decent interval has elapsed.

Spinning. The duration record for spinning a clock balance wheel by hand is 5 min 26.8 sec by Philip Ashley, aged 16, of Leigh, Greater Manchester, England, May 20, 1968.

Spitting. The greatest distance achieved at the annual (July) tobacco-spitting classic (instituted 1955) at Raleigh, Miss is 31 ft 1 in by Don Snyder, 28, on July 26, 1975. In the 3rd International Spittin', Belchin' and Cussin' Triathlon, Harold Fielden reached 34 ft ¼ in at Central City, Colo, July 13, 1973. Distance is dependent on the quality of salivation, absence of cross wind, two-finger pucker and the coordination of the back arch and neck snap. Sprays or wads smaller than a dime are not measured.

The record for projecting a melon seed under WCWSSA (World Championship Watermelon Seed Spitting Association) rules is 59 ft 1½ in by Brian Dunne at Savemore Centre, Yeppoon, Queensland, Australia, Dec 11, 1976. The highest reported distance for a cherrystone is 65 ft 2 in by Rick Krause, at Eau Claire, Mich on July 5, 1980. Spitters who care about their image wear 12-in block-ended boots so practice spits can be measured without a tape.

Stair Climbing. The 100-story record for stair climbing was set by Dennis W. Martz in the Detroit Plaza Hotel, Detroit, Mich on June 26, 1978, at 11 min 23.8 sec.

The record for running a vertical mile in continuous action is 1 hour 25 min 6 sec in ascent and 44 min 39 sec in descent, set by Richard Black, 44, president of the Maremont Corp, in 9 round trips up and down the stairs of Lake Point Tower, Chicago, on July 13, 1978. *These records can only be attempted in buildings with a minimum of 70 stories.*

James B. Rafferty, 26, raced up the 1,575 steps of the Empire State Building, New York City, in 12 min 19.8 sec on Feb 15, 1979.

The record for the 1,760 steps in the world's tallest free-standing structure, Toronto's CN Tower, is 10 min 16 sec by Michael Round.

Standing Up. The longest period on record that anyone has stood up continuously is more than 17 years, from 1955 to Nov 1973, in the case of Swami Maujgiri Maharij while performing the *Tapasya* or penance in Shahjahanpur, Uttar Pradesh, India. He leaned against a plank to sleep.

Stilt Walking. Even with a safety wire, very high stilts are extremely dangerous—25 steps are deemed to constitute "mastery." Eddy Wolf, known as "Steady Eddy," of Loyal, Wisconsin, has mastered aluminum stilts 30 ft 3 in from ground to ankle over a distance of 51 ft in Loyal, Wis, May 18, 1978. Joe Long (*né* Kenneth Caesar), who has suffered 5 fractures, mastered 56-lb 24-ft stilts at the BBC TV Centre, London, on Dec 8, 1978.

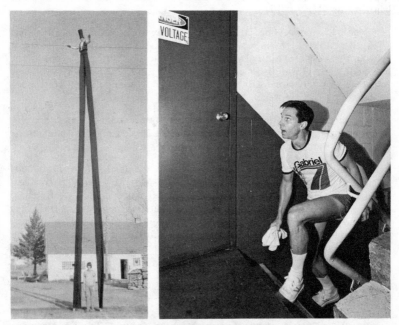

MOVING UP IN THE WORLD: "Steady Eddy" Wolf (left) mastered 30-ft-3-in stilts in Loyal, Wis in 1978. Richard Black (right) set a record for the vertical mile in July 1978 by racing up and down the stairs at Lake Point Tower, Chicago.

STRING BALL: This is one of the two largest in the world. Compiled by Francis Johnson of Darwin, Minn, it measures 11 ft in diameter and weighs 5½ tons.

Hop pickers use stilts up to 15 ft. In 1892 M. Garisoain of Bayonne, France stilt-walked 4.97 miles into Biarritz in 42 min to average 7.10 mph. In 1891 Sylvain Dornon stilt-walked from Paris to Moscow *via* Vilno in 50 stages for the 1,830 miles. Another source gives his time as 58 days.

Emma Sian Disley (b May 17, 1965) walked on stilts up 3,560-ft-high Mt Snowdon in Wales, covering 2,500 vertical ft in 4 hours 5 min 45 sec in aid of the International Fund for Animal Welfare on Aug 19, 1977. Masahami Tatsushiko (Japan), 28, ran 100 meters on 1-ft-high stilts in 14.5 sec in Tokyo on March 30, 1980.

Stowaway. The most rugged stowaway was Socarras Ramirez, who escaped from Cuba June 4, 1969, by stowing away in an unpressurized wheel well in the starboard wing of a Douglas DC-8 in a 5,600-mile Iberian Airlines flight from Havana to Madrid. He survived 8 hours at 30,000 ft where temperatures were −8 °F.

Stretcher Bearing. The longest recorded carry of a stretcher case with a 140-lb "body" is 120 miles in 41 hours 12 min by two 4-man teams from the 1st Field Ambulance, Canadian Forces Base, Calgary, Alberta, Canada, May 5–7, 1979.

String Ball. The largest balls of string on record are both 11 ft in diameter weighing 5½ tons, one of which was amassed by Francis A. Johnson of Darwin, Minn, since 1950, and another by Frank Stoeber of Cawker City, Kans, since at least 1962.

Submergence. The longest submergence under water (excluding the use of diving bells) is 147 hours 15 min established by Robert Ingolia in tests in which the US Navy was the beneficiary of all data in 1961.

The continuous duration record (i.e. no rest breaks) for scuba (self-contained underwater breathing apparatus) without surface air hoses, is 67 hours 44 min by Robert Newton in a charity fund-raising drive in the Holiday Inn swimming pool in Birmingham, England, Apr 4–7, 1980.

Suggestion Box. The most prolific suggestion box stuffer on record is

John Drayton (b Sept 18, 1907) of Newport, Gwent, Wales, who has plied British Rail and the companies from which it was formed with a total of 28,777 suggestions from 1924 to May 1980. One out of every seven was accepted.

The US Postal Service champion, John Kingston, has an acceptance rate of one in 5.3 (284 out of 1,500) to Jan 1976.

Swinging. The record duration for continuous swinging is 185 hours by Mollie Jackson of Tarrytown, NY, March 25–Apr 1, 1979.

Tailoring. The highest speed in making a 2-piece wool suit, starting with shearing the sheep and ending with a finished article, is 1 hour 52 min 18.5 sec to the order of Bud Macken of Mascot, NSW, Australia, Dec 23, 1931. The shearing took 35 sec, the carding and teasing 19 min and the weaving 20 min.

Talking. The record for non-stop talking is 150 hours by Raymond Cantwell at Trust Houses Forte's Travel Lodge, Oxford, England, Dec 4–10, 1977.

The longest continuous political speech on record was one of 33 hours 5 min by Marvin Eakman of Minneapolis, Nov 6–7, 1978.

The women's non-stop talking record was set by Mrs Mary E. Davis, who, Sept 2–7, 1958, started talking at a radio station in Buffalo, NY, and did not draw breath until 110 hours 30 min 5 sec later in Tulsa, Okla.

The longest recorded lecture was one of 59½ hours by James Gray of Evergreen Valley College, San Jose, Calif, Apr 11–14, 1980. The title of the lecture was "Everything You Ever Wanted to Know about Sociology and People."

Historically the longest after-dinner speech with unsuspecting victims was 3 hours, delivered by the Rev Henry Whitehead (d March 1896) at the Rainbow Tavern, Fleet St, London, on Jan 16, 1874. Both Nicholas Parsons and the well-known writer, Gyles Brandreth, spoke for 11 hours from 8 p.m. to 7 a.m. Feb 13–14, 1978, at the Hyde Park Hotel, London, in aid of Action Research, to tie a longest after-dinner speech contest.

Pulling with Teeth. The "strongest teeth in the world" belong to "Hercules" John Massis (b Wilfried Oscar Morbée, June 4, 1940) of Oostakker, Belgium, who on Nov 8, 1978, demonstrated the ability to pull 3 railroad cars weighing 140 tons on a level track outside Stockholm, Sweden, with a bit in his teeth. At Evrey, France on March 19, 1977, he raised a weight of 513⅝ lb to a height of 6 in from the ground with a bit in his teeth. Massis prevented a helicopter from taking off using only a mouth harness in Los Angeles Apr 7, 1979, for the "Guinness Spectacular" ABC-TV show.

Tightrope Walking. The greatest 19th century tightrope walker was Jean François Gravelet, *alias* Charles Blondin (1824–1897), of France, who made the earliest crossing of Niagara Falls on a 3-in rope 1,100 ft long, 160 ft above the Falls June 30, 1859. He also made a crossing with

STRONG MAN, STRONG TEETH: John "Hercules" Massis of Belgium goes all over the world holding down helicopters with his teeth (above), pulling trains (below) that weigh 140 tons, lifting cars (right, above) and twisting iron bars. He has also held back powerboats and motorcycles in action, and performed almost all feats of strength, except eating a bicycle, and his friend, Lotito (M Mangetout) of Belgium has done that.

WIRE WALKING FIRSTS: Charles Blondin (left) of France in 1859 was the pioneer in crossing Niagara Falls on a 3-in rope. He also made a crossing with his agent on his back. Philippe Petit (above), also of France, made the only crossing by wire between the twin towers of NYC's World Trade Center, 1,350 ft above the street, 140 ft across.

Harry Colcord pickaback on Sept 15, 1860, though other artists find it difficult to believe. Colcord was his agent.

The oldest wire walker was "Professor" William Ivy Baldwin (1866–1953) who crossed South Boulder Canyon, Colo on a 320-ft wire with a 125-ft drop, on his 82nd birthday, July 31, 1948.

The tightrope endurance record is 185 days by Henri Rochetain (b 1926) of France on a wire 394 ft long, 82 ft above a supermarket in St Etienne, France, March 28–Sept 29, 1973. His ability to sleep on the wire has left doctors puzzled. During this time, he walked some 310 miles on the wire to keep fit.

The longest tightrope walk by any funambulist was achieved by Rochetain on a wire 3,790 yd long slung across a gorge at Clermont-Ferrand, France, July 13, 1969. He required 3 hr 20 min to negotiate the crossing.

The highest high-wire act was performed by Steve McPeak (b Sept 1945), who made a 300-ft crossing on a wire 1,800 ft above Yosemite Falls, Calif and 2,625 ft above the Yosemite Valley floor July 5, 1976. McPeak also holds the record for the greatest tightrope ascent, with his 2,400-ft-long barefoot walk up a 1.7-in cable with a maximum gradient of 25°, to the top of Sugarloaf Mountain in Rio de Janeiro harbor, Brazil. The climb was 675 ft up, accomplished in 65 minutes. His 35-lb pole was 49 ft long.

Farrell Hettig of Sarasota, Fla beat Steve McPeak by 5 sec in setting the record for the steepest high-wire ascent when they raced up a wire ascending to 57 ft at an angle of 39° in Los Angeles, on "Guinness Spectacular I" ABC-TV show in Apr 1979.

McPeak has also successfully ridden a 41-ft-tall unicycle across a high wire which was itself suspended 40 ft above the ground.

The greatest height above street level in a high-wire performance was when Philippe Petit, 24, of Nemours, France crossed on a wire 1,350 ft above the street in NYC between the newly constructed twin towers of the World Trade Center on Aug 7, 1974. He shot the 140-ft-long wire across by bow and arrow. He was charged with criminal trespass after a 75-min display of at least 7 crossings. The police psychiatrist's verdict was, "Anyone who does this 110 stories up can't be entirely right."

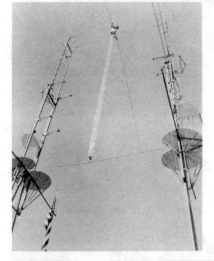

HIGH WIRE SPECIALIST:
Steven McPeak of Las Vegas
holds many tightrope walking
records, such as climbing barefoot
2,400 ft up a cable (above) from
Rio de Janeiro to Sugar Loaf Mt.
Even higher above ground was
his wire walk across Yosemite
Valley, Calif (inset,
below)—2,625 ft up. To astound
55,000 ballgame fans, McPeak
walked 800 ft between Anaheim
Stadium's grand stand roofs on a
wire (below). He rides a tall
unicycle too (left), a 40-ft giant
on a 40-ft-high wire at Circus
Circus Hotel, Las Vegas, from
time to time. (Photos by Franklin
Berger.)

TIRE PILE-UP (left): Geoffrey Capes shows how it's done with 62 tires. His record was broken when another Englishman supported 76 tires. TIGHTROPE ENDURANCE (right): Henri Rochetain spent 185 days on an 82-ft-high tightrope in 1973. He amazed doctors with his ability to sleep on the wire.

Tire Supporting. The greatest number of car tires supported in a freestanding "lift" at one time is 76 by Gary Windebank of Romsey, England on Oct 27, 1979. The total weight was 1111.5 lb. The tires were Esso radials 155 × 13.

Treasure Finding. The most successful treasure hunter has been C. Fred Ahrendt of Dayton, Ohio, who, by Aug 1976, had found with his metal detector 175 class rings (earliest, 1890) and 179 wedding rings of 14 or more carats. Employees of crematoria are officially excluded from the competition.

Tree Climbing. The fastest climb up a 100-ft fir spar pole and return to the ground is one of 31.1 sec by Marvin Trudeau of Honeymoon Bay, BC, Canada, at Haywood, Wis in July 1977. The fastest time up a 40-ft coconut tree barefoot is 8.4 sec by Kini Marawai in Suva, Fiji, on Sept 2, 1977.

Tree Sitting. The duration record for sitting in a tree is 182 days 2 min by Glen T. Woodrich, 23, at Golf N' Stuff Amusement Park, Norwalk, Calif, Jan 1–July 2, 1978.

Typing, Fastest. The highest recorded speeds attained with a ten-word penalty per error on a manual machine are:

One Minute: 170 words, Margaret Owen (US) (Underwood Standard), NYC, Oct 21, 1918.

One Hour: 147 words (net rate per min), Albert Tangora (US) (Underwood Standard), Oct 22, 1923.

The official hour record on an electric machine is 9,316 words (40 errors) on an IBM machine, giving a net rate of 149 wpm by Margaret Hamma, now Mrs Dilmore (US), in Brooklyn, NYC June 20, 1941. Mrs

Barbara Blackburn of Everett, Wash can maintain 150 wpm for 50 min (37,500 key strokes) and attains a speed of 170 wpm using the Dvorak Simplified Keyboard (DSK) system.

In an official test in 1946, Stella Pajunas, now Mrs Garnard, attained a speed of 216 words in a minute on an IBM machine.

Typing, Longest. The duration record for typing on an electric typewriter is 214 hours by Violet Gibson Burns in Cremorne, NSW, Australia Feb 18–27, 1980.

Mrs Marva Drew, 51, of Waterloo, Iowa, between 1968 and Nov 30, 1974, typed the numbers 1 to 1,000,000 (in words) on a manual typewriter. She used 2,473 pages. When asked why, she replied, "But I love to type."

The longest duration typing marathon on a manual machine is 120 hours 15 min by Mike Howell, a 23-year-old blind office worker from Greenfield, Oldham, Greater Manchester, England, Nov 25–30, 1969, on an Olympia manual typewriter in Liverpool. In aggregating 561,006 strokes he performed a weight movement of 2,780 tons plus a further 174 tons in moving the carriage on line spacing.

Walking-on-Hands. The duration record for walking-on-hands is 871 miles by Johann Hurlinger of Austria, who, in 55 daily 10-hour stints, averaged 1.58 mph from Vienna to Paris in 1900.

Thomas P. Hunt of the USAF Academy, Colorado Springs, completed a 50-meter inverted sprint in 18.4 sec in Tokyo, Japan on Sept 22, 1979.

Wheelbarrow Racing. The fastest time reached for a 1-mile wheelbarrow race is 5 min 1.59 sec by Bryan Zellweger ("charger") and Jack Zellweger ("rider") at the Ladner Centennial Sports Festival, Delta, BC, Canada, July 1, 1979.

Whip Cracking. The longest stock whip ever "cracked" (*i.e.* the end made to travel above the speed of sound—760 mph) is one of 97 ft wielded by Noel Harris on the steps of Parliament House, Melbourne, Australia, Aug 7, 1978. The dry weight of the red hide-plaited whip was 26.4 lb.

TYPIST Marva Drew used her hands to type the numbers 1 to 1 million over a period of 6 years. Thomas P. Hunt used his hands to WALK 50 meters in 18.4 sec for a record.

Window Cleaning. The fastest time in the annual Top Shiner contest in England has been 46.5 sec plus three ½-sec smear penalties to equal 48 sec by Richard Baterip for 3 standard 40.94 × 45.39-in office windows with an 11.8-in-long squeegee and 15.83 points of water.

Wood Cutting. The earliest competitions date from Tasmania in 1874. The records set at the Lumberjack World Championships at Hayward, Wis (founded 1960), are:

Power Saw	11.55 sec.	Ron Johnson (US)	1976
One-Man Bucking	23.06 sec.	Ron Hartill (NZ)	1976
Standing Block Chop	26.9 sec.	Ron Wilson (Aust)	1973
Underhand Block Chop	20.3 sec.	Jim Alexander (Aust)	1973
Two-Man Bucking	10.40 sec.	Dave Green and	
		Rudy Dettmer (US)	1976

White pine logs 14 in in diameter are used for chopping and 20 in for sawing.

Writing Small. In 1926 an account was published of Alfred McEwen's pantograph record in which the 56-word version of the Lord's Prayer was written by diamond point on glass in the space of 0.0016 × 0.0008 in.

Frank C. Watts of Felmingham, Norfolk, England, demonstrated for photographers on Jan 24, 1968, the ability, without mechanical or optical aids, to write the Lord's Prayer 34 times (9,452 letters) within the size of a definitive postage stamp (0.84 × 0.71 in).

Writing under Handicap. The ultimate feat in "funny writing" would appear to be the ability to write extemporaneously and decipherably backwards, upside down, laterally inverted (mirror-style) while blindfolded, with both hands simultaneously. Three claims to this ability with both hands and feet simultaneously are under investigation.

Yodeling. The most protracted yodel on record was that of Errol Bird for 10 hours 15 min in Lisburn, N Ireland, Oct 6, 1979.

Yo-Yo. This originates from the Filipino jungle fighting weapon recorded in the 16th century weighing 4 lb with a 20-ft thong. The word means "come-come." Though illustrated in a book in 1891 as a bandalore, the yo-yo did not become a craze until it was marketed by Donald F. Duncan of Chicago in 1926. The most difficult modern yo-yo trick is the "Whirlwind," incorporating both inside and outside horizontal loop-the-loops.

The individual continuous endurance record is 120 hours by John Winslow of Gloucester, Va, Nov 23–28, 1977.

Dr Allen Bussey in Waco, Tex on Apr 23, 1977 completed 20,302 loops in 3 hours (including 6,886 in a single 60-min period). He used a Duncan Imperial with a 34½-in nylon string.

The longest yo-yo ever constructed was one weighing 256 lb, test launched from a 100-ft crane in San Francisco on Oct 13, 1979.

EATING RECORDS

While no healthy person has been reported to have succumbed in any contest for eating or drinking non-alcoholic or non-toxic drinks, such attempts, from a medical point of view, must be regarded as *extremely* inadvisable, particularly among young people. Gastronomic record attempts should aim at improving the *rate* of consumption, rather than the volume. *Guinness* will not list any records involving the consumption of more than 2 liters (approximately 2 quarts) of beer or any at all involving liquor. Nor will this book list records for potentially dangerous categories such as consuming live ants, goldfish, quantities of chewing gum or marshmallows, or raw eggs in shells. The ultimate in stupidity—the eating of a bicycle—has, however, been recorded since it is unlikely to attract competition.

Records for eating and drinking by trenchermen do not match those suffering from the rare disease of bulimia (morbid desire to eat) and polydipsia (pathological thirst). Some bulimia patients have to spend 15 hours a day eating, with an extreme consumption of 384 lb 2 oz of food in 6 days by Matthew Daking, aged 12, in 1743 (known as Mortimer's case). Fannie Meyer of Johannesburg, after a skull fracture, was stated in 1974 to be unsatisfied by less than 192 pints of water a day. By Oct 1978, she was down to 62 pints. Miss Helge Andersson (b 1908) of Lindesberg, Sweden, was reported in Jan 1971 to have been drinking 48 pints of water a day since 1922—a total of 105,120 gallons.

The world's greatest trencherman has been Edward Abraham ("Bozo") Miller (b 1909) of Oakland, Calif. He consumes up to 25,000 calories per day, or more than 11 times that recommended. He stands 5 ft 7½ in tall but weighs from 280 to 300 lb with a 57-in waist. He has been undefeated in eating contests since 1931 (see below).

The bargees (barge sailors) on the Rhine are reputed to be the world's heaviest eaters, with 5,200 calories per day. However, the New Zealand Sports Federation of Medicine reported in Dec 1972 that a long-distance road runner consumed 14,321 calories in 24 hours.

Specific records have been claimed as follows:

Baked Beans. 2,380 cold beans one by one, with a cocktail stick, in 30 min by Martin Moore in Brighton, England on July 29, 1979.

Bananas. 17 (edible weight min 4½ oz each) in 2 min by Dr Ronald L. Alkana at the University of California, Irvine on Dec 7, 1973.

Beer. Steven Petrosino drank one liter of beer in 1.3 sec on June 22, 1977, at "The Gingerbreadman," in Carlisle, Pa.
Peter G. Dowdeswell (b London, July 29, 1940) of Earls Barton, Northamptonshire, England, drank 2 liters in 6 sec on Feb 7, 1975. He also holds the speed record for consuming 2 Imperial pints, in 2.3 sec, on June 11, 1975.

Bicycle. 15 days by Monsieur "Mangetout" (M. Lotito), in the form of tires and metal filings, at Evrey, France, March 17–Apr 2, 1977. No further entries in this category will be accepted.

QUEEN OF THE FRANKFURTER: Lynda Kuerth (left) won the title in a contest by eating 23 in 3 min 10 sec. (Photo by Neil Benson). BEAN EATING CHAMPION (above): Martin Moore is not from Boston but Brighton, England. He ate 2,380 in 30 min—cold.

Champagne. 1,000 bottles per year by Bobby Acland of the "Black Raven," Bishopsgate, London, England.

Cheese. 16 oz of hard English cheddar in 1 min 13 sec by Peter Dowdeswell (see *Beer*) in Earls Barton, England, on July 14, 1978.

Chicken. 27 (2-lb pullets) by "Bozo" Miller (see above) at a sitting at Trader Vic's, San Francisco in 1963.

Clams. 424 Little Necks in 8 min by Dave Barnes at Port Townsend Bay, Wash, on May 3, 1975.

Doughnuts. 37 (weighing 2 lb 14 oz) in 7 min 5 sec by Reggie Graham of Roanoke, Va, May 8, 1980.

Eels. 1 lb of elvers (1,300) in 13.7 sec by Peter Dowdeswell (see *Beer*) at Reeves Club, Bristol, England, on Oct 20, 1978.

Eggs. (Hard-boiled) 14 in 58 sec by Peter Dowdeswell (see above) in Corby, England, on Feb 18, 1977. (Soft-boiled) 32 in 78 sec by Peter Dowdeswell in Northampton, England, on Apr 8, 1978. (Raw, without shells) 13 in 2.2 sec by Peter Dowdeswell in Norwich, England, on Jan 26, 1978.

Frankfurters. 23 (2-oz) in 3 min 10 sec by Lynda Kuerth, 21, at Veterans Stadium, Philadelphia, on July 12, 1977.

Gherkins. 1 lb in 43.6 sec by Rex Barker of Elkhorn, Neb, on Oct 30, 1975.

Grapes. 3 lb 1 oz in 34.6 sec by Jim Ellis of Montrose, Mich, on May 30, 1976.

Hamburgers. 20¾ hamburgers (each weighing 3½ oz, totaling 4½ lb of meat) and buns in 30 min by Alan Peterson at Longview, Wash on Feb 8, 1979.

SPEED EATERS: Bennett D'Angelo (above) ate 3 lb 6 oz of ice cream in 90 sec in Waltham, Mass in 1977. Hamburgers (top, right) are Alan Peterson's favorite. He ate 20¾ in Longview, Wash in 30 min in 1979. Perhaps the biggest eater of all time is Peter Dowdeswell of England (right) who holds records in consuming beer, cheese, eels, eggs (3 ways), milk, pancakes, potatoes, sandwiches (as pictured) and shrimps. He's trying for more.

Ice Cream. 3 lb 6 oz of unmelted ice cream in 90 sec by Bennett D'Angelo at Dean Dairy, Waltham, Mass on Aug 7, 1977.

Lemons. 12 quarters (3 lemons) whole (including skin and seeds) in 15.3 sec by Bobby Kempf of Roanoke, Va on May 2, 1979.

Meat. One whole roast ox in 42 days by Johann Ketzler of Munich, Germany, in 1880.

Milk. One Imperial quart (1.2 US quarts) in 3.2 sec by Peter Dowdeswell (see above) at Dudley Top Rank Club, West Midlands, England on May 31, 1975.

Oysters. 350 (total weight 3.08 lb) in 2 min 32 sec by Shaun Ryan of Russell, New Zealand on Jan 1, 1980.

The record for opening oysters is 100 in 3 min 1 sec by Douglas Brown, 31, at Christchurch, New Zealand, on Apr 29, 1975.

Pancakes. 62 (each 6 in in diameter, buttered and with syrup) in 6 min 58.5 sec by Peter Dowdeswell (see above) in Northampton, England on Feb 9, 1977.

Peanuts. 100 (whole, out of the shell) singly in 46 sec by Jim Kornitzer at Brighton, England on Aug 1, 1979.

Pickled Onions. 91 (total weight 30 oz) in 1 min 8 sec by Pat Donahue in Victoria, BC, Canada, on March 9, 1978.

Potatoes. 3 lb in 1 min 22 sec by Peter Dowdeswell in Earls Barton, England on Aug 25, 1978.

Potato Chips. 30 2-oz bags in 24 min 33.6 sec, without a drink, by Paul G. Tully of Brisbane University, Australia, in May 1969. (Charles Chip Inc of Mountville, Pa produced chips 4 × 7 in from outsize potatoes in Feb 1977.)

Prunes. 144 in 65 sec by Douglas Mein at Dundee University, Tayside, Scotland, on Oct 19, 1978.

Ravioli. 324 (first 250 in 70 min) by "Bozo" Miller (see above) at Rendezvous Room, Oakland, Calif, in 1963.

Sandwiches. 40 (jam and butter, 6 × 3¾ × ½ in) in 17 min 53.9 sec by Peter Dowdeswell (see above) on Oct 17, 1977, at the Donut Shop, Reedley, Calif.

Sausages. 96 1-oz sausages in 6 min by Steve Meltzer of Brooklyn, NY, on Oct 14, 1974.

Shellfish. 81 (unshelled) whelks in 15 min by William Corfield at Helyar Arms, East Coker, Somerset, England, on Sept 6, 1969.

Shrimps. 3 lb in 4 min 8 sec by Peter Dowdeswell (see above) at Earls Barton, England, on May 25, 1978.

Snails. 144 in 11 min 30 sec by Marc Quinquandon, 27, in France, July 1979.

Spaghetti. 100 yd in 28.73 sec by Steve Weldon of Austin, Tex on May 1, 1977.

Tortillas. 74 (total weight 4 lb 1½ oz) in 30 min by Tom Nall in the 2nd World Championship at Mariano's Mexican Restaurant, Dallas, Tex on Oct 16, 1973.

WEALTH AND POVERTY

The comparison and estimation of extreme personal wealth are beset with intractable difficulties. Quite apart from reticence and the element of approximation in estimating the valuation of assets, as Jean Paul Getty (1892–1976) once said: "If you can count your millions, you are not a billionaire." The term "millionaire" was invented *c.* 1740 and "billionaire" in 1861.

The earliest dollar billionaires were John Davison Rockefeller (1839–1937); Henry Ford (1863–1947); and Andrew William Mellon (1855–1937). In 1937, the last year in which all 3 were alive, a billion dollars was worth 10.97 times as much in purchasing power as it is today (1980).

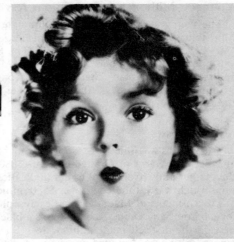

MILLIONAIRE AND MILLIONAIRESS: In 1937 when John D. Rockefeller (above) died, Shirley Temple (right) was just making her first million in the movies at age 9. Dollars in that era were worth 10.97 times as much as in 1980. The dimes that Rockefeller gave away would be worth dollars today.

Richest Men

There is currently only one surviving US dollar billionaire of the seven US citizens so described in the 20th century, namely Daniel K. Ludwig (b South Haven, Mich June 1897) whose fortune was estimated at $3,000 million in 1977. Ludwig reportedly began in business at age 9 by buying a sunken boat for $25, and now has the world's third largest tanker fleet and much real estate in the US and South America.

H. (Henry) Ross Perot (b Texarkana, Tex 1930) was, in Dec 1969, worth in excess of a billion dollars on paper.

The richest man in Great Britain today is reputed to be John Moores (b Eccles, Lancashire, 1896), a football pool operator who pioneered in the field in 1923. In 1973, he was estimated to be worth £400 million (hence £1,020 million in 1980 pounds sterling). His first job after leaving school at 14 was as a telephone operator.

Highest Income

The greatest incomes derive from the collection of royalties per barrel by rulers of oil-rich sheikdoms who have not abrogated personal entitlement. Before his death in 1965, HH Sheikh Sir Abdullah as-Salim as-Sabah (b 1895), the 11th Amir of Kuwait, was accumulating royalties payable at the rate of £2.6 million ($6.5 million) per week or £135 million ($337.5 million) a year.

The highest gross income ever achieved in a single year by a private citizen is an estimated $105 million in 1927 by the Neapolitan-born gangster Alphonse ("Scarface Al") Capone (1899–1947). This was derived from illegal liquor trading and alky-cookers (illicit stills), gambling establishments, dog tracks, dance halls, "protection" rackets and vice. On his business card, Capone described himself as a "Second Hand Furniture Dealer."

Paul McCartney reputedly earned £25 million ($57.5 million) in 1979–80 for the highest gross income in a year by a Briton.

Youngest Millionaire and Millionairess

The youngest person ever to accumulate $1 million was the child film actor Jackie Coogan (b Los Angeles, Oct 26, 1914), co-star with (Sir) Charles Chaplin (1889–1977) in "The Kid," made in 1920.

Shirley Temple (b Apr 23, 1928, Santa Monica, Calif), formerly Mrs John Agar, Jr now Mrs Charles Black, accumulated wealth in excess of $1 million before she was 10 years old. Her child actress career spanned the years 1934–39.

Millionairesses

The world's wealthiest woman was probably Princess Wilhelmina Helena Pauline Maria of Orange-Nassau (1880–1962), formerly Queen of the Netherlands (from 1890 to her abdication, Sept 4, 1948), with a fortune which was estimated at over $550 million.

The cosmetician Madame Charles Joseph Walker (née Sarah Breedlove, b Louisiana Delta, Dec 23, 1867), a black woman, is reputed to have become the first self-made millionairess. She was an uneducated orphan whose fortune was founded on a hair straightener. She had been a scrubwoman and a laundress.

It was estimated in 1979 that 50.4% of the US' 519,834 millionaires are in fact millionairesses, with the highest density in Idaho (262.5 per 1,000) and the lowest in Wyoming (1.9 per 1,000).

Greatest Miser

If meanness is measurable as a ratio between expendable assets and expenditure then Henrietta (Hetty) Howland Green (née Robinson) (1835–1916), who kept a balance of over $31,400,000 in one bank alone, was the all-time world champion. She was so stingy that her son had to have his leg amputated because of the delays in finding a *free* medical clinic. She herself lived off cold oatmeal because she was too thrifty to heat it, and died of apoplexy in an argument over the virtues of skimmed milk. Her estate proved to be worth $95 million.

Richest Families

It has been tentatively estimated that the combined value of the assets nominally controlled by the Du Pont family of some 1,600 members may be on the order of $150,000 million. The family arrived from France on Jan 1, 1800. Capital from Pierre Du Pont (1739–1817) enabled his son Eleuthère Irénée Du Pont to start his explosives company (E. I. Du Pont) in the US.

Biggest Dowry

The largest recorded dowry was that of Elena Patiño, daughter of Don Simón Iturbi Patiño (1861–1947), the Bolivian tin millionaire, who in 1929 bestowed $22,400,000 from a fortune at one time estimated to be worth $350 million.

Longest Pension

Miss Millicent Barclay, daughter of Col William Barclay (GB), was born posthumously on July 10, 1872, and became eligible for a Madras Military Fund pension to continue until her marriage. She died unmarried on Oct 26, 1969, having drawn the pension for every day of her life of 97 years 3 months.

Highest Earnings

The highest remuneration reported for any US business executive in 1979 was $2,202,938 in salary, bonus, stock awards and other benefits to David Tendler, 42, of Englehardt Minerals and Chemicals Corp, and president of Philipps Bros trading division.

Highest Fee

The highest paid investment consultant in the world is Dr Harry D. Schultz, who operates in Western Europe. His standard consultation fee for 60 min is $2,000 on weekdays and $3,000 on weekends. His quarterly retainer permitting companies to call him on a daily basis is $28,125. He writes and edits an information-packed International Newsletter instituted in 1964 now sold at $25 per copy.

Lowest Incomes

The poorest people in the world are the Tasaday tribe of cave-dwellers of central Mindanao, the Philippines, who were "discovered" in 1971 and live without any domesticated animals, agriculture, pottery, wheels or clothes.

Return of Cash

The largest amount of cash ever found and returned to its rightful owners was $500,000 found by Lowell Elliott, 61, on his farm at Peru, Ind. It had been dropped in June 1972 by a parachuting skyjacker.

Greatest Bequests

The greatest bequests in a lifetime of a millionaire were those of the late John Davison Rockefeller (1839–1937), who gave away sums totaling $750 million.

The Scottish-born US citizen Andrew Carnegie (1835–1919) is estimated to have made benefactions totaling $350 million in the last 18 years of his life. These included 7,689 church organs and 2,811 libraries. He had started in a bobbin factory at $1.20 per week.

The largest bequest made in the history of philanthropy was the $500 million-gift, announced on Dec 12, 1955, to 4,157 educational and other institutions by the Ford Foundation (established 1936) of NYC.

2. HONORS, DECORATIONS AND AWARDS

Eponymous Record

The largest object to which a human name is attached is the universe itself—in the case of the "standard" cosmological model devised in 1922 by the Russian mathematician Aleksandr Aleksandrovich Friedman (1888–1925) and known as Friedman's Universe. The model was undermined in Jan 1980 by the quadrupole on-isotropy theory, which denies the Friedmanian model. The new model may eventually be named after F. Melchiori of the University of Florence.

Highest US Decoration

The highest US decoration is the Congressional Medal of Honor. Five marines received both the Army and Navy Medals of Honor for the same acts in 1918, and 14 officers and men from 1863 to 1915 have received the medal on two occasions.

Top Jet Ace

The greatest number of kills in jet-to-jet battles is 16 by Capt Joseph Christopher McConnell (USAF) in the Korean War (1950–53). He was killed on Aug 25, 1954. It is possible that an Israeli ace may have surpassed this total in the period 1967–70, but the identity of pilots is subject to strict security.

Top Woman Ace

The record score for any woman fighter pilot is 12 by Jr Lt Lydia Litvak (USSR) in the Eastern Front campaign of 1941–43. She was killed in action on Aug 1, 1943.

Top Scoring Air Aces

Country	World War I 1914–1918	World War II 1939–1945
World	80 Rittm Manfred Freiherr (Baron) von Richthofen (Germany)	352[1] Major Erich Hartmann (Germany)
US	26 Capt Edward Vernon Rickenbacker, M.H., D.S.C. (7 o.l.c.), L. d'H., C. de G.	40 Major Richard I. Bong, M.H., D.S.C., S.S., D.F.C. (6 o.l.c.), A.M. (11 o.l.c.).
Canada	72 Lt-Col William Avery Bishop, V.C., C.B., D.S.O. and bar, M.C., D.F.C., L. d'H., C. de G.	31½ Sq-Ldr George F. Beurling, D.S.O., D.F.C., D.F.M. and bar.

[1] All but one of the aircraft in this unrivaled total were Soviet combat aircraft on the Eastern Front in 1942–1945.

MOST CLUSTERS AND GOLD STARS

Navy Cross	4 gold stars	Brig Gen Lewis B. Puller, USMC
		Cdr Ray M. Davenport, USN
Distinguished Service Cross	7 clusters	Capt Edward Rickenbacker (d 1973)
Silver Star	8 clusters	Col David H. Hackworth, USA
	2 gold stars	Lt-Col Raymond L. Murray, USMC
Distinguished Flying Cross	11 clusters	Col Francis S. Gabreski, USAF
	8 gold stars	Capt Howard J. Finn, USMC
Distinguished Service Medal (Army)	4 clusters	Gen of the Army Douglas MacArthur (also one Naval award)
		Gen of the Army Dwight D. Eisenhower
Distinguished Service Medal (Navy)	3 gold stars	Fleet Adm William F. Halsey
Legion of Merit	5 clusters	Maj Gen Richard Steinbach
	4 gold stars	Lt Gen Claire E. Hutchin
Purple Heart	9 clusters	Sgt Raymond E. Tirva

WAR HEROES: Audie Murphy (left) was the most decorated soldier in World War II, while Baron Von Richtofen of Germany was the World War I air ace with 80 planes shot down.

Most Decorated Soldier

Audie Murphy (1924–71) was the most decorated soldier in World War II, receiving the Medal of Honor, the Silver Star with 2 oak leaf clusters, the Bronze Star with an oak leaf cluster, the Distinguished Service Cross, the French Croix de Guerre, the Legion of Merit, the Purple Heart with 2 oak leaf clusters, and the French Légion d'Honneur.

Most Statues

The record for raising statues to oneself was set by Generalissimo Dr Rafael Leónidas Trujillo y Molina (1891–1961), a former President of the Dominican Republic. In March 1960 a count showed that there were "over 2,000." The country's highest mountain was named Pico Trujillo (now Pico Duarte). One province was called Trujillo and another Trujillo Valdez. The capital was named Ciudad Trujillo (Trujillo City) in 1936, but reverted to its old name of Santo Domingo on Nov 23, 1961. Trujillo was assassinated in a car ambush on May 30, 1961, and May 30 is now celebrated annually as a public holiday.

The man to whom most statues have been raised is undoubtedly Vladimir Ilyich Ulyanov, *alias* Lenin (1870–1924), busts of whom have been mass-produced. Busts of Mao Tse-tung (1893–1976) and Ho Chi Minh (1890–1969) have also been mass-produced.

Most Honorary Degrees

The greatest number of honorary degrees awarded to any individual is 89, given to Herbert Clark Hoover (1874–1964), former President of the United States (1929–33).

Most Valuable Annual Award

The highest valued annual award is the Templeton Foundation Prize for Progress in Religion inaugurated in 1972 by John M. Templeton of England. The award has been increased from £34,000 to £90,000 ($207,000) for 1981.

Nobel Prizes

The Nobel Foundation of $8,960,000 was set up under the will of Alfred Bernhard Nobel (1833–96), the unmarried Swedish chemist and chemical engineer who invented dynamite in 1866. The Nobel Prizes are presented annually on Dec 10, the anniversary of Nobel's death and the festival day of the Foundation. Since the first Prizes were awarded in 1901, the highest cash value of the award, in each of the six fields of Physics, Chemistry, Medicine and Physiology, Literature, Peace and Economics was $192,775 in 1979.

Most Nobel Prizes by Countries

US citizens have won outright or shared in the greatest number of awards (including those made in 1979) with a total of 148 made up of 41 for Physics, 21 for Chemistry, 53 for Medicine-Physiology, 9 for Literature, 17 for Peace and 7 for Economics.

By classes, the US holds the records for Medicine-Physiology with 53, for Physics with 41, for Peace with 17 and Economics with 7; Germany for Chemistry with 22; and France for Literature with 12.

Individual Nobel Prize Winners

Individually the only person to have won two Prizes outright is Dr Linus Carl Pauling (b Feb 28, 1901), Prof of Chemistry since 1931 at the Calif Institute of Technology, Pasadena, Calif. He was awarded the Chemistry Prize for 1954 and the Peace Prize for 1962. Only two others have won two Prizes. One was Madame Marie Curie (1867–1934), born in Poland as Marja Sklodowska, who shared the 1903 Physics Prize with her husband, Pierre Curie (1859–1906), and Antoine Henri Becquerel (1852–1908), and won the 1911 Chemistry Prize outright. The other was Prof John Bardeen (b May 23, 1908), who shared the Physics Prize in 1956 and 1972. The Peace Prize has been awarded three times to the International Committee of the Red Cross (founded Oct 29, 1863), of Geneva, Switzerland, namely in 1917, 1944 and in 1963, when it was shared with the International League of Red Cross Societies.

Oldest and Youngest Prize Winners

The oldest prizeman was Prof Francis Peyton Rous (b Baltimore, 1879–1970), who worked at the Rockefeller Institute, NYC. He shared the Medicine Prize in 1966, at the age of 87.

The youngest laureate has been Prof Sir William Lawrence Bragg (b Adelaide, South Australia, 1890, d 1971), of the UK, who, at the age of 25, shared the 1915 Physics Prize with his father, Sir William Henry Bragg (1862–1942), for work on X-rays and crystal structures. Bragg and also Theodore William Richards (1868–1928) (US) who won the 1914 Chemistry Prize, carried out their prize work when aged 23. The youngest Literature prizeman was (Joseph) Rudyard Kipling (UK) (1865–1936) at the age of 41, in 1907. The youngest Peace Prize winner was the Rev Dr Martin Luther King, Jr (b Jan 15, 1929, assassinated Apr 4, 1968), of the US, in 1964 at the age of 35.

YOUNGEST LITERATURE PRIZE WINNER: At 41, Rudyard Kipling (above) won the Nobel prize, one of the awards provided by Alfred Nobel (right) upon his death. Nobel made his money by inventing dynamite.

Who's Who

The longest entries of the 66,000 entires in *Who's Who in America* is that of Dr Glen T. Seaborg (b Apr 12, 1912), whose all-time record listing of 97 lines compares with the 16-line sketch on President Carter.

In the British *Who's Who*, the longest entry was that of Winston Churchill, who appeared in 67 editions from 1899 (18 lines) and had 211 lines by the 1965 edition. When he died he was replaced by the romantic novelist, Barbara Cartland, who had 114 lines in the 1980 edition. The youngest entry of those who qualify without hereditary title is Yehudi Menuhin (b NYC, Apr 22, 1916), the concert violinist now living in England, who first appeared in the 1932 edition, aged 15.

Chapter 12

Sports, Games and
Pastimes

Many more sports, records and details can be found in the "Guinness Book of Sports Records, Winners and Champions" published in 1980 by Sterling.

Earliest

The origins of sport stem from the time when self-preservation ceased to be the all-consuming human preoccupation. Archery was a hunting skill in Mesolithic times (by *c.* 8000 BC), but did not become an organized sport until about 300 AD, among the Genoese. The earliest dated evidence for sport is *c.* 2450 BC for fowling with throwing sticks and hunting. Ball games by girls, depicted on Middle Kingdom murals at Beni Hasan, Egypt, have been dated to *c.* 2050 BC.

Fastest

The highest speed reached in a non-mechanical sport is in sky-diving, in which a speed of 185 mph is attained in a head-down free-falling position, even in the lower atmosphere. In delayed drops, a speed of 614 mph has been recorded at high rarefied altitudes. The highest projectile speed in any moving ball game is *c.* 188 mph in pelota (jai-alai). This compares with 170 mph (electronically-timed) for a golf ball driven off a tee.

Slowest

In amateur wrestling, before the rules were modified toward "brighter wrestling," contestants could be locked in holds for so long that a single bout once lasted for 11 hours 40 min. In the extreme case of the 2-hour 41-min pull in the regimental tug o'war in Jubbulpore, India, Aug 12, 1889, the winning team moved a net distance of 12 ft at an average speed of 0.00084 mph.

Longest

The most protracted sporting contest was an automobile duration test of 222,618 miles by Appaurchaux and others in a Ford Taunus. This was contested over 142 days in 1963. The distance was equivalent to 8.93 times around the equator.

The most protracted non-mechanical sporting event is the *Tour de France* cycling race. In 1926 this was over 3,569 miles, lasting 29 days.

The total damage to the French national economy due to the interest in this annual event, now reduced to 23 days, is immense, and is currently estimated to be in excess of $2,000 million.

Largest Field

The largest field for any ball game is that for polo with 12.4 acres, or a maximum length of 300 yd and a width, without side-boards, of 200 yd.

Most Participants

The *Stramilano* 22-km run around Milan, Italy, attracted over 50,000 runners on Apr 16, 1978.

In May 1971, the "Ramblin' Raft Race" on the Chattahoochee River at Atlanta, Ga, attracted 37,683 competitors on 8,304 rafts.

According to a report issued in 1978, 55 million people are actively involved in sports in the USSR, using 3,282 stadiums, 1,435 swimming pools and over 66,000 indoor gymnasiums. It is estimated that some 29% of the East German population participates in sport regularly.

Worst Disasters

The worst disaster in recent history was when an estimated 604 were killed after some stands at the Hong Kong Jockey Club race course collapsed and caught fire on Feb 26, 1918. During the reign of Antoninus Pius (138–161 AD) the upper wooden tiers in the Circus Maximus, Rome, collapsed during a gladiatorial combat, killing 1,112 spectators.

Heaviest Sportsmen

The heaviest sportsman of all time was the wrestler William J. Cobb of Macon, Ga, who in 1962 was billed as the 802-lb "Happy Humphrey." The heaviest player of a ball game was Bob Pointer, the 487-lb tackle, formerly on the 1967 Santa Barbara High School team.

Youngest and Oldest Recordbreakers

The youngest age at which any person has broken a world record is 12 years 298 days in the case of Gertrude Caroline Ederle (b Oct 23, 1906)

MOST PARTICIPANTS: 37,683 people on 8,304 rafts entered the "Ramblin' Raft Race" on the Chattahoochee River.

of the US, who broke the women's 880-yd freestyle swimming world record with 13 min 19.0 sec at Indianapolis, Ind, Aug 17, 1919.

The oldest person to break a world record is Irish-born John J. Flanagan (1868–1938), triple Olympic hammer throw champion for the US, 1900–1908, who set his last world record of 184 ft 4 in at New Haven, Conn, July 24, 1909, aged 41 years 196 days.

Youngest and Oldest Internationals

The youngest age at which any person has won international honors is 8 years in the case of Joy Foster, the Jamaican singles and mixed doubles table tennis champion in 1958. It would appear that the greatest age at which anyone has actively competed for his country is 72 years 280 days in the case of Oscar G. Swahn (Sweden) (1847–1927), who won a silver medal for shooting in the Olympic Games at Antwerp on July 26, 1920. He qualified for the 1924 Games, but was unable to participate because of illness.

Most Versatile Athletes

Charlotte "Lottie" Dod (1871–1960) won the Wimbledon singles title (1887 to 1893) 5 times, the British Ladies Golf Championship in 1904, an Olympic silver medal for archery in 1908, and represented England at hockey in 1899. She also excelled at skating and tobogganing.

Mildred (Babe) Didrikson Zaharias (US) was an All-American basketball player, took the silver medal in the high jump, and gold medals in the javelin throw and hurdles in the 1932 Olympics. Turning professional, she first trained as a boxer, and then, switching to golf, eventually won 19 championships, including the US Women's Open and All-American Open. She holds the women's world record also for longest throw of a baseball—296 ft.

Most Prolific Recordbreaker

Between Jan 24, 1970, and Nov 1, 1977, Vasili Alexeyev (USSR) (b Jan 7, 1942) broke a total of 80 official world records in weight lifting.

Youngest and Oldest Champions

The youngest person to have successfully participated in a world title event was a French boy, whose name is not recorded, who coxed the winning Netherlands pair at Paris on Aug 26, 1900. He was not more than 10 and may have been as young as 7. The youngest individual Olympic winner was Marjorie Gestring (US) (b Nov 18, 1922), who took the springboard diving title at the age of 13 years 268 days at the Olympic Games in Berlin, Aug 12, 1936. Oscar G. Swahn (see above) was aged 65 years 258 days when he won the gold medal in the 1912 Olympic Running Deer team shooting competition.

Longest Reign

The longest reign as a world champion is 33 years (1829–62) by Jacques Edmond Barre (France, 1802–73) at real (royal) tennis.

Greatest Earnings

The greatest fortune amassed by an individual in sport is an estimated $60 million by the boxer Muhammad Ali Haj to Aug 1979. The most for

EARLY AND OFTEN: In 1919, Gertrude Ederle (left) became the youngest record-breaker ever by setting a swimming record when she was only 12 years old. She was also the first woman to successfully swim the English Channel. Vasili Alexeyev (right) has broken 80 world records in less than 8 years.

a single event is a reported purse of $8,500,000 earned by Sugar Ray Leonard (US) when he lost the WBC welterweight title to Roberto Duran (Panama) in the Olympic Stadium, Montreal on June 20, 1980.

The highest-paid woman athlete is ice skater Janet Lynn (*née* Nowicki) (US) (b Apr 6, 1953) who in 1974 signed a $1,500,000 three-year contract. In 1974 she earned more than $750,000.

Largest Trophy

The world's largest trophy for a particular sport is the Bangalore Limited Handicap Polo Tournament Trophy. This massive cup is 6 ft tall and was presented in 1936 by the Raja of Kolanka.

Most Expensive Sport

The most expensive of all sports is the racing of large yachts—"J" type boats and International 12-m boats. The owning and racing of these is beyond the means of individual millionaires and is confined to multi-millionaires or syndicates.

Largest Crowd

The greatest number of live spectators for any sporting spectacle is the estimated 2,500,000 who lined the route of the New York Marathon in Oct 1979. The race was won by Bill Rodgers (US) for the fourth consecutive time. However, spread over 23 days, it is estimated that more than 10 million see the annual *Tour de France* along the route.

GREATEST TV AUDIENCE: The 1978 World Cup final drew the largest TV audience in sports history (excluding the Olympics) with 400 million viewers. Here, Mario Kempes scores for Argentina in their 3–1 victory over Holland.

The largest crowd traveling to any single sporting event is "more than 400,000" for the annual *Grand Prix d'Endurance* motor race on the Sarthe circuit near Le Mans, France. The record stadium crowd was one of 199,854 for the Brazil *vs.* Uruguay soccer match in the Maracaña Municipal Stadium, Rio de Janeiro, Brazil, July 16, 1950.

The largest television audience for a single sporting event (excluding Olympic events) was the 400 million who watched the final of the 1978 World Cup soccer competition.

AEROBATICS

Earliest

The first aerobatic maneuver is generally considered the sustained inverted flight in a Blériot of Célestin-Adolphe Pégoud (1889–1915) at Buc, France, Sept 21, 1913, but Lieut Peter Nikolayevich Nesterov (1887–1914), of the Imperial Russian Air Service, performed a loop in a Nieuport Type IV monoplane at Kiev, USSR, Aug 27, 1913.

World Championships

Held biennially since 1960 (excepting 1974), scoring is based on the system devised by Col José Aresti of Spain. The competitions consist of two compulsory and two free programs. Team competition has been won on 4 occasions by the USSR. No individual has won more than one title, the most successful competitor being Igor Egorov (USSR) who won in 1970, was second in 1976, fifth in 1972 and eleventh in 1968. The most successful in the women's competition has been Lidia Leonova (USSR) with first place in 1976, second in 1978, third in 1972 and fifth in 1970.

Inverted Flight

The duration record for inverted flight is 2 hours 15 min 4 sec by John Leggatt in a Champion Decathlon on May 28, 1974, over the Arizona Desert.

Loops

John "Hal" McClain performed 1,501½ inside loops in a Pitts S-2A over Long Beach, Calif, Dec 16, 1973. He also achieved 180 outside loops in a Bellanca Super Decathlon, Sept 2, 1978, over Houston, Tex.

ARCHERY

Earliest References

Though the earliest evidence of the existence of bows is seen in the Mesolithic cave paintings in Spain, archery as an organized sport appears to have developed in the 3rd century AD. The world governing body is the *Fédération Internationale de Tir à l'Arc* (FITA), founded in 1931.

Flight Shooting

The longest flight shooting records are achieved in the footbow class. In the unlimited footbow division, the professional Harry Drake (b May 7, 1915) of Lakeside, Calif, holds the record at 1 mile 268 yd, shot at Ivanpah Dry Lake, Calif, Oct 24, 1971. The crossbow record is 1,359 yd 29 in, held by Drake and set at the same venue, Oct 14–15, 1967. The unlimited handbow class (*i.e.* standing stance with bow of any weight) record is 1,164 yd 2 ft 9 in by Don Brown (b Nov 13, 1946) at Wendover, Utah, Sept 18, 1977. April Moon (US) set a women's record of 870 yd 1 ft 2 in at Ivanpah Dry Lake, Oct 7, 1979.

Sultan Selim III shot an arrow 1,400 Turkish *pikes* or *gez* near Istanbul, Turkey, in 1798. The equivalent English distance is somewhere between 953 and 972 yd.

Highest Scores

The world records for a single FITA round are: men, 1,341 points (of a possible 1,440) by Darrell Pace (US) at Kumamoto, Japan, Nov 3–4, 1979; and women, 1,321 points (possible 1,440) by Natalia Butuzova (USSR) in Poland, Aug 1979.

There are no world records for Double FITA rounds, but the highest scores achieved in either a world or Olympic championship are: men, 2,571 points (possible 2,880) by Darrell Pace (US) posted at the 1976 Olympics at Montreal, July 27–30, 1976; women, 2,515 by Luann Ryon (US) at Canberra, Australia, Feb 11–12, 1977.

Most Titles

The greatest number of world titles (instituted 1931) ever won by a man is 4 by Hans Deutgen (Sweden), 1947–50. The greatest number won by a woman is 7 by Mrs Janina Spychajowa-Kurkowska (Poland), 1931–34, 1936, 1939 and 1947.

Oscar Kessels (Belgium) participated in 21 world championships.

Olympic Medals

Hubert van Innis (Belgium) (1866–1961) won 6 gold and 3 silver medals in archery events at the 1900 and 1920 Olympic Games.

Greatest Pull

Gary Sentman of Roseburg, Ore, drew a longbow weighing a record 176 lb to the maximum draw on the arrow (28¼ in) at Forksville, Pa, Sept 20, 1975.

Highest 24-Hour Score

The record over 24 hours by a pair of archers is 51,633 during 48 Portsmouth Rounds (60 arrows at 20 yards with a 2-in diameter 10 ring) shot by Jimmy Watt and Gordon Danby at the Epsom Showgrounds, Auckland, NZ, Nov 18–19, 1977.

HIGHEST SCORES: Darrell Pace holds records for both an FITA round and a Double FITA round.

AUTO RACING

Earliest Races

There are various conflicting claims, but the first automobile race was the 201-mile Green Bay-to-Madison, Wis, run in 1878, won by an Oshkosh steamer.

In 1887, Count Jules Felix Philippe Albert de Dion de Malfiance (1856–1946) won the *La Velocipede* 19.3-mile race in Paris in a De Dion steam quadricycle in which he is reputed to have exceeded 37 mph.

The first "real" race was from Paris to Bordeaux and back (732 miles) June 11–13, 1895. The winner was Emile Levassor (1844–97) (France) driving a Panhard-Levassor two-seater with a 1.2-liter Daimler engine developing 3½ hp. His time was 48 hours 47 min (average speed 15.01 mph). The first closed circuit race was held over 5 laps of a mile dirt track at Narragansett Park, Cranston, RI on Sept 7, 1896. It was won by A. H. Whiting, who drove a Riker electric.

The oldest auto race in the world still being regularly run is the R.A.C. Tourist Trophy, first staged on the Isle of Man on Sept 14, 1905. The oldest continental race is the French Grand Prix first held June 26–27, 1906. The Coppo Florio, in Sicily, has been irregularly held since 1900.

Fastest Circuits

The highest average lap speed attained on any closed circuit is 250.958 mph in a trial by Dr Hans Liebold (b Oct 12, 1926) (Germany) who lapped the 7.85-mile high-speed track at Nardo, Italy, in 1 min 52.67 sec in a Mercedes-Benz C111-IV experimental coupé on May 5, 1979. It was powered by a V8 engine with two KKK turbochargers with an output of 500 hp at 6,200 rpm.

The highest average race lap speed for a closed circuit is 214.158 mph by Mario Gabriele Andretti (US) (b Trieste, Italy, Feb 28, 1940) driving a 2.6-liter turbocharged Viceroy Parnelli-Offenhauser on the 2-mile 22-degree banked oval at Texas World Speedway, College Station, Tex, Oct 6, 1973.

The fastest road circuit was the Francorchamps circuit near Spa, Belgium, then 14.10 km (8 miles 1,340 yd) in length. It was lapped in 3 min 13.4 sec (average speed of 163.086 mph) on lap seven of the Francorchamps 1,000-km sports car race on May 6, 1973, by Henri Pescarolo (b Paris, France, Sept 25, 1942) driving a 2,933-cc V12 Matra-Simca MS 670 Group 5 sports car. The race lap average speed record at Berlin's AVUS track was 171.75 mph by Bernd Rosemeyer (Germany) (1909–38) in a 6-liter V16 Auto Union in 1937.

The fastest world championship Grand Prix circuit in current use is the 2.932-mile course at Silverstone, Northamptonshire, England (opened 1948). The race lap record is 1 min 14.40 sec (average speed 141.87 mph) by Gianclaudio (Clay) Regazzoni (Switzerland) (b Sept 5, 1939) driving a Saudia-Williams FW07 on July 14, 1979. The practice lap record is 1 min 11.88 sec (146.84 mph) by Alan Jones (Australia) (b Nov 2, 1946) in a Saudia-Williams on July 12, 1979.

Fastest Races

The fastest race in the world is the NASCAR Grand National 125-mile event (a qualifying race for the Daytona 500) on the 2½-mile 31-degree banked tri-oval at Daytona International Speedway, Daytona Beach, Fla. The record time is 40 min 55 sec (average speed 183.295 mph) by William Caleb "Cale" Yarborough (b March 27, 1939) of Timmonsville, SC, driving a 1969 Mercury V8, on Feb 19, 1970.

The fastest road race was the 1,000-km (621-mile) sports car race held on the Francorchamps circuit. The record time for this 71-lap (622.055-mile) race was 4 hours 1 min 9.7 sec (average speed 154.765 mph) by Pedro Rodriguez (1940–71) of Mexico and Keith Jack "Jackie" Oliver (b Chadwell Heath, Essex, England, Aug 14, 1942), driving a 4,998-cc flat-12 Porsche 917K Group 5 sports car on May 9, 1971.

Toughest Circuits

The Targa Florio (first run May 9, 1906) was widely acknowledged to be the most arduous race in the world. Held on the Piccolo Madonie Circuit in Sicily, it covered 11 laps (492.126 miles) and involved the negotiation of 9,350 corners over severe mountain gradients and narrow rough roads.

The record time was 6 hours 27 min 48.0 sec (average speed 76.141

mph) by Arturo Francesco Merzario (b Civenna, Italy, March 11, 1943) and Sandro Munari (b Venice, Italy, 1940) driving a 2,998.5-cc flat-12 Ferrari 312 P Group 5 sports car in the 56th race on May 21, 1972. The lap record was 33 min 36.0 sec (average speed 79.890 mph) by Leo Juhani Kinnunen (b Tampere, Finland, Aug 5, 1943) on lap 11 of the 54th race in a 2,997-cc flat-8 Porsche 908/3 Spyder Group 6 prototype sports car on May 3, 1970.

The most gruelling and slowest Grand Prix circuit is that for the Monaco Grand Prix (first run Apr 14, 1929), run through the streets and around the harbor of Monte Carlo. It is 3.312 km (2.058 miles) in length and has 11 pronounced corners and several sharp changes of gradient. The race is run over 76 laps (156.4 miles) and involves on average about 1,600 gear changes.

The record for the race is 1 hour 55 min 22.48 sec (average speed 81.338 mph) by Jody Scheckter (b South Africa, Jan 29, 1950) driving a Ferrari 312T4 on May 27, 1979. The race lap record is 1 min 28.65 sec (average speed 83.67 mph) by Andreas-Nikolaus "Niki" Lauda (b Austria, Feb 22, 1949) driving a Brabham-Alfa Romeo BT46 on May 7, 1978. The practice lap record is 1 min 26.45 sec (average speed 85.69 mph) by Jody Scheckter in a Ferrari 312T4 on May 26, 1979.

Le Mans

The greatest distance ever covered in the 24-hour *Grand Prix d'Endurance* (first held May 26–27, 1923) on the old Sarthe circuit (8 miles 650 yd) at Le Mans, France, is 3,315.208 miles by Dr Helmut Marko (b Graz, Austria, Apr 27, 1943) and Jonkheer Gijs van Lennep (b Bloemendaal, Netherlands, March 16, 1942) driving a 4,907-cc flat-12 Porsche 917K Group 5 sports car June 12–13, 1971. The record for the current circuit is 3,134.52 miles by Didier Pironi (b March 26, 1952) and Jean-Pierre Jaussaud (b June 3, 1937) (average speed 130.60 mph) in an Alpine Renault, June 10–11, 1978. The race lap record (8.475-mile lap) is 3 min 34.2 sec

MEN OF LE MANS: Jacky Ickx (left) shares the record of 4 wins in the Le Mans 24-hour race. He recorded the fastest practice lap in 1978, averaging 146.97 mph. Jean Pierre Jabouille (right) holds the race lap record of 3 min 34.3 sec (142.44 mph) over the 8.475-mile lap.

(average speed 142.44 mph) by Jean Pierre Jabouille (b France, Oct 1, 1942) driving an Alpine Renault on June 11, 1978. The practice lap record is 3 min 27.6 sec (average speed 146.97 mph) by Jacques-Bernard "Jacky" Ickx (b Belgium, Jan 1, 1945) in a turbocharged 2.1-liter Porsche 936/78 on June 7, 1978.

The race has been won by Ferrari cars nine times, in 1949, 1954, 1958 and 1960–65. The most wins by one man is 4 by Olivier Gendebien (Belgium), who won in 1958, 1960–62, and by Jacky Ickx (Belgium), who won in 1969, 1975–77.

Indianapolis 500

The Indianapolis 500-mile race (200 laps) was inaugurated on May 30, 1911. The most successful driver has been Anthony Joseph "A.J." Foyt, Jr, who won in 1961, 1964, 1967 and 1977.

The record time is 3 hours 4 min 5.54 sec (average speed 162.962 mph) by Mark Donohue (b NJ, March 18, 1937, d 1975) driving a 2,595-cc 900-bhp turbocharged Sunoco McLaren M16B-Offenhauser on May 27, 1972. The second prize fund was $1,271,954 for the 63rd race on May 27, 1979. The individual prize record is $290,363 by Al Unser (b Albuquerque, NM, May 29, 1939) on May 28, 1978.

The race lap record is 46.71 sec (average speed 192.678 mph) by Danny Ongais of Costa Mesa, Calif, driving a 2.6-liter turbocharged Parnelli-Cosworth DFX on lap 42 of the race held on May 29, 1977. The 4-lap qualifying record is 2 min 58.08 sec (average speed 202.156 mph) by Tom Sneva (b US, June 1, 1948) driving a Penske-Cosworth DFX turbocharged PC6 on May 20, 1978.

Fastest Pit Stop

Bobby Unser (US) took 4 sec to take on fuel on lap 10 of the Indianapolis 500 on May 30, 1976.

Duration Record

The greatest distance ever covered in one year is 400,000 km (248,548.5 miles) by François Lecot (1879–1949), an innkeeper from Rochetaillée, France, in a 1,900-cc 66-bhp Citroën 11 sedan mainly between Paris and Monte Carlo, from July 22, 1935 to July 26, 1936. He drove on 363 of the 370 days allowed.

The world's duration record is 185,353 miles 1,741 yd in 133 days 17 hours 37 min 38.64 sec (average speed 58.07 mph) by Marchand, Presalé and six others in a Citroën on the Montlhéry track near Paris, March–July 1933.

Most Successful Drivers

Based on the World Drivers' Championships, inaugurated in 1950, the most successful driver is Juan-Manuel Fangio y Cia (b Balcarce, Argentina, June 24, 1911), who won five times in 1951, 1954–57. He retired in 1958, after having won 24 Grand Prix races (2 shared).

The most successful driver in terms of race wins is Richard Lee Petty (b Randleman, NC, July 2, 1937) with 190 NASCAR Grand National wins from 1960 to Dec 1979. (See also *Stock Car Racing*.)

The most Grand Prix victories is 27 by Jackie Stewart of Scotland between Sept 12, 1965 and Aug 5, 1973. Jim Clark, (1936–1968) of Scotland

HIGHEST TERMINAL VELOCITY: Shirley "Cha Cha" Muldowney broke her own record with a 255.58-mph run in Jan 1979.

holds the record of Grand Prix victories in one year with 7 in 1963. He won 61 Formula One and Formula Libre races between 1959 and 1968. The most Grand Prix starts is 176 (out of a possible 184) between May 18, 1958, and Jan 26, 1975, by (Norman) Graham Hill (1929–1975). He took part in 90 *consecutive* Grands Prix between Nov 20, 1960 and Oct 5, 1969.

Oldest and Youngest World Champions

The oldest was Juan-Manuel Fangio, who won his last World Championship Aug 18, 1957, aged 46 years 55 days. The youngest was Emerson Fittipaldi (b São Paulo, Brazil, Dec 12, 1946) who won his first World Championship Sept 10, 1972, aged 25 years 273 days.

Oldest and Youngest Grand Prix Winners and Drivers

The youngest Grand Prix winner was Bruce Leslie McLaren (1937–70) of New Zealand, who won the US Grand Prix at Sebring, Fla, on Dec 12, 1959, aged 22 years 104 days. The oldest Grand Prix winner was Tazio Giorgio Nuvolari (1892–1953) of Italy, who won the Albi Grand Prix at Albi, France, on July 14, 1946, aged 53 years 240 days.

The oldest Grand Prix driver was Louis Alexandre Ghiron (Monaco, 1899–1979), who finished 6th in the Monaco Grand Prix on May 22, 1955, aged 55 years 292 days. The youngest Grand Prix driver was Christopher Arthur Amon (b Bulls, New Zealand, July 20, 1943) who took part in the Belgian Grand Prix on June 9, 1963, aged 19 years 324 days.

Land Speed Records

For details of the land speed record see pages 294 and 432.

The most successful land speed record breaker was Major Sir Malcolm Campbell (1885–1948) (UK). He broke the official record nine times between Sept 25, 1924, with 146.157 mph in a Sunbeam, and Sept 3, 1935, when he achieved 301.129 mph in the Rolls-Royce-engined *Bluebird*.

The world speed record for compression-ignition-engined cars is 190.344 mph (average of two runs over measured mile) by Robert Havemann of Eureka, Calif, driving his *Corsair* streamliner, powered by a turbocharged 6,981-cc 6-cylinder GMC 6-71 diesel engine developing 746 bhp, at Bonneville Salt Flats, Utah, in Aug 1971. The faster run was made at 210 mph.

Piston-Engined Dragsters

The lowest elapsed time recorded by a piston-engined dragster is 5.637 sec by Donald Glenn "Big Daddy" Garlits (b 1932) of Seffner, Fla, driving his rear-engined AA-F dragster, powered by a 7,948-cc supercharged Dodge V8 engine, during the National Hot Rod Association's Supernationals at Ontario Motor Speedway, Calif, Oct 11, 1975.

The highest terminal velocity recorded is 255.58 mph by Shirley Muldowney (US) at Pomona, Calif, in Jan 1979.

The world record for two runs in opposite directions over 440 yd from a standing start is 6.70 sec by Dennis Victor Priddle (b 1945) of Yeovil, Somerset, England, driving his 6,424-cc supercharged Chrysler dragster, developing 1,700 bhp using nitromethane and methanol, at Elvington Airfield, England, Oct 7, 1972. The faster run took 6.65 sec.

Rocket or Jet-Engined Dragsters

The highest terminal velocity recorded by any dragster is 377.754 mph (elapsed time 4.65 sec) by Norman Craig Breedlove (b March 23, 1938) of Los Angeles, driving his *English Leather Special* rocket dragster at Bonneville Salt Flats, Utah, in Sept 1973. The lowest elapsed time recorded by any dragster is 3.94 sec by Sam Miller (b Apr 15, 1945) of Wayne, NJ, in Miami, Fla, in Feb 1979.

Terminal velocity is the speed attained at the end of a 440-yd run made from a standing start and elapsed time is the time taken for the run.

Stock Car Racing

Richard Petty of Randleman, NC, was the first stock car driver to attain $1 million lifetime earnings on Aug 1, 1971. His earnings through the 1979 season were over $3,633,502. Petty also holds several NASCAR records, including: most races won (190), most victories in a single season (27 in 1967), most consecutive wins (10 in 1967), and greatest earnings in one year ($531,292 in 1979).

Earliest Rally

The earliest long rally was promoted by the Parisian daily *Le Matin* in 1907 from Peking to Paris, over a route of about 7,500 miles. Five cars left Peking on June 10. The winner, Prince Scipione Borghese, arrived in Paris on Aug 10, 1907 in his 40 hp Itala accompanied by his chauffeur, Ettore, and Luigi Barzini.

Longest Rallies

The world's longest ever rally event was the *Singapore Airlines* London-Sydney Rally run over 19,329 miles starting from Covent Garden, Greater London, on Aug 14, 1977, ending at the Sydney Opera House, passing through 17 countries. It was won Sept 28, 1977, by Andrew Cowan, Colin Malkin and Michael Broad in a Mercedes 280E.

The longest rally held annually is the East African Safari (first run 1953 through Kenya, Tanzania and Uganda), which is up to 3,874 miles

TOAST OF MONTE CARLO: Italy's Sandro Munari (right) has won the famous Monte Carlo Rally a record 4 times. He and partner Silvio Maiga are enjoying a champagne celebration after their victory in 1976.

long, as in the 17th Safari held Apr 8–12, 1971. It has been won a record three times by Joginder Singh (Kenya) in 1965, 1974 and 1976 and Shekhar Mehta (Uganda) in 1973, 1979 and 1980.

Monte Carlo

The Monte Carlo Rally (first run 1911) has been won a record 4 times by Sandro Munari (Italy) in 1972, 1975–77. The smallest car to win was an 851-cc Saab driven by Erik Carlsson (b Sweden, March 5, 1929) and Gunnar Häggbom of Sweden, on Jan 25, 1962, and by Carlsson and Gunnar Palm on Jan 24, 1963.

Pikes Peak Race

The Pikes Peak Auto Hill Climb, Colorado (instituted 1916) has been won by Bobby Unser 13 times between 1956 and 1974 (10 championship, 2 stock and 1 sports car title). On June 30, 1968, in the 46th race, he set an absolute record of 11 min 54.9 sec in his 5,506-cc Chevrolet championship car over the 12.42-mile course, rising from 9,402 to 14,110 ft through 157 curves.

BADMINTON

Origins

A game similar to badminton was played in China in the 2nd millennium BC. The modern game was devised c. 1863 at Badminton Hall in Avon, England, the seat of the Dukes of Beaufort. The oldest club is the Newcastle Badminton Club, England, formed as the Armstrong College Club, Jan 24, 1900.

International Championships

The International Championship or Thomas Cup (instituted 1948) has been won 7 times by Indonesia, in 1958, 1961, 1964, 1970, 1973, 1976 and 1979.

The Ladies International Championship or Uber Cup (instituted 1956) has been won 4 times by Japan (1966, 1969, 1972 and 1978).

Most Titles

The record number of All-England Championship (instituted 1899) titles won is 21 by Sir George Thomas (1881–1972) between 1903 and 1928. The record for men's singles is 8 by Rudy Hartono Kurniwan (b Aug 18, 1948) of Indonesia (1968–74, 76). The most, including doubles, by women is 17, a record shared by Muriel Lucas (1899–1910) and Mrs G. C. K. Hashman (*née* Judy Devlin) (US) (b Oct 22, 1935), whose wins came from 1954 to 1967, including a record 10 singles titles.

Shortest Game

In the 1969 Uber Cup in Djakarta, Indonesia, Noriko Takagi (later Mrs Nakayama) (Japan) beat P. Tumengkol in 9 min.

Marathons

The longest singles match is 73 hours 20 min by Richard P. Cuthbert at Queen Elizabeth's Grammar School, Horncastle, Lincolnshire, England, Apr 23–26, 1979. (*This category will now be confined to two players only.*) Christopher Berry, Stephen Crilley, Christopher Southall, and Gary Wemyss played doubles for 60 hours 36 min at Arnold School, Blackpool, Lancashire, England, Aug 26–28, 1979.

Longest Hit

Frank Rugani drove a shuttlecock 79 ft 8½ in in indoor tests at San Jose, Calif, Feb 29, 1964.

MOST TITLES: Judy Hashman (left) won a total of 17 All-England titles, including a record 10 singles championships. Rudy Hartono (above) has the most men's singles titles with 8.

BASEBALL

Origins

The Reverend Thomas Wilson, of Maidstone, Kent, England, wrote disapprovingly, in 1700, of baseball being played on Sundays. It is also referred to in *Northanger Abbey* by Jane Austen, *c.* 1798.

Earliest Games

The earliest game on record under the Cartwright rules was on June 19, 1846, in Hoboken, NJ, where the "New York Nine" defeated the Knickerbockers 23 to 1 in 4 innings. The earliest all-professional team was the Cincinnati Red Stockings in 1869, who had 56 wins and 1 tie that season.

Home Runs

Henry L. (Hank) Aaron broke the major league record set by George H. (Babe) Ruth of 714 home runs in a lifetime when he hit No. 715 on Apr 8, 1974. Between 1954 and 1974 he hit 733 home runs in the National League. In 1975, he switched over to the American League and in that year and 1976, when he finally retired, he hit 22 more, bringing his lifetime total to 755, the major league record.

The Japanese slugger Sadaharu Oh (b May 20, 1940), of the Yomiuri Giants, hit his 850th career home run on June 12, 1980.

An all-league record of almost 800 in a lifetime has been claimed for Josh Gibson (1911–47) mostly for the Homestead Grays of the Negro National League, who was elected in 1972 to the Baseball Hall of Fame in Cooperstown, NY. Gibson is said to have hit 75 round-trippers in one season, in 1931, but no official records were kept.

FASTEST PITCHER (left): Nolan Ryan's pitches have been electronically timed at 100.9 mph. This blazing fastball has helped Ryan to game and season strikeout records and 4 no-hit games. MOST HOME RUNS (right): Hank Aaron collected more home runs and runs batted in than any other major leaguer.

The most officially recorded home runs hit by a professional player in the US in one season is 72, by Joe Bauman, of the Rosewell, NM team, a minor league club, in 1954. The major league record is 61 by Roger Maris, of the NY Yankees, in 1961.

The most home runs in a professional game is 8, by Justin Clarke of the Corsicana, Tex, minor league team, on June 15, 1902. The major league record is four, by several players.

Frank Robinson (b Aug 31, 1935) hit home runs in the most major league ballparks—at least one in 32 different stadiums during regular season games from 1956–1977.

The longest home run ever measured was one of 618 ft by Roy Edward "Dizzy" Carlyle (1900–56) in a minor league game at Emeryville Ball Park, Calif, July 4, 1929. Babe Ruth hit a 587-ft homer in a Boston Red Sox vs NY Giants game at Tampa, Fla, in 1919.

Fastest Pitcher

The fastest pitcher in the world is L. Nolan Ryan (Houston Astros) who, on Aug 20, 1974, in Anaheim Stadium, Calif, was electronically clocked at a speed of 100.9 mph.

Longest Throw

The longest throw of a 5-5¼-oz baseball is 445 ft 10 in by Glen Gorbous (b Canada) Aug 1, 1957. Mildred "Babe" Didrikson (later Mrs George Zaharias) (1914–56) threw a ball 296 ft at Jersey City, NJ, July 25, 1931.

Do-Nothing Record

Toby Harrah of the Texas Rangers (AL) played an entire double-header at shortstop on June 26, 1976, without having a chance to make any fielding plays, assists or putouts.

Do-Everything Record

Two major league ballplayers, Bert Campaneris (b March 12, 1942) and Cesar Tovar (b July 3, 1940), have the distinction of playing each of the nine field positions in a single major league game. Campaneris did it first, on Sept 8, 1965, when his team, the Kansas City A's, announced he would. He played one inning at each position, including the full eighth inning as a pitcher and gave up just one run. Tovar duplicated the feat on Sept 22, 1968, when he played for the Minnesota Twins. He pitched a scoreless first inning, and retired the first batter, none other than Campaneris.

Hit by Pitch

Ron Hunt, an infielder who played with various National League teams from 1963 to 1974, led the league in getting hit by pitched balls for a record 7 consecutive years. His career total is 243, also a major league record.

Fastest Base Runner

Ernest Evar Swanson (1902–73) took only 13.3 sec to circle the bases at Columbus, Ohio, in 1932, averaging 18.45 mph.

LITTLEST
MAJOR
LEAGUER:
Eddie Gaedel, a
3-ft-7-in stunt
man, walked on
4 pitches in his
only major
league
appearance.

Youngest and Oldest Players

The youngest major league player of all time was the Cincinnati pitcher Joe Nuxhall, who started his career in June 1944, aged 15 years 10 months 11 days.

Leroy Satchel Paige pitched three scoreless innings for the Kansas City Athletics at age 59 in 1965. Baseball's color barrier had kept him out of the major leagues until 1948, when he was a 42-year-old "rookie," and his record of 6 wins and 1 loss helped the Cleveland Indians win the pennant. His birthday is listed as July 7, 1906, but many believed he was born earlier. The Atlanta Braves carried him on their roster in 1968 to allow Paige to qualify for a pension.

Shortest and Tallest Players

The shortest major league player was surely Eddie Gaedel, a 3-ft-7-in, 65-lb midget, who pinch hit for the St Louis Browns vs the Detroit Tigers on Aug 19, 1951. Wearing number ⅛, the batter with the world's smallest major league strike zone walked on four pitches. Following the game, major league rules were hastily rewritten to prevent the recurrence of such an affair.

Fastball pitcher James Rodney Richard (b March 7, 1950) of the Houston Astros is reportedly the tallest ever major league ballplayer at 6 ft 8½ in.

Largest Stadium

The Cleveland Municipal Stadium in Cleveland, Ohio, has a seating capacity of 76,977.

World Series Attendance

The World Series record attendance is 420,784 (6 games with total receipts of $2,626,973.44) when the Los Angeles Dodgers beat the Chicago White Sox 4 games to 2, Oct 1–8, 1959.

The single game record is 92,706 for the fifth game (receipts $552,774.77) at the Memorial Coliseum (no longer used for baseball), Los Angeles, Oct 6, 1959.

Major League All-Time Records
(*including 1979 season*)
Individual Batting

Highest percentage, lifetime (5,000 at-bats)
.367 Tyrus R. Cobb, Det AL, 1905–26; Phil AL, 1927–28

Highest percentage, season (500 at-bats) (Leader in each league)
.438 Hugh Duffy, Bos NL, 1894
.422 Napoleon Lajoie, Phil AL, 1901

Most consecutive games played
2,130 Henry Louis Gehrig, NY AL, June 1, 1925 through Apr 30, 1939

Most runs batted in, season
190 Lewis R. (Hack) Wilson, Chi NL, 155 games, 1930

Most runs batted in, game
12 James L. Bottomley, St L NL, Sept 16, 1924

Most runs batted in, inning
7 Edward Cartwright, St L AA, Sept 23, 1890

Most base hits
4,191 Tyrus R. Cobb, Det AL, 1905–26; Phil AL, 1927–28; 24 years

Most runs batted in, lifetime
2,297 Henry L. Aaron, Mil NL, 1954–65, Atl NL, 1966–74; Mil AL, 1975–76

Most base hits, season
257 George H. Sisler, St L AL, 154 games, 1920

Most hits in succession
12 M. Frank (Pinky) Higgins, Bos AL, June 19–21 (4 games), 1938 Walter Dropo, Det AL, July 14, July 15, 2 games, 1952

Most base hits, consecutive, game
7 Wilbert Robinson, Balt NL, June 10, 1892, 1st game (7-ab), 6-1b, 1-2b

Renaldo Stennett, Pitt NL, Sept 16, 1975 (7-ab), 4-1b, 2-2b, 1-3b

Cesar Gutierrez, Det AL, June 21, 1970, 2nd game (7-ab) 6-1b, 1-2b (extra-inning game)

Most consecutive games batted safely, season
56 Joseph P. DiMaggio, NY AL (91 hits—16-2b, 4-3b, 15 hr), May 15 to July 16, 1941

IRON MAN: Lou Gehrig played in 2,130 consecutive games over a period of 15 years. He also hit 23 grand-slam home runs.

Most total bases, lifetime
6,856 Henry L. Aaron, Mil NL, 1954–65, Atl NL, 1966–74; Mil AL, 1975–76

Most total bases, season
457 George H. (Babe) Ruth, NY AL, 152 g. (85 on 1b, 88 on 2b, 48 on 3b, 236 on hr), 1921

Most total bases, game
18 Joseph W. Adcock, Mil NL (1-2b, 4-hr), July 31, 1954

Most one-base hits (singles), season
202 William H. Keeler, Balt NL, 128 games, 1898

Most two-base hits, season
67 Earl W. Webb, Bos AL, 151 games, 1931

Most three-base hits, season
36 J. Owen Wilson, Pitts NL, 152 games, 1912

Most home runs, season
61 Roger E. Maris, NY AL (162-game schedule) (30 home, 31 away), 161 gs, 1961
60 George H. (Babe) Ruth, NY AL (154-game schedule) (28 home, 32 away), 151 gs, 1927

Most home runs, lifetime
755 Henry L. Aaron, Mil NL, 1954
(13), 1955 (27), 1956 (26), 1957
(44), 1958 (30), 1959 (39), 1960
(40), 1961 (34), 1962 (45), 1963
(44), 1964 (24), 1965 (32); Atl
NL, 1966 (44), 1967 (39), 1968
(29), 1969 (44), 1970 (38), 1971
(47), 1972 (34), 1973 (40), 1974
(20); Mil AL, 1975 (12), 1976
(10)

Most home runs, bases filled, lifetime
23 Henry Louis Gehrig, NY AL,
1927–1938

Most home runs with bases filled, season
5 Ernest Banks, Chi NL, May 11,
19, July 17 (1st game), Aug 2,
Sept 19, 1955
James E. Gentile, Balt AL, May 9
(2), July 2, 7, Sept 22, 1961

Most home runs, with bases filled, same
game
2 Anthony M. Lazzeri, NY AL,
May 24, 1936
James R. Tabor, Bos AL (2nd
game), July 4, 1939
Rudolph York, Bos AL, July 27,
1946
James E. Gentile, Balt AL, May 9,
1961 (consecutive at-bats)
Tony L. Cloninger, Atl NL, July
3, 1966
James T. Northrup Det AL, June
24, 1968 (consecutive at-bats)
Frank Robinson, Balt AL, June
26, 1970 (consecutive at-bats)

Most bases on balls, game
6 James E. Foxx, Bos AL, June 16,
1938

Most bases on balls, season
170 George H. (Babe) Ruth, NY AL,
152 games, 1923

Most consecutive games hitting home
runs
8 R. Dale Long, Pitt NL, May
19–28, 1956

Most home runs, one doubleheader
5 Stanley F. Musial, St L NL, 1st
game (3), 2nd game (2), May 2,
1954
Nathan Colbert, SD NL, 1st game
(2), 2nd game (3), Aug 1, 1972

Most hits, pinch-hitter, lifetime
147 Manuel R. Mota, SF NL, 1962;
Pitt NL, 1963–1968; Mont NL,
1969; LA NL, 1969–1979

Most consecutive pinch hits, lifetime
9 David E. Philley, Phil NL, Sept 9,
11, 12, 13, 19, 20, 27, 28, 1958;
Apr 16, 1959

Most home runs, pinch-hitter, consecutive plate appearances
3 Del Unser, Phil NL, June 30, July
5, 10, 1979

Base Running

Most stolen bases, lifetime
938 Louis C. Brock, Chi-St L NL,
1961–79

Most stolen bases, season since 1900
118 Louis C. Brock, St L NL, 153
games, 1974

Most stolen bases, game
7 George F. (Piano Legs) Gore, Chi
NL, June 25, 1881
William R. (Sliding Billy) Hamil-
ton, Phil NL, 2nd game, 8 inn.,
Aug 31, 1894

Most times stealing home, lifetime
35 Tyrus R. Cobb, Det-Phil AL,
1905–28

Fewest times caught stealing, season (50+
attempts)
2 Max Carey, Pitt NL, 1922 (53
atts)

Pitching

Most games, lifetime
1,070 J. Hoyt Wilhelm, NY-St L-Atl-
Chi-LA (448) NL, 1952–57,
69–72; Clev-Balt-Chi-Cal (622)
AL, 1957–69

Most games, season
106 Mike Marshall, LA NL, 1974

Most complete games, lifetime
751 Denton T. (Cy) Young, Clev-St
L-Bos NL (428); Bos-Clev AL
(323), 1890–1911

Most complete games, season
74 William H. White, Cin NL, 1879

Most innings pitched, game
26 Leon J. Cadore, Bklyn NL, May
1, 1920
Joseph Oeschger, Bos NL, May 1,
1920

Lowest earned run average, season
0.90 Ferdinand M. Schupp, NY NL,
1916 (140 inn)
1.01 Hubert B. (Dutch) Leonard, Bos
AL, 1914 (222 inn)
1.12 Robert Gibson, St L NL, 1968
(305 inn)

Most games won, lifetime
511 Denton T. (Cy) Young, Clev NL
(239) 1890–98; St L NL (46))
1899–1900; Bos AL (193)
1901–08; Clev AL (29) 1909–11;
Bos NL (4) 1911

LONGEST HITTING STREAK: Three-time MVP Joe DiMaggio batted safely in 56 consecutive games in 1941.

Most games won, season
 60 Charles Radbourne, Providence NL, 1884

Most consecutive games won, lifetime
 24 Carl O. Hubbell, NY NL, 1936 (16); 1937 (8)

Most consecutive games won, season
 19 Timothy J. Keefe, NY NL, 1888
   Richard W. Marquard, NY NL, 1912

Most shutout games, season
 16 George W. Bradley, St L NL, 1876
   Grover C. Alexander, Phil NL, 1916

Most shutout games, lifetime
 113 Walter P. Johnson, Wash AL, 21 years, 1907–27

Most consecutive shutout games, season
 6 Donald S. Drysdale, LA NL, May 14, 18, 22, 26, 31, June 4, 1968

Most consecutive shutout innings
 58 Donald S. Drysdale, LA NL, May 14-June 8, 1968

Most strikeouts, lifetime
 3,508 Walter P. Johnson, Wash AL, 1907–27

Most strikeouts, season
 505 Matthew Kilroy, Balt AA, 1886 (Distance 50 ft)
 383 L. Nolan Ryan, Cal AL, 1973 (Distance 60 ft 6 in)

Most strikeouts, game (9 inn) since 1900:
 19 Steven N. Carlton, St L NL vs NY, Sept 15, 1969 (lost)
   G. Thomas Seaver, NY NL vs SD, Apr 22, 1970
   L. Nolan Ryan, Cal AL, vs Bos, Aug 12, 1974

Most strikeouts, extra-inning game
 21 Thomas E. Cheney, Wash AL vs Balt (16 inns), Sept 12, 1962 (night)

Most no-hit games, lifetime
 4 Sanford Koufax, LA NL, 1962–63–64–65
   L. Nolan Ryan, Cal AL, 1973(2)–74–75

Most consecutive no-hit games
 2 John S. Vander Meer, Cin NL, June 11–15, 1938

Perfect game—9 innings

1880	John Lee Richmond, Worcester vs Clev NL, June 12	1–0
	John M. Ward, Prov vs Buff NL, June 17 AM	5–0
1904	Denton T. (Cy) Young, Bos vs Phil AL, May 5	3–0
1908	Adrian C. Joss, Clev vs Chi AL, Oct 2	1–0
†1917	Ernest G. Shore, Bos vs Wash AL, June 23 (1st g)	4–0
1922	C. C. Robertson, Chi vs Det AL, Apr 30	2–0
*1956	Donald J. Larsen, NY AL vs Bklyn NL, Oct 8	2–0
1964	James P. Bunning, Phil NL vs NY, June 21 (1st g)	6–0
1965	Sanford Koufax, LA NL vs Chi, Sept 9	1–0
1968	James A. Hunter, Oak AL vs Minn, May 8	4–0

Special mention
1959 Harvey Haddix, Jr, Pitt vs Mil NL, May 26, pitched 12 "perfect" innings, allowed hit in 13th and lost.

---

†Starting pitcher, "Babe" Ruth, was banished from game by Umpire Owens after giving first batter, Morgan, a base on balls. Shore relieved and while he pitched to second batter, Morgan was caught stealing. Shore then retired next 26 batters to complete "perfect" game.
*World Series game.

WORLD SERIES LEADERS: Mickey Mantle (left) holds career series records for home runs (18), runs batted in (40), and runs scored (42). Yogi Berra (right) collected 71 base hits in 14 World Series, and played for the Yankees when they won a record 5 consecutive championships, 1949–53.

World Series Records

Most series played
14   Lawrence P. (Yogi) Berra, NY, AL, 1947, 49–53, 55–58, 60–63

Highest batting percentage (20 g min.), total series
.391   Louis C. Brock, St L NL, 1964, 67–68 (g-21, ab-87, h-34)

Highest batting percentage, 4 or more games, one series
.625   4-game series, George H. (Babe) Ruth, NY AL, 1928

Most runs, total series
42   Mickey C. Mantle, NY AL, 1951–53, 55–58, 60–64

Most runs, one series
10   Reginald M. Jackson, NY AL, 1977

Most runs batted in, total series
40   Mickey C. Mantle, NY, AL, 1951–53, 55–58, 60–64

Most runs batted in, game
6   Robert C. Richardson, NY AL, (4) 1st inn, (2) 4th inn, Oct 8, 1960

Most runs batted in, consecutive times at bat
7   James L. (Dusty) Rhodes, NY NL, first 4 times at bat, 1954

Most base hits, total series
71   Lawrence P. (Yogi) Berra, NY AL, 1947, 49–53, 55–58, 60–61

Most home runs, total series
18   Mickey C. Mantle, NY AL, 1952 (2), 53 (2), 55, 56 (3), 57, 58 (2), 60 (3), 63, 64 (3)

Most home runs, one series
5   Reginald M. Jackson, NY AL, 1977

Most home runs, game
3   George H. (Babe) Ruth, NY AL, Oct 6, 1926; Oct 9, 1928
Reginald M. Jackson, NY AL, Oct 18, 1977

Pitching in most series
11   Edward C. (Whitey) Ford, NY AL, 1950, 53, 55–58, 60–64

Most victories, total series
10   Edward C. (Whitey) Ford, NY AL, 1950 (1), 55 (2), 56 (1), 57 (1), 60 (2), 61 (2), 62 (1)

All victories, no defeats
6   Vernon L. (Lefty) Gomez, NY AL, 1932 (1), 36 (2), 37 (2), 38 (1)

Most games won, one series
3   games in 5-game series
Christy Mathewson, NY NL, 1905
J. W. Coombs, Phil AL, 1910
Many others won 3 games in series of more games.

Most shutout games, total series
4   Christy Mathewson, NY NL 1905 (3), 1913

Most shutout games, one series
3   Christy Mathewson, NY NL 1905

Most strikeouts, one pitcher, total series
94   Edward C. (Whitey) Ford, NY AL,
1950, 53, 55–58, 60–64

Most strikeouts, one series
23   in 4 games
Sanford Koufax, LA NL, 1963

18   in 5 games
Christy Mathewson, NY NL, 1905

20   in 6 games
C. A. (Chief) Bender, Phil AL,
1911

35   in 7 games
Robert Gibson, St L NL, 1968

28   in 8 games
W. H. Dinneen, Bos AL, 1903

Most strikeouts, one pitcher, game
17   Robert Gibson, St L NL, Oct 2,
1968

Most Series Won
22   New York AL, 1923, 1927, 1928,
1932, 1936–39, 1941, 1943, 1947,
1949–53, 1956, 1958, 1961, 1962,
1977, 1978

SWEET SWING:
Reggie Jackson
stroked 3 first-pitch
home runs in one
World Series game
in 1977.

BASKETBALL

Origins

Ollamalitzli was a 16th century Aztec precursor of basketball played in
Mexico. If the solid rubber ball was put through a fixed stone ring placed
high on one side of the stadium, the player was entitled to the clothing of
all the spectators. The captain of the losing team often lost his head (by
execution). Another game played much earlier, in the 10th century BC by
the Olmecs in Mexico, called *Pok-ta-Pok,* also resembled basketball in its
concept of a ring through which a round object was passed.

Modern basketball (which may have been based on the German game
of *Korbball*) was devised by the Canadian-born Dr James A. Naismith
(1861–1939) at the Training School of the International YMCA College
at Springfield, Mass, in Dec 1891. The first game played under modified
rules was on Jan 20, 1892. The first public contest was on March 11, 1892.

The International Amateur Basketball Federation (FIBA) was
founded in 1932.

Most Accurate Shooting

The greatest goal-shooting demonstration was made by a professional, Ted St. Martin, now of Jacksonville, Fla, who, on June 25, 1977, scored 2,036 consecutive free throws.

In a 24-hour period, May 31–June 1, 1975, Fred L. Newman of San Jose, Calif, scored 12,874 baskets out of 13,116 attempts (98.15%). Newman has also made 88 consecutive free throws while blindfolded at the Central YMCA, San Jose, Calif, Feb 5, 1978.

Longest Field Goal

The longest *measured* field goal in a college game was made from a measured distance of 89 ft 3 in by Les Henson for Virginia Tech vs Florida State, Jan 21, 1980. In an AAU game at Pacific Lutheran University on Jan 16, 1970, Steve Myers sank a shot while standing out of bounds at the other end of the court. Though the basket was illegal, the officials gave in to crowd sentiment and allowed the points to count. The distance is claimed to be 92 ft 3½ in from measurements made 10 years later.

Individual Scoring

Marie Boyd scored 156 points in a girls' high school basketball game for Central HS Lonaconing, Md, vs Ursaline Academy, on Feb 25, 1924. The boys' high school record is 135 points by Danny Heater of Burnsville, W Va, on Jan 26, 1960.

In college play, Clarence (Bevo) Francis of Rio Grande College, Ohio, scored 113 points against Hillsdale on Feb 2, 1954. One year earlier, Francis scored 116 points in a game, but the record was disallowed because the competition was with a two-year school.

Wilton Norman (Wilt) Chamberlain (b Aug 21, 1936) holds the professional record with 100 points for the Philadelphia Warriors vs NY Knicks, scored on March 2, 1962. During the same season, Wilt set the record for points in a season (4,029) and he also holds the career record (31,419).

Pearl Moore of Francis Marion College, Florence, SC, scored a record 4,061 points during her college career, 1975–79. She also holds the AIAW (Association for Intercollegiate Athletics for Women) single-game tournament record with 60 points. The men's college career scoring record is 4,045 points by Travis Grant for Kentucky State, 1969–72.

Tallest Players

The tallest player of all time is reputed to be Suleiman Ali Nashnush (b 1943) who played for the Libyan team in 1962 when he measured 8 ft tall. The tallest woman player is Iuliana Semenova (USSR) who is reputed to stand 7 ft 2 in tall and weigh 281 lb. The tallest NBA player is Tom Burleson, who is 7 ft 4 in tall.

Youngest and Oldest

Bill Willoughby (b May 20, 1957) made his NBA debut for the Atlanta Hawks on Oct 23, 1975, when he was 18 years 5 months 3 days old. The oldest NBA player was Bob Cousy (b Aug 9, 1928), who was 41 years 6 months 2 days old when he appeared in the last of seven games he played for the team he was coaching (Cincinnati Royals) during 1969–70.

LONGEST GOAL (left): Les Henson's 89-ft-3-in basket at the buzzer gave Virginia Tech a 2-point victory. MOST CAREER POINTS (right): Pearl Moore, now with the champion NY Stars pro team, scored the most points in college with 4,061.

Greatest Attendances

The Harlem Globetrotters played an exhibition to 75,000 in the Olympic Stadium, West Berlin, Germany, in 1951. The largest indoor basketball crowd was at the Astrodome, Houston, Tex, where 52,693 watched a game on Jan 20, 1968, between the University of Houston and UCLA.

The Harlem Globetrotters have traveled over 6 million miles, visited 94 countries on six continents, and have been watched by an estimated 80 million spectators. They have won over 12,000 games, losing less than 350, but many were not truly competitive. The team was founded by Abraham M. Saperstein (1903–66) of Chicago, and their first game was played at Hinckley, Ill, Jan 7, 1927.

Olympic Champions

The US won all 7 Olympic titles from the time the sport was introduced to the Games in 1936 until 1968, without losing a single contest. In 1972, in Munich, their run of 63 consecutive victories was broken when they lost 51–50 to the USSR in a much-disputed final game. They regained the Olympic title in Montreal in 1976, again without losing a game.

World Champions

Brazil, the USSR and Yugoslavia are the only countries to win the World Men's Championship (instituted 1950) on more than one occasion. Brazil won in 1959 and 1963; the USSR in 1967 and 1974; Yugoslavia in 1970 and 1978.

In 1975, the USSR won the women's championship (instituted 1953) for the fifth consecutive time since 1959.

Marathon

The longest game is 89 hours by two teams of five at Kwinana High School, W Australia, May 18–21, 1979.

NBA Regular Season Records (including 1979–80)

The National Basketball Association's Championship series was established in 1947. Prior to 1949, when it joined with the National Basketball League, the professional circuit was known as the Basketball Association of America.

SERVICE

Most Games, Lifetime
  1,270 John Havlicek, Bos 1963–78

Most Complete Games, Season
    79 Wilt Chamberlain, Phil 1962

Most Minutes, Lifetime
47,859 Wilt Chamberlain, Phil-SF-LA
      1960–73

Most Minutes, Season
  3,882 Wilt Chamberlain, Phil 1962

SCORING

Most Seasons Leading League
    7 Wilt Chamberlain, Phil 1960–62;
      SF 1963–64; SF-Phil 1965;
      Phil 1966

Most Points, Lifetime
31,419 Wilt Chamberlain, Phil-SF-LA
      1960–73

Most Points, Season
  4,029 Wilt Chamberlain, Phil 1962

Most Points, Game
   100 Wilt Chamberlain, Phil vs NY,
      Mar 2, 1962

Most Points, Half
    59 Wilt Chamberlain, Phil vs NY,
      Mar 2, 1962

Most Points, Quarter
    33 George Gervin, SA vs NO, Apr
      9, 1978

Most Points, Overtime Period
    13 Earl Monroe, Balt vs Det, Feb 6,
      1970
      Joe Caldwell, Atl vs Cin, Feb 18,
      1970

Highest Scoring Average, Lifetime (400+ games)
  30.1 Wilt Chamberlain, Phil-SF-LA
      1960–73

Highest Scoring Average, Season
  50.4 Wilt Chamberlain, Phil 1962

Field Goals Made

Most Field Goals, Lifetime
12,681 Wilt Chamberlain, Phil-SF-LA
      1960–73

Most Field Goals, Season
  1,597 Wilt Chamberlain, Phil 1962

Most Field Goals, Game
    36 Wilt Chamberlain, Phil vs NY,
      Mar 2, 1962

Most Field Goals, Half
    22 Wilt Chamberlain, Phil vs NY,
      Mar 2, 1962

Most Field Goals, Quarter
    13 David Thompson, Den vs Det,
      Apr 9, 1978

Most 3-Point Field Goals, Game
     8 Rick Barry, Hou vs Utah, Feb 9,
      1980

Field Goal Percentage

Most Seasons Leading League
    9 Wilt Chamberlain, Phil 1961; SF
      1963; SF-Phil 1965; Phil
      1966–68; LA 1969, 72–73

Highest Percentage, Lifetime
  .559 Artis Gilmore, Chi 1977–78

Highest Percentage, Season
  .727 Wilt Chamberlain, LA 1973

Free Throws Made

Most Free Throws Made, Lifetime
  7,694 Oscar Robertson, Cin-Mil
      1961–74

Most Free Throws Made, Season
   840 Jerry West, LA 1966

ALL-TIME LEADER: Wilt
Chamberlain (#13)
dominates the NBA record
book. There were 245
fifty-point efforts in the
NBA to Jan 1980, and
Wilt had 122 of them.

FREE THROW LEADER: Jerry West sank 840 free throws in his 1966 season for LA.

Most Free Throws Made, Consecutive, Season
    60 Rick Barry, GS Oct 22–Nov 16, 1976

Most Free Throws Made, Game
    28 Wilt Chamberlain, Phil vs NY, Mar 2, 1962

Most Free Throws Made (No Misses), Game
    19 Bob Pettit, St L vs Bos, Nov 22, 1961

Most Free Throws Made, Half
    19 Oscar Robertson, Cin vs Balt, Dec 27, 1964

Most Free Throws Made, Quarter
    14 Rick Barry, SF vs NY, Dec 6, 1966

Free Throw Percentage

Most Seasons Leading League
    7 Bill Sharman, Bos 1953–57, 59, 61

Highest Percentage, Lifetime
 .900 Rick Barry, SF-GS-Hou 1966–67, 73–80

Highest Percentage, Season
 .947 Rick Barry, Hou 1979

REBOUNDS

Most Seasons Leading League
   11 Wilt Chamberlain, Phil 1960–62; SF 1963; Phil 1966–68; LA 1969, 71–73

Most Rebounds, Lifetime
23,924 Wilt Chamberlain, Phil-SF-LA 1960–73

Most Rebounds, Season
 2,149 Wilt Chamberlain, Phil 1961

Most Rebounds, Game
   55 Wilt Chamberlain, Phil vs Bos, Nov 24, 1960

Most Rebounds, Half
   32 Bill Russell, Bos vs Phil, Nov 16, 1957

Most Rebounds, Quarter
   18 Nate Thurmond, SF vs Balt, Feb 28, 1965

Highest Average (per game), Lifetime
 22.9 Wilt Chamberlain, Phil-SF-LA 1960–73

Highest Average (per game), Season
 27.2 Wilt Chamberlain, Phil 1961

ASSISTS

Most Seasons Leading League
    8 Bob Cousy, Bos 1953–60

Most Assists, Lifetime
 9,887 Oscar Robertson, Cin-Mil 1961–74

Most Assists, Season
 1,099 Kevin Porter, Det 1979

ASSIST SPECIALIST: Oscar Robertson holds the career record for setting up plays with 9,887 assists and an average of 9.5 per game, lifetime.

HIGHEST LIFETIME FREE THROW SHOOTER: Rick Barry has made 90% of his free throws in his NBA career, including 60 in a row.

Most Assists, Quarter
12 Bob Cousy, Bos vs Minn, Feb 27, 1959
John Lucas, Hou vs Mil, Oct 27, 1977

Highest Average (per game), Lifetime
9.5 Oscar Robertson, Cin-Mil 1961–74

Highest Average (per game), Season
13.4 Kevin Porter, Det 1979

PERSONAL FOULS

Most Personal Fouls, Lifetime
3,855 Hal Greer, Syr-Phil 1959–73

Most Personal Fouls, Season
367 Bill Robinzine, KC 1979

Most Personal Fouls, Game
8 Don Otten, TC vs Sheb, Nov 24, 1949

DISQUALIFICATIONS
(Fouling Out of Game)

Most Disqualifications, Lifetime
127 Vern Mikkelsen, Minn, 1950–59

Most Disqualifications, Season
26 Don Meineke, Ft W 1953

Most Games, No Disqualifications, Lifetime
1,045 Wilt Chamberlain, Phil-SF-LA 1960–73 (Entire Career)

Most Assists, Game
29 Kevin Porter, NJ vs Hou Feb 24, 1978

Most Assists, Half
19 Bob Cousy, Bos vs Minn, Feb 27, 1959

BOBSLEDDING AND TOBOGGANING

Origins

The oldest known sled is dated *c.* 6500 BC and came from Heinola, Finland. The first known bobsled race took place at Davos, Switzerland, in 1889. The International Federation of Bobsleigh and Tobogganing was formed in 1923, followed by the International Bobsleigh Federation in 1957.

Olympic and World Titles

The Olympic 4-man bob title (instituted 1924) has been won 4 times by Switzerland (1924, 36, 56, 72). The US (1932, 1936), Switzerland (1936, 1980), Italy (1956, 1968) and W Germany (1952, 1972) have won the Olympic boblet event (instituted 1932) twice. The most medals won by an individual is 6 (2 gold, 2 silver, 2 bronze) by Eugenio Monti (Italy) (b Jan 23, 1928) from 1956 to 1968.

The world 4-man bob has been won 12 times by Switzerland (1924, 1936, 1939, 1947, 1954–57, 1971–73, 1975). Italy won the 2-man title 14

TOBOGGAN CHAMPION: Nino Bibbia of Italy has won 8 Grand National titles, 8 Curzon Cup titles, and the gold medal in the 1948 Olympic Games.

times (1954, 1956–63, 1966, 1968–69, 1971, 1975). Eugenio Monti has been a member of 11 world championship crews, 8 two-man and 3 four-man.

Tobogganing

The word toboggan comes from the Micmac American Indian word *tobaakan*. The oldest tobogganing club in the world, founded in 1887, is at St Moritz, Switzerland, home of the Cresta Run, which dates from 1884, and site of the introduction of the skeleton one-man racing toboggan.

On the Cresta Run, the record from the Junction (2,913 ft) is 42.96 sec (average 63.08 mph) by Poldi Berchtold of Switzerland on Feb 22, 1975. The record from the top (3,977 ft long with a drop of 514 ft) is 53.24 sec (average speed 50.92 mph), also by Berchtold on Feb 9, 1975. Speeds of 90 mph are occasionally attained.

The greatest number of wins in the Grand National (instituted 1885) is eight by the 1948 Olympic champion Nino Bibbia (Italy) (b Sept 9, 1924) in 1960–64, 1966, 1968, 1973. The greatest number of wins in the Curzon Cup (instituted in 1910) is eight by Bibbia in 1950, 1957–58, 1960, 1962–64, 1969, who hence won the double in 1960, 1962–64. The most descents made in a season is 7,915 during 70 days in 1980.

Lugeing

In lugeing the rider adopts a sitting, as opposed to a prone position. Official international competition began at Klosters, Switzerland, in 1881. The first European championships were at Reichenberg (now East) Germany, in 1914 and the first world championships at Oslo, Norway, in 1953. The International Luge Federation was formed in 1957. Lugeing became an Olympic sport in 1964.

Most Luge World Titles

The most successful rider in the world championships is Thomas Köhler (E Germany) (b June 25, 1940), who won the single-seater title in 1962, 1964 (Olympic), 1966, and 1967, and shared in the two-seater title in 1967 and 1968 (Olympic). Margit Schumann (E Germany) (b Sept 14, 1952) has won the women's championship 5 times—in 1973, 1974, 1975, 1976 (Olympic) and 1977.

Highest Luge Speed

The fastest luge run is at Krynica, Poland, where speeds of more than 80 mph have been recorded.

BOWLING

Origins

Bowling can be traced to articles found in the tomb of an Egyptian child of 5200 BC where there were nine pieces of stone to be set up as pins at which a stone "ball" was rolled. The ball first had to roll through an archway made of three pieces of marble. There is also resemblance to a Polynesian game called *ula maika* which utilized pins and balls of stone. The stones were rolled a distance of 60 ft. In the Italian Alps about 2,000 years ago, the underhand tossing of stones at an object is believed the beginnings of *bocci,* a game still widely played in Italy and similar to bowling. The ancient Germans played a game of nine-pins called *Heidenwerfen*—knock down pagans. Martin Luther is credited with the statement that nine was the ideal number of pins. In the British Isles, lawn bowls was preferred to bowling at pins. In the 16th century, bowling at pins was the national sport in Scotland. How bowling at pins came to the US is a matter of controversy. Early British settlers probably brought lawn bowls and set up what is known as Bowling Green at the tip of Manhattan Island in NY but perhaps the Dutch under Henry Hudson were the ones to be credited. Some historians say that in Connecticut the tenth pin was added to evade a legal ban against the nine-pin game in 1845 but others say that ten pins was played in NYC before this and point to Washington Irving's "Rip Van Winkle," written about 1818, as evidence.

Lanes

In the US there were 8,699 bowling establishments with 154,077 lanes in 1979 and about 65 million bowlers.

The world's largest bowling center (now closed) was the Tokyo World Lanes Center, Japan, with 252 lanes.

Organizations

The American Bowling Congress (ABC) comprises 4,800,000 men who bowl in leagues and tournaments. The Women's International Bowling Congress (WIBC) has a membership of 4,200,000. The Professional Bowlers Association (PBA), formed in 1958, numbers nearly 2,000 of the world's best bowlers.

World Championships

The Fédération Internationale des Quilleurs world championships were instituted in 1954. The highest pinfall in the individual men's event is 5,963 for 28 games by Ed Luther (US) at Milwaukee, Wis on Aug 28, 1971.

In the women's event (instituted 1963) the record is 4,720 in 24 games by Bong Coo (Philippines) at Manila, Philippines, Dec 1979.

Longest Career

William H. Bailey (b Jan 4, 1891) has been bowling in the Hamilton City Ten Pin League, Ontario, Canada, for 72 consecutive years.

Marathons

Tom Destowet bowled for 150 hours 15 min in Dublin, Calif, Apr 2–8, 1978. He bowled 709 games with a 16-lb ball.

LEAGUE SCORES

Highest Men's

The highest individual score for three games is 886 by Allie Brandt of Lockport, NY, on Oct 25, 1939. Maximum possible is 900 (three perfect games). Highest team score is 3,858 by Budweisers of St Louis on March 12, 1958.

The highest season average attained in sanctioned competition is 239 by Jim Lewis of Schenectady, NY, in 88 games in a 3-man league in 1975–76.

Highest Women's

The highest individual score for three games is 831 by Anne Splain in Boardman, Ohio, on Dec 7, 1979. Highest team score is 3,379 by Freeway Washer of Cleveland in 1960. (Highest in WIBC tournament play is 737 by D. D. Jacobson in 1972.)

HIGH SCORES: Anne Splain (left) rolled an 831 three-game series. Les Schissler (right) claps his hands as the pins fall for a perfect 300 game in 1967. He is one of three men to win 3 ABC titles in one year.

Most Perfect Scores

The highest number of sanctioned 300 games is 27 (through 1979) by Elvin Mesger of Sullivan, Mo. The maximum 900 for a three-game series has been recorded three times in unsanctioned games—by Leo Bentley at Lorain, Ohio, on March 26, 1931; by Joe Sargent at Rochester, NY, in 1934; and by Jim Murgie in Philadelphia, on Feb 4, 1937.

ABC TOURNAMENT SCORES

Highest Individual

Highest three-game series in singles is 801 by Mickey Higham of Kansas City, Mo, in 1977. Best three-game total in any ABC event is 804 by Lou Veit of Milwaukee, Wis, in team in 1977. Jim Godman of Lorain, Ohio, holds the record for a nine-game All-Events total with 2,184 (731–749–704) set in Indianapolis, Ind, in 1974. ABC Hall of Famers Fred Bujack of Detroit, Bill Lillard of Houston, and Nelson Burton Jr of St Louis, have won the most championships with 8 each. Bujack shared in 3 team and 4 team All-Events titles between 1949 and 1955, and also won the individual All-Events title in 1955. Lillard bowled on Regular and team All-Events champions in 1955 and 1956, the Classic team champions in 1962 and 1971, and won regular doubles and All-Events titles in 1956. Burton shared in 3 Classic team titles, 2 Classic doubles titles and has won Classic singles twice and Classic All-Events.

Highest Doubles

The ABC record of 558 was set in 1976 by Les Zikes of Chicago and Tommy Hudson of Akron, Ohio. The record score in a doubles series is 1,453, set in 1952 by John Klares (755) and Steve Nagy (698) of Cleveland.

Perfect Scores

Les Schissler of Denver scored 300 in the Classic team event in 1967, and Ray Williams of Detroit scored 300 in Regular team play in 1974. In all, there have been only thirty-seven 300 games in the ABC tournament through 1979. There have been 20 perfect games in singles, 14 in doubles, and three in team play.

Best Finishes in One Tournament

Les Schissler of Denver won the singles, All-Events, and was on the winning team in 1966 to tie Ed Lubanski of Detroit and Bill Lillard of Houston as the only men to win three ABC crowns in one year. The best four finishes in one ABC tournament were third in singles, second in doubles, third in team and first in All-Events by Bob Strampe, Detroit, in

1967, and first in singles, third in team and doubles and second in All-Events by Paul Kulbaga, Cleveland, in 1960.

Most Tournament Appearances

Bill Doehrman of Fort Wayne, Ind, has competed in 69 consecutive ABC tournaments, beginning in 1908. (No tournaments were held 1943–45.)

Attendance

Largest attendance on one day for an ABC Tournament was 5,257 in Milwaukee in 1952. The total attendance record was set at Reno, Nev, in 1977 with 174,953 in 89 days.

Youngest and Oldest Winners

The youngest champion was David Chilcott of Butler, Pa, who was a member of the 1970 Booster team champions. The oldest champion was Joe Detloff of Chicago, Ill, who, at the age of 72, was a winner in the 1965 Booster team event. The oldest doubles team in ABC competition totaled 165 years in 1955: Jerry Ameling (83) and Joseph Lehnbeutter (82), both from St Louis.

Strikes and Spares in a Row

In the greatest finish to win an ABC title, Ed Shay set a record of 12 strikes in a row in 1958, when he scored a perfect game for a total of 733 in the series.

The most spares in a row is 23, a record set by Lt Hazen Sweet of Battle Creek, Mich, in 1950.

PROFESSIONAL BOWLERS ASSOCIATION RECORDS

Most Titles

Earl Anthony of Kent, Wash, has won a lifetime total of 31 PBA titles. The record number of titles won in one PBA season is 8, by Mark Roth of North Arlington, NJ, in 1978.

Consecutive Titles

Only three bowlers have ever won three consecutive professional tournaments—Dick Weber in 1961, Johnny Petraglia in 1971, and Mark Roth in 1977.

Highest Earnings

The greatest lifetime earnings on the Professional Bowlers Association circuit have been won by Earl Anthony who has taken home $719,141 through 1979. Mark Roth won a record $134,500 in the 1978 season.

Perfect Games

A total of 119 perfect (300-point) games were bowled in PBA tournaments through 1979. Dick Weber rolled 3 perfect games in one tournament (Houston) in 1965, as did Billy Hardwick of Louisville, Ky (in the Japan Gold Cup competition) in 1968, Roy Buckley of Columbus, Ohio

MOST TITLES: Earl Anthony (left) is the PBA career champion with a lifetime total of 31 titles and earnings of over $700,000. Mark Roth (right) set PBA season marks in 1978 when he won 8 titles and earned $134,500.

(at Chagrin Falls, Ohio) in 1971, John Wilcox (at Detroit), and Norm Meyers of St Louis (at Peoria, Ill) in 1979.

Don Johnson of Las Vegas, Nev, bowled at least one perfect game in 11 consecutive seasons (1965–1975). Guppy Troup, of Savannah, Ga, rolled 6 perfect games on the 1979 tour.

BOXING

Earliest References

Boxing with gloves was depicted on a fresco from the Isle of Thera, Greece, which has been dated 1520 BC. The earliest prize-ring code of rules was formulated in England on Aug 16, 1743, by the champion pugilist Jack Broughton (1704–89), who reigned from 1729 to 1750. Boxing, which had in 1867 come under the Queensberry Rules, formulated for John Sholto Douglas, 9th Marquess of Queensberry, was not established as a legal sport in Britain until after a ruling of Mr Justice Grantham following the death of Billy Smith (Murray Livingstone) as the result of a fight on Apr 24, 1901, at Covent Garden, London.

Longest Fight

The longest recorded fight with gloves was between Andy Bowen of New Orleans and Jack Burke in New Orleans, Apr 6–7, 1893. The fight lasted 110 rounds (7 hours 19 min from 9:15 p.m. to 4:34 a.m.) but was declared a no contest (later changed to a draw) when both men were unable to continue. The longest recorded bare knuckle fight was one of 6 hours 15 min between James Kelly and Jack Smith at Fiery Creek, Dalesford, Australia, Dec 3, 1855. The greatest recorded number of rounds is 276 in 4 hours 30 min, when Jack Jones beat Patsy Tunney in Cheshire, England, in 1825.

Shortest Fight

There is a distinction between the quickest knockout and the shortest fight. A knockout in 10½ sec (including a 10-sec count) occurred on Sept 26, 1946, when Al Couture struck Ralph Walton while the latter was adjusting his mouthpiece in his corner at Lewiston, Me. If the time was accurately taken it is clear that Couture must have been more than halfway across the ring from his own corner at the opening bell.

The shortest fight on record appears to be one in a Golden Gloves tournament in Minneapolis, Minn, Nov 4, 1947, when Mike Collins floored Pat Brownson with his first punch and the contest was stopped, without a count, 4 sec after the bell.

The shortest world heavyweight title fight occurred when Tommy Burns (1881–1955) (*né* Noah Brusso) of Canada knocked out Jem Roche in 1 min 28 sec in Dublin, Ireland, March 17, 1908. The duration of the Clay vs Liston fight at Lewiston, Me, May 25, 1965, was 1 min 52 sec (including the count) as timed from the video tape recordings despite a ringside announcement giving a time of 1 min. The shortest world title fight was when Al McCoy knocked out George Chip in 45 sec for the middleweight crown in NYC, Apr 7, 1914.

Tallest

The tallest boxer to fight professionally was Gogea Mitu (b 1914) of Rumania in 1935. He was 7 ft 4 in and weighed 327 lb. John Rankin, who won a fight in New Orleans, in Nov 1967, was reputedly also 7 ft 4 in.

WORLD HEAVYWEIGHT CHAMPIONS

Longest and Shortest Reigns

The longest reign of any world heavyweight champion is 11 years 8 months and 7 days by Joe Louis (b Joseph Louis Barrow, in Lafayette, Ala, May 13, 1914), from June 22, 1937, when he knocked out James J. Braddock in the 8th round at Chicago until announcing his retirement on March 1, 1949. During his reign Louis made a record 25 defenses of his title. The shortest reign was by Leon Spinks (US) (b July 11, 1953) for 212 days, Feb 15–Sept 15, 1978.

Heaviest and Lightest

The heaviest world champion was Primo Carnera (Italy) (1906–67), the "Ambling Alp," who won the title from Jack Sharkey in 6 rounds in NYC, on June 29, 1933. He scaled 267 lb for this fight but his peak weight was 270 lb. He had the longest reach at 85½ in (fingertip to fingertip) and also the largest fists with a 14¾-in circumference. He had an expanded chest measurement of 53 in. The lightest champion was Robert James Fitzsimmons (1863–1917), (b Helston, Cornwall, England) who, at a weight of 167 lb, won the title by knocking out James J. Corbett in 14 rounds at Carson City, Nev, March 17, 1897.

The greatest differential in a world title fight was 86 lb between Car-

OLDEST HEAVYWEIGHT CHAMPION: Jersey Joe Walcott (left) defeated Ezzard Charles (right) to become heavyweight champion at age 37.

nera (270 lb) and Tommy Loughran (184 lb) of the US, when the former won on points at Miami, Fla, March 1, 1934.

Tallest and Shortest

The tallest world champion was Primo Carnera, who was measured at 6 ft 5.4 in by the Physical Education Director at the Hemingway Gymnasium of Harvard, although he was widely reported and believed in 1933 to be 6 ft 8½ in tall. Jess Willard (1881–1968), who won the title in 1915, was often described as being 6 ft 6¼ in tall, but was in fact 6 ft 5¼ in. The shortest was Tommy Burns (1881–1955) of Canada, world champion from Feb 23, 1906, to Dec 26, 1908, who stood 5 ft 7 in and weighed 179 lb.

Oldest and Youngest

The oldest man to win the heavyweight crown was Jersey Joe Walcott (b Arnold Raymond Cream, Jan 31, 1914, at Merchantville, NJ), who knocked out Ezzard Charles on July 18, 1951, in Pittsburgh, when aged 37 years 5 months 18 days. Walcott was the oldest title holder at 38 years 7 months 23 days when he lost to Rocky Marciano on Sept 23, 1952. The youngest age at which the world title has been won is 21 years 331 days by Floyd Patterson (b Waco, NC, Jan 4, 1935). After the retirement of Rocky Marciano, Patterson won the vacant title by beating Archie Moore in 5 rounds in Chicago, on Nov 30, 1956.

Most Recaptures

Muhammad Ali Haj (b Cassius Marcellus Clay, in Louisville, Ky, Jan 17, 1942) is the only man to regain the heavyweight title twice. Ali first

THREE-TIME CHAMP: Muhammad Ali failed to regain his title from Joe Frazier (left) in their first fight, but 3 years later Ali KO'd George Foreman (right) in Zaire for the first of his two recaptures.

won the title on Feb 25, 1964, defeating Sonny Liston. He defeated George Foreman on Oct 30, 1974, having been stripped of his title by the world boxing authorities on Apr 28, 1967. He lost his title to Leon Spinks on Feb 15, 1978, but regained it on Sept 15, 1978 by defeating Spinks in New Orleans.

Undefeated

Rocky Marciano (b Rocco Francis Marchegiano) (1923–69) is the only heavyweight champion to have been undefeated in his entire professional career (1947–1956). His record was 49 wins (43 by KO) and no losses or draws.

Earliest Title Fight

The first world heavyweight title fight, with gloves and 3-minute rounds, was between John L. Sullivan (1858–1918) and "Gentleman" James J. Corbett (1866–1933) in New Orleans, Sept 7, 1892. Corbett won in 21 rounds.

WORLD CHAMPIONS (ANY WEIGHT)

Longest and Shortest Reign

Joe Louis's heavyweight duration record stands for all divisions. The shortest reign has been 33 days by Tony Canzoneri (US) (1908–59) who was junior welterweight champion from May 21 to June 23, 1933.

Youngest and Oldest

The youngest at which any world championship has been claimed is 17 years 180 days by Wilfredo Benitez (b Sept 8, 1958) of Puerto Rico, who won the WBA light-welterweight title in San Juan, March 6, 1976.

The oldest world champion was Archie Moore (b Archibald Lee Wright, Collinsville, Ill , Dec 13, 1913 or 1916), who was recognized as a light-heavyweight champion up to Feb 10, 1962, when his title was removed. He was then between 45 and 48. Bob Fitzsimmons (1863–1917) had the longest career of any official world titleholder with over 32 years from 1882 to 1914. He won his last world title aged 40 years 183 days in San Francisco on Nov 25, 1903. He was an amateur from 1880 to 1882.

Greatest "Tonnage"

The greatest "tonnage" recorded in any fight is 700 lb, when Claude "Humphrey" McBride of Okla at 340 lb knocked out Jimmy Black of Houston at 360 lb in the 3rd round at Oklahoma City, June 1, 1971.

The greatest "tonnage" in a world title fight was 488¾ lb when Primo Carnera (259¼ lb) fought Paolino Uzcudun (229½ lb) of Spain, in Rome, Italy, Oct 22, 1933.

Smallest Champions

The smallest man to win any world title has been Pascual Perez (1926–1977) who won the flyweight title in Tokyo on Nov 26, 1954, at 107 lb and 4 ft 11½ in tall. Jimmy Wilde (b Merthyr Tydfil, 1892, d 1969, UK), who held the flyweight title from 1916 to 1923, was reputed never to have fought above 108 lb.

Longest Fight

The longest world title fight (under Queensberry Rules) was between the lightweights Joe Gans (1874–1910), of the US, and Oscar "Battling" Nelson (1882–1954), the "Durable Dane," at Goldfield, Nev, Sept 3, 1906. It was terminated in the 42nd round when Gans was declared the winner on a foul.

Most Recaptures

The only boxer to win a world title five times at one weight is Sugar Ray Robinson (b Walker Smith, Jr, in Detroit, May 3, 1920) who beat Carmen Basilio (US) in the Chicago Stadium on March 25, 1958, to regain the world middleweight title for the fourth time. The other title wins were over Jake LaMotta (US) in Chicago on Feb 14, 1951; Randy Turpin (UK) in NYC on Sept 12, 1951; Carl "Bobo" Olson (US) in Chicago on Dec 9, 1955; and Gene Fullmer (US) in Chicago on May 1, 1957. The record number of title bouts in a career is 33 or 34 (at bantam and featherweight) by George Dixon (1870–1909), *alias* "Little Chocolate," of Canada, between 1890 and 1901.

Most Titles Simultaneously

The only man to hold world titles at three weights simultaneously was "Hammerin' " Henry Armstrong (b Dec 12, 1912), now the Rev Henry Jackson, of the US, at featherweight, lightweight and welterweight from Aug to Dec 1938.

Most Knockdowns in Title Fights

Vic Toweel (South Africa) knocked down Danny O'Sullivan of London 14 times in 10 rounds in their world bantamweight fight at Johannesburg, Dec 2, 1950, before the latter retired.

ALL FIGHTS

Largest Purse

The greatest purse received is a reported $8,500,000 by Sugar Ray Leonard (US) (b May 17, 1956) when he lost the WBC welterweight title to Roberto Duran (Panama) in the Olympic Stadium, Montreal, on June 20, 1980.

The largest stake ever fought for in the bare-knuckle era was $22,500 in a 27-round fight when Jack Cooper beat Wolf Bendoff at Port Elizabeth, South Africa, July 26, 1889.

Highest and Lowest Attendances

The greatest paid attendance at any boxing fight has been 120,757 (with a ringside price of $27.50) for the Tunney *vs* Dempsey world heavyweight title fight at the Sesquicentennial Stadium, Philadelphia, Sept 23, 1926. The indoor record is 63,360 for the Spinks vs Ali world heavyweight title fight at the Louisiana Superdome in New Orleans, Sept 15, 1978. The gate receipts exceeded $6 million, a record total. The highest non-paying attendance is 135,132 at the Tony Zale vs Billy Pryor fight at Juneau Park, Milwaukee, Wis, Aug 18, 1941.

The smallest attendance at a world heavyweight title fight was 2,434 at the Clay vs Liston fight at Lewiston, Me, May 25, 1965.

Highest Earnings in Career

The largest known fortune ever made in a fighting career (or any sports career) is an estimated $60 million (including exhibitions) amassed by Muhammad Ali from Oct 1960 to Aug 1979, in 59 fights comprising 529 rounds.

Most Knockouts

The greatest number of knockouts in a career is 141 by Archie Moore (1936 to 1963). The record for consecutive KO's is 44, set by Lamar Clark

THREE GOLD MEDALS: Teofilio Stevenson (right) punishes Duane Bobick enroute to the first of 3 Olympic titles.

of Utah at Las Vegas, Nev, Jan 11, 1960. He knocked out 6 in one night (5 in the first round) in Bingham, Utah, on Dec 1, 1958.

Most Fights

The greatest recorded number of fights in a career is 1,024 by Bobby Dobbs (US) (1858–1930), who is reported to have fought from 1875 to 1914, a period of 39 years. Abraham Hollandersky, *alias* Abe the Newsboy (US), is reputed to have had 1,309 fights in the 14 years from 1905 to 1918, but many of them were exhibition bouts.

Most Fights Without Loss

Hal Bagwell, a lightweight, of Gloucester, England, was reputedly undefeated in 180 consecutive fights, of which only 5 were draws, between Aug 15, 1938, and Nov 29, 1948. His record of fights in the wartime period (1939–46) is very sketchy, however. Of boxers with complete records, Packey McFarland (1888–1936) went undefeated in 97 fights from 1905 to 1915.

Olympic Gold Medals

The only amateur boxers ever to win three Olympic gold medals are the southpaw László Papp (b 1926, Hungary), who took the middleweight (1948) and the light-middleweight titles (1952 and 1956), and Cuban heavyweight Teofilio Stevenson, who has won the gold medal in his division for three successive Games (1972, 1976 and 1980). The only man to win two titles in one meeting was Oliver L. Kirk (US), who took both the bantam and featherweight titles at St Louis, Mo, in 1904, when the US won all the titles. Harry W. Mallin (GB) was in 1924 the first boxer ever to defend an Olympic title successfully when he retained the middleweight crown.

The oldest man to win an Olympic gold medal in boxing was Richard K. Gunn (b 1870) (GB), who won the featherweight title on Oct 27, 1908, in London, aged 38.

BULLFIGHTING

Earliest

In the latter half of the second millennium BC, bull leaping was practiced in Crete. Bullfighting in Spain was first reported by the Romans in Baetica (Andalusia) in the third century BC.

The first renowned professional *espada* (bullfighter) was Francisco Romero of Ronda, in Andalusia, Spain, who introduced the *estoque* and the red *muleta c.* 1700. Spain now has some 190 active matadors. Since 1700, 42 major matadors have died in the ring.

Largest Stadiums

The world's largest bullfighting ring, the Plaza, Mexico City, with a capacity of 48,000, was closed in March 1976. The largest of Spain's 312 bullrings is Las Ventas, Madrid, with a capacity of 24,000.

HIGHEST PAID: El Cordobés received millions of dollars for the high-risk occupation of matador.

Most Successful Matadors

The most successful matador measured by bulls killed was Lagartijo (1841–1900), born Rafael Molina, whose lifetime total was 4,867.

The longest career of any full matador was that of Bienvenida (1922–75) (*né* Antonio Mejías) from 1942 to 1974. (Recent Spanish law requires compulsory retirement at age 55.)

Most Kills in a Day

In 1884, Romano set a record by killing 18 bulls in a day in Seville, and in 1949 El Litri (Miguel Báes) set a Spanish record with 114 *novilladas* in a season.

Highest Paid Matadors

The highest-paid bullfighter in history is El Cordobés (b Manuel Benitex Pérez, probably on May 4, 1936, in Palma del Rio, Spain), who became a multimillionaire in 1965, during which year he fought 111 *corridas* up to Oct 4, receiving over $15,000 for each half hour in the ring. In 1970, he received an estimated $1,800,000 for 121 fights.

Paco Camino (b Dec 19, 1941) has received $27,200 (2,000,000 *pesetas*) for a *corrida*. He retired in 1977.

CANOEING

Origins

The acknowledged pioneer of canoeing as a modern sport was John Macgregor, a British barrister, in 1865. The Canoe Club was formed on July 26, 1866.

Olympic and World Titles

Gert Fredriksson (b Nov 21, 1919) of Sweden has won the most Olympic gold medals with six (1948, 1952, 1956, 1960).

The most by a woman is 3 by Ludmila Pinayeva (*née* Khvedosyuk, b

Jan 14, 1936) (USSR) in the 500-m K1 in 1964 and 1968, and the 500-m K2 in 1972.

The Olympic 1,000-m best performance of 3 min 02.70 sec by the 1980 USSR K4 on July 31, 1980, represents a speed of 12.24 mph.

Yuri Lobanov (USSR) (b Sept 29, 1952) has won a record 11 titles from 1972 to 1979. Ludmila Pinayeva added 6 other world titles to her 3 Olympic golds, from 1966 to 1973, for a female record.

Longest Journey

The longest canoe journey in history was one of 7,516 miles around the eastern US by paddle and portage, from Lake Itasca, Minn, *via* New Orleans, Miami, NYC, and Lake Ontario, by Randy Bauer (b Aug 15, 1949) and Jerry Mimbach (b May 22, 1952) of Coon Rapids, Minn, from Sept 8, 1974 to Aug 30, 1976.

The longest journey without portage or aid of any kind is one of 6,102 miles by Richard H. Grant and Ernest Lassey circumnavigating the eastern US from Chicago to New Orleans to Miami to NYC, returning back to Chicago *via* the Great Lakes, from Sept 22, 1930, to Aug 15, 1931.

Eskimo Rolls

The record for Eskimo rolls is 1,000 in 53 min 5.7 sec by Terry Russell (24) at Swanley, Kent, England, on Apr 20, 1980. A "hand-rolling" record of 100 rolls in 3 min 23 sec was set in the Crystal Palace Pool, London, on Feb 25, 1980, by John Bouteloup (21).

Longest Open Sea Voyage

Beatrice and John Dowd, Ken Beard and Steve Benson (Richard Gillett replaced him mid-journey) paddled 2,170 miles out of a total journey of 2,192 miles from Venezuela to Miami, Fla, via the West Indies from Aug 11, 1977, to Apr 29, 1978, in two Klepper Aerius 20 kayaks.

OPEN SEA VOYAGE (left): This crew paddled 2,170 miles on the open sea. MOST MEDALS (right): Gert Fredriksson displays one of his 6 gold medals, this one for 10,000 m K1, won in Melbourne in 1956.

Highest Altitude

In Sept 1976 Dr Michael Jones (1951–78) and Michael Hopkinson of the British Everest Canoe Expedition canoed down the Dudh Kosi River in Nepal from an altitude of 17,500 ft.

Longest Race

The longest regularly held canoe race in the US is the Texas Water Safari (instituted 1963) which covers the 419 miles from San Marcos to Seadrift, Tex, on the San Marcos and Guadalupe rivers. Robert Chatham and Butch Hodges set the record of 37 hours 18 min, June 5–6, 1976.

CROSS-COUNTRY RUNNING

International Championships

The earliest international cross-country race was run between England and France on a course 9 miles 18 yd long from Ville d'Avray, outside Paris, on March 20, 1898 (England won by 21 points to 69). The inaugural International Cross-Country Championships took place at the Hamilton Park Racecourse, Scotland, on March 28, 1903. Since 1973 the race has been run under the auspices of the International Amateur Athletic Federation.

The greatest margin of victory in the International Cross-Country Championships has been 56 sec, or 390 yd, by Jack T. Holden (England) at Ayr Racecourse, Scotland, March 24, 1934. The narrowest win was that of Jean-Claude Fayolle (France) at Ostend, Belgium, on March 20, 1965, when the timekeepers were unable to separate his time from that of Melvyn Richard Batty (England), who was placed second.

Most Appearances

The runner with the largest number of international championship appearances is Marcel Van de Wattyne of Belgium, who participated in 20 competitions in the years 1946–65.

HIGHEST BICYCLE SPEED: Dr Allan Abbott rode this bicycle at 140.5 mph behind a pacing automobile in 1973.

Most Wins

The greatest number of victories in the International Cross-Country Race is 4 by Jack Holden (England) in 1933–35, and 1939; by Alain Mimoun-o-Kacha (b Jan 1, 1921) (France) in 1949, 1952, 1954 and 1956; and Gaston Roelants (b Feb 5, 1937) (Belgium) in 1962, 1967, 1969 and 1972. England has won 45 times to 1980. Doris Brown-Heritage (US) (b Sept 17, 1942) has won the women's race 5 times, 1967–71.

Largest Field

The largest recorded field in any cross-country race was 7,036 starters in the 18.6-mile Lidingöloppet, near Stockholm, Sweden, on Oct 10, 1978. There were 6,299 finishers.

CYCLING

Earliest Race

The earliest recorded bicycle race was a velocipede race over 2 km (1.24 miles) at the Parc de St Cloud, Paris, on May 31, 1868, won by Dr James Moore (GB) (1847–1935).

Stationary Cycling

David Steed of Tucson, Ariz, stayed stationary without support for 9 hours 15 min on Nov 25, 1977.

Highest Speed

The highest speed ever achieved on a bicycle is 140.5 mph by Dr Allan V. Abbott, 29, of San Bernardino, Calif, behind a windshield mounted on a 1955 Chevrolet over ¾ of a mile at Bonneville Salt Flats, Utah, Aug 25, 1973. His speed over a mile was 138.674 mph. Considerable help is provided by the slipstreaming effect of the lead vehicle. Charles Minthorne Murphy (b 1872) achieved the first mile-a-min behind a pacing locomotive on the Long Island Railroad on June 30, 1899. He took only 57.8 sec, so averaging 62.28 mph.

Fred Markham recorded an official unpaced 8.80 sec for 200 m (50.84 mph) on a streamlined bicycle at Ontario, Calif, May 6, 1979.

The greatest distance ever covered in one hour is 76 miles 604 yd by Leon Vanderstuyft (Belgium) on the Montlhéry Motor Circuit, France, Sept 30, 1928. This was achieved from a standing start paced by a motorcycle. The 24-hour record behind pace is 860 miles 367 yd by Hubert Opperman in Australia in 1932.

The greatest distance covered in 60 min unpaced is 30 miles 1,258 yd by Eddy Merckx at Mexico City, on Oct 25, 1972. The 24-hour record on the road is 515.8 miles by Teuvo Louhivouri of Finland on Sept 10, 1974.

Most Olympic Titles

Cycling has been on the Olympic program since the revival of the Games in 1896. The greatest number of gold medals ever won is 3 by Paul Masson (France) in 1896, Francisco Verri (Italy) in 1906 and Robert Charpentier (France) in 1936. Marcus Hurley (US) won 4 events in the "unofficial" cycling competition in the 1904 Games.

SIX-DAY RACER: Patrick Sercu (above) had won 72 six-day races to March 1980. TOUR DE FRANCE: Eddy Merckx (right) has won the Tour de France 5 times. Merckx also has the greatest distance for 1 hour, unpaced.

Tour de France

The greatest number of wins in the Tour de France (inaugurated 1903) is 5 by Jacques Anquetil (b Jan 8, 1934) of France, who won in 1957, 1961–64; and Eddy Merckx (b Belgium, June 17, 1945) who won five titles (1969–72, 1974).

The closest race ever was that of 1968 when after 2,898.7 miles over 25 days (June 27–July 21) Jan Jannssen (Netherlands) (b May 19, 1940) beat Herman van Springel (Belgium) in Paris by 38 sec. The longest course was 3,569 miles on June 20 to July 18, 1926. The length of the course is usually about 3,000 miles, but varies from year to year.

The fastest average speed was 23.2 mph by Anquetil in 1962. The greatest number of participants was in 1928, when 162 started and only 41 finished.

Six-Day Races

The greatest number of wins in six-day races is by Patrick Sercu (b June 27, 1944), of Belgium, who, by March 1980, had taken his total number of victories to 72.

World Titles

The only 4 male cyclists to have won 7 world titles in any single world championship event are Leon Meredith (GB) who won the Amateur 100-km paced event, 1904–05, 1907–09, 1911, 1913; Jeff Scherens (Belgium) who won the Professional sprint title in 1932–37 and 1947; Antonio Maspes (Italy) who won the Professional sprint title in 1955–56, 1959–62, 1964; and Daniel Morelon (France) who won the Amateur sprint title in 1966–67, 1969–71, 1973, 1975.

Yvonne Reynders (Belgium) won a total of 7 titles in women's events, the pursuits in 1961, 1964–65 and the road title in 1959, 1961, 1963, and 1966. Beryl Burton (GB) equaled this total by winning the pursuits title in 1959–60, 1962–63, 1966 and the road title in 1960 and 1967.

Endurance

Tommy Godwin (1912–75) (GB) in the 365 days of 1939 covered 75,065 miles or an average of 205.65 miles per day. He then completed 100,000 miles in 500 days to May 14, 1940.

The longest cycle tour on record is the more than 402,000 miles amassed by Walter Stolle (b Sudetenland, 1926), an itinerant lecturer. From Jan 24, 1959 to Dec 12, 1976, he covered 159 countries, had 5 bicycles stolen and suffered 231 other robberies, along with over 1,000 flat tires. From 1922 to Dec 25, 1973, Tommy Chambers (b 1903) of Glasgow, Scotland, had ridden a verified total of 799,405 miles. On Christmas Day he was badly injured and has not ridden since.

Ray Reece, 41, of Alverstoke, England, circumnavigated the world by bicycle (13,325 road miles) between June 14 and Nov 5 (143 days) in 1971.

John Hathaway of Vancouver, Canada, covered 50,600 miles, visiting every continent from Nov 10, 1974 to Oct 6, 1976.

Vivekananda Selva Kumar Anandan of Sri Lanka cycled for 187 hours 28 min non-stop around Vihara Maha Devi Park, Colombo, Sri Lanka, May 2–10, 1979.

Veronica and Colin Scargill, of Bedford, England, traveled 18,020 miles around the world, on a tandem, Feb 25, 1974–Aug 27, 1975.

US Touring Records

The transcontinental record is 12 days 3 hours 41 min from Santa Monica, Calif, to NYC by John Marino (b 1948), in June 1980, breaking his own 2-year-old record by almost one full day.

Richard J. DeBernardis of Los Angeles bicycled around the perimeter of the continental US in 180 days, beginning in Seattle, Wash, Sept 10, 1978, and returning on March 8, 1979. His 12,092-mile continuous journey was accomplished without resorting to other means of transportation at any point.

EQUESTRIAN SPORTS

Origin

Evidence of horse riding dates from a Persian engraving dated *c.* 3000 BC. Pignatelli's academy of horsemanship at Naples dates from the 16th century. The earliest jumping competition was at the Agricultural Hall, London, in 1869. Equestrian events have been included in the Olympic Games since 1912.

Most Olympic Medals

The greatest number of Olympic gold medals is 5 by Hans-Günter Winkler (b July 24, 1926) (W Germany), who won 4 team gold medals as captain in 1956, 1960, 1964 and 1972, and won the individual Grand Prix in 1956. The most team wins in the Prix des Nations is 5 by Germany in 1936, 1956, 1960, 1964, and 1972.

The lowest score obtained by a winner was no faults, by Frantisek Ventura (Czechoslovakia) on "Eliot" in 1928, and by Alwin Schockemöhle (W Germany) on "Warwick Rex" in 1976. Pierre Jonqueres d'Oriola (France) is the only two-time winner of the individual gold medal, in 1952 and 1964.

World Titles

The men's world championship (instituted 1953) has been won twice by Hans-Günter Winkler of W Germany in 1954 and 1955, and Raimondo d'Inzeo of Italy in 1956 and 1960. The women's title (instituted 1965) has been won twice by Jane "Janou" Tissot (*née* Lefebvre) of France on "Rocket" in 1970 and 1974.

Jumping Records

The official *Fédération Equestre Internationale* high jump record is 8 ft 1¼ in by "Huaso," ridden by Capt A. Larraguibel Morales (Chile) at Santiago, Chile, on Feb 5, 1949, and 27 ft 2¾ in for long jump over water by "Amado Mio" ridden by Lt-Col Lopez del Hierro (Spain), at Barcelona, Spain, on Nov 12, 1951. "Heatherbloom," ridden by Dick Donnelly, was reputed to have covered 37 ft in clearing an 8-ft-3-in *puissance* jump at Richmond, Va, in 1903. H. Plant on "Solid Gold" cleared 36 ft 3 in over water at the Wagga Show, NSW, Australia, Aug 28, 1936. "Jerry M" allegedly cleared 40 ft over water at Aintree, Liverpool, England, in 1912.

At Cairns, Queensland, "Golden Meade" ridden by Jack Martin cleared an unofficially measured 8 ft 6 in on July 25, 1946. "Ben Bolt" was credited with clearing 9 ft 6 in at the 1938 Royal Horse Show, Sydney, Australia. The Australian record, however, is 8 ft 4 in by Colin Russell on "Flyaway" in 1939 and A. L. Payne on "Golden Meade" in 1946.

LONGEST JUMP: "Heatherbloom" was reported to have made a 37-ft jump. She could also clear barriers over 8 ft high.

NO FAULTS: Alwin Schockemöhle scored no faults in the 1976 Olympics to win the gold medal aboard "Warwick Rex."

The world's unofficial best for a woman is 7 ft 8 in by Katrina Towns (now Musgrove) (Australia) on "Big John" at Cairns, Queensland, Australia, in 1978.

The greatest recorded height reached bareback is 6 ft 7 in by "Silver Wood" at Heidelberg, Victoria, Australia, Dec 10, 1938.

Longest Ride

Aimé Felix Tschiffely (b Switzerland) rode 10,000 miles from Buenos Aires, Argentina, to Wash, DC, in 504 days, starting on Apr 23, 1925, with two horses, "Mancha" and "Gato."

The Bicentennial "Great American Horse Race," begun on May 31, 1976, from Saratoga Springs, NY, to Sacramento, Calif (3,500 miles) was won by Virl Norton on "Lord Fauntleroy"—a mule—in 98 days. His actual riding time was 315.47 hours.

Marathon

Michael Grealy (Australia) rode at all paces (including jumping) for 55 hours 26 min at Blackwater, Queensland, Australia, May 5–7, 1978.

FENCING

Origins

Fencing (fighting with single sticks) was practiced as a sport, or as part of a religious ceremony, in Egypt as early as c. 1360 BC. The first governing body for fencing in Britain was the Corporation of Masters of Defence founded by Henry VIII before 1540, and fencing was practiced as sport, notably in prize fights, since that time. The foil was the practice weapon for the short court sword from the 17th century. The épée was established in the mid-19th century and the light sabre was introduced by the Italians in the late 19th century.

Most Olympic Titles

The greatest number of individual Olympic gold medals won is 3 by Ramón Fonst (Cuba) (1883–1959) in 1900 and 1904 (2) and Nedo Nadi (Italy) (1894–1952) in 1912 and 1920 (2). Nadi also won 3 team gold medals in 1920 making a then unprecedented total of 5 gold medals at one Olympic meet.

Edoardo Mangiarotti (Italy) (b Apr 7, 1919) holds the record of 13 Olympic medals (6 gold, 5 silver, 2 bronze), won in the foil and épée competitions from 1936 to 1960.

The most gold medals won by a woman is four (one individual, three team) by Elena Novikova-Belova (USSR) (b July 28, 1947) from 1968 to 1976, and the record for all medals is 7 (2 gold, 3 silver, 2 bronze), by Ildikó Sagine-Retjöo (formerly Ujlaki-Retjö) (Hungary) (b May 11, 1937) from 1960 to 1976.

Most World Titles

The greatest number of individual world titles won is 4 by Christian d'Oriola (see table below), but note that d'Oriola also won 2 individual Olympic titles. Likewise, of the 3 women foilists with 3 world titles (Helene Mayer, Ellen Müller-Preiss and Ilona Schacherer-Elek) only Elek also won 2 individual Olympic titles.

Most Olympic and Most World Titles

Event	Olympic Gold Medals	World Championships (not held in Olympic years)
Men's Foil, Individual	2 Christian d'Oriola (France) (b Oct 3, 1928) 1952, 56 2 Nedo Nadi (Italy) (1894–1952) 1912, 20	4 Christian d'Oriola (France) 1947, 49, 53, 54
Men's Foil, Team	6 France 1924, 32, 48, 52, 68, 80	12 Italy 1929–31, 33–35, 37, 38, 49, 50, 54, 55
Men's Epée, Individual	2 Ramón Fonst (Cuba) (1883–1959) 1900, 04	3 Georges Buchard (France) (b Dec 21, 1893) 1927, 31, 33
		3 Aleksey Nikanchikov (USSR) (b July 30, 1940) 1966, 67, 70
Men's Epée, Team	6 Italy 1920, 28, 36, 52, 56, 60	10 Italy 1931, 33, 37, 49, 50, 53, 55, 57, 58
Men's Sabre, Individual	2 Jean Georgiadis (Greece) (b 1874) 1896, 1906 2 Dr Jenö Fuchs (Hungary) (b Oct 29, 1882) 1908, 12 2 Rudolf Kárpáti (Hungary) (b July 17, 1920) 1956, 60	3 Aladar Gerevich (Hungary) (b March 16, 1910) 1935, 51, 55 3 Jerzy Pawlowski (Poland) (b Oct 25, 1932) 1957, 65, 66 3 Yacov Rylsky (USSR) (b Oct 25, 1932) 1958, 61, 63
Men's Sabre, Team	9 Hungary 1908, 12, 28, 32, 36, 48, 52, 56, 60	15 Hungary 1930, 31, 33–35, 37, 51, 53–55, 57, 58, 66, 73, 78
Women's Foil, Individual	2 Ilona Schacherer-Elek (Hungary) (b May 17, 1907) 1936, 48	3 Helene Mayer (Germany) (1910–53) 1929, 31, 37 3 Ilona Schacherer-Elek (Hungary) 1934, 35, 51 3 Ellen Müller-Preiss (Austria) (b May 6, 1912) 1947, 49, 50 (shared)
Women's Foil, Team	4 USSR 1960, 68, 72, 76	13 USSR 1956, 58, 61, 63, 65–66, 70–71, 74–75, 77–79

MOST WORLD TITLES: Christian d'Oriola (left) won 4 World Championships and 2 Olympic gold medals.

FISHING

Largest Catches

The largest fish ever caught on a rod is an officially ratified man-eating great white shark (*Carcharodon carcharias*) weighing 2,664 lb, and measuring 16 ft 10 in long, caught by Alf Dean at Denial Bay, near Ceduna, South Australia, on Apr 21, 1959. Capt Frank Mundus (US) harpooned and landed a 17-ft-long 4,500-lb great white shark, after a 5-hour battle, off Montauk Point, LI, NY, on June 6, 1964. He was assisted by Peter Brandenberg, Gerald Mallow, Frank Bloom and Harvey Ferston.

A white pointer shark weighing 3,388 lb was caught on a rod by Clive Green off Albany, W Australia, on Apr 26, 1976, but this will remain unratified as whale meat was used as bait.

The largest marine animal ever killed by *hand* harpoon was a blue whale 97 ft in length, killed by Archer Davidson in Twofold Bay, NSW, Australia, in 1910. Its tail flukes measured 20 ft across and its jaw bone 23 ft 4 in.

Smallest Catch

The smallest fish ever to win a competition was a smelt weighing 1/16 of an oz, caught by Peter Christian at Buckenham Ferry, Norfolk, England, on Jan 9, 1977. This beat 107 other competitors.

Spear-fishing

The largest fish ever taken underwater was an 804-lb giant black grouper by Don Pinder of the Miami Triton Club, Fla, in 1955.

Fishing (Sea and Freshwater fish records taken by tackle as ratified by the International Game Fish Association to Jan 1980.)

Species	Weight in lb	oz	Name of Angler	Location	Date
Amberjack	149	0	Peter Simons	Bermuda	June 21, 1964
Barracuda††	83	8	K. J. W. Hackett 88	Lagos, Nigeria	Jan 13, 1952
Bass (Giant Sea)	563	8	James D. McAdam, Jr	Anacapa Island, Calif	Aug 20, 1968
Black Runner (Cobia)	110	5	Eric Tinworth	Off Mombasa, Kenya	Sept 8, 1964
Carp†	55	5	Frank J. Ledwein	Clearwater Lake, Minn	July 10, 1952
Cod	98	12	Alphonse J. Bielevich	Isle of Shoals, NH	June 8, 1969
Marlin (Black)	1,560	0	Alfred C. Glassell, Jr	Cabo Blanco, Peru	Aug 4, 1953
Marlin (Atlantic Blue)	1,282	0	Larry Martin	St. Thomas, US VI	Aug 6, 1977
Marlin (Pacific Blue)	1,153	0	Greg D. Perez	Ritidian Point, Guam	Aug 21, 1969
Marlin (Striped)	417	8	Phillip Bryers	Cavalli Isles, New Zealand	Jan 14, 1977
Marlin (White)	174	3	Otavia Cunha Reboucas	Vitoria, Brazil	Nov 1, 1976
Pike (Northern)	46	2	Peter Dubuc	Sacandaga Reservoir, NY	Sept 15, 1940
Sailfish (Atlantic)	128	1	Harm Steyn	Luanda, Angola	March 27, 1974
Sailfish (Pacific)	221	0	C. W. Stewart	Santa Cruz I, Galapagos Is	Feb 12, 1947
Salmon (Chinook)§	93	0	Howard C. Rider	Kelp Bay, Alaska	June 24, 1977
Shark (Blue)	437	0	Peter Hyde	Catherine Bay, NSW, Australia	Oct 2, 1976
Shark (Mako)**	1,080	0	James L. Melanson	Montauk, NY	Aug 26, 1979
Shark (White or Man-Eating)	2,664	0	Alfred Dean	Ceduna, South Australia	Apr 21, 1959
Shark (Porbeagle)	465	0	Jorge Potier	Cornwall, England	July 23, 1976
Shark (Thresher)‡	739	0	Brian Galvin	Tutukaka, New Zealand	Feb 17, 1975
Shark (Tiger)	1,780	0	Walter Maxwell	Cherry Grove, SC	June 14, 1964
Sturgeon (White)‡‡	360	0	Willard Cravens	Snake River, Idaho	Apr 24, 1956
Swordfish	1,182	0	L. E. Marron	Iquique, Chile	May 7, 1953
Tarpon	283	0	M. Salazar	Lago de Maracaibo, Venezuela	March 19, 1965
Trout (Lake)‖	65	0	Larry Daunis	Great Bear Lake, Northwest Terr, Canada	Aug 8, 1970
Tuna (Allison or Yellowfin)	388	12	Curt Wiesenhutter	San Benedicto Islands, Mexico	Apr 1, 1977
Tuna (Atlantic Big-eyed)	375	8	Cecil Browne	Ocean City, Md	Aug 26, 1977
Tuna (Pacific Big-eyed)	435	0	Dr Russel V. A. Lee	Cabo Blanco, Peru	Apr 17, 1957
Tuna (Bluefin)	1,496	0	Ken Fraser	Aulds Cove, Nova Scotia, Canada	Oct 26, 1979
Wahoo	149	0	John Pirovano	Cat Cay, Bahamas	June 15, 1962

†† A barracuda weighing 103 lb 4 oz was caught on an untested line by Chester Benet at West End, Bahamas, on Aug 11, 1932. Another weighing 48 lb 6 oz was caught barehanded by Thomas B. Pace at Panama City Beach, Fla, on Apr 19, 1974. 88 Hackett was only 11 years 137 days old at the time. † A carp weighing 83 lb 8 oz was taken (not by rod) near Pretoria, South Africa. A 60-lb specimen was taken by bow and arrow by Ben A. Topham in Wythe Co, Va, on July 5, 1970. § A salmon weighing 126 lb 8 oz was taken (not by rod) near Petersburg, Alaska. ** A 1,295-lb specimen was taken by two anglers off Natal, South Africa, on March 17, 1939, and a 1,500-lb specimen harpooned inside Durban Harbour, South Africa, in 1933. ‡ W. W. Dowding caught a 922-lb thresher shark in 1937 on an untested line. ‡‡ Glenn Howard caught a sturgeon weighing 394 lb on the Snake River, Idaho, in 1954. ‖ A 102-lb trout was taken from Lake Athabasca, northern Saskatchewan, Canada, on Aug 8, 1961.

Freshwater Casting

The longest freshwater cast ratified under ICF (International Casting Federation) rules is 574 ft 2 in by Walter Kummerow (W Germany), for the Bait Distance Double-Handed 30-g event held at Lenzerheide, Switzerland, in the 1968 Championships.

The longest Fly Distance Double-Handed cast is 257 ft 2 in by S. Sheen of Norway, also set at Lenzerheide in Sept 1968.

Longest Fight

The longest recorded fight between a fisherman and a fish is 32 hours 5 min by Donal Heatley (b 1938) (New Zealand) with a black marlin (estimated length 20 ft and weight 1,500 lb) off Mayor Island off Tauranga, New Zealand, Jan 21–22, 1968. It towed the 12-ton launch 50 miles before breaking the line.

FOOTBALL

Origins

The origin of modern football stems from the "Boston Game" as played at Harvard. Harvard declined to participate in the inaugural meeting of the Intercollegiate Football Association in NYC in Oct 1873, on the grounds that the proposed rules were based on the non-handling "Association" code of English football. Instead, Harvard accepted a proposal from McGill University of Montreal, who played the more closely akin English Rugby Football. The first football match under the Harvard Rules was thus played against McGill at Cambridge, Mass, in May 1874. In Nov 1876, a New Intercollegiate Football Association, based on modern football, was inaugurated at Springfield, Mass, with a pioneer membership of 5 colleges.

Professional football dates from the Latrobe, Pa vs Jeannette, Pa match at Latrobe, in Aug 1895. The National Football League was founded in Canton, Ohio, in 1920, although it did not adopt its present name until 1922. The year 1969 was the final year in which professional football was divided into separate National and American Leagues, for record purposes.

Longest Service Coach

The longest service head coach was Amos Alonzo Stagg (1862–1965), who served Springfield in 1890–91, Chicago from 1892 to 1932 and College of the Pacific from 1933 to 1946, making a total of 57 years. He later served as an assistant coach to his son.

College Series Records

The oldest collegiate series is that between Princeton and Rutgers dating from 1869, or 7 years before the passing of the Springfield rules. The most regularly contested series is between Lafayette and Lehigh, who have met 115 times between 1884 and the end of 1979.

Yale University became the only college to win more than 700 games when they finished the 1979 season with a total of 701 victories in 107 seasons.

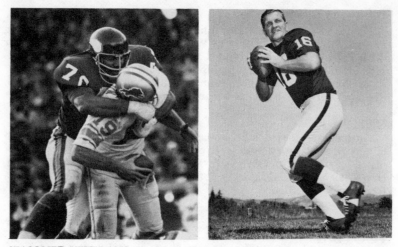

SEASONED VETERANS: Jim Marshall (left) played in 282 consecutive regular-season games, including every game in the history of the Vikings to 1979. George Blanda (right) played in the most games over the most seasons and scored the most points. An excellent quarterback, he passed for 36 td's in 1961.

Modern Major-College Individual Records

(Through 1979 Season)

Points

Most in a Game	43	Jim Brown (Syracuse)	1956
Most in a Season	174	Lydell Mitchell (Penn State)	1971
Most in a Career	356	Tony Dorsett (Pittsburgh)	1973–76

Touchdowns

Most in a Game	7	Arnold Boykin (Mississippi)	1951
Most in a Season	29	Lydell Mitchell (Penn State)	1971
Most in a Career	59	Glenn Davis (Army)	1943–46
	59	Tony Dorsett (Pittsburgh)	1973–76

Field Goals

Most in a Game	6	Frank Nester (West Virginia)	1972
	6	Charlie Gogolak (Princeton)	1965
	6	Vince Fusco (Duke)	1976
Most in a Season	22	Matt Bahr (Penn State)	1978
Most in a Career	56	Tony Franklin (Texas A & M)	1975–78

Season Records

Yards Gained Rushing	1,948 yd	Tony Dorsett (Pittsburgh)	1976
Highest Average Gain per Rush	9.35 yd	Greg Pruitt (Oklahoma)	1971
Most Passes Attempted	509	Bill Anderson (Tulsa)	1965
Most Passes Completed	296	Bill Anderson (Tulsa)	1965
Most Touchdown Passes	39	Dennis Shaw (San Diego St)	1969
Most Yards Gained Passing	3,720 yd	Marc Wilson (Brigham Young)	1979
Most Passes Caught	134	Howard Twilley (Tulsa)	1965
Most Yards Gained on Catches	1,779 yd	Howard Twilley (Tulsa)	1965
Most Touchdown Passes Caught	18	Tom Reynolds (San Diego St)	1969
Most Passes Intercepted by	14	Al Worley (Washington)	1968

Highest Score

The most points ever scored in a college football game was 222 by Georgia Tech, Atlanta, Ga, against Cumberland University of Lebanon, Tenn on Oct 7, 1916. Tech also set records for the most points scored in one quarter (63), most touchdowns (32) and points after touchdown (30) in a game, and the largest victory margin (Cumberland did not score). There were no first downs.

Longest Streaks

The longest winning streak is 47 straight by Oklahoma. The longest unbeaten streak is 63 games (59 won, 4 tied) by Washington from 1907 to 1917.

All-America Selections

The earliest All-America selections were made in 1889 by Caspar Whitney of *The Week's Sport* and later of *Harper's Weekly.*

All-Time Professional Records
(*Through 1979 Season*)

SERVICE

Most Seasons, Active Player
  26 George Blanda, Chi Bears, 1949–58; Balt, 1950; AFL: Hou, 1960–66; Oak, 1967–75

Most Games Played, Lifetime
  340 George Blanda, Chi Bears, 1949–58; Balt, 1950; AFL: Hou, 1960–66; Oak, 1967–75

Most Consecutive Games Played, Lifetime
  282 Jim Marshall, Cleve, 1960; Minn, 1961–79

Most Seasons, Head Coach
  40 George Halas, Chi Bears, 1920–29, 33–42, 46–55, 58–67

SCORING

Most Seasons Leading League
  5 Don Hutson, GB, 1940–44
    Gino Cappelletti, Bos, 1961, 63–66 (AFL)

Most Points, Lifetime
  2,002 George Blanda, Chi Bears, 1949–58; Balt, 1950; AFL: Hou, 1960–66; Oak, 1967–75 (9-td, 943-pat, 335-fg)

Most Points, Season
  176 Paul Hornung, GB, 1960 (15-td, 41-pat, 15-fg)

Most Points, Rookie Season
  132 Gale Sayers, Chi, 1965 (22-td)

MOST ROOKIE POINTS: Gale Sayers (right) scored 132 points, including 36 in one game, as a rookie in 1965. Watching him is the LONGEST SERVING PRO COACH, George Halas (center, in raincoat and baseball hat).

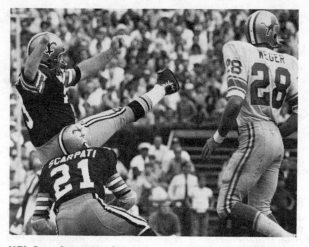

LONGEST PRO FIELD GOAL: Tom Dempsey, who was born with only half a right foot, kicked a 63-yd field goal. In a semipro game, he kicked one barefoot 57 yd.

NFL Records (continued)
Most Points, Game
  40 Ernie Nevers, Chi Cards vs Chi Bears, Nov 28, 1929 (6-td, 4-pat)

Most Points, One Quarter
  29 Don Hutson, GB vs Det, Oct 7, 1945 (4-td, 5-pat) 2nd Quarter

Touchdowns
Most Seasons Leading League
  8 Don Hutson, GB, 1935–38, 41–44

Most Touchdowns, Lifetime
  126 Jim Brown, Cleve, 1957–65 (106-r, 20-p)

Most Touchdowns, Season
  23 O. J. Simpson, Buff, 1975 (16-r, 7-p)

Most Touchdowns, Rookie Season
  22 Gale Sayers, Chi, 1965 (14-r, 6-p, 1-prb, 1-krb)

Most Touchdowns, Game
  6 Ernie Nevers, Chi Cards vs Chi Bears, Nov 28, 1929 (6-r)
     William (Dub) Jones, Cleve vs Chi Bears, Nov 25, 1951 (4-r, 2-p)
     Gale Sayers, Chi vs SF, Dec 12, 1965 (4-r, 1-p, 1-prb)

Most Consecutive Games Scoring Touchdowns
  18 Lenny Moore, Balt, 1963–65

Points After Touchdown
Most Seasons Leading League
  8 George Blanda, Chi Bears, 1956; AFL: Hou, 1961–62; Oak, 1967–69, 72, 74

Most Points After Touchdown, Lifetime
  943 George Blanda, Chi Bears, 1949–58; Balt, 1950; AFL: Hou, 1960–66; Oak, 1967–75

Most Points After Touchdown, Season
  64 George Blanda, Hou, 1961 (AFL)

Most Points After Touchdown, Game
  9 Marlin (Pat) Harder, Chi Cards vs NY, Oct 17, 1948
     Bob Waterfield, LA vs Balt, Oct 22, 1950
     Charlie Gogolak, Wash vs NY, Nov 27, 1966

Most Consecutive Points After Touchdown
  234 Tommy Davis, SF, 1959–65

Most Points After Touchdown (no misses), Game
  9 Marlin (Pat) Harder, Chi Cards vs NY, Oct 17, 1948
     Bob Waterfield, LA vs Balt, Oct 22, 1950

Field Goals
Most Seasons Leading League
  5 Lou Groza, Cleve, 1950, 52–54, 57

Most Field Goals, Lifetime
  335 George Blanda, Chi Bears, 1949–58; Balt, 1950; AFL: Hou, 1960–66; Oak, 1967–75

Most Field Goals, Season
  34 Jim Turner, NY, 1968 (AFL)

Most Field Goals, Game
  7 Jim Bakken, St L vs Pitt, Sept 24, 1967

Most Consecutive Games, Field Goals
31   Fred Cox, Minn, 1968–70

Most Consecutive Field Goals
16   Jan Stenerud, KC, 1969 (AFL)
     Don Cockroft, Cleve, 1974–75
     Garo Yepremian, Mia, 1978

Longest Field Goal
63 yd   Tom Dempsey, NO vs Det,
        Nov 8, 1970

RUSHING

Most Seasons Leading League
8   Jim Brown, Cleve, 1957–61,
    63–65

Most Yards Gained, Lifetime
12,312   Jim Brown, Cleve, 1957–65

Most Yards Gained, Season
2,003   O. J. Simpson, Buff, 1973

Most Yards Gained, Game
275   Walter Payton, Chi vs Minn,
      Nov 20, 1977

Longest Run from Scrimmage
97 yd   Andy Uram, GB vs Chi
        Cards, Oct 8, 1939 (td)
        Bob Gage, Pitt vs Chi Bears,
        Dec 4, 1949 (td)

Highest Average Gain, Lifetime (799 att)
5.2   Jim Brown, Cleve, 1957–65
      (2,359–12,312)

Highest Average Gain, Season (100 att)
9.9   Beattie Feathers, Chi Bears,
      1934 (101–1004)

Highest Average Gain, Game (10 att)
17.1   Marion Motley, Cleve vs Pitt,
       Oct 29, 1950 (11–188)

Most Touchdowns Rushing, Lifetime
106   Jim Brown, Cleve, 1957–65

Most Touchdowns Rushing, Season
19   Jim Taylor, GB, 1962
     Earl Campbell, Hou, 1979

Most Touchdowns Rushing, Game
6   Ernie Nevers, Chi Cards vs Chi
    Bears, Nov 28, 1929

PASSING

Most Seasons Leading League
6   Sammy Baugh, Wash, 1937, 40,
    43, 45, 47, 49

Most Passes Attempted, Lifetime
6,467   Fran Tarkenton, Minn, 1961–66,
        72–78; NY Giants, 1967–71
        (3,686 completions)

TOP GAINER: O. J. Simpson ran for
2,003 yd in 1973. Two years later, he
scored 23 td's for another record.

Most Passes Attempted, Season
572   Fran Tarkenton, Minn, 1978
      (345 completions)

Most Passes Attempted, Game
68   George Blanda, Hou vs Buff,
     Nov 1, 1964 (AFL) (37 com-
     pletions)

Most Passes Completed, Lifetime
3,686   Fran Tarkenton, Minn, 1961–66,
        72–78; NY Giants, 1967–71
        (6,467 attempts)

Most Passes Completed, Season
345   Fran Tarkenton, Minn, 1978
      (572 attempts)

Most Passes Completed, Game
37   George Blanda, Hou vs Buff,
     Nov 1, 1964 (AFL) (68 at-
     tempts)

Most Consecutive Passes Completed
17   Bert Jones, Balt vs NY Jets, Dec
     15, 1974

Passing Efficiency, Lifetime (1,500 att)
59.9   Ken Stabler, Oak, 1970–78
       (2,481–1,486)

Passing Efficiency, Season (100 att)
70.3   Sammy Baugh, Wash, 1945
       (182–129)

Passing Efficiency, Game (20 att)
90.9   Ken Anderson, Cin vs Pitt, Nov
       10, 1974 (22–20)

Longest Pass Completion (all tds)
99 Frank Filchock (to Farkas), Wash vs Pitt, Oct 15, 1939
George Izo (to Mitchell), Wash vs Cleve, Sept 15, 1963
Karl Sweetan (to Studstill), Det vs Balt, Oct 16, 1966
C. A. Jurgensen (to Allen), Wash vs Chi, Sept 15, 1968

Most Yards Gained Passing, Lifetime
47,003 Fran Tarkenton, Minn, 1961–66, 72–78; NY Giants, 1967–71

Most Yards Gained Passing, Season
4,082 Dan Fouts, SD, 1979

Most Yards Gained Passing, Game
554 Norm Van Brocklin, LA vs NY Yanks, Sept 28, 1951 (41–27)

Most Touchdown Passes, Lifetime
342 Fran Tarkenton, Minn, 1961–66, 72–78; NY Giants, 1967–71

Most Touchdown Passes, Season
36 George Blanda, Hou, 1961 (AFL)
Y. A. Tittle, NY, 1963

Most Touchdown Passes, Game
7 Sid Luckman, Chi Bears vs NY, Nov 14, 1943
Adrian Burk, Phil vs Wash, Oct 17, 1954
George Blanda, Hou vs NY, Nov 19, 1961 (AFL)
Y. A. Tittle, NY vs Wash, Oct 28, 1962
Joe Kapp, Minn vs Balt, Sept 28, 1969

Most Consecutive Games, Touchdown Passes
47 John Unitas, Balt, 1956–60

Passes Had Intercepted

Fewest Passes Intercepted, Season (Qualifiers)
1 Joe Ferguson, Buff, 1976 (151 attempts)

Most Consecutive Passes Attempted, None Intercepted
294 Bryan (Bart) Starr, GB, 1964–65

Most Passes Intercepted, Game
8 Jim Hardy, Chi Cards vs Phil, Sept 24, 1950 (39 attempts)

Lowest Percentage Passes Intercepted, Lifetime (1,500 att)
3.31 Roman Gabriel, LA, 1962–72; Phil, 1973–77 (4,498–149)

Lowest Percentage Passes Intercepted, Season (Qualifiers)
0.66 Joe Ferguson, Buff, 1976 (151–1)

PASS RECEPTIONS

Most Seasons Leading League
8 Don Hutson, GB, 1936–37, 39, 41–45

Most Pass Receptions, Lifetime
649 Charley Taylor, Wash, 1964–75, 77

Most Pass Receptions, Season
101 Charley Hennigan, Hou, 1964 (AFL)

Most Pass Receptions, Game
18 Tom Fears, LA vs GB, Dec 3, 1950 (189 yd)

Most Pass Receptions by a Running Back, Game
15 Rickey Young, Minn vs NE, Dec 16, 1979

Longest Pass Reception (all tds)
99 Andy Farkas (Filchock), Wash vs Pitt, Oct 15, 1939
Bobby Mitchell (Izo), Wash vs Cleve, Sept 15, 1963
Pat Studstill (Sweetan), Det vs Balt, Oct 16, 1966
Gerry Allen (Jurgensen), Wash vs Chi, Sept 15, 1968

Most Consecutive Games, Pass Receptions
112 Harold Carmichael, Phil, 1972–1979

Touchdowns Receiving

Most Touchdown Passes, Lifetime
99 Don Hutson, GB, 1935–45

Most Touchdown Passes, Season
17 Don Hutson, GB, 1942
Elroy (Crazy Legs) Hirsch, LA, 1951
Bill Groman, Hou, 1961 (AFL)

Most Touchdown Passes, Game
5 Bob Shaw, Chi Cards vs Balt, Oct 2, 1950

Most Consecutive Games, Touchdown Passes
11 Elroy (Crazy Legs) Hirsch, LA, 1950–51
Gilbert (Buddy) Dial, Pitt, 1959–60

PASS INTERCEPTIONS

Most Interceptions by, Lifetime
81 Paul Krause, Wash (28), 1964–67; Minn (53), 1968–79

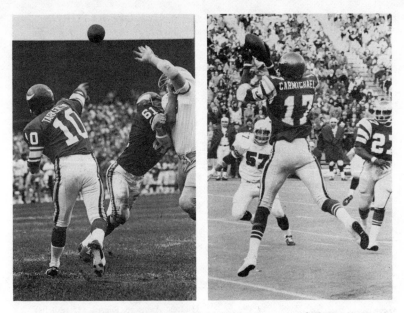

PASS AND CATCH: Fran Tarkenton (left) holds career records for most completions, yd gained passing and td's. Harold Carmichael (right) has caught at least one pass in 112 consecutive games.

Most Interceptions by, Season
14 Richard (Night Train) Lane, LA, 1952

Most Interceptions by, Game
4 By many players

PUNTING

Most Seasons Leading League
4 Sammy Baugh, Wash, 1940–43
Jerrel Wilson, AFL: KC, 1965, 68; NFL: KC, 1972–73

Most Punts, Lifetime
1,072 Jerrel Wilson, AFL: KC, 1963–69; NFL: KC, 1970–77; NE, 1978

Most Punts, Season
109 John James, Atl, 1978

Most Punts, Game
14 Dick Nesbitt, Chi Cards vs Chi Bears, Nov 30, 1933
Keith Molesworth, Chi Bears vs GB, Dec 10, 1933
Sammy Baugh, Wash vs Phil, Nov 5, 1939
John Kinscherf, NY vs Det, Nov 7, 1943
George Taliaferro, NY Yanks vs LA, Sept 28, 1951

Longest Punt
98 yd Steve O'Neal, NY Jets vs Den, Sept 21, 1969 (AFL)

Average Yardage Punting

Highest Punting Average, Lifetime (300 punts)
45.1 yd Sammy Baugh, Wash, 1937–52 (338)

Highest Punting Average, Season (20 punts)
51.4 yd Sammy Baugh, Wash, 1940 (35)

Highest Punting Average, Game (4 punts)
61.8 yd Bob Cifers, Det vs Chi Bears, Nov 24, 1946

PUNT RETURNS
Yardage Returning Punts

Most Yards Gained, Lifetime
2,288 Rick Upchurch, Den, 1975–79

Most Yards Gained, Season
655 Neal Colzie, Oak, 1975

Most Yards Gained, Game
205 George Atkinson, Oak vs Buff, Sept 15, 1968

SUPER BOWL: Quarterback Terry Bradshaw has helped the Pittsburgh Steelers to a record 4 Super Bowl victories.

NFL Records (continued)
Longest Punt Return (all tds)
  98 Gil LeFebvre, Cin vs Brk, Dec 3, 1933
      Charlie West, Minn vs Wash, Nov 3, 1968
      Dennis Morgan, Dall vs St L, Oct 13, 1974

Average Yardage Returning Punts

Highest Average, Lifetime (75 returns)
  13.4 Billy (White Shoes) Johnson, Hou, 1974–78

Highest Average, Season (Qualifiers)
  23.0 Herb Rich, Balt, 1950

Highest Average, Game (3 returns)
  47.7 Chuck Latourette, St L vs NO, Sept 29, 1968

Touchdowns Returning Punts

Most Touchdowns, Lifetime
  8 Jack Christiansen, Det, 1951–58

Most Touchdowns, Season
  4 Jack Christiansen, Det, 1951
     Rick Upchurch, Den, 1976

Most Touchdowns, Game
  2 Jack Christiansen, Det vs LA, Oct 14, 1951; vs GB, Nov 22, 1951
     Dick Christy, NY Titans vs Den, Sept 24, 1961
     Rick Upchurch, Den vs Cleve, Sept 26, 1976

KICKOFF RETURNS
Yardage Returning Kickoffs

Most Yards Gained, Lifetime
  6,922 Ron Smith, Chi, 1965, 70–72; Atl, 1966–67; LA, 1968–69; SD, 1973; Oak, 1974

Most Yards Gained, Season
  1,317 Bobby Jancik, Hou, 1963 (AFL)

Most Yards Gained, Game
  294 Wally Triplett, Det vs LA, Oct 29, 1950 (4)

Longest Kickoff Return for Touchdown
  106 Al Carmichael, GB vs Chi Bears, Oct 7, 1956
       Noland Smith, KC vs Den, Dec 17, 1967 (AFL)
       Roy Green, St L vs Dall, Oct 21, 1979

Average Yardage Returning Kickoffs

Highest Average, Lifetime (75 returns)
  30.6 Gale Sayers, Chi, 1965–71

Highest Average, Season (15 returns)
  41.1 Travis Williams, GB, 1967 (18)

Highest Average, Game (3 returns)
  73.5 Wally Triplett, Det vs LA, Oct 29, 1950 (4–294)

Touchdowns Returning Kickoffs

Most Touchdowns, Lifetime
  6 Ollie Matson, Chi Cards, 1952 (2), 54, 56, 58 (2)
     Gale Sayers, Chi, 1965, 66 (2), 67 (3)
     Travis Williams, GB, 1967 (4), 69, 71

LONGEST PUNTER: Steve O'Neal (NY Jets) kicked 98 yd in 1969.

Most Touchdowns, Season
   4 Travis Williams, GB, 1967
      Cecil Turner, Chi, 1970

Most Touchdowns, Game
   2 Thomas (Tim) Brown, Phil vs
      Dall, Nov 6, 1966
      Travis Williams, GB vs Cleve,
      Nov 12, 1967

FUMBLES

Most Fumbles, Lifetime
   105 Roman Gabriel, LA, 1962–72;
        Phil, 1973–77

Most Fumbles, Season
   17 Dan Pastorini, Hou, 1973

Most Fumbles, Game
   7 Len Dawson, KC vs SD, Nov 15,
      1964 (AFL)

Longest Fumble Run
   104 Jack Tatum, Oak vs GB, Sept
        24, 1972

Most Own Fumbles Recovered, Lifetime
   43 Fran Tarkenton, Minn, 1961–66,
       72–78; NY Giants, 1967–71

Most Own Fumbles Recovered, Season
   8 Paul Christman, Chi Cards, 1945
      Bill Butler, Minn, 1963

Most Own Fumbles Recovered, Game
   4 Otto Graham, Cleve vs NY, Oct
      25, 1953
      Sam Etcheverry, St L vs NY,
      Sept 17, 1961
      Roman Gabriel, LA vs SF, Oct
      12, 1969
      Joe Ferguson, Buff vs Miami,
      Sept 18, 1977

Most Opponents' Fumbles Recovered,
Lifetime
   29 Jim Marshall, Cleve, 1960;
       Minn, 1961–79

Most Opponents' Fumbles Recovered,
Season
   9 Don Hultz, Minn, 1963

Most Opponents' Fumbles Recovered,
Game
   3 Corwin Clatt, Chi Cards vs Det,
      Nov 6, 1949
      Vic Sears, Phil vs GB, Nov 2,
      1952
      Ed Beatty, SF vs LA, Oct 7, 1956
      Ron Carroll, Hou vs Cin, Oct 27,
      1974
      Maurice Spencer, NO vs Atl,
      Oct 10, 1976
      Steve Nelson, NE vs Phil, Oct 8,
      1978

GAMES AND PASTIMES

BRIDGE (CONTRACT)

Bridge (corruption of Biritch) is thought to be of Levantine origin, similar games having been played there in the early 1870's. The game was known in London in 1886 under the title of "Biritch or Russian Whist." Whist, first referred to in 1529, was the world's premier card game until 1930. Its rules had been standardized in 1742.

Auction bridge (highest bidder names trump) was invented c. 1902. The contract principle, present in several games (notably the French game *Plafond, c.* 1917), was introduced to bridge by Harold S. Vanderbilt (US) on Nov 1, 1925, during a Caribbean voyage aboard the SS *Finland*. The new version became a world-wide craze after the US vs GB challenge match between Rumanian-born Ely Culbertson (1891–1955) and Lt-Col Walter Thomas More Buller (1887–1938) at Almack's Club, London, Sept 1930. The US won the 200-hand match by 4,845 points.

Perfect Deals

The mathematical odds against dealing 13 cards of one suit are 158,753,389,899 to 1, while the odds against receiving a "perfect hand" consisting of all 13 spades are 635,013,559,596 to 1. The odds against each of the 4 players receiving a complete suit (a "perfect deal") are 2,235,197,406,895,366,368,301,559,999 to 1.

Highest Possible Scores

(excluding penalties for rules infractions)

Opponents bid 7 of any suit or no trump, doubled and redoubled and vulnerable.

Opponents make no trick.		
Above Line 1st undertrick		400
12 subsequent under-tricks at 600 each		7,200
All Honors		150
		7,750

Bid 1 no trump, doubled and redoubled, vulnerable.

Below Line 1st trick (40 × 4)	160
Above Line 6 overtricks (400 × 6)	2,400
2nd game of 2-Game Rubber	*350
All Honors (4 aces)	150
Bonus for making redoubled contract	50
(Highest Possible Positive Score)	3,110

* In practice, the full bonus of 700 points is awarded after the completion of the second game, rather than 350 after each game.

CHESS

The name chess is derived from the Persian word *shah*. It is a descendant of the game *Chaturanga*. The earliest reference is from the Middle Persian Karnamak (*c.* 590–628), though there are grounds for believing its origins are from the 2nd century, owing to the discovery, announced in Dec 1972, of two ivory chessmen in the Uzbek Soviet Republic, datable to that century. The *Fédération Internationale des Echecs* was established in 1924. There were an estimated 7 million registered players in the USSR in 1973.

World Champions

World champions have been generally recognized since 1886. The longest undisputed tenure was 27 years by Dr Emanuel Lasker (1868–1941) of Germany, from 1894 to 1921. Robert J. (Bobby) Fischer (b Chicago, March 9, 1943) is reckoned on the officially adopted Elo system to be the greatest Grandmaster of all time.

The women's world championship was held by Vera Menchik-Stevenson (1906–44) (GB) from 1927 till her death, and was successfully defended a record 7 times. Nona Gaprindashvili (USSR) (b May 3, 1941) held the title from 1962 to 1979, and defended 4 times.

The youngest world champion was Mikhail Nekhemevich Tal (USSR) (b Nov 9, 1936) when he took the title on May 7, 1960, aged 23 years 180 days.

GRANDEST GRANDMASTER: Anatoli Karpov (left), shown defending his title against Victor Korchnoi, had lost less than 5% of his games to the end of 1977.

Winning Streak

Bobby Fischer won 20 games in succession in Grandmaster chess from Dec 2, 1970 (vs Jorge Rubinetti of Argentina) to Sept 30, 1971 (vs Tigran Petrosian of the USSR). Anatoli Karpov (USSR) (b May 23, 1951) lost only 4.3 per cent of his 597 games between 1966 and Dec 1977.

Longest Games

The most protracted master game on record was one drawn on the 191st move between Herman Pilnik (W Germany, later Argentina) and Moshe Czerniak (Poland, later Israel) at Mar del Plata, Argentina, in Apr 1950. The total playing time was 20 hours. A game of 21½ hours, but drawn on the 171st move (average over 7½ min per move), was played between Vladimir Makagonov and Vitali Chekhover at Baku, USSR, in 1945.

The slowest reported move (before modern rules) was one of 11 hours between Paul Charles Morphy (1837–84), the US champion 1852–1862, and the German chess master Louis Paulsen (1833–91). Grandmaster Friedrich Sämisch (b Germany Sept 20, 1896) ran out of the allotted time (2½ hours for 45 moves) after only 12 moves, in Prague, Czechoslovakia, in 1938.

Marathon

The longest recorded session is one of 165 hours 9 min by Philip Thomas and Andrew Harris of Nottingham University in England, Oct 6–13, 1979.

Most Opponents

The record for most opponents tackled (with replacements as they are defeated) is held by Branimir Brebrich (Canada) who played 575 games (winning 533, drawing 27 and losing 15) in Edmonton, Alberta, Canada, Jan 27–28, 1978 in 28 hours of play.

Vlastimil Hort (b Jan 12, 1944) (Czechoslovakia) in Seltjarnarnes, Iceland, Apr 23–24, 1977, simultaneously tackled 201 opponents and did not lose a game.

Georges Koltanowski (Belgium, later of US) tackled 56 opponents "blindfold" and won 50, drew 6, lost 0 in 9¾ hours at the Fairmont Hotel, San Francisco, on Dec 13, 1960.

FRISBEE®

Competitive play began in 1957, and championships are supervised by the International Frisbee Disc Association.

Distance

The world record for outdoor distance is 444 ft on a throw by John Kirkland of Del Mar, Calif, on Apr 30, 1978, in Dallas, Tex. The indoor distance record is held by Tyrone Hines with a 316-ft toss on June 4, 1980, in Seattle, Wash.

Susane Lempert holds the women's outdoor distance record (283.5 ft, set in Boston on July 24, 1976), while the women's indoor distance record belongs to Monika Lou, who threw 222.5 ft on Aug 24, 1977, in Los Angeles.

The 24-hour group distance record is 428.02 miles set in Vernon, Conn, by the South Windsor Ultimate Frisbee Disc Team, July 8–9, 1977. Dan Roddick and Alan Bonopane of Pasadena, Calif, hold the world record for 24-hour pair distance with 250.02 miles, Dec 30–31, 1979.

The greatest distance any inert object heavier than air has been thrown is 857 ft 8 in in the case of a plastic "Skyro" by Tom McRann, 30, in Golden Gate Park, San Francisco, on June 9, 1980.

Skills

Mark Vinchesi set the record for maximum time aloft by keeping a Frisbee disc in the air for 15.2 sec in Amherst, Mass, on Aug 20, 1978. For women, the time-aloft record is 10.04 sec, set in Santa Barbara, Calif, by Monika Lou.

The greatest distance achieved for throwing a Frisbee disc, running, and catching it is 271.2 ft by Tom Monroe of Huntsville, Ala, on Aug 24, 1979, in Irvine, Calif.

Fastest Guts Catch

Charles Duvall threw a professional model Frisbee disc at a speed of 60 mph and his teammate Steve McClean made a clean catch of the throw on Aug 1, 1979, for the "Guinness Game" TV show in Los Angeles. The throw was electronically timed across a regulation 14-meter Guts court.

Marathons

The Alhambra Frisbee Disc Club of Alhambra, Calif, set the group marathon mark with 1001 hours, May 7–June 18, 1978. The two-person marathon record is held by Ken McDade and Chris Train of Mississauga, Ontario. They played for 100 hours 40 min, March 25–29, 1979, in Toronto.

POOL AND BILLIARDS

Pool

Pool or championship pocket billiards with numbered balls began to become standardized c. 1890. The greatest exponents were Ralph Greenleaf (US) (1899–1950), who won the "world" professional title 19 times (1919–1937), and William Mosconi (US), who dominated the game from 1941 to 1957.

Michael Eufemia holds the record for the greatest continuous run, pocketing 625 balls without a miss on Feb 2, 1960 before a large crowd at Logan's Billiard Academy, Brooklyn, New York.

The greatest number of balls to be pocketed in 24 hours is 11,700 (a rate of one per 7.38 sec) by Gary Maunsey (b 1947) at Hamilton, New Zealand, June 30–July 1, 1979.

The longest game is 201 hours by Frank Drabble and Dave Spence at the Imperial Hotel, Stockport, Cheshire, England, Nov 3–11, 1979.

DOG CATCHER: "Martha Faye" caught a Frisbee 334.6 ft from where it was thrown for a canine distance record in 1978.

3-Cushion Billiards

This pocketless variation dates back to 1878. The world governing body, *Union Mondiale de Billiard,* was formed in 1928. The most successful exponent, 1906–52, was William F. Hoppe (b Oct 11, 1887), Cornwall-on-Hudson, NY; d Feb 1, 1959) who won 51 billiards championships in all forms. The most UMB titles have been won by Raymond Ceulemans (Belgium) (b 1937) with 14 (1963–66, 1968–73, 1975–78), with a peak average of 1,679 in 1978.

SKATEBOARDING

"World" skateboard championships have been staged intermittently since 1966. The highest recorded speed on a skateboard under US Skateboard Association rules is 71.79 mph on a course at Mt Baldy, Calif, in a prone position, by Richard K. Brown, age 33, on June 17, 1979. The stand-up record is 53.45 mph by John Hutson, 23, at Signal Hill, Long Beach, Calif, June 11, 1978. The high jump record is 5 ft 2 in by Trevor Baxter of Burgess Hill, Sussex, England, at the UK Open Championship at Kelvingrove, Glasgow on Sept 22, 1979.

LONGEST RUN: Michael Eufemia pocketed 625 balls consecutively, without a miss, in 1960.

At the 4th US Skateboard Association championships at Signal Hill on Sept 25, 1977, Tony Alva, 19, of Santa Monica, Calif, took off from a moving skateboard, jumped over 17 barrels (12-in diameters) and landed on another skateboard.

Mike Kinney won a marathon contest at Reseda, Calif, on May 26, 1979, with 217.3 miles in 30 hours 35 min.

GLIDING

Emanuel Swedenborg (1688–1772) of Sweden made sketches of gliders c. 1714.

The earliest man-carrying glider was designed by Sir George Cayley (1773–1857) and carried his coachman (possibly John Appleby) about 500 yd across a valley near Brompton Hall, Yorkshire, England, in the summer of 1853. Gliders now attain speeds of 168 mph and the Jastrzab aerobatic sailplane is designed to withstand vertical dives at up to 280 mph.

Most World Titles

The most world individual championships (instituted 1948) won is 3 by Helmut Reichmann (W Germany) in 1970, 1974 and 1978.

Hang-Gliding

In the 11th century, the monk Elmer is reported to have flown from the 60-ft-tall tower of Malmesbury Abbey, Wiltshire, England. The earliest modern pioneer was Otto Lilienthal (1848–96) of Germany who made numerous flights between 1893 and 1896. Professor Francis Rogallo of the US National Space Agency developed a "wing" in the 1950's from his research into space capsule re-entries.

The official FAI record for the farthest distance covered is 95.4 miles by George Worthington (US) in an ASG-21 (Rogallo) over Calif, July 22, 1977.

The official FAI height gain record is 11,700 ft, recorded by George Worthington (US) over Bishop, Calif, July 22, 1978.

GLIDING SPEED: Walter Neubert piloted his Kestrel 604 at a speed of 95.95 mph over a triangular 300-km course.

The greatest altitude from which a hang-glider has descended is 31,600 ft by Bob McCaffrey, 18, who was released from a balloon over the Mojave Desert, Calif, on Nov 21, 1976.

Championships

The First World Team Championships, held at Chattanooga, Tennessee, in Oct, 1978, were won by Great Britain.

Gliding World Records (Single-Seaters)

DISTANCE	907.7 miles	Hans-Werner Grosse (W Germany) in an ASW-12 on Apr 25, 1972.
DECLARED GOAL FLIGHT		
	799.4 miles	Bruce Drake, David Speight. S. H. "Dick" Georgeson (all NZ) all in Nimbus 2s, from Te Anau to Te Araroa, Jan 14, 1978.
ABSOLUTE ALTITUDE		
	46,266 ft	Paul F. Bikle, Jr (US) in a Schweizer SGS 1-23E over Mojave, Calif (released at 3,963 feet) on Feb 25, 1961 (also record altitude gain—42,303 ft).
GOAL AND RETURN		
	1,015.7 miles	Karl H. Striedieck (US) in an ASW-17 from Lock Haven, Pa to Tenn on May 9, 1977.

SPEED OVER TRIANGULAR COURSE

100 km	102.74 mph	Ross Briegleb (US) in a Kestrel 17 over the US on July 18, 1974.
300 km	95.95 mph	Walter Neubert (W Germany) in a Kestrel 604 over Kenya on March 3, 1972.
500 km	88.82 mph	Edward Pearson (GB) in a Nimbus 2 over Namibia on Nov 27, 1976.
750 km	87.69 mph	Georg Eckle (W Germany) in a Nimbus 2 over South Africa on Jan 7, 1978.
1,000 km	90.28 mph*	Hans-Werner Grosse (W Germany) in an ASW-17 over Australia, on Jan 3, 1979.

* Awaiting official confirmation

GOLF

Origins

Although a stained glass window in Gloucester Cathedral, Scotland, dating from 1350 portrays a golfer-like figure, the earliest mention of golf occurs in a prohibiting law passed by the Scottish Parliament in March 1457, under which "golff be utterly cryit doune and not usit." The Romans had a cognate game called *paganica,* which may have been carried to Britain before 400 AD. The Chinese National Golf Association claims the game is of Chinese origin ("*Ch'ui Wan*—the ball-hitting game") from the 3rd or 2nd century BC. Gutta-percha balls succeeded feather balls in 1848, and were in turn succeeded in 1902 by rubber-cored balls, invented in 1899 by Coburn Haskell (US). Steel shafts were authorized in the US in 1925.

Oldest Clubs

The oldest club of which there is written evidence is the Gentleman Golfers (now the Honourable Company of Edinburgh Golfers) formed

LOW SCORES: Sam Snead (left) shot a 59 in 1959 and has won 134 tournaments. Mickey Wright (right) carded a 62 in 1964 and has won 82 tournaments, including 13 in 1963.

in March 1744—10 years prior to the institution of the Royal and Ancient Club of St Andres, Fife, Scotland. The oldest existing club in North America is the Royal Montreal Club (Nov 1873) and the oldest in the US is St Andrews, Westchester County, NY (1888). An older claim is by the Foxbury Country Club, Clarion County, Pa (1887).

Highest and Lowest Courses

The highest golf course in the world is the Tuctu Golf Club in Morococha, Peru, which is 14,335 ft above sea level at its lowest point. Golf has, however, been played in Tibet at an altitude of over 16,000 ft.

The lowest golf course in the world was that of the now defunct Sodom and Gomorrah Golfing Society at Kallia (Qulya), on the northern shores of the Dead Sea, 1,250 ft below sea level. Currently the lowest is the Rotterdam Golf Club's 9-hole course at 26 ft below sea level.

Longest Course

The world's longest course is the 8,101-yd Dub's Dread Golf Club course (par 78) in Piper, Kans.

Longest Hole

The longest hole in the world is the 17th hole (par 6) of 745 yd at the Black Mountain Golf Club, NC. It was opened in 1964. In Aug 1927, the 6th hole at Prescott Country Club in Arkansas measured 838 yd.

Largest Green

Probably the largest green in the world is the 5th green at International GC, Bolton, Mass, with an area greater than 28,000 sq ft.

Biggest Bunker

The world's biggest trap is Hell's Half Acre on the 585-yd 7th hole of the Pine Valley course, Clementon, NJ, built in 1912 and generally regarded as the world's most trying course.

Lowest Scores for 9 and 18 Holes

The lowest recorded score on any 18-hole course with a par of 70 or more is 55 first achieved by Alfred Edward Smith (b 1903), the English professional, at Woolacombe on Jan 1, 1936. The course measured 4,248 yd. The detail was 4, 2, 3, 4, 2, 4, 3, 4, 3=29 out, and 2, 3, 3, 3, 3, 2, 5, 4, 1=26 in.

At least three players are recorded to have played a long course (over 6,000 yd) in a score of 58.

Nine holes in 25 (4, 3, 3, 2, 3, 3, 1, 4, 2) was recorded by A. J. "Bill" Burke in a round of 57 (32 + 25) on the 6,389-yd par 71 Normandie course in St Louis on May 20, 1970. The tournament record is 27 by Mike Souchak (US) (b May 1927) for the second nine (par 35) first round of the 1955 Texas Open, Andy North (US) (b Mar 9, 1950) second nine (par 34), first round, 1975 BC Open at En-Joie GC, Endicott, NY and Jose Maria Canizares (Spain) (b Feb 18, 1947), first nine, third round, in the 1978 Swiss Open on the 6,811 yd Crans-Sur course.

The US PGA tournament record for 18 holes is 59 (30 + 29) by Al Geiberger (b Sept 1, 1937) in the second round of the Danny Thomas Classic, on the 72-par, 7,249-yd Colonial CC, course Memphis, Tenn, June 10, 1977.

In non-PGA tournaments, Sam Snead had 59 in the Greenbrier Open (now called the Sam Snead Festival), at White Sulphur Springs, W Va, on May 16, 1959; Gary Player (South Africa) (b Nov 1, 1935) carded 59 in the second round of the Brazilian Open in Rio de Janeiro on Nov 29, 1974; and David Jagger (GB) also had 59 in a Pro-Am tournament prior to the 1973 Nigerian Open.

The lowest recorded score on an 18-hole course (over 6,000 yd) for a woman is 62 (30 + 32) by Mary (Mickey) Kathryn Wright (b Feb 14, 1935), of Dallas, on the Hogan Park Course (6,282 yd) at Midland, Tex, in Nov 1964.

Wanda Morgan (b March 22, 1910) recorded a score of 60 (31 + 29) on the Westgate and Birchington Golf Club course, Kent, England, over 18 holes (5,002 yd) on July 11, 1929.

Lowest Scores for 36 holes

The record for 36 holes is 122 (59 + 63) by Sam Snead in the 1959 Greenbrier Open (now called the Sam Snead Festival) (non-PGA) (see above) May 16–17, 1959. Horton Smith (see below) scored 121 (63 + 58) on a short course on Dec 21, 1928.

Lowest Scores for 72 holes

The lowest recorded score on a first-class course is 257 (27 under par) by Mike Souchak (b May 10, 1927) in the Texas Open at Brackenbridge Park, San Antonio in Feb 1955, made up of 60 (33 out and 27 in), 68, 64, 65 (average 64.25 per round), exhibiting, as one critic said, his "up and down form." Horton Smith (1908–63), twice US Masters Champion, scored 245 (63, 58, 61 and 63) for 72 holes on the 4,700-yd course (par 64)

LONGEST DRIVE (left): Tommie Campbell hit a 392-yd drive. LONGEST PUTT: Cary Middlecoff (above) sank an 86-ft putt in the 1955 Masters Tournament.

at Catalina Country Club, Calif, to win the Catalina Open, Dec 21–23, 1928.

The lowest 72 holes in a national championship is 262 by Percy Alliss (1897–1975) of Britain, with 67, 66, 66 and 63 in the Italian Open Championship at San Remo in 1932, and by Liang Huan Lu (b 1936) (Taiwan) in the 1971 French Open at Biarritz. Kelvin D. G. Nagle (b Dec 21, 1920) of Australia shot 261 in the Hong Kong Open in 1961.

Most Rounds in a Day

The greatest number of rounds played on foot in 24 hours is 22 rounds plus 5 holes (401 holes) by Ian Colston, 35, at Bendigo GC, Victoria, Australia (6,061 yd), Nov 27–28, 1971. He covered more than 100 miles.

The most holes played on foot in a week (168 hours) is 1,123 by Richard H. Stacey at Paxton Park Golf Club (6,100 yd), Paducah, Ky, Sept 25–Oct 1, 1978.

Longest Drive

In long-driving contests 330 yd is rarely surpassed at sea level.

The world record is 392 yd by a member of the Irish PGA, Tommie Campbell (Foxrock Golf Club), made at Dun Laoghaire, Co Dublin, in July 1964.

The USPGA record is 341 yd by Jack William Nicklaus (b Columbus, Ohio, Jan 21, 1940), then weighing 206 lb, in July 1963.

Valetin Barrios (Spain) drove a Slazenger B51 ball 568½ yd on an airport runway at Palma, Majorca, on March 7, 1977.

The longest on an ordinary course is 515 yd by Michael Hoke Austin (b Feb 17, 1910) of Los Angeles, in the US National Seniors Open Championship at Las Vegas, Nev, Sept 25, 1974. Aided by an estimated

35-mph tailwind, the 6-ft-2-in 210-lb golfer drove the ball on the fly to within a yard of the green on the par-4, 450-yd 5th hole of the Winterwood Course. The ball rolled 65 yd past the hole.

Arthur Lynskey claimed a drive of 200 yd out and 2 miles down off Pikes Peak, Colo, June 28, 1968.

A drive of 2,640 yd (1½ miles) across ice was achieved by an Australian meteorologist named Nils Lied at Mawson Base, Antarctica, in 1962. On the moon, the energy expended on a mundane 300-yd drive would achieve, craters permitting, a distance of a mile.

Longest Hitter

The golfer regarded as the longest consistent hitter the game has ever known is the 6-ft-5-in-tall, 230-lb George Bayer (US) (b Sept 17, 1925), the 1957 Canadian Open Champion. His longest measured drive was one of 420 yd at the fourth in the Las Vegas Invitational in 1953. It was measured as a precaution against litigation since the ball struck a spectator. Bayer also drove a ball pin high on a 426-yd hole in Tucson, Ariz. Radar measurements show that an 87-mph impact velocity for a golf ball falls to 46 mph in 3.0 sec.

Longest Putt

The longest recorded holed putt in a major tournament was one of 86 ft on the vast 13th green at the Augusta National, Ga, by Cary Middlecoff (b Jan 1921) in the 1955 Masters Tournament.

Bobby Jones was reputed to have holed a putt in excess of 100 ft on the 5th green in the first round of the 1927 British Open at St Andrews, Scotland.

Most Titles

US Open	Willie Anderson (1880–1910)	4	1901–03–04–05
	Robert Tyre Jones, Jr (1902–71)	4	1923–26–29–30
	W. Ben Hogan (b Aug 13, 1912)	4	1948–50–51–53
	Jack William Nicklaus (b Jan 21, 1940)	4	1962–67–72–80
US Amateur	R. T. Jones, Jr	5	1924–25–27–28–30
British Open	Harry Vardon (1870–1937)	6	1896–98–99, 1903–11–14
British Amateur	John Ball (1861–1940)	8	1888–90–92–94–99, 1907–10–12
PGA Championship (US)	Walter C. Hagen (1892–1969)	5	1921–24–25–26–27
	Jack W. Nicklaus	5	1963–71–73–75–80
Masters Championship (US)	Jack W. Nicklaus	5	1963–65–66–72–75
US Women's Open	Elizabeth (Betsy) Earle-Rawls (b May 4, 1928)	4	1951–53–57–60
	"Mickey" Wright (b Feb 14, 1935)	4	1958–59–61–64
US Women's Amateur	Mrs Glenna Vare (née Collett) (b June 20, 1903)	6	1922–25–28–29–30–35

Most Tournament Wins

The record for winning tournaments in a single season is 19, including a record 11 consecutively, by Byron Nelson (b Feb 4, 1912) (US), March 8–Aug 4, 1945.

Sam Snead has won 84 official USPGA tour events to Dec 1979, and has been credited with a total 134 tournament victories since 1934.

Mickey Wright (US) has won 82 professional tournaments from 1955 to Dec 1979, including a record 13 in 1963.

Jack Nicklaus (US) is the only golfer who has won all five major titles (British Open, US Open, Masters, PGA and US Amateur) twice, while setting a record total of 19 major tournament victories (1962–80). His remarkable record in the British Open is 3 firsts, 7 seconds and 2 thirds.

US Open

This championship was inaugurated in 1894. The lowest 72-hole aggregate is 272 (63, 71, 70, 68) by Jack Nicklaus on the Lower Course (7,015 yd) at Baltusrol Golf Club, Springfield, NJ, June 12–15, 1980. The lowest score for 18 holes is 63 by Johnny Miller (b Apr 29, 1947) of Calif on the 6,921-yd, par-71 Oakmont (Pa) course on June 17, 1973, and Jack Nicklaus and Tom Weiskopf (b Nov 9, 1942), both on June 12, 1980.

US Masters

The lowest score in the US Masters (instituted at the 6,980-yd Augusta National Golf Course, Ga, in 1934) was 271 by Jack Nicklaus in 1965

MOST WINS: Jack Nicklaus (left) has won 19 major tournaments and has career earnings of about $3.5 million. He set records for 18 and 72 holes in the 1980 US Open. Byron Nelson (right) won 19 out of 31 tournaments, including 11 in a row, in 1945.

and Raymond Floyd (b 1942) in 1976. The lowest rounds have been 64 by Lloyd Mangrum (1914–74) (1st round, 1940), Jack Nicklaus (3rd round, 1965), Maurice Bembridge (GB) (b Feb 21, 1945) (4th round, 1974), Hale Irwin (b June 3, 1945) (4th round, 1975), Gary Player (S Africa) (4th round, 1978), and Miller Barber (b March 31, 1931) (2nd round, 1979).

US Amateur

This championship was inaugurated in 1893. The lowest score for 9 holes is 30 by Francis D. Ouimet (1893–1967) in 1932.

British Open

The Open Championship was inaugurated in 1860 at Prestwick, Strathclyde, Scotland. The lowest score for 9 holes is 29 by Tom Haliburton (Wentworth) and Peter W. Thomson (Australia), in the first round at the Open on the Royal Lytham and St Anne's course at Lytham St Anne's, Lancashire, England, on July 10, 1963, by Tony Jacklin (GB, b July 1944) in the first round of the 1970 Open at St Andrews, Scotland and by Bill Longmuir (b June 10, 1953) in the first round on the Royal Lytham and St Anne's course on July 18, 1979.

The lowest scoring round in the Open itself is 63 by Mark Hayes (US, b July 12, 1949) at Turnberry, Strathclyde, Scotland, in the second round on July 7, 1977, and by Isao Aoki (Japan) in the third round in Muirfield, July 19, 1980. Henry Cotton (GB) at Royal St George's, Sandwich, Kent, England, completed the first 36 holes in 132 (67 + 65) on June 27, 1934.

The lowest 72-hole aggregate is 268 (68, 70, 65, 65) by Tom Watson (US) (b Sept 4, 1949) at Turnberry, Scotland, on July 9, 1977.

British Amateur

The lowest score for nine holes in the British Championship (inaugurated in 1885) is 29 by Richard Davol Chapman (b March 23, 1911) of the US at Royal St George's, Sandwich, Kent (par 70, 6,633 yd) on May 27, 1948. Michael Francis Bonallack (b 1934) shot a 61 (32 + 29) on the 6,905-yd par-71 course at Ganton, Yorkshire, on July 27, 1968, on the 1st 18 of the 36 holes in the final round.

World Cup (formerly Canada Cup)

The World Cup (instituted 1953) has been won most often by the US with 15 victories between 1955 and 1979. The only men on six winning teams have been Arnold Palmer (b Sept 10, 1929) (1960, 62–64, 66–67) and Jack Nicklaus (1963–4, 66–67, 71, 73). The only man to take the individual title three times is Jack Nicklaus (US) in 1963–64, 1971. The lowest aggregate score for 144 holes is 545 by Australia (Bruce Devlin and David Graham) at San Isidro, Buenos Aires, Argentina, Nov 12–15, 1970, and the lowest score by an individual winner was 269 by Roberto de Vicenzo, 47, on the same occasion.

Walker Cup

The US versus Great Britain–Ireland series instituted in 1921 (for the Walker Cup since 1922), now biennial, has been won by the US 26½–2½ to date. Joe Carr (GB–I) played in 10 contests (1947–67).

Ryder Trophy

The biennial Ryder Cup (instituted 1927) professional match between the US and GB (Europe in 1979) has been won by the US 19½–3½. Billy Casper has the record of winning most matches, with 20 won (1961–75).

Biggest Victory Margin

Randall Colin Vines (b June 22, 1945) of Australia won the Tasmanian Open in 1968 with a score of 274, with a margin of 17 strokes over the second-place finisher, and Bernhard Langer (W Germany) won the 1979 World Under-25 tournament at Nimes, France, Sept 30, 1979, also by 17 strokes with a 274 (73, 67, 67, 67).

Highest Earnings

The greatest amount ever won in official USPGA golf prizes is $3,408,827 by Jack Nicklaus to the end of 1978.

The record for a year is $462,636 by Tom Watson (US) in 1979.

The highest career earnings by a woman is $858,461 by Kathy Whitworth (b Sept 27, 1939) through the end of 1979.

Nancy Lopez (now Mrs T. Melton) (b Jan 6, 1957) won a record $197,488 in the 1979 season.

Youngest and Oldest Champions

The youngest winner of the British Open was Tom Morris, Jr (1851–75) at Prestwick, Ayrshire, Scotland, in 1868, aged 17 years 5 months. The youngest winners of the British Amateur title were John Charles Beharrel (b May 2, 1938) at Troon, Strathclyde, Scotland, on June 2, 1956, and Robert (Bobby) Cole (S Africa) (b May 11, 1948) at Carnoustie, Tayside, Scotland, on June 11, 1966, both aged 18 years 1 month. The oldest winner of the British Amateur was the Hon Michael Scott at Hoylake, Cheshire, England, in 1933, when 54. The oldest British Open champion was "Old Tom" Morris (1821–1908) who was aged 46 years 99 days when he won in 1867. In modern times, the 1967 champion Roberto de Vicenzo (b Buenos Aires, Argentina, Apr 14, 1923) was aged 44 years 93 days. The oldest US Amateur Champion was Jack Westland (b 1905) at Seattle, Wash, in 1952, aged 47.

Longest Span

Jacqueline Ann Mercer (*née* Smith) (b Apr 5, 1929) won her first South African title at Humewood GC, Port Elizabeth, in 1948, and her fourth title at Port Elizabeth GC on May 4, 1979, 31 years later.

Richest Prize

The greatest first-place prize money was $100,000 (total purse $500,000) in the 144-hole "World Open" played at Pinehurst, NC, Nov 8–17, 1973, won by Miller Barber, 42, of Texas. The World Series of Golf also carries a prize of $100,000.

Probably the greatest prize for one shot was the £50,000 ($110,000) won by Isao Aoki (Japan) by acing the 155-yd second hole in the World Match Play Championship at Wentworth on Oct 12, 1979.

TEN ACES (left): Joseph Vitullo has scored 10 holes-in-one on the 16th hole at Hubbard GC, Ohio. GREATEST EARNINGS (right): Nancy Lopez-Melton won $197,488 in 1979 to break her own women's yearly earnings record.

HOLES-IN-ONE

In 1979, *Golf Digest* was notified of 29,416 holes-in-one, so averaging over 80 per day.

Longest

The longest straight hole shot in one is the 10th hole (447 yd) at Miracle Hills GC, Omaha, Neb. Robert Mitera achieved a hole-in-one there on Oct 7, 1965. Mitera, aged 21 and 5 ft 6 in tall, weighed 165 lb. A two-handicap player, he normally drove 245 yd. A 50-mph gust carried his shot over a 290-yd drop-off. The group in front testified to the remaining 154 yd.

The longest dogleg achieved in one is the 480-yd 5th hole at Hope CC, Ark, by L. Bruce on Nov 15, 1962.

The women's record is 393 yd by Marie Robie of Wollaston, Mass, on the first hole of the Furnace Brook GC, Sept 4, 1949.

Most

The greatest number of holes-in-one in a career is 44 by Norman L. Manley, 56 years old, of Long Beach, Calif.

Douglas Porteous, 28, aced 4 holes over 36 consecutive holes—the 3rd and 6th on Sept 26, and the 5th on Sept 28 at Ruchill GC, Glasgow, Scotland, and the 6th at the Clydebank and District GC Course on Sept 30, 1974. Robert Taylor holed the 188-yd 16th hole at Hunstanton, Norfolk, England, on three successive days—May 31, June 1 and 2, 1974. Joseph F. Vitullo (b Apr 1, 1916) aced the 130-yd 16th hole at the Hubbard GC, Ohio, for the tenth time on June 26, 1979.

Consecutive

There is no recorded instance of a golfer performing three consecutive holes-in-one, but there are at least 15 cases of "aces" being achieved in two consecutive holes, of which the greatest was Norman L. Manley's unique "double albatross" on two par-4 holes (330-yd 7th and 290-yd 8th) on the Del Valle CC course, Saugus, Calif, on Sept 2, 1964.

The only woman ever to card consecutive aces is Sue Prell, on the 13th and 14th holes at Chatswood GC, Sydney, Australia, on May 29, 1977.

The closest recorded instances of a golfer getting 3 consecutive holes-in-one were by the Rev Harold Snider (b July 4, 1900) who aced the 8th, 13th and 14th holes of the par-3 Ironwood course in Phoenix, Ariz, on June 9, 1976, and Dr Joseph Boydstone on the 3rd, 4th and 9th at Bakersfield GC, Calif on Oct 10, 1962.

Youngest and Oldest

The youngest golfer recorded to have shot a hole-in-one was Coby Orr (aged 5) of Littleton, Colo, on the 103-yd fifth hole at the Riverside GC, San Antonio, Tex, in 1975.

The oldest golfers to have performed the feat are George Miller, 93, at the 11th (116 yd) at Anaheim GC, Calif, on Dec 4, 1970, Charles Youngman, 93, at the Tam O'Shanter Club, Toronto, in 1971, and William H. Diddel, 93, on the 142-yd 8th at the Royal Poinciana GC, Naples, Fla, on Jan 1, 1978. Maude Hutton became the oldest woman to make a hole-in-one when, at age 86, she aced the 102-yd 14th hole at Kings Inn Golf and Country Club, Sun City Center, Fla, on Aug 7, 1978.

GREYHOUND RACING

Earliest Meeting

In Sept 1876, a greyhound meeting was staged at Hendon, North London, England, with a railed hare operated by a windlass. Modern greyhound racing originated with the perfecting of the mechanical hare by Owen P. Smith at Emeryville, Calif, in 1919.

Fastest Dog

The highest speed at which any greyhound has been timed is 41.72 mph (410 yd in 20.1 sec) by "The Shoe" for a track record at Richmond, NSW, Australia, on Apr 25, 1968. It is estimated that he covered the last 100 yd in 4.5 sec or at 45.45 mph. The fastest 500-m *photo*-timing is 28.96 sec or 38.62 mph by "Monday's Bran" on Aug 4, 1979, at Brighton and Hove Stadium, Sussex, England. The fastest photo-timing over hurdles at 500 m is 29.71 sec (37.64 mph) by "Watchit Buster" on Aug 22, 1978, also at Brighton.

Winning Streak

An American greyhound, "Real Huntsman," won a world record 28 consecutive victories in 1950–51.

GYMNASTICS

Earliest References

A primitive form of gymnastics was widely practiced in ancient Greece and Rome during the period of the ancient Olympic Games (776 BC to 393 AD), but Johann Friedrich Simon was the first teacher of modern gymnastics, at Basedow's School, Dessau, Germany, in 1776.

World Championships

The greatest number of individual titles won by a man in the World Championships is 10 by Boris Shakhlin (USSR) between 1954 and 1964. He was also on three winning teams. The women's record is 10 individual wins and 5 team titles by Larissa Semyonovna Latynina (b Dec 27, 1934, retired 1966) of the USSR, between 1956 and 1964.

Japan has won the men's team title a record 5 times (1962, 66, 70, 74, 78) and the USSR has won the women's title on 6 occasions (1954, 58, 62, 70, 74, 78).

Olympic Games

Japan has won the most men's titles with 5 victories (1960, 1964, 1968, 1972, 1976). The USSR has won 8 women's team titles (1952–1980).

The only men to win 6 individual gold medals are Boris Shakhlin (USSR), with one in 1956, 4 (2 shared) in 1960 and one in 1964; and Nikolai Andrianov (USSR) with one in 1972, 4 in 1976 and one in 1980.

The most successful woman has been Vera Caslavska-Odlozil (Czechoslovakia), with 7 individual gold medals, 3 in 1964 and 4 (one shared) in 1968. Larissa Latynina of the USSR won 6 individual and 3

MOST TITLES: Boris Shakhlin (left) has won 10 individual world titles and 6 individual Olympic gold medals. Larissa Latynina (right) has also won 10 individual world titles and 6 individual Olympic golds. In addition, she has won 3 team golds, 5 silvers and 4 bronzes for a record 18 Olympic medals.

team gold medals, 5 silver, and 4 bronze for an all-time record total of 18 Olympic medals.

Nadia Comaneci (b Nov 12, 1961) (Rumania) became the first gymnast to be awarded a perfect score of 10.00 in the Olympic Games, in the 1976 Montreal Olympics. She ended the competition with a total of 7 such marks (4 on the uneven parallel bars, 3 on the balance beam).

Youngest International Competitor

Anita Jokiel (Poland) was aged 11 years 2 days when she competed at Brighton, East Sussex, England, on Dec 6, 1977.

World Cup

In the first World Cup Competition in London in 1975, Ludmilla Tourisheva (now Mrs Valery Borzov) (b Oct 7, 1952) of the USSR won all 5 available gold medals.

Chinning the Bar

The record for 2-arm chins from a dead hang position is 135 by Joe Hernandez (b 1961) at Dysart Junior HS, Cashion, Ariz, on May 22, 1980. William Aaron Vaught (b 1959) did 20 one-arm chin-ups at Finch's Gymnasium, Houston, Tex, on Jan 3, 1976. It is believed that only one person in 100,000 can chin a bar one-handed.

Francis Lewis (b 1896) of Beatrice, Neb, in May 1914, achieved 7 consecutive chins using only the middle finger of his left hand. His bodyweight was 158 lb.

Sit-Ups

The greatest recorded number of consecutive sit-ups on a hard surface without feet pinned or knees bent is 26,000 in 11 hours 44 min by Angel Bustamonte (b Feb 28, 1959) in Sacramento, Calif, on Dec 17, 1977. Vivekananda Selva Kumar Anandan (Sri Lanka) (aged 36) recorded 165 sit-ups in 2 minutes under the same conditions at the Central YMCA Colombo Gymnasium, Sri Lanka, on May 15, 1980.

Rope Climbing

The US Amateur Athletic Union records are tantamount to world records: 20 ft (hands alone) 2.8 sec, by Don Perry, at Champaign, Ill, on Apr 3, 1954; 25 ft (hands alone), 4.7 sec, by Garvin S. Smith at Los Angeles, on Apr 19, 1947.

Parallel Bar Dips

Thomas Gildert performed a record 533 consecutive parallel bar dips on July 1, 1980, at the Colorall Leisure Center, Nelson, England. Jack LaLanne (b 1914) is reported to have done 1,000 in Oakland, Calif, in 1945.

Push-Ups

Tommy Gildert (b 1944) did 9,105 consecutive push-ups in 4 hours 17 min 9 sec at the Burnley Boys Club, Lancashire, England, on July 1, 1979.

Noel Bany Mason did 1,845 push-ups, the most in 30 min, at Burton Sporting Club, Burton on Trent, England, Nov 16, 1979. He also did 267 fingertip push-ups on June 10, 1979. Harry Lee Welch, Jr, 32, performed 392 one-armed push-ups at WTIK Broadcasting Station, Durham, NC, on Apr 17, 1980. Carl A. White did 90 consecutive handstand push-ups in Baltimore, Md, on Dec 7, 1979.

Jumping Jacks

The greatest number of side-straddle hops is 27,000 performed in 6 hours 45 min by Ashrita Furman (b Oct 16, 1954) at Jack LaLanne Health Spa, NY, on Aug 14, 1979.

MOST JUMPING JACKS (left): Ashrita Furman performed 27,000 jumping jacks in 6 hours 45 min. PERFECT SCORE (right): Nadia Comaneci was awarded the first perfect score in the Olympics, in 1976. She was among several gymnasts to receive perfect scores in 1980.

Vertical Jump

The greatest height reached in a vertical jump (the difference between standing and jumping fingertip reach) is 42 in by David Thompson (6 ft 4 in) of North Carolina in 1972. Higher jumps reported by athletes Franklin Jacobs (US) and Greg Joy (Canada) were probably made with an initial run. Olympic Pentathlon champion Mary E. Peters (GB) reportedly jumped 30 in in Calif in 1972.

For a TV show, Shannon Faucher, a 23-year-old college student from Los Angeles, jumped from a flat standing position to a standing position on top of a refrigerator 55 in high to set a jumping stunt record.

Somersaults

James Chelich (b Fairview, Alberta, Canada, March 12, 1957) performed 8,450 forward rolls in 8.3 miles on Sept 21, 1974.

Junior Corporal Phillip N. Richards, of the Pegasus Gymnastic Team, made a successful dive and tucked somersault over 34 men at HMS Vernon, Portsmouth, England, on Sept 22, 1979.

Shigeru Iwasaki (b 1960) backwards somersaulted over 50 m (54.68 yd) in 10.8 sec in Tokyo, March 30, 1980.

Rope Jumping

The longest recorded non-stop rope-jumping marathon was one of 9 hours 46 min by Katsumi Suzuki, in Kumagaya Gymnasium, Saitama, Japan, on March 23, 1980.

Other rope-jumping records made without a break:

Most quintuple turns	5	Katsumi Suzuki	Saitama, Japan May 29, 1975
Most turns in 1 minute	330	Brian D. Christensen	Ridgewood Shopping Center, Tenn Sept 1, 1979
Most turns in 10 seconds	108	A. Rayner	Wakefield, Eng June 28, 1978
Most doubles (with cross)	422	Kevin A. Brooks	Queensland, Australia Dec 15, 1979
Double turns	10,133	Katsumi Suzuki (Japan)	Saitama Sept 29, 1979
Treble turns	381	Katsumi Suzuki (Japan)	Saitama May 29, 1975
Quadruple turns	51	Katsumi Suzuki (Japan)	Saitama May 29, 1975
Duration 1,264 miles		Tom Morris (Aust)	Brisbane-Cairns 1963
Most children single rope (15 turns)	65	Hakoda Nakayoshi team	Tokyo Oct 3, 1979
On a tightrope (consecutive)	55	Bryan Andrew (né Dewhurst)	BBC TV May 5, 1980 Centre, London

HANDBALL (COURT)

Origin

Handball is a game of ancient Celtic origin. In the early 19th century only a front wall was used, but later side and back walls were added. The court is now standardized 60 ft by 30 ft in Ireland, Ghana and Australia, and 40 ft by 20 ft in Canada, Mexico and the US. The game is played with both a hard and soft ball in Ireland, and a soft ball only elsewhere.

HANDBALL MASTER (left): Jim Jacobs has won 6 USHA singles and doubles titles. MOST SUCCESSFUL DRIVER (right): Herve Filion has won over 7,000 races and captured over $29 million in purse money.

The earliest international contest was in NYC in 1887, between the champions of the US and Ireland.

Most Titles

The most successful player in the USHA National Four-Wall Championships has been James Jacobs (US), who won a record 6 singles titles (1955–56, 57, 60, 64–65) and shared in 6 doubles titles (1960, 62–63, 65, 67–68). Martin Decatur has shared in 8 doubles' titles (1962–63, 65, 67–68, 75, 78–79), 5 of these with Jacobs as his partner.

HARNESS RACING

Origins

Trotting races were held in Valkenburg, Netherlands, in 1554. In England the trotting gait (the simultaneous use of the diagonally opposite legs) was known in the 16th century. The sulky first appeared in harness racing in 1829. Pacers thrust out their fore and hind legs simultaneously on one side.

Greatest Winnings

The greatest amount won by a trotting horse is $1,960,945 by "Bellino II" (France) to retirement in 1977. The record for a pacing horse is $1,604,307 by "Rambling Willie" (US) to the end of the 1979 season.

The greatest award won by a harness horse in a single season is $826,542 by "Hot Hitter" during 1979.

Most Successful Driver

The most successful sulky driver in North America has been Herve Filion (Canada) (b Quebec, Feb 1, 1940) who reached a record of 7,079 wins and $29.1 million in purse money by the end of the 1979 season, after a record 637 victories and winnings of $3,474,315 in the 1974 season. Filion won the North American championship for the tenth time in 1978.

RECORDS AGAINST TIME
TROTTING

World (mile track)	1:54.8	"Nevele Pride" (driver Stanley Dancer) (US), Indianapolis	Aug 31, 1969

PACING

World (mile track)	1:52.0	"Steady Star" (driver Joe O'Brien) (Canada), Lexington, Ky	Oct 1, 1971

RECORDS SET IN RACES

Trotting	1:55.0	"Speedy Somolli" (driver Howard Beissinger) (US) at Du Quoin, Ill	Sept 2, 1978
	1:55.0	"Florida Pro" (driver George Sholty) (US) at Du Quoin, Ill	Sept 2, 1978
Pacing	1:53.0	"Abercrombie" (driver Glen Garnsey) (US) at E Rutherford, NJ	Aug 4, 1979
	1:53.0	"Niatross" (driver Clint Galbraith) (US) at E Rutherford, NJ	July 30, 1980

HOCKEY

Origins

There is pictorial evidence of a hocky-like game being played on ice in the Netherlands in the early 16th century. The game probably was first played in 1855 at Kingston, Ontario, Canada, but Halifax also lays claim to priority.

The International Ice Hockey Federation was founded in 1908. The National Hockey League was inaugurated in 1917. The World Hockey Association was formed in 1971 and disbanded in 1979 when 4 of its teams joined the NHL.

Olympic Games

Canada has won the Olympic title six times (1920, 24, 28, 32, 48, 52) and the world title 19 times, the last being at Geneva in 1961. The longest

LONGEST CAREER: Gordie Howe played in the NHL for 26 seasons and collected career records for most games, goals, assists and points. He was selected as an all-star 22 times.

Olympic career is that of Richard Torriani (Switzerland) from 1928 to 1948. The most gold medals won by any player is 3; this was achieved by 4 USSR players in the 1964, 68 and 72 Games—Vitaliy Davidov, Aleksandr Ragulin, Anatoliy Firssov and Viktor Kuzkin.

Stanley Cup

This cup, presented by the Governor-General Lord Stanley (original cost $48.67), became emblematic of world professional team supremacy 33 years after the first contest at Montreal in 1893. It has been won most often by the Montreal Canadiens, with 22 wins in 1916, 24, 30–31, 44, 46, 53, 56–60, 65–66, 68–69, 71, 73, 76–79. Henri Richard played in his eleventh finals in 1973.

Longest Match

The longest match was 2 hours 56 min 30 sec (playing time) when the Detroit Red Wings eventually beat the Montreal Maroons 1-0 in the 17th minute of the sixth period of overtime at the Forum, Montreal, at 2:25 a.m. on March 25, 1936, 5 hours 51 min after the opening faceoff.

Longest Career

Gordie Howe (b March 31, 1928, Floral, Saskatchewan, Canada) skated a record 25 years for the Detroit Red Wings from 1946–47 through the 1970–71 season, playing in a record total of 1,687 NHL games. During that time he also set records for most career goals, assists, and scoring points; was selected as an all-star a record 21 times; and collected 500 stitches in his face. (see also *Individual Scoring*)

After leaving the Red Wings, he ended a 2-year retirement to skate with his two sons as teammates and played for 6 more seasons with the Houston Aeros and the New England Whalers of the World Hockey Association, participating in 419 games.

With the incorporation of the (now Hartford) Whalers into the NHL for the 1979–80 season, Gordie Howe skated in all 80 regular season games in his 26th year in that league, and the remarkable 52-year-old grandfather was again selected as an NHL all-star. Including playoffs, he skated in 2,421 "major league" games. Howe is the first team athlete in modern North American professional sports to have a career that spanned parts of five decades.

Most Consecutive Games

Garry Unger, playing for Toronto, Detroit, St Louis, and Atlanta, skated in 914 consecutive NHL games without a miss during 13 seasons from Feb 24, 1968, through Dec 21, 1979, when a torn shoulder muscle kept him on the bench.

The most consecutive complete games by a goaltender is 502, set by Glenn Hall (Detroit, Chicago), beginning in 1955 and ending when he suffered a back injury in a game against Boston on Nov 7, 1962.

Longest Season

The only man ever to play 82 games in a 78-game season is Ross Lonsberry. He began the 1971–72 season with the Los Angeles Kings where he played 50 games. Then, in January, he was traded to the Philadelphia Flyers (who had played only 46 games at the time) where he finished out the season (32 more games).

Dennis Owchar (with Pittsburgh and Colorado) and Jerry Butler (with St Louis and Toronto) played 82 games in an 80-game season in 1977–78.

Longest Winning Streak

In the 1929–30 season, the Boston Bruins won 14 straight games. The longest a team has ever gone without a defeat is 35 games, set by the Philadelphia Flyers with 25 wins and 10 ties from Oct 14, 1979, to Jan 6, 1980. The Flyers outscored their opponents 153 goals to 98 during the record unbeaten streak which was ended by the Minnesota North Stars on Jan 7, 1980.

Team Scoring

The greatest number of goals recorded in a World Championship match has been 47-0 when Canada beat Denmark on Feb 12, 1949.

The Boston Bruins set all-time records for goal production in the 1970–71 season with a total of 399. Added to a record 697 assists they tallied a record total of 1,096 points. One line alone (Esposito, Hodge, Cashman) accounted for 336 points—a record itself.

Guy Lafleur, Steve Shutt, and Jacques Lemaire of the Montreal Canadiens produced a total of 150 goals in the 1976–77 season—a record for a single line.

The NHL record for both teams is 21 goals, scored when the Montreal Canadiens beat the Toronto St Patricks at Montreal 14-7 on Jan 10, 1920. The most goals ever scored by one team in a single game was set by the Canadiens, when they defeated the Quebec Bulldogs on March 3, 1920 by a score of 16-3.

The Detroit Red Wings scored 15 consecutive goals without an answering tally when they defeated the NY Rangers 15-0 on Jan 23, 1944.

Fastest Scoring

Toronto scored 8 goals against the NY Americans in 4 min 52 sec on March 19, 1938.

The fastest goals that have ever been scored from the opening whistle both came at 6 sec of the first period: by Henry Boucha of the Detroit Red Wings on Jan 28, 1973, against Montreal; and by Jean Pronovost of the Pittsburgh Penguins on March 25, 1976, against St Louis. Claude Provost of the Canadiens scored a goal against Boston after 4 sec of the opening of the second period on Nov 9, 1957.

Kim D. Miles scored a goal after only 3 sec of play for the University of Guelph, playing the University of Western Ontario on Feb 11, 1975.

The fastest scoring record is held by Bill Mosienko (Chicago) who scored 3 goals in 21 sec against the NY Rangers on March 23, 1952.

Gus Bodnar (Toronto Maple Leafs) scored a goal against the NY Rangers at 15 sec of the first period of *his first NHL game* on Oct 30, 1943. Later in his career, while with Chicago, Bodnar again entered the record book when he assisted on all 3 of Bill Mosienko's quick goals.

Individual Scoring

The career record in the NHL for regular season goals is 801 by Gordie Howe of the Detroit Red Wings and Hartford Whalers. Howe has scored 1,850 points in his NHL career, with 1,049 assists. With 68 goals, 92 assists, and 160 points in Stanley Cup competition; and 202 goals, 377 assists, and 579 points in WHA season and playoff games, Howe's unequaled professional career scoring totals are 1,071 goals, 1,518 assists, and 2,589 points.

Guy Lafleur (b Sept 20, 1951), of the Montreal Canadiens, has scored both 50 or more goals and 100 or more points for 6 consecutive seasons from 1974–75 through 1979–80.

Reggie Leach (Philadelphia Flyers) scored a total of 80 goals in the 1975–76 season including the playoffs.

Phil Esposito (Boston Bruins) scored 76 goals on a record 550 shots in the 1970–71 regular season. Esposito also holds the record for most

POINT MEN: Bobby Orr (left) had 102 assists in 1970–71, and 6 consecutive 100-point seasons. He had more career goals and points than any other NHL defenseman. Phil Esposito recorded 76 goals and 152 points in 1970–71, and his 32 career hat-tricks are tops in the NHL.

GREAT GOALTENDERS: Gerry Cheevers (left) had a 32-game unbeaten streak in 1971–72. He draws stitchmarks on his mask whenever it protects him from injury. Terry Sawchuk (right) had 103 shutouts in 971 games.

points in a season at 152 (76 goals, 76 assists), set in the same season. Phil Esposito has also scored 100 or more points in 6 different seasons, and 50 or more goals in 5 consecutive years.

Bobby Orr (b Parry Sound, Ontario, Canada, March 20, 1948) had 6 consecutive 100-or-more-point seasons from 1969–70 to 1974–75. Orr assisted on 102 goals in the 1970–71 season for a record. His average of 1.31 assists per game is also a league record.

Anders Hedberg (b Sweden, Feb 25, 1951) set a WHA mark, scoring 83 goals for the Winnipeg Jets in 1976–77.

Marc Tardif (b June 12, 1949) set a WHA record for most points in a season with 169 (71 goals and 98 assists) for the Quebec Nordiques in 1977–78.

The most goals ever scored in one game is 7 by Joe Malone of the Quebec Bulldogs against the Toronto St Patricks on Jan 31, 1920. Four different men have scored 4 goals in one period—Harvey Jackson (Toronto), Max Bentley (Chicago), Clint Smith (Chicago), and Red Berenson (St Louis).

The most points scored in one NHL game is 10, a record set by Darryl Sittler of the Toronto Maple Leafs, on Feb 7, 1976, against the Boston Bruins. He had 6 goals and 4 assists.

Jim Harrison, playing for Alberta, set a WHA record for points with 10 (3 goals, 7 assists) against Toronto on Jan 30, 1973.

In 1921–22, Harry (Punch) Broadbent of the Ottawa Senators scored 25 goals in 16 consecutive games to set an all-time "consecutive game goal-scoring streak" record.

The most assists recorded in an NHL game is 7 by Billy Taylor of Detroit on March 16, 1947 against Chicago (Detroit won 10-6); and by Wayne Gretzky for Edmonton vs Washington, Feb 15, 1980.

Most 3-Goal Games

In his 17-year NHL career, Phil Esposito of Chicago, Boston and the NY Rangers has scored 3 or more goals in 32 games. Five of these were 4-goal efforts. The term "hat-trick" properly applies when 3 goals are scored consecutively by one player in a game without interruption by either an answering score by the other team or a goal by any other player on his own team. In general usage, a "hat-trick" is any 3-goal effort by a player in one game.

Goaltending

The longest any goalie has gone without a defeat is 33 games, a record set by Gerry Cheevers of Boston in 1971–72. The longest a goalie has ever kept successive opponents scoreless is 461 min 29 sec by Alex Connell of the Ottawa Senators in 1927–28. He registered 6 consecutive shutouts in this time.

The most shutouts ever recorded in one season is 22 by George Hainsworth of Montreal in 1928–29 (this is also a team record). This feat is even more remarkable considering that the season was only 44 games long at that time, compared to the 80-game season currently used.

Terry Sawchuk registered a record 103 career shutouts in his 20 seasons in the NHL. He played for Detroit, Boston, Toronto, Los Angeles, and the NY Rangers during that time. He also appeared in a record 971 games.

The only goaltender to score a goal in an NHL games is Bill Smith (NY Islanders), against the Colorado Rockies in Denver, Nov 28, 1979. After the Rockies had removed their goaltender in favor of an extra skater during a delayed penalty, a Colorado defenseman's errant centering pass skidded nearly 200 ft down the ice into his own untended goal. Goalie Smith was the last Islander to touch the puck and was credited with the goal even though he did not take the actual "shot."

Fastest Player

The highest speed measured for any player is 29.7 mph for Bobby Hull (then of the Chicago Black Hawks) (b Jan 3, 1939). The highest puck speed is also attributed to Hull, whose left-handed slap shot has been measured at 118.3 mph. Also known as the "Golden Jet," Hull is the only player beside Gordie Howe to score over 1,000 goals in NHL and WHA play.

HORSE RACING

Origins

Horsemanship was an important part of the Hittite culture of Anatolia, Turkey, dating from about 1400 BC. The 33rd ancient Olympic Games of 648 BC featured horse racing. The earliest horse race recorded in England was one held c. 210 AD at Netherby, Yorkshire, among Arabians brought to Britain by Lucius Septimius Severus (146–211 AD), Emperor of Rome.

Organized horse racing began in New York State at least as early as March 1668.

The original Charleston Jockey Club, Virginia, was the first in the world, organized in 1734. Racing colors (silks) became compulsory in 1889.

Longest Race

The longest recorded horse race was one of 1,200 miles in Portugal, won by "Emir," a horse bred from Egyptian-bred Blunt Arab stock. The holder of the world's record for long distance racing and speed is "Champion Crabbet," who covered 300 miles in 52 hours 33 min, carrying 245 lb, in 1920.

Victories

The horse with the best recorded win-loss record was "Kincsem," a Hungarian mare foaled in 1874, who was unbeaten in 54 races (1876–79), including the English Goodwood Cup of 1878.

"Camarero," owned by Don José Coll Vidal of Puerto Rico, foaled in 1951, had a winning streak of 56 races, 1953–55, and 73 wins in 77 starts altogether.

Greatest Winnings

The greatest amount ever won by a horse is $2,394,267 by "Spectacular Bid" from 1978 to June 1980.

The most won by a mare is $1,535,443 by "Dahlia," from 1972 to 1976.
The most won in a year is $1,279,334 by "Spectacular Bid" in 1979.

Triple Crown

Eleven horses have won all three races in one season which constitute the American Triple Crown (Kentucky Derby, Preakness Stakes and the

HORSES AND JOCKEYS: Triple Crown winner "Affirmed" (#6) beat "Spectacular Bid" (#3) in the Jockey Club Gold Cup in Oct 1979. Despite the loss, "Bid" broke "Affirmed's" records for yearly and career winnings. The winning jockey was Lafitt Pincay, who won more than $8 million in 1979. Willie Shoemaker (7,766 wins and $74.5 million in purses) rode "Bid."

Belmont Stakes). This feat was first achieved by "Sir Barton" in 1919, and most recently by "Seattle Slew" in 1977 and "Affirmed" in 1978.

The only Triple Crown winner to sire another winner was "Gallant Fox," the 1930 winner, who sired "Omaha," who won in 1935.

Tallest

The tallest horse ever to race is "Fort d'Or," owned by Lady Elizabeth (Eliza) Nugent (*née* Guinness) of Berkshire, England, which stands 18.2 hands. He was foaled in Apr 1963.

Most Valuable Horse

The most expensive horse ever is the 1979 Kentucky Derby winner "Spectacular Bid" (foaled 1976) owned by Harry Meyerhoff. It was announced in March 1980 that he had been syndicated for $22 million, in 40 shares of $550,000 each.

The highest price for a yearling is $1.9 million for a colt by "Lyphard"–"Stylish Genie," bought on July 22, 1980, at Keeneland, Ky, by Stavros Niarchos.

Horses   Speed Records

Distance	Time mph	Name	Course	Date
¼ mile	20.8s. 43.26	Big Racket (Mex.)	Mexico City, Mex	Feb 5, 1945
½ mile	44.4s. 40.54	Sonido (Ven)	‡Caracas, Ven	June 28, 1970
⅝ mile	53.6s. 41.98†	Indigenous (GB)	‡*Epsom, England	June 2, 1960
	53.89s. 41.75††	Raffingora (GB)	‡*Epsom, England	June 5, 1970
	55.4s. 40.61	Zip Pocket (US)	Phoenix, Ariz	Apr 22, 1967
¾ mile	1m. 06.2s. 40.78	Broken Tendril (GB)	*Brighton, England	Aug 6, 1929
	1m. 07.2s. 40.18	Grey Papa (US)	Longacres, Wash	Sept 4, 1972
Mile	1m. 31.8s. 39.21	Soueida (GB)	*Brighton, England	Sept 19, 1963
	1m. 31.8s. 39.21	Loose Cover (GB)	*Brighton, England	June 9, 1966
	1m. 32.2s. 39.04	Dr. Fager (US)	Arlington, Ill	Aug 24, 1968
1¼ miles	1m. 57.4s. 38.33	Double Discount	Arcadia, Calif	Oct 9, 1977
1½ miles	2m. 23.0s. 37.76	Fiddle Isle (US)	Arcadia, Calif	Mar 21, 1970
		John Henry (US)	Arcadia, Calif	March 16, 1980
2 miles**	3m. 15.0s. 36.93	Polazel (GB)	Salisbury, England	July 8, 1924
2½ miles	4m. 14.6s. 35.35	Miss Grillo (US)	Pimlico, Md	Nov 12, 1948
3 miles	5m. 15.0s. 34.29	Farragut (Mex)	Aguascalientes, Mex	Mar 9, 1941

* Course downhill for ¼ of a mile.
** A more reliable modern record is 3min 16.75 sec by *Il Tempo* (NZ) at Trentham, Wellington, New Zealand, on Jan 17, 1970.
† Hand-timed.   †† Electrically-timed.   ‡ Straight courses.

Dead Heats

There is no recorded case in turf history of a quintuple dead heat. The nearest approach was in the Astley Stakes, at Lewes, England, on Aug 6, 1880, when "Mazurka," "Wandering Nun" and "Scobell" triple dead-heated for first place, just ahead of "Cumberland" and "Thora," who dead-heated for fourth place. Each of the five jockeys thought he had won. The only three known examples of a quadruple dead heat were between "Honest Harry," "Miss Decoy," a filly by "Beningbrough" (later named "Young Daffodil") and "Peteria" at Bogside, England, on June 7, 1808; between "Defaulter," "The Squire of Malton," "Reindeer" and "Pulcherrima" in the Omnibus Stakes at The Hoo, England, on Apr 26, 1851; and between "Overreach," "Lady Go-Lightly," "Gamester" and

"The Unexpected" at the Houghton Meeting at Newmarket, England, on Oct 22, 1855.

Since the introduction of the photo-finish, the highest number of horses in a dead heat has been three, on several occasions.

Jockeys

The most successful jockey of all time is Willie Shoemaker (b weighing 2½ lb on Aug 19, 1931) now weighing 98 lb and standing 4 ft 11½ in, who beat Johnny Longden's lifetime record of 6,032 winners on Sept 7, 1970. From March 1949, to the end of 1979 he rode 7,766 winners from some 33,168 mounts. His winnings have aggregated some $74,504,570.

Chris McCarron (US), 19, won a total of 546 races in 1974.

The greatest amount ever won by any jockey in a year is $8,183,535 by Laffit Pincay (b Panama, Dec 29, 1946) in 1979.

The oldest jockey was Levi Barlingame (US), who rode his last race at Stafford, Kan, in 1932, aged 80. The youngest jockey was Frank Wootton (1893–1940) (English Champion jockey 1909–12), who rode his first winner in South Africa aged 9 years 10 months. The lightest recorded jockey was Kitchener (d 1872), who won the Chester Cup in England on "Red Deer" in 1844 at 49 lb. He was said to have weighed only 40 lb in 1840.

Victor Morley Lawson won his first race at Warwick, England, on "Ocean King," Oct 16, 1973, aged 67.

The most winners ridden on one card is 8 by Hubert S. Jones, 17, out of 13 mounts at Caliente, Calif, on June 11, 1944 (of which 5 were photo-finishes), and by Oscar Barattuci at Rosario City, Argentina, on Dec 15, 1957.

The longest winning streak is 12 races by Sir Gordon Richards (GB) who won the last race at Nottingham, Eng, on Oct 3, 1933, 6 out of 6 at Chepstow on Oct 4, and the first 5 races the next day at Chepstow.

Trainers

The greatest number of wins by a trainer in one year is 494 by Jack Van Berg in 1976. The greatest amount won in a year is $3,563,147 by Lazaro S. Barrera in 1979.

Owners

The most winners by an owner in one year is 494 by Dan R. Lasater (US) in 1974, when he also won a record $3,022,960 in prize money.

ICE SKATING

Origins

The earliest reference to ice skating is in Scandinavian literature of the 2nd century, although its origins are believed, on archeological evidence, to be 10 centuries earlier still. The earliest known illustration is a Dutch woodcut of 1498. The earliest skating club was the Edinburgh Skating Club, Scotland, formed in 1742. The first recorded race was from Wisbech to Whittlesea, East Anglia, in 1763. The earliest artificial ice rink in the world was opened at the Baker Street Bazaar, Portman Square, London, on Dec 7, 1842. The International Skating Union was founded in 1892.

Longest Race

The longest race regularly held is the "Elfstedentocht" ("Tour of the Eleven Towns") in the Netherlands. It covers 200 km (124 miles 483 yd) and the fastest time is 7 hours 35 min by Jeen van den Berg (b Jan 8, 1928) on Feb 3, 1954.

Largest Rink

The world's largest indoor artificial ice rink is in the Moscow Olympic indoor arena which has an ice area of 86,800 sq ft. The largest artificial outdoor rink is the quintuple complex of the Fujikyu Highland Promenade Rink, Japan (opened 1967), with an area of 285,244 sq ft.

Longest Marathon

The longest recorded skating marathon is one of 109 hours 5 min by Austin McKinley of Christchurch, New Zealand, June 21–25, 1977.

FIGURE SKATING

World Titles

The greatest number of individual world men's figure skating titles (instituted 1896) is 10 by Ulrich Salchow (1877–1949), of Sweden, in 1901–05 and 1907–11. The women's record (instituted 1906) is also 10 individual titles, by Sonja Henie (Apr 8, 1912–Oct 12, 1969), of Norway, between 1927 and 1936. Irina Rodnina (b Sept 12, 1949), of the USSR, has won 10 pairs titles (instituted 1908)—four with Aleksiy Ulanov (1969–72) and six with her husband Aleksandr Zaitsev (1973–77). The most ice dance titles (instituted 1950) won is 6 by Aleksandr Gorshkov (b Dec 8, 1946) and Ludmilla Pakhomova (b Dec 31, 1946), both of the USSR, in 1970–74 and 1976.

Olympic Titles

The most Olympic gold medals won by a figure skater is 3 by Gillis Grafstrom (1893–1938), of Sweden, in 1920, 1924, and 1928 (also silver medal in 1932); by Sonja Henie (see above) in 1928, 1932 and 1936; and by Irina Rodnina (see above) in the Pairs event in 1972, 1976 and 1980.

MOST TITLES: Irina Rodina has won 10 world titles and 3 Olympic gold medals in pairs competition.

MOST GOLD MEDALS: Lidia Skoblikova (above) won 6 Olympic speed skating gold medals. Eric Heiden (right) swept all 5 speed skating events in the 1980 Olympics.

Most Difficult Jump

The first ever triple Axel performed in competition was by Vern Taylor (b 1958) (Canada) in the World Championships at Ottawa on March 10, 1978.

A quadruple twist lift has been performed by only one pair, Sergei Shakrai (b June 28, 1958) and Marina Tcherkasova (b Nov 17, 1964) of the USSR, in an international championship at Helsinki, Finland, on Jan 26, 1977. They were also the first skaters to accomplish simultaneous triple jumps at that level, at Strasbourg, France, on Feb 1, 1978.

Highest Marks

The highest number of maximum 6 marks awarded for one performance in an international championship was 11 to Aleksandr Zaitsev and Irina Rodnina (USSR) in the European pairs competition in Zagreb, Yugoslavia, in 1974.

Donald Jackson (Canada) was awarded 7 "sixes" (the most by a soloist) in the world men's championship at Prague, Czechoslovakia, in 1962.

SPEED SKATING

World Titles

The greatest number of world overall titles (instituted 1893) won by any skater is 5 by Oscar Mathisen (Norway) in 1908–09 and 1912–14, and Clas Thunberg (b Apr 5, 1893) of Finland, in 1923, 1925, 1928–29 and 1931. The most titles won by a woman is 4 by Mrs Inga Voronina, *née* Artomonova (1936–66) of Moscow, USSR, in 1957, 1958, 1962 and 1965, and Mrs Atje Keulen-Deelstra of the Netherlands (b Dec 31, 1938) in 1970 and 1972–74.

The record score achieved in the world overall title is 162.793 points by Eric Heiden (US) at Oslo, Norway, Feb 10–11, 1979.

Olympic Titles

The most Olympic gold medals won in speed skating is 6 by Lidia Skoblikova (b March 8, 1939), of Chelyabinsk, USSR, in 1960 (2) and 1964 (4). The male record is held by Clas Thunberg (see above) with 5 gold (including 1 tied gold) and also 1 silver and 1 tied bronze in 1924–28; and by Eric Heiden (US) (b June 14, 1958) who won 5 gold medals, all at Lake Placid, NY, in 1980.

World Speed Skating Records
(Ratified by the I.S.U.)

Distance	min sec	Name and Nationality	Place	Date
MEN				
500 m	37.00*	Evgeni Kulikov (USSR)	Medeo, USSR	Mar 29, 1975
1,000 m	1:13.60	Eric Heiden (US)	Davos, Switz	Jan 13, 1980
1,500 m	1:54.79	Eric Heiden (US)	Davos, Switz	Jan 20, 1980
3,000 m	4:04.06	Dmitri Ogloblin (USSR)	Medeo, USSR	Mar 29, 1979
5,000 m	6:56.90	Kay Stenshjemmel (Norway)	Medeo, USSR	Mar 19, 1977
10,000 m	14:26.71	Dmitir Ogloblin (USSR)	Medeo, USSR	Mar 30, 1980
WOMEN				
500 m	40.68	Sheila Young (US)	Inzell, W Ger	Mar 13, 1976
1,000 m	1:23.01	Natalia Petruseva (USSR)	Medeo, USSR	Mar 27, 1980
1,500 m	2:07.18	Khalida Vorobyeva (USSR)	Medeo, USSR	Apr 10, 1978
3,000 m	4:31.00	Galina Stepanskaya (USSR)	Medeo, USSR	Mar 23, 1976

* This represents an average speed of 30.22 mph.

JUDO

Origin

Judo is a modern combat sport which developed out of an amalgam of several old (pre-Christian era) Japanese fighting arts, the most popular of which was *ju-jitsu* (*Jiu-jitsu*), which is thought to be of pre-Christian Chinese origin. Judo has developed greatly since 1882, when it was first devised in Dr Jigoro Kano (1860–1938). World Championships were inaugurated in Tokyo on May 5, 1956.

Highest Grades

The efficiency grades in Judo are divided into pupil (*kyu*) and master (*dan*) grades. The highest awarded is the extremely rare red belt *Judan* (10th *dan*), given only to 7 men. The highest awarded to a woman is 6th *dan*, achieved by 3 Japanese women. The Judo protocol provides for a *Juichidan* (11th *dan*), who also would wear a red belt, and even a *Junidan* (12th *dan*), who would wear a white belt twice as wide as an ordinary belt, and even a *Shihan* (the highest of all), but these have never been bestowed.

Marathon

The longest recorded Judo marathon with continuous play by two of six Judoka in 5-min stints is 200 hours by the Dufftown and District Judo Club, Banffshire, Scotland, July 9–17, 1977.

Champions

Two men have won 4 world titles. Wilhelm Ruska of the Netherlands won the 1967 and the 1971 heavyweight and the 1972 Olympic heavyweight and Open titles, and Shozo Fujii (Japan) (b May 12, 1950) won the middleweight title in 1971, 1973, 1975 and 1979.

KARATE

Origins

Originally *karate* (empty hand) is known to have been developed by the unarmed populace as a method of attack on, and defense against, armed Japanese aggressors in Okinawa, Ryukyu Islands, based on techniques devised from the 6th century Chinese art of Shaolin boxing (Kempo). Transmitted to Japan in the 1920's by Funakoshi Gichin, this method of combat was refined and organized into a sport with competitive rules.

The five major schools of *karate* in Japan are *Shotokan, Wado-ryu, Goju-ryu, Shito-ryu,* and *Kyokushinkai,* each of which places different emphasis on speed, power, etc. Other styles include *Sankukai, Shotokai* and *Shukokai.* The military form of *Tae-kwan-do* with 9 *dans* is a Korean equivalent of *karate. Kung fu* is believed to have originated in Nepal or Tibet but was adopted within Chinese temples *via* India, and has in recent years been widely popularized through various martial arts films.

Wu shu is a comprehensive term embracing all Chinese martial arts.

Most Titles

The only winner of 3 All-Japanese titles has been Takeshi Oishi, who won in 1969–71.

The leading exponents among karatekas are a number of 10th *dans* in Japan.

MOTORCYCLING

Earliest Races

The first motorcycle race was held on an oval track at Sheen House, Richmond, Surrey, England, on Nov 29, 1897, won by Charles Jarrott (1877–1944) on a Fournier. The oldest motorcycle races in the world are the Auto-Cycle Union Tourist Trophy (TT) series, first held on the 15.81-mile "Peel" ("St John's") course on the Isle of Man on May 28, 1907, and still run on the island, on the "Mountain" circuit (37.73 miles).

Longest Circuits

The 37.73-mile "Mountain" circuit, over which the two main TT races have been run since 1911, has 264 curves and corners and is the longest used for any motorcycle race.

Fastest Circuit

The highest average lap speed attained on any closed circuit is 160.288 mph by Yvon du Hamel (Canada) (b 1941) on a modified 903-cc four-

MOST WINS: Giacomo Agostini (above) won 15 world titles, including 19 in 1970. Mike Hailwood (right) shares the yearly winnings title with 19 in 1966.

cylinder Kawasaki Z1 on the 31-degree banked 2.5-mile Daytona International Speedway, Fla, in March 1973. His lap time was 56.149 sec.

The fastest road circuit is the Francorchamps circuit near Spa, Belgium. It is 14.12 km (8 miles 1,340 yd) in length and was lapped in 3 min 50.3 sec (average speed of 137.150 mph) by Barry S. F. Sheene (b Holborn, London, England, Sept 11, 1950) on a 495-cc four-cylinder Suzuki during the Belgian Grand Prix on July 3, 1977.

Fastest Race

The fastest track race in the world was held at Grenzlandring, W Germany, in 1939. It was won by Georg Meier (b Germany Nov 9, 1910) at an average speed of 134 mph on a supercharged 495-cc flat-twin BMW.

The fastest road race is the 500-cc Belgian Grand Prix on the Francorchamps circuit (see above). The record time for this 10-lap 87.74-mile race is 38 min 58.5 sec (average speed of 135.068 mph) by Barry Sheene (UK) on a 495-cc four-cylinder Suzuki on July 3, 1977.

Longest Race

The longest race is the Liège 24 Hours. The greatest distance ever covered is 2,761.9 miles (average speed 115.08 mph) by Jean-Claude Chemarin and Christian Leon of France on a 941-cc four-cylinder Honda on the Francorchamps circuit (8 miles 1,340 yd) near Spa, Belgium, Aug 14–15, 1976.

World Championships

Most world championship titles (instituted by the *Fédération Internationale Motorcycliste* in 1949) won are 15 by Giacomo Agostini (Italy) in the 350-cc class 1968–74 and in the 500-cc class 1966–72 and 1975. Agostini (b Lovere, Italy, June 16, 1942) is the only man to win two world championships in five consecutive years. Agostini won 122 races in the world championship series between Apr 24, 1965, and Aug 29, 1976, including a record 19 in 1970, also achieved by Stanley Michael Bailey "Mike" Hailwood, (b Oxford, England, Apr 2, 1940) in 1966.

Klaus Enders (Germany) (b 1937) won 6 world side-car titles, 1967, 69–70, 72–74.

Joël Robert (b Chatelet, Belgium, Nov 11, 1943) has won six 250-cc moto-cross (also known as "scrambles") world championships (1964, 68–72). Between Apr 25, 1964, and June 18, 1972, he won a record fifty 250-cc Grands Prix. He became the youngest moto-cross world champion on July 12, 1964, when he won the 250-cc championship aged 20 years 8 months.

Alberto "Johnny" Cecotto (b Caracas, Venezuela, Jan 1956) was the youngest person to win a world championship. He was aged 19 years 211 days when he won the 350-cc title on Aug 24, 1975. The oldest was Hermann-Peter Müller (1909–76) of W Germany, who won the 250-cc title in 1955, aged 46.

Most Successful Machines

Italian MV-Agusta motorcycles won 37 world championships between 1952 and 1973 and 276 world championship races between 1952 and 1976. Japanese Honda machines won 29 world championship races and 5 world championships in 1966. In the 7 years Honda contested the championship (1961–67) its annual average was 20 race wins.

Speed Records

Official world speed records must be set with two runs over a measured distance within a time limit (one hour for FIM records, two hours for AMA records).

Donald Vesco (b Loma Linda, Calif, Apr 8, 1939) recorded an average speed of 303.810 mph over the measured mile at Bonneville Salt Flats, Utah, on Sept 28, 1975, to establish an AMA record. Riding a 21-ft-long *Silver Bird* Streamliner powered by two 750-cc Yamaha TZ750 4-cylinder engines developing 180 bhp, he covered the first mile in 11.817 sec (304.646 mph). On the second run his time was 11.882 sec (302.979 mph). The average time for the two runs was 11.8495 sec (303.810 mph) for the

HIGHEST SPEEDS: Henk Vink (left) holds the records for average speed over 2 runs for both 1 km and 440 yd. Russ Collins (right) had the fastest time for a single run at 440 yd.

AMA record. On the same day, he set an FIM record at an average speed of 302.928 mph. Also on the same day, he covered a flying quarter mile in 2.925 sec (307.692 mph), the highest speed ever achieved on a motorcycle.

The world record average speed for two runs over 1 km (1,093.6 yd) from a standing start is 16.68 sec by Henk Vink (b July 24, 1939) (Netherlands) on his supercharged 984-cc 4-cylinder Kawasaki, at Elvington Airfield, Yorkshire, England, on July 24, 1977. The faster run was made in 16.09 sec.

The world record for two runs over 440 yd from a standing start is 8.805 sec by Henk Vink on his supercharged 1,132-cc 4-cylinder Kawasaki, at Elvington Airfield, Yorkshire, England, on July 23, 1977. The faster run was made in 8.55 sec.

The fastest time for a single run over 440 yd from a standing start is 7.62 sec by Russ Collins of Gardena, Calif, riding his nitro-burning 2000-cc 8-cylinder Honda, *Sorcerer*, at the National Hot Rod Association's World Finals at Ontario Motor Speedway, Calif, on Oct 7, 1978. The highest terminal velocity recorded at the end of a 440-yd run from a standing start is 199.55 mph by Russ Collins in the same run.

MOUNTAINEERING

Origins

Although bronze-age artifacts have been found on the summit (9,605 ft) of the Riffelhorn, Switzerland, mountaineering, as a sport, has a continuous history dating back only to 1854. Isolated instances of climbing for its own sake exist back to the 13th century. The Atacamenans built sacrificial platforms near the summit of Llullaillaco in South America (22,058 ft) in late pre-Columbian times, *c.* 1490.

Greatest Wall

The highest final stage in any wall climb is that on the south face of Annapurna I (26,545 ft). It was climbed by the British expedition led by Christian Bonington Apr 2–May 27, 1970, when Donald Whillans, 36, and Dougal Haston, 27, scaled to the summit. They used 18,000 ft of rope.

The longest wall climb is on the Rupal-Flank from the base camp at 11,680 ft to the South Point (26,384 ft) of Nanga Parbat—a vertical ascent of 14,704 ft. This was scaled by the Austro-Germano-Italian Expedition led by Dr Karl Maria Herrligkoffer in Apr 1970.

The most demanding free climbs are in the Yosemite Valley, Calif, with a severity rating of 5.12.

Mount Everest

Mount Everest (29,028 ft) was first climbed at 11:30 a.m. on May 29, 1953, when the summit was reached by Edmund Percival Hillary (b July 20, 1919), of New Zealand, and the Sherpa, Tenzing Norgay (b as Namgyal Wangdi, in Nepal in 1914, formerly called Tenzing Khumjung Bhutia). The successful expedition was led by Col (later Hon Brigadier) Henry Cecil John Hunt (b June 22, 1910).

GOLD MEDALISTS: Al Oerter (left) won the Olympic discuss event at 4 consecutive games, 1956–68. Mark Spitz (right) won 7 gold medals in the 1972 swimming competition in Munich.

Since the first ascent, another 97 climbers have succeeded to the end of 1979, including 3 Sherpas who have done it twice. Franz Oppurg (Austria) was the first to make the final ascent solo, on May 14, 1978. Four women have reached the summit, the first being Junko Tabei (b 1939) (Japan) on May 16, 1975. The oldest person was Dr Gerhard Schmatz (W Germany) (b June 5, 1929) aged 50 years 88 days on Oct 1, 1979.

Highest Bivouac

Douglas Scott and Dougal Haston bivouaced in a snow hole at 28,700 ft on the South Summit of Everest on the night of Sept 24, 1975.

OLYMPIC GAMES

Note: These records include the un-numbered Games held at Athens in 1906.

Origins

The earliest celebration of the ancient Olympic Games of which there is a certain record is that of July 776 BC (when Coroibos, a cook from Elis, won a foot race), though their origin probably dates from *c.* 1370 BC. The ancient Games were terminated by an order issued in Milan in 393 AD by Theodosius I, "the Great" (*c.* 346–395), Emperor of Rome. At the instigation of Pierre de Fredi, Baron de Coubertin (1863–1937), the Olympic Games of the modern era were inaugurated in Athens on Apr 6, 1896.

Most Medals

In the ancient Olympic Games, victors were given a chaplet (head garland) of olive leaves. Leonidas of Rhodos won 12 running titles from 164 to 152 BC.

The most individual gold medals won by a male competitor in the modern Games is 10 by Raymond Clarence Ewry (US) (b Oct 14, 1874, at Lafayette, Ind; d Sept 27, 1937), a jumper (see *Track and Field*). The female record is seven by Vera Caslavska-Odlozil (b May 3, 1942) of Czechoslovakia (also see *Gymnastics*).

The only Olympian to win 4 consecutive individual titles in the same event has been Alfred A. Oerter (b Sept 19, 1936, NYC) who won the discus title in 1956, 60, 64 and 68.

The only man to win a gold medal in both the Summer and Winter Games is Edward F. Eagan (US) (1898–1967) who won the 1920 light-heavyweight boxing title and was a member of the winning four-man bob in 1932.

Most Olympic Gold Medals at One Games

Mark Spitz (US), the swimmer who won 2 relay golds in Mexico in 1968, won 7 more (4 individual and 3 relay) at Munich in 1972. The latter figure is an absolute Olympic record for one celebration at any sport.

Youngest and Oldest Gold Medalists

The youngest woman to win a gold medal is Marjorie Gestring (US) (b Nov 18, 1922) aged 13 years 9 months, in the 1936 women's springboard event. The youngest winner ever was a French boy (whose name is not recorded) who coxed the Netherlands coxed pair in 1900. He was not more than 10 and may have been as young as 7. He substituted for Dr Hermanus Brockmann, who coxed in the heats but proved too heavy.

Oscar G. Swahn was a member of the winning Running Deer shooting team in 1912, aged 65 years 258 days.

National Medals

The total figures for most medals and most gold medals for all Olympic events (including those now discontinued) for the Summer (1896–1980) and Winter Games (1924–1980) are:

	Gold	Silver	Bronze	Total
1. US	664*	515½	443½	1,623
2. USSR (formerly Russia)	402	330	294	1,026
3. GB (including Ireland to 1920)	171½	209½	187	568

* The AAU (US) reinstated James F. Thorpe (1888–1953), the disqualified high scorer in the 1912 decathlon and pentathlon events on Oct 12, 1973, but no issue of medals has yet been authorized by the International Olympic Committee. If allowed, this would give the US 2 more gold medals.

Longest Span

The longest competitive span of any Olympic competitor is 40 years by Dr Ivan Osiier (Denmark) (1888–1965), who competed as a fencer in 1908, 1912 (silver medal), 1920, 1924, 1928, 1932 and 1948, and by Magnus Konow (Norway) (1887–1972) in yachting, 1908–20 and 1936–48. The longest span for a woman is 24 years (1932–56) by the Austrian fencer Ellen Müller-Preiss. Raimondo d'Inzeo (b Feb 8, 1925) competed for Italy in equestrian events in a record 8 celebrations (1948–1976), gaining one gold medal, 2 silver and 3 bronze medals. Janice Lee York Romary (b Aug 6, 1928), the US fencer, competed in all 6 Games from 1948 to 1968, and Lia Manoliu (Rumania) (b Apr 25, 1932) competed from 1952 to 1972, winning the discus title in 1968.

Largest Crowd

The largest crowd at any Olympic site was 150,000 at the 1952 ski-jumping at the Holmenkollen, outside Oslo, Norway. Estimates of the number of spectators of the marathon race through Tokyo on Oct 21, 1964, have ranged from 500,000 to 1,500,000.

Most and Fewest Competitors

The greatest number of competitors in any summer Olympic Games has been 7,147 at Munich in 1972. A record 122 countries competed in the 1972 Munich Games. The fewest was 311 competitors from 13 countries in 1896. In 1904 only 12 countries participated. The largest team was 880 men and 4 women from France at the 1900 Games in Paris.

Most Participations

Four countries have never failed to be represented at the 20 Celebrations of the Games: Australia, Greece, Great Britain and Switzerland.

PARACHUTING

Origins

Parachuting became a regulated sport with the institution of world championships in 1951. A team title was introduced in 1954, and women's events were included in 1956.

Most Titles

The USSR won the men's team titles in 1954, 58, 60, 66, 72 and 76 and the women's team titles in 1956, 58, 66, 68, 72 and 76. No individual has ever won a second world overall title.

Greatest Accuracy

Jacqueline Smith (GB) (b March 29, 1951) scored 10 consecutive dead center strikes (4-in disk) in the World Championships at Zagreb, Yugoslavia, Sept 1, 1978. At Yuma, Ariz, in March 1978, Dwight Reynolds scored a record 105 daytime dead centers, and Bill Wenger and Phil Munden tied with 43 nighttime DCs, competing as members of the US Army team, the Golden Knights. With electronic measuring the official FAI record is 50 DCs by A. Aasmiae (USSR) in Moscow, Oct 1979.

Most Jumps

The greatest number of consecutive jumps completed in 24 hours is 233 by David Parchment at Shobdon Airfield, Hereford, England, on June 19, 1979.

A record 10,000 jumps have been made by Anatoli Ossipov (USSR) to the end of 1979. The women's record is 7,000 by Valentina Zakoretskaya (USSR).

GREATEST ACCURACY: Jacqueline Smith landed a world record with 10 consecutive dead center jumps to win the 1978 World Championships.

POLO

Earliest Games

Polo is usually regarded as being of Persian origin, having been played as *Pulu c.* 525 BC. Other claims have come from Tibet and the Tang dynasty of China 250 AD.

The earliest club of modern times was the Kachar Club (founded in 1859) in Assam, India. The game was introduced into England from India in 1869 by the 10th Hussars at Aldershot, Hampshire, and the earliest match was one between the 9th Lancers and the 10th Hussars on Hounslow Heath, west of London, in July 1871. The earliest international match between England and the US was in 1886.

Playing Field

The game is played (by two teams of four) on the largest field of any ball game. The ground measures 300 yd long by 160 yd wide with sideboards or, as in India, 200 yd wide without boards.

Highest Score

The highest aggregate number of goals scored in an international match is 30, when Argentina beat the US 21–9 at Meadowbrook, LI, NY, in Sept 1936.

Most Olympic Medals

Polo has been part of the Olympic program on five occasions: 1900, 1908, 1920, 1924 and 1936. Of the 21 gold medalists, a 1920 winner, John

Wodehouse, the 3rd Earl of Kimberley (1883–1941) uniquely also won a silver medal (1908).

Highest Handicap

The highest handicap based on eight 7½-min "chukkas" is 10 goals, introduced in the US in 1891 and in the UK and Argentina in 1910. The latest of the 39 players to have received 10-goal handicaps are Alberto Heguy and Alfredo Harriot of Argentina, and in England, Eduardo Moore (Argentina). A match of two 40-goal handicap teams was staged for the first time ever at Palermo, Buenos Aires, Argentina, in 1975.

Most Internationals

Thomas Hitchcock, Jr (1900–44) played five times for the US vs England (1921, 24, 27, 30, 39) and twice vs Argentina (1928, 36).

Largest Trophy

Polo claims the world's largest sporting trophy—the Bangalore Limited Handicap Polo Tournament Trophy. This massive cup standing on its plinth is 6 ft tall and was presented in 1936 by the Indian Raja of Kolanka.

Largest Crowd

Crowds of more than 50,000 have watched floodlit matches at the Sydney, Australia, Agricultural Shows.

A crowd of 40,000 watched a game played at Jaipur, India, in 1976, when elephants were used instead of ponies. The length of the polo sticks used has not been ascertained.

POWERBOAT RACING

Origins

The earliest application of the gasoline engine to a boat was by Jean Joseph Etienne Lenoir (1822–1900) on the River Seine, Paris, in 1865. The sport was given impetus by the presentation of a championship cup by Sir Alfred Harmsworth of England in 1903, which was also the year of the first offshore race from Calais to Dover.

Harmsworth Cup

Of the 25 contests from 1903 to 1961, the US has won the most with 16.

The greatest number of wins has been achieved by Garfield A. Wood (US) with 8 (1920–21, 1926, 1928–30, 1932–33). The only boat to win three times is *Miss Supertest III*, owned by James G. Thompson (Canada), driven by Bob Hayward (Canada), in 1959–61. This boat also achieved the record speed of 119.27 mph at Picton, Ontario, Canada, in 1961. The trophy is now awarded to the British Commonwealth driver with the highest points in the World Offshore Championships.

Gold Cup

The Gold Cup (instituted 1903) has been won 8 times by Bill Muncey (1956–57, 61–62, 72, 77–79). The record speed attained is 128.338 mph

LONGEST POWERBOAT JUMP: Jerry Comeaux jumped his boat 110 ft through the air for the film "Live and Let Die."

for a 2½-mile lap by the unlimited hydroplane *Atlas Van Lines,* driven by Bill Muncey in a qualifying round on the Columbia River, Wash, in July 1977, and again in July 1978.

Highest Speeds

The fastest offshore record, as recognized by the Union Internationale Motonautique, is 97.20 mph by a Class IIIN Cougar, *Miss Toyota,* driven by Robert Cook on Lake Windermere, Cumbria, England, on Oct 15, 1979.

The R6 inboard engine record of 128.375 mph was set by the hydroplane *Vladivar I,* driven by Tony Fahey (GB) on Lake Windermere on May 23, 1977.

The Class ON record is 136.38 mph by J. F. Merten (US) in 1973.

Longest Race

The longest race has been the Port Richborough (London) to Monte Carlo Marathon Offshore International event. The race extended over 2,947 miles in 14 stages, June 10–25, 1972. It was won by *H.T.S.* (GB), driven by Mike Bellamy, Eddie Chater and Jim Brooks in 71 hours 35 min 56 sec (average 41.15 mph).

Longest Jump

The longest jump achieved by a powerboat has been 110 ft by Jerry Comeaux, 29, in a Glastron GT-150 with a 135-hp Evinrude Starflite off a greased ramp on an isolated waterway in Louisiana, in mid-October 1972. The takeoff speed was 56 mph. The jump was required for a sequence in the eighth James Bond film, *Live and Let Die.*

Dragsters

The first drag boat to attain 200 mph was Sam Kurtovich's *Crisis* which attained 200.44 mph in Calif in Oct 1969, at the end of a one-way run. *Climax* has since been reported to have attained 205.19 mph.

RODEO

Origins

Rodeo, which developed from 18th century *fiestas,* came into being with the early days of the North American cattle industry. The earliest reference to the sport is at Santa Fe, NM, on June 10, 1847. Steer wrestling began with Bill Pickett (Tex) in 1900. The other events are calf roping, bull riding, saddle and bareback bronc riding.

The largest rodeo in the world is the Calgary Exhibition and Stampede at Calgary, Alberta, Canada. The record attendance has been 1,069,830, July 8–17, 1977. The record for one day is 148,486 on July 7, 1979. The oldest continuously-held rodeo is that at Payson, Ariz, first held in Aug 1887.

Champion Bull

The top bucking bull was probably "Honky Tonk," an 11-year-old Brahma, who unseated 187 riders in an undefeated eight-year career to his retirement in Sept 1978.

Champion Bronc

Traditionally a bronc called "Midnight" owned by Jim McNab of Alberta, Canada, was never ridden in 12 appearances at the Calgary Stampede.

Most World Titles

The record number of all-round titles is 6 by Tom Ferguson (b Dec 20, 1950) consecutively, 1974–79, and by Larry Mahan (b Nov 21, 1943) (1966–70 and 73). Jim Shoulders (b 1928) of Henryetta, Okla, won a record 16 world championships between 1949 and 1959. The record figure for prize money (including bonuses) in a single season is $131,233 by Tom Ferguson, of Miami, Okla, in 1978. Ferguson also holds the record for the most money won at one rodeo with $16,945 earned at Houston, Tex, in 1979.

YOUNGEST CHAMPION: Metha Brorsen was only 11 years old when she won the 1975 barrel racing title.

MOST TITLES: Tom Ferguson won 6 straight all-round championships, 1974–79. He earned a record $131,233 in 1978 and $16,945 at one rodeo in 1979.

Youngest Champion

The youngest winner of a world title is Metha Brorsen of Okla, who was only 11 years old when she won the International Rodeo Association Cowgirls barrel racing event in 1975.

Time Records

Records for timed events, such as calf roping and steer wrestling, are meaningless, because of the widely varying conditions due to the size of arenas and amount of start given the stock. The fastest time recently recorded for roping a calf is 5.7 sec by Bill Reeder in Assiniboia, Saskatchewan, Canada, in 1978, and the fastest time for overcoming a steer is 2.4 sec by James Bynum of Waxahachie, Tex, at Marietta, Okla, in 1955.

The standard required time to stay on in bareback, saddle bronc and bull riding events is 8 sec. In the now discontinued ride-to-a-finish events, rodeo riders have been recorded to have survived 90 min or more, until the mount had not a buck left in it.

The highest score in bull riding was made by Don Gay on "Oscar" at The Cow Palace, San Francisco, in 1977, when he was awarded 97 points.

ROLLER SKATING

Origin

The first roller skate was devised by Joseph Merlin of Huy, Belgium, in 1760, and was first worn by him in public in London. James L. Plimpton of NYC produced the present four-wheeled type and patented it in Jan 1863. The first indoor rinks were opened in London in 1857. The great boom periods were 1870–75, 1908–12, 1948–54 and 1978 to the present, each originating in the US.

Largest Rink

The largest indoor rink ever to operate was located in the Grand Hall, Olympia, London, England. It had an actual skating area of 68,000 sq ft. It first opened in 1890 for one season, then again from 1909 to 1912.

The largest rink now in operation is the Fireside Roll-Arena in Hoffman Estates, Ill, which has a total skating surface of 29,859 sq ft.

Roller Hockey

Roller hockey was first introduced in England as Rink Polo, at the old Lava rink, Denmark Hill, London, in the late 1870's. The Amateur Rink Hockey Association was formed in 1905, and in 1913 became the National Rink Hockey (now Roller Hockey) Association. Britain won the inaugural World Championship in 1936, and since then Portugal has won the most with 11 titles from 1947 to 1973.

Most Titles

Most world speed titles have been won by Alberta Vianello (Italy) with 16 between 1953 and 1965. Most world pair titles have been taken by Dieter Fingerle (W Germany) with 4 in 1959, 65–67. The records for figure titles are 5 by Karl Heinz Losch in 1958–59, 61–62, 66, and 4 by Astrid Bader, also of W Germany, in 1965–68.

Speed Records

The fastest speed (official world's record) is 25.78 mph by Giuseppe Cantarella (Italy) who recorded 34.9 sec for 440 yd on a road at Catania, Italy, on Sept 28, 1963. The mile record on a rink is 2 min 25.1 sec by Gianni Ferretti (Italy). The greatest distance skated in one hour on a rink by a woman is 21.995 miles by Marisa Danesi at Inzell, W Germany, on Sept 28, 1968. The men's record on a track is 23.133 miles by Alberto Civolani (Italy) at Inzell, W Germany, on Sept 28, 1968. He went on to skate 50 miles in 2 hours 20 min 33.1 sec.

Marathon Record

The longest recorded continuous roller skating marathon was one of 331 hours 20 min by Lou Sergi at the Majestic Rink, Sydney, Australia, June 22–July 6, 1980.

Endurance

Theodore J. Coombs (b 1954) of Hermosa Beach, Calif, skated 5,193 miles from Los Angeles to NYC and back to Yates Center, Kan, from May 30 to Sept 14, 1979. His longest 24-hour distance was 120 miles, June 27–28. For the first 3,200 miles he averaged 66.6 miles per day.

ROWING

Oldest Race

The Sphinx stela of Amenhotep II (1450–1425 BC) records that he *stroked* a boat for some three miles. The earliest established sculling race is the Doggett's Coat and Badge, first rowed on Aug 1, 1716 from London Bridge to Chelsea, and still contested annually. Although rowing regattas were held in Venice in 1300, the first English regatta probably took place

THREE GOLD MEDALS: Vyacheslav Ivanov (left) and Jack Beresford (right) are 2 of the 5 rowers who have won 3 Olympic gold medals.

on the Thames by the Ranelagh Gardens near Putney, London, in 1775. Boating began at Eton, England, in 1793. The oldest club, the Leander Club, was formed *c.* 1818.

Olympic Games

Since 1900 there have been 133 Olympic finals of which the US has won 26, E Germany 25, Germany (now W Germany) 15 and GB 14. Five oarsmen have won 3 gold medals: John B. Kelly (US) (1889–1960), father of Princess Grace of Monaco, in the sculls (1920) and double sculls (1920 and 1924); his cousin Paul V. Costello (US) (b Dec 17, 1899) in the double sculls (1920, 1924 and 1928); Jack Beresford, Jr (GB) (1899–1977) in the sculls (1924), coxless fours (1932) and double sculls (1936); Vyacheslav Ivanov (USSR) (b July 30, 1938) in the sculls (1956, 1960 and 1964); and Siegfried Brietzke in the coxless pairs (1972) and the coxless fours (1976 and 1980).

Sculling

The record number of world professional sculling titles (instituted 1831) won is 7 by William Beach (Australia) between 1884 and 1887.

Highest Speed

Speeds in tidal or flowing water are of no comparative value. The highest recorded speed for 2,000 m on non-tidal water by an eight is 5 min 32.17 sec (13.46 mph) by E Germany at the Montreal Olympics on July 18, 1976. A team from the Penn AC (US) was timed in 5 min 18.8 sec (14.03 mph) in the FISA Championships on the Meuse River, Liège, Belgium, on Aug 17, 1930.

Longest Race

The longest annual rowing race is the Ringvaart Regatta, a 62-mile (100-km) contest for eights held at Delft, Netherlands. The record time is 7 hours 3 min 29 sec by the Njord team on May 31, 1979. The Swedish

Royal Navy's annual race for ten-man ship's boats is over 74.5 miles (120 km).

Cross-Channel Row

The fastest row across the English Channel is 3 hours 50 min by the Rev Sidney Swann (1862–1942) on Sept 12, 1911.

World Records

MEN—Fastest times over 2,000 m course

	min sec	Country	Place	Date
Single Sculls	6:52.46	Sean Drea (Ireland)	Montreal	July 23, 1976
Double Sculls	6:12.48	Norway	Montreal	July 23, 1976
Coxed Pairs	6:56.94	E Germany	Copenhagen	Aug — 1971
Coxless Pairs	6:33.02	E Germany	Montreal	July 23, 1976
Coxed Fours	6:09.17	E Germany	Amsterdam	June 30, 1979
Coxless Fours	5:53.65	E Germany	Montreal	July 23, 1976
Quadruple Sculls	5:47.38	W Germany	Lucerne	June 4, 1980
Eights	5:32.17	E Germany	Montreal	July 18, 1976

WOMEN—Fastest times over 1,000 m course

	min sec	Country	Place	Date
Single Sculls	3:34.31	Christine Scheiblich (E Germany)	Amsterdam	Aug 21, 1977
Double Sculls	3:16.27	USSR	Moscow	July 16, 1980
Coxless Pairs	3:26.32	E Germany	Amsterdam	Aug 21, 1977
Coxed Fours	3:14.03	E Germany	Lucerne	June 14,1980
Quadruple Sculls	3:08.49	E Germany	Montreal	July 19, 1976
Eights	2:57.38	US	Lucerne	June 14, 1980

SHOOTING

Earliest Club

The Lucerne Shooting Guild (Switzerland) was formed c. 1466, and the first recorded shooting match was held at Zurich in 1472.

Olympic Games

The record number of medals won is 11 by Carl Townsend Osburn (US) (1884–1966) in 1912, 1920 and 1924, consisting of 5 gold, 4 silver and 2 bronze. Six other marksmen have won 5 gold medals. The only marksman to win 3 individual gold medals has been Gudbrand Gudbrandsönn Skatteboe (Norway) (1875–1965) in 1906.

Record Heads

The world's finest head is the 23-pointer stag head in the Maritzburg collection, E Germany. The outside span is 75½ in, the length 47½ in and the weight 41½ lb. The greatest number of points is probably 33 (plus 29) on the stag shot in 1696 by Frederick III (1657–1713), the Elector of Brandenburg, later King Frederick I of Prussia.

Largest Shoulder Guns

The largest bore shoulder guns made were 2-bore. Less than a dozen of these were made by two English wildfowl gunmakers c. 1885. Normally the largest guns made are double-barrelled 4-bore weighing up to 26 lb which can be handled only by men of exceptional physique. Larger smooth-bore guns have been made, but these are for use as punt-guns.

Individual World Records
(as ratified by the International Shooting Union—UIT)

Possible Score

Free Rifle	300m	3 × 40 shots	1200–1160	Lones W. Wigger (US) Seoul, S Korea 1978
Standard Rifle	300m	3 × 20 shots	600–577	D. Kimes (US) Seoul, S Korea 1978
Small-bore Rifle	50m	3 × 40 shots	1200–1173	Viktor Vlasov (USSR) Moscow 1980
Small-bore Rifle	50m	60 shots prone	600–599	Six men
Free Pistol	50m	60 shots	600–581	Aleksandr Melentev (USSR) Moscow 1980
Rapid Fire Pistol	25m	60 shots	600–598	Giovanni Liverzani (Italy) Phoenix, Ariz 1970
			600–598	Ian Corneliu (Rumania) Bucharest, Rumania 1977
Center-Fire Pistol	25m	60 shots	600–597	Thomas D. Smith (US) Sao Paulo, Brazil 1963
Standard Pistol	25m	60 shots	600–583	Ragnar Skanaker (Sweden) Seoul, S Korea 1978
Running Target	50m	60 shots 'normal runs'	600–589	Igor Sokolov (USSR) Moscow 1980
Trap	—	200 birds	200–199	Angelo Scalzone (Italy) Munich 1972
			200–199	Michel Carrega (France) Thun, Switz 1974
Skeet	—	200 birds	200–199	J. Clemmons (US) Mexico City 1977
Air Rifle	10m	40 shots	400–393	Olegario Vasquez (Mexico) Mexico City 1975
Air Pistol	10m	40 shots	400–394	Uwe Potteck (E Germany) Graz, Austria 1979

Biggest Bag

The largest animal ever shot by any bird game hunter was a bull African elephant (*Loxodonta africana africana*) shot by E. M. Nielsen of Columbus, Neb, 25 miles north-northeast of Mucusso, Angola, on Nov 7, 1974. The animal, brought down by a Westley Richards 0.425, stood 13 ft 8 in at the shoulder.

In Nov 1965, Simon Fletcher, 28, a Kenyan farmer, claims to have killed two elephants with one 0.458 bullet.

The greatest recorded lifetime bag is 556,000 birds, including 241,000 pheasants, by the 2nd Marquess of Ripon (1852–1923) of England. He himself dropped dead on a grouse moor after shooting his 52nd bird on the morning of Sept 22, 1923.

Trick Shooting

The greatest rapid-fire feat was that of Ed McGivern (US), who twice fired from 15 ft in 0.45 sec 5 shots which could be covered by a silver half-dollar piece at the Lead Club Range, SD, on Aug 20, 1932.

McGivern also, on Sept 13, 1932, at Lewiston, Mont, fired 10 shots in 1.2 sec from two guns at the same time double action (no draw), all 10 shots hitting two 2¼ × 3½ in playing cards at 15 ft.

The most renowned trick shot of all time was Annie Oakley (*née* Mozee) (1860–1926). She demonstrated the ability to shoot 100 of 100 in trap shooting for 35 years, aged between 27 and 62. At 30 paces she could split a playing card end-on, hit a dime in mid-air or shoot a cigarette from the lips of her husband—one Frank Butler.

Bench Rest Shooting

The smallest group on record at 1,000 yards is 6.125 in by Kenneth A. Keefer, Jr, with a 7 mm-300 Remington Action in Williamstown, Pa, on Sept 22, 1974.

Small-Bore Rifle Shooting

Richard Hansen shot 5,000 bull's-eyes in 24 hours at Fresno, Calif, on June 13, 1929.

Clay Pigeon Shooting

The record number of clay birds shot in an hour is 1,904 by Tom Kreckman, 36, at Cresco, Pa, on a Skeet range, Sept 28, 1975. Jerry Teynor shot 1,735 birds on a trapshooting range at Bucyrus, Ohio, on July 30, 1977.

Most world titles have been won by Susan Nattrass (Canada) with 5, 1974–5, 1977–9. The most by a man is 4 by Michel Carrega (France), 1970–1, 1974 and 1979.

Highest Score in 24 Hours

The Central Lancashire Rifle Club team of John Jepson, Graham Sharples, Derek Byron and Joseph Graham, scored 85,752 points (averaging 94.03 per card), Nov 26–27, 1976.

ALPINE ACE (left): Christel Cranz won 12 World Alpine Championships between 1934 and 1939. HIGHEST SPEED (above): Steve McKinney reached a speed of 124.412 mph at Portillo, Chile, on Oct 1, 1978.

Rapid Firing

Using a Soper single-loading rifle, Private John Warrick, 1st Berkshire Volunteers, loaded and fired 60 rounds in 1 min at Basingstoke, England, in Apr 1870.

SKIING

Origins

The most ancient ski in existence was found well preserved in a peat bog at Höting, Sweden, dating from *c.* 2500 BC. A rock carving of a skier at Bessovysledki, USSR, dates from 6000 BC. The earliest recorded military use was in Norway, in 1199, though it did not grow into a sport until 1843 at Tromsø. The Trysil Shooting and Skiing Club (founded 1861), in Norway, claims to be the world's oldest. Skiing was not introduced in the Alps until 1883, though there is some evidence of earlier use in the Carniola district. The earliest formal downhill race was staged at Montana, Switzerland, in 1911. The first Slalom event was run at Mürren, Switzerland, on Jan 21, 1922. The International Ski Federation (FIS) was founded on Feb 2, 1924. The Winter Olympics were inaugurated on Jan 25, 1924.

Highest Speed

The highest speed ever claimed for any skier is 124.412 mph by Steve McKinney (US) (b 1953) at Portillo, Chile, on Oct 1, 1978. The fastest by a woman is 103.084 mph by Catherine Breyton (France) at Portillo on Oct 1, 1978.

The highest average race speed in the Olympic downhill was in 1976 by Franz Klammer (b Dec 3, 1953) of Austria on the Patscherkofel course, Innsbruck, Austria, with 63.894 mph on Feb 5, 1976.

Duration

The longest non-stop Nordic skiing marathon was one that lasted 48 hours by Onni Savi, aged 35, of Padasjoki, Finland, who covered 305.9 km (190.1 miles) between noon on Apr 19 and noon on Apr 21, 1966.

Ahti Nevada (Finland) covered 174.5 miles in 24 hours at Rovaniemi, Finland, on March 30, 1977.

Pat Purcell and John McGlynn (US) completed 81 hours 12 min of Alpine skiing at Holiday Mountain, Monticello, NY, Feb 1–4, 1979.

Most World Titles

The World Alpine Championships were inaugurated at Mürren, Switzerland, in 1931. The greatest number of titles won is 12 by Christel Cranz (b July 1, 1914), of Germany, with 4 Slalom (1934, 37–39), 3 Downhill (1935, 37, 39) and 5 Combined (1934–35, 37–39). She also won the gold medal for the Combined in the 1936 Olympics. The most titles won by a man is 7 by Anton "Toni" Sailer (b Nov 17, 1935), of Austria, who won all 4 in 1956 (Giant Slalom, Slalom, Downhill and the non-Olympic Alpine Combination) and the Downhill, Giant Slalom and Combined in 1958.

MEN'S WORLD CUP: Gustavo Thoeni (left) has won the Alpine World Cup 4 times. He has also won an Olympic gold and 4 other world titles. CROSS-COUNTRY CHAMP: Galina Koulakova (right) has won 9 Nordic world titles, 4 Olympic gold medals and the inaugural Nordic World Cup.

In the Nordic events Sixten Jernberg (Sweden) (b Feb 6, 1929) won 8 titles, 4 at 50 km, one at 30 km, and 3 in relays, in 1956–64. Johan Grottumsbraaten (1899–1942), of Norway, won 6 individual titles (2 at 18 km and 4 Combined) in 1926–32. The most by a woman is 9 by Galina Koulakova (USSR) (b Apr 29, 1942) from 1968 to 1978. The record for a jumper is 5 by Birger Ruud (b Aug 23, 1911), of Norway, in 1931–32 and 1935–37.

The Alpine World Cup, instituted in 1967, has been won 4 times by Gustavo Thoeni (Italy) (b Feb 28, 1951) in 1971–73, and 75. The women's cup has been won 6 times by the 5-ft-6-in 150-lb Annemarie Moser (née Pröll) (Austria) in 1971–75 and 79. From Dec 1972 to Jan 1974 she completed a record sequence of 11 consecutive downhill victories and in 10 seasons, 1970–79, has won a total of 62 individual events. The most individual events won by a man is 51 by Ingemar Stemark (Sweden) in 1974–79, including a record 14 in one season in 1979.

The Nordic World Cup, instituted in 1979, was first won by Oddvar Braa (Norway) with the women's title won by Galina Koulakova (USSR).

Most Olympic Victories

The most Olympic gold metals won by an individual for skiing is 4 by Sixten Jernberg (b Feb 6, 1929), of Sweden, in 1956–64 (including one for a relay); and by Aleksandr Tikhonov (b Jan 2, 1947) (USSR) who won all 4 as a member of the winning team in the 4 × 7.5-km biathlon relay, 1968–80. In addition, Jernberg has won 3 silver and 2 bronze medals. The only woman to win 4 gold medals is Galina Koulakova (b Apr 29, 1942) of USSR who won the 5 km and 10 km (1972) and was a member of the winning 3 × 5-km relay team in 1972 and the 4 × 5-km team in 1976. Koulakova also has won 2 silver and 2 bronze medals, 1968–80.

The most Olympic gold medals won in men's alpine skiing is 3, by Anton "Toni" Sailer in 1956 and Jean-Claude Killy in 1968.

Closest Verdict

The narrowest winning margin in a championship ski race was one hundredth of a second by Thomas Wassberg (Sweden) (b March 23, 1956) over Juha Mieto (Finland) in the Olympic 15 km cross-country race at Lake Placid, NY on Feb 17, 1980. His winning time was 41 min 57.63 sec.

Longest Jump

The longest ski jump ever recorded is one of 181 m (593 ft 10 in) by Bogdan Norcic (Yugoslavia) (b Sept 19, 1953) who fell on landing at Planica, Yugoslavia, in Feb 1977.

The official record is 176 m (577 ft 5 in) by Toni Innauer (Austria) (b Apr 1, 1958) at Oberstdorf, W Germany, on March 6, 1976; Klaus Ostwald (E Germany) (b Aug 26, 1958) at Planica on March 18, 1979: and Armin Kogler (Austria) (b Sept 4, 1959) at Harrachov, Czechoslovakia, on March 28, 1980.

The women's record is 321 ft 6 in by Anita Wold of Norway, at Okura, Sapporo, Japan, on Jan 14, 1975.

The longest jump achieved in the Olympics is 117 m (384 ft) by Juoko Tormanen (Finland) (b Apr 10, 1954) at Lake Placid, NY, on Feb 23, 1980.

Largest Race

The world's greatest Nordic ski race is the "Vasa Lopp," which commemorates an event in 1521 when Gustavus Vasa (1496–1560), later King of Sweden, skied 85.8 km (53.3 miles) from Mora to Sälen, Sweden. The re-enactment of this journey in the reverse direction is an annual event, with a record 11,596 starters on March 5, 1978. The record time is 4 hours 5 min 58 sec by Ola Hassis (Sweden) on March 4, 1979.

WOMEN'S WORLD CUP: Annemarie Moser has won 6 Alpine World Cup titles and 62 individual events in that competition, including 11 consecutively.

Steepest Descent

Sylvain Saudan (b Lausanne, Switzerland, Sept 23, 1936) achieved a descent of Mt Blanc on the northeast side down the Couloir Gervasutti from 13,937 ft on Oct 17, 1967, skiing gradients in excess of 60 degrees.

Greatest Descent

The greatest reported aggregate elevation descended in 12 hours is 416,000 ft by Sarah Ludwig, Scott Ludwig, and Timothy B. Gaffney, at Mt Brighton, Mich on Feb 16, 1974.

Highest Altitude

Yuichiro Miura (Japan) skied 1.6 miles down Mt Everest on May 6, 1970, starting from 26,574 ft.

Longest Run

The longest all-downhill ski run in the world is the Weissfluhjoch-Küblis Parsenn course (7.6 miles long), near Davos, Switzerland. The run from the Aiguille du Midi top of the Chamonix lift (vertical lift 8,176 ft) across the Vallée Blanche is 13 miles.

The longest downhill race is the *Inferno* in Switzerland, 8.7 miles from the top of the Schilthorn to Lauterbrunnen. In 1980 there was a record entry of 1,282, with Heinz Fringen (Switzerland) winning in a record 18 min 15 sec.

Backflip on Skis

Twenty-one skiers at Mont St Saveur, Quebec, Canada, performed a simultaneous back somersault while holding hands on March 12, 1977.

Longest Lift

The longest chair lift in the world is the Alpine Way to Kosciusko Châlet lift above Thredbo, near the Snowy Mountains, NSW, Australia. It takes from 45 to 75 min to ascend the 3.5 miles, according to the weather. The highest is at Chacaltaya, Bolivia, rising to 16,500 ft. The longest gondola ski lift, at Killington, Vt, is 3.4 miles long.

Ski Parachuting

The greatest recorded vertical descent in parachute ski-jumping is 3,300 ft by Rick Sylvester (b Apr 3, 1942) (US), who on July 28, 1976, skied off the 6,600-ft summit of Mt Asgard in Auyuittuq National Park, Baffin Island, Canada, landing on the Turner Glacier. The jump was made for a sequence in the James Bond film *The Spy Who Loved Me*.

Ski-Bob

The ski-bob was invented by a Mr Stevens of Hartford, Conn, and patented (No 47334) on Apr 19, 1892, as a "bicycle with ski-runners." The Fédération Internationale de Skibob was founded on Jan 14, 1961, in Innsbruck, Austria. The first World Championships were held at Bad Hofgastein, Austria, in 1967.

The highest speed has been 103.4 mph by Erich Brenter (Austria) at Cervinia, Italy, in 1964. The only ski-bobbers to retain world championships are Gerhilde Schiffkorn (Austria) who won the women's title in 1967 and 1969, Gertrude Geberth (Austria), who won in 1971 and 1973

MOST GOALS: Pelé celebrates one of his 1,281 goals, this one with the NY Cosmos of the North American Soccer League.

and Alois Fischbauer (Austria) who won the men's title in 1973 and 1975.

Snowmobiling

The record speed for a snowmobile was increased to 135.93 mph by Donald J. Pitzen (US) at Union Lake, Mich on Feb 27, 1977.

SOCCER

Origins

A game with some similarities termed *Tsu-chu* was played in China in the 3rd and 4th centuries BC. One of the earliest references to the game in England refers to the accidental death of a goalkeeper on Feb 23, 1582, in Essex. The earliest clear representation of the game is in a print from Edinburgh, Scotland, dated 1672–73. The game became standardized with the formation of the Football Association in England on Oct 26, 1863. A football game, *Calcio,* existed in Italy in 1410. The world's oldest club is Sheffield FC of England, formed on Oct 24, 1857. Eleven on a side was standardized in 1870.

Highest Team Scores

The highest score recorded in any first-class match is 36. This occurred in the Scottish Cup match between Arbroath and Bon Accord on Sept 5,

1885, when Arbroath won 36–0 on their home ground. But for the lack of nets, the playing time might have been longer and the score possibly even higher.

The highest goal margin recorded in any international match is 17. This occurred in the England vs Australia match at Sydney on June 30, 1951, when England won 17–0. This match is not listed by England as a *full* international.

Individual Scoring

The most goals scored by one player in a first-class match is 16 by Stephan Stanis (*né* Stanikowski, b Poland, July 15, 1913) for Racing Club de Lens vs Aubry-Asturies, in Lens, France, on Dec 13, 1942.

The record number of goals scored by one player in an international match is 10 by Gottfried Fuchs for Germany, which beat Russia 16–0 in the 1912 Olympic tournament (consolation event) in Sweden.

Artur Friedenreich (1892–1969) (Brazil) scored an undocumented 1,329 goals in a 43-year first-class football career. The most goals scored in a specified period is 1,216 by Edson Arantes do Nascimento (b Baurú, Brazil, Oct 23, 1940), known as Pelé, the Brazilian inside left, from Sept 7, 1956, to Oct 2, 1974 (1,254 games). His best year was 1958 with 139. His *milesimo* (1,000th) came in a penalty for his club, Santos, in the Maracaña Stadium, Rio de Janeiro, on Nov 19, 1969, when he was playing in his 909th first-class match. He came out of retirement in 1975 to add to his total with the New York Cosmos of the North American Soccer League. By his retirement on Oct 1, 1977 his total had reached 1,281 in 1,363 games. Franz ("Bimbo") Binder (b 1911) scored 1,006 goals in 756 games in Austria and Germany between 1930 and 1950.

Fastest Goals

The record for an international match is 3 goals in 3½ min by Willie Hall (Tottenham Hotspur) for England against Ireland on Nov 16, 1938, at Old Trafford, Manchester, England.

The fastest goal in World Cup competition was one in 30 sec by Olle Nyberg for Sweden vs Hungary, in Paris, June 16, 1938.

Most Successful National Coach

Helmut Schoen (b 1915) of W Germany coached his teams to victory in the 1972 European championship and the 1974 World Cup, as well as finishing second in the 1966 World Cup and 1976 European championships, and third in the 1970 World Cup. George Raynor's Swedish teams won the 1948 Olympic competition and were second in the 1958 World Cup and third in both the 1950 World Cup and the 1952 Olympic competition.

Longest Match

The world duration record for a first-class match was set in the Copa Libertadores championship in Santos, Brazil, Aug 2–3, 1962, when Santos drew 3–3 with Penarol FC of Montevideo, Uruguay. The game lasted 3½ hours (with interruptions), from 9:30 p.m. to 1 a.m.

A match between the Simon Fraser University Clansmen and the Quincy College Hawks lasted 4 hours 25 min (221 min 43 sec playing time) at Pasadena, Calif, in Nov 1976.

Crowds

The greatest recorded crowd at any football match was 205,000 (199,854 paid) for the Brazil vs Uruguay World Cup final in Rio de Janeiro, Brazil, on July 16, 1950.

The highest attendance at any amateur match is 120,000 at Senayan Stadium, Djakarta, Indonesia, on Feb 26, 1976, for the Pre-Olympic Group II Final between North Korea and Indonesia.

World Cup

The *Fédération Internationale de Football Association* (FIFA) was founded in Paris on May 21, 1904, and instituted the World Cup Competition in 1930, in Montevideo, Uruguay.

The only country to win three times has been Brazil (1958, 1962, 1970). Brazil was also third in 1938 and 1978, and second in 1950, and is the only one of the 45 participating countries to have played in all 11 competitions.

The record goal scorer has been Just Fontaine (France) with 13 goals in 6 games in the final stages of the 1958 competition. The most goals scored in the final is 3 by Geoffrey Hurst (West Ham United) for England vs W Germany on July 30, 1966. Gerd Müller (W Germany) scored 14 goals in two World Cup finals (1970 and 1974).

Antonio Carbajal (b 1923) played for Mexico in goal in the competitions of 1950, 54, 58, 62 and 66.

Receipts

The greatest receipts at a World Cup final were £204,805 ($573,454) from an attendance of 96,924 for the match between England and W Germany at the Empire Stadium, Wembley, Greater London, on July 30, 1966.

WORLD CUP GOALS: Gerd Müller (above) scored 14 goals in 2 World Cup final series. Geoffrey Hurst (right) netted 3 goals in the 1966 final game.

SOFTBALL PITCHING: Ty Stofflet (left) struck out 98 batters in the 1976 men's world championship series. Joan Joyce (right) struck out 76 and pitched 2 perfect games in the women's championships in 1974.

Heaviest Goalkeeper

The biggest goalie on record was Willie J. ("Fatty") Foulke of England (1874–1916) who stood 6 ft 3 in and weighed 311 lb. By the time he died, he tipped the scales at 364 lb. He once stopped a game by snapping the cross bar.

Most Olympic Wins

The only country to have won the Olympic football title three times is Hungary in 1952, 1964 and 1968. The UK won in 1908 and 1912 and also the unofficial tournament of 1900. These contests have now virtually ceased to be amateur. The highest Olympic score is Denmark 17 vs France "A" 1 in 1908.

Heading

The highest recorded number of repetitions for heading a ball (non-stop) is 20,100 in 2 hours 10 min by Mikael Palmqvist at Hällefors, Sweden, on June 6, 1980.

Ball Control

Mikael Palmqvist (20) juggled a regulation soccer ball for 10 hours non-stop at Träffens Sporthall, Gäule, Sweden, on May 8, 1980. He did

80,357 repetitions with feet, legs and head without the ball ever touching the ground.

Marathons

The longest recorded 11-a-side soccer marathon is 52 hours 40 min by the Town 'n' Country Rangers vs the Blackwatch Celtics at Skyway Field, Tampa, Fla, Apr 2–4, 1980.

The longest recorded authenticated 5-a-side games have been (outdoors) 63 hours 21 min by two teams (no substitutes) from the Trustee Savings Bank at Neston Recreation Centre, South Wirral, England, May 15–18, 1980, and (indoors) 100 hours 5 min by two teams (no substitutes) from The Friends of Powys at Yale Sixth Form College, Wrexham, Wales, Apr 4–8, 1980.

SOFTBALL

Origins

Softball, as an indoor derivative of baseball, was invented by George Hancock at the Farragut Boat Club of Chicago, in 1887. Rules were first codified in Minneapolis in 1895 as Kitten Ball. International rules were set in 1933 when the name Softball was officially adopted. The ISF was formed in 1952 as governing body for both fast pitch and slow pitch.

World Championships

The US has won the men's world championship (instituted in 1966) three times, 1966, 68 and 76 (shared). The US has also won the women's title (instituted in 1965) twice, in 1974 and 78.

Joan Joyce set a pair of records by pitching 2 perfect games and notching 76 strikeouts for the US women's team in the 1974 world championships at Stratford, Conn. In the same competition, Miyoko Naruse of Japan set three batting records with 17 hits, a .515 batting average and 11 RBIs (shared with two others). In the men's competition at Wellington, New Zealand, in 1976, pitcher Ty Stofflet (US) struck out a record 98 batters. Bob Burrows of Canada hit the most-ever home runs with 4, and tied a record with 14 RBIs.

Marathon

The longest fast pitch marathon is 55 hours 50 min by two teams of nine (no substitutes) from the YCW Softball Association, Melbourne, Australia, Dec 16–18, 1978. The longest for slow pitch is 74 hours 31 min by two teams of ten players from the USS *John Young*, Apr 11–14, 1980.

SQUASH

Earliest Champion

Although racquets with a soft ball was played in 1817 at Harrow School (England), there was no recognized champion of any country until J. A. Miskey of Philadelphia won the American Amateur Singles Championship in 1907.

World Amateur Title

Australia has won the team title 4 times. Geoffrey B. Hunt (b March 11, 1947) (Australia) took the individual title in 1967, 1969 and 1971.

World Open Title

The World Open championship, instituted in 1976, has been won 3 times by Geoffrey B. Hunt (Australia), in 1976, 77 and 79.

British Open Championship

The most wins in the Open Championship (amateur or professional), held annually in Britain, is 7 by Hashim Khan (Pakistan) in 1950–55 and 1957 and Geoffrey Hunt in 1969, 74, and 76–80. Hashim Khan has also won the Vintage title 3 times, in 1977–78 and 1980.

British Amateur Championship

The most wins in the Amateur Championship is 6 by Abdel-Fattah Amr Bey (Egypt), later appointed Ambassador in London, who won in 1931–33 and 1935–37.

Longest and Shortest Championship Matches

The longest recorded match was one of 2 hours 35 min in the British Amateur Championships at Wembley, England, on Dec 12, 1976, when Murray Lilley (New Zealand) beat Barry O'Connor (GB) 9–3, 10–8, 2–9, 7–9, 10–8. The second game lasted 58 min and there were a total of 98 lets called in the match.

Deanna Murray beat Christine Rees in only 9½ min in a Ladies Welsh title match at Rhos-on-Sea, Clwyd, Wales, on Oct 21, 1979.

Women's Championship

The most wins in the Women's Squash Rackets Championship is 16 by Heather McKay (*née* Blundell) (b July 31, 1941) of Australia, 1961 to 1976. She also won the World Open title in 1976 and 79. In her career from 1959 to 1979 she lost only two matches.

MOST WINS: Heather McKay has won 16 women's championships and both women's World Open titles. Between 1959 and 1979, she lost only 2 matches.

FASTEST SWIMMER: American Joe Bottom covered 50 yd in 19.70 sec (5.19 mph) in March 1977.

Marathon Record

The longest squash marathon has been 120 hours 51 min by Peter Fairlie (b Dec 18, 1957) at the Bridge of Allan Sports Club, Stirling, Scotland, June 30–July 5, 1979. George Deponselle and William de Bruin played for 106 hours 43 min at Sutterheim Country Club, Cape Province, South Africa, Oct 1–5, 1978. (*This category will now be confined to two players only.*)

SWIMMING

Earliest References

Swimming in schools in Japan was ordered by Imperial edict of Emperor Go-Yozei (1586–1611) as early as 1603, but competition was known from 36 BC. Sea water bathing was fashionable at Scarborough, New Yorkshire, England, as early as 1660.

Largest Pools

The largest swimming pool in the world is the salt-water Orthlieb Pool in Casablanca, Morocco. It is 480 m (1,547 ft) long, 75 m (246 ft) wide, and has an area of 8.9 acres.

The largest land-locked swimming pool with heated water was the Fleishhacker Pool on Sloat Boulevard, near Great Highway, San Francisco. It measures 1,000 ft by 150 ft (3.44 acres), is up to 14 ft deep, and can contain 7,500,000 gallons of water. It was opened on May 2, 1925, but has now been abandoned to a few ducks.

The world's largest competition pool is at Osaka, Japan. It accommodates 13,614 spectators.

Fastest Swimmers

Excluding relay stages with their anticipatory starts, the highest speed reached by a swimmer is 5.19 mph by Joe Bottom (US), who recorded

SWIMMING—WORLD RECORDS—MEN

At distances recognized by the Fédération Internationale de Natation Amateur as of Aug 1980. FINA no longer recognizes any records made for non-metric distances. Only performances set up in 50-m pools are recognized as World Records.

FREESTYLE

Distance	min sec	Name and Nationality	Place	Date
100 m	49.44	Jonty Skinner (S Africa)	Philadelphia, Pa	Aug 14, 1976
200 m	1:49.16	Ambrose (Rowdy) Gaines (US)	Austin, Tex	Apr 11, 1980
400 m	3:50.49	Peter Szmidt (Canada)	Toronto, Canada	July 17, 1980
800 m	7:56.49	Vladimir Salnikov (USSR)	Minsk, USSR	Mar 23, 1979
1,500 m	14:58.27	Vladimir Salnikov (USSR)	Moscow, USSR	July 22, 1980
4 × 100 Relay	3:19.74	US National Team (Jack Babashoff, Ambrose Gaines, David McCagg, James Montgomery)	W Berlin, W Germany	Aug 22, 1978
4 × 200 Relay	7:20.82	US National Team (Bruce Furniss, William Forrester, Bobby Hackett, Ambrose Gaines)	W Berlin, W Germany	Aug 24, 1978

BREASTSTROKE

Distance	min sec	Name and Nationality	Place	Date
100 m	1:02.86	Gerald Moerken (W Germany)	Jönkoping, Sweden	Aug 17, 1977
200 m	2:15.11	David Wilkie (GB)	Montreal, Canada	July 24, 1976

BUTTERFLY STROKE

Distance	min sec	Name and Nationality	Place	Date
100 m	54.15	Per Arvidsson (Sweden)	Austin, Tex	Apr 11, 1980
200 m	1:58.21	Craig Beardsley (US)	Irvine, Calif	July 30, 1980

BACKSTROKE

Distance	min sec	Name and Nationality	Place	Date
100 m	55.49	John Naber (US)	Montreal, Canada	July 19, 1976
200 m	1:59.19	John Naber (US)	Montreal, Canada	July 24, 1976

INDIVIDUAL MEDLEY

Distance	min sec	Name and Nationality	Place	Date
200 m	2:03.24	Bill Barrett (US)	Irvine, Calif	Aug 1, 1980
400 m	4:20.05	Jesse Vassallo (US)	W Berlin, W Germany	Aug 22, 1978

MEDLEY RELAY

(Backstroke, Breaststroke, Butterfly Stroke, Freestyle)

Distance	min sec	Name and Nationality	Place	Date
4 × 100 m	3:42.22	U.S. National Team (John Naber, John Hencken, Matthew Vogel, James Montgomery)	W Berlin, W Germany	Aug 22, 1978

19.70 sec for 50 yd in a 25-yd pool at Cleveland, Ohio, on March 24, 1977.

The fastest by a woman is 4.42 mph by Sue Hinderaker (US) who clocked 23.14 sec for 50 yd in Pittsburgh, Pa, on March 16, 1979.

Most World Records

Men: 32, Arne Borg (Sweden) (b 1901), 1921–29. Women: 42, Ragnhild Hveger (Denmark) (b Dec 10, 1920), 1936–42. Under modern conditions (only metric distances in 50-m pools) the most is 26 by Mark Spitz (US), 1967–72, and 23 by Kornelia Ender (E Germany), 1973–6.

World Titles

In the world swimming championships (instituted in 1973), the greatest number of medals won is 10 (8 gold, 2 silver) by Kornelia Ender of E Germany. The most by a man is 7 (6 gold, 1 bronze) by James Montgomery (US).

The most medals in a single championship is 6 by Tracy Caulkins (US) (b Jan 11, 1963) in 1978 with 5 gold and a silver.

Most Olympic Gold Medals

The greatest number of Olympic gold medals won is 9 by Mark Andrew Spitz (US) (b Feb 10, 1950), as follows:

100 m freestyle	1972
200 m freestyle	1972
100 m butterfly	1972
200 m butterfly	1972
4 × 100 m freestyle relay	1968 and 1972
4 × 200 m freestyle relay	1968 and 1972
4 × 100 m medley relay	1972

All but one of these performances (the 4 × 200 m relay of 1968) were also new world records at the time.

FASTEST BACKSTROKE (left): John Naber set 2 world records to win 2 gold medals in the 1976 Olympics. MOST TITLES (right): Tracy Caulkins won 6 medals (5 gold) in one world championship. At 16, she was the youngest recipient of the Sullivan Award (1978), honoring the outstanding amateur athlete.

SWIMMING—WORLD RECORDS—WOMEN
(As of Aug 1980)

Distance	min sec	Name and Nationality	Place	Date
FREESTYLE				
100 m	54.79	Barbara Krause (E Germany)	Moscow, USSR	July 21, 1980
200 m	1:58.23	Cynthia Woodhead (US)	Tokyo, Japan	Sept 3, 1979
400 m	4:06.28	Tracey Wickham (Australia)	W Berlin, W Germany	Aug 24, 1978
800 m	8:24.62	Tracey Wickham (Australia)	Edmonton, Canada	Aug 5, 1978
1,500 m	16:04.49	Kim Linehan (US)	Ft Lauderdale, Fla	Aug 19, 1979
4 × 100 Relay	3:42.71	E Germany	Moscow, USSR	July 27, 1980
		(Barbara Krause, Caren Metschuck, Ines Diers, Sarina Hulsenbeck)		
BREASTSTROKE				
100 m	1:10.11	Ute Geweniger (E Germany)	Moscow, USSR	July 24, 1980
200 m	2:28.36	Lina Kachushite (USSR)	Potsdam, E Germany	Apr 6, 1979
BUTTERFLY STROKE				
100 m	59.26	Mary Meagher (US)	Austin, Tex	Apr 11, 1980
200 m	2:06.37	Mary Meagher (US)	Irvine, Calif	July 30, 1980
BACKSTROKE				
100 m	1:00.86	Rica Reinisch (E Germany)	Moscow, USSR	July 23, 1980
200 m	2:11.77	Rica Reinisch (E Germany)	Moscow, USSR	July 27, 1980
INDIVIDUAL MEDLEY				
200 m	2:13.00	Petra Schneider (E Germany)	Magdeburg, E Germany	May 24, 1980
400 m	4:36.29	Petra Schneider (E Germany)	Moscow, USSR	July 26, 1980
MEDLEY RELAY				
4 × 100 m	4:06.67	E German National Team	Moscow, USSR	July 20, 1980
		(Backstroke, Breaststroke, Butterfly Stroke, Freestyle)		
		(Rica Reinisch, Ute Geweniger, Andrea Pollack, Sarina Hulsenbeck)		

FREESTYLE RECORD (left): Cynthia Woodhead holds the 200 m freestyle record. MOST MEDALS AND RECORDS (above): Kornelia Ender won 8 world titles, captured 8 Olympic medals (4 gold) and broke 23 world records in her career.

The record number of gold medals won by a woman is 4 shared by Mrs Patricia McCormick (*née* Keller) (US) (b May 12, 1930) with the High and Springboard Diving double in 1952 and 1956 (also the women's record for individual golds); by Dawn Fraser (later Mrs Gary Ware) (Australia) (b Sept 4, 1937) with the 100 m freestyle (1956, 60, 64) and the 4 × 100 m freestyle relay (1956); and by Kornelia Ender (now Matthes) (E Germany) (b Plauen, E Germany, Oct 25, 1958) with the 100 and 200 m freestyle (1976), the 100 m butterfly (1976) and the 4 × 100 m medley relay (1976). Dawn Fraser is the only swimmer to win the same event on three successive occasions.

Most Olympic Medals

The most medals won is 11 by Spitz, who in addition to his 9 golds (see above), won a silver (100 m butterfly) and a bronze (100 m freestyle), both in 1968.

The most medals won by a woman is 8 by Dawn Fraser, who in addition to her 4 golds (see above) won 4 silvers (400 m freestyle 1956, 4 × 100 m freestyle relay 1960 and 1964, 4 × 100 m medley relay 1960); by Shirley Babashoff (US) who won 2 golds (4 × 100 m freestyle relay 1972 and 1976) and 6 silvers (100 m freestyle 1972, 200 m freestyle 1972 and 1976, 400 m and 800 m freestyle 1976, and 400 m medley 1976); and by Kornelia Ender (E Germany) who, in addition to her 4 golds (see above), won 4 silvers (200 m individual medley 1972, 4 × 100 m medley 1972, 4 × 100 m freestyle 1972 and 1976).

Most Individual Gold Medals

The record number of individual gold medals won is 4 shared by four swimmers: Charles M. Daniels (US) (1884–1973) (100 m freestyle 1906 and 1908, 220 yd freestyle 1904, 440 yd freestyle 1904); Roland Matthes (E Germany) (b Nov 17, 1950) with 100 m and 200 m backstroke 1968 and 1972 and Spitz and McCormick (see above).

Closest Verdict

The closest victory in the Olympic Games was in the Munich 400 m individual medley final on Aug 30, 1972, when Gunnar Larsson (Sweden) won by 2/1,000ths of a sec in 4 min 31.981 sec over Tim McKee (US)—a margin of less than ⅛ in, or the length grown by a fingernail in 3 weeks. This led to a change in international rules with timings and places decided to hundredths.

Olympic Medals for Diving

Klaus Dibiasi (Italy) won a total of 5 medals (3 gold, 2 silver) in 4 Games from 1964 to 1976. He is also the only diver to win the same event (highboard) at 3 successive Games (1968, 1972, and 1976). Pat McCormick (see above) won 4 gold medals.

World Diving Titles

Phil Boggs (US) (b Dec 29, 1949) has won 3 gold medals, in 1973, 75 and 78, but Klaus Dibiasi of Italy won 4 medals (2 gold and 2 silver) in 1973 and 1975. Trina Kalinina (USSR) (b Feb 8, 1959) won 5 medals (3 gold, 1 silver, 1 bronze) in 1973, 75 and 78.

DIVING MEDALIST: Klaus Dibiasi has dominated men's diving competition with 5 Olympic medals and 4 world championship medals between 1964 and 1976.

Perfect Dive

In the 1972 US Olympic Trials, held in Chicago, Michael Finneran (b Sept 21, 1948) was awarded a score of 10 by all seven judges for a backward 1½ somersault 2½ twist free dive from the 10-m board, an achievement without precedent.

Long Distance Swimming

A unique achievement in long distance swimming was established in 1966 by Mihir Sen of Calcutta, India. He swam the Palk Strait from Sri Lanka to India (in 25 hours 36 min, Apr 5–6); the Straits of Gibraltar (Europe to Africa in 8 hours 1 min on Aug 24); the Dardanelles (Gallipoli, Europe, to Sedulbahir, Asia Minor, in 13 hours 55 min on Sept 12) and the entire length of the Panama Canal in 34 hours 15 min, Oct 29–31. He had earlier swum the English Channel in 14 hours 45 min on Sept 27, 1958.

The longest ocean swim claimed is one of 128.8 miles by Walter Poenisch (US) (b 1914), who started from Havana, Cuba, and arrived at Little Duck Key, Fla (in a shark cage and wearing flippers) 34 hours 15 min later, July 11–13, 1978.

The greatest recorded distance ever swum is 1,826 miles down the Mississippi from Ford Dam, near Minneapolis, to Carrollton Avenue, New Orleans, July 6 to Dec 29, 1930, by Fred P. Newton, then 27, of Clinton, Okla. He was in the water a total of 742 hours, and the water temperature fell as low as 47° F. He protected himself with petroleum jelly.

The longest duration swim ever achieved was one of 168 continuous hours, ending on Feb 24, 1941, by the legless Charles Zibbelman, *alias* Zimmy (b 1894), of the US, in a pool in Honolulu, Hawaii.

The longest duration swim by a woman was 87 hours 27 min in a salt water pool at Raven Hall, Coney Island, NY by Mrs Myrtle Huddleston of NYC, in 1931. Margaret "Peggy" Byrne (US) (b Dec 17, 1949), a Minnesota State Representative, swam 60 hours 15 min in a freshwater pool at Saint Paul, Minn, Dec 18–20, 1978.

The greatest distance covered in a continuous swim is 292 miles by Joe Maciag (b March 26, 1956) from Billings to Glendive, Mont, in the Yellowstone River in 64 hours 50 min, July 1–4, 1976.

Bertrand Malègue (France) (21) swam 54.38 miles in 24 hours in a pool at St Étienne, France, May 31–June 1, 1980.

Earliest Channel Swimmers

The first man to swim across the English Channel (without a life jacket) was the merchant navy captain Matthew Webb (1848–83) (GB), who swam breaststroke from Dover, England, to Calais Sands, France, in 21 hours 45 min, Aug 24–25, 1875. Webb swam an estimated 38 miles to make the 21-mile crossing. Paul Boyton (US) had swum from Cap Gris Nez to the South Foreland in his patent lifesaving suit in 23 hours 30 min, May 28–29, 1875. There is good evidence that Jean-Marie Saletti, a French soldier, escaped from a British prison hulk off Dover by swimming to Boulogne in July or Aug 1815. The first crossing from France to England was made by Enrico Tiraboschi, a wealthy Italian living in Argentina, who crossed in 16 hours 33 min on Aug 12, 1923, to win a $5,000 prize.

The first woman to succeed was Gertrude Ederle (b Oct 23, 1906) (US) who swam from Cap Gris Nez, France, to Deal, England, on Aug 6, 1926, in the then record time of 14 hours 39 min. The first woman to swim from England to France was Florence Chadwick of California, in 16 hours 19 min on Sept 11, 1951.

Youngest and Oldest Channel Swimmers

The youngest conqueror is Marcus Hooper (b June 14, 1967) of Eltham, England, who swam from Dover to Sangatte, France, in 14 hours 37 min, when he was aged 12 years 53 days. The youngest woman was Abla Adel Khairi (b Egypt, Sept 26, 1960), aged 13 years 326 days when she swam from England to France in 12 hours 30 min on Aug 17, 1974.

The oldest conqueror of the 21-mile crossing has been James Edward "Doc" Counsilman (b Dec 28, 1920), head coach of the 1976 US Olympic Swim team, who was 58 years 260 days when he swam from Dover to Cap Gris Nez on Sept 14, 1979. The oldest woman to conquer the Channel was Stella Taylor (b Bristol, Avon, England, Dec 20, 1929), aged 45 years 350 days when she swam it in 18 hours 15 min on Aug 26, 1975.

FASTEST DOUBLE CROSSING: Cynthia Nicholas (left) swam the fastest double crossing of the English Channel, breaking her own record. She had conquered the channel 10 times to Sept 1979. MOST CONSECUTIVE TITLES: Rumania's Angelica Rozeanu won 6 straight table tennis titles, 1950–55.

Fastest and Slowest Channel Crossings

The official Channel Swimming Association record is 7 hours 40 min by Penny Dean (b March 21, 1955) of California, who swam from Shakespeare Beach, Dover, England to Cap Gris Nez, France on July 29, 1978.

The slowest crossing was the third ever made, when Henry Sullivan (US) swam from England to France in 26 hours 50 min, Aug 5–6, 1923. It is estimated that he swam some 56 miles.

Channel Relays

The two-way record is 16 hours 5½ min by Six Saudi Arabian men on Aug 11, 1977. They completed the return journey from France to England in a record 7 hours 58 min.

Double Crossings of the English Channel

Antonio Abertondo (Argentina), aged 42, swam from England to France in 18 hours 50 min (8:35 a.m. on Sept 20 to 3:25 a.m. on Sept 21, 1961) and after about 4 minutes' rest returned to England in 24 hours 16 min, landing at St Margaret's Bay at 3:45 a.m. on Sept 22, 1961, to complete the first "double crossing" in 43 hours 10 min.

Cynthia Nicholas, a 19-year-old from Canada, became the first woman to complete a double crossing of the English Channel, Sept 7–8, 1977. Her astonishing time of 19 hours 55 min was more than 10 hours faster than the previous mark. She achieved a still faster time of 19 hours 12 min, Aug 4–5, 1979.

Most Conquests of the English Channel

The greatest number of Channel conquests is 17 by Michael Read (GB), to Oct 28, 1979, including a record 6 in one year. Cindy Nicholas made her first crossing of the Channel on July 29, 1975, and her tenth on Sept 1, 1979.

Underwater Channel Swim

The first underwater cross-Channel swim was achieved by Fred Baldasare (US), aged 38, who completed a 42-mile swim from France to England with scuba in 18 hours 1 min, July 10–11, 1962.

Relay Records

The longest recorded mileage in a 24-hour relay swim (team of 5) is 89 miles 1,455.3 yd by a team from Loughborough University, Leicestershire, England, May 13–14, 1980.

The fastest time recorded for 100 miles in a pool by a team of 20 swimmers is 22 hours 8 min 15 sec at Menzieshill High School, Dundee, Scotland, Feb 23–24, 1980.

Treading Water

The duration record for treading water (vertical posture in an 8-ft square without touching the lane markers) is 64 hours by Norman Albert at Pennsylvania State University, Nov 1–4, 1978.

TABLE TENNIS

Earliest Reference

The earliest evidence relating to a game resembling table tennis has been found in the catalogues of London sporting goods manufacturers in the 1880's. The old Ping-Pong Association was formed there in 1902, but the game proved only a temporary craze until resuscitated in 1921.

Fastest Rallying

The record number of hits in 60 sec is 162 by Nicky Jarvis and Desmond Douglas in London, England, on Dec 1, 1976. This was equaled by Douglas and Paul Day at Blackpool, England, on March 21, 1977. The most by women is 148 by Linda Howard and Melodi Ludi at Blackpool, Lancashire, England, on Oct 11, 1977.

With a paddle in each hand, Gary D. Fisher of Olympia, Wash, completed 5,000 consecutive volleys over the net in 44 min 28 sec on June 25, 1979.

Longest Rally

In a 1936 Swaythling Cup match in Prague between Alex Ehrlich (Poland) and Paneth Farcas (Rumania), the opening rally lasted 1 hour 58 min.

Robert Siegel and Donald Peters of Stamford, Conn, staged a rally lasting 8 hours 33 min on July 30, 1978.

Longest Match

In the Swaythling Cup final match between Austria and Rumania in Prague, Czechoslovakia, in 1936, the play lasted for 11 hours, beginning Sunday, March 15, and completed the following Wednesday.

Marathon

The longest recorded time for a marathon singles match by two players is 132 hours 31 min by Danny Price and Randy Nunes in Cherry Hill, NJ, Aug 20–26, 1978.

The longest doubles marathon by 4 players is 101 hours 1 min 11 sec by Lance, Phil and Mark Warren and Bill Weir at Sacramento, Calif, Apr 9–13, 1979.

Highest Speed

No conclusive measurements have been published, but in a lecture M. Sklorz (W Germany) stated that a smashed ball had been measured at speeds up to 105.6 mph.

Youngest International

The youngest international (in any sport) was Joy Foster, aged 8, when she represented Jamaica in the West Indies Championships at Port of Spain, Trinidad, in Aug 1958.

TENNIS

Origins

The modern game of lawn tennis is generally agreed to have evolved as an outdoor form of Royal Tennis. "Field Tennis" was mentioned in an English magazine (*Sporting Magazine*) on Sept 29, 1793. The earliest club for such a game, variously called Pelota or Lawn Rackets, was the Leamington Club, founded in 1872 by Major Harry Gem. In Feb 1874, Major Walter Clopton Wingfield of England (1833–1912) patented a form called "sphairistike," but the game soon became known as lawn tennis.

Amateurs were permitted to play with and against professionals in Open tournaments starting in 1968.

Most Davis Cup Victories

The greatest number of wins in the Davis Cup (instituted 1900) has been (inclusive of 1979) by the US with 26.

Individual Davis Cup Performance

Nicola Pietrangeli (Italy) (b Sept 11, 1933) played 164 rubbers, 1954 to 1972, winning 120. He played 110 singles (winning 78) and 54 doubles (winning 42). He took part in 66 ties.

Greatest Domination

The "grand slam" is to hold at the same time all four of the world's major championship titles: Wimbledon, the US Open, Australian and French championships. The first time this occurred was in 1935 when

GRAND SLAM WINNERS: The only men to win all 4 major titles in the same year were Rod Laver (left) of Australia who performed the feat twice in 1962 and 1969, and Don Budge (right) of the US who did it once in 1937–38.

Frederick John Perry (GB) (b 1909) won the French title, having won Wimbledon (1934), the US title (1933–34) and the Australian title (1934).

The first player to hold all four titles simultaneously was J. Donald Budge (US) (b June 13, 1915), who won the championships of Wimbledon (1937), the US (1937), Australia (1938), and France (1938). He subsequently retained Wimbledon (1938) and the US (1938). Rodney George Laver (Australia) (b Aug 9, 1938) achieved this grand slam in 1962 as an amateur and repeated as a professional in 1969 to become the first two-time grand slammer.

Two women players also have won all these four titles in the same tennis year. The first was Maureen Catherine Connolly (US). She won the US title in 1951, Wimbledon in 1952, retained the US title in 1952, won the Australian in 1953, the French in 1953, and Wimbledon again in 1953. She won her third US title in 1953, her second French title in 1954, and her third Wimbledon title in 1954. Miss Connolly (later Mrs Norman Brinker) was seriously injured in a riding accident shortly before the 1954 US championships; she died in June 1969, aged only 34.

The second woman to win the "grand slam" was Margaret Smith Court (Australia) (b July 16, 1942) in 1970.

Olympic Medals

Lawn tennis was part of the program at the first 8 celebrations of the Games (including 1906). The winner of the most medals was Max Decugis (1882–1978) of France, with 6 (a record 4 gold, 1 silver and 1 bronze) in the 1900, 1906 and 1920 tournaments.

The most medals won by a woman is 5 by Kitty McKane (later Mrs L. A. Godfree) of GB, with 1 gold, 2 silver and 2 bronze in 1920 and 1924. Five different women won a record 2 gold medals.

Greatest Crowd

The greatest crowd at a tennis match was the 30,472 who came to the Houston Astrodome in Houston, Tex, on Sept 20, 1973, to watch Billie Jean King beat Bobby Riggs, over 25 years her senior, in straight sets in the so-called "Tennis Match of the Century."

The record for an orthodox match is 25,578 at Sydney, Australia, on Dec 27, 1954, in the Davis Cup Challenge Round vs the US (1st day).

Highest Earnings

The greatest reward for playing a single match is the $500,000 won by Jimmy Connors (US) (b Sept 2, 1952) when he beat John Newcombe (Australia) (b May 23, 1944) in a challenge match at Caesars Palace Hotel, Las Vegas, Nev, Apr 26, 1975.

According to the USTA, the record winnings for a year, not including special restricted events and team tennis salaries, is $1,019,345 by Bjorn Borg (Sweden) in 1979. The women's record is $747,548 in 1979 by Martina Navratilova (b Prague, Oct 18, 1956).

Fastest Service

The fastest service ever *measured* was one of 163.6 mph by William Tatem Tilden (1893–1953) (US) in 1931. The American professional Scott Carnahan, 22, was electronically clocked at 137 mph at Pauley Pavilion in Los Angeles during the third annual "Cannonball Classic" sponsored by *Tennis* magazine, and reported in the fall of 1976.

Some players consider the service of Robert Falkenburg (US) (b Jan 29, 1926), the 1948 Wimbledon champion, as the fastest ever produced.

HIGHEST EARNINGS: Both Bjorn Borg (left) and Martina Navratilova (right) set records in 1979 for greatest winnings in one year. Borg earned over $1 million. In addition, he won his 5th straight Wimbledon singles title in 1980.

Tennis Marathons

The longest recorded tennis singles match is one of 105 hours by Ricky Tolston and Jeff Sutton at Bill Faye Park, Kinston, NC, May 7–11, 1979.

The duration record for doubles is 84 hours 7 min by Daryl Murray, Richard Monao, Stephen Duerden and Stephen Foord at the Racquet Centre, Silverwater, NSW, Australia, Jan 7–10, 1980.

Longest Game

The longest known singles game was one of 37 deuces (80 points) between Anthony Fawcett (Rhodesia) and Keith Glass (GB) in the first round of the Surrey championships at Surbiton, Surrey, England, on May 26, 1975. It lasted 31 min.

Longest Career

The championship career of C. Alphonso Smith (b March 18, 1909) of Charlottesville, Va, extended from winning the US National Boy's title at Chicago on Aug 14, 1924, to winning the National 70-and-over title at Santa Barbara, Calif, in Aug 1979. Smith has won 31 US National titles in all.

WIMBLEDON RECORDS

The first Championship was in 1877. Professionals first played in 1968. From 1971 the tie-break system was introduced, which effactually prevents sets proceeding beyond a 17th game, i.e., 9–8.

Most Appearances

Arthur W. Gore (1868–1928) (GB) made 36 appearances between 1888 and 1927, and was in 1909 at 41 years the oldest singles winner ever. In 1964 Jean Borotra (b Aug 13, 1898) of France made his 35th appearance since 1922. In 1977 he appeared in the Veterans' Doubles, aged 78.

Most Wins

Six-time singles champion Billie Jean King (*née* Moffitt) has also won 10 women's doubles and 4 mixed doubles during the period 1961 to 1979, to total a record 20 titles.

The greatest number of singles wins was 8 by Helen N. Moody (*née* Wills) (b Oct 6, 1905) (US), who won in 1927–30, 1932–33, 1935 and 1938.

The greatest number of singles wins by a man since the Challenge Round (wherein the defending champion was given a bye until the final round) was abolished in 1922 is 5 consecutively by Bjorn Borg (Sweden) (b June 6, 1956) in 1976–80. The all-time men's record was seven by William C. Renshaw in 1881 and 1889.

The greatest number of doubles wins by men was 8 by the brothers Doherty (GB)—Reginald Frank (1872–1910) and Hugh Lawrence (1875–1919). They won each year from 1897 to 1905 except for 1902. Hugh Doherty also won 5 singles titles (1902–06) and holds the record for most men's titles with 13.

The most wins in women's doubles was 12 by Elizabeth "Bunny" Ryan (US) (1894–1979). The greatest number of mixed doubles wins was 7 by Elizabeth Ryan, giving her a record total of 19 doubles wins.

MOST WIMBLEDON VICTORIES: Billie Jean King tosses her racket in the air to celebrate one of her record 20 Wimbledon titles.

The men's mixed doubles record is 4 wins, shared by Elias Victor Seixas (b Aug 30, 1923) (US) in 1953–56, Kenneth N. Fletcher (b June 15, 1940) (Australia) in 1963, 65–66 and 68, and Owen Keir Davidson (Australia) (b Oct 4, 1943) in 1967, 71 and 73–74.

Youngest Champions

The youngest champion ever at Wimbledon was Charlotte (Lottie) Dod (1871–1960), who was 15 years 9 months old when she won in 1887.

The youngest male singles champion was Wilfred Baddeley (b Jan 11, 1872), who won the Wimbledon title in 1891 at the age of 19 years 175 days.

Richard Dennis Ralston (b July 27, 1942), of Bakersfield, Calif, was 25 days short of his 18th birthday when he won the men's doubles with Rafael H. Osuna (1938–69), of Mexico, in 1960.

The youngest-ever player at Wimbledon is reputedly Miss Mita Klima (Austria), who was 13 years old in the 1907 singles competition. The youngest of modern times is Tracy Austin (US) (b Dec 12, 1962) who was only 14 years 7 months in the 1977 tournament.

Greatest Attendance

The record crowd for one day a Wimbledon is 38,295 on June 27, 1979. The total attendance record was set at the 1979 Championships with 343,091.

TRACK AND FIELD

Earliest References

Track and field athletics date from the ancient Olympic Games. The earliest accurately known Olympiad dates from July 776 BC, at which celebration Coroibos won the foot race. The oldest surviving measurements are a long jump of 23 ft 1½ in by Chionis of Sparta c. 656 BC, and a discus throw of 100 cubits (c. 152 ft) by Protesilaus.

Oldest Race

The oldest continuously held foot race is the "Red Hose Race" held at Carnwath, Scotland, since 1507. First prize is a pair of hand-knitted knee-length red stockings. Michael Glen, of Bathgate, won a record 14 times, 1951–66.

Earliest Landmarks

The first time 10 sec ("even time") was bettered for 100 yd under championship conditions was when John Owen, then 30 years old, recorded 9 4/5 sec in the AAU Championships at Analostan Island, Wash, DC, on Oct 11, 1890. The first recorded instance of 6 ft being cleared in the high jump was when Marshall Jones Brooks (1855–1944) jumped 6 ft 0⅛ in at Marston, near Oxford, England, on March 17, 1876. The breaking of the "4-minute barrier" in the one mile was first achieved by Dr Roger Gilbert Bannister (b Harrow, England, March 23, 1929), when he recorded 3 min 59.4 sec on the Iffley Road track, Oxford, at 6:10 p.m. on May 6, 1954.

Most Records in a Day

The only athlete to have his name entered in the record book 6 times in one day was J. C. "Jesse" Owens (US) (1913–80) who at Ann Arbor, Mich, on May 25, 1935, equaled the 100-yd running record with 9.4 sec at 3:15 p.m.; long-jumped 26 ft 8¼ in at 3:25 p.m.; ran 220 yd (straight away) in 20.3 sec at 3:45 p.m.; and 220 yd over low hurdles in 22.6 sec at 4 p.m. The two 220-yd runs were also ratified as 200 m world records.

Fastest Runners

Robert Lee Hayes (b Dec 20, 1942), of Jacksonville, Fla, may have reached a speed of over 27 mph at St Louis, on June 21, 1963, in his then

ONE DAY'S WORK: Jesse Owens (left) performed the incredible feat of setting 6 world records in 45 min in 1935. EVEN TIME 100: In 1970, Chi Cheng (right) ran the first women's 10-sec 100 yd. In the same year, she won all 63 races she entered and set 5 world records.

WORLD RECORDS—MEN

The complete list of World Records for the 32 scheduled men's events (excluding the walking records, see under Walking) passed by the International Amateur Athletic Federation as of Aug 1980. Those marked with an asterisk* are awaiting ratification. Note: On July 27, 1976, IAAF eliminated all records for races measured in yards, except for the mile (for sentimental reasons). All distances up to (and including) 400 m must be electrically timed to be records. When a time is given to one-hundredth of a second, it represents the official electrically-timed record. In one case, a professional performance has bettered or equaled the IAAF mark, but the same highly rigorous rules as to timing, measuring and weighing are not necessarily applied.

RUNNING

Event	min sec	Name and Nationality	Place	Date
100 m	9.95	James Ray Hines (US)	Mexico City	Oct 14, 1968
200 m (turn)	19.72	Pietro Mennea (Italy)	Mexico City	Sept 12, 1979
400 m	43.86	Lee Edward Evans (US)	Mexico City	Oct 18, 1968
800 m	1:42.4*	Sebastian Newbold Coe (GB)	Oslo	July 5, 1979
1,000 m	2:13.4*	Sebastian Newbold Coe (GB)	Oslo	July 1, 1980
1,500 m	3:32.1	Steven Michael James Ovett (GB)	Oslo	July 15, 1980
	3:32.1	Sebastian Newbold Coe (GB)	Zurich	Aug 15, 1979
1 mile	3:48.8*	Steven Michael James Ovett (GB)	Oslo	July 1, 1980
2,000 m	4:51.4	John Walker (NZ)	Oslo	June 30, 1976
3,000 m	7:32.1	Henry Rono (Kenya)	Oslo	June 27, 1978
5,000 m	13:08.4	Henry Rono (Kenya)	Berkeley, Calif	Apr 8, 1978
10,000 m	27:22.4	Henry Rono (Kenya)	Vienna	June 11, 1978
20,000 m	57:24.2	Jos Hermens (Netherlands)	Papendal, Netherlands	May 1, 1976
25,000 m	1 hr. 14:11.8	William Rodgers (US)	Saratoga, Calif	Feb 21, 1979
30,000 m	1 hr. 31:30.4	James Noel Carroll Alder (UK)	Crystal Palace, London	Sept 5, 1970
1 hour	13 miles 24⅔ yd	Jos Hermens (Netherlands)	Papendal, Netherlands	May 1, 1976

HURDLING

110 m (3′6″)	13.00	Renaldo Nehemiah (US)	Westwood, Calif	May 6, 1979
400 m (3′0″)	47.13	Edwin Corley Moses (US)	Milan	July 3, 1980
3,000 m Steeplechase	8:05.4	Henry Rono (Kenya)	Seattle, Wash	May 13, 1978

DECATHLON

8,649 points*		Guido Kratschmer (W Germany)	Burghausen, W Germany	June 13–14, 1980

(First day: 100 m 10.58 sec, long jump 25 ft 7¼ in, shot put 50 ft 9¼ in, high jump 6 ft 6¾ in, 400 m 48.04 sec; second day: 110 m hurdles 13.92 sec, discus 149 ft 4 in, pole vault 15 ft 1 in, javelin 218 ft 0½ in, 1,500 m 4 min 24.15 sec.)

THE MARATHON

There is no official marathon record because of the varying severity of courses. The best time over 26 miles 385 yd (standardized in 1924) is 2 hours 08 min 33.6 sec (average 12.24 mph) by Derek Clayton (b 1942 at Barrow-in-Furness, England) of Australia, at Antwerp, Belgium, on May 30, 1969.

The fastest time by a female is 2 hours 27 min 33 sec (average 10.31 mph) by Grete Waitz (Norway) (b Oct 1, 1953) in NYC on Oct 21, 1979.

FASTEST 100 M (left): The record set at the 1968 Olympic Games by Jim Hines has now stood for over 10 years. FOUR RECORDS fell to Henry Rono (right) in 3 months, as he set new marks at 3,000 m, 5,000 m, 10,000 m, and 3,000 m steeplechase in spring 1978.

IN THE DISTANCE: Sebastian Coe (left) holds the world records at 800, 1,000 and 1,500 m. He picked up an Olympic gold medal in Moscow in 1980. Derek Clayton (above) ran the fastest marathon ever, at Antwerp, Belgium in 1969.

Men's World Records *(continued)*

FIELD EVENTS

Event	ft	in	Name and Nationality	Place	Date
High Jump	7	8¾	Gerd Wessig (E Germany)	Moscow	Aug 1, 1980
Pole Vault	18	11½*	Wladyslaw Kozakiewicz (Poland)	Moscow	July 30, 1980
Long Jump	29	2½	Robert Beamon (US)	Mexico City	Oct 18, 1968
Triple Jump	58	8½	Joao de Oliveira (Brazil)	Mexico City	Oct 15, 1975
Shot Put	72	8	Udo Beyer (E Germany)	Gothenburg, Sweden	July 6, 1978
Discus Throw	233	5	Wolfgang Schmidt (E Germany)	E Berlin	Aug 9, 1978
Hammer Throw	268	4½*	Yuri Sedykh (USSR)	Moscow	July 31, 1980
Javelin Throw	317	4	Ferenc Paragi (Hungary)	Tata, Hungary	Apr 23, 1980

Note: One professional performance which was equal or superior to the IAAF marks, but where the same highly rigorous rules as to timing, measuring and weighing were not necessarily applied, was the Shot Put of 75 ft by Brian Ray Oldfield (US), at El Paso, Tex, on May 10, 1975.

RELAYS

Event	min sec	Team	Place	Date
4 × 100 m	38.03	US Team (William Collins, Steven Earl Riddick, Clifford Wiley, Steven Williams)	Düsseldorf, W Germany	Sept 3, 1977
4 × 200 m	1:20.3†	University of Southern California (US) (Joel Andrews, James Sanford, William Mullins, Clancy Edwards)	Tempe, Ariz	May 27, 1978
4 × 400 m	2:56.1	US Olympic Team (Vincent Matthews, Ronald Freeman, G. Lawrence James, Lee Edward Evans)	Mexico City	Oct 20, 1968
4 × 800 m	7:08.1	USSR Team (Vladimir Podoliakov, Nikolai Kirov, Vladimir Malosemlin, Anatoli Reschetniak)	Podolsk, USSR	Aug 12, 1978
4 × 1,500 m	14:38.8	W German Team (Thomas Wessinghage, Harald Hudak, Michael Lederer, Karl Fleschen)	Cologne, W Germany	Aug 17, 1977

† The time of 1:20.2 achieved by the Tobias Striders at Tempe, Ariz on May 27, 1978 was not ratified as the team was composed of varied nationalities.

world record 9.1 sec for 100 yd. Marlies Göhr (*née* Oelsner) (b E Germany, March 21, 1958) reached a speed of over 24 mph in her world record 100 m in 10.88 sec at Dresden, E Germany, on July 1, 1977.

Oldest and Youngest Recordbreakers

The greatest age at which anyone has broken a standard world record is 41 years 196 days in the case of John J. Flanagan (1868–1938), who set a world record in the hammer throw on July 24, 1909. The female record is 35 years 255 days for Dana Zátopkova (*née* Ingrova) (b Sept 19, 1922) of Czechoslovakia, who broke the women's javelin record with 182 ft 10 in at Prague, Czechoslovakia, on June 1, 1958.

Ulrike Meyfarth (b May 4, 1956) (W Germany) equaled the world record for the women's high jump at 6 ft 3½ in winning the gold medal at the Munich Olympics, 1972, when she was aged 16 years 123 days. Barbara Jones (US) was aged 15 years 123 days when she was part of a record-setting 4 × 100 m relay team in the 1952 Olympics.

Highest Jumper

There are several reported instances of high jumpers exceeding the official world record height of 7 ft 8 in. The earliest of these came from unsubstantiated reports of Watusi tribesmen in Central Africa clearing up to 8 ft 2½ in, definitely, however, from inclined take-offs. The greatest height cleared above an athlete's own head is 23¼ in by Franklin Jacobs (US), who cleared 7 ft 7¼ in despite a physical height of only 5 ft 8 in, at NY on Jan 28, 1978.

The greatest height cleared by a woman above her own head is 10¼ in by Tamami Yagi (Japan) (b Nov 15, 1958), who stands 5 ft 4½ in tall and jumped 6 ft 2¾ in at Matsumoto, Japan, on Oct 19, 1978.

Longest Career

Duncan McLean (b Gourock, Scotland, Dec 3, 1884) won the South African 100-yd title in Feb 1904, in 9.9 sec, and at age 91 set a world age-group record for 100 m in 21.7 sec in Aug 1977—more than 72 years later.

Dimitrion Yordanidis completed a marathon race in 7 hours 33 min at the age of 98 in Athens, Greece, on Oct 10, 1976.

OVER THEIR HEADS: The greatest heights cleared over their own heads by a man and a woman are, respectively, 23¼ in by Franklin Jacobs (left) and 10¼ in by Tamami Yagi (above).

WORLD RECORDS—WOMEN

RUNNING

Event	min sec	Name and Nationality	Place	Date
100 m	10.88	Marlies Oelsner (now Göhr) (E Germany)	Dresden	July 1, 1977
200 m (turn)	21.71	Marita Koch (E Germany)	Karl Marx Stadt, E Germany	June 10, 1979
400 m	48.94	Marita Koch (E Germany)	Prague	Aug 31, 1978
800 m	1:53.5*	Nadyezhda Olizarenko (*née* Mushta) (USSR)	Moscow	July 27, 1980
1,500 m	3:55.0*	Tatyana Kazankina (USSR)	Moscow	July 6, 1980
1 mile	4:21.7††	Mary Decker (US)	Auckland, NZ	Jan 26, 1980
3,000 m	8:27.2	Ludmila Bragina (USSR)	College Park, Md	Aug 7, 1976

HURDLES

100 m (2'9")	12.36*	Grazyna Rabsztyn (Poland)	Warsaw	June 13, 1980
400 m (2'6")	54.28*	Karin Rossley (E Germany)	Jena, E Germany	May 17, 1980

FIELD EVENTS

Event	ft in	Name and Nationality	Place	Date
High Jump	6 7	Sara Simeoni (Italy)	Brescia, Italy	Aug 4, 1978
Long Jump	23 3¼	Vilma Bardauskiene (USSR)	Prague	Aug 29, 1978
Shot Put	73 7†	Ilona Slupianek (*née* Schoknecht) (E Germany)	Potsdam	May 11, 1980
Discus Throw	235 7*	Marica Vergoni (Bulgaria)	Sofia	July 13, 1980
Javelin Throw	229 11*	Tatyana Biryulina (USSR)	Minsk, USSR	July 12, 1980

† Helena Fibingerova (Czech) set an indoor record of 73 ft 10 in at Jablonec, Czechoslovakia, on Feb 19, 1977.
†† Decker ran an indoor mile in 4:17.6 in Houston, Feb 16, 1980. No official record was set as the track was "oversize."

PENTATHLON

5,083 points*	Nadyezhda Tkachenko (USSR) (100 m hurdles 13.29 sec, shot put 55 ft 3 in, high jump 6 ft 0¼ in, long jump 22 ft 1 in, 800 m 2 min 5.20 sec.)	Moscow	July 24, 1980

RELAYS

Event	min sec	Team	Place	Date
4 × 100 m	41.60*	E Germany (Romy Müller, Barbara Wöckel, Marlies Göhr, Ingrid Auerswold)	Moscow	Aug 1, 1980
4 × 200 m	1:28.2	E Germany (Marlies Göhr, Romy Müller, Barbara Wöckel, Marita Koch)	Jena, E Germany	Aug 10, 1980
4 × 400 m	3:19.2	E German National Team (Doris Maletzski, Brigitte Rohde, Ellen Streidt, Christina Brehmer)	Montreal	July 31, 1976
4 × 800 m	7:52.3	USSR National Team (Tatyana Providokhina, Valentina Gerasimova, Svetlana Styrkina, Tatyana Kazankina)	Podolsk, USSR	Aug 16, 1976

RUNNING RECORDS: Mary Decker (left) bettered her mile record by nearly 4 sec in an unofficial run on an "oversize" indoor track. Marita Koch (above, right) holds sprint records at 200 m and 400 m. Here, she is running with Irena Szewinska, who has won 7 Olympic medals (3 gold, 2 silver, 2 bronze).

HIGHEST JUMP: Sara Simeoni cleared 6 ft 7 in in Italy in 1978 to set a women's high jump record. She won the high jump competition in the 1980 Olympics.

Most Olympic Gold Medals

The most Olympic gold medals won is 10 (an absolute Olympic record) by Ray C. Ewry (US) (b Oct 14, 1873, d Sept 29, 1937) with:

Standing High Jump	1900, 1904, 1906, 1908
Standing Long Jump	1900, 1904, 1906, 1908
Standing Triple Jump	1900, 1904

The most gold medals won by a woman is 4, a record shared by Francina E. Blankers-Koen (Netherlands) (b Apr 26, 1918) with 100 m, 200 m, 80 m hurdles and 4 × 100 m relay (1948) and Betty Cuthbert (Australia) (b Apr 20, 1938) with 100 m, 200 m, 4 × 100 m relay (1956) and 400 m (1964).

Most Olympic Medals

The most medals won is 12 (9 gold and 3 silver) by Paavo Johannes Nurmi (Finland) (1897–1973) with:

1920 Gold: 10,000 m; Cross-Country, Individual and Team; silver: 5,000 m
1924 Gold: 1,500 m; 5,000 m; 3,000 m Team; Cross-Country, Individual and Team.
1928 Gold: 10,000 m; silver: 5,000 m; 3,000 m steeplechase.

The most medals won by a woman athlete is 7 by Shirley de la Hunty (*née* Strickland) (Australia) (b July 18, 1925) with 3 gold, 1 silver and 3 bronze in the 1948, 1952 and 1956 Games. A recently discovered photo-finish indicates that she finished third, not fourth, in the 1948 200 m event, thus unofficially increasing her total to 8. Irena Szewinska (*née* Kirszenstein) of Poland has also won 7 medals (3 gold, 2 silver, 2 bronze) in 1964, 1968, 1972 and 1976. She is the only woman ever to win Olympic medals in track and field in 4 successive Games.

Most Wins at One Games

The most gold medals at one Olympic celebration is 5 by Nurmi in 1924 (see above) and the most individual is 4 by Alvin C. Kraenzlein (US) (1876–1928) in 1900 with 60 m, 110 m hurdles, 200 m hurdles and long jump.

Oldest and Youngest Olympic Champions

The oldest athlete to win an Olympic title was Irish-born Patrick J. "Babe" McDonald (US) (1878–1954) who was aged 42 years 26 days when he won the 56-lb weight throw at Antwerp, Belgium, on Aug 21, 1920. The oldest female champion was Lia Manoliu (Rumania) (b Apr 25, 1932) aged 36 years 176 days when she won the discus at Mexico City on Oct 18, 1968.

The youngest gold medalist was Barbara Jones (US) (b March 26, 1937) who was a member of the winning 4 × 100 m relay team, aged 15 years 123 days, at Helsinki, Finland, on July 27, 1952. The youngest male champion was Robert Bruce Mathias (US) (b Nov 17, 1930) aged 17 years 263 days when he won the decathlon at London, Aug 5–6, 1948.

Standing Long Jump

Joe Darby (1861–1937), the famous Victorian professional jumper from Dudley, Worcestershire, England, jumped a measured 12 ft 1½ in *without* weights at Dudley Castle, on May 28, 1890. Johan Christian Evandt (Norway) achieved 11 ft 11¾ in as an amateur in Reykjavik, Iceland, on March 11, 1962. The best long jump by a woman is 9 ft 5½ in by

MOST MEDALS: Paavo Nurmi (left) won 12 Olympic medals (9 gold, 3 silver) and might have won more had he not been controversially banned as a "professional" after 1928. Betty Cuthbert (far right) shares the women's record with 4 gold medals.

Oddron Lange-Hokland (Norway) (b Nov 29, 1942) at Stavanger, Norway, on March 6, 1966.

Standing High Jump

The best amateur high jump is 6 ft 2¾ in by Rune Almen (b Oct 20, 1952) (Sweden) at Karlstad, Sweden, on May 30, 1980. Joe Darby (see above), the professional, reportedly cleared 6 ft with his ankles tied at Church Cricket Ground, Dudley, England, on June 11, 1892. The best high jump by a woman is 4 ft 5¼ in by Inger Abrahamsen (Norway) at Heroya, Norway, on March 14, 1965.

Running Backwards

The fastest time recorded for running 100 yd backwards is 13.1 sec by Paul Wilson in Tokyo, Sept 22, 1979. He clocked 14.4 sec for 100 m.

Three-Legged Race

The fastest recorded time for a 100-yd three-legged race is 11.0 sec by Olympic medalists Harry L. Hillman and Lawson Robertson in Brooklyn, NYC, on Apr 24, 1909.

Ambidextrous Shot Put

Allan Feuerbach (US) has put a 16-lb shot a total of 121 ft 6¾ in (51 ft 5 in with his left hand and 70 ft 1¾ in with his right) at Malmö, Sweden, on Aug 24, 1974.

Blind 100 Meters

The fastest time recorded for 100 m by a blind man is 11.4 sec by Graham Henry Salmon (b Sept 5, 1952) of Loughton, Essex, England, at Grangemouth, Scotland, on Sept 2, 1978.

MARATHONERS: The largest field for a marathon was the 11,405 registered runners who ran the 1979 NYC Marathon. Nearly 92% finished the race, including Roger Bourban who ran in a waiter suit and carried a bottle of mineral water (it did not spill) on a tray. Claiming to be the world's fastest waiter, he ran the race in 3 hours 21 min.

One-Legged High Jump

Arnie Boldt (b 1958), of Saskatchewan, Canada, cleared a height of 6 ft 6¾ in indoors in 1977, in spite of the fact that he has only one leg.

Longest Race

The longest race ever staged was the 1929 Transcontinental Race (3,665 miles) from NYC to Los Angeles. The Finnish-born Johnny Salo (1893–1931) was the winner in 79 days, from March 31 to June 18. His elapsed time of 525 hours 57 min 20 sec gave a running average of 6.97 mph. His margin of victory was only 2 min 47 sec.

Endurance

Ernst Mensen (1799–1846) (Norway), a former seaman in the British Navy, is reputed to have run from Istanbul, Turkey, to Calcutta, in West Bengal, India, and back in 59 days in 1836, so averaging an improbable 92.4 miles per day. The greatest non-stop run recorded is 352.9 miles in 121 hours 54 min by Bertil Järlåker (Sweden) at Norrköping, Sweden, May 26–31, 1980. He was moving 95.04% of the time. Max Telford (b Hawick, Scotland, Feb 2, 1935) of New Zealand ran 5,110 miles from Anchorage, Alaska, to Halifax, Nova Scotia, in 106 days 18 hours 45 min from July 25 to Nov 9, 1977.

The 24-hour running record (on a standard track) is 161 miles 545 yd by Ron Bentley, 43, at Walton-on-Thames, Surrey, England, Nov 3–4, 1973. The best by a woman is 123 miles 675 yd by Sue Ellen Trapp (US) (b March 3, 1946) at Miami, Fla, Feb 29–March 1, 1980.

The fastest recorded time for 100 miles is 11 hours 30 min 51 sec by Donald Ritchie (b July 6, 1944) at Crystal Palace, London, on Oct 15, 1977. The best by a woman is 16 hours 50 min 47 sec by Ruth Anderson (b 1929) at Woodside, Calif, June 15–16, 1978.

The greatest distance covered by a man in six days (*i.e.* the 144 permissible hours between Sundays in Victorian times) was 623¾ miles by George Littlewood (England), who required only 141 hours 57½ min for this feat on Dec 3-8, 1888, at the old Madison Square Garden, NYC.

The fastest time for the cross-America run is 53 days, 7 min for 3,046 miles by Tom McGrath (N Ireland) from Aug 29 to Oct 21, 1977.

The greatest racing mileage is the 5,926 miles in 192 races of marathon distance or more by Ted Corbitt (US) (b Jan 31, 1920) from Apr 1951 to the end of 1978.

Jay F. Helgerson (b Feb 3, 1955) of Foster City, Calif, ran a certified marathon (26 miles 385 yd) or longer, each week for 52 weeks from Jan 28, 1979 to Jan 19, 1980, totalling 1,418 racing miles. He claims the secret of his success is that he does not do much mileage during the rest of the week.

The greatest lifetime mileage recorded by any runner is 195,855 miles by Earle Littlewood Dilks (b Sept 24, 1894) of New Castle, Pa, through 1977.

Mass Relay Record

The record for 100 miles by 100 runners belonging to one club is 7 hours 56 min 55.6 sec by Shore AC of New Jersey, on June 5, 1977.

The women's mark is 10 hours 47 min 9.3 sec by a team from the San Francisco Dolphins Southend Running Club, on Apr 3, 1977.

The best time for a 100 × 400 m relay is 1 hour 29 min 11.8 sec (average 53.5 sec) by the Physical Training Institute, Leuven, Belgium, on Apr 19, 1978.

Twelve runners from the Rochester Institute of Technology, NY, ran 2,846.5 miles in relay from Will Rogers State Beach Park, Santa Monica, Calif to Chesapeake Bay, at Annapolis, Md, in 14 days 4 hours 8 min from Nov 22 to Dec 6, 1979.

The longest relay ever run, and the one with the most participants, was by 1,607 students and teachers who covered 6,014.65 miles at Trondheim, Norway, from Oct 21 to Nov 23, 1977.

Pancake Race Record

The annual Housewives Pancake Race at Olney, Buckinghamshire, England, was first mentioned in 1445. The record for the winding 415-yd course (three tosses mandatory) is 61.0 sec, set by Sally Ann Faulkner, 16, on Feb 26, 1974. The record for the counterpart race at Liberal, Kansas, is 58.5 sec by Sheila Turner in the 1975 competition.

TRAMPOLINING

Origin

The sport of trampolining (from the Spanish word *trampolin,* a springboard) dates from 1936, when the prototype "T" model trampoline was developed by George Nissen (US). Trampolines were used in show business at least as early as "The Walloons" of the period, 1910–12.

Marathon Record

The longest recorded trampoline bouncing marathon is one of 1,248 hours (52 days) set by a team of 6 in Phoenix, Ariz, from June 24 to Aug 15, 1974. The solo record is 240 hours (with 5-min breaks per hour permissible) by Darlene Blume, at Matraville RSL Youth Club, NSW, Australia, May 8–18, 1980.

Most Titles

Four men have won a world title (instituted 1964) twice; Dave Jacobs (US) in 1967–68, Wayne Miller (US) in 1966 and 1970, Richard Tison (France) in 1974 and 1976, and Evgeni Janes (USSR), 1976 (shared) and 1978. Judy Wills won 5 women's titles (1964–68).

VOLLEYBALL

Origin

The game was invented as Minnonette in 1895 by William G. Morgan at the YMCA gymnasium at Holyoke, Mass. The International Volleyball Association was formed in Paris in Apr 1947. The ball travels at a speed of up to 70 mph when smashed over the net, which measures 7 ft 11½ in. In the women's game it is 7 ft 4¼ in.

World Titles

World Championships were instituted in 1949. The USSR has won 5 men's titles (1949, 1952, 1960, 1962 and 1978). The USSR won the women's championship in 1952, 1956, 1960 and 1970. The record crowd is 60,000 for the 1952 world title matches in Moscow, USSR.

Most Olympic Medals

The sport was introduced to the Olympic Games for both men and women in 1964. The only volleyball player to win four medals is Inna Ryskal (USSR) (b June 15, 1944), who won a silver medal in 1964 and 1976 and golds in 1968 and 1972.

The record for medals for men is held by Yuriy Poyarkov (USSR), who won gold medals in 1964 and 1968, and a bronze in 1972.

Marathon

The longest recorded volleyball marathon by two teams of six is 75 hours 30 min by 12 players from Kinston, NC, Jan 31–Feb 3, 1980.

WALKING

Longest Annual Race

The Strasbourg-Paris event (instituted in 1926 in the reverse direction) over 313 to 344 miles is the world's longest annual walk event. Gilbert Roger (France) has won 6 times (1949, 53–54, 56–58). The fastest performance is by Roger Pietquin (b 1938) (Belgium) who walked 315 miles in the 1980 race in 60 hours 1 min 10 sec, so (deducting 4 hours of compulsory stops) averaging 5.25 mph.

Longest in 24 hours

The best official performance is 133 miles 21 yd by Huw Neilson (GB) at Walton on Thames, Surrey, England, Oct 14–15, 1960. A distance of 142 miles 448 yd is claimed by Jesse Castañeda (US) at the New Mexico State Fair in Albuquerque, Sept 18–19, 1976. The best by a woman is 118.5 miles by Ann Sayer (GB) at Torcy, France, May 4–5, 1980.

Most Olympic Medals

Walking races have been included in the Olympic schedule since 1906, but walking matches have been known since 1589. The only walker to win 3 gold medals has been Ugo Frigerio (Italy) (1901–68) with the 3,000 m and 10,000 m in 1920 and the 10,000 m in 1924. He also holds the record of most medals with 4 (having additionally won the bronze medal in the 50,000 m in 1932), which total is shared with Vladimir Golubnitschiy (USSR) (b June 2, 1936), who won gold medals for the 10,000 m in 1960 and 1968, the silver in 1972 and the bronze in 1964.

One Hour

The greatest distance covered on the track in one hour is 9 miles 696 yd by Daniel Bautista (Mexico) at Monterey, Mexico on March 27, 1980.

Most Titles

Four-time Olympian Ronald Owen Laird (b May 31, 1938) of the NYAC, won a total of 65 US National titles from 1958 to 1976, plus 4 Canadian championships.

Official World Records (Track Walking)

(As recognized by the International Amateur Athletic Federation)

Distance	hr	min	sec	Name and Nationality	Date	Place
20,000 m	1	20	06.8	Daniel Bautista	Oct 17, 1979	Canada
30,000 m	2	08	00.0	José Marin (Spain)	Apr 8, 1979	Spain
50,000 m	3	41	39.0	Raul Gonzalez (Mexico)	Apr 8, 1979	Norway
2 hours		17 miles 881 yards		José Marin (Spain)	May 25, 1979	Spain

Women's Unofficial World Records (Track Walking)

Distance	min	sec	Name and Nationality	Date	Place
3,000 m	13	25.2	Carol Tyson (GB) (b Dec 15, 1957)	July 6, 1979	Hofgangens, Sweden
5,000 m	23	11.2	Carol Tyson (GB)	June 30, 1979	Östersund, Sweden
10,000 m	48	11.0	Marion Fawkes (GB) (b Dec 3, 1948)	July 8, 1979	Hanosand, Sweden

Road Walking

The world's best road performances are: 20,000 m, 1 hour 18 min 49 sec by Daniel Bautista (Mexico) at Eschborn, W Germany, on Sept 29, 1979; 50,000 m, 3 hours 41 min 19.2 sec by Raul Gonzalez (Mexico) at Podebrady, Czechoslovakia on June 11, 1978.

Greatest Mileage

Dimitru Dan (b July 13, 1890, *fl.* 1976) of Rumania was the only man of 200 entrants to succeed in walking 100,000 km (62,137 miles), in a contest organized by the Touring Club de France on Apr 1, 1910. By March 24, 1916, he had covered 96,000 km (59,651 miles), averaging 27.24 miles per day.

Walking Backwards

The greatest exponent of reverse pedestrianism has been Plennie L. Wingo (b Jan 24, 1895) then of Abilene, Tex, who started on his 8,000-mile transcontinental walk on Apr 15, 1931, from Santa Monica, Calif, to Instanbul, Turkey, and arrived on Oct 24, 1932. He celebrated the walk's 45th anniversary by covering the 452 miles from Santa Monica to San Francisco, Calif, backwards, in 85 days, aged 81 years.

The longest distance recorded for walking backwards in 24 hours is 80.5 miles by Veikko Matias (b Apr 23, 1941) of Kangasala, Finland, at Kankaapää Airfield, Niinisalo, Finland, Oct 7–8, 1978.

"Non-Stop" Walking

Thomas Patrick Benson (b 1933) of GB walked 314.33 miles at Moor Park, Preston, England, in 123 hours 28 min, Apr 11–16, 1977. He did not permit himself any stops for resting and was moving 99.41% of the time.

Walking Around the World

The first person reported to have "walked around the world" is George M. Schilling (US), Aug 3, 1897–1904, but the first verified achievement was by David Kunst, who started with his brother John from Waseca, Minn, on June 10, 1970. John was killed by Afghani bandits in 1972. David arrived home, after walking 14,500 miles, on Oct 5, 1974.

Tomas Carlos Pereira (b Argentina, Nov 16, 1942) spent 10 years, Apr 6, 1968, through Apr 8, 1978, walking 29,825 miles around all 5 continents.

The Trans-Asia record is 238 days for 6,800 miles from Riga, Latvia, to Vladivostok, USSR, by Georgyi Bushuyev, 50, 1973–74.

Walking Across America

John Lees, 27, of Brighton, England, Apr 11–June 3, 1972, walked 2,876 miles across the US from City Hall, Los Angeles, to City Hall, NYC, in 53 days 12 hours 15 min (53.746 miles per day).

Walking Across Canada

The record trans-Canada (Halifax to Vancouver) walk of 3,764 miles is 96 days by Clyde McRae, 23, from May 1 to Aug 4, 1973.

WATER POLO

Origins

Water polo was developed in England as "Water Soccer" in 1869 and was first included in the Olympic Games in Paris in 1900.

ACROSS AMERICA: John Lees (left) still holds the record for the fastest walk across the US. AROUND THE WORLD: George Shilling (right) was reportedly the first man to walk around the world.

Olympic Victories

Hungary has won the Olympic tournament most often with 6 wins, in 1932, 36, 52, 56, 64 and 1976. Five players share the record of 3 gold medals: George Wilkinson (1879–1946) in 1900, 08 and 12, Paulo (Paul) Radmilovic (1886–1968) and Charles Sidney Smith (1879–1951) in 1908, 12 and 20—all GB; and the Hungarians Deszö Gyarmati (b Oct 23, 1927) and György Kárpáti (b June 23, 1935) in 1952, 56 and 64.

Radmilovic also won a gold medal for the 4 × 200 m freestyle relay in 1908.

Marathon

The longest match on record is one of 70 hours 17 min between two teams of 15 from the Sedbergh School Swimming and Water Polo Club, Cumbria, England, July 14–17, 1979. (*In future this category will be restricted to two teams of 7 only.*)

WATER SKIING

Origins

The origins of water skiing lie in plank gliding or aquaplaning. A 19th century treatise on sorcerers refers to Eliseo of Tarentum who, in the 14th century, "walks and dances" on the water. The first report of aquaplaning was from the Pacific coast of the US in the early 1900's.

A photograph exists of a "plank-riding" contest in a regatta won by a Mr H. Storry at Scarborough, Yorkshire, England, on July 15, 1914. Competitors were towed on a *single* plank by a motor launch. The present-day sport of water skiing was pioneered by Ralph W. Samuelson on Lake Pepin, Minn, on two curved pine boards in the summer of 1922, though claims have been made for the birth of the sport on Lake Annecy (Haute Savoie), France, in 1920. The first World Water Ski Organization was formed in Geneva, Switzerland, on July 27, 1946.

Jumps

The first recorded jump on water skis was by Ralph W. Samuelson, off a greased ramp at Lake Pepin in 1925. The longest jump recorded is one of 194 ft by Michael Hazelwood (GB) at Moomba, Australia, on March 9, 1980. The women's record is 129 ft by Deana Brush (US) at Tyler, Tex, on July 9, 1979.

Slalom

The world record for slalom on a particular pass is 4 buoys (with a 37-ft rope) at 36 mph by Kris LaPoint (US) at Horton Lake, near Barstow, Calif, on July 15, 1975, and also by his brother, Bob LaPoint, in Miami in Aug 1976.

The women's record is 4 buoys on a 39-ft line by Cindy Hutcherson Todd (US) at Calloway Gardens, Ga, in 1978.

Tricks

The highest official point score for tricks is 8,200 points by Patrice Martin (France) at Thorpe Water Park on June 29, 1980.

The women's record of 6,200 points by Natalia Rumyontzeva (USSR) at Castel Gandolfo, Italy on Sept 2, 1979.

Longest Run

The greatest distance traveled is 1,124 miles by Will Coughey (New Zealand) on Lake Karapiro, New Zealand, in 30 hours 34 min, Feb 26–27, 1977.

Highest Speed

The unofficial water skiing speed record is 128.16 mph by Craig Wendt (US) at the Long Beach Stadium, Calif, on Aug 19, 1979. Donna Patterson Brice (b 1953) set a feminine record of 111.11 mph at Long Beach, Calif, on Aug 21, 1977.

Most Titles

World overall championships (instituted 1949) have been twice won by Alfredo Mendoza (US) in 1953 and 1955, Mike Suyderhoud (US) in 1967 and 1969, and George Athans (Canada) in 1971 and 1973, and three times by Mrs Willa McGuire (*née* Worthington) of the US, in 1949–50

LONGEST JUMP: Mike Hazelwood jumped 194 ft on water skis in March 1980.

and 1955, and Elizabeth Allan-Shetter (US) in 1965, 1969, and 1975. Allan-Shetter has also won a record eight individual championship events.

The US has won the team championship on 12 successive occasions since 1957.

Barefoot

The first person to waterski barefoot is reported to be Dick Pope, Jr, at Lake Eloise, Fla, on March 6, 1947. The barefoot duration record is 2 hours 42 min 39 sec by Billy Nichols (US) (b 1964) on Lake Weir, Fla, on Nov 19, 1978. The backwards barefoot record is 39 min by Paul McManus (Australia). The best officially recorded barefoot jump is 52 ft by Keith Donnelly at Baronscourt, Northern Ireland, on July 9, 1978. The official barefoot speed record (two runs) is 110.02 mph by Lee Kirk (US) at Firebird Lake, Phoenix, Ariz, on June 11, 1977. His fastest run was 113.67 mph. The fastest by a woman is 61.39 mph by Haidee Jones (now Lance) (Australia).

WEIGHT LIFTING

Origins

Amateur weight lifting is of comparatively modern origin, and the first "world" championship was staged at the Café Monico, Piccadilly, London, on March 28, 1891. Prior to that time, weight lifting consisted of professional exhibitions in which some of the advertised poundages were open to doubt. The first to raise 400 lb was Karl Swoboda (1882–1933) (Austria) in Vienna, with 401¼ lb in 1910, using the continental clean and jerk style.

Greatest Lift

The greatest weight ever raised by a human being is 6,270 lb in a back lift (weight raised off trestles) by the 364-lb Paul Anderson (US) (b 1932), the 1956 Olympic heavyweight champion, at Toccoa, Ga, on June 12, 1957. (The heaviest Rolls-Royce, the Phantom VI, weighs 5,936 lb.) The

MOST MEDALS: Norbert Schemansky (left) has won 4 Olympic medals. STRONGEST WOMAN: Jan Todd (right) set a women's powerlifting record with a squat of 529 lb in London in May 1980.

greatest by a woman is 3,564 lb with a hip and harness lift by Mrs Josephine Blatt (*née* Schauer) (US) (1869–1923) at the Bijou Theatre, Hoboken, NJ, on Apr 15, 1895.

The greatest overhead lifts made from the ground are the clean and jerks achieved by super-heavyweights which now exceed 560 lb.

The greatest overhead lift ever made by a woman is 286 lb in a continental jerk by Katie Sandwina, *née* Brummbach (Germany) (b Jan 21, 1884, d as Mrs Max Heymann in NYC, in 1952) *c.* 1911. This is equivalent to seven 40-lb office typewriters. She stood 5 ft 11 in tall, weighed 210 lb, and is reputed to have unofficially lifted 312½ lb and to have once shouldered a 1,200-lb cannon taken from the tailboard of a Barnum & Bailey circus wagon.

Power Lifts

Paul Anderson as a professional has bench-pressed 627 lb, achieved 1,200 lb in a deep-knee bend, and deadlifted 820 lb, making a career aggregate of 2,647 lb.

Precious McKenzie (b June 6, 1936) was the first man to total 11 times his body weight (121 lb) with 1,339 lb at Honolulu, Hawaii on May 5, 1979. Lamar Grant (US) deadlifted five times his body weight (123½ lb) with 617¼ lb at Dayton, Ohio on Nov 2, 1979.

The newly instituted two-man dead lift record was raised to 1,439 lb by Clay and Doug Patterson in El Dorado, Ark, on March 3, 1979.

Hermann Görner (Germany) performed a one-handed dead lift of 734½ lb in Dresden on July 20, 1920. He once raised 24 men weighing 4,123 lb on a plank with the soles of his feet, and also carried on his back a 1,444-lb piano for a distance of 52½ ft on June 3, 1921.

Peter B. Cortese (US) achieved a one-arm dead lift of 370 lb—22 lb over triple his body weight—at York, Pa, on Sept 4, 1954.

GREATEST LIFT: Paul Anderson once back-lifted 6,270 lb—the heaviest weight ever raised.

The greatest by a woman is a squat of 529 lb by Jan Suffolk Todd (b May 22, 1952) (US) at BBC TV Centre, London, on May 6, 1980. The official record for the three-lift total is 1,179 lb by Ann Turbyne (US) at Culver City, Calif, on Jan 27, 1980.

A dead lift record of 2,204,622 lb in 24 hours was set by the Hreod Burna Weightlifting Club, Swindon, England, March 1–2, 1980.

Most Olympic Medals

Winner of most Olympic medals is Norbert Schemansky (US) with 4: gold, middle-heavyweight 1952; silver, heavyweight 1948; bronze, heavyweight 1960 and 1964.

Most World Titles

The most world title wins is 8 by John Davis (US) (b Jan 12, 1921) in 1938, 1946–52; by Tommy Kono (US) (b June 27, 1930) in 1952–9; and by Vladimir Alexeyev (USSR) (b Jan 7, 1942) 1970–7.

FLYWEIGHT CHAMP: Alexander Voronin (above) has the highest total in the lightest weight class.
MOST TITLES: Tommy Kono won 8 world titles.

Official World Weight Lifting Records

(As of Aug 4, 1980)

Flyweight
(114½ lb—52 kg)

Snatch	249¾	Han Gyong Si (N Korea)	USSR	July 20, 1980
Jerk	314	Alexander Senchine (USSR)	USSR	May 14, 1980
Total	545½	Alexander Voronin (USSR)	W Germany	Sept 18, 1979

Bantamweight
(123¼ lb—56 kg)

Snatch	275½	Daniel Nunez (Cuba)	USSR	July 21, 1980
Jerk	347	Yuri Sarkisian (USSR)	USSR	July 21, 1980
Total	606¼	Daniel Nunez (Cuba)	USSR	July 21, 1980

Featherweight
(132¼ lb—60 kg)

Snatch	292	Viktor Mazin (USSR)	USSR	July 6, 1980
Jerk	368	Viktor Mazin (USSR)	USSR	July 6, 1980
Total	655¾	Viktor Mazin (USSR)	USSR	July 6, 1980

Lightweight
(148¾ lb—67.5 kg)

Snatch	326¼	Yanko Rusev (Bulgaria)	Yugoslavia	Apr 28, 1980
Jerk	429¾	Yanko Rusev (Bulgaria)	USSR	July 23, 1980
Total	755	Yanko Rusev (Bulgaria)	USSR	July 23, 1980

Middleweight
(165¼ lb—75 kg)

Snatch	354¾	Nedelcho Kolev (Bulgaria)	Bulgaria	Feb 3, 1980
Jerk	453	Asen Zlatev (Bulgaria)	USSR	July 24, 1980
Total	793½	Asen Zlatev (Bulgaria)	USSR	July 24, 1980

Light-heavyweight
(181¾ lb—82.5 kg)

Snatch	391¼	Yurik Vardanyan (USSR)	USSR	July 26, 1979
Jerk	490½	Yurik Vardanyan (USSR)	USSR	July 26, 1980
Total	881¾	Yurik Vardanyan (USSR)	USSR	July 26, 1980

Middle-heavyweight
(198¼ lb—90 kg)

Snatch	398	David Rigert (USSR)	Czech	June 16, 1978
Jerk	491½	Yurik Vardanyan (USSR)	USSR	July 6, 1980
Total	881¾	David Rigert (USSR)	USSR	May 14, 1976

(220½ lb—100 kg)

Snatch	403¼	Igor Nikitine (USSR)	USSR	June 27, 1980
Jerk	506¾	David Rigert (USSR)	USSR	July 6, 1980
Total	892¾	David Rigert (USSR)	USSR	Nov 23, 1979

Heavyweight
(242½ lb—110 kg)

Snatch	419¾	Vyacheslav Klokov (USSR)	USSR	July 6, 1980
Jerk	529	Leonid Taranenko USSR)	USSR	July 29, 1979
Total	931¼	Leonid Taranenko (USSR)	USSR	July 29, 1980

Super-heavyweight
(Over 242½ lb—110 kg)

Snatch	442	Sultan Rakhmanov (USSR)	USSR	Apr 25, 1978
Jerk	564¼	Vasili Alexeyev (USSR)	USSR	Nov 1, 1977
Total	981	Vasili Alexeyev (USSR)	USSR	Sept 1, 1977

World Powerlifting Records

(as recognized by the International Powerlifting Federation as of June 1, 1980)

		Lb	Date	Place of Competition
	52 Kg			
SQT	Chuck Dunbar (US)	490.5	Apr 19, 1980	Auburn, Ala
BP	Chuck Dunbar (US)	303	Aug 18, 1979	Bay St Louis, Mo
DL	Hideaki Inaba (Japan)	496	Nov 3, 1979	Dayton, Ohio
TOT	Hideaki Inaba (Japan)	1189	Nov 3, 1979	Dayton, Ohio
	56 Kg			
SQT	Precious McKenzie (NZ)	507	May 5, 1979	Honolulu, Hawaii
BP	Lamar Gant (US)	319.5	Apr 19, 1980	Auburn, Ala
DL	Lamar Gant (US)	633.5	Apr 19, 1980	Auburn, Ala
TOT	Lamar Gant (US)	1366.5	Apr 19, 1980	Auburn, Ala
	60 Kg			
SQT	Joe Bradley (US)	573	Apr 19, 1980	Auburn, Ala
BP	Joe Bradley (US)	363.5	Apr 19, 1980	Auburn, Ala
DL	Lamar Gant (US)	622.5	Nov 3, 1978	Turku, Finland
TOT	Joe Bradley (US)	1466	Apr 19, 1980	Auburn, Ala
	67½ Kg			
SQT	Mike Bridges (US)	622.5	Nov 3, 1978	Turku, Finland
BP	Armington Rafael (US)	413	Feb 16, 1980	Tollhouse, Calif
DL	Troy Hicks (US)	639	Jan 27, 1979	Cleveland, Tenn
TOT	Mike Bridges (US)	1609	Nov 3, 1979	Turku, Finland
	75 Kg			
SQT	Mike Bridges (US)	722	Apr 19, 1980	Auburn, Ala
BP	Mike Bridges (US)	462.5	Apr 19, 1980	Auburn, Ala
DL	Rick Gaugler (US)	694	Feb 10, 1979	Ft Worth, Tex
TOT	Mike Bridges (US)	1840.5	Apr 19, 1980	Auburn, Ala
	82.5 Kg			
SQT	Dennis Wright (US)	749.5	Apr 19, 1980	Auburn, Ala
BP	Mike MacDonald (US)	512.5	Feb 17, 1979	Brookings, SD
DL	Veli Kumpuniemi (Finland)	788	May 17, 1980	Zurich, Switzerland
TOT	Ron Collins (GB)	1884.5	May 17, 1980	Zurich, Switzerland
	90 Kg			
SQT	Jerry Jones (US)	782.5	May 5, 1979	Honolulu, Hawaii
BP	Mike MacDonald (US)	551	May 5, 1979	Honolulu, Hawaii
DL	Vince Anello (US)	815.5	Nov 4, 1978	Turku, Finland
TOT	Walter Thomas (US)	1951	Apr 19, 1980	Auburn, Ala
	100 Kg			
SQT	Chip McCain (US)	785.5	Aug 18, 1979	Bay St Louis, Mo
BP	Mike MacDonald (US)	573	Aug 21, 1977	Santa Monica, Calif
DL	Vince Anello (US)	804.5	June 19, 1977	Culver City, Calif
TOT	Larry Pacifico (US)	2061	Nov 4, 1977	Perth, Australia
	110 Kg			
SQT	Marvin Phillips (US)	843	Apr 19, 1980	Auburn, Ala
BP	Mike MacDonald (US)	573	Nov 22, 1975	Duluth, Minn
DL	John Kuc (US)	865	Mar 15, 1980	Honolulu, Hawaii
TOT	John Kuc (US)	2154.5	Mar 15, 1980	Honolulu, Hawaii
	125 Kg			
SQT	Ernie Hackett (US)	822.5	Aug 19, 1979	Bay St Louis, Mo
BP	Doug Young (US)	585	Aug 19, 1979	Bay St Louis, Mo
DL	Dave Shaw (US)	806.5	July 15, 1979	Inglewood, Calif
TOT	Larry Kidney (US)	2149	Mar 15, 1980	Honolulu, Hawaii
	Over 125 Kg			
SQT	Paul Wrenn (US)	954.5	Aug 19, 1980	Bay St Louis, Mo
BP	Bill Kazmier (US)	633.5	Apr 19, 1980	Auburn, Ala
DL	Don Reinhoudt (US)	881.5	May 3, 1975	Chattanooga, Tenn
TOT	Don Reinhoudt (US)	2420	May 3, 1975	Chattanooga, Tenn

Note: SQT = Squat; BP = Bench Press; DL = Dead Lift

MOST TITLES: Aleksandr Medved, here taking down India's Maruti Mane, has won 10 world titles, including 3 Olympic gold medals.

WRESTLING

Earliest References

The earliest depictions of wrestling holds and falls on the walls of the tomb of Ptahhotep (5th Dynasty Egypt) indicate that organized wrestling dates from before *c.* 2350 BC. It was introduced into the ancient Olympic Games in the 18th Olympiad *c.* 708 BC. The Graeco-Roman style is of French origin and arose about 1860. The International Amateur Wrestling Federation (FILA) was founded in 1912.

Sumo Wrestling

The sport's origins in Japan certainly date from *c.* 23 BC. The heaviest performers were probably Dewagatake, a wrestler of the 1920's who was 6 ft 7¾ in tall and weighed up to 430 lb, and Odachi, of the 1950's, who stood 6 ft 7½ in and weighed about 441 lb. Weight is amassed by over-eating a high protein stew called *chankonabe*. The tallest was probably Ozora, an early 19th century performer, who stood 7 ft 3 in tall. The most successful wrestlers have been Koki Naya (b 1940), *alias* Taiho ("Great Bird"), who won 32 Emperor's Cups until his retirement in 1971; Sadaji Akiyoshi (b 1912), *alias* Futabayama, who won 69 consecutive bouts in the 1930's; and the *ozeki* Torokichi, *alias* Raiden, who in 21 years (1789–1810) won 240 bouts and lost only 10 for the highest ever winning percentage of .962.

The youngest of the 56 men to attain the rank of *Yokozuna* (Grand Champion) was Toshimitsu Obata (*alias* Kitanoumi) in July 1974, aged 21 years 2 months. He set a record in 1978 winning 82 of the 90 bouts that top *rikishi* fight annually. Jesse Kuhaulua (b Hawaii, June 16, 1944), *alias*

Takamiyama, was the first non-Japanese to win an official tournament in July, 1972 and has had a record of 1,140 consecutive top division bouts through June, 1980.

Best Records

In international competition, Osamu Watanabe (b Oct 21, 1940) (Japan), the 1964 Olympic freestyle featherweight champion, was unbeaten and unscored-upon in 187 consecutive matches.

Wade Schalles (US) has won 668 bouts from 1964 to 1980.

Most World Championships

The greatest number of world championships won by a wrestler is 10 by the freestyler Aleksandr Medved (USSR), with the light-heavyweight titles in 1964 (Olympic) and 1966, the heavyweight 1967 and 1968 (Olympic), and the super-heavyweight title 1969, 1970, 1971 and 1972 (Olympic). The only wrestler to win the same title in 6 successive years has been Abdollah Movahed (Iran) in the lightweight division in 1965–70. The record for successive Graeco-Roman titles is 5 by Roman Rurua (USSR) with the featherweight 1966, 1967, 1968 (Olympic), 1969 and 1970.

Most Olympic Titles

Three wrestlers have won three Olympic titles. They are:

Carl Westergren (Sweden) (1895—1958)		Ivar Johansson (Sweden) (b Jan 31, 1903)	
Graeco-Roman Middleweight A	1920	Free-style Middleweight	1932
Graeco-Roman Middleweight B	1924	Graeco-Roman Welterweight	1932
Graeco-Roman Heavyweight	1932	Graeco-Roman Middleweight	1936

Aleksandr Medved (USSR) (b Sept 16, 1937		The only wrestler with more medals is Imre Polyák (Hungary) who won the
Free-style Light-heavyweight	1964	silver medal for the Graeco-Roman
Free-style Heavyweight	1968	featherweight class in 1952, 56–60
Free-style Super-heavyweight	1972	and the gold in 1964.

HEAVIEST WRESTLER: Chris Taylor weighed over 420 lb when he won an Olympic bronze medal in 1972.

Heaviest Heavyweight

The heaviest wrestler in Olympic history is Chris Taylor (1950–79), bronze medallist in the super-heavyweight class in 1972, who stood 6 ft 5 in tall and weighed over 420 lb.

Longest Bout

The longest recorded bout was one of 11 hours 40 min between Martin Klein (Estonia, representing Russia) and Alfred Asikáinen (Finland) in the Graeco-Roman middleweight "A" event in the 1912 Olympic Games in Stockholm, Sweden. Klein won.

NEWLY VERIFIED RECORDS

The following pages include records which were received and verified too late to be included in the main sections of this book.

Chapter 1

Tallest Giantesses (page 15). In May 1978 a height of 7 ft 7¾ in was recorded for 17-year-old Hu Qunzhang living near Shasi, China. She was never anthropometrically assessed again, but was reportedly still growing at the time of her death in Aug 1979.

Oldest Living Twins (page 31). On June 16, 1980, identical twin sisters, Naemi Bomanson and Elin Hagmark of Mariehamn, Finland, celebrated their 100th birthday.

Human Computer (page 37). Mrs Shakuntala Devi of India demonstrated the multiplication of two 13-digit numbers, 7,686,369,774,870 × 2,465,099,745,779 (picked at random by the Computer Department of Imperial College, London, on June 18, 1980) in 28 sec. Her correct answer was 18,947,668,177,995,426.

Memorizing Pi (page 37). Creighton Carvello recited Pi to 20,013 places on June 27, 1980, in 9 hours 10 min at the Saltscar Comprehensive School, Redcar, Cleveland, England.

Longest Finger Nails (page 37). Romesh Sharma's longest finger nail had grown to 26½ in by Apr 7, 1980.

Shouting (page 40). Joanne Brown, 14, of Dronfield Woodhouse, Sheffield, England, attained 113 decibels on June 15, 1980, at the Yorkshire Television Centre, Sheffield. Peter Van de Vooren twice achieved 112 decibels while whistling, on Radio 2SM, Sydney, Australia, on Feb 9, 1980.

Sword Swallowing (page 45). Count Desmond swallowed thirteen 23-in-long blades to below his xiphisternum. *This category will now be retired and no further entires will be considered.*

Chapter 2

Highest Dog Jumps (page 77). There is no photographic evidence to substantiate the 11-ft-6-in claim. On March 19, 1980, "Max of Pan-

TELETHON (above):
Jerry Lewis' 1979 Telethon
raised over $30 million.
SWORD SWALLOWING
(right): "Count
Desmond" swallowed 13
swords in 1980.

goula," a 2-year-old German shepherd dog scaled an 11-ft-5⅛-in smooth
wooden wall at Chikurubi prison's dog training school near Salisbury,
Zimbabwe.

Largest Pet Litters (page 79). On Feb 28, 1974, a golden hamster
owned by Loryn and Sheri Miller of Baton Rouge, La, produced a live
litter of 26 (18 killed by mother). A gerbil belonging to Heather James of
High Wycombe, England, matched the record litter of 11 on May 4,
1980.

Longest Snakes (page 91). "Cassius" died on Apr 3, 1980. The preserved skin measures 29 ft.

Oldest Goldfish (page 98). "Ted" died on Aug 1, 1980, aged 41 years.

Chapter 5

Most Expensive Wine (page 81). The highest price paid for any bottle
of wine is $31,000 for a bottle of 1822 Chateau Lafite by John Grisanti at
an auction in San Francisco on May 28, 1980.

Most Accurate Device. The accuracy capability of the cesium beam
frequency standard can approach 1 part in 10^{13} compared to 5 parts in
10^{12} for the methane stabilized helium-neon laser and 1 part in 10^{12} for
the hydrogen maser.

Chapter 6

Painting: Auction Prices (page 194). The record for a 20th century painting was set at $3 million at Sotheby Parke Bernet, NYC, on May 12, 1980, by Picasso's 1923 portrait of an acrobat *Saltimbanque* bought by Tokyo's Bridgestone Museum.

Most Expensive Manuscript (page 208). The highest price ever paid for a manuscript at auction has been £850,000 ($1,955,000) at Sotheby's, London, on July 8, 1980, for one of the two surviving copies of the Persian illustrated *History of the World* written in the Rashid al-Din scriptorium in 1314 AD on the orders of the Mongol ruler Uljaytu.

Most Publishers' Rejections (page 211). Gilbert Young's number of rejections has now reached 110.

Most Durable Pen Pals (page 216). Mrs Ida McDougall of Tasmania, Australia, corresponded with Miss R. Morton of Sevenoaks, Kent, England, for 75 years from Nov 11, 1904 until Mrs McDougall's death on Dec 24, 1979, aged 86 years.

Longest Musical March. The longest recorded musical march is one of 37.9 miles from Lillehammer to Hamar, Norway, in 15 hours when, on May 10, 1980, 26 of 35 members of the Trondheim Brass Band survived the playing of 135 marches.

Most Successful Telethons (page 241). The Jerry Lewis Labor Day Telethon on Sept 4, 1979, raised $30,075,227 in pledges for the Muscular Dystrophy Association from an audience estimated at 93 million. The East African Emergency Appeal, broadcast on BBC-TV by Sue Lawley on June 19, 1980, reached $12,047,400 in actual contributions by July 19 for the five distributing charities.

Chapter 7

Most Expensive Hotel Room (page 256). The rent for the Celestial suite was raised to $3,000 a day in June 1980.

Longest Pleasure Pier (page 261). It was reported on July 29, 1980 that Southend Pier would be demolished at the end of the 1980 summer season.

Chapter 8

Snowmobiling (page 302). Tony Lenzini of Sylvania, Ohio drove his Ski-Doo Citation 4500, 5,627 miles from Houghton Lake, Mich to Anchorage, Alaska in 62 days, from Jan 7 to March 6, 1980.

Most on One Motorcycle (page 304). A team of 19 Royal Signal White Helmets, weighing 3,099 lb 9 oz, rode a Triumph motorcycle at Catterick Camp, North Yorkshire, England on July 14, 1980. Roy Castle, 140 lb, was number 20 and top-mounter.

Unicycle Records (page 305). Cathy Fox of Marion, Ohio, set a speed record for 100 miles in 10 hours 37 min 10 sec on June 7, 1980.

Most Powerful Computer (page 335). On June 2, 1980, Control Data Corporation announced the CYBER Model 205-444 system from Arden Hill, Minn, which has a memory of 4 million 64-Bit words and will cost $16.5 million for delivery in Jan 1981.

Chapter 9

Cigars (page 352). Jon Zealando smoked 15 cigars simultaneously, while whistling, at Henderson Square, Auckland, NZ on Oct 19, 1979.

Cigarettes (page 353). Jim Purol and Mike Papa each smoked 135 cigarettes simultaneously for 5 min on Oct 5, 1978 at Rameys Lounge, Detroit, Mich.

Pistols (page 359). The highest price paid at auction for a pistol is £110,000 ($253,000) at Christie's London on July 8, 1980 for a Sadeler wheel-lock holster pistol from Munich, dated 1600.

Chapter 10

Earliest Elected Female Head of State. President Vigdis Finnbokdottir (b 1930) became the first democratically elected female head of state on June 30, 1980 and was scheduled to take office on Aug 1, 1980.

Most Successful Criminal Lawyer (page 391). Sir Lionel Luckhoo obtained his 232nd acquittal by July 14, 1980.

Longest Working Week (page 405). A case of a working week of 142 hours was recorded in June 1980 by Dr Paul Ashton, 32, the anesthetics registrar at Birkenhead General Hospital, Merseyside, England. This left an average each day of 3 hours 42 min 51 sec for sleep. Some non-consultant doctors are actually contracted to work 110 hours a week.

Largest Chocolate Easter Egg (page 409). An egg weighing 4.737 lb and measuring 12 ft high was made outside The Royal Oak, Winterbourne, Bristol, England.

Candy (page 411). From May 1913 to June 30, 1980, the total US sales of Life Savers was 29,651,840,000 rolls. A tunnel formed by the holes in the middle, placed end to end, would be 6 times longer than the distance from the earth to the moon.

Coffee (page 411). The people of Sweden consumed 25.78 lb of coffee per person per year in 1979–80.

Postal Services (page 417). In 1979 in the US, people posted 98,828.9 million letters and packages, at an average of 455 letters per person per year. The US Postal Service employed 663,067 employees in 1979.

Chapter 11

Marine Circumnavigation Records (page 438). The smallest boat to make a successful circumnavigation is the *Super Shrimp,* an 18-ft 4-in Bermudan Sloop. Shane Acton of England, and crew, started in Cambridge, England in Aug 1972 and returned to the same city in Aug 1980.

Transatlantic Marine Records (page 440). The fastest woman solo transatlantic marine record was set by Dame Naomi James, on the 53-ft *Kriter Lady,* from Plymouth, England to Newport, RI, in 25 days 19 hours 12 min in 1980.

Eric Tabarly of France and a crew of 2 set the record for fastest-ever transatlantic sail in the 52-ft 2-in *Paul Ricard* (trimaran) (hydrofoil) in 10 days 5 hours in July 1980, sailing from Sandy Hook, NJ to Lizard, Cornwall, England.

The fastest solo east-west (Northern) (multihull) was set in 1980 by

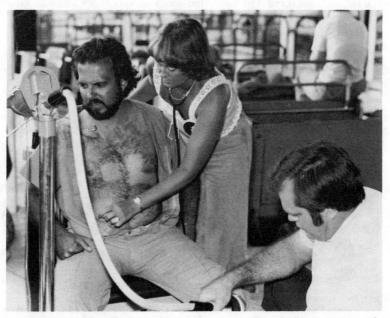

ROLLER COASTER KING: Jim King broke his own record with a 368-hour ride.

Philip Weld of the US on the 51-ft *Moxie,* from Plymouth, England to Newport, RI, in 17 days 23 hours 12 min.

The fastest solo east-west (Northern) (monohull) was set in 1980 by Kazimierz Jaworski of Poland on the 56-ft *Spaniel II,* from Plymouth, England to Newport, RI, in 19 days 13 hours 25 min.

Longest Marriage (page 443). John and Harriet Orton celebrated their 80th wedding anniversary on July 9, 1980.

Baton Twirling (page 446). A team of 5 from the Academy of Baton and Dance in Holland, Ohio, twirled for 72 hours 15 min, Apr 8–11, 1980.

Beard of Bees (page 446). A beard of bees estimated at not less than 21,000 swarmed on the chest and throat of Dan Cooke, Ohio on June 20, 1980.

Bed of Nails (page 446). The Rev Ken Owen spent 81 hours 8 min 32 sec non-stop lying on a bed of nails at the YMCA, Port Talbot, W Glamorgan, Wales, July 21–24, 1980.

Bell Ringing (page 448). The Whitnash Handbell Ringers of Leamington Spa, Warwickshire, England gave a handbell-ringing recital 45 hours 25 min long, July 18–20, 1980.

Champagne Fountain (page 449). Robert D. Mers of Wauconda, Ill, assisted by M. G. Ryan of McHenry, Ill, equalled the champagne fountain record with 20 glasses on Apr 12, 1980.

Coin Balancing (page 452). Bruce McConachy (b 1963) of West Vancouver, BC, balanced 170 Canadian coins on top of a Canadian com-

RUNNING RECORD (left): Tatyana Kazankina (in the lead) broke her own world record for 1,500 m. CRAWLING RECORD (right): Jim Purol crawled 25 miles to raise money for the March of Dimes.

COIN BALANCING: Bruce McConachy balanced 170 Canadian coins on the edge of a freestanding Canadian penny.

memorative penny which was freestanding vertically on another coin in Vancouver on Aug 24, 1979.

Crawling (page 453). Jim Purol of Livonia, Mich, completed 25 miles, Oct 22–23, 1979.

Grape Catching (page 458). Arden Chapman of Pioneer, La, caught a grape thrown in his mouth from 319 ft 8 in on July 18, 1980. The thrower was Jerry "Pete" Mercer.

Human Fly (page 462). Lead climber Jean-Claude Droyer (b May 8, 1946) of Paris, France, and Pierre Puiseux (b Dec 2, 1953) of Pau, France, climbed up the outside of the Eiffel Tower to a height of 984 ft in 2 hours 18 min on July 21, 1980.

Ramp Jumping (page 470). Jean-Pierre Vignau completed a T-bone dive of 196 ft 5 in in a Ford Capri 2600 at Montlhéry autodome near Paris, France on July 20, 1980.

Roller Coasting (page 470). Jim King completed 368 hours at the Miracle Strip Amusement Park, Panama City, Fla, June 22–July 7, 1980.

Spitting (page 473). Randy Ober of Bentonville, Ark spat a tobacco wad 44 ft 6 in at the Calico 3rd Annual Tobacco Chewing and Spitting Championships north of Barstow, Calif on March 30, 1980.

Stilt Walking (page 474). John Russell of Ringling Brothers and Barnum & Bailey Circus mastered 31-ft aluminum stilts, with 30 steps at the Riverfront Coliseum, Cincinnati, Ohio on Apr 17, 1980. The stilts weighed 35 lb each.

Prunes (page 486). Peter Dowdeswell ate 144 prunes in 53.5 sec in Paris, France on July 21, 1980.

Shellfish Eating (page 486). John Fletcher ate 82 whelks in 5 min 26 sec at the Castle Inn, Dover, Kent, England on July 27, 1980.

HIGH JUMP: Trevor Baxter took off from a moving skateboard and jumped over a bar set at 5 ft 3 in.

EQUESTRIAN MARATHON: Paulette Stoudt rode at all paces (including jumping) for 58 hours 15 min at Mohnton, Pa, June 13–16, 1980.

Chapter 12

Bowling: Most Perfect League Scores (page 525). Bob Brown bowled a 900 series for three unsanctioned games at Roseville Bowl, Calif, on Apr 12, 1980.

Games and Pastimes: Skateboarding (page 557). Trevor Baxter broke his own world record for the skateboard high jump when he cleared 5 ft 3 in at Skatepark, Southsea, England, on July 6, 1980.

Track and Field: Women's World Records (page 632). Tatyana Kazankina (USSR) set a world record of 3 min 52.47 sec in the women's 1,-500-m run in Zurich on Aug 13, 1980, shattering her own previous record by over 2 sec.

INDEX

Index prepared by Henry W. Engel

PICTURE CREDITS

The editors and publishers wish to thank the following people and organizations for pictures which they supplied:

Cover photographs: All-Sport Photographic; Franklin Berger; Janis Kursman.

Color photographs: All-Sport Photographic; Tony Duffy; Yotis Georgi; Graham Hind; Tommy Mardell; NASA.

Text photographs: Mrs. Addison; Aero-Camera; Aero-Pic; Ernest W. Albright; Allen Photographers; All-Sport Photographic; Amateur Softball Association; Bill Amatucci; American Broadcasting Companies, Inc.; American Museum of Natural History; *Anaheim Bulletin;* Ardea Photographic: Donald D. Burgess; John Arden; *Argosy* Magazine; Bill Ashe; Associated Newspapers Ltd.; Associated Press; Atlanta Braves; Stephen Austin Newspapers Ltd.; Australian News and Information Bureau; Harold Bastin; Denis Bekett; Bell, Howarth Ltd.; Bell Labs; Bensen Aircraft Corp.; Neil Benson; Franklin Berger; Lawrence Berkeley Laboratory; Bethlehem Steel Corp.; Bettmann Archive; Big Fights Inc.; Bilderdienst; Birmingham Post & Mail; Peter J. Bish; Border Press, Carlisle; Boston Bruins; Boston Celtics; Boston Gardens; Boving and Co. Ltd.; Braniff International; *Brighton Evening Argus;* British Airways; British Broadcasting Corporation; British Information Services; Jerry Brooks; Buffalo Bills; Camera Press; *Canberra Times;* J. Allan Cash; *The Catholic News;* Central Photographic Agency; Central Press Photos Ltd.; Victor Chambi; Chesapeake Bay Bridge and Tunnel Commission; Chicago Bears; Peter Chiodo; Christie's; Chip Clark; Coca-Cola Inc; *Coffeyville Journal;* R. J. Collovick; M. Colomban; *Connacht Tribune; Contra Costa Suns,* California; Jerry Cooke; Gordon Counsell; Gerry Cranham; Crown Copyright; F. E. Curran; Sandra Dahringa: *Daily Mail,* London; Dept. of Supply, Antarctic Division; "Discovery" Committee, Colonial Office, London; Roy Doran Photography; Tony Duffy; Alfred Dunhill Ltd.; A. Dupont; Editorial Photocolor Archives; Eljay Photo Service; Embassy of Syrian Arab Republic; Jim England; *Enquirer and News,* Battle Creek, Mich.; Europix; *Evening News,* London; *Express Star,* Wolverhampton, England; John Fairfax and Sons Ltd.; Fairleigh Dickinson University; *Family Doctor;* F.A.O.; The Federal Reserve Bank of N.Y.; Flight International; Ralph Fogelman; *Fort Worth Star Telegram;* Robert L. Foster; Fox Photos Ltd.; French Embassies, London and Washington; French Government Tourist Office; Marvin Frost; General Photographic Agency; Gilbreath Collection; Global Olympic Picture Association; Golden State Warriors, Step One Productions, San Francisco; Golding Farms; Goodyear Inc.; Government of India; Grace's Gardens; Greek Tourist Office; Bob Hagopian; Charles Hammarstein; Robert Harding Associates; Harmsworth Photo Library; Hartford Whalers; Harvard University; Michael R. Hatfield; Ralph Helfer; *F. R. Herald News;* George Herringshaw; Herts Pictorial, Hitchin, England; Hill and Knowlton; Wilson Hitchings; Hong Kong Government Information Services; David Hossingers; Hsinhua News Agency;

Edwin G. Huffman; Huntsville *Times;* Impact Photo, Inc.; Imperial War Museum, London; Indonesian Consulate General; International Nickel Co., Inc.; International Rodeo Association; Irvin Industries; Japanese National Railways; Japan Railway Construction Public Corp.; Ellerton M. Jette; Marion Kaplan; *Kentish Mercury South East;* Keystone Press Agency; R. Kinne/B. Coleman Ltd.; George Konig; Norman Kunstforlag A.S.; E. D. Lacey; Clive Landen; Frank Lane; Las Vegas News Bureau; Ann Li Mongello; Loffland Drilling Co.; London Features International Ltd.; Arthur MacCannell; Alfredo MacDondo; Bob Madden; Ed Mahan; William C. Mann, Sr.; Mansell Collection; March Five Inc.; John Marshall; E. W. Marwick; McCulloch Oil Corporation; Gary McMillin; Metropolitan Photo Service, Inc.; *Middletown Journal;* Manny Milan; *Minneapolis Tribune;* Minnesota Vikings; R. N. Misra; Monitor Press Features Ltd.; Dr. S. Moorbath; A. P. Moose; Don Morley; *Morning Telegraph Sheffield;* Moroccan National Tourist Office; *Montreal Star-Canada Wide;* Mt. Wilson & Palomar Observatory; Museum of Science, Boston; NASA; National Baseball Hall of Fame; *National Enquirer;* NCAA; New York Cosmos; *New York Daily News* Photo; New York Racing Association; New York Rangers; New York Road Runners Club; New York Stars; *The New York Times;* New York Yankees; New York Zoological Society; New Zealand Consulate; *New Zealand Herald Weekly News;* Nippon Steel Corp.; Norsk Polarinstitutt; NorskTelegram byra; *Northern Advocate,* N.Z.; Nova Scotia Information Service; Novosti; Nucolorvue Productions Ltd.; Oakland Raiders; Oak Ridge National Laboratory; Oberthur Collection; Office du Film de la Province de Québec; Oklahoma Publishing Co.; Pacific Telephone & Telegraph Co.; Gerry Paknadel; J. P. Coates Palgrave; Svante Palme; Panagra; Peabody Museum of Salem; D. E. Pedgley; *Peekskill Evening Star;* Dane Penland; Lani Pettit; *The Philadelphia Inquirer;* Philadelphia Phillies; Photo Cern; Photo-Reportage Ltd.; Picture Post; Planet News Ltd.; Clotilde Poisson; Hank Pollard; Popperfoto; The Port Authority of N.Y. & N.J.; Steve Powell; Kenneth Prater, A.I.I.P.; Press Association Photos; W. R. Proctor Associates Inc.; Product Support, Ltd.; Professional Bowlers Association; Professional Rodeo Cowboys Association; Pro Football Hall of Fame; Provincial Sports Photography; Queens Nassau Pix; W. T. Rabe; Radio Times Hulton Picture Library; David Rauns; RCA Records; Reaction Dynamics, Inc.; Record House Glasgow; Republican Publications; Reuter; Ringsport; Ruth Robertson; R. Rodden; Bernard Ronget; Royal Canadian Mint; Royal Greenwich Observatory; Royal Society of London; Al Ruelle; *Saint Petersburg Times;* Henry Salameh; Santa Fe Railway; Ugo Sarto; Ugo Sbaraglia; Dale Scherfling; Toni Schneiders; Eddie Schuurling/Frank W. Lane; Scientific Instrument Centre; *The Seattle Times;* Sea World, Inc.; Sporting Pictures; H. H. Seiden; Shell Photographic Service; Robert L. Smith; Smithsonian Institution; Jerry Soalt; Rick Sorrell; Sotheby Parke Bernet & Co.; Spanish Tourist Office; A. G. Spalding & Bros.; Sperryn's; Sport and General; *Sports Illustrated; Springfield Union; Sun;* Tate & Lyle Ltd.; Thomson Newspapers Ltd; Triborough Bridge and Tunnel Authority; T.R.W. Corp.; Twentieth-Century Fox; UNATIONS; United Artists; Universal Photographers; Universal Pictorial Press; University Museum; University of Denver; UPI; U.S. Air Force; U.S. Army; U.S. Coast Guard; U.S. Dept. of Commerce; U.S. Forest Service; U.S. Information Service; U.S. Lawn Tennis Association; U.S. National Park Service; U.S. Navy; USTA; Vanguard Photography, Hollywood, California; Virginia Tech Photo; Ernest P. Walker; M. T. Walters & Associates Ltd.; Peter Ward; *Waterloo Courier,* Iowa; Wayne Corporation; Otho Webb; Bob Wendt; Werkfoto; Westminster Press Ltd.; Ron Wheeler; Charles Wherry; Wide World Photos; Wilson Sporting Goods Co.; Hanns Wolters Theatrical Agency; G. L. Wood; Roger C. Wood; Hamilton Wright; Wyman-Gordon Press; Norman Zeisloft; Zoological Society of London; Zoological Society of Philadelphia.